LANCELOT-GRAIL

THE OLD FRENCH ARTHURIAN VULGATE AND POST-VULGATE IN TRANSLATION

LANCELOT-GRAIL

LANCELOT-GRAIL

THE OLD FRENCH ARTHURIAN VULGATE AND POST-VULGATE IN TRANSLATION

NORRIS J. LACY, GENERAL EDITOR

VOLUME II

THE STORY OF MERLIN
translated by Rupert T. Pickens

D. S. BREWER

Published by arrangement with Routledge, Inc., part of Taylor & Francis Group LLC

First published 1993-1996
Garland Publishing Inc., New York

New edition 2010
D. S. Brewer, Cambridge

ISBN 978 1 84384 234 7

Set ISBN 978 0 85991 770 4

D. S. Brewer is an imprint of Boydell & Brewer Ltd
PO Box 9, Woodbridge, Suffolk IP12 3DF, UK
and of Boydell & Brewer Inc.
668 Mt. Hope Avenue, Rochester NY 14620, USA
website: www.boydellandbrewer.com

A catalogue record for this book is available
from the British Library

This publication is printed on acid-free paper

Printed in Great Britain by
CPI Antony Rowe, Chippenham and Eastbourne

CONTENTS

PREFACE

Norris J. Lacy

THE VULGATE AND POST-VULGATE CYCLES

During the second half of the twelfth century, Chrétien de Troyes developed and fixed the form of the Arthurian episodic romance. In the process he popularized King Arthur in French, as Geoffrey of Monmouth had done in Latin, but he also contributed to the legend new characters and themes unknown to Geoffrey. These include in particular the love story of Lancelot and Guenevere and the quest for the Grail. Several texts, notably the works of Robert de Boron, from the end of that century, transformed the mysterious Grail into the "Holy Grail," the Chalice of the Last Supper and the vessel in which Christ's blood was collected after the crucifixion.

Then, between 1215 and about 1235, an anonymous author or group of authors composed the Lancelot-Grail Cycle (also called the Vulgate Cycle, the Prose *Lancelot,* or the Pseudo-Map Cycle) of Arthurian romance. This cycle of five imposing romances can only be termed monumental, owing in equal measure to its enormous length, its complexity and literary value, and its influence. The romances run to several thousand pages of text, and they offer many hundreds of characters and countless adventures intricately interlaced with one another. Most important, they constitute the most extended attempt to elaborate the full story of the Arthurian era and to set that era in a framework of universal history.

The two romances that stand first chronologically were actually composed after the other three. The *Estoire del saint Graal* (translated in this set as *The History of the Holy Grail*) opens the cycle by tracing the early history of the Grail, from Joseph of Arimathea to his son Josephe, who becomes the first Christian bishop, and eventually to Alain, the first Fisher King, who places the Grail in Corbenic Castle and begins the wait for the arrival of the chosen Grail Knight. *The Story of Merlin* depicts the role of the seer and magician in Arthur's conception and birth, in his designation as king following the Sword in the Stone revelation, and in the establishment of the Round Table, a replica of the Grail Table (itself modeled after the table of the Last Supper). Merlin also directs Arthur's major victories over his rebellious barons.

These two romances are followed chronologically (but preceded in order of composition) by the *Lancelot Proper, La Queste del saint Graal* (*The Quest for the Holy Grail*)*, and *La Mort Artu* (*The Death of Arthur*)*. The first of these, constituting fully half of the entire cycle, presents Lancelot's youth, his love for Guenevere, and a long series of exploits that he performs in her service. The second depicts the Grail Quest undertaken by a number of knights (Gawain, Bors, Perceval, and others) but finally accomplished by the chosen hero, Galahad. Concluding the cycle, *The Death of Arthur* traces the tragic decline and dissolution of the Arthurian world, due in large part to the sin of Lancelot and Guenevere, and closes with an account of the death of the king.

The Vulgate Cycle was soon followed by an anonymous Post-Vulgate, based on the earlier cycle but characterized by the omission of the *Lancelot Proper* and, consequently, of the emphasis on Lancelot and Guenevere. The second cycle thus focuses squarely on the Grail quest and related pious themes. It includes versions of the other four romances represented in the Vulgate and even borrows the text of the *Merlin* intact; on the other hand, the Post-Vulgate *Death of Arthur* romance is a significantly abridged adaptation of its model. Without a *Lancelot Proper,* the second cycle is far shorter than the first, but it remains daunting nonetheless in its dimensions and in its complexity.

The Post-Vulgate Cycle is further complicated for modern scholars and readers— and this is a complication almost beyond resolution—by the fact that some portions of the Old French text have long since disappeared, whereas others have survived only in fragments or in translations into Portuguese and Spanish. Extraordinary scholarly efforts, especially by Fanni Bogdanow, have made it possible to reconstitute significant portions of the texts.

The importance of the Vulgate Cycle and, to a only slightly lesser extent, of the Post-Vulgate is almost incalculable. Portions of them (most often the Vulgate *Lancelot-Quest-Death of Arthur*) were translated or adapted into a number of other languages. Authors rendered much of the Vulgate narrative into German and Dutch, while the *Quest* was translated into Irish and Welsh. Italian and Hispanic authors too translated it or drew on it, although, as suggested, the Post-Vulgate proved more influential on the Iberian Peninsula than did the Vulgate.

But for English-speaking readers, the importance of the Vulgate is indicated most clearly by its influence on Sir Thomas Malory, who took the cycle as the principal of his numerous sources: although each part of his work has multiple sources, his first, third, sixth, seventh, and eighth tales were drawn largely or principally from the Vulgate Cycle. He even gave his work, *Le Morte Darthur,* a title that indicates his indebtedness not only to related English romances like the Alliterative *Morte Arthure* and the Stanzaic *Le Morte Arthur* but to the final component of the Old French cycle.

THE STORY OF MERLIN

The Story of Merlin depicts the role of the seer Merlin in the conception and birth of Arthur, who is to rescue Britain from the Saxons and establish an ideal kingdom. It follows Arthur's career as he is designated king by the magical sign of the Swolrd in the Stone, triumphs over his rebellious barons and drives out the Saxons. With his narriage to Guinevere, he acquires the Round Table, and sets up the famous order of knighthood which is at the centre of his power.

The *Merlin* was writtne after the last three romances of the Vulgate Cycle were already complete, and serves as a prologue to the history of Arthur, just as the *History of the Holy Grail* is the prologue to the adventures of the Grail.

See the introduction in volume I for a full discussion of the Vulgate Cycle. The volumes in the set are listed oposite the title page. A complete chapter summary of the cycle and an index of names is to be found in volume X.

THE STORY OF MERLIN

TRANSLATED BY RUPERT T. PICKENS

THE STORY OF MERLIN

1. MERLIN'S CONCEPTION AND CHILDHOOD DEEDS.*

[3] In this part the story says that the devil grew very angry after Our Lord had gone to Hell and freed Adam and Eve and as many others as He pleased, so that when the devils saw it they were very much afraid and they were greatly astounded by it.

So they met and said, "Who is this who so overwhelms us that no power we have can stop Him from doing whatever He pleases? We did not believe that any man born of woman could fail to belong to us, yet He overwhelms us! How can He have been born? For we have not seen in Him any leanings for earthly delights such as we have seen in all other people."

Another devil then answered them and said, "He has been able to harm us because we thought that we could overcome Him. Remember, the prophets said that the Son of God would come to earth to save sinners, descendants of Eve and Adam, as many as He pleased. And we went and took those who said this and tormented them more than the others. Yet, it seemed that our torture did not hurt them, rather they brought solace to the other sinners by telling them that the One who would deliver them would come down to earth.

"What the prophets said has now happened, and He has taken from us all those we had won for ourselves, so that we cannot lay claim to any of them, and He has also taken away all the others with such might that we cannot understand it. Don't you know that He washes them in water in His own name and that they are baptized in that water in the name of the Father and the Son and the Holy Ghost? By this we should know that we have lost them, and we have no power over them until they come back to us through their own deeds. So our strength fails, for He has taken it from us. What's more, He has left ministers on earth who will go on saving souls, so long as they do not do our works, if they are willing to repent and give up our works and do what their teachers command. This is how they are utterly lost to us.

---

* Corresponds to Sommer II, 3-20. This translation is based primarily on the second volume of Sommer's edition of the Vulgate (see bibliography following introduction), but it also makes use of Micha's edition of *Merlin,* which includes the material contained in approximately the first eighty-eight pages of Sommer. The main source is cited in the notes simply as "Sommer," with vol. II understood.

"He has indeed provided spiritual substance who came down to earth to save humankind and lowered Himself to be born of a woman and suffer the torments of the world. He came without our knowledge and not through the fleshly lust of a man or a woman, though we saw Him and assailed Him in every way we could. When we had put Him to the test and seen that we could not find any of our works in Him, He was willing to die to save human creatures. He loved them greatly indeed, [4] since He wanted to undergo such great suffering to have them for Himself and take them from us.

"And we must work very hard to get them back,* so that He will not have taken anything from us that is ours by right, and we must trick Him and work our way so that they cannot find their way back or even speak with those through whom they might have forgiveness."

Then they all said together, "We have lost everything, since He can forgive sins until the end of humankind, if He can find people doing His works, whereby they are His. And even though they do our works all the time, they will be lost to us if they repent. Thus, we have lost everything!"

Then they began talking all at the same time and said, "The ones who have hurt us most are those who tell the news of His coming down to earth: they are the ones through whom the great harm has come to us. The more they said it, the more we tortured them, so it seems that He came all the more quickly to help them and to save them from the torments we worked on them. But how can *we* have someone who might speak out and tell about our aims, our deeds, and our ways of life—who might have the power, like us, to know things done and said and past? If we had someone who had that power and who knew those things, and if he were on earth with other folk, then he could help us trick them just as the prophets who were with us tricked us, those who told us what we did not believe could happen. And he could also foretell things that were to come about and be said soon and far in the future, so that he would be believed by everybody. Anyone who can bring about such a thing will have worked wonders!"

Then one of them said, "I don't have the power to conceive or to cause a woman to conceive. But if I had that power, I would do it well! For I know of a woman who gladly does everything I want. And there is among us," he went on, "one who can take on the likeness of a man and lie with a woman, so long as he does it as secretly as he can." They undertook to engender a man who would teach the others. The devils were mad for thinking that Our Lord did not know this plan.

Thus the devil undertook† to engender a man in his likeness and mind in order to ensnare the people‡ of Jesus Christ. We can be very certain that the devil is evil and deceitful.

So the council ended, and all of them agreed to the plan. The one who said that he had power over the woman did not tarry, but came to where she was as fast as he could, and he found her just as he had hoped. She granted the devil what belonged

---

*   *"Avoir* ("to have") in Sommer's text (4, l. 1), *ravoir* ("to get back") in Micha (1, l. 47).

†   Supplied from Micha (1, l. 89); Sommer's text has *aprinst* ("learned, taught.") (4, l. 29).

‡   Sommer's text, along with several manuscripts consulted by Micha, has *lomme ihesu crist* ("the man Jesus Christ." or "the man of Jesus Christ.") (4, 30), while Micha's text bears *le Jhesu Crist* (1, ll. 90-91), unusual because of the article "the."

to him: everything she had and all she did. She was the wife of a very rich man who had a great plenty of livestock and other goods. He had three daughters and one son by the woman of whom the devil had his share.

The devil did not forget what he was about. He yearned to trick the man, so he went to the fields. He had asked the woman how he might ensnare him, and she said that he could not do so in any way unless he upset him: "If you take what belongs to him, he will be distraught."

The devil then went straight to the fields where the good man's cattle were, [5] and he killed quite a lot of them. And when the herdsmen saw the livestock dying in the fields, they were quite astonished, so they went to their lord and told him about their livestock's sickness. And when the gentleman heard that, he was bewildered that his animals were dying, and he asked the herdsmen if they knew why this was, but they did not.

Thus ended what happened that day. And when the devil saw that the man was so upset for so little, it seemed to him that if he could do him such great harm that he was truly distraught, then he could do with him as he wanted. So he came back to the livestock. There were ten beautiful horses belonging to the worthy man; he killed them all at once. And when the good man saw that things were going so badly for him, he was deeply shaken, and, overcome with grief, he said something very foolish, for he commended to the devils all he had owned and all he had left.

When the devil learned that he had bestowed such a gift, he was very happy. And he tried all the more to do him worse harm, so that the worthy man was bereft of all his livestock and became utterly distraught. And in his great anger, he fled human fellowship and cared nothing for anyone.

When the devil saw that he had taken from him the companionship of his fellows, he knew that he could do with him what he wanted. Then the devil visited the good man's most fair son and strangled him in his bed, and when morning came he was found dead. When the father saw that he had lost his little boy, he lost all hope and went grievously awry in his beliefs. The devil then saw that the gentleman had lost his faith and that he could not get it back, and he was very glad about it.

And the devil made the woman through whom he had won everything climb upon a chest in her cellar. She lashed a rope about the joist and tied it around her neck; she then jumped down, hanging herself and strangling herself to death. In the morning she was found hanging, and when the worthy man learned that he had lost his wife as well as his son, his sorrow was so great that he was stricken with an illness that killed him.

The devil does such things to those whom he wants to trick into doing his will. And when he had done all that, he was quite gladdened, and he began thinking how he might beguile the three daughters who were left. There was a young squire who very often did this devil's bidding. He took him to where the maidens were, and he became acquainted with one of them. He spent so much time with her that, by his deeds and words, he was at last able to seduce her. When he had done so, he was very happy. And the devil did not want to hide his victory; rather, he wanted to flaunt it openly before people so the shame would grow; thus the devil made known what he had done by his efforts alone, and many people found out about it

In that time it was a custom that a woman taken in adultery would be brought to justice unless she yielded herself fully to all men. And because the devil always wants to shame those who belong to him, he made what had happened known far and wide. The squire fled, and the woman was seized and brought to trial before the judges. The judges were filled with sorrow because of the love they bore the worthy man whose daughter she was, and they said, "You can be amazed at what has happened to the good man whose daughter this was, how she has fallen in such a short time! Not long ago he was one of the wealthiest men in this country, and what dreadful things have befallen him!"

They said that they would have her buried [6] alive at night for the shame she had brought to her friends. This is how the devil treats those who consent to do his will.

In that land there was a good confessor, a worthy man, who heard about those wonders. He came to the two sisters who were left, the eldest and the youngest, and he comforted them and told to them how what had happened to their father, their mother, their brother, and their sister had come about. And they answered that they did not know anything about it, only that we believe God hates us, so He allows us to undergo this torment."

And the worthy priest said to them, "What you say is not true or fitting. God hates no one, rather He is sorry when sinners hate themselves. You must understand that what has happened came about through the devil's work. And did you know that your sister, whom you have lost so shamefully, was as she was?"

They answered, "We knew nothing about it."

The good priest said to them, "Keep yourselves from evil works, for evil works take the sinner to a bad end."

The good man taught them a great deal and instructed them in many things. The youngest daughter wanted him to be burned to ashes, but what the worthy priest had said meant a great deal to the eldest. He taught her the creed and how to believe in the powers of Jesus Christ. She put great stock in it and bent her mind to what the good man taught her. He said to her, "If you believe truly what I teach you and tell you, many good things will come to you. You will be my daughter and my friend in God. As long as you behave in accordance with my advice, I'll never fail to help you in any hour of need, with the aid of Our Lord. Don't be afraid, for God will help you if you stay with Him. Come to me often, for my abode will not be far from here."

Thus the wise priest counseled the two daughters; he set them on the right path, and they put their faith in him because of the good words he spoke to them. And when the devil became aware of this, he was sorely grieved and feared that he might lose the two daughters. So he worked out a way to ensnare them. Nearby lived a woman who many times had done what he wanted. The devil took that woman and sent her to the youngest daughter—the woman did not dare speak to the eldest because she saw that she behaved so humbly. She took the younger sister aside to speak to her and asked her a great deal about the way she lived and what she did. She also asked her, "What kind of life does your sister lead? Is she happy or sullen?"

And she answered, "My sister is so worried about the misfortunes that have befallen us that she does not show a cheerful face to me or to anyone else. And a good priest who always speaks to her about God has so turned her to his ways that she does nothing but what he wishes."

The woman then said to her, "What a waste that your fair body was ever born! For it will never know delight as long as you are with your sister. God! if you only knew, dear friend, the joy that other women have, you would scorn what you are now! For we have such joy when we are with our lovers that, if we lived only on handouts, we would be happier than you are even if you had all the wealth in the world. God! a woman's pleasures are worthless if she does not have a man's company. Dear friend," she went on, "I tell you this because otherwise you will never [7] have that or know what it's like to take delight from a man. And I will tell you why. Your sister is older than you, and she will have a man first. And when she has one for herself, she won't care about you. So you have lost all chances of knowing the pleasures of your lovely body, and that's a shame!"

When the maiden understood the meaning of what the woman had told her, she answered, "How would I dare do what you say? My sister was put to death!"

And she answered, "Your sister behaved very foolishly. But if you trust me, you will know your body's every delight and not be condemned for it."

"I don't know how," said the maiden, "nor would I ever dare talk about it."

When the devil heard this, he was glad indeed; he was sure that he would have her just as he wanted, so he sent his woman away. When the woman had gone, the girl thought about what she had said. That night, as she was going to bed, she looked at her lovely body and said, "The good woman indeed told me the truth when she said that I was being wasted."

In the morning, when she got up, she did not dally, for the devil had taken hold of her, and she sent for the woman. When she came, she said to her, "You told me the truth when you said that my sister doesn't care about me."

And she answered, "I was sure of it, and she will care even less about you when she has fulfillment. We women are made for just one thing: taking our delight from men."

Then the girl said, "I would very willingly do so if I were not afraid of being put to death."

"They would do that only if you behaved as foolishly as your sister. But I will teach you how to do what you want."

Then she answered, "Tell me and I will believe your counsel."

The woman said to her, "You will give yourself up to all men, this is how you will avoid your worries. And you will say that you can't live with your sister any longer. You will do what you will with your lovely body; no judge can say anything about it, and you will be out of harm's way. But after you have led such a life for a while, you will find a good man who will be very glad to have you because of your great inheritance. Thus you will have every kind of enjoyment in this world."

The girl promised her that she would do just as she said, and she did. She left her sister and gave her body up to all men at the bidding of that woman, and the devil was very gleeful about it.

When her sister found out that she was behaving so, she went to the wise priest, sure that he would tell her what to think about it, for she was quite worried and felt great sorrow for her sister whom she had lost in such a way. When the good man saw how sorrowful she was, he felt great sadness and said to her, "Cross yourself and commend yourself to God, for I see that you are very much afraid."

She said, "I have a right to be, for I have lost my sister."

She told him what she knew and said to him outright that her sister had given herself up to all men. When the good man heard this amazing news, he grew frightened and said to her, "The devil is still around you, and he will not stop until he has ensnared both of you, unless God takes care of you."

She asked him, "Sir, how could I avoid it? There is nothing in this world that I fear more than being tricked by him."

The good man said to her, "If you believe me, he will not trick you."

She answered, "I will believe everything you [8] tell me."

And he said, "Then don't you believe in the Father and the Son and the Holy Ghost? Don't you believe that these three Beings are one and the same in God and in the Trinity? And that Our Lord came to earth to save the sinners who wanted to believe in baptism and in Holy Church's and her ministers' other sacraments that He left on earth to save those who would believe in His name and to keep them on the right path?"

She said, "Just as you have taught me, so I believe it, and may He truly protect me so that no devil can entrap me."

The good man said, "If you believe it as truly as you say, no kind of devil or evil thing can harm you. And I bid you, do not let yourself be wrathful, for the devil likes most to be where wrath is. This is why you must guard against evil deeds and all stumbling blocks that come your way, and against every kind of anger. My dear friend, come to me and tell me everything, just as it happens to you, that makes you guilty before Our Lord, before all saints, and before all creatures who believe in God. And every time you go to bed and get out of bed, cross yourself in the name of the Father and the Son and the Holy Ghost, and in the name of that cross where He suffered death, because of the devil, to keep sinners from the death of Hell.

"If you do this," said the good man, "you will not have to worry about any devil. And make sure that there is light wherever you lie down, for a devil does not willingly come where light is."

Thus the wise priest taught the maiden, who was very much afraid that the devil would ensnare her. Afterwards the young woman went away to her house, strongly believing* and lowering herself before her Creator and before the poor of the land.

And the good men and women came to her and said, "In faith, dear friend, you must truly be worried about your dead brother and the torment that has befallen your father and mother and sisters. But take our counsel to heart, for you are a very wealthy woman and you have a very good inheritance, and some gentleman will be very glad to have you."

And she answered them, "May Our Lord uphold me according to what He knows I need."

---

*   Supplied from Micha (5, ll. 51-52), not in Sommer's text (8, l. 23).

This is how the young woman behaved for two good years or more, so that the devil could not trick her, nor did he learn of any evil thing she might have done, and he was most distraught. He knew that he could not entrap her unless he made her forget what the worthy priest had taught her and become upset, for she did not care about doing such things.

Then it happened that on a Saturday night her sister went into the house where she was in order to upset* her and to see if she could ensnare her for the devil. And it was very late in the night when she came, and she brought with her a crowd of lowborn young men, and they all came into the house. When the elder sister saw her, she grew very angry and said to her, "Dear sister, as long as you want to lead this kind of life, you must not come here, for people would cast blame on me, and I don't need that."

When the younger heard her sister say that she would be blamed because of her, she grew angry in turn [9] and spoke like a woman in whom the devil dwelled. She threatened her sister, and she said that the good priest loved her in sin and that, if people found out about it, she would be burned alive.

When the elder heard her sister accuse her of such devilry, she grew even angrier and told her to leave the house, but the younger said that she was as much her father's daughter as her sister was and she would not leave. The elder saw that she refused to leave, so she took her by the shoulders, meaning to throw her out, but she defended herself, and the young men who had come with her took hold of her sister and beat her dreadfully. But as soon as she could get away, she ran into a room all by herself, lay down on her bed with all her clothes on, and wept bitterly.

When the devil saw her alone and so upset, he was very glad and said, "Now this woman has turned out well!"

And he reminded her of times before the deaths of her father and mother and sister† and brother. When she recalled all these things, she began to weep and to show her deep sorrow and great anger, and in this distress, she fell asleep. When the devil was sure that she had forgotten everything the good priest had told her, he said, "Now has this woman been led away from her teacher's watchful eye. Now we can put our man into her."

This one devil had the power to lie with a woman and get her with child. Then he was all ready, and he lay with her carnally as she slept, and she conceived. After this had been done, the young woman awoke. As she was awakening, she remembered the wise priest, so she crossed herself and said, "Holy Lady Mary, what has happened to me? I feel so much worse than when I went to bed. Fair, glorious Mother of God, pray your dear Son to keep my soul and defend my body from torment and from the might of the devil."

Then she got up and began looking for the one who had done this thing to her, for she thought she could find him. She ran to the door of the room, but found it locked; she looked everywhere in her room, but found no one. It was then that she understood that she had been tricked by a devil. She began wailing, softly

---

*   *Concheuoir* ("conceive") in Sommer's text (8, l. 26), *couroucier* (the reading adopted) in the other manuscripts.
†   The text has the plural *ses suers* (9, l. 11), but the death of only one sister is actually depicted.

calling out to Our Lord and entreating him not to allow anyone to shame her in this world.

Night went by and day came. As soon as it was light, the devil took the younger sister away, for she had done well in what he had brought her there to do. When she and the young men had gone, the elder sister came out of her room in great distress. She called her manservant and told him to bring two women. As soon as they had come, she left and made her way until she found her confessor.

When he saw her he said to her, "You are in trouble, for I see that you are very frightened."

"Sir," she told him, "something has happened to me that has never happened to any other woman. I come to you so that you'll tell me what to do, for you have said to me that people cannot commit such a great sin that, if they confess it and repent of it and do whatever their confessor tells them, it will not be forgiven. Sir," she went on, "I have sinned, and you should know that I've been ensnared by a devil."

Then she told him how her sister came to the house, how she grew angry with her, how she and the young men beat her, how she went to her room burning with wrath and closed the door against her, and how, because of her great anger and the distress she felt, she forgot to cross herself "and all the commands you gave me as well. When I awoke I found myself shamed and deflowered. My room was closed as fast as when I locked it myself, and I did not find a soul there, [10] so I do not know who did this to me. Sir, I have been betrayed, and I beg you, have pity. If my body suffers torment, please pray for my soul so that it will not be lost."

When the good man had heard everything she had to tell him, he was greatly astounded, and he did not believe anything she told him, for he had never heard tell of such a wonder. So he answered her* and said to her, "You are all full of devils and devils dwell in you! From what you tell me, how can I hear your confession and give you penance, since I truly believe that you are lying?† For never was a woman deflowered when she did not know by whom, unless she could not see the man who did it to her. And you want me to believe that such a wonder happened to you!"

She answered, "May God keep me from torment, I've told you the truth."

And the worthy priest said to her, "If it is as you say, you will find out well enough. Yet you did a great sin when you broke the vow I gave you to take. And because you transgressed, I will impose a penance on you today: that for as long as you live you will eat only once on Fridays. And for what you tell me about lustful behavior, although I do not believe you, I must impose another penance for all the days you will live henceforth, if you are willing to accept it just as I say."

She said, "Sir, you will never order me to do anything that I won't do my utmost to accomplish."

And he answered, "God grant it to you. Do you mean," he went on, "to abide in the counsel of God and Holy Church and in the mercy of Jesus Christ, who redeemed us with the worthy ransom of His own precious blood and death? Is

*   Supplied from Micha (7, ll. 22-25); Sommer's text omits everything after "heard" (10, l. 3).
†   Supplied from Micha (7, ll. 27-28); Sommer's text omits the reference to lying (10, l. 5).

this a true confession and a sincere repentance, sworn to on your body and soul—everything you have told me by your own mouth? Do you hold it in your heart and body to be true in every way, in word and in deed?"*

She answered, "I will very willingly hold to everything just as you have said it, God willing."

"As I believe in God," he said, "I believe that if what you have told me is true, you need not be afraid."

"Sir," she said, "What I have said to you is true, may God keep me from an unworthy death and from any rebuke."

And the good man answered, "You have sworn to me to do your penance and to avoid sin."

"Sir, that is true."

And he said to her, "Then you have forsworn lasciviousness, and I forbid you for all time to engage in it, except for that which comes while you are asleep; no one can keep from that. Now see if you can."

She answered, "Yes, indeed I will. If you pledge yourself as a guarantee that I am not damned for that one time, then never will any other overwhelm me."

"For this," he answered, "I will stand as your pledge before God by His command, just as surely as He put you on this earth."

The woman accepted her penance just as he imposed it, and she wept because she repented mightily. The worthy priest made the sign of the cross and blessed her, and he sent her on her way as he knew best, in the love of Christ Jesus. And he worried about how what she had told him could be true, and at last he understood that she must have been ensnared by the devil. So he called her and took her to the holy water and had her drink of it in the name of the Father and the Son and the Holy Ghost; he also sprinkled it on her and said, "Do not forget the commandments I have given you. And any time you need me, come back."

Again he blessed her with the sign of the cross and commended her to God, and she set out on the way back to her house. And she led a very good and simple life. When the devil saw that he had lost her—and he did not see that she was behaving otherwise than she always had—he became very angry.

So she was until the seed she bore in her body could no longer be hidden. She grew so big that the other women noticed it and stared [11] at her belly. They asked her if she was with child and who the man was that had done it to her. She answered, "May God bring me into joy, but I don't know and I never knew."

They said to her, "Have so many men lain with you that you don't know which one to accuse?"

But she answered, "May it not please God that I give birth to the child if ever to my knowledge anything happened to me that should bring me to this."

When they heard this they crossed themselves and said, "Dear friend, that could not be, nor did that ever happen to you or anyone else. Perhaps you love the man who did this to you so much, as much as or more than you love yourself, so that you're not willing to name him. But what a shame for you that, as soon as the judges learn about it, you will have to die!"

---

* The last sentence is supplied from Micha (7, ll.. 48-50), not in Sommer's text (10, l.19).

When she heard that she would have to die because of it, she was filled with great dread, and she said, "God save my soul, but I never saw or knew the one who has done this to me."

The women laughed at her* and thought she was crazy, and they said, "What a shame about your lovely homestead, its good land and fine buildings, for it will soon be lost."

When she heard this she was greatly frightened, and she went off to her confessor and told him what the women had said to her. The good man saw that she was pregnant with a living child, and he was quite amazed. "Dear sister," he said to her, "have you faithfully kept the penance I imposed on you?"

"Yes, sir," she answered, "and I have done nothing wrong."

"And did this wonder ever happen to you more than one time?"

She answered no, and he was astounded and wrote down the hour and the night just as she had told to him, and he said that she had to be quite sure about it:

"And when the child who is in you is born, I am bound to know if you have lied to me. And I have strong faith in God that, if it is just as you have told me, you will not have to fear death. But you will have reason to be afraid when the judges find out, for they will arrest you just to have your buildings and your good land, yet they will say that they are bringing you to justice. And when you have been arrested, let me know and I will come to comfort you and help you if I can. God will help you: He will be with you if things are as you say."

Then he said, "Go home and don't worry; lead a good life, for a good life helps bring people to a good end."

So the young woman went back home that night and lived very quietly until the judges came to the region. And when they found out what had happened to her, they sent men to her house to get her; they arrested her and took her away with them. As soon as she was taken prisoner, she sent for the same good priest who had always counseled her; and when he found out about her, he came to her as fast as he could.

When he had come there, they called for him, and he found that the judges had already had the young woman brought before them. The good man gave them the young woman's testimony, and he said that she did not believe she needed to fear anyone. But the judges said to him, "Do you think a woman can become pregnant and have a child without lying with a man?"

The good man answered, "I won't tell you everything I know about it, but I can certainly tell you this: if you will believe me, you won't bring her to justice until she has had the child. It would not be right or just otherwise: the child has not deserved death, since it did not commit the sin, and the child has done nothing wrong in the sins of the mother."

The judges answered, "We will do as you advise."

And the good man said, "If you follow my advice, you [12] will keep her well guarded and locked in a tower where she cannot do anything foolish. Lock two women up with her to help her give birth when she needs it, and don't let them

---

*   Supplied from Micha (8, 1l. 27-28); instead of *s'en rient* ("laughed at her about it."), Sommer's text has *sen vont* (11, l. 12): "go away."

out either. My advice is to leave her there until she has the child and until the child can eat by itself and ask for what it needs. And then, if you are bent* on doing something more, do what you please. If you have faith in me, you will do as I advise; if you want to do otherwise, I can't do any more about it."

And the judges answered, "It seems to us that what you say is right."

They did everything just as the good man had set it forth. They put the young woman in a very strong stone house and had all the doorways walled up. And they locked up two women with her, the most skilled they could find for doing what had to be done. High up they left one window open through which they could pull up whatever they needed. When the good man saw this, he spoke to the young woman through the window and said to her, "When your child is born, have it baptized as soon as you can. And when you are put outside, the judges will want to try you, so send for me."

So she stayed a long time in the tower. The judges took care of everything she needed and had it brought to her. She was inside there so long that at last she had her child as it pleased God. And when he was born, he unavoidably had the power and the mind of a devil, and the cunning, because he was sired by one.

But the devil had behaved most unwisely, for Our Lord had bought true repentance with His death. The devil had ensnared the young woman through deceit and trickery while she was asleep. As soon as she felt that she had been beguiled, she confessed and cried out for mercy where she ought. And when she cried out, she put herself under the mercy and the commandments of the Lord God and Holy Church. This is why God did not want the child to lose, because of the devil, anything that belonged to him; rather He allowed the child to have what was his by right. Therefore, He bestowed on him the devils' art of knowing things that are done, said, and past—all this he knew. And Our Lord, who is all-knowing, knew, by the mother's repentance, by her good confession, by the cleansing of confession, and by the true repentance he knew to be in her heart, that she had not wanted or willed what had happened to her. By the power of the baptism with which the child was washed in the font, Our Lord willed that the sin of the mother should not harm him. And He also gave him the sense and the power to know the future.

This is the reason why he knew the things that were done, spoken, and past: he inherited this from the devil. Moreover, he knew things that were to come; Our Lord willed that he should know things contrary to those he knew from the other side. Now he could turn to whichever side he wanted, for if he wished, he could give the devils their due, or else His to God just as well.

Thus was he born. And when the women had received him, they were all deeply frightened, for they saw that he was hairier than they had ever seen any other child. After they had shown him to his mother she crossed herself and said, "This child frightens me very much."

And the [13] other women said, "And we are so afraid of him that we can scarcely hold him."

She said to them, "Send him down and have him baptized."

---

* In Sommer's text (12, l. 5), *vaer/veer* ("to forbid") is confused with *baer/beer* ("to strive, be intent."). Sommer needlessly negates the verb (see his n. 1, and Micha, 9, l. 28, and note).

They asked her, "What do you want him named?"

And she answered, "The same as my father's name."

Then they put him into a basket and sent him down with a rope, then they gave orders to have him baptized: "let him bear the name of his grandfather on his mother's side; that good man was called Merlin by his father."

Thus the child was baptized and named Merlin after his grandfather. He was then given to his mother to be nursed, for no other woman dared do so. His mother nursed him until he was nine months old. The women who were with her told her many times that they were quite amazed that the child, who was so hairy, was only nine months old, yet he looked as if he were two years old or more.

Then, some time later, after the child was eighteen months of age, the two women said to the mother, "Lady, we must leave this place; it seems to us that we have been here long enough."

And she answered, "As soon as you are gone they will bring me to trial."

"We can do no more, and we can't stay here forever."

She wept and cried out for mercy: for God's sake, could they not bear to stay awhile longer?

They went off to a window while the mother held her child in her arms and sat and wept very bitterly and said, "Dear son, I will be put to death because of you, and I haven't deserved it; no one knows the truth, yet I am not believed, so I will have to die."

She spoke these words to her son and said that it was a great shame that God had allowed him to be born.

And while she wept and wailed to Our Lord, the child looked at her and said with a smile, "Never will you die for what has happened to you because of me."

When the mother heard him, her heart nearly stopped beating, and she became frightened. Her arms went limp and she dropped him; he fell to the floor and screamed. The women who were at the window ran to her, for they were afraid she wanted to kill the child. When they came to her, they both asked her, "Why did your child fall? I think that you want to kill him!"

She answered, "I never meant to do that, but he fell out of my arms because of a great wonder. He spoke to me; my arms grew weak, and my whole body too, and that is why he fell."

They asked her, "Then what did he say to you?"

"He told me that I would never be put to death because of him."

Very shaken, they answered her: "He will say yet other things."

Then they took him with them and began to speak to him in order to find out whether he would talk, but it did not seem that he would. He uttered not a word, until at length the mother said to the two women, "Threaten me and say that I will be burned because of my son, and I will hold him in my arms and you will hear whether he is willing to speak."

Then his mother took him, for she yearned for him to speak so that the women could hear him, and she began to weep and cry out. The women said, "It will be a great shame for you who are so beautiful to be burned because of this creature; it would have been better if he had not been born."

And he answered, "You are lying. My mother has made you say this."

When they heard him speak, they ran away very frightened and said, "He is not a child, but a devil who knows what we have said."

Then they began to ask him things and tried to get him to speak, but he only said to them, "Leave my mother in peace, for [14] you are foolish and more sinful than she is."

When they heard this, they were greatly amazed and said, "This wonder cannot be hidden. We will tell the people down there that he talks."

They then went to the window, called the people, and told them what they had heard. And when they heard this wonder, they said that it was high time for the woman to be brought to trial. So they had letters written and summoned every judge to be there within forty days to hold court. When the letters had been sent out, and the mother knew the day of her execution, she became very frightened and sent word about it to the good man who was her confessor.

And so things were until seven days before the time she was to be burned, when the child was walking about the tower and saw his mother weeping. He began to smile and to look very happy. And the women said to him, "Now you care very little that she weeps because within the week she will be burned on your account. It was a cursed hour, unless it was God's doing, when you were ever born, for she is being put to death because of you."

He answered, "Dear mother, they are lying. No one will ever be so bold as to dare lay a hand on you as long as I am alive, much less put you to death—except God."

When his mother and the women heard him, they were very glad and said, "The child who can say this will in time be very wise."

So it was until the day that had been set. The women were taken out of the tower, and the mother carried the child in her arms. The judges talked to the two women away from the others. They asked them if it was true that the child could speak, and they told them everything they had heard him say. When the judges heard this, they were very greatly amazed and said that he would have to know many words to save his mother. So they came back to where the others were. And the young woman's confessor had come.

Then one of the judges said to Merlin's mother, "Get yourself ready, for you must be put to death."

She answered, "Sir, please, I would like to talk alone with this good man." And they gave her leave to do so.

She and the wise priest went into a room while the child stayed outside (and many people tried to get him to speak, but he would have nothing to do with it). The mother spoke very pitifully to her confessor and wept. And the good man asked her, "Is it true that your child talks, just as they say?"

"Yes, sir," she said, and she told him everything she had heard him say.

After the good man had listened to her, he said, "Something wonderful will come of this."

Then they came out and went over to the judges, and the young woman wore nothing but her shift, which had a mantle. She found her child outside the chamber, took him in her arms, and went before the judges. When the judges saw her, they asked her, "Who is the father of this child? Be careful not to hide anything."

And she said, "I see full well that I am condemned to die! May God never take pity on me or grant me mercy if I ever saw the father or knew him, or if ever I gave myself to any man so that I should have a child by him."

The judge answered, "We don't think that could be true, so we'll ask the other women if what you would have us believe could be true. For no one has ever heard such a wonder!"

The judges drew to one side and called the women over to meet with them (and there were many of them there that day), and one of the judges spoke out and said, "You ladies who [15] have come here, has it ever happened to any of you, or to any other woman you have ever heard about, that a woman could conceive and have a child without being with a man?"

And they said that no woman could have a child or get pregnant unless she had known a man carnally. When the judges heard that, they went back to Merlin's mother and told what they had found from the other women and said that justice should be done. For what she would have them understand did not seem just or right.

Then Merlin sprang forward and said that she would not be burned so soon, "for if all those who have been with someone other than their husbands or wives were brought to justice," he went on, "then he would already have burned half* or more of the men and women who are here. I know about their behavior just as well as they themselves do. If I wanted to talk about it, I would have everything brought out into the open right here. You can be sure that my mother is not guilty of what you accuse her of. The guilt she did have in it this good man took upon himself. If you do not believe me, ask him."

The judges then called the wise priest and asked him whether it was true "that she told you that it had happened to her in such and such a way."

He answered that she had done nothing in the world wrong: "She herself told me how she was tricked, and she told me about the wonder of this child with whom she became pregnant. It happened to her while she was asleep and with no feelings of pleasure, nor does she know by whom the child was fathered. She confessed everything and has been repentant for so long that it cannot by rights harm her, if her conscience is clear, before God or before the world."

The child then went forward and said to the good man, "You have written down the hour and the night when I was conceived, and you can reckon when I was born and at what time. By this you can show most of the things my mother has done."

And the good priest said to him, "I don't know how you happen to know more than all of us together."

The two women were called, and they told before the judges when the conception happened, how long the pregnancy lasted, and when the birth took place. By this† and what the good man had written down, they found it to be as Merlin had said. But the judge answered that she would not be acquitted unless she said who the father was "in such a way that we can believe it."

---

    *   Sommer's text reads *.ii. pars* (15, l. 11): "two parts"; the intent in the expression is to suggest a very significant portion.

    †   Not in Sommer's text (15, l. 27), where the comparison is only implicit.

The child grew angry and said to the judge, "I know my father better than you know yours, and your mother knows better who sired you than mine knows who fathered me."

The judge grew angry and said, "If you have anything to say about my mother, I will certainly hold it to be the truth!"

He answered, "I can say enough about her so that, if you made the right judgment, she would deserve death more than my mother. And if I make you admit this, you must leave my mother in peace, for she is not guilty of what people blame her for, and everything she said about my conception was true."

And when the judge heard this, he became very angry indeed, and said, "You have truly rescued your mother from being burned! You can be sure that if you cannot say enough about my mother to make me believe you and leave your mother in peace, I will burn you with her!"

Then they set a day to meet again in two weeks, and the judge sent for his mother. And he had the child and his mother guarded well; he himself went with the guards many times, and many times he tried to get the child to talk about his mother, but [16] never during the whole two weeks could they draw a word out of him. And when the judge's mother came, they brought them out of prison and took them before the people.

Then the judge said, "Here is my mother, about whom you must speak."

The child answered, "You are not nearly as clever as you think you are. Go, take your mother into a house by yourselves and call your most intimate counsellors, and I will call the counsellors of my mother, that is, the almighty God and her confessor."

Those who heard him were so astonished that hardly anyone could find an answer, but the judge recognized that he spoke wisely. Then the child asked one and all, "If I free my mother from this man justly, need she fear the others?"

And they all answered, "If she is freed by him, no one else will ever hold her accountable for anything concerning this."

Then they went into a room: the judge took his mother there and two men among his closest friends, and the child took his mother's confessor. After they had gathered, the judge said, "Now say what you will about my mother whereby your mother will be acquitted."

The child answered, "I will never say anything about your mother whereby mine should be acquitted—I will not say whether she has done any misdeed—for I am not willing to defend my mother against what is wrong. Rather, I mean to uphold the right of the Lord God—and hers. You can be sure that my mother has not deserved the torment you wish to give her; if you will believe my advice, you will acquit my mother and let yours be tried."

The judge answered, "You won't get away from me like that, for you must say more."

The child said, 'You promised me and my mother too that I could defend her."

"This is true," answered the judge, "and we are gathered here to hear what you will say concerning my mother."

"You want," said the child, "to burn my mother and me as well because she will not say and does not know who my father is. But if I wanted her to, she could say that better than you can say who your father is."

And the judge said, "Dear mother, was I not the son of your lawful husband?"

The mother answered, "For God's sake, dear son, whose son would you then be but my husband's who is now dead?"

"Lady, lady, you must tell the truth," said the child. "Nevertheless, if your son were willing to acquit my mother and me, I would be satisfied."

But the judge answered, "*I* will not be satisfied!"

"What you'll learn from your mother's testimony," said the child, "is that your father is still alive."

When those who were there heard him, they were amazed. Then the child said to the judge's mother, "You must tell your son whose son he is."

The lady crossed herself and said, "The devil Satan, and I never told him!"

The child answered her, "You know it's true that he is not the son of the man he thinks."

The lady was abashed and asked him, "Whose then?"

And he said to her, "By these signs you know very well indeed that he is the son of your priest, that the first time you had intercourse with him you said that you were afraid of getting pregnant, that he told you you would never have a child by him, that he said he would write down all the times he lay with you because he was himself afraid that you might go to bed with another man, and that your husband was estranged from you at the time. And when your son* was conceived, hardly any time passed before you told him† that you were pregnant by him. Now say whether it is true just as I have told you. And if you don't admit it, I will tell you [17] still other signs."

The judge was very angry, and he asked his mother whether what he had said was the truth. The mother was terrified, and she said, "Dear son, do you believe that devil?"

But the child said, "If you don't admit this thing, I will tell you yet another that you well know is true."

And the lady fell silent.

The child said, "I know everything that happened. It is true that when you felt that you were pregnant, you begged the priest to make peace between your husband and yourself‡ in order to hide that you were already pregnant. He did his best, until in the end he got you two to lie together. You led your husband to believe that the child was his, and many people thought it was so, and your son, the very one who is here, thought it was true. From then until now you have led this life and you still do. The night you left to come here the priest§ lay with you. In the morning he rode

* The text has an ambiguous *il* ("he").
† It is unclear whether *li* ("him") refers to the lady's husband or her lover, however, the insistent "by him" *(de lui)* suggests it may have been the priest.
‡ From Micha's text (15, ll. 84-85). In Sommer's text, Merlin says that the mother made her husband make peace with the priest (17, l. 6).
§ The text again has the ambiguous *il* ("he"), which would logically, according to context, refer to the lady's lover-priest, as is translated, but which has as an implicit antecedent the husband.

along with you quite a way, and before leaving you he said to you alone, smiling, 'Take care to do and say whatever my son wishes,' for he well knows that he is his son because of what he had written down."

When the lady heard him out, she knew well that everything he said was true, so she sat down and was very distraught. She knew full well that she had to tell the truth.

Her son looked at her and said to her, "Dear mother, whoever my father may be, I am your son and I'll treat you as a son should. Tell me whether or not he spoke the truth about what we have heard here."

The lady answered, "For God's sake, dear son, have mercy! Surely I cannot hide it: everything happened just as he has said."

When the judge heard her, he said, "This child told the truth, for he knew better who his father was than I mine. Therefore, it is not right that I should bring his mother to justice when I do not condemn my own. But for God's sake, for your honor, and so that I might prove you innocent before the people, you and your mother, please tell me who your father is."

He answered, "I will tell it more for your love's sake than because I fear your power. I want you to know and believe that I am the son of a devil who ensnared my mother. Know also that one kind of devil is called incubi, and they live in the air. God allowed me to have their intelligence and their memory, so I know things that are done, said, and past; this is how I know what your mother has done. And Our Lord has permitted and wills me to have this in my memory because of my mother's goodness. And because of her holy and true repentance, the penance that this worthy man imposed on her, and the commands of Holy Church which she believed, God has given me such power that I know the things that are to come. And this you can see by what I'm about to tell you."

Then he took him aside so that they were by themselves, and he said to him, "Your mother will go off and will tell what I have said to her to the man who fathered you. And when he hears that you know it, he will be so frightened that his heart will not be able to bear it, and he will run away out of fear of you. And the devil, whose works he has always done, will lead him to a spring, and he will drown himself. This way you can prove that I know the things that are to come."

And the judge answered, "If it happens thus, I will never doubt you."

Then they left their private meeting and went back before the people, and the judge said within the hearing of everyone that the child had indeed justly saved his mother from being burned: all those who would see him should know that "to my mind they will never see so wise a man."

And they answered, "Praise God!"

This is how Merlin's mother was saved and the [18] judge's mother found guilty. Merlin stayed with the judges while the judge sent two men with his mother to find out whether what the child had said would turn out to be true. As soon as she reached her house, she spoke to the priest and told him about the wonder she had heard. When he heard this, he was so terrified that he could not utter a word. In his heart he imagined that the judge would kill him as soon as he came there. Thus brooding, he went out of the town, saying to himself that it would be better for him to drown himself than for the judge to give him an unworthy death. The devil, whose works he had done, egged him on until he made him jump into a pond and drown himself. The men who had been sent with the lady saw it.

This is why this story forbids anyone ever to flee other people, for the devil abides more often with a man by himself than in a crowd.*

Those who saw this wonder went back to the judge and told him what had happened just as they had seen it. The priest had drowned the third day they were there. When the judge heard it, he was astounded; he came to Merlin and told him.

When Merlin heard it, he smiled and said, "Now you can know whether I say the truth. And I bid you, tell it to Blaise." (This Blaise was the good man who was his mother's confessor.) So the judge told him the wonder just as it had happened to the priest.

Then Merlin went away with his mother and Blaise while the judges went their separate ways elsewhere. This Blaise was a very good, sharp-witted clerk. When he heard Merlin saying those things, he was greatly amazed that such keen intelligence should come to one so young, less than two and a half years old. So he undertook with great earnestness to test him in many ways, until Merlin said, "Blaise, stop testing me. The more you test me the more astonished you will become. But do what I'll ask, and believe as much as you can† of what I'll tell you. I will teach you easily how to have the love of Jesus Christ and everlasting joy."

Blaise answered, "I have heard you talk, and I really believe that you are the devil's son, so I am afraid that you will trick me."

Merlin said, "Evil hearts usually recognize evil rather than good. Just as you heard it said that I was sired by the devil, so you heard me say that Our Lord had given me knowledge and memory of the things that were to come. So, if you are clever, you should try to find out which one I would claim. You can be sure that since Our Lord willed that I should know these things, the devils have lost hold of me, but I have not lost their craft or their artifice, rather I hold from them what I ought.

"I do not claim this to further their cause. They were unwise, when they sired me, to put me in a vessel that was never to be theirs, for the good life of my mother has hurt them a great deal. If they had begotten me in my grandmother, then I would not have the power to recognize that God exists, for she led a very evil life— through her came all the suffering my mother had because of her father and the other wrongs you have heard about. But believe what I'll tell you about the creed and the faith, and I'll tell you something that no one but God could tell you. Make a book out of it so that the many people who hear it will be the better for it and will all the more keep from sinning. Thereby you will do an act of charity, and you will put [19] your work to good use."

Blaise answered him, "I will do what you say, and I'll gladly make the book, but let it be done in the name of the Father and the Son and the Holy Ghost—for just as truly I believe and know these three parts to be a single thing in God—and in the name of the blessed lady who bore the Son of God, all the holy apostles, all the

* It is worthwhile to recall that Merlin's grandfather, in his despair, fled human company and that, having driven him to this, the devil pursuing him knew that he could work his will on him.
† The text reads *croi grant partie* ("believe a large part.").

angels and archangels, all the saints, all the prelates of Holy Church, all good men and women, and all creatures who love and honor God, so that you will not be able to deceive me or trick me or do anything that would displease Our Lord."

Merlin answered, "May all these creatures you have mentioned damn me before God if I have you do anything that is against the will of Jesus Christ my Savior."

"Now tell me what you will," said Blaise, "for from now on I'll do everything good you order me to do."

And Merlin said to him, "Now run get ink and parchment quickly, for I will tell you many things that you would not think anyone could tell you."

Then Blaise went to get what he needed. And after he had looked for it and found it, Merlin began to recount the love between Jesus Christ and Joseph of Arimathea, just as it had been, and to tell about Joseph and his offspring and those people who had the vessel called the Grail and all their accomplishments, just as they had been, of Alan and his companions, how he left his father's house, how Petrus had departed, how Joseph disposed of his vessel, and how he died.* Afterward he told him about the devils, how they had gathered together because they had lost the power they had enjoyed over humanity before, and he told him how the prophets had done them harm and how, for this reason, they had conspired to make a man. "And they said they would make me. You heard all about it and you learned from my mother and other people about their deeds and tricks—and then the foolishness they are all so full of, for they have lost me and every other advantage."

Thus did Merlin set out the plan for the work that he ordered Blaise to undertake. And Blaise was amazed at the wonders that Merlin told, but they seemed to be nonetheless true and good and beautiful, so he devoted himself to writing them down, so much so that one day Merlin said to Blaise, "You must suffer a great deal for this undertaking, and I will suffer more than you."

And he asked him how that was.

"People will come from the west to seek me out. And those who will come to find me will have promised their lord that they would kill me and bring him my blood. But when they see me and hear me, they won't want to kill me. But when I go away with them, you will go to the place where the people are who possess the holy cup, the Grail. Forever thereafter, your work and your book will be told about, and your book will be gladly heard everywhere. But it will not have authority, because you cannot be among the apostles, who never put anything down in writing about Our Lord that they had [20] not seen or heard, and you do not put down what you have seen or heard except as I tell you to. And just as I will remain obscure except concerning those things wherein I wish to reveal myself, so will your book remain hidden. In a short while it will come about that no one will thank you for it, and you will take it away with you when I go off with those who are to come for me.

"You will go to Western parts, and the book of Joseph will be put together with yours. And when you have fulfilled your task, and when you are, as you should be, in the company of the Grail, then your book will be joined to Joseph's book, and everything will have been proved true concerning my labors and yours, and God

* The preceding lines, beginning with "Joseph and his offspring," are supplied from Micha's text (16, ll. 65-71). Sommer's text truncates.

will bless it if it pleases Him. And those who hear it will pray to Our Lord on our behalf. And when the two books are put together, there will be one beautiful book, and the two will be one and the same thing, except that I cannot say or recount the intimate words between Jesus Christ and Joseph.

"In England there had not yet been a Christian king, and about those who had come before, I do not care to tell anything except what has bearing on this story."

2. MERLIN EXPLAINS WHY VORTIGERN'S TOWER WILL NOT STAND.*

In this part the story says that there was a king in England named Constant, and this Constant ruled for a long time. He had children. One son was named Maine,[†] the second Pendragon, and the third Uther.[‡] This Constant had a liegeman on his land called Vortigern; he was very shrewd in the ways of the world, clever, and a good knight. Constant was quite old, and in time he died. And when he was dead, the folk of the land asked whom they should make lord and king of the country. Many agreed that they would make the son of their overlord king. He was young, but it was not right to make anyone else king and leave him aside. Vortigern himself agreed to this, and they all deliberated until they made him king.

After Maine became king, war broke out, and Vortigern was his seneschal. It was the Saxons who made war against Maine, and those who were of the pagan Roman religion also came often to fight against the Christians. Vortigern, who was seneschal of the land, did there as he pleased. The old king's son and his brothers, all of whom were quite ignorant, were not so wise or worthy as they needed to be. Vortigern had taken for his own use much of the land's wealth, and he had the hearts of the people. He knew that they held him to be worthy and wise, so pride rose up in him, and he said that, because he saw that no one could do what he could do, he would no longer take care of the king's land, so he would withdraw from it.

When the Saxons saw that he meant to leave, they gathered together and came upon the Christians in a great horde. The king went to Vortigern and said, "Dear friend, help defend the land, and I and all those who belong to it will do as you will."

Vortigern answered, "Sir, let others go defend it, for I cannot now go there, as there are people in your [21] service who hate me. I want them to have this battle, for I will never commit myself to it."

When King Maine and those who were with him heard that they could accomplish nothing more, they left and made ready to fight the Saxons. And the Saxons moved against them and routed them. After they had been defeated, they gathered and

---

*   Corresponds to Sommer, 20-35.
†   Named Constant like his father in Geoffrey of Monmouth (6, 5-8), he had withdrawn from the world as a monk (Old French *moine/maine.*) Apparently an epithet such as "the Monk" attached to his name (cf. Geoffrey of Monmouth, 6, 6) became confused, in the French tradition, with a proper name.
‡   In Geoffrey of Monmouth (6, 5) the sons are, in addition to Constant the Monk, Aurelius Ambrosius and Uther Pendragon. In the French tradition the second name is dropped and the third divided.

said that they had lost a great deal, but they would not have suffered this loss if Vortigern had been there. The boy stood there, unable to defend the land as he needed to, so they greeted him with shouts of scorn and said that they would no longer put up with him.

Then they came to Vortigern and said to him, "Sir, we have no king or lord, for he is worthless. For God's sake, please be our king; govern us and keep us. For there is no man in this land who could or should do this as you can."

And he answered, "I cannot and I must not, not as long as my lord is alive."

And they said that they would rather he were dead.

Vortigern said to them, "If he were dead and if you and the others wanted me to be king, I would gladly do so, but as long as he lives I cannot and must not."

They listened to Vortigern's words and understood them as they saw fit. They took leave of him and went away into their country. And when they had got there, they sent for their friends and told them how they had spoken to Vortigern and the answer he had given them. When they had heard it, they said, "It is best for us to kill the king, and then Vortigern will be king as soon as we have killed him. Ever after he will do just what we will: thus we will find a way to make ourselves lords over him!"

They then agreed which among them should kill Maine. They chose twelve, and those twelve went to the place where King Maine was, while the others stayed behind in town to learn whether anyone meant to hurt their cause or harm them, so that they might help their friends. And those twelve came to the place where they found King Maine; they ran upon him with knives and swords and killed him.

After they had killed him, they found no one who would talk about it very much at all. And they came to Vortigern and said to him, "Now you will be king, for we have killed King Maine."

And when Vortigern heard that they had killed him, he seemed to be greatly distraught. And he then said to them, "You have done an evil deed in killing your lord. I advise you to flee because of the worthy men of the land, for if they find you they will kill you. I am sorry that you have come here."

And they went away.

Afterward it happened that the folk of the kingdom gathered together and talked about whom they would make their king. Vortigern had the hearts of many of the folk in the kingdom, and they agreed all together that he should be king. At this gathering were two worthy men who were in charge of the other two boys, Pendragon and Uther. These two boys were sons of Constant and brothers of King Maine. When they heard and learned that Vortigern would be king, they began to suspect that he had had King Maine killed.

The two men who protected the boys took counsel and said, "Since Vortigern has had our lord killed, as soon as he is king he will have these two boys in our charge killed. We dearly loved their father, for he did us [22] many great favors, and thanks to him we still have what we have. We would be wicked to allow those under our protection to come to grief. We are sure that when Vortigern is king he will have them killed, because he knows full well that the kingdom should be theirs."

The two worthy men agreed that they would flee and take the two boys to a faraway land to the east; their forebears had come from there, and they would save them in this way. And they did just as they had planned.

Vortigern was chosen and proclaimed king. After his crowning, the twelve who had killed King Maine came to him, and when Vortigern saw them, he did not make any signs of having ever seen them before. They rushed to him and rebuked him, for it was thanks to them that he was king, since they had killed King Maine. When Vortigern heard that they had killed their lord, he ordered them to be taken prisoner, and he said to them, "You have judged yourselves in admitting that you have killed your lord, whom you could not have a right to kill. You would do the same to me if you could, but I'll know how to protect myself against you."

And when they understood what he was saying, they were aghast and said, "Sir, we did it for your good and because we thought you would love us all the more for it."

When Vortigern heard them he said, "I will show you clearly how one must love people like you."

Then he had all twelve of them taken, tied to the tails of twelve horses, and pulled and dragged about for so long that little was left of them. They were of noble stock and had many kinsmen who said to Vortigern, "You shamed us mightily when you killed our kinsmen and friends so unworthily. We will no longer serve you willingly as our overlord."

And when Vortigern heard them threatening him, he grew angry and told them that if they did not hold their tongues, he would do the very same thing to them. When they heard that he was threatening them, their scorn for him grew, and they answered very angrily that they had little fear of his authority: "King Vortigern, threaten us all you will, but we say this to you: as long as we have one friend left on earth you will surely have war. From this moment on we break our faith with you; you are not our lord and you do not hold this land lawfully, for you have it against the will of God and Holy Church. You can be sure that you will die the same death you gave our kinsmen."

They then went away. And when Vortigern heard them threatening him with death, he grew even angrier than he had been before.

Thus ill will was born among them, and the killers' kinsmen gathered together some men-at-arms and invaded the land. Vortigern fought against them a great number of times until he drove them back out of the country. And after they had been driven out, he behaved so wickedly toward his people that they rose up against him. When he saw that, he was very frightened that they would drive him from the land. He then sent his messengers to hunt out the Saxons, and when they heard that he was suing for peace, they were very glad.

One of them was named Hengist; he was more fearsome than any of the others. This Hengist had served Vortigern for a very long time, and he served him so well in the war that he led the triumph. When the war was over, Hengist told Vortigern that his own people sorely hated him. I have heard so much said about this that I cannot [23] tell you everything, but I can tell you this much, that Hengist spoke for so long and so persuasively that Vortigern took Hengist's daughter as his wife. And all those who hear this story should know that she was the first in that kingdom to say "Wassail!"* I must not recount to you everything about Hengist and his deeds and estate, but all Christians grieved when Vortigern took Hengist's daughter, and it was quite often said that Vortigern ignored a great part of his religious belief because of the woman, who did not believe in Jesus Christ

After all this, Vortigern knew that he was not well loved by his liegemen. He learned as well that Constant's two sons had been taken away to faraway lands and that they would come back as soon as they could; he was sure that if they did come back, it would be for his downfall. He therefore decided to build a tower so big and so strong that he need not fear anyone. Then he sent for all his master masons, ordered limestone and mortar, and began building the tower. When they had worked up to twenty or so feet above the ground,† it all fell down. And the same thing happened again three or four times.‡

And when Vortigern saw that his tower§ could not hold up, he became very distraught and said that he would never be happy if he could not find out why his tower kept falling. So he sent throughout all his land for all the wise men who could be found. When they had gathered together, he told them the wonder of his falling tower, which would not stand no matter what he did. And he asked them all their advice about it. When they heard the wonder and saw the tower fallen down in the midst of the place, they were greatly amazed, and said, "It is our opinion that no one but a learned man, a clerk, can find out why this building keeps falling down, for clerks know a great deal about things, thanks to their clerkly learning and training, that the rest of us are ignorant of. So if you want to find out why, you can do so only through them."

And Vortigern said, "It indeed seems to me that you speak the truth."

Then he called together all the learned clerks in his land. And when they had gathered, he showed them the wonder; and when they had seen it, they were greatly amazed, and they said to one another, "This is a very great wonder the king has told us about!"

And then the king summoned his wealthiest vassals. He took them aside and said to them, "Will you be able to advise me by yourselves or in consultation with others? I would bid you, make every effort so that I might learn why the tower falls down, for I have been told that I cannot know it unless you tell me."

When they heard that the king was asking them so earnestly, they said, "Sir, we know nothing about it, but it may well be that there are clerks right here who can

---

*   The translation follows Micha's text (17, ll. 18-19), a reading Sommer gives as a variant (23, n. 1). Sommer's manuscript reads, illogically, "that it was she who first held the kingdom." The story of the bride's contribution to English culture is amplified in Geoffrey of Monmouth (6, 12).

†   Sommer's text reads "three or four *toises*" (23, l. 13), a *toise* being a measure of about six feet. Micha's text, however, speaks of the length of time they had worked: "twenty days or three weeks" (19, ll. 33-34).

‡   "The translation combines Sommer's text—"and thus it fell back down" (23, l. 15)—and Micha's—"and thus it happened" (19, l. 35).

§   Micha's text bears the doublet *sa tors ne s'euvre* ("his tower and his work") (19, l. 35), while the scribe of Sommer's base apparently garbled the second element: *sa tor ne sere* ("his tower and ?") (23, l. 16). As editor, Sommer draws attention to the apparent error, but does not correct it.

learn about it through an art called astrology,* and there are clerks here who know it."

And the king said, "You clerks know who you are, so get together and talk about the matter. Find out which ones among you know how to work astrology, and let them come forward boldly. And they will never ask me for anything, if they can tell me what I want to know, that will not be theirs."

Then they drew aside and asked one another if they knew anything about that art. Two of them stepped forward and said that they knew enough about it [24] to find out the answer.

"We have here two clerks who know about it."

And the wealthy men said, "Go find your fellow astrologers and come talk to us all together."

They said they would do so gladly, so the two looked about until there were seven of them; and among these seven was not one who did not believe that he was the master of the others. So they went before the king, and the king asked them if they could say why his tower kept falling down.

And they answered, "Yes, if it can be known by anyone."

The king told them that if they could tell him, he would give them all they wanted.

This is how the king engaged his clerks. And after they entered his service, they worked hard to find out why that tower was falling down and how it could be made to stand. Each and every one put forth his greatest efforts. But the more they worked, the more they wasted their effort, for they found out just one thing, and that had nothing to do with the tower, it seemed to them, so they were terrified. At last the king called them before him and asked them, "Why do you not tell me news about my tower?"

They answered, "This is a very great thing you are asking of us, and we still need nine more days."† The king answered, "We grant you the respite, but make sure that you can tell me at the end of the nine days."

Then the clerks went away to take counsel together, and each one asked the others, "What do you say about this thing the king asks of us?"

So they asked one another, but not one of them would tell the others what he had found out. In the end, there was one who knew more than the others, and he said, "You will do well to tell me privately, each without the others, what you have found out. I will not reveal anyone's secret unless all of you give me leave to do so."

And they said that they were willing to do that. Then he took each one aside privately and asked them in turn what they had found out about the tower. And they all said that they knew nothing about it, nor could they see how it could happen. But they all saw another wonder, for they saw a boy seven years old who had been born with no man on earth as his father, yet conceived in a woman, who would tell about the tower. Every one of the six‡ told him this same thing.

---

* Old French *astronomie* (Sommer, 23, l. 35). As proved by ensuing events, the clerks do not practice astronomy in the modem sense, but are seers. Cf. 73, l. 26, and 102, l. 28.

† Sommer's text twice reads *.xj.*, perhaps a printing error for *.ix.*, since his summary speaks of a "respite of nine days" (24, ll. 16-17). Micha prints the preferred reading (20, ll. 27, 29).

‡ Thus Micha's text; Sommer repeats *.vij.* (24, l. 28).

And when he had heard everyone's opinion, he said to them, "Come back, all of you." And they did so. And when they were all together, he said to them, "You have all told me one thing and hidden one thing."

They answered, "Tell us now what we said to you and what we hid from you."

And he said, "You all told me that you know nothing about that tower, but you see a boy seven years old born with no man on earth as his father, yet conceived in a woman, but you told me nothing more. I will tell you this: believe me, there is not one among you who has not seen that he is to die because of that boy. I myself have seen it just as plainly as any of you. But if you will believe me, we will come to grips with this since we know about it so long before our deaths. Do you know what we'll do? We will all agree on one thing and say that the tower cannot stand and never will, unless some of the blood of the boy born fatherless is put into the mortar in the foundation: if anyone could take some of his blood and put it into the mortar, the tower would stand, and it would be good and strong forever. Let everyone say this each in his own way [25] so that the king will not find out what we really saw. This is how we can save ourselves from death by the death of the one by whom we have seen we are to die. Let us also convince the king to order those who will go out looking for him to kill him on the spot as soon as they find him and to bring away his blood."

Thus they agreed on what to say. And when they came before the king, they said that they would not speak their minds all together, but each one separately: then he would know who spoke best. And they pretended that no one knew anything about the others.

And so each one told the king what his reckoning had been, and he heard five men, each one by himself. When the king and his men had heard these wonders, they were greatly amazed and said, "How can a man be born without a father?"

The king then called all the clerks together before him and said to them, "You all say the same thing, yet each one says it in his own way."

They said to him, "Sir, now tell us what it was."

And he told word for word just what they had said. They all said to him, "If what we have told you is not true, then do with us as you will."

And the king asked them, "Can it be true that a man was born without conception by a father?"

They answered, "Sir, we have never heard it said of anyone except this boy. But we can assure you of this: he was born fatherless and he is seven years of age."

And the king said, "I will have you put under a strong guard, then I'll send people to fetch some of the boy's blood."

They said all together, "Sir, we are very willing for you to have us guarded, but you should not talk to the boy or even see him; rather, order him to be killed and his blood to be brought back to you. This way, your tower will stand, if it is to stand, without fail."

The king had all seven put into a very strong house and provided them with everything they needed. He then gathered his messengers and sent them out two by two. There were twelve in all, and the king had them swear on saints' relics that the one who found the boy first would kill him and bring his blood to him; they also swore not to come back before he had been found.

Thus the king sent people out to look for the boy, and his messengers left two by two. And they looked for him in many lands, until two messengers came upon two of their fellows and they agreed to go along together for a while. One day they happened to pass by a big field at the entrance to a town, and in that field a band of children were playing ball. And Merlin, who knew all things, was there. He saw those who were looking for him, so he drew up to one of the wealthiest boys in the town, because he was sure that he would say ugly things about him, raised the stick he was holding, and struck the boy in the leg. The boy burst into tears and began to call Merlin names, accusing him of being born fatherless. And when the messengers heard this, they went all four to where the boy was weeping.

They asked him, "Who is the one that struck you?"

He said to them, "He is the son of a woman who never knew who sired him, and he has never had a father."

When Merlin heard this, he came to them smiling and said to them, "I am the one you are looking for, the one you have sworn to kill, and you must take my blood to King Vortigern." [26]

When they heard the boy speak they were dumbfounded, and they asked him who had told him that. And he answered, "I know for a fact that you swore to kill me."

They asked him, "Will you come with us if we carry you on horseback?"

And he answered, "I would be afraid you'd kill me." He knew that they did not want to, but he said it to worry them all the more. And he said to them. "If you will promise not to harm me, I will go away with you and I will also tell you why the tower for which you want to kill me cannot stand."

When they heard this, they were utterly amazed and asked him who had told him that. And he answered, "I know it for a fact, since you swore to kill me."

And they said to one another, "This boy tells us wonders, and whoever killed him would commit a grievous sin." Each one of them said, "I would rather break my oath than kill him."

Then Merlin said to them, "You will come take lodging where my mother lives. I could not go with you without her leave or that of a worthy man who lives in my mother's house."

"We will go where you wish."

Thus Merlin took the messengers who had come to kill him to his mother's house in a community of nuns where the good priest had sent her to retire. When they came there, Merlin ordered those within to give them a warm welcome. And after they had got down from their horses, Merlin took them before Blaise and said to him, "Look, here are the ones I told you were looking for me to kill me."

And he said to the messengers, "Please admit to this good man, without lying, the truth in what I am going to say about what you have undertaken. I want you to know that if you lie, I am sure to know it."

"We will never lie to you," they said. "Just make sure that you do not lie to us."

And Merlin said to Blaise, "Now listen closely to what we are about to tell you. I say," said Merlin to the messengers, "that you are King Vortigern's men. That king wants to build a tower, but when they have gone up twenty feet or so,* the tower cannot stand, and everything that has been finished crumbles in an hour's time, and the king gets very angry because of it.

"He has summoned clerks, but not one of them could figure it out. They told him they would explain to him why the tower could not stand and how to get it to hold. They cast their lots, but they saw nothing about the tower. But they did find out that I had been born, and it seemed to them that I could hurt them, so they agreed to have me killed. They would tell the king that the tower would stand if some of my blood were in it. And they told him so. When Vortigern heard it, he took it for a great wonder and believed it to be true. They advised him to send out men to look for me, but they should kill me when they found me and bring him my blood to put into the tower, in the mortar for the foundation, and this is how, they said, the tower would stand. And Vortigern chose twelve messengers and made them all swear on holy relics that they would kill me and bring him my blood. So he sent these twelve out, and four of the twelve came here, to the big field where other children and I were playing ball. And knowing that they were looking for me, I struck one of the boys because I knew for certain that he would say the worst things about me he could think of and that he would scold me for being born fatherless. I did it because I wanted these worthy men to find me, and so they have found me. And so I bid you, dear Master [27] Blaise, ask them if I have spoken the truth."

And he asked them whether the wonder he had told was true. They answered that everything had happened just as he told it, "and he did not lie to you in a single word."

The master crossed himself and said that Merlin would be most wise if he lived long enough, "and it would be a very great shame if you killed him."

They answered, "Sir, we would sooner be perjurers all our days—we would sooner the king seized all our possessions—than kill him. And he himself, who knows all other things, knows full well whether we wish to."

And Blaise said, "You speak the truth. And I will ask him this and other things in front of you, and you will be greatly astounded by what he will say."

Then they called him back, for he had left them earlier because he wanted them to speak privately. And when he had come back, Blaise asked him, "Now tell me, Merlin, do these messengers want to kill you?"

And Merlin flashed a smile and said, "I know surely, thanks be to God and to them, that they do not wish to at all."

And they said to him, "You have spoken the truth."

Then they asked him, "Will you come with us?"

And he answered, "Yes, without fail, if you swear a binding oath to me that you will take me before the king and that you will allow no harm to come to me before I have talked to him, for I am sure that after I spoken to him, I will have no need to fear."

And they promised him.

---

* Here Micha's text (22, l. 15) agrees with Sommer's (26, l. 25): "three or four *toises*." See above, p. 25n.

Then Blaise spoke and said, "Now I see clearly that you wish to leave me. Tell me then what you want me to do with this work you have had me begin."

And he answered, "What you ask me, I will tell you aright. For you see that Our Lord, who rightly and justly endowed me with such intelligence and memory that the one who thought he could have me for his own use has lost me—so God has chosen me to work in His own service, for no one but I can do it and no one knows things as I know them. And I must go to that land which they left to come look for me. I will do and say such things that more people will believe me than any man who has ever been on this earth except God.

"And you will go away to bring to an end the work you have undertaken; you won't come with me, but you'll go off by yourself and ask the way to a land called Northumberland. That land is full of great forests, and it is forbidding even to those who belong there, for there are places where no one has yet been. And you will live there. And I'll come to you and tell you the things you will need to make the book you have begun. You must work hard at it, for you will have great rewards from it: during your life you will have a full heart, and at the end, everlasting joy. And the story will forever be told and gladly heard for as long as the world lasts.

"Do you know where this grace will come from? It will come from the grace that Our Lord accorded Joseph from the cross. And when you finish laboring for Joseph's sake and all his descendants and kindred, and have done such good work that you deserve to be their companion, then I will show you where they are, and you will see the glorious vessel and the glorious services that Joseph performed for the body of Jesus Christ which was given to him.

"And I want you to know, to make you more [28] certain, that God has given me such intelligence and such memory that I will make the whole kingdom where I am going, the worthy men and noble women, suffer grief along with the one who is to be of that kindred so beloved of God* — Oh, God! I'll have so much to do! But I truly want you to know that the great troubles will not come before the fourth king. That king because of whom my great troubles will come about will be named Arthur.

"And so you will go to the place I have told you, and I'll come to you often and bring you the things I want you to put into your book. And you should know that your book will be much loved and greatly prized by many people. And when you finish it, you will bring it into the company of those good folk who have the glorious services I have told you about. There will be no noble man or worthy woman in the place where I am going some part of whose life I will not have you write down.†
You should also know that never have the lives of royal personages or the righteous been so gladly listened to as will be those of King Arthur and the people who in that time will live and rule. When you have finished everything and recounted their lives, then you will deserve the joy they have who are in the company of the holy vessel called the Grail. And your book that you have made will be called *The Book of the Grail* for as long as the world lasts. And people will hear it gladly."

---

*   The epithet is supplied from Micha's text (23, l. 39).
†   The final clause is supplied from Micha's text (23, ll. 51-52).

Thus spoke Merlin to his master, and he showed him what he had to do. (He called him Master because he had been his mother's teacher.) And when the good man heard him say those things, he was very glad and said, "If I can, I will do everything you order me to do."

This is how Merlin instructed Blaise. And he spoke to the messengers who had come for him, and said, "Come with me, for I want you to hear my mother's and my leave-taking."

Then he took them to the place where his mother was, and he said to her, "Dear mother, I have been summoned from faraway, foreign lands, but I will go only by your leave. I must render to Jesus Christ the service for which He gave me the power, and I cannot accomplish this unless I go to the land where these men want to take me. Your master Blaise also has to leave, so you must let go of both of us."

And his mother said to him, "Dear son, I commend you to God, for I am not so clever that I would dare hold you back. But please, I would truly like Blaise to stay here."

But Merlin said that could not be.

Thus did Merlin take leave of his mother, and he left with the messengers. Blaise went off another way, toward Northumberland, where Merlin had ordered him to go.

Merlin rode with the messengers until they went through a town that had a market, and after they had left the town, they came upon a peasant who had bought a pair of stout shoes, and he carried with him the leather to mend his shoes with when he wore holes in them, for he meant to go on a pilgrimage. When Merlin drew close to the peasant, he began to laugh, and the men leading him asked him why he had laughed. And he said to them, "Because of the peasant you see here. Now ask him what he means to do with that leather he's taking with him, and he will say that he will need to mend his shoes. Then follow him, for I tell you truthfully [29] that he will be dead before reaching home."

When they heard this, they took it for a great wonder, and they said, "We will try to see whether or not that is true." So they went over to the peasant and asked him what he meant to do with that leather, and he said that he wanted to go on a pilgrimage and would need to mend his shoes when he wore holes in them.

And when they heard him say just what Merlin had told them he would, they were greatly astounded and said, "This man looks hale and hardy. Two of us will follow him and the other two will take the straight road and wait for us where they'll spend the night, for it would be good to know all about the wonder the boy has told."

And two of them followed the peasant and had not gone more than a league when they found the peasant dead right in their path, with his shoes in his arms. And when they saw this, they turned about and caught up with their companions and told them what they had seen. And when the others heard it, they said, "Our clerks behaved like complete fools when they ordered this clever little boy to be killed."

And the first ones said that they would rather suffer great harm to their persons than kill him; they said this among themselves in secret, for they did not think that Merlin would know it. When they came to where Merlin was, he thanked them for what they had said, and they asked him, "What have we said that you should thank us for it?"

He repeated what they had said word for word, and when they heard it they were astonished and said, "We can't say or do anything that this boy doesn't know about."

So they rode many days until they came to Vortigern's kingdom.

One day they happened to be going through a town, and people were taking a child to be buried. There were all about the body men and women wailing bitterly. And when Merlin saw the sorrow and the priests and clerks chanting and bearing the body to be buried, Merlin stopped at once and began to laugh. The men who were leading him asked him why he was laughing, and he said, "For a great wonder that I see."

And he told them, "Do you see that good man over there who is mourning so and that priest who is chanting?"

And they said, "Yes, of course."

So Merlin said, "The priest ought to be doing the other man's grieving. I want you to know that the child was his son, yet the man to whom he did not belong at all mourns so much for him. And the one whose son it is, is singing! That's why this seems to me to be a great wonder."

And the messengers asked him, "How can we find this out?"

And he answered them, "Go to the woman over there who is mourning so much and ask her why she is weeping. She will tell you, for her son who is dead. And you will answer her, 'I know just as well as you that this is not your husband's son, but the son of that priest who has chanted over him so much today. And the priest himself is aware of it, for he told you himself and reckoned the day when he was conceived.'"

When the messengers had understood clearly what Merlin had said, two of them[*] approached the woman and said to her just what Merlin had told them.[†] And when she heard it, she was very much afraid and said to them, "My lords, by God's mercy, I know that I can't hide it from you, so I'll admit the whole truth. It is just as you have said, but for God's sake, do not tell my husband, for he would kill me."

And when they heard her, they came back to their companions and recounted [30] to them what the woman had told them. Then they said among the four of them that never in the world had there been such a good seer.

So they rode until they were a day's journey from where Vortigern was. Then the messengers asked Merlin to advise them what they could say to their lord, because they had not killed him as soon as they found him as he had ordered them to do. When Merlin heard them talk in that way, he knew that they wanted what was best for him, so he said to them, "You will do just as I advise you and you will never be blamed for it. Go to King Vortigern and tell him that you have found me, and tell him the truth about what you have heard me say. And tell him that I'll show him truly why his tower falls down and why it cannot stand—provided that he do to those who wanted to have me killed just what they wished done to me. And tell him

---

[*]   Supplied from Micha (25, l. 29); Sommer's text does not specify the number, which is necessary because not all four go to speak to the woman.

[†]   Supplied from Micha (25, l. 30); Sommer's text reads ("him") (29, l. 39).

that I will explain to him why they want to have me killed. And when you have said all this, do confidently what he orders you to do."

Then the messengers turned away from Merlin and went to the king. And when he saw them, he was very glad and asked them what they had done with his mission. And they answered, "The best we could."

Then they asked him to see them alone, and they told him everything just as it had happened, just how they found Merlin. "If he had wished, we would never have found him, and he comes to you very willingly."

And the king said to them, "What Merlin are you telling me about? Is he the boy who was born fatherless whose blood you were to have brought me?"

One of them said, "He is the very Merlin we are telling you about. And you can be sure that he is the wisest and best seer who ever was in the world, but for God. Sir, he told us exactly how you made me swear and gave your orders, and he said outright that the clerks know nothing about why your tower keeps falling, but he will tell you why and show you, if you want, before your very eyes. And he told us other wonders, very great ones, and he has sent us to you to learn whether you will speak to him. If not, we'll kill him right where he is, for two of our companions are with him guarding him."

And the king answered, "If you will pledge to me that he will show me why my tower keeps falling, then it is not my will to have him killed."

And they said, "We do indeed pledge this."

The king said, "Go fetch him, for I truly wish to speak to him."

Then the messengers left, and the king himself rode after them. And when Merlin saw the two messengers, he said to them, "You have vouched for me with your lives."

"You have told the truth," they said. "We would rather put ourselves in jeopardy than kill you, and we must do one or the other."

Merlin answered, "I will be your guaranty against this peril."

Then they rode until they met the king. And when Merlin saw him, he greeted him and said, "Vortigern, speak with me in private."

And he took him aside and called those who had brought him. And when they were together by themselves, Merlin said,* "Sir, you had me sought out because of your tower that cannot stand, and you ordered me to be killed on the advice of your clerks, who said that the tower would hold up with my blood, but they lied. Yet if they had said that it would stand by my intelligence, they would have told the [31] truth. And if you promise me to do to them what they wanted you to do to me, then I will show you why the tower keeps falling down. And I will show you, if you are willing to do it, how it will stand up."

And Vortigern answered, "If you show me what you say, I will do with the clerks what you wish."

And Merlin said to him, "If one word of what I say is a lie, do not believe me ever again. Let's go and call the clerks together, and you will hear that they themselves can't explain."

---

* Thus Micha (27, l. 4). Sommer's text adds *lor* (30, l. 39): "to them"; however, the remarks are addressed to the king alone.

So the king took Merlin to the place where the tower had been started and kept falling down. And the clerks were sent for and came before Merlin; and when they got there, he had one of the messengers who had brought him ask them, saying, "Sir clerks, what is the reason you say that the tower falls down?"

And they answered, "We know nothing about its falling down, but we have told the king how it will stand."

The king said to them, "You have told me wonders. For you advised me to summon a fatherless man, but I don't know how he will be found."

Merlin began to speak to the clerks and said to them,* "Sirs, do not take the king for a fool. You had him seek the boy born fatherless not out of concern for him, but because you foresaw that by the boy born fatherless you would die. It was because you were afraid he would kill you that you made the king believe that he should have him killed and put his blood in the mortar in the tower's foundation, and then the tower would hold up and never give way. So you brooded about how you could have the one killed by whom you would die, according to your forecasts."

And when they heard that the boy was telling this wonder, which they thought no one but they knew, they were terrified and knew that they would have to die. And Merlin said to the king, "From now on you can be sure that these clerks wanted to have me killed not for the sake of your tower, but because they had foreseen that they would die because of me. Please ask them if this was so, for they will never be so bold as to dare lie to you in front of me."

The king asked them whether he was telling the truth.

"Sir," they said, "may God save us from our sins as truly as he has spoken the truth. But we do not know by whom he knows these wonders. We ask you as our rightful overlord, please let us live so long that we may see whether he will tell the truth about the tower and whether it will stand because of him."

Then Merlin spoke and said to them, "You need not fear dying† until you have seen why the tower falls down."

And they thanked him profusely.

Then Merlin said to Vortigern, "Do you want to know why your tower will not stand and who knocks it down? If you will do what I tell you, I will show you plainly. Do you know what is beneath this tower? There is a great pool of water. And beneath that great pool there are two dragons that can't see a thing.‡ One of them is red and the other white. They are under two great rocks. Each senses the other's presence,§ and they are very big. And when they feel the water growing heavier above them and the work going on, they turn over, and the pool makes such a great uproar that whatever is built over it must fall down. So your tower falls because of the dragons. Take a look for yourself, and if you don't find it just

---

*   Supplied from Micha (27, l. 29). Sommer's text reads *lors* ("then") for *lor* ("to them") (31, l. 14).

†   Supplied from Micha's text (27, l. 52): *Vos n'avez garde de morir.* In substituting *m* for *n*, Sommer's text provides a meaning inappropriate for the passage (31, l. 31): *Vous maues garde de morir* ("You have kept me from dying").

‡   That is, are asleep (as in Geoffrey of Monmouth)?

§   Supplied from Micha (28, l. 7): *sentent* [sic] *bien li uns l'autre,* where Sommer's text reads *seit* (for *sent*? or for *sait*?) (31, l. 37).

as I have said, then have me burned to death. And if you find it to be so, then let my guarantors* be absolved and the clerks proved guilty since they know nothing about all this."

And Vortigern answered, "If what you tell me is true, I'll hold you to be the wisest man in the world." [32]

Then the king said to Merlin, "Now show me how I can have the earth taken away."

And Merlin told him, "With horses and carts and men with yokes to carry things a long way."

And the king ordered workmen to be put to the task and called together as many as were needed for the job. The people all around took this to be a great wonder and a great folly. And Merlin recommended that the clerks be well guarded.

So the king had the work underway for a long time to take out all that dirt, and the people worked at it until they found the pool. And after they had found it, they uncovered it and sent word to the king that they had found it. And the king came there gladly to behold the wonder, and he took Merlin with him. And when they came there, they found the pool to be very large. The king called two of his advisers and said to them, "Very wise indeed is this man who knew that this pool was under the ground. And he also said that beneath this pool there are two very great rocks and beneath these two rocks are two dragons! From now on, anything he tells me to do I'll do."

Then he called Merlin and said to him, "You have spoken the truth about this thing, for the workmen have found the pool. But I do not yet know whether you told the truth about the two rocks and the two dragons."

And Merlin answered, "You can't know it before you see it."

The king asked him, "How can we be rid of that water?"

And Merlin said, "They will drain it away in good ditches."

Then ditches were ordered dug and the water drained away. And Merlin said to Vortigern, "Those dragons that are beneath the pool, as soon as they smell each other, they will fight until they kill each other. Send for all the foremost men in the land to see the fight, for the battle between those two will have a very great meaning."

And Vortigern said that he would. Then he sent out through all his land for the great men, both clerics and laymen. And when they had gathered together, Vortigern recounted to them all the wonders that Merlin had told and how the two dragons were to fight. Then they said to one another, "That will be very good to see!"

They asked the king if he had said which one would win, and the king answered, "Not yet."

Then the water was drained away, and they could see the two rocks that were at the bottom of the pool. And when Merlin saw them, he said, "Do you see these two great rocks?"

And the king answered, "Yes."

"Sir," he said, "beneath these two rocks are two dragons."

And the king asked, "How will the dragons be got out?"

---

* That is, the messengers who have staked their lives on Merlin's truthfulness.

Merlin said to him, "Very easily, for the dragons will not move before they smell each other, and as soon as they smell each other, they will fight until one of them must die."

And the king said to him, "Merlin, will you tell me which one will be defeated?"

Merlin answered, "In their fight and in their victory there is very great meaning. And what I can tell you I'll tell you in private before three worthy men who are your close advisors."

Then Vortigern called three of the liegemen in his kingdom he most trusted, and he told them what Merlin had said to him. And they advised him to ask when they were alone which of the two dragons would be defeated: he should say it before he saw them and before the fight began.

And he said to them, "You have spoken well and I agree. After the fight he could make people think whatever he wanted." [33]

Then he called Merlin and asked him which one of the two dragons would win. And Merlin asked him, "Those three* liegemen of yours, are they in your confidence?"

And Vortigern said to him, "Yes, more than anyone else I know of."

"Then can I indeed say in front of them what you ask me?"

And the king said, "Yes, indeed."

And Merlin told them, "I want you to know that the white one will kill the red one. And be assured that he will have a great deal of trouble before he kills him. That he will kill him will have very great meaning for him who will know how to recognize it. But I will not tell you any more about it until after the fight."

Then the people were brought together, and they came to the two rocks; they broke them and dragged out the white dragon. And when they saw that it was so large and ugly and fearsome, they became frightened of it and drew back. Then they went to the other one and brought it out. And when the people saw this one they were more terrified than they had been before, for it was larger and uglier than the other one and even more fearsome. So it seemed to the king that this one would defeat the other.

Merlin said to Vortigern, "Now my guarantors should be absolved."

And he said that they were indeed.

Then they dragged one dragon near the other, and they smelled each other's backsides. As soon as one smelled the other, they both turned about and grabbed each other with their teeth and feet. Never have you heard of two animals fighting so fiercely. They fought in this way all that day and all that night and the next day until midday. And all the people who were watching them truly believed that the red one would kill the white one. But in the end, fire and flames shot out of the white dragon through its nose and mouth, and he burned the red one up. And when the red one was dead, the white one withdrew, lay down, and lived no more than three days longer. And those who saw that said that no one had ever seen such a wonder.

---

*   Sommer text has *.iiij.* (33, l. 2).

And Merlin said to Vortigern, "Now you can build your tower as high as you wish, and it will never be so high that it will fall down."

Then Vortigern ordered his workmen to go to work, and he built it as high and as strong as he could.

And he asked Merlin many times to tell him the meaning of the two dragons and how it could be that the white one killed the red one, since the red one had had the better of the fight for such a long time. And Merlin answered, "These things are all signs of what is to come. If I told you what you ask me to, you would grow angry with me. But you will assure me that you will not harm me."

And Vortigern answered that he would give him all the assurance he could wish.

And Merlin said to him, "Go now and send for your council, and have the clerks come before me who have left* this tower and who wanted to have me killed."

Vortigern did as Merlin advised. And when the council and the clerks had come, Merlin spoke to the clerks and said to them, "You are very foolish when you think you can work with the occult arts and not be so good or pure or noble as you ought. And because you are foolish and wicked, what you tried to find out eluded you; and because of the other art, the art of first principles, you did not see what you were asked about. You are not ones to see it. But you saw better that I had been born. And the one who showed me to you made it seem that you [34] were to die because of me—and he did it out of sorrow that he had lost me so that you would have me killed. But I have a Lord who will guard me against devils' tricks, if it pleases Him. And I will show them to be liars, for I will do nothing whereby you might die, if you will swear to me what I order you to."

And when they heard that they could be reprieved from dying, they said, "We will do anything you ask us to do, for we see plainly that you are the wisest man in the world."

And Merlin said to them, "You will swear to me that you will never traffic in this art. And because you have already practiced it, I order you to confess it to a priest, for whoever repents of a sin and does not give it up is lost. So put your flesh into such subjection that your souls will not be damned. If you will promise me this, I will let you go."

And they thanked him many times over and swore to him that they would do as he ordered.

This is how Merlin freed the clerks who had had him sought out. And all those who saw that he had proved himself so well were most thankful to him. And Vortigern came to him with his council and said to him, "You must tell me the meaning of the two dragons, for you have spoken the truth to me about all the other things, and I consider you the wisest man in the world. This is why I beg you to tell me the meaning of the two dragons."

And Merlin answered, "I will tell you. The red dragon stands for you, and the white one represents the sons of Constant."

---

* Supplied from Micha's text (29, l. 74): *sortirent*. Sommer's text introduces an irrelevant meaning by shifting a letter, *sartirent* (33, l. 35): "cut, adjusted."

And when Vortigern understood his meaning, he was ashamed. Merlin took note of this and said to him, "If you wish, I'll stop telling you this thing; please do not hold it against me."

And Vortigern answered, "There is no one here whom I do not trust, and I want you to tell me the meaning plainly, and spare me nothing that has to do with it."

And Merlin said, "I have told you truly that the red dragon means you, and I'll tell you why. You certainly know that Constant's sons were left alone, after their father's death; and you must admit that if you behaved as you ought, you should protect them and counsel them and defend them against all men on earth. And you also recognize that it is with their landholdings and their liegemen that you won the allegiance of the people of the kingdom. As soon as you saw that the people of the kingdom loved you, you withdrew from their doings because you understood that they would have troubled times. And when the people of the kingdom came to you to say that Maine should not be king and to ask you to take his place, you answered them like a weakling and said that you could not be king as long as Maine was alive.

"So you hid behind your misleading words. And those to whom you spoke them understood that you truly wanted Maine dead, and so they killed him. After they had killed him, two more were left, but they fled the country because they were afraid of you, so you were made king and you still hold their birthright.

"When those who had killed King Maine came before you, you had them killed to make it seem that you were sorry about his death; but this was not true sorrow, for you took the kingdom and you still hold on to it And you have built your tower for your own protection and to safeguard yourself against your foes. But the tower cannot save you because you do not want to save yourself."

Vortigern clearly heard what Merlin told him, and he understood that he had spoken the whole truth. So he said to him, "I acknowledge that you are the wisest man in the world, [35] and I beseech you to counsel me as to what I can do in the face of these things and to tell me how I will die."

And Merlin answered, "If I were not telling you how you would die, I would not be telling you the meaning of the two dragons."

So he begged him to tell him without hiding anything.

And Merlin said to him, "I want you to know that the great red dragon stands for your wicked heart, and that its body was so huge means your great power. And the white dragon stands for the birthright of the youths who have fled because they fear your rule. That they fought for such a long time means that you have long held their kingdom. That you saw the white one burn the red one with fire coming out of its body means that the youths will burn you with their fire. And so I do not think that your tower or any other stronghold will keep you from dying."

When Vortigern heard him, he was terrified. He asked Merlin where the youths were. And Merlin said to him, "They are at sea, and they have gathered a great army to invade their kingdom and to bring you to justice. And they say in truth that you had their brother murdered. I will tell you that they will come ashore three months* from now in the port of Winchester."

Greatly distraught was Vortigern when he heard this news and found out that those people were coming. So he asked Merlin if it could not be otherwise. And he answered, "No, it is not possible for you not to die from the fire of Constant's children, just as you saw the white dragon burn the red one."

Thus Vortigern spoke to Merlin, who told him the meaning of the two dragons. On the day Merlin told him, he called together all his people to go against the youths who were at sea, and Vortigern led his men-at-arms to Winchester, where the youths were to land.

And after they had all gathered, Merlin went off to Northumberland where Blaise was, and he told him that he had indeed done what he had been sent to do. And Blaise put everything into his book, which is how we still know it.

3. Uther Pendragon and the Round Table; the Perilous Seat.[†]

Here the story says that Merlin stayed for a long time with Blaise, until Constant's sons sent for him.

And Vortigern was at the port with a great host of men, and he waited for the day Merlin had told him about. And that very day the folk in Winchester saw on the sea the sails of the boats that Constant's sons were leading. As soon as Vortigern saw them, he ordered his men to take their arms and defend his port. They came to the port to defend it, while Constant's sons came there to go ashore. And when those who were on land saw the banners of King Constant, they were greatly amazed. And when the boat carrying Constant's sons touched shore, the men on land asked them, "Whose boats are these?"

Those on board answered, "They belong to Pendragon and his brother Uther, Constant's two sons who are coming back to their land, which Vortigern, a false and unfaithful man, took from them a long time ago. He had their brother killed, and they have come to bring him to justice."

And when the men by the harbor heard [36] that it was the sons of Constant their rightful lord who were leading such a great host, they saw clearly that they had lost the contest and that if they fought them, great harm could come to them, and they told Vortigern so. And when he saw that most of his men were deserting him and that they were already going over to Pendragon's and Uther's side, he was afraid; and he told his men who would not desert him to fortify the tower, and they did.

The boats came to port, and when they had touched shore, the horses came out, covered with armor, and all the men-at-arms as well; and when they had all left the boats, they went toward the castle. Some of the people, when they saw their

---

* Supplied from Micha (30, l. 66): *d'ui en .III. mois* ("three months from today"); Sommer's text has *.iij. iors* ("three days").

† Corresponds to Sommer, 35-58.

rightful lords, came over to them and their men-at-arms, and welcomed them as their lords.* And those who stayed with Vortigern had fled into the castle and defended themselves, for the men outside were storming them.

Thus the ones attacked and the others defended themselves, until Pendragon set fire to the castle on one of the great assaults, and as soon as the fire had overtaken them, a great part of the castle was burned up. And Vortigern was burned in that fire.

This is how the boys came back to their land, and they let it be known throughout the kingdom that they had returned. And when the people learned of the arrival of their lords, they were overjoyed and came to them and greeted them as their rightful lords. So the two brothers came back to what was theirs by birthright.

Pendragon was made king, and he was a very good and faithful lord to the people. And the Saxons whom Vortigern had brought to the land held on to their castles, which were very strong,† and every day they waged war against Pendragon and the Christians, and they fought for so long that sometimes they lost and sometimes they won. At last Pendragon laid siege to the castle of Hengist,‡ and he stayed there for most of the year.

At last he took counsel, and on the council were many men, and they deliberated as to how they could take the castle. Five of them had been privy to the meeting where Merlin had explained to Vortigern the meaning of the dragons and had told him about the boys and his death. They called Pendragon and his brother Uther aside and told them the wonder that Merlin had recounted, and said that he was the best seer who ever was, and if he was willing, he would say plainly whether this castle would be taken. When Pendragon heard this, he asked where the good seer could be found.

And one of them answered, "We don't know where. But we do know very well that when someone talks about him, he knows it, and if he wanted to, he would surely come, for I know that he's in this country."

"Then I will find him," said Pendragon.

Then he called for his messengers and sent them throughout the whole land to seek Merlin. And Merlin, who had known that the king was summoning him since he spoke to Blaise, went as quickly as he could to the town where the messengers were who had gone out looking for him. And he came like a woodsman into the town, with a great axe at his neck and stout shoes on his feet, dressed in a short tunic torn to shreds; his hair was standing out and his beard was quite long. He looked very much indeed like a wildman. He came so to the house where the messengers were eating, and when they saw him they stared at him in wonder.

They said to one another, "This one looks like a very bad man."

And he went forward and said to them, "You are not doing your lord's work very well. For he ordered you [37] to look for the seer named Merlin."

---

*   In the text references to the overlords are in the singular. Later, before one of the brothers is named king, the text reverts to the plural.

†   Supplied from Micha (31, ll. 58-59). Sommer's text refers imprecisely only to *le chattel, car moult estoit fors* (36, l. 20): "the castle, for it was very strong." See following note.

‡   Supplied from Micha (31, l. 62). Sommer's text continues to refer without specifics to *le chastel* (36, l. 23): "the castle."

When they heard it, they said to one another, "What devil has told that to this peasant, and what business is it of his?"

And he answered, "If it had been my job to look for him, I would have found him sooner than you have."

Then they stood all around him and asked if he knew who Merlin was and if he had ever seen him. And he answered, "I have seen him and I know where he lives. He is aware that you are looking for him, but you will not find him unless he is willing. And he ordered me to tell you that you are wasting your effort looking for him, and even if you did find him, he would not go with you. Say to the men who told your lord that he was in this country that they spoke the truth. And when you come to your lord, tell him that he will not take the castle that he is besieging until Hengist has died.

"You should also know that it was only five men from the army who told your lord to send people to look for Merlin, but when you go back you will find only three of them. And tell your lord and these three that if they came to this land and looked for Merlin in these woods, they would find him. But if the king himself does not come, he will find no one to bring Merlin to him."

They understood very well what he had told them. Merlin turned about, and as he turned they lost him from sight. And they crossed themselves and said that they had spoken to a devil. "What shall we do about what he has told us?"

They agreed among themselves that they would go back and tell this wonder to their lord and those who had sent them there. "Then we will find out whether those two have died, and we will tell the king what we have seen and heard."

So they rode back until, after many days, they came to the army where the king was. And when the king saw them he asked them, "Have you found the man you went to look for?"

And they answered, "Sir, we will tell you something that has happened to us. Call for your council and those who told you about the seer."

And the king sent for them. When they had come, they drew aside to meet privately. The messengers told the wonder that had happened to them and all the things the peasant had told them, including the two men he said would be dead before they came back. And they asked about them and were told that they had indeed died. When the men who had told about Merlin heard this, they were very amazed at the loathsome man they spoke about, and they wondered who he could be. They did not know that Merlin could take on a likeness other than his own, yet it seemed to them that no one could say that but Merlin himself.

So they said to the king, "We truly believe that it was Merlin himself who spoke to your messengers. No one else could have told about the two who have died, and no one but Merlin would have dared talk about Hengist's death."

Then they asked the messengers in what town they had found that man, and they said that they had found him in Northumberland, "and he came to our lodging."

Then they said very plainly that it had been Merlin. "And he said," the messengers went on, "that the king himself should come for him."

Then the king said that he would leave his brother Uther at the siege, and he would go off to Northumberland and take with him those who he thought knew Merlin. And he did as he said he would. And when they came to Northumberland, he asked news [38] of Merlin, but he found no one who could tell him anything. So he said that he would go look for him deep in the forest. And he rode through the forest looking for Merlin. One of the king's men* happened to find a great herd of cattle and a very ugly, misshapen man who kept them.

The one who found him asked him where he was from, and he said that he was from Northumberland and worked for a gentleman "who told me that the king would come looking for him in the woods today."

And the king's man said to him, "It is true that the king is looking for him. Could you tell me about him?"

He answered, "I would tell the king things I wouldn't say to you."

And he said to him, "Come along. I will take you where the king is."

The herdsman replied, "Then I'd be doing a bad job keeping my livestock! I have no need of him! But if he came to me, I would surely tell him where he'd find the man he's looking for."

And he said, "I'll bring him to you."

Then he left him and went looking for the king until he found him, and he told him what he had found. And the king said, "Take me to him now."

And he took the king to the place where he had found the peasant, and he was still there. And he said to the peasant, "Here is the king whom I bring to you. Tell him what you told me just now."

And he said, "I know for a fact that you are looking for Merlin, but you can't find him until he himself wishes you to. But go off to one of your towns near here, and he will come to you as soon as he knows you are waiting for him."

Then the king said, "How will I know that you are telling me the truth?"

And he answered, "If you don't believe me, don't do anything I tell you, for it is madness to believe bad advice. But you should know this much: I give you better advice than anyone else could."

And the king said, "Then I'll believe you."

So the king rode off to his town nearest the forest. After he had settled in there, it happened one day that a highborn man, well dressed and well shod, came to his lodging. And he said to those he found inside, "Take me before the king."

And they did. When he came before the king, he said to him, "Sir, Merlin sends me to you. And he declares that he was the herdsman who spoke to you in the woods, and the proof is that he told you he would come to you when it was his will. He told you the truth, but you still do not need him, and he has never wanted to see any great man unless that man had something for him to accomplish."

The king said, "Dear friend, I would very gladly see him now."

And he said to him, "Since you have said this, he sends you some very good news by me: Hengist is dead, and Uther your brother has killed him."

When the king heard this, he was greatly amazed, and he said, "Can what you tell me be true?"

---

*   The first part of the sentence is supplied from Micha (33, ll. 5-6, and his note). Sommer's text (38, ll. 2-3), like that of most manuscripts, including Micha's base, omits the reference to the other man and presents Pendragon as coming upon the hideous herdsman; this is illogical, as the man who finds the herdsman wants to take him back to the king and eventually brings the king to him.

And he answered, "You are behaving like a fool if you do not believe it before you prove otherwise. Now send there to find out whether or not what I told you is true. And if it is true, believe it yet again."

And the king replied, "You speak well."

Then the king took two messengers and sent them on the two best horses he had, and he ordered them not to stop riding, on the way there or back, until they knew for certain whether Hengist was dead. And they left and went as fast as they could, and after they had ridden a day and a night, they met Uther's messengers who were coming with the news of Hengist's death. When the messengers met, they gave their messages, and they all went back to the king.

The man who had brought Merlin's message [39] to the king had left. And the king's and Uther's messengers all went before the king and told him in private how Uther had killed Hengist. When the king heard it, he ordered them, if they valued their lives at all, not to speak of this thing, and so it was. And the king was greatly astounded because Merlin had known about Hengist's death.

So the king began waiting for Merlin in his town to find out whether he would come, and he thought in his heart that if he did come, he would ask him how Hengist had been killed, for few people even knew about his death. Thus the king waited for Merlin; then one day the king happened to be leaving the church when a very handsome, well-dressed man came along who certainly looked like a gentleman.

And he came straight before the king and said to him, "Sir, whom are you waiting for in this town?"

And the king answered, "I was waiting for Merlin to come speak to me."

"Sir," he said, "you are not so clever that you can recognize him when he is talking to you! Now, call those you have brought who should know who Merlin is and ask them if I could ever be this Merlin."

And when the king heard him, he was amazed. He sent for the ones who ought to recognize Merlin and said to them, "My lords, we are waiting for Merlin, but there is no one here among us who, to my knowledge, knows what he looks like. If you know him, tell me."

"Sir," they said, "it would be impossible for us *not* to recognize him, if we saw him."

And the gentleman who was with the king spoke and said, "My lords, how can people who don't know themselves know another?"

And they answered, "We do not see him here, and if we did, we would know him by his looks."

The gentleman said to them, "I'll show him to you."

Then he called the king into a room all by themselves and said to him, "Sir, I want very much to be friends with you and your brother Uther. And you should know that I am that Merlin whom you have come looking for, but those who think they know me do not know anything about me. I will show you this soon. Go out there and bring me the ones who say they know me well. And as soon as they see me, they will tell you that you have found me and that if I had willed it so, they would never have found me."

When the king heard this he was very glad, and he said to him, "I'll do whatever you want."

So he went out of the room as quickly as he could and brought those who he thought would recognize Merlin. And when they were there, Merlin took on the likeness in which they had seen him. As soon as they saw him, they said to the king, "Sir, it is indeed true that you have found Merlin."

When the king heard it, he smiled and said, "Be sure you know who he is."

They answered, "We know in truth that it is he."

And Merlin said, "Sir, they are telling the truth. Now tell me what you will."

The king said to him, "I would beseech you to be my faithful friend, if that can be, and to let me be your friend in return, for worthy men have often told me that you are very learned and wise."

And Merlin answered him, "Sir, you will never ask me for anything, advice or anything else, that I will not tell you if I know it."

The king said, "Would you please tell me whether I ever spoke to you after I came to this town [40] looking for you?"

And he answered, "Sir, I am the man whom you found keeping the livestock, and I am he who told you that Hengist was dead."

When the king and those who were with him heard this, they were astonished. And the king said to the others, "You knew Merlin badly when he came before us and we could not recognize him."

And they answered, "Sir, we never saw him do such things, but we believe that he can say and do what we other mortals could not."

Then the king said to Merlin, "How did you know about Hengist's death?"

"Sir, I knew when you came here that Hengist wanted to murder your brother, and I went to your brother and told him so, and he believed me, thanks be, and he was on the alert I also told him about all Hengist's strength and bravery and what could come from them. And Hengist stole into the midst of your army, in front of your brother's pavilion, to kill him. Your brother could hardly believe all that I told him, but thanks be, he did stand watch that night all alone without telling anyone, and he put on his armor without anyone knowing it. At last Hengist came carrying the knife to kill him with. When Hengist went into the tent, your brother began to stalk him; then, when he did not find him there, he went to the tent's opening. There your brother fell upon him and fought with him. He had him quickly; he was wearing armor and Hengist was not for he had come only to kill your brother and then to get back out as quickly as possible."

When the king heard this wonder, he asked him, "What shape did you take when you talked to my brother? For I am amazed that he believed you."

"Sir, I took the likeness of an old wretch, and I talked to him alone. I told him plainly that unless he was very much on his guard that night he would have to die."

And the king asked him, "Did you tell him who you were?"

He answered, "He does not yet know who spoke to him, and he will not know until you tell him yourself. And this is why I sent you word that you would not take the castle before Hengist died."

And the king said to him, "Dear friend, will you come away with me? For I have great need of your counsel and your help."

"The sooner I go, the sooner your barons will be upset about it. But if you can see what is worthwhile for you, and if you are wise, you will never, because of them, stop believing me,* and it will be for your own good."

And the king said, "You have already done enough for me and told me enough, if what you have showed me is true—that is, that you have saved my brother's life—so that I should never doubt your word."

Merlin said to him, "Sir, you will go ask your brother who told him what I have said to you, and if he cannot tell you, do not ever disbelieve me on any subject. What is more, I want you to know how to recognize me when I speak to your brother. I will have the character and likeness I had when I told him to beware of Hengist."

The king said to him, "Please let me know when you will speak to my brother."

And Merlin answered, "I will gladly tell you. But as you hold my love dear, be careful not to tell anyone else, for if I ever learned that you have betrayed me, I would never again have faith in you, and you would be hurt far worse than I."

"If I ever lie to you one time, never believe me again, and I will test you in [41] many ways†—this I tell you plainly."

Merlin answered, "I am glad for you to test me in as many ways as you like. And I want you to know that I will speak to you and your brother on the eleventh day after you come to him."

Then Merlin took leave of King Pendragon and went off to Blaise, and he told him these things. And Blaise put them all in writing, and this is how we still know them.

Pendragon rode until, after many days, he found his brother Uther. When each saw the other, they were overjoyed. And Pendragon took his brother to one side and told him about the death of Hengist just as Merlin had recounted it to him, and he asked him if it had been so.

And Uther answered, "Sir, God help me, you have said something that I never thought anyone could know but God and an old man who told me in secret, and I did not think that any other man could know it. So I bid you, tell me who told you this, for I am amazed that you could know it."

Pendragon said to him, "You can acknowledge fully that I truly know. But I beg you, tell me if you know who the old man is who saved you from death, for it seems to me that if it hadn't been for him, Hengist would have killed you."

And Uther answered, "Sir, by the faith I owe you as my brother and my lord, I do not know who he was, but he seemed to me to be a very worthy and wise man. And because he seemed so, I believed him. He told me something that was not to be believed, for Hengist behaved foolishly when he tried to kill me in the midst of our army and in my own tent."

---

*   Word supplied from Micha (35, l. 37).

†   The passage follows Micha (35, ll. 53-57). Sommer's text attributes this clause to Merlin: *Et merlins li dist ie vous assaierai* (40, ll. 41-43): "And Merlin said to him, 'I'll test you. ...'" Accordingly, the rejoinder is attributed to the king: *& li rois respont ore massaies en toutes les manieres que vous uoldres* (41, ll. 1-2): "And the king answers, 'Now test me in all the ways you wish.'" In Sommer's text the last sentence in Merlin's reply is correctly attributed to him. Later Merlin tells Blaise that the king wishes to test him (41, ll. 29-30), contrary to what Sommer's text affirms here.

Pendragon asked him, "Would you ever know this man if you saw him again?"
And he answered, "Yes, sir, I think so."

Pendragon said to him, "I assure you—and you can be certain of this—that he will speak to you eleven days from now. But for the love of me, do all you can to be with me all that day until the day is over, so that I can see all those who speak to you, that is, so I can see whether I can recognize him."

So the two brothers swore their oath one to the other. And Merlin, who knew all these things, brought this about so that they might be friends, and so that he might have their companionship.

And he told Blaise how the two brothers had spoken about him and how the king wanted to test him. Blaise asked him, "What do you mean to do about this?"

And Merlin said to him, "They are young and fickle, so I could hardly draw them into friendship with me* except by telling them at least a part of what they crave to know. And to give them joy and smiling faces, I know about a lady whom Uther loves. I'll go to him and bring on behalf of the lady a letter that you will write for me, so that he may believe me in what I tell him. We will talk about these things on the eleventh day, when they'll see me and not know who I am. And when the following day comes, I will become their true friend, and they will be all the more grateful to me."

Merlin did as he said he would. And he came on the eleventh day to the city where the brothers were. He took on the likeness of one of the serving boys in the lady's train, and so he came to the place where he found the two brothers. And he said to Uther, "Sir, my lady greets you and sends you this [42] letter."

And Uther, to whom the letter gave great joy, took it. He truly thought that the lady had sent it to him, so he had it read to him. The letter said that he should believe what the boy had to say. And Merlin told him what he knew he would be most glad to hear. And so, on that day until the evening, he was before the king, and Uther was overjoyed.

And when evening drew near, the king was amazed at Merlin, who had promised him that he would come that day to speak with Uther. When evening had finally fallen, the two brothers talked together and said that Merlin had lied to them. But Merlin withdrew a little and took on the likeness in which he had spoken to Uther, and he came before Uther and his brother. And when the king saw him, he asked Uther whether he was the gentleman who had saved him from death, and Uther recognized him and showed him how glad he was to see him, and he spoke to him about many things.

And he said, "Sir, you have saved me from death and from much else, but I am very astonished that you should say what I did after you had left me. And my brother told me that you would come today to speak to me. He asked me, if you spoke to me, to let him know. And I am amazed that my brother should have known what you told me."

Merlin answered, "He could not know it if someone hadn't told him."

---

*   Supplied from Micha: *m'amor* ("love for me") (37, l. 8), where Sommer's text reads *amor* ("love, faith") generally (41, l. 32).

The king had gone out of the pavilion, and Merlin told Uther, "Now go look for your brother and bring him here, and ask him what he said in my presence."

And Uther went out of the tent and ordered those who were outside to take care that no one went in. As soon as he was outside, Merlin took on the likeness of the serving boy who had brought the letter. When they came back, they found the boy, and when they saw him they were greatly taken aback.

Uther said to the king, "Sir, I see wonders, for just now I left the gentleman here I had told you about, and now I find here only this serving boy. Now, stay here and I'll ask my men-at-arms out there whether they saw the gentleman leave and the boy come in."

So Uther spoke to his men outside the pavilion. And the king began to laugh out loud. Uther asked those outside if they had seen anyone go in or out "after I went to fetch my brother."

And they said, "After you left, no one went in but the king and you."

Then Uther came back and said to the king, "Sir, I do not know what can have happened." And then he asked the serving boy, "And you, when did you come in here?"

He answered, "I was already here when you spoke to the gentleman."

And Uther raised his hand and crossed himself and said, "God help me, I am utterly bewitched; nothing like this has ever happened to anyone but me."

The king took great delight in this, and he was sure in his heart that it was Merlin who had done these things. Then he said, "Dear brother, I wouldn't have thought that you could lie!"

He answered, "Sir, I am so amazed I don't know what to say."

And the king asked him, "Who is this boy?"

And Uther said, "This is the boy who brought me the letter today* right in your presence!"

The king asked, "Did you recognize him?"

And he said, "Yes, very well."

And the king said to him, "Does it seem to you that this could be the gentleman who told you to come fetch me?"

He said, "Sir, this could not be he!"

And the king said to him, "Well, let's go along outside, and if he wants us to find him, we'll soon find him."

Then they went outside and stayed there a little while. Then the king said to [43] a knight, "Go inside to see who is there."

And he went in and found the gentleman sitting on a bed; then he came back to the king and told him.

When Uther heard it, he was struck with wonder, and he said, "Thank God! now I see what I did not believe anyone could know. Here is the very gentleman who warned me that Hengist would kill me!"

When the king heard this, he was greatly delighted, and he welcomed the gentleman. Then he asked him, "Sir, do you want me to tell my brother who you are?"

---

*   Sommer's text has *iui* (42, l. 38) for *hui* ("today").

Merlin answered, "Yes, indeed."

Then the king, who knew much about the things Merlin did, said, "Dear brother, where is the serving boy who brought you the letter?"

And Uther answered, "Sir, he was here just now. What do you want him for?"

The king and Merlin began to laugh and to share delight in what was happening. Merlin took the king aside and told him what he had said to Uther about his sweetheart, and he told him to repeat it in front of him. Then the king, laughing all the while, called his brother and said to him, "Dear brother, you have lost the boy who brought you a letter from your sweetheart."

"And how do you know," said Uther, "what letter he brought me and from whom?"

And the king answered, "I'll tell you if you want to hear what I know."

He replied, "I do," for he thought that no one on earth would know it.

And the king told him everything word for word that Merlin had said to him.

When Uther heard it he was greatly amazed and said, "How could I believe that you knew so much about it unless the boy told you?"

And the king said to him, "In God's name, this gentleman told me! And you can be sure that he was the serving boy who let you know that Hengist was about to kill you. This is Merlin, whom I went to look for in Northumberland, and this man has such power that he knows everything done and past, and of all the things that are to come he knows a great deal."

And Uther answered, "Sir, if it is your pleasure, this man could be very useful to us."

Then both brothers begged him to stay with them for the love of God and because they would believe whatever he wanted them to.

And Merlin answered, "You must both know that I know everything I want to know. And you, sir," he said to the king, "are you still not sure whether or not what I have told you about the things you asked me is true?"

And the king said, "I have never caught you in a lie."

"And you, Uther, did I not tell you the truth about Hengist and about your love for a lady?"

Uther answered, "You have told me so much that I will never disbelieve you. And because I know you are so worthy and clever, I would like you always to be with my brother."

"I will very gladly stay," he said. "But I want you to know, just the two of you, about my ways. I must, by the force of my nature, be away from people at times. But you can be sure that everywhere I am, I will be mindful of you more than anyone else and of what you do. And just as soon as I know that you are in any kind of trouble, I will come to help you and give you counsel. If you want to keep me as a friend, you must not be upset whenever I go away, and whenever I come, show everyone how glad you are to have me back, so that the worthy people who love you will love me all the more. The evildoers and those who hate you will hate me, but if you show me a cheerful face, they will not dare do otherwise. And you can be sure [44] that I will not change my shape for long except in private with you. I'll always come to your lodging in my right likeness, and those who have seen me before will run to tell you that I have come. As soon as you hear this, show

how happy you are, and they will tell you what a good seer I am! In all trust, ask whatever your mind bids you ask, and I will counsel you in everything."

So Merlin stayed with Pendragon and his brother Uther, and he became fast friends with them. He asked their permission to take back* the likeness in which the people knew him. And when he came before those who had seen him with Vortigern, they were very happy and ran to tell the king that Merlin had come. And when the king heard it, he went out to greet him, welcomed him joyfully, and took him to his lodging.

As soon as he came inside, the king's advisers took him aside and said to him, "Sir, there is Merlin, who we know for a fact is the best seer there is. Ask him to tell you how we will take this castle and how the war between you and the Saxons will end. You know that if he wants to, he will surely tell you."

And the king said that he would very gladly ask him. Then they let the matter drop because the king wanted to honor Merlin beforehand. When the third day came, the king's council was gathered together, and the king said to Merlin, "Dear friend, I have heard it said that you are very wise and a very good seer, so I beg you, so that I may be† always in your good graces, please tell me how I can take this castle and, as for the Saxons who have invaded my land, whether I can ever drive them out."

And Merlin answered, "Now you can test me to see how clever I am! I want you to know that ever since the Saxons lost Hengist, all they want is to give up your land and flee. Find this out for yourself tomorrow: you will send messengers to them seeking a truce, and you will call on them‡ to leave you the land that belonged to your father; you will give them passage out, and you will give them boats in which they can leave."

The king answered, "You have spoken well, and I will do what you say."

Then the king sent them Ulfin, one of his counselors, and other knights with them. He entrusted his message to them, and they left for the castle. When those within the castle saw them, they came out to meet them and asked what they wanted.

Ulfin said to them, "The king seeks a truce with you for three months."

"We will talk about it among ourselves," said the Saxons.

Then they drew to one side and took counsel together: "We are in a bad way because of Hengist's death, and we don't have the food to hold out here for as long as the king is giving us. But we'll tell him that if he lifts the siege and leaves us the castle, we will hold it as a fief from him, and we will give him each year ten§ knights, ten maidens, ten falcons, a hundred greyhounds, a hundred warhorses, and a hundred palfreys."

They all agreed to everything. So they came back to the messengers and told them, and the messengers went back to the king and told him. And [45] the king

---

* Verb supplied from Micha: *revenir en* ("to come back into") (39, l. 68); Sommer's text has *reveoir en ("to* see again in") (44, l. 8).

† Sommer's text has *sour estre* for *pour estre* ("in order to be, that I may be") (44, l.20).

‡ Supplied from Micha's text, which reads *et lor faites querre que* ("and you will entreat them to") (40, l. 23-24); Sommer's text has *lors vous requerront* ("then they will call on you") (44, l. 26). In the latter tradition, the text became garbled as, apparently, it was truncated.

§ Supplied from Micha (40, l. 42); Sommer's text reads *.ij.* (44, l. 38).

asked Merlin what he would do about it. Merlin answered that the king should not become entangled in such a truce, for great harm would yet come to the country because of it, "but tell them straightway, without waiting any longer, that they must withdraw from the castle. And they will do it very willingly, for they have nothing to eat. And tell them that they will never come to terms with you if they do not come out, but you will hand boats over to them so that they can leave. And if they are not willing to do this, then every one of them you take prisoner will die a dreadful death. And I pledge my life that if you let them go with their lives, they will be overjoyed as never before, for they think they are doomed to die."

The king did just as Merlin had set it out. He sent his messengers to them in the morning to deliver his terms. And when the Saxons heard that they could leave safe and sound, they were happier than they had ever been since they had lost Hengist. So the Saxons withdrew from the castle. The king had them taken to the harbor, and he gave them boats. Thus King Pendragon sent them out of his land on Merlin's advice. Merlin stayed on as head of the king's council. He was there a long time, until one day he spoke to the king about a matter of great import.

One of the king's barons grew very troubled about Merlin, and he went to the king and said to him, "Sir, it is a wonder how you can trust this man so much, for all the wisdom in what he tells you and all the intelligence he has come from the devil. If you like, I will test him,* and you will see very clearly that he knows nothing on his own."

And the king said to him, "I advise you to leave this alone, for I would not like at all for him to get upset."

He said, "Sir, I would never touch him, nor would I ever say anything to him that could bother him."

And the king granted him what he asked. When he had the king's leave, he was very happy. He was, in the eyes of the world, a very clever man, deceitful and full of wickedness, and a wealthy man, powerful and well born.

One day he came to Merlin. He seemed to be delighted to see him and looked very cheerful. He called Merlin before the king for private counsel and took him aside with a gathering of only four men, and he said to the king, "Sir, here is one of the wisest men in the world and one of the most trustworthy, for I have heard that he told Vortigern about his death and said that he would die from your fire, and so he did. Sir, I therefore entreat you and all who are here, for God's sake, since you see clearly that I am ill, please to ask him to tell me what my death will be, if he knows. I am sure that if he is willing, he will indeed tell me."

They all begged Merlin, and he answered them; and, speaking to the man who was testing him, for he knew well the jealousy and ill will he bore him, he said, "You have asked me to tell about your death, and I will tell you. You can know for a fact that on the day you die, you will fall from a horse and break your neck. This is how you will leave this life on that day."

And when he heard this, he said to the king, "Sir, you well know what this man has said, God keep me!"

---

*   Supplied from Micha (41, l. 7). Sommer's text has *iel laissaroie* ("I would let him") (45, l. 19) for *iel assaieroie* or *essaieroie* ("I would test.").

He then called the king aside and said to him, "Sir, now remember well what Merlin has told me, and I'll test him in yet another way."

And he went off to his own lands, dressed himself in different clothing as fast as he could, came back to the town where the king was, and made out to be ill. He secretly sent word to the king to come see him and bring Merlin with him in such a way that he would know [46] nothing. And the king said that he would go very gladly and that Merlin would not find out anything from him.

Then the king came to Merlin and said to him, "Let us go, just the two of us, to see a sick man in the town, and we will take along with us whomever you will."

And Merlin answered, "My lord, a king must not go anywhere alone or so privately that he does not have twenty men with him."

Then the king called those whom he wanted, and he went to see the sick man. And when they came there, he had got his wife ready to fall at the king's feet, and she did so. And she said to him, "Sir, for God's sake, have your seer say about my husband here, whom I care for in his sickness, whether he will some day get well."

And the king had a very pitiful look on his face, and he looked at Merlin and said to him, "Could you know anything about what this woman asks concerning her husband's death and whether or not he will get well?"

And Merlin said, "I truly want you to know that the sick man lying here cannot die in this bed from this illness."

And the sick man tried hard, so it seemed, to speak and said, "Sir, for God's sake, what will be my death when I leave this bed?"

"The day when you die," said Merlin, "you will be found hanging, and you will be hanging in the place where you die."

Then Merlin turned about and made a look as though he were upset, and so he left the king in the house. He did this because he wanted those inside to speak to the king.

When Merlin had gone, the baron said to the king, "Sir, if you know anything, you must know that he is mad, and there is nothing in what he has told me, for he has set out for me two kinds of death that cannot go together. I'll test him yet a third time before you. I'll go off tomorrow to an abbey, and I'll play the sick man. I'll send the abbot to find you, and he'll tell you that I am one of his monks, I am in a dreadful state, and he is very much afraid that I will die. He will beseech you, for the sake of God and for your own good, to come there with your seer,* and I swear to you that I will test him harder than today."

And the king promised that he would go there and bring Merlin with him.

So the king left that man and went off with Merlin. And the baron went straight to the abbey and did everything he had told the king he would do. He sent the abbot for the king, and the king went there and took Merlin. Before the king had heard Mass,† the abbot came to him with a good twenty-five monks and entreated the

---

*   The last phrase is elaborated on the basis of Micha's text (42, l. 11): *que vos i amenez vostre devin* ("that you bring your seer there"); the clause in Sommer's text is truncated (46, l. 25): *que vous i soies* ("that you be there").

†   Other manuscripts, as in Micha's text (42, ll. 17-20), add that they rode to the abbey, arriving there early in the morning before Mass was sung; after the king had heard Mass, the abbot came, etc.

king to come see one of his brother monks who was very ill and to bring his seer so that they might know if the efforts they were devoting to him would be worthwhile. The king asked Merlin if he would go with him, and he said that he would gladly do so, but he first wanted to talk to Uther his brother in his presence.

And Merlin called both of them privately to an altar, and he said to them, "The better I know you, the madder I think you are. Do you believe that I do not know how this madman who is testing me will die? Yes, I truly do know. And I will tell him today another death than the other two he has asked me for twice."

The king answered, "Can it be true that a man can die as you have said?"

"If he does not die that way," said Merlin, "then never believe me in anything I say to you. I truly know what his death will be and yours, too. When you have seen his death, you will ask me about your own. And I say to Uther right now that I will see him king [47] before I am separated from his company."

Then they went to the sick man, and the abbot said to the king, "Sir, for God's sake, have your seer tell me whether this worthy man can get well."

And Merlin looked as if he were upset and said, "He certainly can get up, for he isn't sick at all. He is testing me for nothing, for he will indeed have to die in both the ways I have told him, and I will tell him the third way even stranger than the other two. He should know for a fact that on the day he dies, he will break his neck, hang, and drown.* Whoever is alive then will see his death and will see these things happen, and you can surely test me to see whether I am telling the truth! He can stop pretending from now on, for I know all his ill will, and I know what his foolish heart thinks."

The baron got up and said, standing, "Sir, now you can plainly recognize his madness, for he does not know what he's saying. How can he possibly say that on the day I die I will break my neck and I will drown and I will hang, and that all that will happen on the day I die? I know very well that this could not happen to me or anyone else. Now look at how wise you are to believe such a man, to make him lord over you and head of your council!"

And the king answered, "I will never forsake him for this and certainly not before I know how you have died."

Then the baron grew angry when he heard that the king would not oust him from the council until after his death.

This is how things stayed for a while, and everyone in the land learned what Merlin had said about this man's death, and they were all eager to know how Merlin could be telling the truth about it.

One day a long time afterward, the man who was to die as Merlin had foretold was riding with a great crowd of people, and he came to a stream. Over the stream

---

Apparently, a rewriter in the tradition of Sommer's manuscripts (assuming that his text does not reflect the original) responded to a certain logic in the context developing from the fact that in the original plan, which the text says was followed, the abbot was to tell the king about the ill monk from the very beginning; moreover, subsequent details might seem redundant if the king were already at the abbey so close to the presumably dying man. In this light, the details constitute a kind of amplified repetition of the previous summary statements.

* The order of the last two is supplied from Micha (43, ll. 47-48); they are reversed in Sommer's text (47, l. 7).

was a wooden bridge, and his palfrey stumbled on the bridge and fell to its knees. The baron who had been on the horse was thrown forward and fell on his neck and broke it, and his body twisted and fell into the water in such a way that it was caught by his mantle on one of the old uprights that had been on the bridge: his backside was up in the air, and he kept hanging with his head and shoulders in the water.

He had three gentlemen with him who saw that he had fallen in this way, and the cry rose up so that all the people heard it* and came as fast as they could across the bridge or by boat in the water. When they had all come there, the three gentlemen said to those who pulled him from the water, "Look carefully to see if his neck is broken."

They looked and said, "It is broken beyond any doubt."

And when they all heard it, they were amazed, and they said, "Merlin indeed spoke the truth when he said that this man would break his neck, hang, and drown. Anyone who does not believe Merlin in everything he says is mad, for it seems to us that all his words are true."

Then they did with his body what was fitting. And Merlin, who knew all these things, went straight to Uther, whom he greatly loved, and told him about that man's death, just the way he had died. He asked him to tell the king, and he did. When the king heard it, he was quite amazed and said to him, "Who told you this?"

And he said, "Merlin."

The king told him to ask him when† this had happened. And when Uther came to Merlin, he asked him when it had happened, and he said, "It happened yesterday. And [48] those who will tell the king about it will come six days from now. I am going away, for I do not want to be here when they come. They would make‡ many speeches to me and ask me things I would not want to answer. From now on, I will not speak within the hearing of the people except so obscurely that they will not understand what I have said before they see it happen."

This is what Merlin said to Uther, and Uther came straight to the king and told him. The king believed that Merlin was upset, and he was very sorry about it, and he said, "Where has he gone?"

And Uther said, "I don't know. But he said that he did not want to be here when the news came."

So the king was left alone. And Merlin went off to Northumberland, to Blaise, to tell all these things to provide material for making his book.

And the king waited until the sixth day, when those bringing the news about the baron came. And when they were there, they told the king the wonder they had seen happen to that man. Then the king and all those who had heard Merlin's words said that there had never lived such a wise man as he. Then they said that they would write down everything they ever heard him say would come about.

---

*   Supplied from Micha, 43, n. 14 (omitted in Micha's text). Sommer's text, along with other manuscripts, reads *le uirent* (47, l. 30): "saw it."

†   Supplied from Micha (43, l. 31). Sommer's text reads *comment* ("how") (47, l. 41).

‡   Supplied from Micha (43, ll.. 35-36): *me metroient* ("would put."). Sommer's text has *me croient* ("believe me") (48, l. 2).

This is how they all ordained it, and thus was begun *The Story of the Prophecies of Merlin* from what he said about the kings[*] of England and all the other things he spoke about afterwards. This is why that book does not say who Merlin is or who he was,[†] for they put[‡] down in writing only the things he said to them.

And this is how the king was for a long time.

In that time Merlin was like a lord over Pendragon and his brother Uther. And when Merlin found out that they had said they would write down his every utterance, he told Blaise. And Blaise asked him if they would make another book like the one he was to make.

And Merlin answered, "No. They will write down only what they can come to know after it has happened."

Merlin came back to the court. And when he was there, he told them the news as though they knew nothing about it. And then Merlin began to speak those murky words from which was made *The Book of Prophecies,* the ones that cannot be understood until after they have come about. And after that, Merlin came to Pendragon and Uther, and he told them with great feeling that he loved them very much and wanted what was good for them and for their honor. And when they heard it, they were awestruck, and they told him to tell them in trust as much as he was willing to say and to hide nothing from them that had to do with them.

And Merlin said, "I will never hide from you anything that I am bound to tell you. And I'll tell you a great wonder. Do you recall the Saxons whom you threw out of the land after Hengist's death?"

And they answered that they did indeed. And he said that the ones who left were telling in Saxony the news of Hengist's death. He was of very noble stock, and his kinsmen were saying that they would never find happiness until they avenged Hengist's death. And they thought they could overpower this land and the whole country.

When the brothers heard this, they were astonished. They asked, "Have they then such a great army that they can bear up against ours?"

And he answered, "For every man you have ready to fight they will have two. And if you do not act cleverly, they will destroy you and win your kingdom from you."

And they said, "We will do everything you tell us to do, and with your help we'll never fail to do anything you order."

And he [49] said to them, "You must know that the enemy horde will come against you on the eleventh day of June. No one in your kingdom will know about it unless you send them word, and I forbid either of you two to utter a word about it. But do as I tell you. Send for all your liegemen and all your knights, rich and poor, and show them the best time you can, for it is a wise thing to be mindful of a man's well-being, so keep them nearby you. Then call them all together and bid them do their utmost to be with you the last week of June at the gates of Salisbury. And there gather all your forces on the riverbank so that you can defend yourselves."

"What?" said the king. "Shall we then let them come ashore?"

---

[*]   Supplied from Micha (44, l. 12); Sommer's text reads *del roi* in the singular (48, l.16).
[†]   The reference to Merlin as a character is supplied from Micha (44, l.14).
[‡]   Supplied from Micha (44, l. 15). Sommer's text has the verb in the conditional (48, l. 17).

And Merlin said, "Yes, take my word for it. And you will let them get a long way in from the water, and they will not yet know that you have gathered your forces. After they have gone in quite a way, you will send some of your men to their boats to make it seem that you want to stop them from getting back. When they see that, they will be disheartened. Then one of you two must go there with your army, and you will move so near them that you will force them to camp away from the water.* When they have set up their encampment, they will suffer from a lack of water, and the boldest among them will be distraught. You will hold them there two days, then on the third you will fight them. And if you do just this, then I tell you truly that the people of your kingdom will have the victory."

Then the two brothers said to him, "For God's sake, Merlin, please tell us if we will die in that battle."

And Merlin answered, "Everything that has a beginning must come to an end, and no one may run away from death, but all accept it as they have to. All people alive must learn that they will die, and you two surely know that you will die and that no amount of wealth can save you."

And Pendragon said to him, "You told me one time that you knew about my death just as you knew that of the man who was testing you. As for his, I was sure that you were telling the truth about it. This is why I beseech you, please tell me about my death."

And Merlin answered, "I want both of you to have the very most holy things and the most powerful relics you own brought out, and I want both of you to swear by the saints that you will do everything I tell you for your welfare and for your honor. And when you have done this, I can tell you in greater trust the things I know that you will need to know."

And they did everything that Merlin set out. And when they had sworn their oath, they said to him, "Merlin, we have done what you ordered. Now please tell us why you made us do it."

And Merlin answered the king: "You asked me about your own death and what will come of this battle. I'll tell you enough about it so that you won't need to ask any more.

"Do you two know what you have sworn? I'll tell you: you have sworn that in this battle you will be worthy men and faithful to yourselves and to God, and you may be sure that no man can be upright and faithful to himself if he is not so first to God. I will show you how to be faithful and worthy men. Confess to a priest; you must do so now more readily than at any other time, because you know that you have to go into battle against your foes. If you are as I have told you to be, they will be beaten, for they do not believe in the Trinity or in the trials that Jesus Christ suffered on earth, and you will be defending your birthright, which is yours by law and by religion. All who [50] die so upholding their rights will be reconciled to the law of Jesus Christ by the authority of Holy Church, and they need hardly fear death. I want you both to know that since holy Christianity was brought to this

---

* Supplied from Micha (44, ll. 76-77), where the location of the Saxon encampment at a distance from a water source is stated more clearly—*ou plain sanz riviere* ("in the plain without a stream")—than in Sommer's text (49, l. 15): *ensus de la rive* ("above," even "adjoining the bank").

island there has never been, nor will there be again in our time, such a great battle as this one.

"Each of you has sworn that he will work for the other's welfare and honor. I want you to know something that I will tell you openly:* one of you two must leave this world. And the one who will come back alive will make, on the spot where the battle will take place, the handsomest and richest burial ground he can with my help, and I swear to you to work so hard that what I build there will be seen as long as Christendom lasts.

"I have told you that one of you must die. Now strive to be worthy men who can in heart and in body carry through with what I have said. May each of you be clothed in greatest honor when he goes before his Lord. One of you two will come back. I will not tell you which one will die, because I want both of you to be strong-hearted and upstanding, as you both need to be. Now both of you, remember to show a happy, cheerful face, and treat each other in good faith for the love of Jesus Christ."

This is how Merlin ended his speech. They understood thoroughly what he told them and what in good faith he advised them to do, and they did so with resolve. They called for their liegemen and their barons in every land. When they had come together, Uther and Pendragon gave them of their great wealth, and they gladdened the barons' hearts. And they entreated each one to bid† those under him to take arms and horses and to send word throughout the land that the last week of June all should gather at the head of Salisbury Plain on the banks of the Thames in order to defend the kingdom. All who heard the news said they would be there most willingly.

Time went by and the day of the summons came. The two brothers had personally taken care to do everything that Merlin told them. And so they came to hold their Whitsuntide court on the riverside, and the whole people gathered there. Much wealth was given out there, and there were many cheerful faces. And they waited there until they heard that the boats had landed. When Uther found out that they had landed right on the eleventh day of June, he knew for a fact that Merlin had told him the truth. So he sent word to his bishops and to other leaders of Holy Church that every man in the host was to confess and that each was to forgive the other his anger and ill will; and if there was a piece of chattel over which any were in disagreement, it would be given back to the rightful owner. The orders were given throughout the army.

And the Saxons had left their boats and gone ashore, and they camped for a week. The next day they rode out.

King Pendragon knew very well what they were about. He had his spies in their army and knew that they would ride out, so he went to Merlin and told him, and he said it was true. He then asked him what he had in mind for him to do.

And Merlin answered, "You will send your brother to them tomorrow with a great many men-at-arms. And when he sees that they have got far away from the river and the sea, and have come to the middle of the plain, then he must keep his

---

*   Thus Micha (45, l. 28), whereas in Sommer's text (50, l. 6) the verb is negated.

†   The subordinate *que il comendassent* ("that they bid") is lacking in Sommer's text (50, l. 21) and is supplied from Micha (45, l. 50).

troops so near them that he forces them to halt and make camp. And when [51] the Saxons have encamped, then your brother and his men should draw back. Next morning, when they want to go on, he should hem them in so tightly that they cannot ride forth. Then there will be none among them so bold that he wouldn't wish to be back where he came from. Your brother should keep them there for two days. And on the third day, with your own army, as soon as it is daylight, you will see a red dragon moving in the air, and it will run from the sky to the earth. When you see the embodiment of your own name, you can safely begin to fight, for the victory will belong to your men."

At that meeting there were only Pendragon and Uther, and when they heard it they were struck with wonder, and they were very glad.

Then Merlin said, "I will go away now. Trust what I have told you, and be worthy men and good knights."

So they went their ways. Uther got his equipment and his men-at-arms ready to march between the river and the Saxon army.

Merlin took Uther aside and told him, "Strive to prove your worth, for you need not fear death in this battle."

When Uther heard this, his heart was filled with gladness.

Merlin went away to Northumberland, to Blaise, to work this story out and make it just right.

And the two brothers did just as Merlin had set it out. Uther came between the boats and the Saxon army and drove them into the plain far from the water. And he and his men ran against them so forcefully that they made them pitch camp, like it or not, right in the middle of the plain far from any water. Uther held them there for two days, and they could not ride out. And on the third day King Pendragon came with his army. When they saw those in the encampment lined up in battalions to fight Uther, the king ordered his battalions to form. This was done quickly, for each man knew beside whom he was to fight, and Pendragon's army drew near to the encampment.

When the Saxons saw both armies, they were stricken with fear, for they saw plainly that they could not get back to their boats without a fight. Then the wondrous thing appeared up in the sky—a red dragon that breathed fire and smoke from its nose and mouth, so it seemed to those in the army. The Saxons were disheartened and overcome with dread.

Pendragon and Uther said to their men, "Let us attack them!" (And they did so, because the Saxons were utterly undone.) "For we have seen all the signs Merlin told us about."

Then Pendragon's men* ran against them as fast as their horses could go. And when Uther saw that his brother's men had engaged in battle, he fell upon the Saxons with his men. Thus began the Battle of Salisbury. I cannot tell you everything, who fought well there and who poorly, but I can tell you this much: King Pendragon was killed there and many other barons. And the story says that Uther won the battle and that many of his liegemen rich and poor died there. But of the Saxons who

---

* Thus Micha (46, ll. 58-60); Sommer's text does not specify whose men attack first (51, ll. 30-31).

were there, we find none that got out alive; they died right there or were drowned at sea. Thus ended the Battle of Salisbury.

After Pendragon died, Uther was left lord of the kingdom. He had all the bodies of the Christians brought together on one plot of ground, and there all the men took their friends' bodies and laid them near the others by troops. Uther had his brother's body taken there along with the others. And he had written on his headstone who each one was. [52] Uther had his brother buried higher up than all the others, but he said that he would not have his name written above him, for anyone would be mad to see his grave and not recognize that it belonged to the lord of all the others who lay there.

And when he had done this, he went to London and called together* all his chief vassals and all the prelates of Holy Church who were under him, and he had himself crowned and anointed king; and he wore the crown and ruled as king after his brother. And after he had been anointed and given the crown, Merlin came to him two weeks later. And the king was very glad to see him.

And Merlin said to him, "I want you to tell your people about the signs I told you would come to this land and the pledge you and your brother made to me and the oath that each of you swore to the other."

So Uther told his people everything, how the brothers had tried to do everything Merlin had told them about, except the dragon, which he knew no more about than any of the others. Then Merlin explained the meaning of the dragon and said that the dragon had come to signal the death of Pendragon and Uther's survival, and he told what ill fortune had befallen the king because of his brother's death and the meaning ascribed to the battle. And because of the dragon's wondrous appearance, the new king bore for evermore the name Uther Pendragon, and thereafter that was the name he wanted all to call him.

And thus everyone knew that the things Merlin had shown the two brothers how to do, and the things he counseled them to do, were good.

So Merlin stayed for a long time: he was King Uther Pendragon's chief adviser, and the king confided in him. At last, a long time later, Merlin called Uther Pendragon and said to him, "Why don't you do more for your brother Pendragon, who lies on the Plain of Salisbury?"

And he answered, "What do you want me to do with him? I will do whatever you advise me to do."

And Merlin said, "You swore to do as I wish, and I promise you that we will build something that will be seen as long as this world lasts. Do as you have promised, and I will keep my word."

And Uther Pendragon answered, "Tell me what I can do and I will very gladly do it."

And he said to him, "Now learn how to do something that no one has ever known before, and it will be spoken of ever hereafter."

Uther Pendragon answered, "I will do so very gladly."

"Now send someone for great stones that are in Ireland, and send along two boats in which to bring them, and they will not be able to bring so many back that

*   The verb, supplied from Micha (46, l. 84), lacks Sommer's text (52, l. 4).

I cannot set them all up. And I will go to show them which ones I want so they can bring them back."

And the king said that he would very gladly send them there, and he sent a great many boats. And when they got there, Merlin showed them some great stones, long and wide. And he said to them, "Here are the stones we came to find."

When they saw them, they thought it was all madness, and said that all together they could hardly turn one of them over, "and we will never put such stones on our boats at sea."

And Merlin said, "If you don't wish to do this, then you have come for nothing."

They turned about and went back to the king and told him the wonder Merlin had ordered them to perform, which they knew no man on earth could do. And the king said to them, "Now wait until he comes." [53]

When Merlin came, the king told him the story his men had brought back to him. And Merlin answered, "Since they have all let me down, I will do what I have promised all by myself."

Then by the power of magic he had the stones brought from Ireland which are still in the burial ground at Salisbury.* And when they had come, the king went to see them and took many of his people to see the wonder of the stones. When they saw them, they said that all of them together could not move one of them, and they wondered at how he got them there, for no one had seen it or heard about it. And Merlin said that someone should set them upright, for they would be more beautiful standing straight up than lying down.

And the king answered that no man could do that but God, "unless you did it."

And Merlin said to him, "Now you go away and I will set them up, and I will have fulfilled my pledge to Pendragon; otherwise, I would have begun something for his sake that can never be brought to an end."

So Merlin stood the stones up. They are still in the burial ground at Salisbury and will be there as long as the world lasts. And so this work was over, and Merlin came back to King Uther Pendragon; he served him a great deal and loved him. A long time had gone by since he had come to understand in whom he had put his love, and he knew that he would believe him in everything he said.

One day it happened that Merlin came to the king and said to him privately, "I must talk to you about the highest secrets I know. For I see that all this land is yours; you are firmly in command of it as lord, and no one could rule it better. It is because I love you that I want to tell you something. Don't you remember that Hengist would have killed you if it hadn't been for me? Thus it seems to me that you ought well to believe me and love me."

Uther Pendragon answered, "There is nothing that you would say that I would not believe and do all in my power to bring about."

"Sir, if you do this, it will all be for your own good, for I will teach you something that will hardly distress you, and you could never do anything whereby you might so easily have the love of God."

---

* The reference, clearly, is to Stonehenge.

And the king answered, "As surely as you say it, if it can be done by any man, I will do it."

Then Merlin said, "What I will tell you will be a very strange thing to you, and I bid you, keep it hidden and do not say it to your courtiers or your knights, for I mean for all the worth and honor and thanks to be yours."

And the king said that he would never talk about it except through him alone.

He then said to the king, "Sir, you must take it as truth that I know everything that is past, gone by, and spoken, and I want you to know that this skill came to me from a devil. Sir, Our Lord, who is powerful over all things, has given me the intelligence and the knowledge to recognize and to know things that are to come. And thanks to that sovereign power, the devils lost me, for I will never, God willing, be subject to their will. Sir, now do you know where my power to do the things I do comes from?

"I will tell you what I know Our Lord wants you to do. And when you know it, be sure to honor Him according to His will. Sir, you must believe that Our Lord came to earth to save the world and that He sat down at the Last Supper and said to His disciples, 'There is one of you who will betray me.' Sir, everything was true just as He said, and the one who did Him wrong left His fellowship, just as He said he would.

"Sir, after this it happened that Our Lord [54] suffered death for our sake. And a knight* asked to take Him down from the cross, and He was given to him in place of his wages. Sir, this hired soldier loved Our Lord very much, for he wanted Him and agreed to have Him given to him. Sir, His disciples bore many hardships and many fearsome things afterwards. And it happened a long time after Our Lord was raised from the dead that the knight was in a wilderness along with some of his kin and a great many others who had gone along after him. Sir, a very great famine overcame them, and they complained to the knight, who was their leader. And he prayed to Our Lord to give them a sign telling them why He wanted them to suffer this trial.

"Our Lord ordered him to make a table in the name of the table that was at the Last Supper and to put a vessel he had on that table† after he had covered it with a white cloth, and he was to cover the vessel fully as well. Sir, Jesus Christ gave that cup to him, and with this cup. He divided the fellowship of the good from the wicked. And, sir, anyone who could sit at that table could fulfill his heart's desires in every way.

"Sir, at that table there was always an empty seat that stood for the place where Judas sat at the Last Supper when he understood what Our Lord was saying on his account and he left the fellowship of Jesus Christ. And his seat was left empty until Our Lord put another man there to take his place to bring the count to twelve. And the empty seat at the new table stands for that place. Thus these two tables are very much alike, and Our Lord perfects men's hearts at the second table. And they call the vessel, from which they have that grace, the Grail.

---

*   That is, Joseph of Arimathea.

†   The text beginning "in the name …" supplied from Micha (48, ll. 57-58), a scribe in the source of Sommer's text (54, l. 10) having telescoped it (see Micha 184, n. to ll. 57-58).

"If you will believe me, you will set up the third table* in the name of the Trinity, and by these three tables will the Trinity be signified in its three Persons, the Father, the Son, and the Holy Ghost. I promise you that if you do this, great good will come to you from it and great honor to your soul and your body, and in your time will happen things that will utterly amaze you. If you will do this, I will help you, and I promise you that if you do, it will be one of the most talked about things ever. For Our Lord has indeed granted grace to those who will know how to speak well of it. And I tell you also that this vessel and the people who keep it have drawn westward, by the will of Jesus Christ, to these parts. And even those who do not know where the vessel is have come here, and Our Lord, who brings good things to pass, led them. If you believe me, you will do what I advise you to do about these things. If you do this, and if you will believe me, you will be very glad indeed."

Thus spoke Merlin to Uther Pendragon, and the king was very glad about it. And he answered, "I do not want Our Lord to lose, because of me, any part of the thing that must be done according to His will. Indeed, I want you to know that I love Him. I put it all onto you, and I will do anything you order me to do, if I can."

So King Uther Pendragon put the whole burden onto Merlin, who was very glad to bear it. And Merlin said, "Sir, now look to the place where you would like most to do what you must."

And the king answered, "I want it to be done where you would most like it done, where you know it can best be done according to the will of Jesus Christ."

Merlin replied, "We will do it at Carduel in Wales, so have your people gather there to meet you on Whitsunday, and you will be ready to give out great gifts and to be of good cheer. And I will go before you and have the table built, and you will give me silver and [55] men who will do what I order them to do. And when you get there and your people are gathered, I will pick out the ones who are to stay there."

As Merlin set it out the king ordered it done, and he sent word throughout his kingdom that he would hold his court at Whitsuntide at Carduel in Wales, and all knights and all ladies were to be there to meet him. This is what the king made known everywhere. Merlin went off and had the table built and everything done there that needed to be done. And so it was until the week before Whitsunday, when the king came to Carduel.

And when he had got there, he asked Merlin how he had fared, and he answered, "Very well."

So the people gathered that Whitsuntide at Carduel, a great many knights and ladies and other folk.

Then the king said to Merlin, "Which ones will you choose to have sit at that table?"

And he said, "Tomorrow you will see happen what you never thought you would see. For I will seat there the worthiest men in your kingdom, and never, once they have sat there, will they want to leave this place to go back to their lands and domains. Then you will see for yourself who the worthiest are."

And the king answered, "That I will very gladly do."

---

* It is not explicit until much later that the third table is the Round Table.

And the next day Merlin did just as he had said. It was Whitsunday, and Merlin chose fifty knights, and he bade them, and had others do likewise, to sit at that table and eat the food that was there, and they did so very willingly. And then Merlin, who was full of powerful craft, went among them and called to the king, when they had sat down, and showed him the empty seat. Many others saw it, but they did not know what it meant or why it was empty, except for the king and Merlin. When he had done this, Merlin told the king to go take his seat. And the king said that he would not sit until he had served all who were at the table, and when he had done this he went to sit down. So they were for a whole week, and during the season of that feast the king gave away much wealth and many lovely jewels to ladies and unmarried gentlewomen.

And when it came time for leave-taking, the king went to his worthy companions and asked them how they were. And they answered him, "We have no wish ever to leave here, and we want always to be at this table at the hour of terce, so we will have our wives and children come to this town. And so we will live here at our lord's pleasure, for this is what our hearts tell us to do."

The king asked, "Do you all feel this way?"

And they all said, "Yes indeed! And yet we wonder at how this can be. For many of us have no bonds with any among us; others have not seen one other before, and few of us were friends before. And now we all love one other as much as a son should love his father, or more, and it does not seem to us that we will ever be parted unless it is by death."

When the king heard them speak in this way, he took it for a very great wonder, as did all those who heard it. And the king was most glad and ordered everyone in the town to love, believe, and honor them just as they would his own self. And so Uther Pendragon founded that table in his own time.

Then he came to Merlin and said to him, after [56] the crowds had gone, "You told me the truth indeed, and now I really believe that Our Lord wills this table to be founded, but I wonder at the empty seat. I would like you please to tell me, if you know, who is the one that will sit there."

And Merlin answered, "I can tell you only that the place will not be taken in your time, and the one who will sit there has not yet been conceived. The one who will take that seat must fulfill the adventures of the Grail. This will not be in your time, but in the time of the king who will rule after you. And I bid you, hold all your gatherings and all your high courts in this town, and I ask you please to stay here and hold your court here three times every year."

And the king told him that he would gladly do this, and Merlin said to the king, "Sir, I will go away, and you will not see me again for a very long time."

The king asked him where he was going. "Then you will not be in this town for all the feast days I will keep here?"

And he answered, "I will not. I do not want them to believe what they will see happening, for I want no one to say that I have brought about what will happen."

So Merlin left Uther Pendragon and came into Northumberland to Blaise, and he told him these things, the founding of that table and many other things which you will hear in his book. And so Merlin stayed more than two years, when he did not go to court.

And those who did not love him, or only put on a show of loving him, came one day to the king, who was at Carduel to hold his Christmas court. And they asked him about the empty seat. Why could a worthy man not sit there and so fill up the table?

And he answered, "Merlin told me a great wonder about the empty seat no man could take it in my time, and he who is to sit there has not yet been born."

And they smiled scornfully, for they were falsehearted, and said to the king, "Sir, you don't believe that any man could ever be better than we are! Or even that there is any in your land as good as those who sit there already!"

The king said, "I do not know. But *he* told me as much."

And they said, "Now you are worth nothing if you do not try it."

"I will not try it now," said the king, "for I would fear doing a great wrong, and Merlin would be angry."

They answered, "We are not telling you to try it now. But you say that Merlin knows what people do. If he does, then he knows well enough that we are talking about him and what he does. And if he knows it, he will come here, if he is alive, and he will not allow that place to be filled because of the great lie he has told you about it. And if he doesn't come between now and Whitsunday, please let us try it, and we will do so very willingly, and there are many worthy men among your kinsmen who will be very happy to undergo the test, if you want, and you will see whether they can stand it there!"

And the king answered them, "If I did not think it would disturb Merlin, there is nothing I would do more gladly."

"If Merlin is alive," they said, "and if he knows about it, he will come without fail before anyone can try it. But please, when it's Whitsunday, if he doesn't come, let us test it."

And the king granted them what they asked for, and they were very glad and thought they had done very well indeed.

So it was until Whitsunday. And the king let it be known throughout all the land that everyone should meet him at Carduel, for he would hold his Whitsuntide court there. And Merlin, who knew all these things, told Blaise about the wicked [57] thoughts of those who had undertaken this business, and he said he would not go there, since he knew that they would try the seat. He had rather they do it for their evil reasons than for good, and if he went there, they would say that he had come to upset the court. And the ones who had brought this plan to a head would in no way understand what they needed* to about it This is why Merlin said that he would not go there, so he bore up and waited until the eleventh day after Whitsunday.

The king went off to Carduel and took a great crowd with him. And the ones who came to try the seat spread the word everywhere that Merlin was dead and that peasants had killed him in a wood where they said they had found him behaving like a wildman. And they told the story so often and had it repeated so much that the king himself believed it, because Merlin had taken so long to come and seemed not

---

*   Supplied from Micha. Sommer's text has *quil ni mistrent .j.* ("that they did not put one there") (57, l. 5) for *tant com lor est mestier* ("as much as they need") (Micha 50, l. 49).

to care about the test for the seat. And when the evening before Whitsunday came, the man who wanted to try the place came forward.

He was a highborn and very wealthy man, and he said to the king, "Sir, we must try the seat."

And the king answered, "Who is the one to do it?"

"No one but I will sit there," he said.

Then he came to the table where the fifty worthy men were sitting, and he said to them, "I come to sit with you to share your fellowship."

And these men did not answer a single word, but bore themselves in a kindly way and watched what he wanted to do. And the king was there with a great crowd of people gathered about.

The man went forward to the place, moved in between two of the gentlemen, and sat down. He had just the time to put his thighs onto the seat when he melted away just like a ball of lead, and was lost from sight right before everyone, so that they did not know what had become of him. And when they saw that he had thus perished, everyone else wanted to sit in the place. But the king ordered the worthy gentlemen to stand up, so that after they had got up from the table no one would know which was the place, and they all rose straightway.

The sorrow in the court was great, and the court was utterly distraught by this wonder. The king was more aghast than anyone else, and he thought he had been made a fool of. He said for all to hear that* Merlin had plainly told him before that no one should take that seat, and that that man did not want to believe him; the king himself had forbidden it, but the man would not give up just for that—so did the king explain himself.

And when, two weeks later, Merlin came to court, and after the king had been told that he was there, the king was most happy and went out to greet him. As soon as Merlin saw the king, he said that he had behaved most unwisely about the place, for he had allowed someone to sit there. And the king said to him, "He tricked me."

"So has it happened to many who mean to trick others and trick themselves instead," said Merlin. "You know this because he spread the word that peasants had killed me."

The king said, "It is true that he said so."

And Merlin said to him, "You ought now to have learned your lesson not to try the seat anymore, and I warn you that if you do, you could be badly hurt. For the place and the table have great meaning; they are very high and most worthy, and they will bring great good to those who are in this kingdom."

The king asked him please to tell him what had happened to the man who sat at the place, "for I am awestruck."

And Merlin answered, "It is not your place to ask, and it would be worthless to you even if you knew. Think instead about those who still sit at the table and how to keep up [58] in the most honorable way you can what you have started. Come hold all your high feasts and joyful celebrations in this town in honor of this table. For you know without doubt, thanks to the test you have seen, how worthy it is, for

---

*   Supplied from Micha (50, l. 92), not in Sommer's text (57, 1 .27).

you cannot honor it too much. So I will leave you. Be careful to do just as I have told you."

The king said that he would very willingly do so.

4. Uther's Love for Ygraine; Arthur's Conception and Birth.[*]

So the king and Merlin parted company. And when the king knew that Merlin was gone, he ordered handsome buildings and houses to be built in the town, for he would henceforth hold his courts and his other gatherings there. And he sent word throughout all his land that all in his kingdom should know that he would be in Carduel on all feast days, such as Christmas, Whitsunday, and All Saints, and they should come there without being summoned again. So for a long time the king by custom held all his courts in Carduel.

At length the king happened, one certain time, to wish to call his barons together, and, for the honor and love of him, he wanted them to bring their wives and noble vassals and knights. He had them summoned and sent his letters everywhere, and they did everything the king had asked. So there were a great many married and unwed ladies, and many knights.

I cannot begin to tell you who all the people at that court were. But I must tell you about those my source story speaks of one after the other. And I want you to know in truth that the duke of Tintagel was there and Ygraine his wife. And when he saw Ygraine,[†] the king loved her deeply, but he did not show it, except that he more willingly looked at her than any of the other women. And she herself took note of it and knew in her heart that the king did indeed love her. When she fully understood this, she was slow in coming before him, and avoided it if she could, for she was very beautiful and utterly faithful to her husband. And the king, for love of her, but so that no one[‡] would take notice, sent jewels to all the ladies at the feast; he sent Ygraine some she was sure to like. She knew that he had sent them to all the ladies, and she did not want hers, but she dared not refuse them; instead she took them, and she knew in her heart that the king had given jewels to the other ladies only because of her, but she made no sign of this.

Thus King Uther Pendragon held his court, and every man was there with his wife, but he did it all for love of Ygraine, who had so overwhelmed him that he did not know what to do. The holiday court ended, but before the people left, the king entreated all his barons to be with him again on Whitsunday as they had been at that time, and he asked them to bring their wives as they had just done. And they all swore they would.

That was the end of it. And when the duke of Tintagel left court, the king rode along with him and did him great honors. The king then said to Ygraine, the duke's

* Corresponds to Sommer, 58-80.
† Supplied from Micha (52, l. 14), not in Sommer's text (58, l. 21).
‡ Supplied from Micha (52, l. 22); the verb is not negated in Sommer's text (58, l. 25).

wife, that she was taking his heart away with her, but she did not show that she had understood him. So the duke went off and took leave of the king, as did his wife. The king stayed in Carduel and gladdened the worthy men of the table who were left behind, and he brought cheer to the table, but his heart belonged wholly to Ygraine, and he pined for her until Whitsuntide.

Then the barons [59] gathered again and their wives too, and the king was very glad when he knew that Ygraine had come. At that feast he gave many gifts to the knights and ladies, and the king had the duke and Ygraine sit with him to eat. The king gave so many gifts and looked at her in such a way that Ygraine knew in truth that he loved her, and she was sorely distressed; as all could see, she was deeply worried, but she dared not talk about it. So the king was very cheerful at the feast, and he took delight in his barons. But when the holiday was over, all wanted to go back to their lands and took their leave. And the king begged them to come back to court and bring their wives when he sent for them, and they said they would.

So the people in the court scattered, and all year the king bore the misery of his love for Ygraine. At the end of the year he could hide it no longer, and he told two of his closest friends about his distress and the agony he felt because of Ygraine.

And they said, "What do you want us to do about it?"

And the king asked them, "How could I be with her more often?"

They told him that if he went to the land where she was, he would be blamed because people would take note of it.

So he asked, "What advice will you give me?"

And they said to him, "The best advice we know is for you to call together a great court at Carduel. Send word to all who will come there that they must not leave for two full weeks, and everyone must come ready to stay for the two weeks. Tell all your barons to bring their wives. So you will have a long time to spend with Ygraine, and you can take delight in your love."

When the king heard this, it seemed to him that they were giving him good advice, so he did as they had told him. He sent word to his barons to be at Carduel on Whitsunday, to bring their wives, and to come all ready to stay two weeks. And they came there and brought their wives, just as the king had ordered.

On that Whitsunday the king was of a mind to wear his crown, so he did, and he had many handsome gifts bestowed on his barons and wherever else he thought it worthwhile. On the day the king gave the feast he spoke to one of his advisers, named Ulfin, whom he very much trusted, and he asked him what to do, for love of Ygraine was killing him and he could neither sleep nor rest. He was at his wits' end, for he thought he would die, and he would be utterly unable to live without some kind of help.

And he answered him "Sir, you are very silly if you think you will die of craving a woman. I am a poor man beside you, but if I loved her as you do, I would never believe I would die. I've never heard tell of a woman, if she was entreated and sought after enough, and if a man gladly did everything he could to give jewels to all the men and women about her, to love and honor them by doing, and telling each one of them, what they want and what pleases them—I've never heard tell of a woman who, in face of that, could forbid the man to talk to her! And you who are a king are terrified! This is happening to you because you are fainthearted."

The king answered, "Ulfin, you speak very well, and you certainly know what has to be done in these matters. And I beg you, help me in all the ways you can. Please take from my room everything you will and give it to all the men and [60] women about her. Strive to do whatever pleases her, and speak to Ygraine in ways you know will be useful to me."

"Now let it be," said Ulfin, 'and I will do what I can." This is how the king spoke to Ulfin, and Ulfin answered, "Sir, love has no regard for reason when reason works against love's will. As for yourself, be careful to win the duke's good will and to be with him as much as you can. I will do my best to find a way to speak to Ygraine."

The king told him that he would surely know how to do that, and so they set to work. The king regaled the duke and was his companion for a full week, and he said to him and did whatever might please him, and he endowed him and his companions with many a lovely jewel. And Ulfin spoke to Ygraine: he told her things he believed would please her the most, and many times he brought her beautiful jewels. But Ygraine turned them down and refused to take any.

At length it happened one day that Ygraine was talking privately with Ulfin and said to him, "Ulfin, why do you want to give me these jewels and these lovely gifts?"

And Ulfin answered, "For your great beauty and for the beautiful way you look. And I cannot give you anything, since all the wealth in the kingdom of Logres* is yours and every worthy gentleman is at the mercy of your will and pleasure."

And Ygraine said to him, "How?"

Ulfin said to her, "Because you have the heart of the one to whom everyone else swears fealty. This heart belongs to you and obeys you. This is why all the other hearts are under your sway."

Ygraine asked him, "What heart are you telling me about?"

"The king's."

And she raised her hand and crossed herself and said, "God! what a traitor the king is to make a show of loving my husband and me, yet he means to shame him! Ulfin," she went on, "take care not to let it happen that you should ever say such words to me! For I want you to know that I would tell my husband, and if he knew it, you would have to die! I will hide† it from him just this one time."

And Ulfin answered, "It would be an honor for me to die for my lord. Never has a lady ever forbidden such a thing as you have when you forbid the king to love you, the king who loves you more than all things that can live and die. But perhaps you are jesting with us! Please, lady, for God's sake, take pity on the king your lord and on yourself! For if this is something in which you cannot be merciful, then great harm could yet come from it. Neither the duke your husband nor you could stand up against his will."

---

* The traditional name of the kingdom, but in the *Merlin* Logres is a city from which the kingdom takes its name, as is clear in Sommer's text (79, ll. 6-9). Eventually (Sommer, 96) the city is identified with London.

† Supplied from Micha (54, l. 27): *celerai* ("I will hide"). In Sommer's text (60, l. 25) the future has become a preterite with the loss of the interior syllable: *chelai* ("I hid").

Ygraine answered, weeping, "God willing, I'll protect myself: I'll never be anywhere he can see me."

So Ulfin and Ygraine parted. And Ulfin came straight to the king and told him everything Ygraine had said.

And the king said, "That is how a worthy lady should answer, so I will not stop beseeching her, for a good lady was never won over so quickly."

On the eleventh day after Whitsunday, the king was sitting at table, and the duke of Tintagel was sitting very close by. The king had in front of him a very handsome golden goblet. Ulfin knelt before the king and said to him, "Send this goblet to Ygraine, and tell the duke to bid her take it and drink from it for love of you. Have one of his knights take it to her full of good wine."

The king said that he would very gladly do so, and he said to the duke what [61] Ulfin had advised.

The duke thought there was no harm in it, so he answered, "Sir, many thanks! She will very gladly take it."

And the duke called a knight of his with whom he was very friendly and said to him, "Bretel, take this goblet to your lady on behalf of the king and tell her I bid her drink from it for love of the king."

Bretel took the goblet and came to the table where Ygraine was sitting, and he knelt before her and said, "Lady, the king sends you this goblet, and my lord asks you to take it and drink from if for love of the king."

When she heard this, she was deeply shamed and she blushed, but she dared not refuse her husband the duke's order. She took the goblet and drank from it, then she told Bretel to take it back to the king.

But Bretel said, "My lady, my lord orders you to keep it, and the king himself asked him to do this."

When she heard this she understood clearly that she would have to accept it, and Bretel went back and thanked the king for it on behalf of Ygraine, who had not said a word about it. The king was very happy that she had kept the goblet. And Ulfin went to the table where Ygraine was sitting to see what look she had, and by the look of her he thought she was most upset and brooding in thought.

After the tables had been taken down, she called him and said to him, "Ulfin, it was most unfaithful of your lord to send me a goblet. But you may be certain that he will win nothing by it, for before daylight tomorrow I will bring shame down on him. I will tell my husband about the treachery the king and you are trying to bring about."

Ulfin answered, "You are not so mad you do not know that, once a woman tells her husband such a story, he will never believe her again! This is why you will keep it to yourself."

And she answered, "A curse on any woman who does."

Ulfin left Ygraine straightway.

And the king, who had eaten and washed his hands, was very cheerful. He took the duke by the hand and said to him, "Let's go see the ladies."

And the duke said he would very gladly.

They went into the room where Ygraine had eaten along with all the other ladies. As soon as Ygraine saw the king, she was certain that he had come there only for her. The king talked and enjoyed himself for a while with the ladies, and Ygraine stayed there until nightfall. And when night had come, she went off to her lodging, and the duke went after her and found her weeping bitterly. When he saw her tears he was greatly amazed. He took her in his arms, because he loved her very much, and asked her what the matter was. She told him she wanted to die, and the duke asked her why.

And she said to him, "Husband, I will not hide the reason from you, for I love you more than anything."

"Sir," she went on, "the king says he loves me. And all these courts you see him holding with these other ladies whom he orders to come here—he says he does this only for love of me and to have a reason for you to bring me here. I have known this since the last court; that day I refused his gifts, and I took nothing from him until today. Now you made me take his goblet, and you ordered me through Bretel to drink from it for love of him! This is why I would like to be dead, for I cannot hold out against him or his friend Ulfin. Now I am sure, since telling you this, that he cannot for long keep himself from doing something harmful. So I beg you as my husband, please take me back [62] to Tintagel, for I don't want to stay in this town any more!"

When the duke heard this, he was deeply angered, for he loved his wife very much, more than anyone could. Then he sent through the town for his knights, and when they had gathered, they saw him and recognized how angry he was.

He said to them, "Get ready to ride out in secret, and let no one know a thing about it. I am leaving, and don't ask me why* before I tell you."

And they said, "Just as you order."

And the duke said to them, "Leave behind all your gear except for your armor, and your horses will follow you out in the morning, for I don't want the king or anyone else to know that I am leaving."

The duke's knights did just as he ordered. The duke, his wife, and their household got on their horses and went back toward his country. In the morning, when they found out that the duke had left, there was much ado about it among those who were still with the king.

And when the king found out that the duke had gone off, he was sorely distressed and upset that he had taken Ygraine away with him. He called the barons of his council together and showed them the shameful thing the duke had done to him, and they said that they were amazed that he had done it, and he had done a very foolish thing. And the king asked them to advise him as to how the duke could be made to make amends.

They did not know why the duke had left, so they said, "Sir, you will have your payment in any way you please."

The king told them how he had honored the duke more than any of his other barons, and they said that was true, and they were amazed that he should have done him such a great outrage.

---

* The sentence to here, apparently telescoped in Sommer's text (62, l. 5), is supplied from Micha (56, l. 29).

And the king said to them, "I will order him, if you say so, to come make amends for the wrong he has done me. And as he went back home, so let him come back here to be brought to justice."

And the whole council agreed to this.

Two worthy men went on behalf of the king to take this message, and they rode until, after many days, they came to Tintagel, where they found the duke. And they gave their message just as they had been ordered to. And when the duke heard that he had to go back to court with his wife Ygraine, he told the messengers that he would not.

"For the king and his people," he said, "have done such a wrong to me that I can no longer trust him, nor should I go to his court under his protection, nor will I ever speak otherwise about it. As God is my witness, he did everything in his power to make me lose faith in him."

And the messengers left the duke when they could not find any other arguments. After they had gone, the duke sent for the worthy gentlemen of his private council and told them why he had left Carduel, and he recounted to them the king's treachery and the dishonor he sought to bring him when he wanted to shame his wife.

When they heard about these matters, they were amazed, and they said that, God willing, it would never be allowed to happen, and misfortune should come to anyone who would try to do such a thing to his liegeman.

Then the duke said, "I beseech all of you, for God's sake and for your honor, and because it is your duty, to help me defend my land if he attacks me."

And they said that they would, even if it meant they would lose their heads.

So the duke took counsel with his liegemen. And the messengers went back to Carduel, where they found the king, and they told him and his council what they had found out. Then they all said together that they were astounded by the duke's madness, for they held him to be a very shrewd man.

And the king [63] asked them, as his liegemen and friends, to help him avenge the shameful thing the duke had done to him. They answered that they could not refuse him that, but they begged him all of one voice, so that he might keep the law, to defy him forty days beforehand.

The king did this, and he asked them to come back together at the end of the forty days. They said that they would very gladly do so.

And the king straightway sent his messengers to challenge the duke of Tintagel, and when the duke heard that he was being defied for forty days, he answered that he would defend himself if he could. He sent word to his liegemen telling them about the breech of faith the king had declared. He entreated them to help him, for he had very great need of it. And they told him that they would very willingly help him.

Then the duke took stock, and he said that he had only two castles that might be defended against the king, and he would not lose these two, he said, as long as he lived. So he made a plan to leave his wife in Tintagel along with ten knights, for he knew that the castle did not have to fear an attack from any man, and those ten knights and the townsfolk would keep the gate well guarded. And they did as he had ordered.

And he went off to the other castle that would be harder to take, and he said that he could not defend the rest of his land against the king.

This is how the duke behaved. And the messengers who had delivered the breech of faith came back to the king and told him that the duke was preparing to defend himself against any who would attack him.

When the king heard his messengers, he was very happy. And he sent word throughout his whole kingdom calling his barons together, and he had them gather on the border of the duke's land in a meadowland beside a great river. And when his army and all his barons had gathered, the king told them about the shame, the scorn, and the outrage against the court that the duke had inflicted, and the barons said that it was indeed right that he should make amends.

So the king invaded the duke's country, and he took his castles and his towns and laid waste his lands. Then he was told that the duke was in one of his castles and his wife was in the other. The king spoke to his council and asked them which of the two castles he should storm, and his council advised him to attack the duke where he was, for if he could take the duke, he would have the whole countryside and all his lands. And the king agreed, and they rode there.

The king called Ulfin and said to him, "Ulfin, what shall I do, now that I cannot see Ygraine?"

And he answered, "What a man cannot have he must do without. But you must make every effort to take the duke, for if you had taken him prisoner, all would have come to a good end; but if you had gone first to the place where Ygraine is, your doings would have come out into the open all too soon."

So the king besieged the duke in his castle, and he launched a heavy attack. The duke held out for a long time, and the king could never take the castle. The king was sorry and distraught, and he was most upset because of his love for Ygraine. At length he was in his pavilion one day and began to weep very bitterly. When his men-at-arms saw him weeping, they took themselves far off and left him alone. And Ulfin, who had been outside, went into the tent when he learned of the king's state and found him in tears.

So he asked him [64] why he was weeping, and the king answered, "You should know why, for you are well aware that I am dying for love of Ygraine. And I see plainly that I will have to die because of it. I have lost the will to drink, to eat, to sleep, to rest—this is how I know I will die, for I can see no other way out of this. And so I am sorry for myself."

When Ulfin heard this, he answered, "You are very fainthearted to think that you will die for love of a woman. But I will give you some good advice. Send word to Merlin to come to you, and he cannot fail to give you counsel, and you will do to the utmost whatever his heart wills and not be stubborn about it."

And the king answered, "I would do anything that anyone told me to do. But I know already that Merlin is aware of my distress, and I am afraid that I made him angry when the seat at the table was tested, for it has been a very long time since he has come anywhere I was, or perhaps he is bothered because I love the wife of my liegeman. But I certainly can't do anything more, for I cannot stop my heart from loving her. And I am well aware that he forbade me to send for her."

Ulfin answered, "I am certain of one thing: that if he is hale and hardy, if he still loves you as he has, and if he knows the distress you are in, he will not be slow in letting you hear from him."

This is how Ulfin comforted the king, and he told him to look cheerful and be glad; if he sent for his men and spent some time with them, he would forget much of his distress. And the king answered that he would very willingly do so, but he could never forget his pain or his love. So the king was consoled for a while, and he renewed the assault on the castle, but could not take it.

One day Ulfin happened to be riding in the midst of the army when he met a man he did not know.

And this man said to him, "My lord Ulfin, I would like very much to speak with you away from here."

And Ulfin answered, "And I with you."

Then they went off outside the encampment, the man on foot and Ulfin on horseback. The man was old, and Ulfin got down to talk to him and asked him who he was.

And he answered, "I am an old man, as you can see for yourself. Once, when I was young, I was thought to be wise, but now people say about many things I say that I am driveling. But I will tell you just between us that I was in Tintagel not long ago, and I came to know a worthy man who told me that your King Uther Pendragon loved the duke's wife, and he is laying waste the duke's lands because he took her away from the court at Carduel. If the king and you want to give me a little reward, I know of a man who could bring you to talk to Ygraine and advise the king about his love life."

When Ulfin heard the worthy man speak in this way, he wondered about where he had got what he had said, and he asked him kindly to point out the one who might advise the king about his love life.

And the old man answered, "I will hear first about the reward the king would like to give me."

Ulfin said to him, "Where will I find you again after I have spoken to the king?"

The old man answered, "Tomorrow you will find either me or my messenger on the way between here and the army."

And he commended him to God and went away, saying that he would talk to him the next day without fail and tell him something that would gladden him.

Ulfin left and came straight to the king [65] as fast as he could, and he told him all about how he had spoken with that man. When the king heard what he had to say, he asked Ulfin when he had seen the man.

And he answered, "I saw him just now, and he told me that I would talk to him again tomorrow, and I had to be able to tell him what reward you wished to give him."

The king said, "You will take me when you go to speak to him." And Ulfin said he would very gladly do so. "And if you speak to him without me," said the king, "offer him everything of mine he wants and more."

So they dropped the matter until the next day.

That evening the king was happier than he had been in a long time. And the next day, after Mass when Ulfin was ready, he rode with the king through the encampment to the place where Ulfin thought he would find the old man. After they had gone forward a little, they saw a cripple who also seemed to be blind.

And when the king passed in front of him, he said, "May God fill your heart with the thing you most long for. Give me something I can thank you for."

The king looked at him and said to Ulfin smiling, "Ulfin, will you do what I order as a service to me, for love of me, and to do what I will?"

Ulfin answered, "I want nothing more than to do your will."

And he asked him, "Did you hear what this cripple said and what he asked me for? He has reminded me of the thing in the world that I love most and crave most. Go sit beside him and tell him that I have given you to him and that there is nothing I own that I love more."

Ulfin did not answer him, but went to sit down beside the cripple and gave himself to him.

And when the cripple saw Ulfin, he asked him, "What have you come looking for?"

And he said, "The king sends me to you so that I may be of service to you."

When he heard this, he smiled and said, "The king has taken note and recognized me better than you have. I would like you to know that the old man you spoke to yesterday has sent me to you here. But I will not tell you what he told me. Instead, go to the king and tell him that I see clearly that he would do great harm if he had his way, and I advise him that the sooner he understands this the better off he'll be."

Ulfin said to him, "Could I dare ask you about yourself?"

And he answered, "Ask the king and he will tell you."

And Ulfin got on his horse and rode after the king.

When the king saw him, he turned aside, called Ulfin and said to him, "How can you have come here after me? I just gave you to the cripple."

"Sir, he wants you to know that you are more observant than I am, and he wants you to tell me about him, for he would not, but said that you would."

When the king heard this, he turned about and rode back very fast until they came to the spot where they had found the cripple.

Then the king said to Ulfin, "Do you know who talked to you yesterday in the likeness of an old man? It is the same man whom you saw crippled today."

And Ulfin said, "How could a man disfigure himself so? And who is he?"

The king answered, "You can be sure that it is Merlin playing tricks on us, and when he wants to, he will let us know who he is."

With that, they let the matter drop and rode down through the encampment

And Merlin came straight to the king's tent in his true likeness, so that people would know him for who he was, and [66] he asked where the king was. A messenger came in to the king and told him that Merlin was asking for him. When the king heard this, he was happier than anyone, and he came straightway to Ulfin.

He said to him, "Now you will see what I was telling you, for Merlin has come. And I was sure that they were looking for him in vain!"

Ulfin answered, "Now we'll see whether you can honor him and do what he wants, for no man alive could better help you in your love for Ygraine."

And the king replied, "You speak the truth, and I will do everything he orders."

So they rode to the king's tent, where they found Merlin. And when the king saw him, he was filled with joy and said that Merlin was welcome indeed.

He took him in his arms, embraced him tenderly, and said, "Why should I tell you of my suffering, when you know just as well as I how I am? I have never been so eager for any man to come! And I beseech you, in God's name, for myself and on behalf of what you know my heart craves!"

And Merlin answered, "I will never listen to anything you have to say without Ulfin."

Then the king had Ulfin summoned. He took him aside so that they could talk alone, and said, "Here is the old man you saw yesterday and the cripple."

Ulfin looked very hard at Merlin and said to him, "Could what the king told me be true?"

And Merlin said, "Yes indeed! And as soon as I saw that he sent you to me, I was sure that he had understood everything."

Ulfin said to the king, "Sir, now you should talk to Merlin about your troubles, and not shed tears when you are alone."

And the king answered, "I do not know what to say or what to ask him, for he knows my whole heart and my feelings, and I could not lie to him without his finding it out. But I beg him for God's sake please to help me so that I can have Ygraine's love. And I will do anything that he sets out for me to do."

Merlin answered, "If you dared give me what I asked of you, I would arrange it so that you could have her love and lie in her room naked beside her in her bed."

When Ulfin heard this, he smiled and said, "I'll now see what a man's heart is worth!"

And the king answered, "Anything you ask me for that can be found, you will have it."

"I will be sure of it," said Merlin.

And the king said, "Let everything be as you propose."

"Will you swear by the saints, and will you make Ulfin swear, that what I ask you for the morning after you have lain with her all night and done with her all you will—that you'll give me what I ask you for and not take it back?"

And the king said to him, "Yes, very willingly."

Merlin asked Ulfin if he would swear likewise.

And he said, "I am sorry that I have not already sworn so."

When Merlin heard what they said, he smiled and said, "When the oath is taken, I will tell you how this can happen."

Then the king had relics brought in and the holiest things he had, and he swore to him just what he had laid out. And he agreed to give Merlin in good faith, and with no deceit, what he would ask him for. After the king, Ulfin swore that, with the help of God and all the saints, the king would hand over to him what he had said and sworn in good faith that he would. Thus were the oaths made, and Merlin accepted them.

Then the king said to Merlin, "Now I beg you to tell me about my business, for I am the man in the world who most needs to have it over and done with, and I have the strongest will to satisfy my yearning." [67]

Then Merlin told the king, "You will have to go there very boldly, for she is a most honorable lady and very faithful to God and her husband. But soon you will see what power I have to deceive her. I will bestow on you the likeness of the duke, and it will be so good that all people there will take you for their lord. The duke has two knights who are closer to him, and to Ygraine as well, than anyone could be. One is called Bretel and the other Jordan. I will make Ulfin look like Jordan, and I will take Bretel's shape. I will have the gates opened for you, and thanks to these shapes, I will get you inside there to go to bed, along with Ulfin and myself. But you will have to leave there very early in the morning when Ulfin and I go out, for we will hear very strange news there. Get your army ready to leave your barons in charge,* and give orders forbidding anyone to go toward the castle before we get back. And be careful to tell no one where you are going but the two of us who are here."

The king and Ulfin answered that they would do everything he ordered. Merlin made things ready for what he had to do.

And he said to them, "I will give you your new likenesses on the way."

And the king hurried to do as fast as he could what Merlin had ordered. When he had done, he came straight to Merlin and said to him, "I have done what I had to do. Now tend to your business."

Merlin said to him, "The only thing left to do is to leave."

They got on their horses and rode until they came to Tintagel.

Then Merlin said to the king, "Now wait here a little, and Ulfin and I will go over there."

He and Ulfin went to one side, separated, and went straight back to the king. Merlin brought a herb, and the king took it and rubbed himself with it; and after he put it on himself, he looked unmistakably just like the duke.

And Merlin said then, "Do you recall ever having seen Jordan?"

The king answered, "I know him very well."

And Merlin showed him Ulfin in the likeness of Jordan.

When Ulfin saw the king, he said, "Good Lord God! how can any man be changed to look like another?"

And the king asked him, "What do you think about me?"

Ulfin answered, "I recognize you as no one but the duke."

And the king told him that he looked just like Jordan. After they had spoken thus for a while, Merlin came, and it seemed to them that he was Bretel. So they talked together and waited until night came. Just after darkness began to fall, they came straight to the gate of Tintagel. Merlin, who looked just like Bretel, knocked at the gate, and the gatekeeper and those who guarded the gate came out to him.

And he said, "Open the gate. See, this is the duke coming!"

They opened the gate and saw clearly, so it seemed to them, Bretel, the duke, and Jordan, and they let them in. And Bretel forbade them to tell anyone that the duke had come.

---

* Supplied from Micha (64, l. 18): *a laissier a voz barons* ("to leave to your barons"). Sommer's text reads (67, l. 11) *a loisir, & vos barons* ("at leisure, and your barons").

Several of them ran to tell the duchess that the duke had come. And they rode until they came to the great hall, and they got down from their horses. Merlin told the king privately that he should behave like the duke, cheerfully. Then all three went up to the room where Ygraine was already lying in bed. [68]

As fast as they could, they had their lord's boots taken off, and they put him to bed with Ygraine. This is how the good king called Arthur was conceived. The lady took great delight in the king, for she thought that he was surely her husband the duke, whom she loved very much, and they lay together until daylight the next morning.

Then news came to the town that the duke was dead and his castle taken. When the two companions, who had got up, heard the news, they went straight to their lord where he lay and said to him, "Sir, get up and go to your castle, for news has come to your people that you are dead."

And he jumped up and said, "It is no wonder they think so, for I left the castle and no one knew it."

Then he took leave of Ygraine and kissed her in plain sight of all who were there when he left. And the three of them went out of the castle as quickly as they could, and no one recognized them. When they were outside, they were very happy.

And Merlin came up to the king and said, "Sir, I have done all I promised you. Now be sure to keep the oath you swore to me."

The king answered, "You have made me far happier and served me far better than any man ever did another, and I will certainly hold to our bargain."

And Merlin said to him, "I am laying claim to my reward, and I want you to give it to me. You should know that you have fathered a male child in Ygraine: this is what you have given me, and you must not have him. Any power you have over him you have yielded to me. Have the hour and night you sired him written down, and you will know whether I am telling the truth."

"And I swear to you," said the king, "that I will do everything you have told me, and I surely owe it to you."

So they rode as far as a river, and Merlin had them wash in that river. After washing, they lost the shapes they had taken on, and they looked as they had at first. Then the king rode as fast as he could and came straight to his army. As soon as he had got there, his liegemen and his men-at-arms gathered around him and told him how the duke had been killed.

They said that the day after he had gone, the army grew very still and quiet. "And the duke noticed that you weren't in the encampment. So he had his men put on their armor and had his foot soldiers come out through one gate and his knights through another. They ran against us and did us great harm before our men could get their arms. The cry was raised and the din grew louder. Our people armed themselves, ran against them, and pushed them back to their gate. There they turned about and fought very hard until the duke's horse was killed beneath him and he was struck down. There the duke was killed among your foot soldiers, for they did not recognize who he was. And we broke through after the others inside the gate: they defended themselves very poorly after losing the duke."

And the king answered and told them that he was very sorry about the duke's death.

This is how the duke was killed and his castle taken, and the king spoke to his liegemen and told them that he was very sorry about the duke's ill luck, and he asked their advice as to how he could make up for such a loss so that his vassals would not blame him. For he did not hate the duke so much that he wanted him dead, and he was quite distraught about the mishap that had befallen him, "so I will make up for it as best I can."

Then Ulfin, [69] who was very close to the king, spoke and said, "Since this thing is over and done with, amends must be made in the fairest way we can."

Then Ulfin took a great many barons aside,* and he said to them, "How do you advise the king to take news of this death to the lady and to the duke's friends? He begs you to give him counsel, and you must advise him as best you can, because he is your overlord."

And they answered, "We will very gladly advise him. And we bid you, tell us the thing it would be most worthwhile to ask for, so that the king will not refuse us, for we know that you are his dear friend."

And Ulfin answered, "Since I am a friend of the king, if I knowingly counseled something behind his back that I would not want said to him in front of everyone, then you would take me for a traitor, and I would be. Now if it were up to me to give counsel about the lady's friends and† peace, I would advise something that you would not dare think about."

They answered all together, "We believe everything you say and we yield to you, for we are well aware that you are a wise man and a trustworthy adviser. So we entreat you, help us to make up our minds about this matter."

Ulfin answered, "I will tell you what I think, and if you know anything better, say so. I would advise the king to send word everywhere that the lady's friends are to come to Tintagel. The king should be there, and he should call the lady and her friends to come before him. After they have gathered, the king should make so much ado about the duke's death that people would think that any there who refuse to make peace are mad, and they would say that the king is an upstanding and faithful man of honor and that we his counselors are, too. This is how anyone who wants to make peace should do so."

And the worthy barons said, "We will hold to your counsel, and there will be no other."

So they came to the king and gave him the counsel they had decided upon, but they did not say to him that Ulfin had given it to them.

After they had proposed it all to the king, he answered, "I willingly agree to this, and I want it to be just as you have said."

So the king sent word by letters to all the duke's kinsmen that they should come to Carduel under a truce, for he wished to make amends for everything they held against him.

And Merlin came straight to the king and said to him, "Do you know who has given that counsel?"

---

  *   Supplied from Micha (67, ll. 9-10); in Sommer's text the barons come and take Ulfin aside (69, ll. 2-3).

  †   The conjunction is not in Sommer's text (69, l. 11), where the punctuation suggests that a scribe may not have understood the exemplar.

And the king answered, "No, just that all my worthy barons advised me to do this."

Merlin said, "They did not dare make such a recommendation by themselves, but Ulfin, who is very shrewd and faithful, thought out in his heart the best and most honorable peace there could be. I do not believe anyone knows this but me," he went on, "and I have now told you."

And the king asked Merlin please to tell him just how Ulfin worked it out and Merlin told him all Ulfin's train of thought. When the king heard this, he was very gladdened in his heart and very happy.

And the king said to Merlin, "What would you have me do about this?"

"I could not give you," said Merlin, "better or more faithful advice. This way, you will have everything your heart yearns for. I want to go away, but first I want to talk to you with Ulfin there. After I am gone, you can surely ask Ulfin how he came up with this peace."

And the king said he would do so.

Then Ulfin was called before them, and when he had come before them, Merlin spoke and [70] said to the king, "Sir, you have sworn to me that you will give me, insofar as you can, the heir you have begotten, and you have written the hour and the date he was conceived. You know for a fact that you fathered him thanks to me. So the sin would fall on me if I did not help him, for his mother may yet be shamed because of him: she has no way to hide from the world. So I want Ulfin to write out the documents, and he should put there* the time, the hour and the night when he was conceived. You will not see me before the hour and day he is born. And I entreat you, as my overlord, to believe Ulfin in what he tells you, for he loves you, and he will never say anything to you or advise you in anything that is not for your welfare and for your honor.

"I will not speak to you or to him again for six months, and I will talk first to Ulfin. What I tell you to do through him, please believe in it and do it,† if you want to be my friend and his and if you mean to safeguard from now on what is lawfully yours."

So Ulfin recorded the child's conception.

And Merlin took the king aside by himself and said to him, "Sir, you will take Ygraine as your wife,‡ and you will be careful not to let her know that you have lain with her or that she is with child by you. It is with respect to this that you will most have her at your mercy, for if you ask her about her pregnancy and try to find out by whom she is with child, she will be unable to name the father, and she will feel ashamed toward you. This is how you can best help me have the fruit she is bearing."

So Merlin left the king and Ulfin and came straight to his master Blaise; he told him these things and had him write them down, and it is through the writing that we still know them.

---

* Sommer's text has *quil oie* (70, l. 6): "let him hear" (?), while Micha reads *que il ait* (68, l. 34): "let there be."
† Supplied from Micha (68, l. 42); the verbs are reversed in Sommer's text (70, ll. 11-12).
‡ The clause is supplied from Micha (68, l. 46).

And the king and his barons went off toward Tintagel. And when he had come there, he sent for his liegemen and his council and asked them what to do about the things that had happened.

They answered, "We advise you to make peace with the duchess and the duke's friends, and you will have great honor in it."

The king ordered them to go straight to Tintagel to speak to the duchess and show her that she could not defend herself against him, and tell her that if she and her liegemen throughout her land wanted peace and her advisers counseled it, he would gladly work it out just as she wished. So the barons went to Tintagel, and the king stayed behind and took Ulfin aside privately and asked him what he advised about the peace. He led him to understand that he was well aware who had urged it.

"Then you surely know, sir," he said, "whether or not you like it."

The king answered, "I like it very much indeed, and I would like even better for it to be brought about just as you thought it through in your heart."

And Ulfin said to him, "All you need do is grant it, and I will bring it about."

And the king bade him to do so. So their talk ended.

And messengers came to Tintagel and found the duchess there and the duke's friends, and they showed how the duke had died because of the wrong he did. They said that the king was very sorry about it, and he would gladly make peace and come to terms with the lady and all the duke's friends. The duke's wise barons clearly saw that they could not hold out against the king, so they advised the lady and her friends to make peace with the king. And the lady and her friends said that she would take counsel about it, and they withdrew to a room together. [71]

When they gathered in private, the lady's and the duke's friends said, "Lady, those gentlemen are telling the truth: we cannot hold out against the king. Listen to them and find out what kind of peace the king wishes to make with you and your liegemen. They can offer peace in such a way that it cannot be refused: one must choose the lesser of two evils—we advise you to do this."

And the lady answered and said, "I never shunned my husband's counsel, nor will I ever forgo anything you advise me, for I do not know anyone whom I should believe better than you."

Then they came straight out, and one of the worthiest and wisest of the gentlemen spoke and relayed the lady's words to the king's messengers.

"My lady has taken counsel," he said, "and wishes to know what amends the king will make to her for her dead husband."

The messengers answered, "Dear sir, we do not know the king's will, but he clearly said that he will take counsel with his barons and will make everything up to her as they dare judge fit."

And they replied, "Then he will make amends fairly, if that is the case, and we need not ask any more of him. You are all such worthy gentlemen that you will grant her just redress, if it is God's will, and you will urge him to do what is good and what is honorable for him."

So they set a day at the end of two weeks when the lady and her friends would come before the king to hear what he wanted to say. If he had nothing to say that suited the lady and her friends, then they would have safe conduct to go back to Tintagel. So the day was set, and the messengers went straight back to the king and told him what they had found and the counsel the lady had taken. And the king said that she and all her people who came with her would be very well taken care of, and that he would gladly hear them out if they sought from him what was right.

So the king bided his time for two weeks, and he and Ulfin spoke together of many things. And when the appointed day came, the king sent an escort for the lady. After she had come into his encampment, the king called all his liegemen and counselors together, and he sent word to the lady and her counselors asking them what they meant to request with respect to the peace.

And the lady's counselors said, "Sir, the lady has not come here to ask for anything, but to find out what she will be offered in amends for her husband's death."

And the messengers went straight to the king and told him. When the king heard this, he held them to be very shrewd, and he took his council to one side and asked them what they would advise in this case.

They answered him, "Sir, no one can know better than you what kind of peace you want to make with them or what you mean to offer."

"I have already told you my thoughts and feelings on the matter," said the king. "You are all my liegemen and we are friends, so I put myself wholly in your hands. Anything you advise me I will do."

And they answered, "No one could ask more of you. But sir, this is a very weighty case, and we would not dare undertake it unless we were sure that you would not hold a grudge against anyone."

And Ulfin spoke up: "It seems that you take the king for a madman, and you don't believe anything he tells you."

The barons answered, "Ulfin, you are right. But we beg you to join us in our deliberations, and the king to allow it. You will report our finding to the king, and you yourself will do your best to show us what to do, for you know how by your worth and by right." [72]

When the king heard what they asked Ulfin, he looked happy, and he said to him, "Ulfin, I have raised you up and made you a wealthy man, and I know that you are clever. Go counsel them, on my orders, the best you know how."

And Ulfin answered, "I will do so since you send me there, but I want you to know that no king or any ruler can be loved too much by his liegemen, nor can he lower himself too much to them to win their hearts."

This is what Ulfin told the king when he went to the council of the barons, and they withdrew by themselves. They asked Ulfin what he would have them do in this matter.

And Ulfin answered, "You hear that the king is leaving it all up to us. Let us go to the lady and her friends and ask them if they will defer to us as well."

And they answered that he had spoken well, like a learned man.

So they went to speak to the lady and her council, and when they came before her, they told her that in everything the king had put himself into their hands, that he would keep the peace and do what they told him, "and we have come to you to ask you and your council if you will also yield to us."

They answered, "We should take counsel on this."

So they deliberated and said that the king could not make a better offer than to leave everything up to his barons.

Thus the lady and her counselors and all the dead man's kin agreed to yield to them, and everyone on both sides took heart.

Then the king's barons withdrew to deliberate by themselves, and they asked one another what they advised. After they had spoken among themselves and everyone had given his views, they all asked Ulfin what he would have the king do.

And Ulfin answered, "I will tell you what I think, and what I say here I would say anywhere else. You are well aware that the duke was killed by the king and his army. Whatever wrong he may have done the king, he did nothing against him for which he deserved to die. Isn't what I'm telling you true? And you should know that the duke's wife has been left with child, while the king has utterly laid waste her lands. You may also be sure that she is the best lady in the world, the fairest and the most honorable. And you should know that the duke's kinsmen have lost a great deal through his death, so it is right and just that the king should give back to them a large measure of their losses, according to what they are, so that he may win their love.

"On the other hand, you know that the king has no wife. So I say in my judgment that the king cannot make up for her loss unless he weds her, and it is my view that he should do so to make amends and win your friendship and for the sake of all those in this kingdom who will have restitution. And when he has granted all this, he should as soon wed the duke's elder daughter to King Lot of Orkney, who is right here, and do for the lady's other friends what he must so that each and every one will take him as their lord and lawful king.

"Now you have heard my advice," said Ulfin, "and you may say something else if you cannot agree to it."

And they answered all together, "You have spoken the boldest counsel that any man could think of. And if you dare report it just as you have said it here, and if we see that the king agrees, then we will very willingly agree to it."

And Ulfin said, "You don't say very much at all, but if you agree to it plainly and openly, then I will report our words to the king. Here is King Lot of Orkney, about whom I have said a great deal. Let him say what he thinks."

"Never, whatever you may have said about me," answered the king, "would I want to put off making peace."

When the others heard that, they all agreed as one to Ulfin's counsel. [73]

Then they all went straight to the tent where the king was staying. And the lady was called along with the gentlemen of her council, and when they had all gathered, they all sat down. Ulfin stood and reported the terms of the peace just as they had talked them out.

And when he had said everything, he asked the barons, "Do you not advise what I have just said and agree to it?"

And they all answered that they did.

Ulfin turned toward the king and said to him, "Sir, what do you say? Do you agree to these gentlemen's terms?"

And the king answered, "Yes, Ulfin, if the lady and her friends agree to them and if, for my sake, King Lot will take the duke's daughter as his wife."

King Lot said, "Sir, you will never ask me to do anything for the sake of your love and peace that I would not do very gladly."

Then, within earshot of everyone, Ulfin spoke to the man who had reported these words to the lady and asked him if he recommended this peace. And he answered like the able, learned man he was. He looked at his lady and her council, who were so sad and wretched that the water from their hearts had welled up in their eyes, and behind him they were weeping from sorrow and said through their tears that never had a lord made such an honorable peace with his liegeman. So he asked the lady and the duke's kinsmen if they recommended the terms.

The lady did not speak, but her kinsmen spoke and said all together, "Everyone should agree to them, and we do indeed. For we know that the king is such a worthy and faithful man that we put ourselves into his hands."

Thus it was sworn to on both sides, and the king took Ygraine, and King Lot of Orkney wed her daughter.

The wedding of the king and Ygraine was on the thirtieth day after he had lain with her in her room.

And of the lady's elder daughter and King Lot were born Sir Gawain, Agravain, Guerrehet, Gaheriet, and Mordred.* And King Neutres of Garlot took the other daughter, a bastard† named Morgan. On the advice of his kinsmen, Neutres put her in a nunnery to learn to read and write, and she learned so much so well that she mastered the arts. She became wonderfully skilled in an art called astrology,‡ and she worked hard all the time and knew a great deal about the healing arts. For her mastery of knowledge,§ people called her Morgan the Fay. The king behaved justly toward all the other children, and he loved all the duke's kinfolk.

So the king took Ygraine, and at length it showed that she was with child. The king lay one night beside her and put his hand on her belly. He asked her by whom she was pregnant, for she could not be carrying his child: since he had married her, he had not lain with her without having it written down; and she could not be pregnant by the duke, for she had not seen him since a long time before his death.

And as the king kept heaping guilt on her, she grew frightened and ashamed, so she said, weeping, "Sir, I cannot deny what you already know. For God's sake, please take pity on me, for I will tell you things that are amazing but true, if you promise me that you will not leave me."

The king said, "Speak confidently, for I will not leave you for anything you might say."

When she heard this she was greatly cheered, and she said to him, "Sir, I will tell you amazing things."

---

*   On these sons, see below, Sommer, 96.

†   Supplied from Micha (72, ll. 6-7). Sommer's text introduces a third daughter as Neutres's wife and does not mention that Morgan was a bastard (73, l. 23). Later, the text explicitly mentions five daughters (96, ll. 27-30), none of whom is singled out as a bastard.

‡   On astrology/astronomy, see ch. 2, p. 28 n..

§   Supplied from Micha (72, l. 12). Instead of *clergie* ("book learning"), Sommer's text repeats *fusique/fisique* ("medicine," "medical arts," "natural science") but goes on to mention as well her great intelligence (*sens*) (73, l. 27).

So she told him how a man had lain with her in her husband's shape, and he had brought two men with him who looked like the two men her husband most loved in all the world. Thus he came into my room in front of all [74] my liegemen, and he lay with me, but I thought certainly that he was my husband. That man fathered this child with whom I am pregnant, and I know for a fact that he was conceived on the very night my husband was killed. And when the news came to me the next morning, that man was still lying in my bed. He gave me to understand that he was my husband and that his men didn't know what had become of him, and he left right away."

When she had given her account, the king answered and said, "Dear friend, take care to hide this from every man and woman you can, for you would be shamed if anyone knew it. And I want you to know that this child you are carrying is neither yours nor mine by rights. Neither you nor I will have him, nor will we keep him near us. Rather I beg you to hand him over to the one I'll recommend you give him to, so that we will never hear of him again."

And she answered, "Sir, you may do what you will with me and all that is mine. I am at your beck and call."

The next morning the king came to Ulfin and reported to him all his and the queen's words.

When Ulfin had heard them, he said, "Now you can see clearly how honorable and faithful my lady is, for she did not dare lie to you even about such an upsetting matter. You have carried out very well what Merlin gave you to do, and he could not have it any other way."

So the king waited until the sixth month, when Merlin had promised him to come. And he did come, and he spoke to Ulfin in private and asked him to tell him about many things, and Ulfin told him the truth as he knew it. Then he came to the king, and the king told him how he had spoken with Ygraine, how Ulfin had negotiated the peace, and how he had accepted it.

And Merlin answered, "Ulfin has to a degree atoned for his sins in abetting your love-making. But I have not atoned for my sin in helping to deceive the lady about the child fathered in her womb and she does not know by whom."

The king answered, "You are so learned and so worthy that you will know how to atone for this."

And Merlin replied, "You will have to help me."

The king said that he would help him in any way he could. "And the child," said the king, "I will see that you have him."

And Merlin said, "In the nearby country there is one of the worthiest men in your kingdom, the best endowed with all good traits. He has a wife who has just given birth to a son, and she is very worthy and faithful. This good man is not at all wealthy, so I want you to send for him and tell him that you will give him of your own wealth if he and his wife swear on saints' relics that a child who will be brought to them will be nursed with the woman's very milk, that they raise him as their own and give their son over to another woman to be nursed."

The king answered, "I will do just as you have said."

Then Merlin took leave and went off to Blaise.

And the king had the worthy gentleman sent for, and when he had come, the king welcomed him with great gladness. He was quite amazed that the king was so happy to see him.

And the king said, "Dear friend, I must reveal to you a wonder that has happened to me. You are my liegeman, and I would ask, by the faith you owe me, that you help me in what I am about to tell you and do your best to keep it hidden."

And he answered, "Sir, you could order me to do nothing I wouldn't do [75] if I could. And if I cannot do it, I will keep it a secret."

And the king said to him, "A wondrous thing happened to me. While I was asleep, a gentleman came to me and told me that you were the worthiest man in my kingdom, the most upright and faithful to me. He told me that you have a newborn son by your wife. He also told me to ask you to take your son from your wife and give him to another woman to be nursed, and to ask your wife, for love of me, to suckle and raise a child who will be brought to her."

The good man answered, "Sir, this is a very weighty thing, for you are asking me to cut my child off and disown him, and to have him nurse on milk that is not his. Sir, I will get my wife to agree if I can, so I beg you, tell me when this child will be brought."

And the king answered that, God help him, he did not know.

And the gentleman said to him, "Sir, I would do anything in the world you ordered me to do, if I could."

Then the king gave him such a handsome gift that he was dumbfounded. And he left the king and came straight to his wife and told her what the king had said. And when she heard it, it seemed a very strange thing to her.

"How could I stop nursing my son," she said, "to nurse another?"

And the good man answered, "There is nothing we should not do for our lord. He has done so much for us and given us so much, and he promises to do so much, that we should do as he wills, and I want you to swear to me that you will."

And she replied, "I am yours and so is the child, so do with us as you will. And I grant what you want, for I ought in no way to be against you."

Then the gentleman was very gladdened that his wife would do whatever he wanted. He told her to find a woman who could nurse her child so that they might be ready when the other one was brought to her.

This is how the worthy man spoke to his wife. And it happened that the queen was ready to give birth. The day before she gave birth, Merlin stole back to court and spoke to Ulfin.

He told him that he was proud of the king because he had spoken wisely to Antor "just as I asked him to. Now tell him to go tell the queen that she will have a child tomorrow after midnight and that she must hand him over, or have someone else give him, to the first man they find on the way out of the hall."

And Ulfin said, "Then you will not speak to the king?"

Merlin said, "I will not speak to him at this time."

Then Ulfin came to the king and told him what Merlin had bidden.

And when the king heard him, he was very happy, and he rejoiced with great gladness. He said to Ulfin, "Will he not then speak to me?"

And Ulfin answered, "No, but do as he orders."

The king then came to the queen and said to her, "Lady, I will tell you something. Believe me and do as I ask you." And he went on, "Lady, tomorrow night, after midnight, you will give birth to the child that is inside you. And I beg, I beseech, I order you to have one of the women closest to you give him, just as soon as he is born, to the first man she will find on the way out of the hall. And let none of your maids tell anyone that you have had a child, for it would bring great shame to me and to you if anyone knew that you had borne a child so soon, and many people would say that he was not mine, nor does it seem to me that he could be." [76]

When the lady heard her husband, she said to him, "Sir, what I told you a while ago is true, for I don't know who fathered him. I will do with him whatever you order, since I am very much ashamed of the mishap that has befallen me. But I am utterly astounded that you know the time of the birth."

And the king answered, "I beg you, please do what I have said."

"Sir, I will indeed, God willing."

Thus the king's and queen's meeting ended. And she waited as long as it pleased God until the next evening, after the hour of vespers, she was stricken with the birth pains. And she was in labor until the hour the king had told her. She gave birth right at that hour, after midnight and before daybreak.

As soon as the child had been born, she called one of her women, whom she most trusted, and said to her, "Dear friend, take this little boy and carry him to the door to the hall, and if you find a man who asks for him, hand him over to him. And you will look carefully to see who this man is."

She did just as the queen had ordered. She wrapped the child in the richest and best clothes she had and carried him to the door to the hall. When she had opened it, she saw a man who seemed very old and weak.

So she asked, "What are you waiting for?"

He answered, "The thing you are bringing me."

And she asked, "What kind of man are you? To whom shall I tell my lady I have given her little boy?"

He replied, "That is none of your business. Just do what you have been ordered to do."

And she held the child out to him, and he took it. What became of him after he took the child she never knew. She came straight back to her lady and told her that she had handed the child over to an old man, "but nevertheless, I do not know who he is."

And the queen began to weep because she was filled with great sorrow.

The man to whom she had given up her child went off as fast as he could to Antor, and he found him just as he was leaving to go hear Mass. He had taken on the likeness of an old man, so he called Antor and said to him, "Antor, I want to talk to you."

And Antor looked at him, and he seemed to be a wonderfully worthy gentleman, so he said to him, "Sir, I would very gladly speak with you."

"I bring you a little boy, and I bid you have him nursed in as loving a way as if he were your own. You can be sure that if you do this, many good things will happen to you and your children, such that if anyone told you now what they were, you would not believe it."

"Is this the child the king asked me to have my wife nurse," asked Antor, "the one I disowned my own son for?"

And he answered, "In truth, it is he. And the king and all worthy gentlemen and noble ladies should entreat you to take him, just as I do myself. You can be sure that my entreaty is not worth less than a wealthy man's."

Then Antor took the child and saw that he was most handsome, and he asked him if he had been baptized. He answered that he had not been and begged him to have him baptized at once in that church. And Antor said that he would.

Then he took him and asked the man who had handed him over to him, "What do you want his name to be?"

And he answered, "If you want to have him baptized as I would have it, his name will be Arthur. Now I am going away, for I have nothing more to do here. You can be sure that great good will come to you because of this, and after you and your wife have had this child for just a little while, you will not know whether you love him or your own son better."

And Antor asked him, "Who shall I tell the king gave him to me?"

He answered, "You won't know any more about me now." [77]

Then each went his own way. And Antor had the child baptized. Then he took him to his wife and said to her, "Lady, this is the child I have asked you to care for."

"He is very welcome indeed," she said.

She asked him whether he had been baptized, and he said he had and that his name was Arthur. Then the lady took him and nursed him, and she put her own little boy in the care of another woman.

King Uther Pendragon held the land for a long time afterwards. At length he happened to fall gravely ill with a crippling of his hands and feet, and then upheavals broke out in many places throughout the land, and the rebels* were so bothersome to him that he appealed to his barons. His barons advised him to strike back against them if he could. But the king then entreated them, for God's sake and for love of him, to go together without him, as worthy liegemen should do for their lord, and they said that they would very willingly do so. So they went and found the king's foes, but they saw that they had already drawn much of the land over to their side. The king's men moved as a body against them, but they were an army without a leader, so they were overwhelmed and the king lost many of his liegemen.

When the news that his men had been routed was brought to the king, he was most distraught. Those who had got away from the battle came straight to him, but the numbers of those who won had grown many times. And the Saxons who had been left in the land in a wretched state all drew together and greatly strengthened their ranks. And Merlin, who knew all these things, went straight to Uther Pendragon, who was dreadfully weakened by his illness, and his time had almost run out.

When the king found out that Merlin had come, he was very glad, and thought in his heart that he would yet have solace. And Merlin came straight to him, and the king turned a cheerful face to him.

---

*   Implicit in Micha's text (77, ll. 4-5). In Sommer, the Saxons are responsible for the initial threats (77, l. 8).

Merlin said to him, "Sir, you are very frightened."

And the king answered, "That is right, for you well know that my own liegemen, without my taking notice of them, have destroyed my kingdom and killed my people and routed them in battle."

And Merlin replied, "Now you can see that no one is worth anything without a good overlord."

"For God's sake, Merlin," said the king, "advise me as to what to do!"

"I will tell you something meant for you alone that I want you to believe. Have your army called together. And when they are all gathered, have yourself put on a horse-drawn litter and go out to fight your foes. I can assure you that you will defeat them. And after you have won the battle, you will understand what it means to say that a land without an overlord is worth less than a land that has one. When you have done that, in the name of God and for your soul's sake, share your wealth, for I want you to know that you will not have long to live.

"You must understand this: people who have great wealth and die with it whole cannot then share it to save their souls, for it is no longer theirs, but belongs to those left behind after them, who are hardly at all charitable toward those who have depended on them.* It would be better [78] for a wealthy man to have had nothing than not to share his gifts, as it is fitting, in this earthly life. The wealth and favors that people have in this world are a hindrance to the soul only if they do not share them as they should. And since you know beforehand that you are to die, you must share them well and in such a way that you will not lose the bliss of the other world. For happiness in this world is worthless, and I will tell you why in a single word: in this world there is no happiness that does not come to an end, but the joys you earn in the other world cannot end or grow wearisome or turn bad. And whatever people have in this mortal world, God allows them to have it in order to try them for the next world.

"Now, it is therefore fitting that, if a man wishes to be sensible with the things God has lent him, he should strive for everlasting life. And you, who have had so many of the good things in this world, what have you done for Our Lord, who has graciously lent them to you? I have loved you a great deal, and I still do, but you should know that no one can or should love you better than you yourself, and no one can hate you more than you yourself.†I tell you truly that, after you have won this battle, you cannot live for very long.‡ And I want you to know that all the works a man does in his lifetime cannot be better for him than a good end. If you had done all the good things in the world and came to a bad end, you would be at risk of losing everything, and if you had done many evil things and came to a good end, you would have forgiveness. I want you to know that you cannot take

* Thus Sommer's text (77, l. 37-38). In Micha, and the majority of manuscripts he consulted, it is a question of a single survivor, who is explicitly identified with Satan (78, ll. 18-19): *ainz est a celui qui nul bien n'en laisse faire: et tu saiches que ce est li deables* ("rather it belongs to the one who allows no good to be done with it—you may know for a fact that this is the devil").

† Supplied from Micha (78, ll. 38-40). Sommer's text substitutes *mais bien saces que nus ne se puet miex hounir que li homs lui misme* (78, ll. 13-14): "but you should know that no one can bring shame to a man better than he himself."

‡ Supplied from Micha (79, ll. 40-42); the sentence is not in Sommer's text.

anything away from this world but honor and works of charity. And because I know that there can be no honor without good works and no charity without honor, I have explained to you where you are and what you must do.

"You know that Ygraine your wife is dead and you cannot have another, so your land will be left without an heir because you must strive to do the right thing. I will go away, for I have nothing more to do here, but please tell Ulfin to believe me when he must."

And the king said to Merlin, "You said dreadful things to me when you told me that I would defeat my enemies and what I must do to repay Our Lord."

Merlin answered, "Only to a good end. I am going away, but I implore you to keep in mind what I have said would happen to you after your battle."

The king then asked for news of the little boy he had taken away, and Merlin said to him, "You needn't ask anything about that, but I will tell you that the child is handsome and big and well fed."

The king asked Merlin, "Will I ever see you again?"

And Merlin said, "Yes, one more time."

So Merlin left the king. And the king had his men-at-arms summoned and said that he would go against the enemy. When his army had gathered, he had himself put on a litter, and he moved out with his troops. And the others moved against them forthwith and fought with the king's army, and the king's men routed them thanks to the king's encouragement. So the victory was the king's, and his land was then left in peace.

And the king recalled what Merlin had told him, so he went back to Logres. When he had got there, he called for his hoards and his treasures and then sent for his worthy gentlemen and noble ladies and the poorest people in his kingdom, and he gave them of his wealth and did acts of charity. And what was left over he distributed according to the counsel and will [79] of the ministers of Holy Church and his confessors. Thus did the king share what belonged to him, and there was none of his wealth that he could think of that he did not give away on God's behalf because of the advice Merlin had given him. And he humbled himself so meekly before God and His ministers that all of his people were moved to tears.

So he was for some time, when at length his illness grew more painful. And his people gathered in Logres, because they were distraught over his death, for they saw plainly that he would have to die; and he was so ill and weakened that he could not talk and had not spoken for three days. Then to the town came Merlin, who knew all these things.

And when the gentlemen of the land saw him, they said, "Merlin, now the king has died whom you loved so much."

And Merlin answered, "You are not saying it right. No one dies who has come to such a good end as he has. In fact, he is not even dead yet."

They said that he would never speak, but Merlin said he would indeed, if it was God's will. "Come with me now and I will soon have him talking to you."

They said that it would be the greatest wonder in the world, so they went with Merlin to the room where the king lay, and they had all the windows opened. The king looked at Merlin, and when he had caught sight of him, he turned toward him as best he could and gave a look of recognition.

And Merlin said to the barons who were there and to the prelates of Holy Church, "Anyone who wishes to hear the last words the king will speak, let him draw near."

They all asked him, "How do you think you'll get him to speak?"

And he answered, "You will see."

Merlin then turned around to the head of the king's bed and whispered quietly in his ear, "You have come to a very beautiful end, if your conscience is as your looks say it is. And I tell you that your son will be head of your kingdom after you through the power of Jesus Christ, and he will perfect the Round Table you have founded."

When the king heard this, he pulled toward him and said, "For God's sake, bid him pray* to Jesus Christ for me."

Then Merlin said to those who were there, "Now you have heard what you did not believe could be. And you may be sure that these are the last words the king will ever say."

Then Merlin went away along with all the others, who had been amazed that the king had spoken, and not even one of them could hear what the king had said except Merlin.

The bishops and archbishops held for him the most beautiful service they knew how. And the next day, after the king had been buried, all the barons gathered and took counsel as to how the kingdom would be ruled, but they could never come to terms. Then they said by common agreement that they would seek Merlin's advice, for he was a trustworthy counselor, and they had never heard it said that he had misguided them. So they sent for him.

And when he had come before them, they said to him, "Merlin, we know very well that you are very learned, and you always loved the king. The land is left without an heir, and a land without an overlord is almost worthless. Therefore, we beg you for God's sake to help us choose a king who may rule the kingdom for the good of Holy Church and the welfare of the people."

Merlin said, "I am not one who should give advice in this matter or choose a man to rule. But if you are willing to agree [80] with my view, I will tell you; and if I do not speak well, then do not agree with what I say."

They said, "God grant that we bring about what is good and profitable for the people."

And Merlin said, "I have greatly loved this kingdom and all who are in it. If I said that you should choose a certain one I know about who is capable, I would be taken at my word and he would straightway be king. But a most wondrous thing has happened to you, if you would only recognize it: the king died two weeks after St. Martin's day,† and it is not long before Christmas. If you believe me, I will give you then good and faithful counsel, following the will of God and following reason."

They answered all of a voice, "We will do what you wish."

---

* Supplied from Micha (79, l. 51). Sommer's text has *prieche* (79, l. 25): "preach."

† The feast of St. Martin of Tours is observed November 11. Micha's text, in agreement with the manuscripts he consulted, has *au cinquieme jor* ("on the fifth day" [80, l. 28]) and not *des la quinzaine saint martin* ("on the fifteenth [day] of St. Martin," i.e., a fortnight afterward [Sommer, 80, l. 6]).

And he said to them, "You are aware that the holy day is coming when He who is Lord of all things was born. And I stand as your pledge, if you pray to Him and have the people one and all do the same,* since they need a rightful lord and ruler, that God, in His mercy and His great and noble goodness, on that feast day that is called Christmas, when He condescended to be born, will choose for us as king and lord;† just as truly as He did condescend to be born that day and is King of Kings and Lord of the whole world, he will be a man by whom the people will be ruled according to His will. And he will be chosen in such a way that they will themselves see and recognize that he is king by God's choice and no one else's. And you should know that if you do as I have said, you will see a sign that he is the choice of Jesus Christ."

Then they all said one to another, "This is the best counsel anyone could have given us."

So they agreed to it. Then they asked the bishops to have orders sent out to the common folk and throughout all of Holy Church that everyone will make prayers to God and swear to keep the commandments of Holy Church and all that God manifests therein. This is how they agreed to Merlin's counsel.

And Merlin took leave of them, and they entreated him to come back to them, if he would, so that they might know whether what he had told them was true. But Merlin said, "You will not see me until after the king has been chosen."

So Merlin left them and went straight to Blaise. He told him these things which were yet to come. And it is because he told it to Blaise that we still know it.

Then the barons and the prelates of Holy Church sent word out that all the gentry in the kingdom should come to Logres at Christmas.

And Antor had raised the child named Arthur until he reached the age of sixteen, and he was handsome and big, and he had had no other milk than that of Antor's wife, while her own son had been nursed by a peasant girl. And Antor did not know which he loved better, Arthur or his own son. He had never called Arthur anything but his son, and Arthur truly thought that he was. Antor had had his own son, Kay, knighted on All Saints' Day, and he took him to Logres‡ with him, and Arthur, too.

---

*   Supplied from Micha (80, ll. 35-36). Sommer's text, which appears to be somewhat confused, reads *se vous le faites otroier al pueple communaument quil attendront iusques dont que diex vous conseillera se chascuns prie* (80, ll. 10-12): "if you allow the people one and all to wait until then, when God will give you counsel, if each one prays."

†   Supplied from Micha (80, l. 41). Sommer's text, losing sight of the fact that God is the subject of the verb, reads *que vous puissies auoir* (80, l. 16): "that you will have."

‡   Supplied from Micha (81, l. 22). Here (80, l. 38) and elsewhere in this vicinity, Sommer's text replaces Logres with London.

5. THE YOUTH OF KING ARTHUR; THE SWORD IN THE STONE.*

On Christmas Eve, all the clergy in the kingdom and all the barons of worth were gathered in Logres, for they had very well sent out the orders and done all else Merlin had told them to do. After they had all come, they lived very humbly and [81] very uprightly, and they waited there for the midnight Mass, and they prayed Our Lord to give them an overlord who was worthy to uphold the religion of Christendom. But there were many men who said that they were mad to believe that Our Lord meant to choose their king.

As they were talking, they heard the bells ringing for the first Mass of the day, so they went to the service. And when they had all come together, a holy man from the countryside got ready to sing the Mass.

But before he began the service, he spoke to the people and said to them, "You are gathered here for three things that are for your welfare, and I'll tell you what they are: to save your souls, first and foremost; to bring honor to your lives;† and to see the wonders and amazing displays of His might that Our Lord will bring about among you this day, if it is His will to give you a king and leader to safeguard and keep Holy Church and to uphold all folk. We are gathered here to choose a king, but we don't know which man would be best for our well-being, and we cannot know this by ourselves, so let us pray the King of Kings to show us His will as truly as He was born this day, and this each one of us will pray as best we know how."

They did just as the good man had bidden them, and he went on to sing the Mass. And after he had sung as far as the offertory, certain people went to the open space outside the church. Dawn had broken, and they saw a huge stone in front of the church, and they could not tell what kind of rock it was. In the middle of the stone was an iron anvil at least half a foot high, and a sword was sticking through the middle of the anvil down into the rock.

When those who had left the church saw it, they were amazed, so they ran to the archbishop and told him. When he had heard it, he took some holy water, went to the stone, and sprinkled it with the water. Then he leaned down and saw on the stone writing that was all of gold, and he read it. The writing said that the one who pulled this sword out would be king of the land by the choice of Jesus Christ. And when he had read the writing, he told the people. Then the stone was entrusted to ten worthy knights to be guarded, and everyone said that God had given them a great sign. And they went back inside the church to hear Mass, and they thanked Our Lord.

When the good man had come before the altar, he turned toward the people and said to them, "My dear lords, now you can see that there is something good among us, since by your prayers and entreaties Our Lord has given you a sign. And I beseech you, by all wonders that Our Lord has wrought on earth, that no one go against God's choice for any high rank or wealth that God may have endowed him with. For Our Lord who has given us a sign will show us the way to do the rest."

---

*   Corresponds to Sommer, 80-101.
†   Supplied from Micha (82, ll. 17-18). The second is missing in Sommer's text (81, l. 9).

Then the worthy archbishop sang his Mass. And when he had sung all of it, they went to the stone, and each one asked the other who should try it first. Then they all agreed that no one would try it unless the ministers of Holy Church allowed it. With these words, there was a very great uproar, [82] because the highest-born and wealthiest men who had the strength to do so said that they would try it first. Many a word was then spoken that must not be remembered or set down.

And the archbishop spoke so loudly that they all could hear him, and said, "My lords, you are not so wise or so worthy as I thought. I want you to know this: that Our Lord, who* knows and sees all these things, has† chosen one man, but we do not know who he is. I can tell you for the truth that wealth and high rank and nobility will have nothing to do with it, but only the will of Jesus Christ. And I have such trust in Him that, if‡ the one who is to draw the sword out were not yet born, it would never be drawn out until he was born and he himself drew it out."

The worthy nobles and the learned men were all of one mind that he spoke the truth, and they swore to abide by the agreement they had made with the bishop. And when he heard this, he was very glad, and he wept with feeling.

And he said to them, "I mean for you all to know that I will do my utmost to work according to the will of Jesus Christ for the welfare of Christendom, so that I will have no blame, God willing."

He then showed the people the great wonder that Our Lord had wrought for them as a sign that there would be a true election of a king, "for when Our Lord established law and order on the earth, He set them in the sword. The rule that was over the laity must come from a layman and must be by the sword, and the sword§ was, at the beginning of the three orders, entrusted to knighthood¶ to safeguard Holy Church and uphold true law and order. And by this sword Our Lord has ordained for us this election.

"You can all be sure that He has kept in His sight the one He wills to rule. High-ranking men should not boast that the sword will be drawn out by wealth or pride, but the poor should not be upset if the highborn try it before they do, for it is fitting that the wealthy should go first. There is no one here who would not, if he knew how, choose the worthiest one among us to make him king."

They said all of one voice that they would agree to whatever he advised. The archbishop went on to sing a solemn Mass. After it was sung he chose two hundred and fifty of the worthiest gentlemen he knew of, and he had them try pulling the sword out, but it was all for nothing. When they had tried it, he then ordered the others to put themselves to the test.

Then they all tried it one after the other, but there was no one who could ever move that sword. They then entrusted ten worthy knights to guard it, and they were told to let anyone undertake the test who wanted to and to watch carefully to see the one who would draw the sword out. The sword held fast for a week, when all the

---

*   Supplied from Micha (84, l. 8), not in Sommer's text (82, l.5).

†   Supplied from Micha (84, l. 9), not in Sommer's text (82, l. 6).

‡   Supplied from Micha (84, l. 13), not in Sommer's text (82, l. 8).

§   The text beginning "from a layman" supplied from Micha (84, ll. 34-35); not in Sommer (82, l. 17).

¶   Supplied from Micha (84, l. 35): *au chevalier* ("to the knight."); not in Sommer's text (82, l. 18).

barons went to High Mass on the Feast of the Circumcision.* And the archbishop said to them, "My lords, I told you so: you would all in time come to try pulling the sword out. Now you can truly understand that no man will ever draw it out but the one whom Our Lord wills to be king."

And they all said that they would not leave the town before knowing on whom Our Lord wanted to bestow His grace.

When Mass had been sung, all the barons went to their lodgings to eat. After eating, the knights went jousting, as they usually did, outside the town, and many people went out to see [83] the games. When the knights had fought for a long time, they gave their shields to their serving men and began to joust again. And they fought among themselves so hard that a free-for-all broke out, and everyone from the town, armed and unarmed, ran there.

Antor's son Kay, who had been knighted earlier, on All Saints' Day, called his brother Arthur and said to him, "Go get me my sword at our lodging."

Arthur was always willing to be helpful, so he answered, "Very gladly!"

He then spurred his horse and rode to their lodging. He looked for his brother's sword or another one, but he could not find any, because the lady of the house had hidden them all in her room and gone off to see the fighting with the other ladies. When Arthur saw that he could not find a sword, he turned back and went by the church where the stone was. The thought came to him that he had never tried the test, and if he could pull the sword out he would take it to his brother. So he came straight back, and, still on horseback, he took the sword by the hilt, drew it out, and covered it with the bottom of his tunic. But the men who were to guard the sword had run to the melee.

Kay ran up to meet his brother and asked him for his sword. He answered that he could not find it, but that he had brought him another, so he gave him the sword from the anvil. Kay asked him where he had found it, and he told him that it was the sword from the stone. Kay took it and hid it under his tunic, and went looking for his father.

When he found him, he said to him, "Sir, I will be king. Here is the sword from the stone."

When his father saw it, he was thunderstruck, and he asked him how he had got it. Kay answered that he had taken it out of the stone. When Antor heard this, he did not believe him, but said to him that he knew very well that he was lying about it. Then they both went to the church, and the lad followed after them.

Antor said to his son, "Dear son, don't lie to me. Tell me how you came to have this sword. If you lie to me, I'll know it and I will not love you for it."

And he answered, for he was very much ashamed, "I won't lie to you. My brother Arthur brought it to me when I told him to bring me mine, but I do not know how he got it."

When Antor heard this, he said to him, "Give it to me, for you have no right to it."

---

* The *iour des estraignes* (82, l. 25), that is, New Year's Day.

And Kay gave it to him. Antor looked around and saw Arthur. He called to him and said, "Come here, dear son. Take this sword and put it back where you took it."

He took it and put it into the anvil, and it held there just as fast as before. Antor ordered his son Kay to take it, and he leaned down, but could not get it out. Then Antor went into the church and called both of them inside.

He took Arthur in his arms and said to him, "Sir, if I could see to it that you were king, what advantage would there be for me?"

And Arthur answered, "Sir, I cannot have that or any other worthwhile thing and not have you as my lord, for you are my father."

Antor answered him, "I am your father for having raised you, but in truth I do not know who sired you or who your mother was."

When Arthur heard the man he believed to be his father disown him as his son, he was grief-stricken and began to weep. And he said, "Dear Lord God, how shall I ever have anything when I am fatherless?"

Antor said to him, "Sir, you are not fatherless, for you must have been sired by a father. Now, dear [84] sir, if Our Lord means you to have His grace, and if I help you become king, what advantage will there be for me?"

And Arthur said, "Sir, whatever you please."

Then Antor told him about the favor he had done for him and how he had raised him. He had his own son taken away from his mother and given to another woman to be nursed, while Arthur had his wife's milk. "Thus you should return the favor to me and my son, for never was a child reared more lovingly than I have reared you. So I entreat you, if God bestows this grace on you, and if I can help you out, please reward my son."

And Arthur said, "I beg you not to disown me as your son, for I would not know where else to go. And if God grants me this honor, I will give you anything you ask."

Antor said, "I will not ask you for any of your land. I ask only that my son Kay be your seneschal for as long as he lives and that he never lose his stewardship for anything he might do to any man or woman of your land or to you yourself. If he is wicked and foolish, you will have to bear with him, for his ways of thinking and behaving must have come to him from the peasant girl who nursed him. So that you might be reared properly, he lost his birthright. This is why you must humor him more than others. So I beg you, please give him what I ask."

Arthur said, "I very willingly grant you this."

Then they took him to the altar, and he swore that he would faithfully keep his word. And when he had so sworn, they came back out in front of the church. By then the melee had come to an end, and the barons came back to the church to hear vespers. Antor then called his friends and told them that Arthur had drawn the sword out, and they told the archbishop.

"Sir, this is one of my sons," said Antor. "He is not a knight, but he begs me to let him try the test of this sword. Please call the barons together."

And he did. Then they all gathered at the stone. And when they had come together, Antor ordered Arthur to take the sword and give it to the archbishop, and he did.

And when the archbishop saw this, he took him in his arms and began to sing the *Te Deum* very loudly. Then they took him into the church.

The barons who had seen it were most upset and distraught, and they said it could not be that an upstart boy was their king. But the archbishop grew angry and said, "Our Lord knows better than we what everyone is!"

Antor and his kinsmen stood by Arthur, and the common folk did too, but the barons were against him. Then the archbishop made a bold speech. "If everyone in this world," he said, "wished to stand against this election and God alone wanted it to be, it would be.* And I will show you what faith I have in God."

Then the archbishop said to Arthur, "Dear son, go put the sword back into the stone."

And he took it in plain sight of all, and after he had put it back, the archbishop spoke and said, "Never has a more perfect election been carried out or witnessed. Now go, my wealthy lords, and see if you can pull it out again."

And they went and tried the test [85] one after the other, but they could not draw it out.

And the archbishop said, "Anyone who wants to go against the will of God is a madman. Now you understand the will of the Lord God!"

And they answered, "Sir, we do not go against His will, but it is very strange to us that a mere boy should be lord over us."

The archbishop said to them, "The One who chose him knows him better than we do and better than we know ourselves."

The barons begged the archbishop to leave the sword in the stone until Candlemas, when many others might try it who had not yet done so, and the archbishop allowed it. So the sword stayed there until Candlemas. Then the people were all gathered, and all who wanted underwent the test. When they had all tried it, the archbishop said, "It would be right for you to do the will of Jesus Christ. Go, dear son Arthur. If Our Lord wills you to be king and guardian of this people, show us."

And he went forward and pulled out the sword and gave it to the archbishop.

When they saw it, the common folk wept for joy, and they all asked, "Is there anyone who means to go against this election?"

And the barons answered, "Sir, we beg you, please leave the sword until Easter. If between now and then no one but he draws it out, we will submit to him as you have ordered. And if you mean to do otherwise, then each of us will do the best he can."

The archbishop said to them, "Will you all submit to him wholeheartedly if I let it go until Easter and postpone crowning him?"

And they all said together that they would and that he could always do with the kingdom what he wanted.

And the archbishop said, "Arthur, brother, put the sword back, for, God willing, you will not go without the favor God has promised you."

He went forward and put the sword back. And when it was back in its place, it held just as fast as it ever had. And the archbishop, who had taken the young man under his own care, said to him, "You can be sure that you will be king and lord

* The main clause is supplied from Micha (87, l. 49), not in Sommer's text (84, l. 35).

over this people. Put your heart and mind always to being a worthy man. And from now on, keep your eye on people and choose some with whom you want to share your private thoughts and words. Give out your honors and choose those who will be of your household, just as though you were already king, for you will surely be king, with God's help."*

And Arthur answered, "Sir, I entrust myself and everything God gives me to the care and counsel of Holy Church. Please, you be the one to choose and watch over such people as will be best for me in doing God's will for the welfare of Christendom, and please call my father into your confidence."

Then the archbishop called Antor and told him about the seemly words that Arthur had spoken. They chose all such† counsellors as he wanted, and they made Kay steward of the land, as the archbishop advised. So things were until Easter.

When Eastertide came, everyone came together in Logres on Easter Eve. And the archbishop called them all into his great hall for a meeting. When they had gathered, he told them what he saw the will [86] of Jesus Christ to be, and it was that the lad should have the kingdom; and he told them about the good qualities he had seen in him since he had known him. "We must not be against the will of God," he said.

And the barons answered, "It is very distressing to us that such a young man, and one of such low birth, will be our overlord."

And the archbishop said to them, "You are not good Christians if you mean to go against the will of Jesus Christ."

They answered, "Sir, we do not mean to go against the will of Our Lord. But please do in part what we want. You have seen this lad to be upstanding and learned in many things. We have not got to know him, and we know nothing about him or his ways. There is someone among us who would recognize whether or not he will be worthy."

The archbishop replied, "Do you then mean for us to postpone proclaiming his election and crowning him?"

They said, "Sir, in truth we would like to postpone the election until tomorrow. And if he is not such that he should not be elected king, we ask you to put off his coronation until Whitsuntide. And we beg you to do it."

And the archbishop answered, "I would not lose your allegiance for such a thing."

So they left this meeting. And the next morning, after Mass, they came back to the election of the lad, and he drew the sword out again just as he had done other times. And they took him and raised him up and recognized him as their overlord. Then they all begged him to put the sword back and afterwards to speak to them, and he said he would do this very willingly, and there was nothing they could ask him to do that, unless it was to his dishonor, he would refuse them. Then he put the sword back, and the barons took him into the church for a meeting.

And they said, "Sir, we know well, and we see it, that Our Lord wills you to be lord over us, and since that is His will, it is ours also. So we now hold, and will

---

*   "Wording after "household" supplied from Micha (88, ll. 36-37), not in Sommer's text (85, l. 29).

†   "Supplied from Micha (88, l. 45); Sommer's text specifies two (85, l. 35).

hold, you to be our overlord, and from you we wish to hold our fiefs and what is ours by birthright and the honors that are ours. So we bid you as our lord, please put off your coronation until Whitsuntide, and you will not be any the less lord over us and this kingdom. And we mean you to answer according to your will and without counsel from anyone."

And Arthur said to them, "From what you say, I am to accept your homage and bestow honors on you, and you will hold everything from me. I cannot do this, nor should I. For I cannot bestow honors on you or anyone else, nor can I rule, before I come into my own honor. You tell me that I am to be lord of the kingdom, but that cannot be before I am anointed and given the crown and the honors of the empire. But the delay you request [87] before the coronation I will grant very gladly, for I do not mean to have anointment or honors but by God's will and yours."

Then the barons said among themselves, "If this one lives long enough, he will be very wise and reasonable, and he has answered us very well."

Then they said to him, "Sir, it would be good for you to be anointed and crowned on Whitsunday."

And he said that he was very willing to do what they wanted. Thus was the delay until Whitsunday agreed upon, and in the meantime they would all submit to the archbishop.

Then they had everything of worth brought out, all kingly things and things that a man might lust after or love, to test whether his heart was greedy or grasping. And he asked those who were close to him the value of each thing, and he followed their counsel. When he had accepted everything of worth they had, he gave it all out just as the book tells it. He gave horses to the good knights, and to those who were light-hearted, cheerful, and in love, he gave jewels and coins and silver. As for worthy gentlefolk and the learned, he asked people from their countries what they liked best, and he gave it to them. Thus he shared the gifts bestowed on him by those who wanted to test what kind of man he was. And when they saw that he had borne himself so well, there were none who did not esteem him in their hearts. They all whispered behind their hands that he was surely of high birth, for they found no greed in him: as soon as anything of worth came his way, he put it to good use, and all his gifts were fair according to what each one deserved.

This is how they tested Arthur, and in no way could they find any bad traits in him. So they waited until Whitsuntide. Then all the barons gathered at Logres, and all who wanted tried the sword-test, but no one could draw it out. And the archbishop had made the crown ready for the coronation. On Whitsun Eve, following everyone's wholehearted counsel and all the barons' agreement, the archbishop made Arthur a knight. And Arthur kept watch in the church all that night until day broke the next morning.

When the barons had come to the main church, the archbishop spoke to them and said, "My lords, here is a worthy knight whom Our Lord has chosen for us in the election you have witnessed again and again since Christmas. Here are the kingly raiment and the crown. Now, in this royal meeting with you, I want to know whether there is any of you who means to oppose the election. If so, let him speak."

Then they all answered aloud, "We agree to it, and we wish him to be crowned, in the name of God! In case there are any among us toward whom he has any ill will because they have been against his election and coronation until now, may he forgive them all together at one time!"

They all knelt down and cried for his mercy. And Arthur wept with deep feeling and knelt down to them and said to them in his loudest voice, "I earnestly and faithfully forgive you all, and I pray the Lord who has willed to bestow this honor on me that He may forgive you."

They then rose in a body and took Arthur in their arms and led him to the place where the kingly raiment was, and they attired him with it. And when he was dressed, the archbishop was ready to sing Mass.

And [88] he said to him, "Arthur, go get the sword— the justice with which you will defend Holy Church and Christendom in every way as best you can."

Then the procession went to the stone. And when they had come there, the archbishop said, "Arthur, if you are willing to swear and promise all the saints that you will safeguard the rights of Holy Church, keep lawful order and peace in the land, give help to the defenseless as best you can, and uphold all rights, feudal obligations, and lawful rule, then step forward and take the sword with which Our Lord has shown that you are His elect."

When Arthur heard this, he wept for joy, and many others wept for him.

And he said, "As truly as God is Lord of all things, may He give me the strength and the might to do what is right and to uphold all the things that you have told me and I have heard."

He went down on his knees and took the sword in both his hands. He raised it out from the anvil as easily as if the sword had not been held fast by anything. He bore the sword upright in his hands, and they took him to the altar and set him down there. And when he was seated, they anointed him and crowned him and did everything that must be done to a king. And when he was crowned and the Mass sung, they all left the church; and when they looked, they did not see the stone, nor did they find out what had become of it.

This is how Arthur was made king, and he held the land and the kingdom of Logres in peace for a long time.[*]

At length he sent word one day throughout his land that he would hold a high court. To that court came King Lot of Orkney, who held the land of Loonois and part of the land of Orkney. He came with five hundred knights of great worthiness. From another direction came King Urien of the land of Gorre. He was a young knight of great worth, and he came with five hundred others. Afterwards came King Neutres of Garlot, who had married Arthur's sister, with seven hundred knights. After that came King Caradoc Shortarm, who was one of the knights of the Round Table. He brought six hundred knights. After that came King Aguisant, very well fitted out, who was king of Scotland. He was a young knight and skillful at arms, and he brought five hundred knights. And when they had all come together, King Arthur gave them a fitting welcome and showed that he was very glad to see them.

---

[*]   "The *Merlin* proper attributed to Robert de Boron ends at this point, where the so-called *Merlin* Continuation (the remainder of Sommer's vol. 2) begins as a link to the *Prose Lancelot*. Micha's text continues with a "bridge" linking the prose *Merlin* to the *Didot-Perceval* (91, ll. 59-69), an anonymous prose Perceval romance that is not part of the Vulgate Cycle.

Because they were men of high estate, he bestowed on them beautiful gifts and costly jewels that he had stored up for them beforehand.

When the barons saw the rich gifts and costly jewels that King Arthur was giving them, they looked on him with very great scorn. Some who were there said that they were mad to have made such a lowborn man king and lord over them and so wealthy a land as the kingdom of Logres, and they said that they would not tolerate him at all. They refused the gifts that the king meant them to have, so that he would understand that they did not take him for a king and they wanted him to leave the land forthwith and make sure that they never saw him again. If he did not leave the country, they promised him death if they could get their hands on him.

When King Arthur heard these threats, he withdrew from the main [89] stronghold of Carlion, where they were, for he was very much afraid of their treason. And the other kings stayed in the town of Carlion for two weeks, but no one did any wrong to anyone else. Then it happened that Merlin came into the town and showed himself to all the people, for he meant them all to recognize him.

When the barons heard that Merlin had come, they sent word to him to come before them, and he came there all happy and smiling. And when they saw him coming, they all rose to meet him and were very glad to see him. They took him to a great hall that sat beside the River Thames, and when the barons were gathered there, they spoke to Merlin and asked him what he thought of the new king whom the archbishop had crowned without their leave or the assent of the common folk of the land.

"To be sure, dear lords," said Merlin, "he did well, and it was the right thing, for you should know in truth that he is higher-born than any of us. He is not the son of Antor or the brother of Kay, whom he has made steward over everything but food."

"What?" said the barons. "Merlin, what you are telling us now troubles us more than we were before."

"I tell you," said Merlin, "that you should send for King Arthur. You will call him to come before you by right of truce. You will also summon Ulfin, who was counsellor to King Uther Pendragon, and Antor, who raised King Arthur. Then you will hear the truth about what happened from beginning to end. You can be sure that I would not lie to you about anything."

And the barons said that they would gladly send for King Arthur and that they would grant him safe conduct, "since you have asked us to. But who will go get him for us?"

They sent Bretel on Merlin's advice, and they entrusted him with the message. And Merlin told him to tell the king that he should bring along with him the archbishop of Brice and the archbishop of Logres. Bretel answered that he would very gladly tell him.

Right away Bretel left and came straight to the king and told him everything just as it had been entrusted to him. And the king said that he would go very willingly. Then Bretel left and came straight to Ulfin's lodging and told him that the barons and Merlin were summoning him.

When Ulfin heard that Merlin had come, he was very happy and filled with joy, for he knew then that the truth about the king would be disclosed and spread far and wide. So he went to the great hall. He and Merlin were very glad to see each other, and they talked just between themselves about many things.

Very soon King Arthur came with the archbishop of Brice and Antor, and King Arthur had put on a good, short hauberk over his tunic before he left the keep in the main stronghold. When they had come before the barons, they found a great many other people who had come to hear what Merlin would say publicly. When the barons saw King Arthur coming, they got up to meet him because he was the anointed king and for love of the archbishop of Brice, a holy man who led a good life.

Then everyone sat down but the archbishop, who continued to stand and spoke to them thus: "My dear lords, I want to convince you for God's sake to take pity on Christendom, lest it fall into decline because of you and be put to shame, for that would be a great loss! Every one of you is just a man, and the wealthy man will die soon enough just like the poorest of this town, if it is God's will."

"Sir," said the [90] barons, "Wait awhile until we have spoken to Merlin. Then you can take up your speech again. For Merlin has told us something that has bewildered us more than we were when we came here."

And the archbishop said that he would yield to them, so he sat down.

And Merlin rose to his feet and said to them, "My dear lords, I had started to tell you whose son King Arthur was. You may know for a fact that he was the son of King Uther Pendragon, who fathered him with Queen Ygraine on the very night her husband was killed on the bridge when he stormed King Uther Pendragon's army. The next morning, when King Uther Pendragon went back to his army, I asked him for the child he had sired with the duchess in return for the favors and services I had done him. And he agreed to have him handed over to me as soon as he was born. He had me write this down in a letter bearing his seal. Ulfin still has it, and he himself was witness to the contract, as he can testify.

"And when it happened afterwards that the king married Ygraine, she grew very big with the child the king had sired in her before they were wed. When the king found out that she was with child, he told her that it was not his or the duke's, for it couldn't be. The lady was taken aback, and she admitted that the child had been conceived on the night the duke was killed. When the king heard that she had disclosed the truth to him, he loved her more for it than he had before, because he saw her great faithfulness.

"And he said to her, 'Lady, the child is therefore not mine, so it would not be right for him to inherit this land or be king after I die. This is why I ask you, as you hold me dear, that as soon as he is born, please have him handed over to the first man who will be found on the steps to the great hall.' And the lady swore to him that she would very gladly do this, since he wanted it to be so, and she would have it done just as he had set it out, for she did not wish in any way to be at odds with him.

"I tell you the truth. The child was given over to me on the very night he was born. And as soon as I had him, I went straight to this worthy man named Antor. I entrusted the child to him and told him to have him nursed by his own wife, who had a little boy of her own barely half a year old, and he did it. And he made his own son Kay go to another woman for nursing. So Kay, Arthur's brother, was torn from his mother's breast,* for Arthur nursed at the breast of Antor's wife. For King Uther Pendragon, before the child was brought to him, had implored Antor to do as I had ordered, and so he did, and I thank him for it. And he had the child baptized and named him Arthur.

"This is why I tell you, my dear lords, Our Lord does not forget the sinner, provided he wishes to serve Him with a good heart. Our Lord means to give back to the son what is rightfully his by the seed that issued from his father,† for he sent the stone and the sword, as you saw, to show in the trial before all the people that he was and is the lawful heir. You may know in truth that everything is just as I have told you, and you may ask Antor, who reared Arthur, and Ulfin too, if you don't believe me."

Then they asked Antor if he had spoken the truth, and he said, God help him, that he had not lied in one word.

And Ulfin sprang forward and said, "Look, here is the sealed letter that Uther Pendragon had [91] Merlin draw up about the agreement."

The barons took the document and read it, and they found it to be word for word just as Merlin had told it. And when the common people in the land heard this, they began to weep all around, and they cursed those who sought to harm Arthur.

When the common folk saw that the clergy were taking Arthur's side, they said that they would, too. But the barons said that it was nothing but a cover. They also said that, God willing, they would never have as their overlord a man who was not lawfully conceived; never would there be a bastard whom, God willing, they would allow to hold a land or so high a kingdom as the kingdom of Logres. And the archbishop answered them and said that Arthur would be king, and he would hold the kingdom and all the land of Logres, regardless of who was upset, for Our Lord willed it. For, since he had become involved in the election, he would not fail to help Arthur keep the land.

When the archbishop and the common people saw the barons' faithlessness, they stood together of one accord with King Arthur. And the barons walked out in anger and said, for any who cared to listen, that they did not hold Arthur to be their lord and that thenceforth their faith with him and those who upheld him was broken. They went off to their lodgings, put on their own armor, and armed their liegemen.

And King Arthur went straight to the keep and had as many of his men as he could find arm themselves. When they had all got together, there were a good seven thousand, clerics and commoners, but very few knights indeed. Such knights as were there were poor men to whom Arthur had given horses and money, and all told there were about three hundred and fifty who said they would fight to the death to help Arthur. When King Arthur and his men-at-arms had been fitted out on their horses, they rode into the bailey, the walled yard around the keep, and they were all ready to fight for their lives.

And the barons, all in their armor, had mounted their horses on the other side, and they had gathered about their banners. There were a good four thousand knights,

---

* The participle is missing in Sommer's text (90, l. 32).

† Sommer's text has *que de lui issi* (90, ll. 37-58): "that issued from him."

not counting squires, serving men, and crossbowmen, who were there in great numbers. And when they had come together, they talked about whether they should storm the castle where King Arthur was, and there were some who thought so, but others said that they should lay siege to the bailey and starve to death those who were inside. "No one," they said, "will dare come out of the keep."

While they were so deliberating, Merlin came up to them and said to them, "My dear lords, what are you trying to do? You should know that if you mean to ruin the king, you will lose more than you win. Our Lord, who is all-powerful, will take such vengeance that you will all be brought to shame, for you are wrong to go against the election Our Lord made as you have witnessed it."

"How well the wizard has just spoken!" said the barons, and they began to mock him.

And when Merlin saw that they were laughing at him, he told them that they had behaved wickedly. He went straight to the king and told him not to be frightened of anything and not to be worried about any of the barons, for he would help him yet that very day in such a way that even the bravest one of all his enemies would wish to be back in his own country stripped naked. [92]

Then King Arthur took Merlin by the hand, and they went off to one side, along with the archbishop, Antor, Ulfin, Kay, and Bretel, to a private meeting. And the king said for all of them to hear, "My very dear friend Merlin, I have heard it said that you were very close to my father as long as he lived, so I would beseech you, for God's sake, please advise me what to do about this matter, for you certainly know what I need to do, and you see clearly that the people of this country are doing me wrong. I would like very much for you to be my friend just as you were my father's, if you will. You can be sure that I would strive to my utmost not to do anything that would displease you. You helped me when I was young, so you should help me now to hold on to my land. It is with God's help, and yours and the archbishop's and Antor's who reared me, that I have come to where I am now, so please take pity on me and the folk who will be ruined if God is not mindful of them!"

"Now, don't be afraid, dear sir," said Merlin, "for you needn't worry about them. But as soon as you are rid of the barons who come to attack you, you must do as I advise.

"It is true that the knights of the Round Table, which was founded in the time of your father Uther Pendragon, have gone away to stay in another land because of the faithlessness they saw springing up in this country. And they went to the kingdom of King Leodagan of Carmelide. His wife is dead, he is an old man, and his only child is a daughter to whom the kingdom will go after her father. King Leodagan is fighting a very great war with King Rion, who is king of the Land of Grasslands and Giants, where no one dares dwell because so many strange things happen there day and night.

"This King Rion is very powerful, wealthy in land and people, and he is skilled at arms and a ruthless man as well. He has defeated twenty-five crowned kings, and, out of spite, he had their beards torn off with their skin and made into a coat which he has a knight always hold before him every day he holds court, and he says that he will not stop until he has defeated thirty kings. This king is waging war against King Leodagan, and he is wreaking havoc in his land.

"Now, Leodagan's land borders on your kingdom, and you can be certain that if he loses his land you will lose yours soon after. And he would have lost his land some time ago had it not been for the companions of the Round Table, who have kept up the war for him, for he is very old. This is why I advise you to go serve King Leodagan for a while, and he will give you for a wife his daughter, who stands to inherit the kingdom. She is very beautiful and young, and she is one of the cleverest women in the world.

"Don't be afraid, for your land will not be in danger. The barons who are now waging war against you will have so much trouble for themselves that they will bring but little harm to you in your land, unless they do it by unlawful encroachment. But before you go, you will stock the main strongholds in every city and castle with food and arms. And the archbishop of Brice* will have all those who do any wrong to you in your lands excommunicated in every church. And he will himself pronounce the excommunication of all barons in the land, and he will order the knights to shun them likewise.

"And today you will see such a strange thing happen, when I give you my help, that the boldest of men will be utterly frightened. And you can be sure [93] that whenever you need me, you have my services and you will want for nothing. And just as soon as I cry out to you 'Now at them!' have your gates opened, let your horses run toward the barons, and storm into their midst. I tell you, they will be so astounded that they will run away bewildered in utter defeat!"

"Sir," said King Arthur to Merlin, "many thanks!"

So they left their meeting. And the archbishop of Brice climbed high up on the walls and excommunicated all those outside who were doing any kind of wrong to King Arthur and were seeking his ruin. And King Arthur had his men armed and fitted out with armor, and they waited in readiness. And Merlin gave King Arthur a banner that was full of meaning. There was a dragon on the banner, which he had fixed on a lance; it seemed to breathe out fire and flames through its mouth, and it had a very long, twisted tail. That dragon I have just told you about was made of brass, and no one ever knew where Merlin had got it; it was wonderfully light in weight and easy to handle. And Arthur handed it over to Kay the Seneschal to carry, and such was the custom that ever afterwards, all the days of his life, he was the head standard-bearer to the kingdom of Logres.

Thus did Merlin outfit King Arthur's household. And they waited before the gate, at the ready on horseback.

And the barons outside had their pavilions set up in the meadow below, which was very wide and beautiful. Merlin climbed high up in the keep and cast a spell on them, so that all their tents caught fire, and they were so bewildered that they ran back out into the middle of the meadow. But by the time they got there, there were many injured and burned.

And Merlin came straight to the king and said to him, "Sir, now at them!" And they opened the gates and rode out as fast as their horses could run, holding their

---

* Sommer's text has *brete* ("Britain"?) for *brice* (92, l. 39).

lances under their arms and their shields before their chests, and as many as could get there drove into the midst of the barons. And they were so astounded and frightened that even the bravest would not have wanted to be there for all the gold in the world, for they had not known that so many people were inside. And Arthur's men attacked them with their lances; they brought down a great number of them and killed many, for they were so dazed from the heat of the fire that had struck them that they defended themselves poorly.

When those outside saw the great damage that Arthur's men were doing to them, they all gathered on one side and said that they would be greatly shamed if Arthur got away from them. They were very good knights, skilled and brave, and they were fast friends. King Neutres of Garlot said that he would free them from Arthur very soon. For if King Arthur were killed, the war with the others would be quickly ended.

"Then go right now," said the other barons, "and if you need help, we will come quickly to save you."

King Neutres left his companions at once. He was very tall and very brawny, a good knight and wonderfully strong. He took a short, thick lance with a sharp iron tip, and he rode straight out to meet King Arthur. When King Arthur saw him coming, he reigned in his horse, holding a short, thick lance of ash with a [94] sharp steel tip; he spurred his horse and ran against him so fast and with such an uproar that all the barons who saw him riding so were amazed: he stood so solidly in the stirrups that his horse reared under him. As they met riding very fast, they traded such hard blows that their shields flew into splinters. King Neutres broke his lance on King Arthur, but King Arthur struck him so hard when he came alongside him that he drove King Neutres's shield into his arm and his arm into his side. The blow was so hard that it brought King Neutres to the ground over his horse's rump, and the ground shook with the sound of his falling. But he hurt him no more than that.

When King Lot of Orkney saw him thrown to the ground, he was very upset and sorrowful, for they were first cousins and their wives were sisters. He spurred his horse to ride against King Arthur, whose lance was still whole. When King Arthur saw him coming, he rode very boldly to meet him, as if he did not fear him at all. They traded such strong blows that when each one's lance struck the other's shield, their lances broke apart. And when they meant to go on by, their bodies and shields crashed together so hard that King Lot was stunned. He flew back over his horse's rump and fell to the ground. Then a great hue and cry rose up from both sides, and a very great and awesome battle began, for King Neutres's men struggled hard to come to his rescue, and King Lot's did likewise, while King Arthur's men made every effort to help him and block the others' way. So the great and wondrous slaughter began on both sides, and both kings were put back on their horses.

After King Arthur had been brought back to his senses, he drew his sword from its scabbard, and it cast a great light, as though two tapers had been lit This was the sword he had pulled out of the stone. And the letters that were written on the sword said that it was named Excalibur—this is a Hebrew word that means in French "cuts through iron and steel and wood,"* and the inscription told the truth, as you will hear in the story a little farther along. When the king had drawn the sword, he struck out into the greatest part of the throng and hit one knight between the shoulders so hard that he cut his body in two. The blow was great, and the good sword cut through the saddle blanket and sliced through the horse's backbone from one end to the other, so that knight and horse fell down into one heap. Then he struck right and left and stirred up such an awful fracas that all who saw him were terrified. They did not dare face up to him, but fled and yielded the ground to him.

When the six kings saw the damage and loss they had borne because of King Arthur, they grew very distraught and sorrowful. They said to one another, "Now let's get him! Let's drive him to the ground. Otherwise, we won't defeat him."

They all agreed, and they took strong, straight lances, and they rode against him as fast as they could drive their horses. They struck him on the shield and on his hauberk, but it was so strong that [95] not one link broke. And they drove against him so hard that they bore him and his horse to the ground, and they fell in a heap.

When Kay, Bretel, Antor, Ulfin, and their kinsmen saw that King Arthur had been thrown down, they spurred their horses to help him. And the six kings rode to where he was in order to block the way. But Kay struck King Aguisant of Scotland, who had stopped right next to King Arthur, and he broke through his shield and hauberk right at his left shoulder, and he drove his lance all the way through and brought him from his horse to the ground. He was impaled by the lance, and the ground shook with the sound of his falling.† Kay struck King Caradoc and his horse so hard that he brought him to the ground head over heels. Ulfin and King Neutres knocked each other down, so that their horses fell on top of them, but King Yder and Bretel broke their lances on each other's shield without doing any more harm.

The barons had stopped right next to Arthur, who was still lying on the ground, and they rained harsh blows down on his helmet. When Kay saw them attacking him so dreadfully, he drew his sword and rode to where King Arthur lay beaten down. He struck King Lot on his helmet so hard that he thrust him forward over his saddle horn, then he hit him again and again, put him in such a state that he did not know where he was, and knocked him senseless from his horse to the ground. There the fighting was fierce, and many men were slain on both sides.

King Arthur's men struggled until they got him up from the ground and back on his horse. Then the common folk came out of the city carrying axes, cudgels, and sticks. The cry rose up all around the countryside, and they killed and brought down as many as they could reach. They all said that they would rather die on the spot than that King Arthur should be harmed when they could have defended him. They struck such blows against the six kings' men that they killed or wounded many of them, so they sent them on their way whether they wanted to go or not.

---

*   Lacy relates the name Excalibur to Geoffrey of Monmouth's Caliburn (9, 4) derived from Latin and Greek *chalybs* ("steel"); see Norris J. Lacy, ed. *The New Arthurian Encyclopedia* (New York: Garland, 1991), s.v. Excalibur.

†   In Sommer's text the reference to the ground's shaking is missing; however, the full expression occurs earlier (94, l. 10).

The townspeople said that they would not be satisfied until they had taken their revenge, and the only ransom they would take would be their heads.

And King Arthur, who had become enraged, angrily charged after them ahead of all the others. He happened to come upon King Yder. He raised his sword and meant to strike him on the helmet, but his horse carried him farther forward than he wanted, so the blow fell on the neck of Yder's horse and cut it all the way through just above the chest armor, so that he brought both rider and horse to the ground in a heap. Yder's men were afraid to see him wounded, so they turned around to come help him. There the fighting and the uproar were wondrously fierce, for the ones were struggling to help King Yder, while the others tried to block the way, and more harm was done there than in the battle just before. For King Arthur inflicted great damage on men and horses with his sword Excalibur, and he was covered with so much blood and gore and dirt that none of the paint or varnish on his armor showed through. Nevertheless, Yder's men could at last put him back on his horse, and they rode away in defeat.

The pursuit lasted for a long time, and the six kings lost a great deal. Of all the goods they had brought there, they took back with them scarcely two pence worth, for everything had been burned up in the fire that Merlin brought down on their tents, except for their gold and silver dishes and their coins. [96]

When King Arthur had routed the six kings with Merlin's help, just as you have heard, he went back to Carduel in Wales. He sought out fighting men everywhere he knew them to be and bestowed on them clothing, money, and horses, and the poor knights throughout the country took him in such love that they swore never to fail him even in the face of death. And King Arthur had the main strongholds in cities and castles well fortified.

It happened one time that he held court in the city of Logres, which is now called London in England, on the feast of Our Lady in September. At that court King Arthur made many a new knight with his own hand. All of them paid him homage and swore fealty to him, and he gave them incomes from lands and such other gifts that they had the means to live. They accepted him in such love that never afterwards did they fail him even for fear of death, and the king later had very great help from them, as you will hear me tell.

After this, Merlin took King Arthur aside, along with Ulfin, and said to him, "Sir, there is something I want to show you and teach you about myself and what I do. In truth, there is a worthy man in the forest of Northumberland, in the wildest place there is, and he is a hermit and my very dear friend, because he once saved my mother from being burned to death, and I will tell you how."

So he began to tell his life's story and his mother's and how she was almost burned for a crime she had been accused of; how Vortigern sent people out looking for him; how his mother took the veil in a nunnery where he left her; how the tower that Vortigern had built stood up and the meaning of the two dragons that killed each other; how, after Vortigern's death, he became a friend of Pendragon and Uther, Arthur's father; how he foretold to them the great battle in which Pendragon was slain; how afterwards he was very close to Uther, how he helped him lie with the duchess Ygraine in the castle of Tintagel ("And there," he said to the king, "you were conceived"); how Ulfin thought up the way Uther could wed the duchess

Ygraine, who had five daughters, three by her husband the duke and two by her first husband, one of whom King Lot took as his wife, King Neutres another, King Urien the third, and Caradoc, who was father of King Aguisant of Scotland, the fourth, who had died, while the fifth was in school in Logres.*

"And you should know that King Lot has five sons by his wife, one of whom you sired in London when you were a squire. They are handsome young men, and the eldest is Gawainet,† the second Agravain, the third Guerrehet, the fourth Gaheriet, and the youngest Mordred. You can be sure that, of all knights ever born, Gawainet will be the most faithful to his lord, and he will be one of the best in the world. He will love you the most of any, and, as long as he lives, he will raise you up above everyone else, even his own father. There can be no doubt that through him you will have all your lands back, and out of fear of him all your liegemen will bow down to you and yield to your will.

"King Neutres has a son, a very handsome lad, named Galescalain. Urien has one named Yvain the Great, whose heart will be filled with every kindness, [97] and he and Gawainet will love you and serve you until they die. They will not be dubbed knights by any man before you do so yourself, and they will bring over to you many sons of highborn barons who will serve you for love of them and their fellowship.

"Across the water in Little Brittany are two kings who are brothers, and their wives are sisters. Those two kings will have sons, and they will be good knights; no one could find better anywhere. The elder of the brothers who are kings is called King Ban of Benoic, and the other's name is Bors of Gaunes. They have a very wicked neighbor, also a king, who will yet bring them trouble and grief out of envy and because he cannot overpower them.

"Since they are such worthy and faithful men, I would like very much for you to send them word that you wish to see them and that you beg them to be here on All Saints' Day, because you will hold court in Logres and are sending for all throughout the land who mean to swear fealty to you. Some will come for the sake of good, others for ill, but those two will come for their inborn kindness, because they are worthy and faithful men. So you will become their friend and offer to serve them, and they will think themselves rewarded and will be most grateful for it, and they will gladly swear fealty to you.

"And when it is time for your court to end, you will tell them in trust that you are set on going to Carhaix in Carmelide to serve King Leodagan. Take them with you, for they are very worthy men and good knights, and they will prove to be very useful to you when you are ready to come back into your land, for your enemies will do their utmost to keep you from coming back in, but they will not be able to withstand you, because of the help you will have from the two kings who will be your companions.‡

---

*   Earlier (Sommer, 73), only two (or three) daughters are mentioned. See also above, p. 84n.

†   The form is a diminutive, which obviously reflects Gawain's youth and inexperience. Similar diminutive endings are attached for a time to the names of Yvain and Sagremor but then dropped, whereas with rare exceptions the *Merlin* uses it for Gawain until the end.

‡   The phrase beginning "because of" represents an incomplete sentence in Sommer's text (97, ll. 21-22) consisting only of a subordinate clause introduced by *car* ("for"). A variant reading supplied by

"And I want you to know that I want to keep going back to the woods, and this is by the nature that came to me from the one who sired me, for he does not seek out any companionship that might come about from God. But I do not go into the woods for fellowship with him, but to keep company with Blaise, the holy man. You can be sure that you will never have need of me but that I will come to counsel you. But you will very often see me in another likeness from what you see now, for I don't want everybody to know who I am every time I come to talk to you. But I want you to swear to me that you will reveal to no one anything I tell you, for if you gave me away, more harm than good would come to you."

King Arthur swore this very willingly, for he truly wanted to have his love and friendship, and he swore never to say anything, if he could help it, that went against Merlin's will. And Merlin assured him of his love, and he said that he would help Arthur so well that he would be forever grateful.

This is how the pact was made between the king and Merlin. And the people rejoiced throughout the city for their new king, who was such a good knight at arms, for they had never seen in his time such a good knight for so young a man. The burghers had a dummy set up in the middle of the meadow for a target, and the new knights tilted at it for a long time, their shields at their necks. The merrymaking lasted a good, full week.

When it was over, the king began preparing for the great festival he was to lead on All Saints' Day. He sent orders to all who were to hold lands from him to come swear fealty and pay him homage. [98] Some of them came and some stayed away, and the king made known to the ones who did not come that they would have to make amends.

And King Arthur sent Ulfin and Bretel for King Ban of Benoic and his brother King Bors of Gaunes, and he bade them, if they held his love dear and wanted to be his friend forever, come to him in Logres in Great Britain on All Saints' Day. Ulfin and Bretel were very friendly with the two kings they were going to find, for they had come to love one another in the time of Uther Pendragon. They crossed the sea and went straight to Little Brittany. They made their way through Little Brittany and rode through a land laid waste where they found many a town burned to the ground. At length they came to a city named Benoic, which is now called Bourges in Berry, and it had belonged to King Claudas of the Land Laid Waste.

This Claudas I am telling you about was laying claim to a castle that King Ban had had built on his own land, and he contested the claim by saying that the piece of land where he was strengthening his hold belonged to him, while King Claudas said that it did not. This is how the war began between them, for King Ban did not stop building the stronghold when Claudas had forbidden it. So Claudas overran King Ban's land without even challenging him. He inflicted great damage, taking plunder throughout the land, and he set fire to the towns he found without walls and left charred ruins. But he could do nothing to harm the stronghold that King Ban had had built, because it was well fortified with soldiers and crossbowmen whom King Ban had put in the keep. He had also posted there one of his stewards, a very worthy man named Gratian, whom King Ban had made his fellow godfather

---

Sommer from the Harley manuscript is not helpful in correcting the apparent scribal error.

of a little boy* he had had baptized, and the child's name was Banin. This Banin was afterwards well known for his very great prowess in King Arthur's court, but the story does not tell about him right here, but rather it speaks of King Ban, who was very sorrowful and distraught at the harm Claudas had done him without first challenging him. So he rounded up a great army and went against him as quickly as he could, for he knew very well how to get through the countryside all about.

When the two armies had gathered, each one ranked against the other, there was a very great battle with fierce fighting and many slain on both sides. King Ban killed so many with his own hand that the heaps lay scattered through the fields as though they were sheep or swine. King Ban did so much on his own and with the help of his men that King Claudas turned in flight and lost all his equipment and plunder, and the prisoners who were being taken away were brought to safety.

Furthermore, King Bors, who was King Ban's brother, moved into the land of Gaunes, and he burned a great deal of King Claudas's land and set fire to many of his towns, and he took as much booty as he could, for he laid waste the country so that you could not find shelter under cover anywhere within fifteen leagues other than beside rocks or in cellars below ground. And King Claudas had been brought so low and made so poor that he kept quiet. He did not dare move into King Ban's land for a long time afterwards, but then he brought very grievous harm to the two brothers, as you will hear in the story farther along.

This is why [99] King Arthur's two messengers found that the land had been laid waste, and they were amazed that it could be so and wondered how it could have happened. They rode until they came to Trebe, which was the castle King Ban had had built. It was very strong, and it sat on a high piece of land. In this stronghold was Queen Elaine, King Ban's wife, who was a very worthy lady of great beauty, and she was not yet twenty-six years old; King Bors had wed her sister, who was a very noble and worthy lady.

When Ulfin and Bretel had come to Trebe, they asked for King Ban. And they were told that he had gone to Benoic to take counsel with his brother, King Bors. After they heard this, they took leave of lady Elaine and left Trebe wearing their armor, for the land they had to go through was not at all safe, for there were many outlaws roving about the land. And when they had ridden about five leagues, they saw seven knights of the household of King Claudas who were coming from the wilderness, and they were going about looking out for anything they might win for themselves, but the countryside had been so stripped of anything of worth that they found nothing to take, for all the folk had fled into the cities and strongholds with everything they owned.

When the seven knights saw the two messengers, they said to one another, "Look at those two horses they are riding! We would be bad indeed if we let them take them away!"

"It doesn't seem to me," said one, "that they are from this country, for they are not wearing armor like what is made in this kingdom."

---

* The words *dung petit enfant* ("of a little child") are missing in Sommer's main text (98, l. 22) and are supplied from the Harley manuscript as quoted in Sommer's note.

"In truth, whoever they are," said another, "they look like worthy men-at-arms. If they have served someone else, it certainly must have been a very noble man."

"What do I care whom they served?" said a third. "Let's go take their arms and horses from them, for we could surely use them!"

Straightway one of them spurred his horse and rode away from his companions after the messengers, shouting, "Stand still! Don't go on, or you are dead, if you belong to King Ban or his brother Bors. But if you are King Claudas's men, you needn't worry, for we guard the roads and ways through this borderland, so that none may pass who serves anyone else. This is why we ask for your toll. You haven't paid it yet, so you must leave your arms and horses! What's more, we mean for you to be grateful that we are letting you go without killing you or taking you prisoner."

When Ulfin heard him shouting at them and threatening them, he said to him, "Now, don't be in such a hurry. I don't know who you are, but by your speech, you are a loud-boasting blockhead! Curses on a low-life knight who asks for a toll from a knight errant! And you don't even ask courteously!"

When Bretel heard Ulfin speaking in this way to the knight, he said, "Knight, you'll be sorry for even thinking that!"

And he spurred his horse toward him, and when the knight saw him coming, he fastened his shield on his arm with the armbands and fixed his lance in its holder. They traded such hard blows on their shields that they broke through them, so that the knight's lance came to a stop on Bretel's hauberk. And Bretel spurred his horse forward and dealt him such a great blow that he drove the iron tip of his lance right through his left shoulder, so that the broken pieces of his shield came out the other side [100] more than a yard, and he hit him so hard that he bore him from his horse to the ground impaled on his lance, and the knight fainted from the pain. Bretel withdrew his lance still all in one piece, then he said to the knight, "Now you can stay here as long as you like and guard the road so that no one passes from whom you don't get the toll that is rightfully yours!"

With that, he galloped away after Ulfin, giving free rein to his horse and brandishing his lance. Ulfin had seen the fight between the two men; he was very glad, and he held Bretel in higher esteem than he had before.

When the other knights saw their leader fall down wounded, they were very distraught, and they said that they would never be happy until they had avenged him. Two of them broke away from the others and took off after Bretel and Ulfin as fast as their horses would go. And when the messengers caught sight of them, they turned their horses' heads and bent down behind their shields like the good, fearless knights they were, and when they met they traded hard blows with their lances. Bretel, who bore his weapon high, drove his lance through the other man's throat and knocked him down dead from his horse. Ulfin hit his man so that the tip of his lance went through his hauberk and came out the other side between his shoulder blades; he brought him down to the ground from his horse with the lance still in him.

After this two of the four knights who were left broke away from the others and shouted to the messengers that they would avenge their companions or die trying. When the messengers saw them coming, they turned their horses' heads, and each urged the other to do well. Ulfin rode to meet the one who came in front, and Bretel met the other one. The two knights broke their lances on the messengers. Bretel struck his man and drove his lance through his shield and hauberk right into his body, and he bore him down from his horse and left him laid out on the ground dead and covered with blood. Ulfin came against his man so hard that he brought both the rider and his horse down in one heap; the rider broke his neck in the fall. And when the last two knights saw what had happened to their companions, they turned tail and took to their heels.

Then Bretel said to the dead men words that were heard far and wide: "My lords," he said, "go ahead and threaten us! Now we give you leave to guard the roads!"

The two messengers then made their way until the evening, when they came to the castle of Benoic, where they saw a good many people whom the two kings had ordered to come. The two messengers came straight to the main hall, got down from their horses, and gave them to be looked after by a squire they had brought with them. Then they went up into the hall and asked for King Ban and his brother. They were told that they were in another room in a private meeting. When the messengers heard this, they were very glad to know that they had found them together, so they stayed there until the meeting ended.

While they were waiting, a knight named Pharian came up to them, and when he saw who they were, he welcomed them joyfully. He asked them if they wanted to speak to the two kings, and they said they did. Then he took them by the hand and led them into the room where the brother kings were.

When the two kings saw them coming, they rose to meet them. With them was a knight named Leonce of Payerne. They all embraced the messengers and welcomed them. Then they went to sit down on a bed, and King Ban asked them [101] what business had brought them there, for surely they had come there for an important reason. The messengers then told them the whole truth from beginning to end: they told them what had happened between King Arthur and the six kings, the awful havoc Merlin had wreaked on them with the fire, and the young king's awesome feats of arms. One of them told them that King Arthur was summoning them on Merlin's advice and said that they should make up their minds very soon.

The two kings answered that they were sorely distressed by a war they were waging against King Claudas. "And we are afraid," they said, "that when we leave this country they will storm us and we will suffer very great harm."

"My lords,"* said the messengers, "we would not want that to happen. But Merlin sends word that you will not have to worry while you are away."

When the two kings heard what the messengers told them, they were greatly astonished that Merlin would know things that had yet to happen. Then they promised the messengers that they would go with them three days later without delay, and they thanked them wholeheartedly. And King Ban had a servant take their armor off, for he would not allow them to take lodging anywhere but with him. Then the two kings asked them where their shields had got so beat up, and they entreated them, on their allegiance to King Arthur, to tell the truth. They told them how they had been set upon by seven knights and how it had all gone. And when

---

*   Sommer's text has the singular, as though only one of the kings were being addressed (101, l. 9).

the two kings heard how they had rid themselves of the seven knights, they held them in very high esteem. They were very well served with many good things to eat, and Leonce of Payerne and Pharian were at pains to care for them because they had done them great honor in Great Britain in the time of King Uther Pendragon.

King Ban got himself ready to leave in three days, and King Bors did, too. They entrusted Leonce of Payerne to keep their lands—he was their first cousin, a faithful, worthy man—and Pharian stayed behind with him, along with the stewards of Benoic and Gaunes. And the two kings told them to send for them if they needed to, for they did not know what would happen, and King Ban gave him his ring as his token. Then they took to the road and made their way for many days until they reached the sea, where they took a boat and crossed to the other side, and they had no trouble or disturbance.

But now the story stops talking about them for a while and will tell about King Arthur.

6. The Brother Kings, Ban and Bors, Pay Homage to Arthur.*

Here the story says that when the messengers had left King Arthur, the king fortified all his strongholds with fighting men and crossbowmen. Then Merlin went to the king and told him that he was happy that his messengers had done their job well. And Merlin told him everything that had happened to them along their way and how they had rid themselves of the seven knights. He said that the two kings had already started across the sea, "so think about how to do them honor and welcome them in a fitting way. Go out to meet them, for, although they are your liegemen, they are of higher birth than you, and their wives are as well. So I recommend that you have all the streets of Logres overhung with damask and samite wherever they are to go, and have the maidens and young ladies of this town go out to meet them dancing and singing. [102] And you will go out yourself with a throng of knights. They will get here Sunday before the hour of tierce."

And when King Arthur heard Merlin, he said that he would do everything as he had explained it.

Then King Arthur prepared to welcome the two kings, and he waited until Sunday. Then the king, his barons and household, and the archbishop of Brice mounted their horses and went out to meet them in a grand procession. When they met, they traded kisses and showed how glad they were to see each other, and they came back into the city with all kinds of dancing and with great merrymaking. When they had come to the main hall, King Arthur bestowed gifts of great worth on those in the two kings' households according to their rank, and he gave them warhorses, saddle horses, and beautiful, costly arms. The king did this all on Merlin's advice, and he did so much for everyone around him that they all loved him and held him in great esteem, and they swore that they would never, ever in their lives, let him down.

---

*   Corresponds to Sommer, 101-109.

That day the archbishop of Brice sang Mass, and when it was over, they all went up into the main hall, where a great meal, rich and bountiful, was ready. The three kings sat at one table, and the archbishop of Brice and Antor, who had reared King Arthur, were with them. And Kay served at the tables, as was right. Two new knights served with him. They were very skilled and worthy young men, sons of two castellans: one was named Lucan the Wine Steward, and the other Girflet, son of Doon from Carduel, who had been Uther Pendragon's woodman; and they served with Kay the Seneschal, with Ulfin, and with Bretel, all of whom were very capable. Everyone there was served with the highest courtesy, and they had rich, plentiful food.

After the meal a target dummy was set up, and the young knights held a tilting match. Later they put together a tournament with some knights on one side and others on another, and each side had about seven hundred. Three hundred from the kingdom of Benoic alone fought on one side. As the tourney was getting underway, King Ban and King Bors came to a window to see,* along with one of their brothers, a very learned clerk who knew more about astrology† than anyone except Merlin; and King Arthur was leaning at the window with them and the archbishop of Brice and Antor. They watched the tournament take shape on each side, the banners waving in the wind, the warhorses prancing about and whinnying beneath their riders, so that the mountains and valleys resounded with the din.

When the two sides were close enough to meet, one knight left the formation. He was named Girflet, son of Doon of Carduel, and he sat on a great gray warhorse that ran wonderfully fast. On the other side, a knight from Benoic rode to meet him. His name was Ladinas, and he was very skilled at arms. They traded such hard blows that they broke their lances, for they were both strong and brave, and they were good knights. One was eager to win acclaim, and the other wanted his fame to spread, so each landed such smashing blows on the other's shield and body that they thought their eyes would fly out of their heads. They took each other's horses to the ground on top of them, and they lay in a faint [103] without moving, so that everyone believed they were dead. They all said that they had never seen such a hard-fought combat between two knights.

With that, knights broke out of the formation on each side to come rescue their companion. They fought with one another and jousted so beautifully that all were glad to watch. Some unhorsed one another and broke their lances without falling, and after their lances were broken they drew their swords and began the wondrously violent battle. One knight worked wonders all by himself, and he was known for this far and wide throughout the country. His name was Lucan the Wine Steward, and he was the cousin of Girflet the son of Doon, who had been in the hard-fought single combat. Lucan brought knights and horses down, and he began to wield his weapons so well that none could withstand his blows. He tore helmets from heads and shields from necks, and at last he was able to get Girflet on his horse, while the other knight got back on his. When they had got their wind and cleared their heads, they went back into the fray. Then Girflet began to fight alongside Lucan the

---

* The verb phrase is lacking in Sommer's text (102, l. 27).

† The Old French word is *astrenomie* (Sommer, 102, l. 28). See above, ch. 2 p 26n..

Wine Steward, and they did so well that they won ground from the knights from Benoic.

Then three hundred knights came in; they were all fresh and had not yet struck a blow. The battle was awesome and hard-fought! When lances were broken, knights grabbed their swords, and the fighting started yet again and lasted a very long time. They saw many a fine example of knightly skill on both sides, for there were many good bachelor-knights who fought well. Girflet the son of Doon and Lucan the Wine Steward were clearly the best of all who were there.

When the hour of nones came, the tournament had died down somewhat. And Kay the Seneschal, who had not yet struck a blow there, sprang out with five or so companions from where they had been lying in wait. They were riding horses of great worth and had their shields at their necks and their lances in their grasp. When they drew near the formation, they rushed in headlong, just as the falcon or hawk swoops down on starlings, and they bore the first ones they met to the ground. After their lances had been broken, they drew their swords and began to fight so skillfully that Kay won the tourney prize along with Girflet and Lucan the Wine Steward. And just below them came Duke Malruc of the Rock, Guinan the Pale, Drians of the Wild Forest, Belias the Amorous from the Castle of the Maidens, Flandrin the White, Gratian the White the Castellan, Drulios of the Hamlet, Blioberis of the Wilderness, Meliaduc the Pale, Median the Curly-Haired, and Placides the Merry. These did so well that after they began fighting, no one in the tournament could withstand them.

But later King Ban's companions were able to push the whole throng back to where everyone had started out, for the companions of the kingdom of Logres had withdrawn to change their helmets, which had been broken in and smashed to bits. When they saw that the tide had turned against them, they hurried to take up new lances and rode straight back into the throng as fast as their horses could run, and they rushed into the thickest fray they saw there. Kay came spurring his horse ahead of all his companions, for he was very eager to do well, and he came into the ranks [104] brandishing his lance. He was a wondrously good knight—if only he had been a man of few words! He spoke too much, and his slanderous speech kept him from the good graces of his companions and strangers who heard about him and later refused to go with him on the adventures of the kingdom of Logres, as the story will explain farther on.

Kay received the bad trait, which the story says he had, from the nurse who suckled him, and not from his mother, who was a good lady, wise and faithful. But those who knew his ways did not mind what Kay said, for he did not do it out of any ill will he harbored toward anyone; it was his way that, when he started to say something, he did not know the words he was going to speak before they flew out of his mouth. Those who knew him would very often laugh about it, for his speech could be quite witty; furthermore, he was of the best fellowship that anyone could have.

And when he came to the tournament, as you have just heard, he met Ladinas. Ladinas had fought very well that day, and he and his companions tried very hard to drive the men of Logres off the field, and they had already distressed them somewhat. And when Kay saw this, he was very sorrowful. He drove his spurs into his horse and lowered his lance, and struck Ladinas so hard in his shield that he went all the way through it, and the tip of his weapon came to a stop against his hauberk. Then he thrust at him again very fast and knocked him down to the ground, where he lay all stretched out, and in the same bound Kay rode on and struck Gratian of Trebe and brought him and his horse down in a heap, and he broke his lance. Then he put his hand to his sword and shouted "Clarence!" (the king's battlecry). And those of the side of Logres took heed and saw that they were being helped by their companions, all of whom they believed they had lost, and they found their strength again and began to fight better than they had all day.

King Arthur, King Ban, and King Bors saw Kay's joust clearly, and they said that the seneschal was a very skilled knight, and they gladly watched him. And when Lucan the Wine Steward saw that Kay was fighting so well, he said that he would hold himself to be unworthy if he did not go help him. Then he drove his spurs into his horse and rushed into the thickest fray, and he struck Blioberis so hard that he brought him to the ground and laid him out, and his lance flew into bits. Then he drew his sword and jumped into the midst of them and began to fight so well that he was praised for it by many people, and he began to push the throng back in order to rescue his companions.

Then Girflet came, his lance in its holder, as fast as his horse could run, and he saw three* knights who were bringing Kay up short in a sword fight, and he needed help, for there were three of them and Kay was all alone, and those three were the best knights on the other side. Placides had already hit him so hard on his helmet that he had bent him down over his saddlebow. And when Girflet saw that, he was filled with dread, so he went to strike Blioberis and rained such blows down on him that he brought him and his horse down in a heap. Girflet's lance flew into bits, then he drew his sword and struck Placides on his helmet so hard that he leaned [105] over his saddlebow, and he hit him again and again until he was so stunned that he fell to the ground head over heels. And Kay, who was in great danger, got up again and was able to see that it was Girflet who had helped him, and he deemed that he should reward this good deed if he could, and so he did, and he did not tarry long, just as the story will set it down. This is how they first became companions, and they loved each other with great love ever afterward all the days of their lives.

When Girflet had freed Kay, as you have heard, he looked all around and saw Geroas, who had sorely bothered him throughout the fight that day. He then drew his sword and rode against him in great anger. He dealt him such a hard blow on his helmet that the blade† flew off and hit the ground, and if his sword had not twisted in his grasp, he would have killed him. The sword went down onto his left shoulder so hard that his hauberk broke and the mail came apart, and it cut the strap of his shield. He drove the sword down to his shoulder blade, and he flew to the ground all covered with blood. Then there arose a hue and cry, because those who saw the blow thought that he had been killed with no chance to recover. Then his companions came to the rescue. And from the other side came Kay the Seneschal's companions, and there began such a dreadful tumult that many men were unhorsed

---

*   Sommer's text has *.ij.* here (104, l. 35), but *iij.* and the number spelled out (*troi*) two lines below.
†   Sommer's text has *fus* ("hilt.") (105, l. 10).

or wounded before they could come to help their companions and get them back on their horses. And when the six companions I told you about before saw the fray, they drove to that side so hard that the first six knights they met flew to the ground. Then they rushed in and started such a good fight that those who saw it wondered how they could hold out so long.

There the tournament heated up on both sides, and the six* and the others as well fought long and hard until night came. The three kings went down from the great hall and came straight to the field where the tourney was, and they saw that everyone was showing himself to be as good as the others, so that no one knew which one would prevail. So they separated the two sides and said that it was high time to stop, since it was very late for fighting. So they left the field, and each one went back to his lodging to rest, which they all needed badly.

And the three kings went to hear vespers, and afterwards they went to supper. After supper talk grew lively, and they asked one another who it seemed to them had done the best. They said that King Ban had sixteen knights who had done better than all the others, and these sixteen had fought wonderfully and should be highly praised. But all of a voice they awarded the top prize to Kay the Seneschal, Lucan the Wine Steward, and Girflet the son of Doon; these three had done the best of all.

When the tables had been taken away, the three kings got up, along with the archbishop, Antor, and the clerk Guinebal, and they went into some side rooms off the main hall that looked out over the garden along the river, and they talked together about many things. Then the king looked at Ulfin and Bretel, and he began to laugh out loud because he recalled what Merlin had told them when they went on their mission and how they had been attacked by seven knights in the wilderness and fought them off. Then he called the two knights over and implored them by the faith they owed him to tell him how they had done on their mission. When they heard this, they were certain that the king knew it already from [106] Merlin, so they answered him, "Sir, why should we tell you what you already know? Our words would be wasted for nothing."

"What?" said King Ban. "Who told you this?"

"In truth, sir," said Bretel, "the wisest man in the world."

"And what is his name?" asked King Ban.

"Sir," answered Bretel, "his name is Merlin, and he is in this room, right over there resting. By his advice my lord sent for you."

"Ah! sir," said King Ban to King Arthur, "let us see him, for we have wanted to for a very long time because of the wonders we have heard about him."

And he said he would gladly do so. He sent Ulfin, and as soon as Ulfin moved away to go get him, he met him. Merlin told him to go back to the king and ask him why he was sending for him, and he did so. And King Ban crossed himself for the wonder he felt. Then Merlin went in and told him not to worry that he was bewildered. Then he began to tell him a part of his life's story and some of his ways.

---

* Sommer's text has .*vij.* (105, l. 23).

The clerk Guinebal stepped forward and asked him many things, for he was very learned, and Merlin answered everything he asked. The disputation between the two of them lasted a long time, until at last Merlin told him that there would be no end to his endeavors: the more he asked about, the more he would find out! And Merlin told those all around that he had never found a clerk who had talked to him on so high a level; not even Blaise, who was a very learned and holy man, could ever ask him so much for so long. Why should I go on telling any more? The two of them talked together and became fast friends. Then Merlin went up to the two kings who were brothers and said to them, "My lords, you are very worthy and faithful men indeed. Look, here is King Arthur. He is my lord and he should be yours. You must hold your two kingdoms from him, and he must uphold you and help you against all men, if need be."

They asked him to tell them how he had been chosen king. They also asked whether Antor knew that Arthur was the son of Uther Pendragon, and he answered, "Yes, indeed." Then Merlin told them the truth about the results of the sword test, and the archbishop of Brice and Ulfin bore witness to it.

"Merlin," said King Ban, "we would like you to assure us of one thing we ask. We know that you are such a worthy man that you would not lie for all the land that belongs to the crown."

"Ah! sir," said Merlin, "you want to have my oath that what I have told you is true."

And they began to smile and said that, indeed, no one was more learned than Merlin. And Merlin told them that he would very gladly swear it if they waited until the next day. With that, they went their own ways to go to sleep. The three kings lay in one room. Merlin and Guinebal became better and better acquainted: Merlin taught him many a fine trick, and Guinebal remembered them all like the intelligent clerk he was; he worked some of them many times later, and people talked about it for a long time afterwards, as the story will spell it out. [107]

The next morning they all got up and heard Mass. After Mass Merlin swore them the oath that King Arthur was the son of Uther Pendragon and that he had fathered him on Queen Ygraine the night the duke was killed, and Ulfin swore the same thing. When the two kings had accepted these two men's oaths, they swore fealty to Arthur very graciously, as was fitting, and King Arthur, in tears, received their homage very kindly. Then there was such rejoicing as there had never been before, and they went to eat and were very well served with all things befitting the highborn.

After they had eaten, King Arthur, the two brother kings, and Merlin went to confer by themselves, and Ulfin, Bretel, and Kay the Seneschal were there as well. Then Merlin said to them, "You are all very worthy gentlemen, and I know you as well as you know yourselves. Here is King Arthur your lord, who is a very young man, and he will be quite a good knight in his own right, and he already is. You are aware that he is having trouble with the barons of his land, for they will not accept him as their lord or swear fealty to him as they ought, but mean to do him as much harm as they can, if they ever can. Therefore I beg you, do as I advise."

And they all said that they would very gladly do so.

And Merlin said to them, "My lords, you know very well that King Arthur has no wife. I know of a maiden who is the daughter of a king and a queen. She is highborn and beautiful, and no maiden could be more worthy. She is the daughter of King Leodagan of Carmelide, who is an old man and has no other children than this girl, whose name is Guenevere. His land must fall to her. But he is now waging war against King Rion, who comes from a line of giants, and he is a very wealthy and very powerful man. If he should happen to defeat the kingdom of Carmelide, which borders on King Arthur's kingdom, you can be sure that King Arthur will never again hold his kingdom in peace, so many wars will he have on so many sides. And if it weren't for the knights of the Round Table who are helping King Leodagan defend his land against the giants, he would already have lost his land some time ago. So I beg you, take King Arthur there as your leader in battle, and stay there with him a year or two until you have got to know him well, and it will not be long before he loves you more than those who are with him now. And you should know for a fact that Leodagan will bid King Arthur to take his daughter as his wife; thereby he will be able to hold his kingdom free and clear."

Then King Ban said to Merlin, "Dear, kind friend, if we go to faraway lands and leave our own lands as they are, what will happen to them? Right now we have ruthless neighbors who lay waste our lands, and the very country where we are now is not very safe, for the barons who ought to be the king's liegemen are waging war against him. It is very dangerous to leave one's lands to go off to defend another's."

"Ah! sir," said Merlin, "you are speaking from the way things seem to you. But one must back up before taking a long jump. And you can be sure that for every penny you lose over here, you will earn a hundred over there. And for all your outriders who come over here, you will not lose a single castle or [108] city, and you will win over there a kingdom that will forever defend this kingdom as long as King Arthur is alive."

"I don't know," said King Ban, "what to say, but I'll do everything you advise, for you are more clever than all of us put together. Now all we have to do is get ready, and we will set out when you wish."

"We have time," said Merlin, "to get everything ready, for we will not set out before we have fought a battle against the barons of this land, for they are gathering a great army. And you will summon all the men you can find as stealthily as you can, and you will set up their camp in a heath within Bredigan Forest. Don't be afraid, for you will do far more harm to our enemies than they will to you."

"Merlin," said King Ban, "if my brother and I sent for men in our country, could they get here in time?"

"Yes," said Merlin, "you can be certain."

"Then we will send out the call," said King Ban.

"That is good," said Merlin. "And I will go myself, for I can get there faster than any messenger you might send. We must hurry, for the battle will be fought on Candlemas in the Bredigan meadows. Your army will have to ride day and night to come fast enough. You can know for a fact that I will be in Gaunes by tomorrow night."

And when the two kings heard this, they were utterly astounded. They threw their arms around his neck and showed him how glad they were.

Then Merlin said to King Arthur, "Sir, now, as quietly as you can, send for as many knights, men-at-arms, and crossbowmen as you can find, then have a great plenty of food taken to the heath I have told you about, and have it divided among the people, for they will be in dire need of it, and you will give each man enough food for forty days. And you, sir," he said to King Ban, "entrust me with your ring, and I will carry it to your cousin Leonce of Payerne so that he may believe me when I talk to him."

When the two brothers heard Merlin talking that way, they were quite bewildered, for they did not believe that any man alive could know what he was telling them.

"What is wrong, my dear lords?" said King Arthur. "Don't be amazed or troubled about what he told you, for you should know that he knows everything he wants at a single word, and nothing can be hidden from him."

And they said to him, "Since this is so, we will entrust the ring to him, and may he do what is right for us and for you, for we are well aware that he loves you more than anything."

"By my head," said Merlin, "you have spoken like shrewd and learned men. And you will win enough to know how much I love you."

With that, King Ban gave him the ring. He took it and commended them to God, and he left that place and went off, as I have told you. And he came straight to Blaise and told him all those things, and Blaise put them all down in writing, and this is how we still know them.

And Merlin left Blaise and went the next morning at the hour of prime to the city of Gaunes. He told Leonce what the two brother kings had sent him to do, and he showed him the king's ring with his seal, and he believed everything Merlin told him. He sent far and wide for so many men that, a week before Christmas, fully ten thousand came to the city of Benoic all armed, riding their horses. Then they set up guards in the towns, as was needed. One of the guards was Lambegue, a young nobleman [109] who was faithful and valiant of body. He was posted in the main stronghold of Gaunes, and Pharian, whose nephew he was, entreated him to do his job well, and he said he would do the best he could. And in the city of Benoic they posted the Lord of the High Wall, who was a tall man and good knight with his first growth of beard. And in the city of Trebe they left Banin, son of Gratian, who was King Ban's godson, and the two sister queens were there because it was the best and strongest castle in the two kingdoms. And in Montlair, a stronghold that belonged to King Bors, they posted Placides, one of Leonce's nephews, who was a good knight, wonderfully skilled, brave, and faithful.

When they had thus fortified all the land and countryside, they started out and made their way to the sea, where they took boats. On the other side of the sea, King Arthur made ready just as Merlin had ordered him to do, and at length he gathered a good ten thousand fighting men all mounted on good horses, for he did not want to call in footsoldiers. Furthermore, wagons from throughout the land made up a train that carried the food. And the king had the army led as stealthily as he could to the heath within Bredigan Forest, for it was one of the most out-of-the-way places anyone knew about. And Arthur did what Merlin held to be very wise: as soon as

the army and the wagon train had moved into the heath, he had good guards posted
on every road throughout his land so that no one might pass by who was not taken
and led before the king, because they did not want any spy to go in there who might
tell the enemy anything about what the king was doing.

And throughout King Arthur's land it was forbidden for anyone who owed him
fealty to ride down the countryside until after Candlemas had passed: if anyone
disobeyed, he could be taken captive, and all should know that they would lose
life or limb, for the king had ordered it so. Everyone in his land kept still and
did not move, and the common folk were amazed that it could happen. Thus the
movements were so well hidden that no one ever found out where the horses were
going, excepting only those who were privy to the king's counsel.

But here the story falls silent about them and comes back to the six kings and
their companions, all of whom were routed at Caerlion, just as you have heard it
told before now in the story.

7. The Six Kings' Renewed Forces; the Brother Kings' and Arthur's Victory over the Saxons.*

Here the story says that the six kings were most upset that they had been routed and
had lost all their equipment, so they swore all together that they would never be
happy until, if they could, they had taken vengeance on King Arthur and his wizard,
through whom they had suffered such harm. So the six kings went away filled with
sorrow and downcast about the misfortune that had befallen them; because of that,
they would be worse off for the rest of their lives. Some of them had themselves
carried in a litter if they could not bear riding, so they made the trip at a slow gait
until they got back to their lands, and they stayed there until they had been healed
and brought back to health.

At the end of a month, they held a meeting in a borderland between the kingdom
of Gorre and the kingdom of Scotland, and there everyone [110] swore that he
would send for as many friends and kinsmen as he had, and then they would move
against King Arthur; they would take away his land and dispossess all his liegemen
before driving him out. And they set a day when their army would gather in the
meadows of Bredigan, and they summoned their liegemen and friends.

Duke Escant of Cambenic came to help them with five thousand armed men.
Furthermore, King Tradelmant of North Wales came with six thousand men, as
did the King of Northumberland, whose name was Clarion, with three thousand,
the King of the Hundred Knights, King Lot of Loonois and Orkney with seven
thousand, King Caradoc Shortarm of the land of Estrangorre with eight thousand,
King Neutres of Garlot with six thousand, and King Urien came with six thousand.
They all rode short distances each day because they meant to plunder the countryside,
and they sent out their spies throughout the land to find out what King Arthur was

* Corresponds to Sommer, 109-121.

up to. But the guards, who were everywhere in the land, took them all and sent them to King Arthur, and they were shut up in prison, never to come out again, nor were they ever heard from.

And the armies rode on and eventually encamped beneath the castle of Bredigan, and they were gladdened because they believed they had won everything. They sent their raiders throughout the countryside, but they found little there to take, since everything that could be plundered had been taken away to the castles and cities. When they saw that nothing was left, they set fire everywhere and laid waste the land wherever they went. So they had to supply food from their own lands, and at length they had got a great deal. When the armies at last came together, they were more than forty thousand strong.

But here the story falls silent about them for a while, and we will tell you about Merlin and the help he brought, for he had gone to sea, as the story will set it forth from here on. [111]

Here the story says that when Merlin set out on the sea along with the company he had brought from the land of the two brother kings, they sailed until they landed in Great Britain. After they had come ashore, Merlin ordered all their equipment to be packed away in trunks, for he did not want them to encamp, but they made their way day and night until they came to the place where they wanted to be, and they made camp on Merlin's orders. So they rode on until, on the fifth day, they came into Bredigan Forest, where they found King Arthur's army, and the two armies greeted each other joyfully when they saw each other. Then they settled in in tents and pavilions, and they rested until the next morning. They stayed there for a full week.

Merlin was with the kings, and they were making merry. Ulfin said to him in jest, "Merlin, beware of the men on the other side, for they have slandered you dreadfully."

"I am well aware," said Merlin, "that they don't like me very much, and they are right! But they will never get their hands on me! And they have no worse enemy than I or one who will do them as much harm, as long as they keep bothering King Arthur—and I won't have to start *this* fight!

"But be careful not to let anyone leave this army, for we could never make up for the loss. The king's enemies are encamped in the meadows beneath Bredigan, and there are at least forty thousand men-at-arms on horseback. We must work with very great intelligence, otherwise we will all be killed by them."

Then Merlin took the three kings aside by themselves and said to King Arthur, "Sir, now listen to what I have to tell you. You are a very young man, and you have a very big kingdom to keep up, and the barons have no regard for you at all. The common folk would have dire misgivings about you if it [112] weren't for the huge gifts you have bestowed on them. This is why I tell you to be more generous from now on than you have ever been before, for you cannot ever enjoy your people's high praise or win their hearts if you are not unstinting in giving. You will have everything you need in return, and I will tell you how that will be, if you wish to hear it.

"I want you to know that this piece of ground holds the greatest treasure there ever was, but you won't take any of it until you come back from the battle. For you will have a great many other things to share among yourselves. You will take a hard look at the lie of the land so that you will know how to get back here again."

Then he took them* to the spot where the treasure was. They put a marker there, and the three kings were greatly amazed at what he had told them. Then they went back to the army.

King Arthur's tent was beside a most beautiful, clear spring. The weather was very cold, for it was the month of January, a week before Candlemas, and they had been encamped there for two days. On the third day Merlin came to the three kings and told them that it was then time to go against their enemies and to tell their men-at-arms who would go in front and who behind. For you will go," he said, "in such a way that the enemies will not know a word about it before you are on top of them. You have two leagues to go before daylight. If they catch sight of you too soon,† there are so many of them that you can't hold out against them. But don't worry, for they won't be able to hold out against you!"

Then the three kings put on their armor and got ready, so that all they would have to do was get on their horses. They split their army into battalions and gave Kay the Seneschal the king's standard to bear, and he led the first battalion, and Girflet, Lucan the Wine Steward, Malruc of the Rock, Guinan the Pale, Drians of the Wild Forest, Belias the Amorous, and Flandrin the Noble‡ were also leaders in the first battalion, which was four thousand strong. The second battalion was led by Bretel, a man of very great worth, faithful, and skilled with his hands, and he had three thousand men all well armed and riding good horses. Ulfin led the third battalion, and King Arthur was in this battalion with four thousand worthy men who would never forsake their lord even if it meant their death. The battalions formed as they had been chosen, and they all left riding at a slow gait, in tight formation, just as Merlin, who led them riding in front on a great black horse, had ordered them to.

Next King Ban split up his and his brother's men. He gave Pharian the first battalion to lead and his brother King Bors's standard to carry, for he was a very worthy man, clever and wise, and a good knight, and with him were Ladinas, Moret of the Way, Palet of Trebe, Gratian the Pale, Blioberis, and Meliaduc the Black,§ and three thousand knights all on horseback were with them. The second of King Ban's battalions was led by Leonce of Payerne, a very good and worthy knight, and it was a good four thousand men strong. King Bors of Gaunes led the third battalion; he was a skilled leader, and at least four thousand men all on horseback were with him. The fourth battalion was led by King Ban of Benoic, who was the best knight in the whole army, and he gave his standard to his seneschal Alelme, a very good knight, to carry; there were four thousand men with them, [113] wonderfully mounted on horseback, and they would not forsake him even if it meant their death. And when they were all on horseback, they set out on their way riding at a slow gait, keeping their ranks in order. It was almost midnight; the moon was shining very bright, and it was still and calm.

---

*   Sommer's text has the singular (112, l. 9).
†   Not in Sommer's text (112, l. 18), but the urgency of "too soon" is implicit.
‡   Called Flandrin the White above (Sommer, 103).
§   Called Meriaduc the Pale above (Sommer, 103).

Here the story falls silent about them and speaks about the Saxons from Ireland and the Irish, whose lands bordered the lands belonging to the kings who were waging war against King Arthur.

When King Brandegorre, King Margarit, and King Hargadabran, who were the nephews of Aminaduc, king of the Saxons, uncle of Hengist, whom King Arthur's father killed, just as the story tells it earlier—when they heard that the six kings had left their lands and gone against King Arthur, they gathered an army from far and wide, until there were a good thirty thousand men all riding horses, not counting the footsoldiers, and there were a great many of them. So they moved into the lands of the kings who were waging war against King Arthur, and they took plunder, burned towns, and laid waste the countryside everywhere they went, and they killed many people. They besieged a castle named Vandalior in Cornwall, and they were there for a very long time, and the siege could not be broken by the forces that the ten barons had after King Arthur had driven them out, when the barons reached an agreement against him with the Saxons.[*]

Now the story falls silent about them and does not say anything more right here; rather we will tell you about King Arthur and Merlin and their companions, how they fared in the battle against the six[†] kings, who were in the meadows before the castle of Bredigan.

Here the story says that after King Arthur and King Ban had put their battalions in order—and the story has told before just how they had started out on their way to meet their enemies—the six kings never mounted watches to guard their army that night, but everyone went to sleep. In fact, it happened that all the chief leaders slept in the tent of the King of the Hundred Knights, and they did not believe that they had to be on the lookout for anyone.

As they were sleeping, it happened that King Lot had a very vivid, fearsome dream. It seemed to him that he saw a wind rising so great and so strong that it brought down all their houses and the church bell tower. Afterward thunder and lightning came so strong that everyone shook with fear. After that a great, loud flood came that swept all the houses and a great many people away downstream, and he himself was in danger of drowning in the flood. And while the king was in such a fright, he awoke and crossed himself, for he was terrified by his dream.

He got up, dressed, and went to his companions, woke them, and told them his dream just as it had happened. They asked him what direction he had seen the water coming from, and he told them that the whole storm came from the forest, so it seemed to him. They told him that they knew for a fact that soon they would surely fight a great and fearsome battle, so they got up and woke all the knights who were there, and ordered them to mount their horses and ride out through all the countryside. And the king himself put on his armor and arrayed himself very well.

And Merlin [114] ordered King Arthur's army to hurry, for he knew what was happening in the enemy camp. And Arthur's men moved so fast that before they knew it, they were rushing against them. Merlin was the first one the enemy knights met, and they asked him who was attacking them. And Merlin answered that

<hr/>

[*] An allusion to the aftermath of the Battle of Salisbury?
[†] Sommer's text has *x.* (113, l. 20), carried over from the recent discussion of the ten barons.

they belonged to King Arthur, who was coming to claim the land of anyone who harbored anything against him.

When they heard what he said, they turned about, spurring their horses, and they came back to their army and began shouting, "We've been betrayed! Lord knights! get your armor on! You'll need it now more than ever before, for the enemy is coming!"

They sprang from their beds and ran to get their arms first and not their clothes. Luckily, their horses were saddled, but, for all their rushing, they could not get themselves armed and ready before the enemy was at their throats. They were hampered all the more by a great wind and storm that Merlin sent against them, for all their tents fell in on their heads, and a fog came down on them so thick that they could not see one another without great effort, and it hindered them so much as they tried to arm themselves that they suffered great harm. For King Arthur's men rushed headlong into their midst and brought down or killed as many as they got to.

But the six* kings had got away and come back together in the open field beyond the tents. They had a trumpet blown loud and clear to rally their men so that they might get away from the enemy, who were merciless against them; and many of them had been slain, and the enemy had done away with about a third of them before they could tell one man from another in daylight.

And when enough light came for them to recognize each other and see that the enemy had a very great army, they turned about and fled toward their standard, where they heard the horn blowing; for the kings had stopped at the edge of the forest beside a small stream, and all who could slip out of the enemy's hands gathered there. Their numbers grew little by little until there were about twenty thousand, while the others who could not get to where the standard was fled here and there in utter disarray; they were distraught and upset, bewailing their losses and the harm that had come to them.

When King Arthur saw that the whole camp was left to them, he came straight to Merlin and asked him what he should do. "I will tell you what you'll do," said Merlin. "You will go along this side of the stream to a ford, where more than twenty thousand men have stopped. And you will fight there with them, and you will make them come to terms with you. King Ban and his brother will cut through the forest and storm them from behind when you hit them from the front. And they will be so bewildered that they will no longer have it in them to defend themselves."

With that, each went his own way, and King Arthur found that the six† kings had stopped. They thought they had nothing to fear from anyone and that they could defend themselves well against a bigger army than theirs.

And King Ban turned to go through the forest, while King Arthur rode until he came to the place where the barons had blown the horn. When King Arthur got to the ford, he and his men struck helter-skelter into their midst. There you would have seen shields and lances shattered, knights' heads lying in the ford so that

*   Sommer's text has *.x.* (114, l. 18).
†   Sommer's text has *.x.* (114, l. 37).

the water was all red from their blood. And Kay struggled so hard [115] with the standard he was carrying that his men went on beyond him.

And the six* kings saw that very few men had broken through them and put them to flight, for they were only three thousand against their more than twenty thousand; they were deeply ashamed and began to defend themselves very forcefully. They held together so tightly that no one could break through. King Arthur's men could not hold out for long, but Ulfin brought help and comfort to his companions, and they rushed across the ford.

When they got to the other side, they rushed into the enemy so hard that people could hear the din more than half a league away. The fighting there was ruthless and fierce, with hammer blows on helmets and shields; many brave knights lay dead and wounded, and the loss was huge. King Arthur's men were becoming exhausted, when Bretel came bringing them help. He saw that Ulfin had fallen in the midst of the throng, but he was still brandishing his sword and defending himself forcefully. When Bretel saw him he let his horse run, and he struck the man he was fighting so hard that he bore him from his horse to the ground.

When King Clarion saw him lying on the ground, he was sorely distressed, and he said that he would avenge him if he could, so he spurred his horse to that part of the battlefield. And when Bretel saw him coming, he spurred his horse to meet him, and they struck each other's shields so hard that they broke through them, for the worthy knights were strong, healthy, and full of anger, and they shattered their lances as they went past. Then they traded such mighty blows with their shields, bodies, and helmets that they were stunned; they were so dazed that they flew down from their horses onto the ground, and they did not know whether it was night or day.

The men who were looking on thought they had killed each other, so they rushed to the rescue from both sides. When Kay the Seneschal came to help out, his side could not suffer very great loss. The three kings came from the other side. The fighting was fierce when they came together, for those from King Arthur's side numbered eight, and there were twelve from the other side. Girflet was struck down and Lucan the Wine Steward, King Brandegorre, King Yder, King Aguisant, and King Urien. Then the struggle to rescue them grew so mighty and fearsome that no one would believe it! Kay did a wondrous thing there when, with his sheer strength, he brought Girflet up onto King Neutres's horse, and he struck King Lot with the stump of a lance so hard that he wounded him.

Into the fray came the King of the Hundred Knights, and with him he had forty knights he had chosen. When he saw that Kay the Seneschal had struck down King Lot, he was very distraught and said to himself that Kay would think himself worthless if he let him get away after that. He then sped to where Kay was and struck him so hard that he bore him from his horse to the ground, where he lay motionless, and he took his horse, led it to King Lot, and said, "Sir, take this horse, and set your mind to taking vengeance for our distress, for you have lost a great deal today." And King Lot got on the horse.

---

* Sommer's text has *x*. (115, l. 2).

And when Girflet and Lucan saw Kay on the ground, they were most distressed.
They had found new lances, so they spurred their horses and struck two of the
enemy down to the ground. They took one of the horses and gave it to Kay to ride.
And the King of the Hundred Knights and King Lot fought for so long that the three
enemy kings and Escans of Cambenic had time to get back on horseback. [116]

When these kings had got back on horseback, they said that they would bring
grief and harm to the enemy around them or die trying, so they spurred their horses
and sped all together toward the fray, and the eight worthy fighters on King Arthur's
side rode them down. But they might soon have suffered dreadful losses, had King
Arthur not arrived to bring them welcome help, for as soon as he had crossed the
ford he spurred his horse and found Bretel on foot and Ulfin grievously wounded
on a horse, and he was sorely distressed. So he grasped his lance hard and held it
straight, and he flew against the formation wherever he saw the thickest fighting.
He met Tradelmant, king of North Wales, who had come fresh into the battle, and
he struck him so hard through his shield and hauberk that he grievously wounded
him in the left side, and he bore him to the ground so fiercely that he broke all his
bones, and his own lance flew into pieces. And King Arthur took his horse by the
gilded reins and handed him to Ulfin. He very gladly mounted the horse and said to
King Arthur, "Sir, thank you very much."

As soon as he had got back on horseback, he rushed into the fray and began
to strike out and fight so hard that he broke up the press. Meanwhile,* King Ban
and his men had come fresh from their march through the forest, and those on the
other side were quite distraught, although they were half again as numerous, so
they attacked them all in a body, and the fighting grew all the harder and more
dangerous. There King Arthur wrought wonders on his own, and even those who
had never seen him before recognized who he was, and even the bravest gave him
wide berth, for they did not dare face up to him.

When the King of the Hundred Knights saw King Tradelmant thrown to the
ground, he was filled with awful sorrow, for he loved him a great deal. He spurred
his horse and met King Arthur, who was wonderfully seated on his horse, and he
struck him so hard on his helmet that he dazed him. When King Arthur felt the
blow, he was very worried indeed, and Kay, who was with him, was as well. And
the king rode against the King of the Hundred Knights first, grasping his sword,
and he raised his arm to strike him on his helmet. When the King of the Hundred
Knights saw him, he thrust his shield between them, but King Arthur hit him so
hard that half of it flew into the middle of the field, and the blow bore down on his
helmet, shattering it utterly, then glanced down onto his horse's head and cut him
just behind the ears, and horse and rider fell to the ground.

Kay looked about and saw a horse running riderless, so he gave it to his father,
Antor, who was on foot. And he got on, took hold of a lance, and struck Marganor,
the seneschal of the King of the Hundred Knights, so hard that he lodged the iron
tip between his shoulders and sent him to the ground spit on the lance; then his
lance split. He took the horse and handed it by the rein to Bretel, who was very
glad to have it, and he mounted quickly. When he was on the horse, he looked in

*   Not in Sommer's text (116, ll. 14-15).

the middle of the fray and saw Lucan the Wine Steward being trampled beneath the horses' hooves, and Girflet had stopped near him and was defending him so fiercely that Lucan found him most worthy and praised him, for there were still fourteen men on top of him and he was fighting all alone, yet they could not take him or drive him away despite their strength.

When Bretel saw him in such distress, he spurred his horse over to where he was and hit the first man he came to so hard on his helmet that he split his head down to his teeth; he struck off the second man's arm and sent it flying still strapped to his shield, and then he hit [117] the third man so hard on his left shoulder that he tore it off his body. And when Girflet saw that he was helping him, he struck one man so hard that he split his head open down to the neck, and he fell down dead on the ground. Then Girflet took his horse and gave it to Lucan, who was very upset about being shamed and was very eager to avenge it.

He then took a strong, hard lance and headed toward King Aguisant of Scotland, who had run down Malruc of the Rock, and with all his might he struck him so hard on the collar of his hauberk that he sent him to the ground all in a daze. When Malruc saw that he was freed, he quickly got on his horse, and ran headlong into the throng, where the fighting only got more heated, and found Belias and Flandrin, who were in dire straits because they were having trouble getting two of their companions onto their horses, and the press was so great there that they could not do it. So they fought and landed blows so hard that it was nothing short of awesome, and they both struggled until at last they had put their two companions back on their horses.

Elsewhere King Arthur and his men were also fighting, and a great hue and cry went up for the two kings they had brought down. Knights spurred their horses in from both sides, the ones to rescue the two kings and hamper King Arthur, and the others to hamper the two kings and help King Arthur. There was hard fighting there in the fray, and they killed and maimed one another. Nevertheless, the two kings were able to get back on their horses, but not before a very hard struggle, for King Arthur held them pinned down and they could not throw him back. Had it not been for a stroke of luck that befell him, they could never have got him away from them for all their strength. But he happened to run to help Kay the Seneschal and Girflet, whom King Lot, King Neutres, King Brandegorre, and King Urien had thrown off their horses and were trampling dreadfully; only Lucan the Wine Steward was there to defend them, and they were so hard-pressed that they were very badly off.

When King Arthur saw that they needed help, he turned toward where they were and rushed into their midst raging like a lion. He struck blows to the right and the left and killed as many as he hit, until at last they gave way to him. Kay and Girflet spurred to the king, who was fighting fiercely. Furthermore, Ulfin, Bretel, and Antor were fighting against the duke of Cambenic, against Tradelmant, and against the king of Northumberland, and they brought them down right where King Arthur was fighting and working wonders of knightly skill.

There was much jousting, for the main battle was being fought there. But for the single-handed help that King Arthur gave, his men would have been cut to bits, for those on the other side were very good knights, and there were more of them by half. And they were not far from suffering dreadful harm when King Ban of Benoic and his brother King Bors took the enemy by surprise from the forest.* They were then spreading out along the edge of the forest, where they did not believe they needed to be on their guard against anyone. When the brother kings' men saw them, they let out such a loud yell that the whole forest and riverside resounded with it, and when the enemy heard this they knew that they would have to suffer the brunt of a dreadful attack.

Then the rebellious barons gathered at the edge of the meadow, and they worked out among themselves what they could do. "I don't know," said King Lot, "what each one of you [118] will do, but I am sure of what I'll do as long as I can find four or five men to joust against: I'll take vengeance for the trouble and harm that have come to me, for I have lost everything."

When the King of the Hundred Knights heard what King Lot said, he was very sorrowful, and he said that he would do likewise. And King Caradoc, King Neutres, Duke Escant of Cambenic, and King Clarion of Northumberland said the same thing.

"Now I'll tell you," said King Lot, "what we will do. Six of us should go to meet those who have come fresh from the march through the forest, and five will stay in the fighting here. Let the battle last as long as they can hold out. Half of our men will go against the ones who are coming in just now, and the other half will stay here. We will keep fighting close to the wood, near this river, until nightfall, so that they can't close in on us. This way, we will be able to mount a better assault than we could now, for if we took to the road and fled right now, we would lose more than if we stood our ground."

All the barons agreed to do what King Lot had said. They drew aside and then split their army in two. King Lot, the King of the Hundred Knights, King Aguisant, and Duke Escant of Cambenic took twelve thousand men with them, and they made up six battalions with two thousand men in each one, and they rode out at a slow gait, all drawn up tight together, until they came to the narrow place between the forest and the river that King Lot had told them about. And his was the best advice that anyone could have given them. Six barons got ready to defend them.

And the other five were locked in battle and were forcefully defending themselves against King Arthur's men. Among the five barons who had been left behind were King Brandegorre, King Urien, King Neutres, King Clarion of Northumberland, and King Tradelmant of North Wales, and they had with them seven thousand men. They all held themselves a little hunched over, and they defended themselves very fiercely against men who were most worthy. What a great shame that such ill will came between them and King Arthur! There the hand-to-hand fighting was dreadful, and it lasted until the hour of vespers.

On the other side came King Ban, King Bors, Leonce of Payerne, and Gratian, who led the first battalion, and they rode close together at a slow gait, and they could hardly wait to meet the enemy in combat. From another direction King Yder rode out against them, and when the two sides drew near to each other, they ran against each other so hard that you could have heard the blows from a half league

---

*   Sommer provides the predicate in a note completing the sentence from the Harley manuscript (117, n. 1).

away. The fighting was wondrous there and the fray was dreadful, and there was a great slaughter of men and horses. King Yder's men could not withstand the onslaught, and in the rout they were driven back into the troop of King Aguisant of Scotland, who rescued them.

The fighting was hard and fearsome to behold. Pharian's battalion was charged again and again, and they would have come to a bad end if Leonce of Payerne had not come to help them. They joined forces and hit the enemy so hard that not one of them could keep his ground, and they drove them back into the duke of Cambenic's men, [119] who helped them out very well indeed. When he saw the enemy coming in pursuit, he let out his battlecry and ran hard against them, and those who had been fleeing recovered, turned about against those who were routing them, and struck back, fighting without stopping until both sides were utterly tired out, and the fray lasted for so long that the blows they were trading had little effect.

All at once King Bors came brandishing his lance, and his standard was indigo with little red diagonal bands edged in gold as finely wrought as anyone could do, and it had streamers that blew against him as far down as the horse's neck.* And when King Yder saw him coming, he said, "Ah! my lord duke, defend yourself so that God may keep us this day from death and harm. I see plainly that we are all in danger of dying, for I see over there the standard of the man who is the least willing in all the world to yield ground for fear of being slain; moreover, he is such a good knight that all our men are like footsoldiers beside him, except his brother, whom no one can match in knightly skill, and this man is a very good and bold knight."

When the King of the Hundred Knights saw and heard King Yder's speech, he asked him who it was. And he said that it was King Bors of Gaunes, "and I don't know when he came to this land."

"So help me God," said King Lot, "I don't know, but today it will be clear who is a good knight or not."

"I don't know what each of you will do," said King Caradoc, "but I am going out to meet him. And if I need help, please give it to me."

And they said that they would do so. "Go with God, and may He keep you from harm."

Then King Caradoc left the others, and he avoided all the battalions and went off at a slow gait right up to King Bors's company. And when they were as near to each other as a bowman could shoot an arrow, they began running at each other as fast as their horses could go. They broke their lances when they met, and it looked as if they might have inflicted deadly wounds on each other;[†] then they drew their swords and began to fight with wondrous fierceness.

Then King Bors went to a godson of his whose name was Blaris, and entrusted his standard to him; he was a good knight and did not dare refuse. And the king said that he wanted to know how well the British could fight on horseback. Then he took a lance and rushed into their midst so hard that the whole formation shuddered. He struck one knight so fiercely that all his armor could not keep the tip and shaft of the lance from going straight through his body and bearing him to the ground so

---

* The clause describes a heraldic ensign in the form of a pennant which has long tails *(langhes)* with ends *(baligot)* (119, ll. 6-8). Compare with the description of King Ban's standard just below.

† As Sommer notes (119, n. 1), his text is unclear.

that he broke his neck and the weapon flew into bits. Then King Bors took hold of his sword, drew it out of the scabbard, and began to fight with such strength that all who saw him were amazed, and they ran out of his way when they saw him coming toward them. King Caradoc would have lost everything, but the King of the Hundred Knights came to his rescue with two thousand very worthy knights who were very skilled at bearing arms. As soon as they gathered, they held themselves to be more than King Bors's equals, but his prowess surpassed that of all others, and he worked wonders there. On the other side, King Caradoc and the King of the Hundred Knights matched him very well, but they suffered a great deal of damage on each side, and the fighting went on for a very long time without stopping. [120]

All at once came King Ban of Benoic, who was very eager to join the fray. The standard in the hands of his steward had crowns of gold and indigo, with bands going across of green like meadow grass, and its six tails blew against Alelme the Seneschal down to his wrists and flew over the ears of his horse and all around its neck. And when the barons saw King Ban's standard, it was very plain to them that soon they would have to fall back or die if they held out for too long; indeed, as soon as the fight began, they never held their ground, and then King Lot came to the fight with tears in his eyes, for he saw plainly that they had lost everything. Then you would have seen lances broken on both sides, shields driven through, and the ground shaking beneath the warhorses, and the woods resounded with the blows they traded, which could be heard clearly for half a league.

When King Ban came into the fight the barons held out for only a short time, and he drove them back on the six kings* and their companies. There was very great anguish and slaughter on both sides, for King Ban began to kill so many fighting men that they fled in all directions, and he rode through the ranks with his sword in his hand and struck right and left, meaning to cut down the whole company of troops. Then came King Lot, the King of the Hundred Knights, and Marganor, and they moved against King Ban, and their troops rushed into the fray and became mixed up with each other.

When the barons saw that King Ban was dealing them great harm, they were highly upset. Then the King of the Hundred Knights spurred his horse, his sword in his hand; he was a very good and bold knight, and he struck King Ban across the top of his shield with such a mighty blow that he sent a piece of it flying to the middle of the field. When King Ban saw that, he was most distraught; then he lifted his sword in anger and raised it high to strike the King of the Hundred Knights through his helmet; but the man, who feared this blow, leaned down and hit his horse with his spurs, and King Ban struck the horse on the mail blanket that covered it and cut it all the way through, sending it to the ground all in a heap. And when the King of the Hundred Knights found himself on the ground, he sprang up at once, his sword in his grasp and his shield over his head. And when King Brandegorre saw the King of the Hundred Knights hit the ground, he ran against King Ban and struck him across the shield with such a fierce blow that he split it in two and knocked a big piece to the ground, and King Ban struck him back on the

---

*   Sommer's text has .v. (120, l. 14).

helmet with such a strong blow that he sliced through the metal band and the mail coif, right flat against the head. If his sword had not glanced off, he would have killed him, but he sent him sprawling to the ground.

After the two kings had got back up, the great fight began against King Ban, but King Ban defended himself so well that he brought worse harm to them than they did to him, and both of the other kings lost a great deal of blood, and both of them would have been grievously hurt, but the general battle moved into their midst and separated them in spite of their efforts.

Then King Arthur happened to find King Ban afoot, because they had killed his horse, and he was defending himself so fiercely that no one dared face up to him, for he was a large, uncommonly strong knight. [121] He rushed on them right in the middle of the fray, but they gave him wide berth and let him go past, so much did they fear his blows, and there was none so bold that he waited for them to fall.

And when King Arthur saw him, he went to the side where he was, his sword in his hand smeared with the blood of men and horses, for he was making awesome shows of fighting. And King Arthur reached one knight who was richly armed on a horse of great worth. He struck him through his helmet with such a fierce blow that he split him down to his teeth, and he fell down dead to the ground. King Arthur took his horse by the rein, led him to King Ban, and said to him, "Here, my friend, get on. Our enemies are having a bad day, and soon you will see them give way."

King Ban quickly got on the horse, and he and King Arthur rushed headlong into the enemy formation. And when they saw the great damage they were doing to their fighting men, they were so amazed and bewildered that they lost all will to fight, and they turned their backs and ran to the woods. But there many of them were slain or wounded, and they were pressed so hard between the army and the stream that they were almost utterly routed. There they stopped and made a stand, for they knew that if they ran any farther they would all be killed.

When King Neutres and all the other kings saw this, they drew aside together, and Marganor told them, "Hold out until nightfall; otherwise we are all as good as dead."

And they said that was the plain truth.

Thus King Ban and King Arthur, riding ahead of all the others, ran after them, until they came to a thundering torrent, where the fleeing army had built a bridge out of branches and logs and crossed over in droves. King Arthur and King Ban came to the bridge and wanted to set out after them. But Merlin came to them and said, "King Arthur, what are you trying to do? Isn't it enough that you have thoroughly beaten your enemies? Go back to your land, take your friends with you, serve them and do them honor as best you can. I must go away into the woods to do what I must to be in the company of my master Blaise, who is also my very dear friend."

He suddenly left King Arthur and went away into the forest, where he found Blaise, who had been waiting and wishing for him for a long time. And he asked him where he had been for so long, and Merlin told him that he had been with King Arthur in order to give him counsel. And Blaise told him that he was mad not to stay there with him, unless it was simply good for him to counsel the new king. Then Merlin told him everything that happened since he had left him, and he told how the Saxons had invaded the barons' lands and how they were fighting them. And Blaise put it all down in writing, and thanks to him we still know it.

But now the story falls silent about Merlin and Blaise and speaks of King Arthur and the other kings who were their companions.

8. MERLIN AS A BIRD CATCHER.[*]

Here the story says that when King Arthur had routed the six kings[†] and the duke of Cambenic on Merlin's advice, just as you have heard, King Arthur started back gladly, heartened that Our Lord [122] had given him victory over his enemies. And he made his way back to Logres, and they all encamped in the meadow outside and set up their tents and pavilions. They posted the watch and slept until daybreak.

And when it was daylight, they heard Mass and then went to eat. After they had eaten, King Arthur had all the goods and other spoils of war they had taken put into a heap, and the three kings divided it up among those they knew needed it the most, more to some, less to others, according to their standing, and they gave it out to the poor knights and poor men-at-arms, and not one penny was left. Then they divided up the riding horses and warhorses and silk cloth, and gave out everything until there was nothing more to be given. Then they sent all of their knights and men-at-arms back home, except for only forty, who were to go with them to the kingdom of Carmelide. Pharian and Leonce of Payerne took their armies back to their country to protect their lands and see to it that King Claudas did them no wrong. The knights who had got generous gifts bought fiefdoms and holdings back in their lands, and they lived very honorably from them all the days of their lives. And King Arthur stayed with the two kings at Bredigan, which was the chief city of Great Britain and Carmelide, and there they awaited Merlin, who was to come to them.

The day after King Arthur had come, and he had eaten, there was great merry-making. The three kings went into the galleries that stood by the river in order to look at the meadows and gardens. Then they looked downstream and saw a huge peasant, a lowborn freeman, coming through the meadows along the river; he carried a bow in his hands, and he had arrows. There were wild ducks on a brook bathing, as their nature bids them to do, and the freeman strung his bow and shot one of them, breaking its neck. Then he let fly another arrow and killed a mallard. Then he picked them both up, hung them by their necks on his belt, and went off toward the galleries where the three kings were looking out, and they had watched his shooting.

When he had got within an arrow shot of the pavilions, he called King Arthur, and as he drew still nearer the king asked him if he wanted to sell the birds he had killed, and the freeman said, "Yes, very gladly."

[*]   Corresponds to Sommer, 121-124.
[†]   Sommer's text has *.x.* (121, l. 38).

"And how much are they worth to you?" asked the king, and he did not answer a word.

The freeman had great cowhide shoes on his feet and was dressed in a tunic and coat of burlap and a cape, and around his waist was a knotted sheepskin belt. He was big and tall, black, and hairy, and he looked ruthless and evil, and he said, "I do not respect a king who loves his treasure too much and brings sorrow. Curses on a woebegone king who does not make a poor man wealthy when he can! I'll give you the birds," he said, "for I have nothing else that is worth anything, as you can see. You don't have the heart to give a third of your wealth, which, in any case, will rot in the ground before you can dig it up! You can be sure that this weakens your honor and glory."

When King Arthur heard the freeman's speech, he looked at the other two kings and said to them, "What devils have told this freeman that I have buried treasure?"

Then King Ban called the freeman over and asked him who had told him that. He answered not a word, but told King Arthur to have someone take the birds and he would go away.

"Now [123] tell us," said King Ban, "for the sake of your soul, who told you that the king had buried treasure?"

And the freeman answered, "A wildman named Merlin told me, and he said that he would come today to talk to the king."

While they were talking, Ulfin came out of a room and went straight to where the king was pleading with the freeman.

"Say, now," said the king, "how could I ever believe that you have spoken with Merlin?"

"If you want to," said the freeman, "believe me; if you don't want to, don't believe me! I have got nothing from you, so let's say we're even."

When Ulfin heard him, he began smiling, for he knew right away that it was Merlin. And when the freeman saw Ulfin, he said to him, "Steward, take these birds and give them to your king to eat tonight. He doesn't have the heart to make a rich man from a poor man who could still reward him well! You may be sure that today he has spoken to a man to whom wealth means very little, even though he is among the greatest on earth!"

Then Ulfin began to laugh out loud, and he said to him, "Sir, if you like, I would very gladly talk with you."

And he said that he would very willingly do so. The king looked at Ulfin and saw him smiling broadly, and he asked him why he was laughing, and he answered that he would know in time.

And the freeman went inside dressed as he was and said to Kay, "Here, my lord seneschal, now you can have these birds plucked, and may your king eat them as gladly as I give them to him."

"Sir," said Ulfin, "this is not the first gift you have given him!"

At these words came Bretel, who had heard what Ulfin had told him, and he recognized straightway that it was Merlin. So he began smiling, and the king asked him why he had smiled, and he answered that he would indeed tell him if the freeman wanted him to. And the freeman said that he did. Then Ulfin said to the king, "Sir, don't you know your friend Merlin? And wasn't he to talk to you today just like this freeman?"

"Yes," said the king. "Why do you say this?"

"Sir," said Ulfin, "I say it because you do not know him so well as I would like. You can see people two or three times and not recognize them, and I am amazed!"

When the king heard Ulfin, he was so bewildered that he did not know what to say, except to entreat him to tell him who the freeman was if he knew. "Sir," said Ulfin, "don't you know Merlin?"

"Of course I do," said the king.

"Then look closely at this good man," said Ulfin, "and see if you have ever laid eyes on him. But he can well say to you that he has wasted his time serving you, for this is Merlin who has served you and loved you and helped you as much as he could against all those who wished you ill."

And King Arthur crossed himself, and the other two kings were greatly astounded, and they asked him, "Merlin, is this you then? We never saw you in such garb!"

And he answered that it might well be so.

"My dear lords," said Ulfin, "don't be astonished. He will surely show you the likeness he had when you saw him the first time."

And they said that they would like that.

"Now come into this room," said Ulfin, and they went in with him. And Ulfin said, "Dear lords, don't be bewildered by the things Merlin does. He'll show you many likenesses. Whenever he wants to he changes himself by the powers of the art of necromancy, which he is full of."

And Guinebal, who was there, bore witness to the fact. And then Ulfin said that Merlin changed shape because there were many people in the country who wanted him dead. "Now let's all go [124] to him and see him in his true likeness."

And they went out and found Merlin in the hall in his true likeness. Then they ran to him and showed him that they were glad to see him because they loved him, and they began to laugh at the way he had looked and the words he had spoken to the king. Then King Arthur said to Merlin, "Now I am certain that you love me, for you willingly gave me your birds, and I will eat them for love of you!"

And Merlin said that he would like that very much.

So they stayed together, gladdened and finding solace in their companionship, until mid-Lent. And it happened that King Arthur, following Merlin's advice, became friends with a maiden, the most beautiful ever born. Her name was Lisanor, and she was the daughter of Earl Sevain, and she was born at the castle called Quimper-Corentin.

This maiden came to swear fealty to King Arthur, and other barons came with her, because they feared that he might take their lands away, so they came to him of their own free will. And as soon as King Arthur saw the maiden, he liked her very much, and, thanks to Merlin, he could at last talk to her alone, and they lay together all night. There Loholt was conceived: he was later a good knight and a companion of the Round Table. When it was mid-Lent, the king took leave of the young lady and got ready to go into the kingdom of Carmelide along with a body of forty knights.

But the story does not tell any more about them right here, but it goes back to speaking about the six* kings who had been driven from the field of battle, and we will tell what became of them and where they went.†

9. REBELS' DEFENSES AGAINST THE SAXONS.‡

Here the story says that the barons were sorely distressed by their loss. They rode all night bewailing their losses and the harm that had come to them, and they suffered from hunger and cold. The next day they came to a city called Sorhaut, which belonged to King Urien, and he welcomed them most joyfully. They rested and took their ease, which they very much needed to do, and the sick and wounded stayed there until they were brought back to health. But they had been there only three days when messengers came from Cornwall and Orkney telling their lords about the damage and destruction the Saxons were wreaking in their lands; they had laid siege to the castle of Vambieres, and they had settled so many of their own people in the countryside that they would never be driven out of the land.

When the barons heard this news, none was so bold that his flesh did not crawl from fear. They spent two weeks there in all. [125]

After one week, they all gathered in King Urien's great hall, and King Brandegorre said to them, "My lords, you have heard that the Saxons have invaded your lands. They have plundered and laid waste a great part of them, and they have besieged the castle of Vambieres. This is why we must quickly decide how they might be thrown out of the country. You know very well that we have lost in our march against King Arthur. We do not look for any help from him or his lands, any more than we do from King Leodagan of Carmelide, who would very gladly help us if he could, but King Rion, who is so strong, has been fighting a war against him for two years. We do not hope for help from King Pelles of Listenois, for he is watching over his brother Pellinor, who lies stricken with a sickness he will never be cured of until the one comes there who will put an end to the adventures of the Holy Grail. Nor do we look for any help from King Alan, who lies ill, before the best knight in the world comes to him and asks him where his sickness came from and what the Grail is that he is served from.

"So we cannot decide what to do by ourselves unless Our Lord in His mercy helps us. What we need very much to do is to look to ourselves and see what we can do. You can be sure that the damage that was our lot when we fought against King Arthur happened because of Merlin's sway, for he went to get King Ban of Benoic and his brother King Bors, who are the best knights in the world, and they have become King Arthur's liegemen. And you should know that as long as Merlin is against us, we can never hold out against King Arthur; no one, no matter how

---

* Sommer's text has *x*. (124, l. 18).
† Sommer's text summarizes *ou il deuindrent* (124, l. 19): "where they became."
‡ Corresponds to Sommer, 124-128.

strong or clever he is, can make himself safe against him, for he knows all things that are to come and that are done, said, and past.

"This is why it behooves us to take care of our lands by ourselves and to see how we might strengthen them against those heathen enemies."

And when he had said this, he sat back down, and it was a very long time before any of the barons uttered a single word.

Then King Tradelmant of North Wales rose and said, like the wise man he was, "My lords, the best advice I can give you is that we should go fortify the lands bordering the country where the Saxons are coming from. Let us send there as many of our knights as we can gather, and we will guard the roads and tracks so that no supplies or any kind of help can reach them. In the meantime, let us summon our friends, kinsmen, and men-at-arms from every land, and we will fight them as soon as we are all gathered together. I don't see any other way to break the siege."

When the barons heard King Tradelmant's speech, they found it praiseworthy, and they agreed to do what he had advised. Then they asked which border lands they should fortify. And he told them that as many men as [126] they had left would go to the city of Wissant and to Nantes,* which is a great, strong city, but they would send the first ones they could bring together to the city of Garles, which was not to be forgotten. "And if we can dishearten them and starve the besiegers, then we will win wealth and land."

And King Lot stood up and said to them, "Certainly, my lords, I do not see how we can fortify the border lands through which they come and go unless we take into account King Arthur and the help he gets from the two kings and Merlin, who knows so much about what we do and say."

And the King of the Hundred Knights got up and said, "My dear lords, King Lot says that he is afraid of King Arthur and those who help him running up and down the countryside, but we don't have to fear them! Yesterday a messenger came to me and said that King Arthur, King Ban, and King Bors were getting ready to go into the kingdom of Carmelide to help King Leodagan against King Rion who is waging war against him. They are going to fight under King Leodagan's command, and you can be sure that they are doing this at Merlin's behest. They have well fortified the strongholds throughout his land, and they are aware of the great trouble that has overcome us, which is why they are going off all the more boldly. If King Arthur weren't leaving, I would advise making peace between us and him so that he might strengthen our numbers to help us drive the Saxons out, for they will never be thrown out unless God sees to it. And we must yet take a very strong castle the Saxons have in this land which they call Saxon Rock: its lady is a maiden who is very courtly, and she is the sister of King Hargadabran, who will surely help them out if we don't take the castle quickly."

When the barons heard that King Arthur was going away and leaving his kingdom, they thought long and hard about why this was, but the only reason they were able to think of was that it could only be because of Merlin. At last they agreed to fortify the border lands of Galone and Gorre and the ones near Cornwall and Orkney. Then they sent for all their men who could bear arms and as many men-at-arms from

---

*   Sommer's text has *nalanc* (126, l. 1), which is later corrected to *nantes en bertaigne* (127, l. 1).

other countries as they could gather, and all who were eager for the spoils of war drew together little by little. But not a single one came from the lands belonging to King Arthur and those who held them from him; they did not want their wealth, for their lord had given them very much of his own and promised them still more. [127]

The very first city the barons fortified was Nantes in Brittany, near Cornwall, because it was in the land where the Saxons had come to dwell. King Yder went there with three thousand men, all fitted out with iron armor, who had got away from the rout. And when King Yder came there, the people in the castle were very glad, for they had been quite frightened by the Saxons, who were overrunning the country. And King Yder recruited so many men that he had eight thousand or more following his standard, and they kept watch very well all around the countryside. They often fought with the Saxons, and they won a great deal. Their fame even reached the army of the Saxons, who did not dare ride out where they were without a great company of men.

The other city which they sent out to fortify was called Wissant. King Neutres of Garlot went there, and he took with him three thousand men of those who had come through the rout with him. When he got there, the people welcomed him joyfully, for they had been greatly distressed by the great army of Saxons whom they had seen ride by in front of the city, taking away with them the plunder they had won thereabouts, for they had burned and laid waste all the cities. And as soon as King Neutres got there, he stocked the city well with foodstuffs; then he called in men-at-arms, freemen as well as serfs, until he had over eight thousand, on foot and on horseback, not counting the burghers, who could have been as many as five thousand.

They guarded the border land around them so well that hardly any supplies got through to the Saxons, and they very often fought the Saxons in battles where they lost more than they won, for King Neutres was a very good knight, bold and resourceful. And he had by his wife a son who was sixteen years old, and he was wondrously handsome. King Neutres's wife was the half-sister of King Arthur, from his mother Ygraine, who had been daughter of Duke Hoel of Tintagel, and her name was Blasine. By her King Neutres had a son who was later a companion of the Round Table; his true name was Galescalain, and he later became Duke of Clarence, which King Arthur granted him after marrying Guenevere, his wife.

That Galescalain I am telling you about heard the news that King Neutres had fought against his uncle, King Arthur, and he had heard about the great worth that was in King Arthur. So he came to his mother and said to her, "Dear mother, weren't you the daughter of the Duke of Tintagel and Queen Ygraine? Her second husband was King Uther Pendragon, who fathered on her, as I have heard it told, his offspring whose name is King Arthur. He is so worthy and such a good knight that he routed eleven princes with just a few men, as I have heard it told. For God's sake, tell me the truth! Is he the son of Uther Pendragon, who was in his time the worthiest knight in the world?"

When the mother heard her son talking to her in this way, her eyes began to fill with tears, and she spoke, all the while weeping because her heart was breaking for the brother whom her son had brought to mind. "Dear son," she said, "you can be certain that he is my brother and your uncle, and he is your father's close kinsman on King Uther Pendragon's side, as I have heard my mother say many times. The barons of this country did not want to accept him as their king, but Our Lord, who is so gentle and noble-hearted, showed in a miracle that he had chosen him."

Then she told him the adventure of the stone that had appeared with the sword, and she told him everything as it had happened. When Galescalain heard his mother's words, [128] he said that he bore no good will toward any who were against King Arthur. "And may God never let me die," he said, "before King Arthur has made me a knight. And it is a fact that, if I can do so well that he should be willing to gird my sword on me, I will never leave him as long as I live, provided he wants to keep me as his companion."

Then he left his mother and went into a room to think about what he might do to get to King Arthur, and he decided to send word to his cousin Gawainet asking him to come speak to him at New Castle in Broceliande* and telling him to come as secretly as he could and take care to be there without fail on the third day after Easter. Then Galescalain left the room, went to find a messenger, and sent him to his cousin Gawainet to tell him what you have just heard.

But now the story falls silent about him right here, and we will tell you about the kings who stayed behind at Sorhaut

10. KING LOT'S YOUNG SONS; MORDRED'S PARENTAGE.†

Here the story says that after King Neutres had left the barons at Sorhaut, just as you have heard, King Lot took‡ three thousand fighting men who had survived the battle in which he had been routed, and came straight to the city of Orkney, where he was welcomed very joyfully, for everyone had been afraid of the Saxons, who had the run of the countryside and were burning the towns. And King Lot sent orders to as many as he could muster and raised an army more than ten thousand strong, with foot soldiers and knights, not counting the burghers, of whom there were a good four thousand. So King Lot was able to protect the city and the countryside all about, and he very often fought the Saxons when he got word that they had come on raids, and the poor, young knights won a great deal in spoils; they needed it sorely, and he let them keep everything they took. This is why his fame spread far and wide and his honor grew.

It is also true that his wife was one of King Arthur's half-sisters, his mother's daughter. This lady gave birth to Gawainet, Agravain, Guerrehet, and Gaheriet, who were all King Lot's sons. Furthermore, she also bore Mordred, who was the offspring whom King Arthur fathered. And I will tell you how, for the history will

---

*   In Sommer's text, *la noeve ferte de borceliande* (128, l. 7; cf. 133, l. 28): "the new stronghold of the Forest of Broceliande." Sommer translates as "the New Ford" (133, marginal summary).

†   Corresponds to Sommer, 128-131.

‡   Sommer's text has *sen ala a vne cite a* (128, ll. 14-15): "went to a city with/that had."

be more worthwhile if I make you understand how Mordred was sired by him, for many people would find King Arthur less worthy because of it if they did not know the truth.

As it happened, when the barons of the kingdom of Logres were gathered at Carduel to choose a king after the death of Uther Pendragon, King Lot brought his wife with him, and many other barons had brought theirs as well. King Lot happened to have a very beautiful hall for himself and his household. Antor, his son Kay, and Arthur had a part of that very same house off by themselves, as far from the others as they could get. But when King Lot learned that Antor was a knight, he asked him to eat with him, and he had him sit at his own table with his son Kay, who was newly knighted. And King Lot had a room made up where he slept with his wife, while Antor slept in the hall with his son Kay. Arthur had set up his bed [129] in a corner near the door to King Lot's room, for squires should sleep away from knights.

Arthur was a very handsome lad, and he was very clever. He had noticed everything about the lady. He had seen that she was beautiful and plump; he strongly desired her in his heart and loved her for it. But the lady did not heed this, for she was very faithful to her husband.

It happened that the barons had agreed to set a day when they would come to court, conferring together at Black Cross. And the night before he was to leave in the morning, King Lot told his household, as quietly as he could, to saddle their horses at midnight and to get their arms ready. They did as they were bidden, keeping what they did under wraps as best they could; the king did not even speak to his wife about it, but got up as quietly as he could at midnight so that she never knew what was happening. So the king went off to Black Cross, and his wife stayed behind all alone in her bed.

And Arthur, who had noticed that the king had gone away, got up and went to the lady's bed and lay down with her. And after he had got in bed with her, he turned his back to her, for he did not dare do anything else. And it so happened that the lady awoke and, still half asleep, turned toward him, for she truly thought that he was her husband, and she put her arms around him. When Arthur saw that she had embraced him, he understood that she had not noticed who he was, so he put his arms around her and lay with her fully, and the lady gave him much pleasure, and she did it willingly, for she thought that he was her husband. And this is how Mordred was conceived.

And when Arthur had done to the lady what gave him such great delight, he did not have to wait a very long time before she went back to sleep. He went back to his own bed very quietly, so that no one realized what he had done until the next day, when he happened to tell it himself when he was serving the noonday meal, cutting meat on his knees. And the lady happened to say to him, "Get up, my dear young man; you have knelt long enough."

And he told her in a low voice that he could never deserve the good things she had done for him, and she asked him what that was all about. He told her that he would not say unless she swore to him that she would not tell anyone or try to find a way to cast blame on him or do anything harmful to him. She answered that no harm could come to her from that, and she very willingly swore to what he asked, for she had no reason to worry. And he told her how he had lain with her the night before, and the lady was deeply ashamed and blushed, but no one knew what their secret was. So that is how Arthur lay with his sister, and it never happened again, but the lady knew that she was with child by him.

When it was time for the child to be born, the news had spread through the country that the one who was Uther Pendragon's son would be king. And in her heart the lady loved him better for it than anyone could ever say, but she did not dare show it because of her husband King Lot, and the war between King Arthur and those of her country sorely distressed her.

One day it happened that Gawainet came home from the hunt. He was finely dressed in a homespun robe that was lined with ermine, and he was holding onto three greyhounds by the leash, and he was leading two hunting dogs behind him. Everything he did suited him very well, for he was the most handsome and best-shaped man for his size that anyone had ever seen. When he got up in the morning, he had the strength of the best knight in the world; by the time the hour of prime came, [130] it had grown twofold; at tierce, the same thing. At midday, he went back to the strength he had at first, and at nones and all the nighttime hours, he always still had his first strength.

When Gawainet went into the hall, looking just as I have told you, his mother was lying down in a room by a hearth where there was a great roaring fire. When the lady saw Gawainet, who was a big, handsome lad, and it was high time for him to be knighted, she began to weep. The lad was very sorry for her, so he asked her what was wrong. And she answered, "Dear, sweet son, I am right to weep, for I see you and your brothers waste time doing foolish things, when you should already be knights at King Arthur's court. He is your uncle and the best knight in the world, they say, and you should serve him and work for peace between him and your father. What a great shame it is for there to be such hatred between those two and between him and the other barons who should be serving him and loving him. In their pride they do not deign to recognize him as their overlord, and it certainly seems that Our Lord is grieved by it because they have lost more in the warfare than they have won. Furthermore, the Saxons have invaded this country. They will utterly destroy us if God does not show us a way out, and we will not have help from the man who could drive them out, that is, King Arthur, who will have a hard time loving your father and the other barons! And you and your brothers are much to blame, for right now you should be working for peace between your uncle and your father, so that they might be good friends, but all you do every day is play around with these greyhounds! You are wasting your time and your youth, and I tell you that you ought to be ashamed of yourselves!"

When Gawainet heard his mother, he said to her, "Lady, are you telling me the truth? This King Arthur who is so worthy, is he your brother and my uncle?"

"Dear son," she said, "there is no doubt about it. He truly is your uncle."

Then she told him from beginning to end how it had all happened. And when Gawainet had heard it, he said very courteously, "Dear mother, now don't you worry. By the faith I owe you, I will never wear a sword at my waist or a helmet laced on my head before King Arthur girds me with arms, if he finds me worthy

of being a knight. And we will go to court and help him defend his land against all
those who would do him harm."

"Dear son," said the lady, "I will not keep you from that, for I would be very glad
to see the day when you could do that. And may Our Lord grant that your father and
your uncle also become friends."

"Lady," said Gawainet, "Let it be for now. You can be sure that I will never come
back into my father's house, once I have left to go to King Arthur's court, until
he and my father have come to terms with each other, even if I should have to go
against my own father."

While he and his mother were talking, his three brothers came in and saw that
their mother was weeping. And Agravain said to Gawainet, when he found out why,
"You are more to blame than the rest of us, for you are the eldest, and you should
have taken us to serve the one who makes all those around him better than they
were before. Here we do nothing but waste our time in foolishness, and we are not
looking ahead to a time when we'll be in trouble, [131] just like the bird caught in
a trap.* The Saxons, who have laid waste the whole country, are a day's ride away
from here, and there is no army hereabouts and no way to drive them out except by
the knightly valor of King Arthur. So let's go and ask him to give us our arms, and
we will help him defend his land against his enemies. This is the best thing I see for
us to do, and here the game is so rich that we can win nothing."†

When Gawainet heard his brother's speech, he thought him all the more worthy,
and he praised him and told him that he would do just that. "Now all there is to do
is get ready, for we'll leave within the next two weeks."

When their mother saw what they were undertaking, she was most glad, and she
told them not to worry about anything, for she would fit them out with horses and
armor, and they were very happy.

But here the story falls silent for a while about them and their mother, and we will
tell you about the kings who had stayed behind at Sorhaut.

11. YOUNG SAGREMOR; DISPERSAL OF THE ROUTED REBEL LEADERS.‡

In this part the story says that the three kings had left Sorhaut to fortify strongholds,
just as you have heard. King Clarion left after they did and came to Belande, one of
his cities, and he took three thousand knights with him. After that the King of the
Hundred Knights left and took three thousand armed men with him and went off to

---

* Agravain's wording is *nous ... serons pris ausi comme li oisiaus au brai* (130, l. 43; 131, l. 1):
"we'll be caught like the bird in glue." The use of glue was a common means of trapping small birds.
The reference to a bird caught in a trap is proverbial: *A tart crie li oisiaus quand il est pris* ("The bird
cries out too late when it is already caught."). See Joseph Morawski, *Proverbes français anteriéurs au
XV siècle* (Paris: Champion, 1925), no. 147.

† Another indication of Agravain's tendency to use proverbial language. Cf. Morawski, no. 646:
Endementres que li geus est biaux le fait bon laissier ("While the game is rich, it is well to leave it.").

‡ Corresponds to Sommer, 131-133.

the city of Malehaut, where there was a noble lady. This city bordered on his land, but he withdrew there because it was closer to the way the Saxons were coming in: this is what the barons begged him to do. He did for them what they wanted, and he protected the border land around them very well.

After him King Tradelmant left the city of Sorhaut, and he went off to his stronghold, North Wales,* with three thousand men outfitted with armor, and his liegemen were very glad to welcome him, because they were along the way to Saxon Rock, which had done them great harm.

And after him King Brandegorre left with three thousand armed men and went straight to Estrangorre, his main stronghold, because it was close to Saxon Rock. He called in knights and men-at-arms from far and wide until he had gathered together a great many of them. This King Brandegorre had a wife, a very noble woman, who was the daughter of Hadrian,† emperor of Constantinople. This lady had formerly had a husband who was king of Vlask‡ and Hungary, but he died only five [132] years after he had wed the lady and left a son, the most handsome child ever to be born of a man. This lad was handsome, worthy, and intelligent, and he was at the age when he should become a knight. People called him Sagremor. Afterwards he did many highly worthy deeds in the kingdom of Logres, which the story will tell you about farther on. Now I will tell you what happened to this Sagremor.

Renown, who runs everywhere, went throughout the land and countryside, and people talked about no one but King Arthur and his openhandedness. And the stories spread as far as Constantinople, so that Sagremor heard about him. He was no more than fifteen years old, and he was the most handsome boy in the world, strong of limb and trim of body. When he had heard the news about King Arthur, he yearned for the time when he would be made a knight by his hand. And he often said to himself that only the very worthiest of men could be given the order of knighthood. His grandfather, King Hadrian, who was then still alive, wanted him to become a knight,§ for he was the next male heir who would hold the empire after his death, but he told him that he would never be a knight until King Arthur made him one with his own hand. They talked about it from day to day until at last King Hadrian had his baggage made ready and sent him very richly off to Britain.

But here we will stop talking about him for a while, until it is the right time, and we will tell about the kings who left Sorhaut to protect the border lands.

Here the story says that, after King Brandegorre had left Sorhaut, King Caradoc had his baggage made ready and left Sorhaut with three thousand armored men, and he went straight to Estrangort,¶ his main stronghold, and very boldly set up garrisons there, for he was a worthy, fearless fighter. After him left King Aguisant of Scotland, and he was richer in lands than any other king in those parts, and he was the youngest, but he knew less about fighting than the others. He went off to

---

*   In Sommer's text, treated as the name of his city (131, l. 21). See also 160, ll. 32-33.

†   Soramer's text has *audeans* here (131, l. 27) and *audeans* elsewhere (132, l.15).

‡   Sommer's text has *blasque* (131, l. 28).

§   The clause is not in Sommer's text (132, l. 13). Supplied from the Harley manuscript, as quoted in his n. 2.

¶   Not to be confused with Estrangorre, the city belonging to King Brandegorre (131, l. 24; etc.), or the birthplace of Goswain of Estrangot (153, l. 39).

Corentes in Scotland, which was a very great and wealthy city, and it was very much bothered by the Saxons, for they often went back through that neighborhood; it was only twenty Scottish leagues from there to the castle of Vambieres, where there were so many laying siege that the fighting men who gathered there every day were beyond counting.

As soon as King Aguisant had set himself up in the city of Corentes, the burghers, of whom there were five thousand, were very glad. And he sent throughout the land for knights, mounted men-at-arms, and footsoldiers to come defend the stronghold, and about ten thousand, not counting the burghers, gathered there. They fought the Saxons who ran up and down the countryside, and King Aguisant and the other princes won and lost many times there, but they held out for a very long time.

And after the kings, the Duke of Cambenic left Sorhaut with four thousand armed men, on [133] foot and on horseback. He made his way until at last he got to Cambenic, his stronghold, which was wealthy and well stocked with all kinds of goods. There were a good four thousand of his men in the city, and they were very glad when they saw their lord. And the duke sent far and wide for fighting men, and he got at least eight thousand, not counting those who were garrisoned in the city. So the duke lived very well indeed.

And so, just as you have heard, the eleven leaders left and fought many times against the Saxons. The countryside grew ever poorer, for no wheat had been harvested for five years, and there was none anywhere except that which the Saxons and Christians took from each other, unless by chance a merchant ship came; and this is how they got through it all.

And the Saxons overran King Arthur's land, and they inflicted great damage until God sent help there in the form of handsome, noble, young men. I will tell you who they were who held King Arthur's land until he came back from the kingdom of Carmelide. And the barons, as well as the Saxons, lost a great deal more than King Arthur, but the barons were angry with the king because he did not defend his land himself.

But now the story falls silent for a while about them all, and it comes back to Galescalain, son of King Neutres of Garlot.

12. YOUNG GALESCALAIN AND KING LOT'S SONS; BATTLE WITH THE SAXONS.[*]

Now the story says that when Galescalain had learned the news about King Arthur, just as the story has spelled it out, he sent a messenger to his cousin Gawainet telling him to come confer with him as secretly as he could and to bring his brothers with him; he should take care to be there the third day after Easter. And the messenger made his way for long days at a time until he came to Wales, in the border land of

[*] Corresponds to Sommer, 133-137.

Orkney, and at last he found the means to talk to Gawainet and his brothers and to tell them that Galescalain had sent for them.

When they heard the messenger's speech, they were very glad indeed, and they said that they would be there without fail, for they were well aware that he would not send for them unless they were needed. So they gave the messenger a good horse, and he made his way back to Galescalain and told him the answer of his four first cousins on his mother's side. And he equipped himself and, the day after Easter, went straight to New Castle in Broceliande.*

When he got there, Gawainet and his brothers had not yet come. So he waited for them, and when he did see them coming, he greeted them heartily. And Gawainet said to him, "Dear cousin Galescalain, you sent a messenger to ask my brothers and me to come confer with you. But I want you to know that, if I hadn't wanted to ask your leave, I would have gone to a place where I have much to do; I yearn for nothing more than to be there."

"Sir," said Galescalain, "where do you need to go?"

"You should know," said Gawainet, "that I am on my way to see the embodiment of all worthiness, all [134] wondrous things, all noble generosity in the world; I have never heard more good things said about anyone else."

For God's sake," said Galescalain, "who is this then? God grant that it be the one for whom I have asked you to come."

"In truth," said Gawainet, "his name should not be hidden, but declared before all worthy men. His name is King Arthur, and he is our uncle and yours. But all the barons of this land have done him wrong by fighting him, yet they are the ones who should most love him and hold him dear. As God is my witness," he went on, "I will never have a sword at my side before he girds it on me himself."

When Galescalain heard him, he had never been happier. He ran to him with open arms, and he showed him as much joy as if the whole world belonged to him. He said to him that he had sent for him for no other reason! And he told him word for word how his mother had encouraged him, and Gawainet told him in return what his own mother had said to him. Then they made their plan to set out together within two weeks' time.

And they all hurried back home to get their armor and horses ready, as was fitting for young men who were the sons of kings. Why should I say any more about it? Galescalain worked until he had mustered two hundred of the best-armed knights and squires he could have chosen to his liking, and he left without his father knowing anything about it, and they rode, taking the most out-of-the-way roads they knew, until they came to New Castle in Broceliande. Galescalain stayed there until Gawainet and his brothers came. And they had been able to muster five hundred men on horseback, knights and squires, who were all sons of earls and knights. But they had only nine knights, and of the men Galescalain had brought, there were only twenty.

When they came together, they greeted each other very joyfully, then they talked about where they would go. They agreed to go to Logres in Britain, King Arthur's chief city, "and we will hear news there sooner than anywhere else, and we can

---

*   See above, p.135n.

avoid the Saxons who are about in the countryside, for if we met them, we would suffer great harm."

It was at the beginning of May, in the springtime when the birds sing clear and sweet and all things are kindled with joy, when the woods and gardens are in bloom and the meadows turn green again with new grass shoots and all kinds of sweet-smelling flowers among them, when smooth waters again flow in their beds and newly-awakened love gladdens youths and maidens whose hearts are made merry and gay by the sweetness of this time of renewal. Then it happened that Gawainet, Agravain, Guerrehet, Gaheriet, Galescalain, and those who had come with them got up early because the weather would be very hot at midday and they wanted to ride during the morning when it was wondrously cool and calm and the air was soft. They were still young and unhardened against discomfort. They were fully armed and wore iron helmets on their heads like foot soldiers, and they had their swords hanging from their saddle horns, for the countryside was unsafe because of the Saxons who rode about plundering to get food, which was plentiful at that time, and it was a great shame to see such a rich land destroyed so wrongfully. [135]

On the third day they had been riding, just as you have heard, they met King Leodebron, King Senigran, King Maldalet, and King Servagat of the Land of the Irish, who had laid waste the countryside, and they were bringing back much booty and plenty of food, enough so that the army would be well stocked with bread, wine, and meat for a long time to come, for they had stripped the countryside and the ports where ships came to dock, and there was so much food that five hundred pack horses and seven hundred carts were all loaded with it, and the train was so long and the dust they raised wherever they went was so amazing that one man could not tell who another was without looking into his face. And the fire and smoke were so thick throughout the countryside that people a half day's ride away could see that a fire was burning.

When the youths had got close to the train, they could hear the common folk weeping and wailing because of the harm the Saxons had done them. And there were fully ten thousand Saxons on horseback, not counting those on foot, who ran up and down setting fire to all the towns and mistreating everyone.

When the youths saw the sorrow and bereavement, they asked the peasants, who they saw were very frightened, where King Arthur was. And they said that he had gone off to the kingdom of Carmelide in mid-Lent, and he had fortified the border lands and the strongholds in his own land so that no one could harm them. "But the Saxons are so distressed by the hindrances that they have laid waste the whole country, as you can see."

When the youths heard that the king was away, they said that they would fight the Saxons for his land and the plunder that they were taking off, and they would keep the country until the king had come back. When the peasants heard them saying these things, they asked them who they were, and they told them, and when they heard who they were, they were very glad to know them; they truly thought that King Arthur would win back his lands thanks to them and, through the sons who had come there out of noble generosity, he would have back the love of the fathers.

Then the peasants joined them. And as soon as the youths saw the great harm the Saxons were doing throughout the country, their hearts grew heavy, and they cried out, 'To arms now, noble squires! We'll soon see who is worthy, for we are fighting for what belongs to us. We must defend our rights against all who lay waste what is ours and plunder it."

Right away the squires ran to put their armor on. They got on their horses and lined up by rows and then squeezed tight together, just as the knights showed them to do. There were about eighty* who were good, faithful knights, and the peasants who had come along numbered more than five hundred, on horseback and on foot, and they went off together like a flock of starlings.

The first thing they did was fall on the foodstuffs the Saxons were having driven back to their army, and there were more than three thousand who were to lead the train. And the story says that it was well after midday, and it was so hot and the dust had been raised so high that the men could not see each other a stone's throw away. And as soon as the youths saw their enemies, they ran their horses over them; they hit, struck down, and wounded as many as they reached, so that none might get away from them. That day Gawainet killed more of them than all the others, and he and his horse were all covered with blood. He wielded an axe, and right away, any man he went after could do nothing to avoid [136] being split open down to his bowels. And his brothers fought so well that none dared face up to them. And Galescalain was always with Gawainet, and he fought wonderfully; he killed or struck down all he met in his path, and no one got away from him without having a foot or a hand or a leg or his head or some other part of the body cut off. But above them all, it was awesome to see the death and destruction that Gawainet meted out, for no iron or steel or man's body, no matter how strong, could withstand his blows.

They fought so long up and down the train that of the three thousand who were taking the plunder back toward the army, barely twenty got away. Ten of these fugitives turned back toward their cavalry, which was following behind. There were more than eight thousand of them, but they were not well armed, for they had had the squires pack their armor away because of the heat that was bothering them. And the ten runaways came in and shouted to them that everyone taking the plunder had been killed.

When the Saxons heard that they had lost their plunder, those who had arms ran to get them. They put on their armor and made themselves ready as best they could. But a good third of them could not get to their armor, because their squires had gone off with the wagon train which the youths had taken, and they were having it taken back to Logres, driven by the very peasants who had joined them. Then the youths had followed the runaways and at last stormed them headlong. There they fought a fierce battle, harsh and wicked, that was a wonder to see and hear! There Gawainet killed King Thoas of Ireland, striking him hard with his axe, which he held two-handed, right through the helmet and splitting him down to his teeth. And Galescalain struck King Segrain so hard that he sent his head flying to the middle of the field. And Agravain rushed into the midst of the fray and began striking

* Previously, Sommer's text gives the total number of knights as 29 (134, l. 22).

left and right. And Gaheriet had run after Guinebal an arrow shot away from his companions, because he had struck his brother Guerrehet down with his lance (he had not looked closely, and Gaheriet thought he was dead); he ran on him, with his sword drawn, as fiercely as if he were a wild boar.

When Guinebal saw Gaheriet coming, he turned in flight, for he did not dare face up to him because of the wonders and the slaughter he had seen him do, and without doubt he was of very wonderful prowess. For the account of the histories says that he applied himself just as tirelessly as his brother Gawainet when he was old enough to be a knight. And when he saw the Saxon who was fleeing farther away from him, he swore to God and His Mother that he would not fail, in woods or on the plain, to avenge his brother. So he spurred his horse to a full speed and ran after Guinebal until he had left his own men behind him farther than a crossbow could shoot, and he caught up with him in a convoy of Saxons. Gaheriet hit him so hard right on his helmet that he knocked off a big piece of it and sent him slumping over his horse's neck; then he sliced between his body and his shield right through the shield's straps and cut his arm off, sending it flying to the middle of the field. And when Guinebal saw that he was so dreadfully wounded, he fell to the ground in a faint.

Then Gaheriet twisted his head out of his helmet, for he was very [137] glad to have avenged his brother, and he prepared to go back, but the Saxons who saw him strike the blow would not allow it. King Guinebal shouted, "Now at him!" And straightway hundreds and then thousands of them broke their formation and closed in around him on all sides, and they struck at him with lances and brought him and his horse down in a heap. Gaheriet sprang to his feet after the lances had been broken, for he was very strong and he still had his wind, and he defended himself fiercely. None of the Saxons was so bold as to dare face up to him or take him, but they stood back and threw lances, spears, and sharp knives at him until they had brought him to his knees two or three times.

He was close to being killed or taken prisoner when a squire who had seen him run after the Saxon shouted to Gawainet, "What are you doing here? You will soon lose your brother Gaheriet unless you help him right away! He had given chase to a Saxon and he caught him in that valley, where that fighting is, and they have brought him down and killed his horse. What a shame it would be to lose him like that!"

When Gawainet heard him, he said, "Ah! Lady Mary, Holy Virgin, maiden Mother of Jesus Christ, please don't let my brother be lost to me! I would never again have joy in my heart if I lost him." Then he shouted to his companions to follow him. "Now we'll see who loves me!"

"Dear cousin," said Galescalain, "why do you go on preaching? When there is such need, we shouldn't wait! Ride out fast, for I am afraid that they may kill him before you can get to him!"

Then the youths broke out of their formation all together and rode off as fast as their horses could carry them. Gawainet ran ahead of them and took his axe in both hands, just as he had done in the slaughter before, when the whole field was covered with gore, and he looked until he had found Gaheriet lying sprawled on he ground. The Saxons had knocked his helmet from his head, and they tried to pull his mail coif away in order to cut off his head, but then they thought that they could take him alive if they could bring him to the Saxons' army. They had laid him out on the ground and were trying to tie his hands behind his back when Gawainet came spurring his horse, wielding his axe, and he rode headlong into their midst as fast as he could make his horse run. He struck left and right and quickly killed or wounded every one he hit.

When those who were holding his brother saw the wonders he did, they did not dare face up to him, and they took flight. And when Gaheriet saw his brother, he jumped to his feet and quickly put his helmet back on his head; he picked his sword up and made ready to defend himself. And Agravain brought him a horse and said to him, "Dear brother, get on! You were unwise to go so far away from us." And Gaheriet climbed on the horse, happy and smiling.

And the Saxons gathered their forces over the whole countryside, and they formed their battalions. But now the story falls silent about the youths and the Saxons, and it speaks about the peasants whom the youths had sent back to the city of Logres with the plunder and the wagon train they had won back.

13. GAWAINET AND HIS BROTHERS DEFEAT THE SAXONS.[*]

Here the story says that the peasants who were to take the food the youths had won back from the Saxons went straight to the city of Logres, and they had a very hard time getting there safely, even though the city of Logres was only four Scottish leagues away from the place where the food had been won back. [138] When the burghers saw the valuable plunder and the foodstuffs, they asked to whom they belonged. And the peasants told them that Gawainet, King Lot's son, and his three brothers, along with their cousin Galescalain, the son of King Neutres of Garlot, had come to help King Arthur, and they had left their own lands and countries, and they said that they would not let King Arthur down a single day of their lives. They had come with seven hundred companions, "and they met three thousand foragers who were taking this plunder, and they fought with them until they had killed them all and cut them to pieces, and the Saxons had taken the goods from us to feed their army. And they fought with seven thousand Saxons who were taking this plunder away with them. Open the gates and take it back, and we'll go help them, for it would be a great shame if they were cut off before their prime, for we think they are very worthy and valiant fighters."

And they opened the gates and welcomed them into the city. Afterward they all agreed that some of them would go help the youths, and they had a horn blown atop the highest tower. It was their custom that as soon as they heard the horn, throughout the town they would all put on their armor, so they all took up their arms and went out through the main gate. Then they waited for the castellan, Doon of Carduel, who was a very worthy man and faithful to his lord. And when he came

---

*   Corresponds to Sommer, 137-141.

out, he found that up to seven thousand men had gone out of the town. Then he came to them and said to them, "Dear sirs, it would not be well for the town to be left stripped of all fighting men, for we do not know what is to come of us or where we might find others." And they answered that he had spoken well.

Then he chose five thousand, and two thousand stayed to keep the town from being overtaken by anyone. Then they took to the road in the direction where the youths were and rode until they saw the battle raging wonderfully hot, but the youths were in great distress, for they had with them only eighty knights, five hundred squires, and twenty who had not yet been dubbed, along with three hundred men on foot and on horseback who were from the countryside and had joined them, and in truth, they all said that, for as long as they lived, they would rather die than let them down.

But Medelant and Guinemant had split their army into two companies with four thousand men in each one, for the Saxons who lived on the land had joined the invaders. The first to come was Guinemant, brandishing his lance, and he was large and strong and very bold. And Gawainet came out ahead of his companions; he held his sharp-cutting axe, and he rode against them. Guinemant spurred his horse toward him and hit him in the chest with his lance so hard that the weapon flew into splinters, for his hauberk, which was strengthened with double mail, saved him. And the brave youth, so worthy and bold, did not move from the blow he had dealt him, but he made straight for him and gave him such a blow with his axe below his helmet that he sent him head over heels over his horse's backside, and with the stroke glancing off his helmet, Gawainet cut the horse from one end to the other down across its back, so that man and horse spilled down together in a single heap.

When the Saxons saw the blow, they shook with dread all around, for they were afraid that King Guinemant had been killed. Then all the men from one side spurred to his rescue, [139] and Gawainet flew headlong into their midst. They hurled their weapons at him and killed his horse under him. But he jumped up very fast and struck left and right. He was so lively, and twisted and turned so fast, that no one dared face him. Help came to him from every side, and the fray began all about Gawainet; it was very great and lasted for a long time, for the Saxons were eager to get Guinemant back on a horse and to hold Gawainet and take him prisoner.

When Gawainet saw that they were bent on taking him, he said they would not take him "any time today" if he could help it. Then he came brandishing his lance toward a Saxon who was holding his brother Agravain hunched over his horse's neck and trying hard to cut off his head. When Gawainet saw that, he almost went mad. He put his feet together, leapt through the fighting toward the Saxon, and raised his axe to strike him. When the Saxon saw that he could not get out of the way, he thrust his shield out, but Gawainet struck him so hard that he split the shield in half, and the blow came down on his left shoulder and sliced him down to the waist, and he fell to the ground. Gawainet took his horse and very quickly sprang into the saddle, and he shouted to his companions, "Now we'll see who is worthy! As for me, I won't let them get away in the woods or on the plain."

Then they charged into their midst, and they began such a slaughter that they left heaps of Saxons lying in the fields like piles of dung. Even so, the Saxons were at last able to get Guinemant back on a horse, and when he was dressed in his armor, he took a stout, straight lance and drove toward Agravain, who had killed one of his nephews right before his eyes, and with his lance he struck him a very hard blow below the armpit, and it went between the two layers of mail, grazing his side, so that the tip and shaft stuck out an arm's length on the other side. And he brought man and horse down in a heap.

When Gaheriet and Galescalain saw Agravain fall, they were very much afraid that he would be killed, so they very quickly rode over to help him. Galescalain was ahead, and with his sword he hit Guinemant so hard on the helmet that he made him hunch forward over the saddle horn. Gaheriet struck him on the arm so hard that he sent it flying to the middle of the field, then he hit him again, going between his neck and his shield, and sent his head flying to the middle of the field, and Galescalain kicked his body off the horse onto the ground. Then he took the horse and led it to Agravain, who was fighting hard to defend himself on foot, and he got on the horse as fast as he could.

Then they began fighting wondrously well together, but of Gawainet they knew nothing, for he had fought his way into the midst of the Saxons, and it would not be an easy thing to find him. But when the Saxons saw King Guinemant dead, they were quite taken aback, and they rode in flight into King Medelant's division. There Gawainet was taken along with them.* He had been coming and going so much that he had lost track of his brothers, but when he saw that the Saxons were being routed, he stopped until he saw his companions, and they gathered in order around him.

Medelant was riding with a great many men, a good eight thousand all drawn tightly together. He could only inflict great harm, which would have been grievous for the kingdom of Great Britain. But help came from the city of Logres: there were a good five thousand of them riding good horses and well armed, for they had equipped themselves very well. [140]

When the young men saw help coming from Logres and the standard that Doon of Carduel was bearing, the peasants who had joined with the youths said to them, "Now you can be safe and glad and joyful, for soon you will have help! Here come the men of Logres bringing you help!"

They tightened their horses' saddles again, mounted, fell into order, and rode in close formation. And the Saxons rode on toward them full of anger because of King Guinemant, who was dead. Then they all began striking one another, shattering their lances on bodies and shields, and the battle began great and fearsome! The young men were having the worst of it, when the reinforcements came and rushed headlong into the Saxons as fast as their horses could take them. There so many lances splintered against one another that people could hear the pounding for half a league. And when the lances were broken, they drew their swords and began a great and wondrous fray. There so many men and horses were slaughtered, so many feet and hands cut off, so many arms split away from bodies, that the blood ran down

---

*   Sommer's text is unclear in light of what follows (139, ll. 37-38): *iluec rechurent li fuiant gauainet* ("there the fleeing men received Gawain").

through the valley, and the dust was raised so thick that one man could hardly see or recognize another. And the fighting lasted all day, from first light until evening.

There Gawainet fought so well that the men of Logres looked at him in wonder, for he struck down and killed men and horses so hard and fast that no one dared at all to face up to him. Then he happened to meet King Medelant, who had struck down Doon of Carduel. He was down on the ground, and he was holding Doon by the helmet trying to cut his head off, but Gawainet rode over and struck King Medelant right through the helmet with his axe, which he wielded with two hands, and the blow was so hard that he split him open down to his teeth, and he fell dead to the ground.

When the Saxons saw King Medelant dead, they were so aghast that they turned in flight, scattering here and there, but they headed straight for Vambieres, where the great siege was. Then the pursuit began, and the dust was so thick that one man could not see another. The clatter was very great, for as soon as Doon had got back on his horse, he rode after them with all his might, but still the youths were out ahead, and they used their weapons so hard that the beating lasted for five leagues. Doon and the others struck down so many of the twelve thousand there had been at the beginning that not even three thousand got away. This is how the Saxons were routed.

The pursuit lasted until nightfall, and then they happily turned back toward Logres. There they took winnings wonderful to behold, for the Saxons had brought together everything they had plundered and stolen from the countryside; so they took it all back to Logres with them. And when they got there, those inside welcomed the youths very joyfully when they recognized them. The men then brought out all the goods they had won and said to Gawainet, whom they held to be lord over them all, that he should divide them as he willed. And he told them that he would not put his hand to it ahead of Doon of Carduel, "for he can divide it up and distribute it better than I can, for he knows better than I do who the leading men are and the worthiest So let him do it as he sees fit."

When they heard him speaking this way, they held him in high esteem; they praised him and said that he could not fail to be a worthy man, and they began to love him all the more for the great noble qualities they found in him. So the youths stayed and rested in the city of [141] Logres, and the Saxons did them no harm.

Now the story falls silent about the youths right here and about their companions, and it goes back to King Arthur, King Ban, King Bors, and their companions, who were going into the kingdom of Carmelide to serve King Leodagan.

14. Arthur's Support of King Leodagan Against the Saxons.[*]

Now the story says that when King Arthur and his two kings had left Bredigan, along with their companions, they rode for many days until they came to Carhaix

---

[*]   Corresponds to Sommer, 141-145.

in Carmelide, where King Leodagan was staying, on Easter Eve. And when they got to the city, they rode until they came to the high hall, and they found King Leodagan.

He was very frightened because King Rion had invaded his land with fifteen crowned kings; they had already routed him and driven him from his defenses. And they had laid siege to Aneblayse, which was a great, wealthy city. King Leodagan could not think of a way to drive them out, for he did not have enough fighting men in his lands. So he sought advice from the barons from his lands and those from the kingdom of Logres who had stopped there, and he asked them how he should go about driving King Rion out. And while he was talking this way with his knights, King Arthur came into the hall with his companions. They all took one another by the hand and came before King Leodagan one after the other; King Arthur was the forty-first in line, with Merlin. They were all very richly dressed, young knights with their first growth of beard, except for the two brother kings, who had gone first and were somewhat older. The knights were big and handsome, and all who were there looked at them with wonder, for they were so finely attired. And when they had come in and King Leodagan had seen them, he got up to meet them, for it seemed to him that they were important men of high birth.

King Ban spoke first, and he greeted King Leodagan as courteously as he could. And the king told him that he was welcome, if he meant him no wrong. "To be sure," said King Ban, "we did not leave our lands to harm you, rather we have come to serve you, and we will ask nothing of you that you will find burdensome. We beg you not to bother asking us our names or who we are before we tell you of our own free will. If you do not find this agreeable, then we will commend you to God, may He keep you from shame and distress! And we will very soon find someone who will take us on our terms, but we have heard that you accept any fighting men who come to you. Now all together, we implore you to tell us what it will please you to do with us."

Then King Leodagan answered that he would take counsel, if they did not object, and they said they did not. Then he called the knights of the Round Table in private and asked them their thoughts about what that knight had asked him for, and they said that there could be no harm in engaging them, for to them they seemed to be brave men, "So please accept them, for God's sake. And beg them for love of [142] you to tell you who they are, as soon as it is time and place, and to let you get to know them."

With that, the king left them and came straight to the place where the barons were awaiting him, and he said to them, "Dear sirs, I am amazed that you have asked me to let no one know your names; I have never heard such a thing. But to me you seem to be worthy gentlemen, by the looks of you, and I would in no way deny you what you ask. So, I welcome you, and I engage you as fellow noble lords and as my companions, but you must swear to me that you will help me faithfully and lawfully for as long as you are in my company. But I also ask you by your mercy please to tell me who you are as soon as you can, and I will tell you why I ask—you could be such that I might be ashamed for not having served you as fittingly as you deserve. For perhaps you are higher men than I am."

And they said that they would never do anything that would not be to his liking, and King Ban swore to him that he would tell him their names when the time was right. Then they all swore to King Leodagan that they would help him in his war faithfully and well.

Afterward they left King Leodagan and went off into the town to take the best lodging they could find. And Merlin took them to the house of a vavasor, a very worthy man, a wealthy young knight, and their lodgings were luxurious, beautiful, and pleasant. And the knight had a beautiful wife, good in things heavenly and worldly. The vavasor was a very worthy man, and he led a good life. His name was Blair, and his wife's was Leonelle.

When they came to the door of his house, Blair ran outside to meet them, and he said that they were very welcome. They asked God to grant him good fortune. Then they got down from their horses and went up into the hall, which was beautiful and elegant, while boys fed and stabled their horses. They stayed there for a full week, but they did nothing there that should be recalled in the book.

And King Leodagan sent messengers to his people and summoned all those who could bear arms to be at Carhaix on Ascension Day without fail, armed and ready to fight as though their lives depended on it. And any who did not come put themselves and their wealth in jeopardy, for they would be brought to justice like murdering thieves. So he sent for his friends and kinsmen and as many men-at-arms as he could buy for gold and silver, and a great many of both kinds came there, and there were a good forty thousand of them on foot and on horseback; they were lodged in tents and pavilions. And in the town were more than six thousand, all in full armor.

While King Leodagan was sending word to his people, it happened, on a Tuesday, in the evening before the first day of May, that King Roolant, King Plarion of Ireland, King Sornegrieu of the Land of the Irish, and King Sorhalt had left the main army with fifteen thousand armed men, and they were running down through the land foraging for food, which they sorely needed. So it happened that they came laying waste the countryside about Carhaix, where King Leodagan of Carmelide was lodged waiting for his men whom he had summoned. Then a hue and cry went up against those taking [143] plunder and robbing and stealing throughout the countryside. When those in the city found out what was happening, they closed the gates so that no one could get in who wished them harm. Then the knights who were staying there ran for their arms. They put on their armor, mounted their horses, and gathered just inside the main gate.

Then the knights of the Round Table came out all armed, and Hervi of Rivel and Males the Dark were their leaders, and there were two hundred and fifty of them by count, all of whom were good, faithful knights, and they were so skilled at fighting that there was no need to look for better knights. They made up a company all by themselves, for they did not want to be with the knights of the country.

The knights who lived in the city also got ready, and there were at least four thousand of them. The seneschal led these, for he was a worthy man, and his right name was Cleodalis of Carhaix. It had been his duty to carry the king's great standard, but ever since the knights of the Round Table had come there, no one but Hervi of Rivel had ever borne it. But Cleodalis carried a small, red banner with two long red bands in an indigo field with golden crowns. And the great standard that Hervi bore had four streamers of gold on an azure field.

And when everyone was fully armed, they gathered in order at the gate and waited for the orders of the king, who was still putting on his armor. When King Leodagan was ready, he mounted a big warhorse of great worth and rode up to the standard borne by Hervi of Rivel, and they all waited until they saw a good seven thousand Saxons coming well mounted on good horses.

Elsewhere, King Arthur and his companions were also on their horses, arrayed in rich armor. Merlin carried the standard that day, and he told them that if they held their lives dear, they should always follow his banner wherever he went; and they said they would. With that, they made their way down through the city, and they were more handsome and more richly armed than anyone else, and there were forty of them, not counting Merlin, who carried the standard, which one and all beheld that day with great amazement. The banner had on top a fairly small dragon with a twisted tail a yard and a half long; its mouth gaped open so wide that you would think its tongue always quivered inside, and fiery sparks shot out of its throat into the air.

Just then, the giants and the Saxons came, and they struck at the gates of the town with their lances, then they turned about and rode into the meadows, where they gathered up the cattle that were near the town, for no one was there to defend them. And Merlin got away from those who were in the streets of the town, and he put himself between them and one of the gates along with his whole company. He then went to the gatekeeper and said to him, "Let's go out from here, for it is high time."

And he said that they would not go out before the king had ordered it.

"Then may it be your bad luck," said Merlin, "to lord it over us about something I understand better than you!"

Then he went to the bar on the gate, put his hand on it, and pulled it off. And immediately, the gate moved away from the wall as if it did not have a lock. Then they rode out of the city, whether anyone liked it or not, and took off after the Saxons. [144]

When the forty-one companions were outside the city, the gate closed behind them as though it had never been opened, and King Ban and King Bors crossed themselves. And Merlin rode at great speed until he caught up with a company of Saxons a good two thousand strong, and they were taking away a great lot of plunder. And as soon as Merlin saw them, he rushed into their midst, carrying his banner, along with his companions. They struck and brought down as many as they came to, and in no time at all they had routed them before they had ridden half a league.

But they had gone only a little farther when they saw the four kings coming with fifteen thousand men all in armor who were leading a great wagon train with a great deal of plunder they had stolen, and it was astounding how much they had. When Merlin saw them, he said to his men, "Follow me." And they did so.

It happened that as soon as Merlin had let out a whistle, the wind rose, and a mighty and amazing whirlwind and dust storm blew from the direction of the city, and it came down on the heads of the Saxons and giants so thick and fast that they hardly knew each other. And the forty-one companions rushed headlong into them and killed or brought down so many that it was amazing.

Then the king ordered the gates opened, and it was done, and the seneschal went out first with four thousand men in armor, and they found the gate closed behind the men who were fighting the Saxons outside so hard that it was a wonder. Then came Cleodalis with the banner, and he rushed hard into them. There lances banged together and swords rang down on helmets and shields, and the burghers in the city heard the noise as clearly as if they were in the middle of the battle. There was such a din of men and horses that no one could have heard God Himself thundering. And King Arthur and his companions did wonders.

When the four kings saw that they had been attacked, they split their army into two halves, and eight thousand stayed in that fight and the other eight thousand moved out against King Leodagan's banner, which they saw coming closer. They rode until they met them in a fierce battle. On both sides, they lowered their lances and traded hard blows on their shields; they knocked holes in them, they went through hauberks and broke the links of mail. Some were knocked from their horses and brought to their knees by a lance blow, and others came through unscathed. When the lances were worn out, they drew their swords, and the great and fearsome fray began. The companions of the Round Table did wonders, and there were only two hundred fifty of them fighting against seven thousand or more who came to grief. They had to waver, in spite of themselves, and give ground. But they held themselves tightly together, and no one could break through them at all.

And when King Roolant and King Plarion* saw that so few fighting men were holding up such a great crowd as they were, they grew very bitter. Then they shouted their battlecries and said that their opponents would be damned if they got away. Then they mounted a great and dreadful attack, and on one thrust they brought down [145] more than forty of the enemy, and they did all they could to wound and maim them. But their companions stayed near them, for they were loath to leave them as long as they could fight with their swords. Then it happened that King Leodagan was struck down very dreadfully, and they took him and led him off to be imprisoned. They entrusted him to five hundred of their own who would take him to the army of King Rion of Ireland, and they carried him off gleefully, for they believed they had put an end to their war against King Leodagan, and so they took him away in defeat, and they rode hard to get there as fast as they could.

When King Leodagan saw that so dire a stroke had befallen him that his foes had taken him and were leading him off against his will, he kept fainting away for the distress he felt from his wretched, woeful state. And they made their way far from the city, two leagues or more.

Very great indeed was the hue and cry from the seven thousand fighting men and the weeping and wailing from the two hundred fifty knights of the Round Table mourning for King Leodagan, whom they had lost. And they said among themselves that, since they had lost everything, they could not find help anywhere, and they promised to avenge their own deaths before they died. So they drew tightly together, the ones up against the others, and began defending themselves

---

*   Sommer's text has *placiens* (144, l. 40).

wondrously, and they slaughtered a great many men and horses all about them without even changing places. But they suffered such strife and hardship that the people who saw them from the windows of the great hall wept hot tears from the pity they felt for them.

And when Guenevere, King Leodagan's daughter, saw her father being taken away by his enemies, she was so stricken by the sorrow in her heart that she nearly killed herself.

But right now, for a while, the story falls silent about her and her sorrow, and it will tell you about King Arthur and his companions and how they fared in the battle against the seven thousand men.

15. GUENEVERE WITNESS TO THE BATTLE BELOW CARHAIX; THE TWO GUENEVERES.*

Now the story says that the fighting was fierce and dreadful where King Arthur and his forty companions were, and the four thousand who were the companions of Cleodalis the Seneschal had attacked the eight thousand Saxons whom Sornegrieu and Sapharin were leading, and there were many dead and wounded. King Arthur's companions had been fighting together for a long time, when Merlin rode away from them with the standard at a full gallop and shouted to them, "Follow me!" And they did so as fast as their horses could carry them, and they rode until they had all got away from the fray. They rode faster and faster straight for the siege, where the Saxons and giants were already. They rode until they came to a great, deep valley, and there they caught up with the five hundred who were taking King Leodagan away.

And as soon as Merlin saw them, he shouted, "Now at them, noble knights! For you are as good as dead if a single one gets away!"

And Arthur's men charged them at full speed and struck them like worthy warriors. They brought down and killed as many as were in their path, and there every one of them killed or maimed his man. There you would have seen the forty-one companions† making such a slaughter of men and horses that it was hard for any to get away without being overtaken and brought to a frightful end, except for five who took to their heels [146] in flight.

This is how they rescued King Leodagan. And when the king saw the killing and the slaughter that so few men had done against so many, he was deeply puzzled as to who they could be. Then he looked about and saw that Merlin was carrying the

---

* Corresponds to Sommer, 145-149.

† Sommer's text has *xl.* (145, l. 39), the first instance of confusion about the number of companions. There are in fact forty knights including Arthur and not counting Merlin (124, l. 17, and especially 143, l. 27 [*.xl. sans merlin*]). Just above, the group "King Arthur and his forty companions" includes Merlin (145, l. 26), and the number forty obviously excludes Arthur. Later Sommer's text compounds the confusion by referring to the forty-two companions, as though the original number had been forty excluding both Merlin and Arthur (147, ll. 32, and especially 148).

dragon standard. He recognized it and knew for certain that these were the men he had engaged, and he praised God and thanked Him for the help that He had sent him. And Merlin rode up to him and stopped at his side, and Ulfin and Bretel got down from their horses, untied him, and gave him arms. Then they had him mount a strong, fast warhorse, and Ulfin and Bretel got back on their own horses, and the king thanked them for the service they had done him. Then Merlin shouted, "Noble knights, what are you doing? Now follow me quickly, for I am off!"

With that, Merlin spurred his horse around and rode back toward the city, where the knights of the Round Table were having a bad time of it, for of the two hundred fifty, only twenty were still on their horses, while the others were defending themselves on foot just like wild boars. And Merlin was ahead of the others with the standard, and he and his companions rode at full speed, so that their horses were dripping with sweat. And the dragon he was carrying kept throwing out such huge flames from its throat that they rose high into the air, and those standing on the walls of the city saw the light from half a league away and more, it seemed to them. And when they looked and saw that it was the forty-one companions the king had engaged, and that King Leodagan, whom they had rescued, was coming with them, they were gladdened mightily.

When Guenevere, the daughter of King Leodagan, saw who they were, she leapt with joy, and she was greatly amazed at who the knights were in that fellowship. And they came along roaring like thunder and rushed headlong into the enemy, and they struck down as many as they found in their path. As soon as the forty-one companions and King Leodagan had fought their way through the giants, the hammering sound of the sword fight grew so loud that the maiden leaning at one of the windows of the great hall could hear the blows very plainly.

There King Ban of Benoic landed many a fine blow with his sword Wrathful;[*] he always went against the first man he saw, and no matter how strong his shield, hauberk, and helmet, he could not keep King Ban from slicing through them in a single stroke. And King Ban struck there many times such fierce blows that he would cut through a knight and his horse and send them down in a heap. His brother King Bors did likewise. And the Saxons held them in high esteem for the wonders they did. And King Arthur also did wonders with Excalibur, his good sword: against that sword, I tell you in truth, no kind of armor could withstand, for its time was all used up as soon as he hit it with the right blow.

While he was bent on breaking his way through the fray, King Arthur happened to meet King Caelenc, who was striving mightily to rout the companions of the Round Table. As soon as King Arthur saw him, he ran at him. He was very big and strong, and the story says that he was fourteen feet tall, in the feet they used then to measure. And King [147] Arthur bore down on him and landed a fearsome blow with his sword between his shoulders right above his shield, and he struck him so hard with his sword Excalibur that he split him through down to the navel, and his horse turned in fright and flew away with the body. The onlookers at the castle saw the stroke, and King Leodagan's daughter Guenevere, who was standing high up

---

[*]   Old French *coreuseuse* (146, 1. 29).

at the windows of the great hall, saw it very plainly. They all talked about it to one another, and they wondered who he was.

The battle was very fierce in the meadows below Carhaix, where the two hundred fifty and the forty-one* companions gathered against eight thousand Saxons, and they fought so well that the eight thousand were reduced to five thousand, who were so upset that they had lost King Caelenc that they almost went out of their minds.

And then it happened that King Ban made for King Clarion,† the biggest man in the army of the giants. And the story says that King Ban was big and strong, quick and bold, and he held fast to his good sword Wrathful and struck King Clarion so hard through his helmet that he sliced through him all the way from his ear down; his sword fell on his left shoulder and cut down along his side to his waist, so that his liver and lungs showed. And King Bors struck Sarmedon, their standard-bearer, and cut off his arm holding his shield, and the flag fell to the ground. King Leodagan of Carmelide saw the stroke and said, "Now all their knights who are left will have to help themselves out of dire trouble."

When the giants saw their lord dead and their flag on the ground, they turned in flight, some here, some there. Then rode out from the city knights and men-at-arms, as many as three thousand all wearing armor; thus began the pursuit of those who were fleeing. But Merlin did not go where they were running, but he went straight to where Cliodalis, the seneschal of Carmelide, was fighting very fiercely with four thousand men against seven thousand led by the two kings Sornegrieu and Sapharin. And when Merlin came to the battleground, he found Cleodalis unhorsed and back on his feet, and he was holding the standard straight up, for he would not willingly let go of it or lose it. And his men were in place around him, and they defended themselves very well like the worthy knights they were, but they were in great distress. They were about to suffer great losses, and that would come very soon, when Merlin rushed in among them with his standard and the forty-one companions who were with King Arthur. They came in thundering like a storm, such very good horses did they ride. And King Leodagan was still with them because he never wanted to leave them after they had rescued him.

There was such bellowing there, such hammering, and such a din, just as if they were all carpenters working on wood. There you would have seen knights and horses falling thick and fast; there you would have seen horses running, dragging their reins between their legs because there was no one willing to take hold of them or stop them; there you would have heard such an uproar and such shouting that no one could have heard God Himself thundering. There the forty-one companions fought so well that people in the countryside and throughout the land talked about it long after they were dead, and the history says that they slaughtered and cut up so many that anyone could follow the trail for a whole day without having to ask where they had been heading, so clearly was it marked by the bodies of men and horses that died where they fell. [148]

---

* Sommer's text has *.xlij.* here (147, l. 8) and elsewhere. The new count may include King Leodagan, but his name is not included in the list below.

† Not to be confused with King Clarion of Northumberland.

So it is right and just that the story should tell you the names of the forty-one and who they were, for it is fitting to name them ahead of all other worthy men:

The first was King Ban of Benoic,* the second King Bors his brother, the third King Arthur, the fourth Antor, the fifth Ulfin, the sixth Bretel, the seventh Kay, the eighth Lucan the Wine Steward, the ninth Girflet, son of Doon of Carduel, the tenth Malruc of the Rock, the eleventh Drians of the Forest, the twelfth Belias the Amorous, the thirteenth Flandrin the Short, the fourteenth Ladinas of Benoic, the fifteenth Amores the Swarthy, the sixteenth Alcalec the Red, the seventeenth Whitehead of the Hamlet, the eighteenth Blioberis of Gaunes, the nineteenth Canodes, the twentieth Melaldon of Blois, the twenty-first Jesmeladant, the twenty-second Placides the Merry, the twenty-third Lampades of the Flatland, the twenty-fourth Gervais the Slender, the twenty-fifth Christopher of the Gray Rock, the twenty-sixth Aiglin of the Vales, the twenty-seventh Calogrenant, the twenty-eighth Agusale the Long-Awaited, the twenty-ninth Agraveil, son of the Wise Lady of the Forest of No Return, the thirtieth Cliacles the Orphan, the thirty-first Kehedin the Fair, the thirty-second† Meralgis of Portlesquez, the thirty-third Gornain Cadrus, the thirty-fourth Clariet of Gaul, the thirty-fifth the Ugly Worthy,‡ the thirty-sixth Amadan the Proud, the thirty-seventh Osenain the Stouthearted, the thirty-eighth Galesconde, the thirty-ninth Gales the Bald, the fortieth Blaris, godson of King Bors of Gaunes, and the forty-first Merlin, who led them; and King Leodagan was with them, and he did not in any way want to leave them.

These worthy men went all together to rescue Cleodalis, the seneschal of Carmelide, who was a very worthy gentleman, a faithful and fearless knight, and it was very clear that, for any base deed his lord the king may have wrongfully done against him, he would not willingly forsake him, whatever trouble he might be in; rather, he bore himself in such a way that others did not leave him who otherwise might have done so. And I will tell you why.

In truth, King Leodagan's wife was a very highborn lady of great beauty. When he had taken her from her father's house and married her, the lady took one of her maidens with her who was very beautiful. This maiden greatly loved the seneschal, so that at last he asked her to be his wife. The king liked her a great deal because she had served him wholeheartedly; she was faithful in her service, and the king gave her to him most willingly.

When the seneschal married her, she was sitting at table among the ladies eating. She was dressed very richly, and the king found her to be very beautiful; he fell so deeply in love with her that he could not get her out of his heart. Without any doubt, she was one of the most beautiful ladies in the world. But he put off doing anything about it right then. At length, one Saint John's Day, the king happened to have sent Cleodalis to ride against the Irish, who were waging war against him at that time. And the lady had stayed with the queen to keep her company, for they loved each other very deeply.

---

*   The list is set off in Sommer's text by a section change (148, l. 3).

†   Extending the confusion as to the number of companions, Sommer's text continues to insist on the number forty-two; however, the list skips from the thirty-first to the thirty-third knight before going on through the "forty-second." The apparent error is corrected in the translation.

‡   Old French *li lais hardis* (148, ll. 19-20): "the disagreeable bold man."

King Leodagan had fathered on his wife a little girl whose name was Guenevere, who [149] later grew to be very beautiful. And King Leodagan's wife was a very good lady who lived a very holy life, and there were very few nights indeed when she did not get up and go to matins and listen to the service until after Mass. On the very night her daughter Guenevere had been conceived, she went to matins and came to find the seneschal's wife, but she found her sleeping and did not want to awaken her, so she left her alone and went off to the church, which was nearby. And King Leodagan, who had for a long time yearned to lie with that lady, got up as soon as the queen had gone, put out the candles, then went to lie with the seneschal's wife.

When the lady felt him getting into bed with her, she asked him fearfully who he was. He said that it was he, and he told her to keep quiet: if she shouted a single word, he would kill her with his sharp sword, or if she thrashed about in the least. The lady defended herself with words as much as she could, but she did not dare speak out loud, so her arguments availed her very little. The king lay with her and fathered a daughter on her, and it was the very night his daughter was conceived by his wife.

And it happened that, when the queen had given birth, she found a little mark in the small of her daughter's back that looked like a king's crown. And as soon as she was born, the seneschal's wife began to scream from the pain in her belly, and she gave birth to a very beautiful daughter who looked like the queen's daughter, and no one could tell the one from the other but for the mark of the crown the queen's daughter had on her back. And each one was baptized Guenevere, and they were always nursed together.

And until his wife the queen died, King Leodagan never cooled of his love for the wife of his seneschal Cleodalis. He took her and locked her up in a castle because he did not want the seneschal to speak to her, and he held her for more than five years, until the seneschal's friends came to speak to him about it. He told them that the seneschal would not have her as long as he was unfriendly toward the king, yet for all that, the seneschal never stopped serving him.

But now the story falls silent from talking about this, and it begins speaking again about Cleodalis the Seneschal and how he was on foot in the midst of the giants and the forty-one companions had stopped near him.

16. Rout of the Saxons at Carhaix.[*]

Now the story says that where the seneschal Cleodalis was on his feet, there was a great and awesome fight. There you would have seen one dead man falling over onto another and many a good, running warhorse flying through the fields with their reins between their legs because their masters lay dead on the ground, and

---

[*]   Corresponds to Sommer, 149-156.

many noble ladies wept for their brothers, their sons, and their husbands. And all the while the giants were being thrown back, like it or not, by Merlin's powers.

When Sornegrieu and Sapharin saw the great damage and slaughter that so few men were wreaking on them, they were very angry, for they had many times more men than the others. They blew their trumpets and beat their drums to rally their men, and Sornegrieu kept his men about him. And while he was getting them together, Kay the Seneschal, Girflet, and Lucan the Wine Steward broke out of the formation and ran headlong into their midst, for each one had got a new lance, good and strong. And Kay the Seneschal struck Sornegrieu so hard that he bore him from his horse to the ground, [150] where he lay for a long time sprawled out without moving a foot or a hand, and Girflet and Lucan struck two others down dead and bleeding.

When the Saxons saw Sornegrieu on the ground, they turned and rode that way to rescue him, but the forty-one companions stopped near him with their swords drawn. The Saxons came there to put him back on his horse, but the companions defended themselves so well that the Saxons could not get him out. And the king was trampled upon many times before he could get back on his horse, because the great throng of Saxons was gathering so close by.

And Merlin, who bore the standard, came to help the three companions who might soon have come to harm. The midst of the battle came to be there. Cleodalis had got back on a big gray horse, and he held the king's banner in his hands and very fiercely let out his battlecry. He and his men struck out into the fray as fast as their horses could carry them. There they fought a wondrous battle, hard and fierce, but there were so many Saxons that they could not break through their formation, so they struck blows and fought endlessly.

And then it happened that the eight thousand who had been routed before Carhaix fled back to where Sornegrieu was and came in among Sapharin's troops. The men stopped their flight and began to drive the king's men back, so that Sornegrieu was able to get back on his horse; he was so racked with pain and so battered by the blows he had taken that every part of his body hurt, and his men were keen to avenge the shame the others had brought him. And he and his men ran against them and struck them so hard with their lances and swords that they did them great harm.

Then Merlin dashed headlong into the fray, carried by the strength of his horse, holding the standard in his hand. And the two hundred fifty knights of the Round Table, all of whom had got fresh horses and armed themselves anew, rode slowly back into the battle, drawn tightly together, never breaking their formation. And when they saw ahead of them the dragon standard Merlin was carrying, they swung over to follow it, for it had been of very great help to them when their lives were in jeopardy. Then they rode headlong into the fray so hard that they struck to the ground as many as blocked their way, and when their lances had broken, they drew their swords, and the fighting became so fierce and so bloodthirsty it was a wonder to behold.

Meanwhile, Cleodalis the Seneschal and his men were keeping up their fight. But strong as they were, they could not hold their ground, and Sapharin was ruthlessly driving them back toward the city. The three thousand* from the city came to help them—those who had driven the fleeing Saxons back into Sapharin's battalion, where they stopped their flight. And when they saw the seneschal's standard and the great crowd of men running after it, they turned toward it and struck out into the fray so hard that they brought down more than a thousand right at the first. Then Cleodalis's men stopped giving ground, and the renewed fighting was so fierce that the din could be heard for half a league, and on both sides they fought so hard that no one could tell which were better; although on King Sapharin's side there were many more than on the other, they behaved as though they were the same.

Elsewhere, the knights of the Round Table were fighting alongside the forty-one companions, against Sornegrieu's men, who were a good eight thousand strong, and they were in very great jeopardy because they were only three hundred eight† men against eight thousand. They could not last much longer when Merlin called to [151] King Ban and said to him and the other knights, "What are you waiting here for? Why don't you send them on their way?"

"Sir, how would we do that?" they asked.

"I'll tell you," said Merlin. "On the battlefield are only ten‡ giants who can keep you in at all, and I tell you that, if you can rid yourselves of them, you will soon see the rest of them gone from the field."

"Where are they?" asked King Ban.

"In truth," said Merlin, "Ulfin, Bretel, Lucan, Girflet and Kay have already started fighting them. Now follow me, and soon we will see who can do the best in this company."

Then Merlin spurred his horse, which carried him away forthwith, and he flew headlong into the fray, which was very fierce, with six knights fighting against ten giants who were big and strong beyond belief. And King Ban, who was a big knight and bold, came in ahead of the others, and he happened to meet Sornegrieu first of all. King Ban held up his sword, which was filthy with blood and gore, and struck him right on top of the helmet and cut through the steel ring; the stroke came down along his face, and the blade sliced through his lips, and it was so strong that the blade went on down to cut the strap of his shield along with the left wrist that held it, and his hand went flying into the middle of the field. And when Sornegrieu felt himself so badly wounded, he swung about and took flight; he let out a loud, dreadful bellow and went away moaning in agony.

King Bors struck Marganant through the helmet so that he split him down to the teeth. King Arthur hit Sinelant so hard that he knocked off a fourth of his helmet, and his sword slid down to his left shoulder and cut all the way through, and he flew from his saddle to the ground. And Ulfin struck Balanc so that he brought him

---

*   Sommer's text has *.iiij.* with a superscript *m* (150, l. 31), but earlier, when the company leaves the city to engage the Saxons, they number three thousand (147, l. 22). Confusion arises because these are knights and men-at-arms summoned by Leodagan from all over his kingdom who are lodged in the city, of whom there are six thousand in all (142, l. 37), while Cleodalis's four thousand men, also *de la cite* ("from the city"), actually live there (143, l.10).

†   The official count is, of course, two hundred ninety-one, since the knights of the Round Table number two hundred fifty.

‡   Sommer's text has *.v.* here (151, l. 3), but *.x.* occurs just below (l. 10), and ten in all are named just afterward.

down dead and bleeding. Bretel hit Cordant and Kay Candenart, and Lucan Malec; Girflet slew Mendamp, and Meralgis Sardup, and Gornain Cadrus Dorilas.

As soon as the Saxons saw them brought down, they were so thunderstruck that for a long time they did not move from where they had been making their stand, and they said among themselves that anyone was a fool to keep on fighting, "for those are not people, but devils come from Hell. No armor we have can hold up under their blows, no matter how strong or tightly made."

When the knights of the Round Table and the forty-one companions saw that the Saxons were so bewildered, they began slaying them and cutting them up, and all the Saxons whose horses could carry them away took flight and rushed into the fray where King Sapharin was fighting Cleodalis the Seneschal. And they came in so hard and fast that they drove everyone from the battlefield right up to the gate of the city of Carhaix. And the men from the city were very frightened when they saw their people being treated so ruthlessly, for they did not see the standard of King Leodagan, which the knights of the Round Table were carrying; they truly believed that they had lost him for good, for they thought that he had been killed or taken prisoner. Furthermore, they did not see the dragon that the knights had been carrying, and that filled them with very great dread indeed. Since they saw their foes at the gate, it was no wonder that those from the city took flight, for their lives were in jeopardy, and there were only seven thousand of them and twelve thousand Saxons. They were also very much afraid for the knights of the Round Table, about whom they [152] had no news.

And that is why they came across to the gate that was right at the first bridge; then they drew tight together, closing their ranks, and the Saxons swept upon them very boldly. There was an awesome fight there, and the fray lasted a very long time. And you should know that about a thousand fell in the fray and the throng, and they could never get up again. And so the fighting was dreadful and ruthless.

When the knights of the Round Table and the forty-one* companions had routed Sornegrieu and his army and sent them flying, Merlin drew them to one side of the field and said to them, "Dear lords, let them go now, and don't bother about running after them, for you can do that in due time. But withdraw and dismount from your horses. Get your harness straightened out and let your horses rest, then saddle them again." And they did as he ordered.

When the knights of the Round Table saw that they had stopped, Hervi of Rivel said that they would not go on until they could go with them. They got off their horses and got their gear in order, for they very badly needed to. And King Leodagan came to Merlin and said to him, "Sir, are you willing to keep company with those good men?"

"Certainly, sir," said Merlin, "we truly are, and they are very welcome, for we would be worth all the more if we were in an echelon together."

"Sir," said the king, "many thanks!"

Then King Leodagan went up to Hervi of Rivel, who was carrying the standard, and said to him, "Dear friend, come along with us, you and your companions; you will be the companions of those good men, and you will be much worthier for it."

---

* The number in Sommer's text has increased to forty-three (*.xliij.;* 152, l. 6).

"Sir," said Hervi, "Very gladly, if they are willing."

"In truth," said the king, "they want very much to be peers and companions with you from now on."

"May it so please God," said Hervi. "Fellowship with such worthy men should not be refused."

Then they all got on their horses and gathered themselves into a single body. And Merlin set out ahead of them, and they followed him everywhere he went.

While they were riding as you have heard, Cleodalis the Seneschal was fighting with six thousand men in his company against King Sapharin, who had more than twelve thousand in his. Cleodalis's men were in disarray and struck out here and there, wherever they thought their blows might fall the best, so they had been brought to grief and suffered great harm; they had already undergone so much that some of them were being put to rout, and they were all on the verge of leaving the battlefield, for their bold fighting availed them little, and they yearned for nothing better than to flee.

And then they saw the dragon coming that Merlin was carrying. It threw smoke and fire out of its throat, from time to time, in such great billows that the air was all red. And when the ladies who stood on the walls saw it all, they said to Cleodalis, "Put your mind to fighting well! Look toward the shadowy valley and see the help they are bringing you!"

When Cleodalis heard what the ladies told him, he looked and saw what he longed for so much, and then he knew for certain that in time he would be helped, and he praised God for it. Then he called his men back together, gathered them in order, and said to them, "Now take heart, for you see the help coming to us that we have longed for so much!"

And when they saw help coming, no one had to ask whether they were overjoyed. Then they ran against [153] the Saxons and stormed into their midst, and another great and fearsome battle began. And all this time, Merlin rode at a slow gait, keeping his companions in order, until they came within a stone's throw of the battle. Then he led his companions charging into their formation so fiercely that they brought down more than three hundred who would never get up again, and they drove so deeply into them that they were as lost as if they had fallen into a bottomless pit, but they went on boring their way through them until they came to Cleodalis's standard. And when they had come together with them, Merlin shouted, "Now we'll see how you will fight, for now you are all put to the test!"

When King Arthur heard Merlin shouting, he smiled and said to King Ban and King Bors that there was never one better to wake you up.* And Merlin yelled to him, "Now stop making fun! You'll be able to joke and laugh soon enough!"

And when they heard him, they rushed in among their enemies, wild and full of anger. There the fighting was fierce and awesome, and the fray was more ruthless than any other had been all day. There King Arthur worked wonders all by himself, for he made such efforts because of Merlin's banter that everyone looked at him in amazement. And King Leodagan's daughter and all the ladies and maidens raised

---

*   *... onques mais si boins viellars ne fu* (153, l. 10). Simply calling Merlin a *viellars* ("old man") might not elicit Arthur's smile (or laughter) or Merlin's retort. Perhaps Arthur is playing on Old French *vieillart* ("old man") and *veillier* ("watch, be vigilant, stay awake").

their hands up to Heaven and prayed the Savior of the world to keep him from death and danger. And they wept in pity for him and his companions and the torments of warfare they were suffering, for they were astounded that he could take so much for so young a lad as King Arthur was. For he struck left and right with his sword Excalibur. He cut off arms, hands, and heads, he struck down knights and horses, and he worked wonders all by himself. And he had taken notice of all those round about him who were helping him and keeping him out of all kinds of trouble, for the two kings who were his companions were very worthy men. Against all of them no armor could hold up, nor were they ever hemmed in so badly that they could not cut their way through with their sharp swords. All the renowned knights who had come with him fought very well indeed, and the knights of the Round Table are not to be forgotten.

When Sapharin saw that he had lost so much and that so many of his men had been slain, he swore on his faith that he would never leave until he had hurt them in return. Then he called Sortibran, Clarion,* Iguedon, Senebalt, Malore, and Freelenk—these were all his kinsmen, and they were worthy and bold. And he said to them, "Now we'll see who the real knights are!"

Then twenty knights, big and brawny, rode out and ran into the fray as fast as their horses could go, and Sapharin struck Hervi of Rivel so hard that he bore him sprawling from his horse to the ground, and afterward he gave Antor such a stinging blow that he brought him and his horse down in a heap. Then he hit Girflet in the side and knocked him flat on the ground. And each of his companions struck down his man, but there was not one among those who fell who was killed or wounded. Lucan the Wine Steward was one, Meralgis another, Gornain the third, then Blioberis, Gales the Bald, Guiret of Lambale, Goswain of Estrangot, and Bretel was the eighth† —all these fell because they were struck by a lance or because their horses were hit.

There was a most dreadful din. And the Saxons all stopped near the fallen men and tried their best to kill them, but they were worthy fighters and strong of heart, and they sprang to their feet holding their naked swords, [154] and they fought hard to defend themselves. But their efforts were coming to naught, when Merlin came to help them bearing the dragon standard in his hand. And Sapharin, who was striving to hurt them, let loose and struck King Leodagan through his shield, and he bored right through him; then he lowered his lance and struck his horse in the side through the blanket, and he brought the king and his horse to the ground in a heap. When those from the city saw the king struck down, they started to quake because they were afraid he had been killed, so they rode very hard to the rescue.

When King Arthur saw the giant who jousted so hard that he brought down three worthy knights, he swore that he would test himself against him. Then he left the formation and went to get a stout lance with a sharp iron tip, then came back at a fast gallop. King Ban came to meet him and said to him, "Sir, what do you mean to do? Whom do you want to joust against? Don't fight that giant, he's too strong for

---

*   Not to be confused with the Christian king Clarion of Northumberland.
†   Sommer's text has *li noefismes* ("the ninth") (153, l. 40), but only eight names are listed.

you! You are too young to try such a thing! Let me go against him. I am older than you are, stronger and bigger."

"May God never help me," said King Arthur, "if I send in someone besides myself. The more he does to make everybody dread him, the more gladly will I pit myself against him! I'll never know my worth if I don't pit myself against each and every one of them!"

When Merlin saw him he shouted, "Who is this coward? Why don't you do quickly what you've started out to do? Everyone can see that you are afraid!"

When Arthur heard Merlin calling him a coward, he was deeply ashamed, and he spurred his horse toward the enemy formation. And King Ban said to Merlin that he was wrong to send a man as young as King Arthur to fight against such a huge devil. "He has nothing to worry about," said Merlin, "but take a lance and go after him with your brother and Ulfin." And they did what he said and rode off after King Arthur with all the speed they could get from their horses.

When King Sapharin saw King Arthur coming, he rode hard to meet him. And when those in the formation saw him riding toward the young lord, who was so youthful and small compared to him, they were very frightened for him, and they rode out as fast as their horses could run against the enemy and split their shields with their lances. The iron tips of the lances stopped against their hauberks, which had very tight mail that held together. Sapharin broke his lance and wounded King Arthur a little on his left side, but Arthur hit him so hard that he broke through his shield and his hauberk and drove the tip of his lance right through his body from one side to the other, so that the tip and an arm's length of the shaft stuck out his back; and he had thrust so hard, when he came at him at such great speed, that he bore him sprawling from the horse to the ground already dead and broke his lance as it went through him.

That joust was seen by Guenevere, the daughter of King Leodagan, who was standing by the windows of the great hall, which was somewhat close to the walls of the town. They all praised the young lord and held him in high esteem, and they asked those who were with him who he was, but they could not tell them except to say that he was one of the knights her father had engaged. "In truth," said the maiden, "whoever he is, he comes from good stock. For no man [155] of low birth would dare undertake such a battle unless he had a very noble heart. He and those worthy gentlemen over there have all done wonders with their fighting!"

The maiden spoke of the knights at great length.

King Ban and King Bors had ridden into the formation, and each had a strong, stout lance, and they spurred their horses on. King Ban struck Sortibran, King Bors struck Clariel, and Ulfin attacked Iguedon, and each one unhorsed his man and brought him to the ground dead. And in the same charge, one hit Morat, another Landon, and the third Senebalt so hard that they died before they could be taken from the battlefield.

King Arthur had drawn his sword, and he struck Malore very hard on his helmet, for he had stopped right on top of King Ban along with Freelenk, who was trying to chop off his head, for one was holding him by the helmet and the other was pounding him between the shoulders with a huge cudgel. When the king saw them, he spurred his horse toward them, grasping his sword. And he hit Malore so hard that he sent his head flying to the middle of the field. When Freelenk saw his cousin and companion slain, he raised his cudgel high in the air to hit King Arthur on the head, but the king thrust his shield to ward off the blow and struck him so hard that he flew to the ground. It was a mighty blow, and it had come down so hard on his left shoulder that he hunched over his horse's neck; but he had raised his cudgel again and meant to strike again, but King Arthur, who was lively and quick, spurred his horse, went past him, grasping his sword, then swung around toward him and struck Freelenk so hard that he split him down to his teeth.

The Saxons' yelling and shouting grew louder, for this attack frightened them mightily, and they saw that their only hope for help was Randol,* who bore their standard. And King Ban went straight for him and struck him so hard that he sliced his arm off still holding the standard, and he went flying to the ground.

Then the hue and cry went up that all should turn in flight, and the pursuit began that lasted for a long time, from before vespers until nightfall. There were many killed and wounded; of the fifteen thousand there had been at the start of the battle, only five thousand got away, and they went straight to King Rion and the siege. They told him about the harmful losses they had taken and the killing they had suffered. And when King Rion heard the news, he swore his oath that they would never leave that land until they had taken vengeance on King Leodagan and led him away as their prisoner.

Then he sent word to the land of Denmark that all men high and low should come to him and bring enough food to last two hundred thousand men for two whole years, for now he wanted, he said, to pursue this war even more vigorously than they had done before. And they all began coming, and more and more gathered every day, until before the month was out two hundred fifty thousand had come together there, with twenty crowned kings not counting King Rion. And they had a great wagon train bringing their food from everywhere, and the army was so well supplied that they never again rode out to forage for food, for they had a great plenty coming from the lands of the twenty kings who were in the army, and the weather was [156] good for them. And attacks against the city of Aneblayse came thick and fast, but it was so strong that it had nothing to fear but being .starved out. They asked King Leodagan many times to come help them because they were in a great deal of trouble.

But now the story falls silent about King Rion and his siege, which was very harsh, and about those who were inside the city of Aneblayse, and it begins speaking again about King Arthur and his companions.

---

* Sommer's text has *ralidol* here (155, l. 23), but *randol* in l. 24. West prefers the form Raldol (259a-b); see G.D. West, *An Index of Proper Names in French Arthurian Prose Romances.* (Toronto: University Press, 1978).

17. THE VICTORIOUS ARTHUR FALLS IN LOVE WITH GUENEVERE.[*]

In this part, the story says that those of the kingdom of Carmelide were very glad
and joyful about the Saxons, who were routed, as you have heard, and driven from
the battlefield by as few men as were there. For at the beginning, they numbered no
more than six thousand three hundred, and there were more than fifteen thousand
Saxons, and they were routed thanks to the wisdom of Merlin, who helped out a
great deal, and the help of the knights of the Round Table and the forty-one fighting
men engaged by King Leodagan.

And the story says that after they had run after the Saxons until nightfall, they
came back rejoicing to Carhaix and found the king, whose men had got him back
on his horse. And when he found out that the men he had taken on were coming
back, he went out to meet them and offered them the greatest feast in the world.
They found Antor, Girflet, Kay the Seneschal, Lucan the Wine Steward, and all
their other companions safe and sound, and they had been very much afraid that
they were dead or in prison. There they were all awarded winnings wonderful to
behold that the king gave out to the knights he had engaged. For he could not put it
to better use, he said, for they were the ones who had won it all, and "as for myself,
they rescued me from certain death and imprisonment."

When they saw the great honors the king was bestowing on them, they thanked
him heartily and said that they would take nothing from him and would make up
for it another time, if they took enough plunder and earned enough gifts. And King
Leodagan said that, since he wanted none of the spoils, they should split them up
and give them out wherever they saw fit.

Then Merlin came to the three kings and told them to take their winnings, and
they took them and gave them out where Merlin told them to, keeping nothing for
themselves worth a single penny, and they praised Merlin and held him in greater
esteem. And they stayed in the land for so long that thanks to their generosity—
and Merlin's urging—people throughout the countryside spoke of no one else
but them. And Arthur gave his host and his host's wife riding horses and palfreys,
robes, and so many goods that for all the days of their lives they were wealthier
and more powerful thanks to him. King Leodagan would not allow them to take
lodging anywhere but with him, and thereafter he would never let them be without
companionship above all with the knights of the Round Table.

And when their armor had been taken off, King Leodagan had his daughter
brought in arrayed in the richest clothing she owned, and he had her take the hot
water in silver basins, bring it before the kings, and serve them. But Arthur would
not allow her to serve him until King Leodagan and Merlin bade him to. Then the
young lady herself washed his face and neck and very gently dried him with a
towel, and then she did the same to the two kings; afterwards, King Leodagan had
the other Guenevere, daughter of the seneschal's wife, and the rest of the maidens
serve the other companions. [157]

[*]   Corresponds to Sommer, 156-159.

When King Leodagan's daughter had served the three kings, she served her father; and when they had all washed, the young lady dressed each of them in a mantle tied at the neck. King Arthur was filled with great beauty, and the maiden stared at him and he at her. And she said softly to herself that a lady had reason to be very happy if such a good and handsome knight as he asked her for her love, and shame on her who refused him.

No sooner had the tables been set up than the food was ready, and the knights all sat down. But the knights of the Round Table sat side by side at a table off to themselves with the knights whom the king had engaged, and King Bors and King Ban seated Arthur between themselves, for they did him the highest honors they could. And King Leodagan took notice of who was sitting beside whom at that table, and in his heart he thought, from the honor they bore Arthur and the service they did him, that he was lord over them all, and he wondered mightily who he could be; he would have given anything to know who he was. "And may it please you now, Lord God," he said, "that he should wed my daughter! In truth, I would not have believed that such a young lad could have the worthy knighthood there is in him, and he could not have it at all unless he were a very highborn man indeed! And I might just as well believe that he is a spiritual being whom Our Lord has sent to me to fight for this kingdom and keep it safe, not for love of me, but to raise up Christendom and Holy Church and keep them, and that is how they were able to leave this city against the gatekeeper's will."

This is what King Leodagan thought to himself long and hard as he was eating, and he brought to mind how the forty-one companions had saved him in the deep valley against five hundred knights when they were taking him away as their prisoner, and he recalled all the worthy deeds he had seen him do. He pondered so hard that he half forgot himself and stopped eating, and Hervi of Rivel took notice of this and was greatly distressed by it. He went angrily up to the head of the table, moved in beside King Leodagan, and told him that he had never seen him do anything so discourteous, and he had never been so upset, "for you should be bringing gladness to those worthy men, but instead you are worried and lost in thought, and I wonder what has happened to your mind."

And the king came to his senses, looked at him, and said to him, "Hervi, I was thinking about something having to do with myself and about the worthiest man in the world, and I couldn't keep from it. If you knew what my mind was on, you wouldn't blame me at all."

And he answered, "Sir, that could well be. But for now, let it be, and think about it when and where you ought to, for this is not the right time or place; you should be showing these gentlemen a good time and enjoying yourself. In truth, right now you are behaving wrongly toward them."

"I beg you, dear friend," said the king, "please go take your seat. I am ashamed of myself." Then Hervi went straight back to sit with his companions, and the king began talking to this one and that one.

King Leodagan's daughter served King Arthur wine in her father's goblet, and King Arthur looked at her long and hard, and he very much liked what he saw before him. For she was the most beautiful woman in all Britain at that time, and she was endowed with a very fine [158] body.* On her head she wore a golden coronet with precious stones. Her face was bright and so naturally made up with white and red that she needed not more nor less. Her shoulders were straight, and the skin lustrous, and her body was very well put together, for her waist was slender and her hips low, and they suited her wonderfully. Her feet were pale and well arched, her arms were long and rounded, and her hands were white and plump. Why should I go on telling you about the maiden's great beauty? If she was indeed beautiful, then she was endowed with even greater goodness, generosity, courtesy, sense, worthiness, sweetness, and nobility.

When King Arthur saw the maiden, who was of such great beauty, kneeling before him, he was very eager to look at her, first of all because her breasts were firm and hard like little apples, and her skin was whiter than new-fallen snow, and she was neither too plump nor too thin. And King Arthur so yearned for her that he lost himself in thought and stopped eating, and he turned his face away because he did not want the two kings or anyone else to notice anything. And the maiden bade him drink and said to him, "Young lord, sir, drink up! And please don't be bothered if I do not call you by your right name, for I don't know what else to call you. You should not be shy at table, for you indeed are not on the battlefield, and that was clear today when you were being watched by five thousand people who did not know you except by sight."

And he turned toward her and said to her, "Dear maiden, I was glad to do that. Many thanks for your fair service, and God give me the strength and the ability to reward you."

"Sir," she said, "you have already given me back a hundredfold, more than I could ever deserve; you gave it to me when you and your companions rescued my father when they were taking him away as their prisoner." And the king fell silent.

"There's still more," she said. "Before the gate, at the foot of the bridge, you showed that you were sorry for his troubles when he was struck down in the midst of his enemies and his horse was slain under him, for you killed the one who had brought him down. You risked your life to save him, and you did everything to get him back on his way."

This is how King Leodagan's daughter spoke to King Arthur, but not a word came out of his mouth. Instead, he took the goblet and drank very gladly. And he told the young lady to sit, for she had been kneeling for a very long time, but her father the king would not allow it; rather, they were served in all the ways tongue could tell. When it was time to take away the tablecloths, King Ban asked King Leodagan, who was sitting beside him, "Sir, I am quite amazed that you, whom everyone takes to be such a worthy man, have not wed your daughter a long time since to some highborn man. She is well brought up, and clever, and you have no other children your land could go to after your death; yet you could have given yourself heirs long before now wherever you put her."

"In truth, sir," said King Leodagan, "I have put it off only because of the war, which has lasted so long and done me so much harm. King Rion of Denmark and

---

* Sommer's text seems somewhat garbled, and he notes that it "is not clear" (158, n. 1). The text of the Harley manuscript, reproduced in that note, is translated.

Ireland has not stopped waging war against me for more than seven years, and never since then has any man come into my land to whom I might give her, and no one has sent me word asking for her. But, God help me, if I [159] could find a worthy knight who could stand toil and hardship, and who would keep up my war for me, I would give him my daughter and all my land, if he wanted to have it after my death, and I would not care about his birth or his wealth. Please God, if such a man as I have in mind, and in my heart, were here right now, in truth not three days would go by before she would be wed to a young knight, handsome and worthy, and I truly believe that he is of higher birth than I."

And Merlin began to smile, and he looked at King Bors and gave him a sign that he had said these things about King Arthur, and indeed he had. Then they all began to speak about many things, but steered their talk away from what King Leodagan had said, for they did not wish to speak further of it at that time. King Leodagan understood that they were unwilling to hear about it, although he would very much have liked them to draw him out on the subject, so he fell silent and tried to see if he could learn, from anything in their looks and behavior, where they came from. And he was heedful of their merriment and the joy they took in Arthur, and this was what bothered him the most, and the two worthy gentleman and their companions were so happy to be with him that all who saw them were amazed and bewildered.

And Arthur loved and yearned for the daughter of King Leodagan, and he was daydreaming so about her that he forgot where he was; he very much wanted to have her as his wife and helpmeet, if he could. And the story says that she was the wisest woman in Great Britain, the fairest and best loved who was in that whole land, excepting only Elaine the Peerless, wife of Persides the Red of the Castle of Gazevilte and daughter of King Pelles of Listenois of the Castle of Corbenic; she was the niece of the Fisher King and the king ailing from his wounds. The first was called Alan of the Isle in Listenois. The second was ill and had been wounded with the Avenging Lance, which is why he was called the Maimed King, and he had been wounded through both his thighs; his right name was King Pellinor of Listenois. King Alan and Pellinor were brothers. The maiden I told you about was their niece and the daughter of King Pelles, who was the brother of the two I have just named for you. That maiden was the most beautiful woman who had ever been in any land, and the noblest, and she kept the Most Holy Grail until Galahad was conceived.

But now the story falls silent about her and says no more about her for a while, but you will be enlightened as to how it was taken away from her and why, and how the adventures of the Holy Grail drew to an end; rather it will speak about the companions of the Round Table seated at supper in the city of Carhaix in Carmelide in the great hall of King Leodagan.

18. News of the Young Heroes; the Battle Before Arundel.[*]

Now the story says that they had sat relaxed at supper and had been served meats and wines. And when the high and low tables had been taken away, Merlin took the three kings by the hand and led them aside and said to them, "Do you want me to tell you what has happened in Great Britain?"

"Of course," said King Arthur, "I would like very much to know, if you will."

"In truth," said Merlin, "there has been a great battle, hard and wondrous, in the plain before Logres against the Saxons, who had plundered the countryside and laid waste the whole [160] seaside and the ports as far as Dover. And when they were coming to the stronghold of Logres, they had a huge wagon train that was being driven along with the army, and there were ten thousand Saxons on horseback. And as they were riding, they met with five young men, who are your nephews."

And he told them how the youths had come there, how they had left their mothers without their fathers' knowing anything about it, how they had met the foragers, just as you have heard in the story, and how the battle had been when the Saxons were put to flight, the rich spoils they had won, the rout they had dealt the Saxons, the joyful celebration the burghers made with the youths, and how the boys had said that they would not be made knights "until you yourself armed them with your own hand. Now you don't have to worry about defending your own lands, for they will be safeguarded until you come back.

"Now be happy and make merry, and think about doing right, for the help that is coming to you is growing stronger all the time. The grandson of the emperor of Constantinople is coming into your land with three hundred squires, sons of princes and high barons, to serve you so that you will make them knights."

"Merlin," said the king, "who are those boys who have come to Logres, and what are their names?"

"Sir," said Merlin, "King Lot has four sons. The eldest is named Gawainet, the next Agravain, the third Guerrehet, and the fourth Gaheriet. Those four are your nephews, sons of your sister and King Lot. And there is another one called Galescalain, and he is the son of King Neutres of Garlot and another of your sisters.[†] And the grandson of the emperor of Constantinople is called Sagremor; he will be of wondrous prowess. And still others will come very soon who will have your well-being at heart and be your friends."

While Merlin was saying these things, all of their companions came around him, and when they had heard the news Merlin told, they were very glad and very joyful. With that, all the knights left there and went straight to their lodgings and went to bed for a good rest. And they stayed in the town for a very long time and did nothing but eat and drink. Meanwhile, their armies were gathering.

But now the story stops speaking about King Leodagan and the fighting men he engaged, all of whom were heartened and gladdened and overjoyed by the news that Merlin told them about the young men who had gone into the kingdom of

---

[*]   Corresponds to Sommer, 159-164.

[†]   Sommer's text reads, ambiguously, *& de uostre seror ausi* (160, l. 20): "and of your sister as well."

Logres as he said; and it begins speaking again about King Tradelmant of North Wales.

Here the story says that when King Tradelmant had come into North Wales, his fortified city, he called so many men together that they numbered fully ten thousand, and with them he held the land and the countryside as best he could. And one evening a spy who had gone close to Saxon Rock came to him and said that at least ten thousand Saxons had invaded his land, and they were driving a very long wagon train with food supplies. And the king asked him where they could be. And he told him that they were between the Rock and Arundel. Then the king ordered his men to get their armor on quickly, and he told them to be on their horses right after the bedtime hour and to ride out of the town fully armed as though their lives depended on it, and they did as he said. [161]

And when they were in the fields, they were a good ten thousand strong, and they rode in tight formation, keeping their ranks straight, until they came upon the Saxons. Then they split their army in two. And Pollidamas, who was the king's nephew, led one part; he was a young knight, worthy and bold. And as soon as the army had been split, the main division made straight for Arundel, which King Arthur had garrisoned before he left the country.

After Pollidamas's division had broken away from his uncle's, they both found themselves close to the Saxons' tents, and they rode headlong into the midst of them as fast as their horses could run. That day the Saxons' lookouts served them badly, for they were aware of nothing before their enemies were on top of them. There many Saxons were brought down and many were slain, for they were set upon from two sides; they were unarmed and sleepy, for they were weary from riding, so there was a great slaughter of them. And Tradelmant's men knocked down and toppled tents and pavilions. The Saxons did not have time to take up their arms, but turned in flight toward the Castle of the Rock on foot and on horseback, setting out through the nearby forests. Tradelmant's men brought down and killed as many as they caught up with, so that at least fifteen thousand of them were slain before they could get to their stronghold.

And when the knights inside saw the great rout, the men fleeing everywhere, and the great slaughter of the Saxons, they shouted "Now to arms!" And all in the castle armed themselves as well and strongly as they could, and they rode out as quickly as they could. They made a huge army, and they were all highborn men and powerful, and they were on very fine horses. And when they were outside the stronghold, they numbered a good fourteen thousand.

All at once, they let their horses run against Tradelmant's army, and each side struck out very fiercely against the other. And there was a wild and wondrous slaughter of men and horses. While they were fighting, all the men in Arundel who belonged to King Arthur rode out, and there were a good five hundred of them, all of them strong and swift young men. They seized the foodstuffs, of which they found a good lot in the army, and they won a great deal of booty. Then they rode back into the castle and shut the gates and watched to see what would happen. So they had withdrawn to one side.

And Pollidamas and King Tradelmant kept fighting fiercely, but they suffered great hardship because the fleeing Saxons had drawn together, and there were at least seven thousand of them mounted and armed very richly; meanwhile, fourteen thousand had come out of the Castle of the Rock. So the Saxons ran hard against them, for they were very sorrowful about the harm they had done them, and they drove them back hundreds of yards, and King Tradelmant's men did not stop withdrawing until they had come below Arundel, where they had to hold their ground by main force or die trying. There they started to defend themselves mightily, and there a great many men and horses were brought down and slaughtered on both sides. And King Tradelmant lost a great deal in that attack, for of the ten thousand men he had at the beginning, he lost at least three thousand; and the Saxons lost a good four thousand of their men who had ridden out of the Castle of the Rock.

It would not have taken long for King Tradelmant and his companions to be utterly routed, when the King of the Hundred Knights came to help him; he had heard the news [162] that the Saxons were riding about throughout the land and plundering everything. And his men came straight into the battle, and they struck hard. And the knights from the stronghold at Arundel had ridden out before the King of the Hundred Knights came into the battle, for they felt great sorrow for King Tradelmant and his men, because they were so overwhelmed; and without a doubt, if they had not gone out to help him, King Tradelmant would have been killed or taken prisoner.

And when the King of the Hundred Knights had come there, the shouting, the screaming, and the uproar grew to be so loud that the Saxons were dumbfounded, so much so that they stopped defending themselves, for they saw that they could not hope for a rescue, so far were they from the Valley of Vambieres, where help was. And they were well aware that in the Castle of the Rock there were not left even two hundred men who could defend themselves, for they had all come out when the cry was raised. So they saw clearly that they could not do anything to help themselves but flee.

When the King of the Hundred Knights, his seneschal Marganor, King Tradelmant, and Pollidamas saw that the Saxons were withdrawing, they rode hard against them. The Saxons did not dare make a stand, but made their way toward Saxon Rock. But before they could get there, they were being pursued so closely that not four thousand of their men got away without being killed or wounded. And when those from the castle of Arundel saw that the Saxons were routed and had taken flight, they withdrew from the pursuit on the counsel of a young man who was named Yvonet of the White Hands, and went back to where the fighting had been. And they took horses and coins, gold and silver, food and armor, all they wanted of the best they could find. And they provided themselves so well with everything that they lacked for nothing as long as they were in the stronghold.

And when they had gone back inside, they closed the gates and raised the bridges. Then they climbed high up on the walls to see how the others would fare. And the Saxons fled to the Castle of the Rock, and they rushed inside where they knew the entrance was. But before they could all get [163] in, many were killed and wounded. And when they had gone inside, the two kings saw that they had got away from them, and they drew back, for they were afraid of the arrows the crossbowmen inside were shooting down on them.

And when they had put about half a league between themselves and the stronghold, the two kings greeted each other joyfully, and they took off their helmets and kissed and embraced each other. When they had spent a long time delighting in each other's company, King Tradelmant said to the King of the Hundred Knights, "Sir, I am greatly amazed at how you came here today! And I can thank God for it! For if you had tarried the slightest bit, I could not have avoided being killed or taken prisoner, and all my men with me."

"Sir," said the King of the Hundred Knights, "our Lord God, who is so loving and noble-hearted, will not forget His friends wherever they may be. But it sometimes happens that the ills and griefs we suffer please Him mightily, and we undergo such hardships in order to raise up His true religion. This is why He has sent the Saxons to us in this country, and they do nothing but grow stronger and more plentiful every day, so that we see plainly that they will never be driven out of the country by any army we can raise; and for as long as we live, let us avenge our dead. This is the best I can make out of what is happening; and if anyone believes me, we should do just as I say, and we will come out of it better than any other way."

"How?" said King Tradelmant "What do you have in mind?"

"I'll tell you," said the King of the Hundred Knights. "My advice would be to send word to our companions that every one of them should come with his armed men, as secretly as he can, to the Castle of Lindesores in Broceliande, and then we should call together as many of our people as we can. And then let us ride against the Saxons and fight them in God's name. And to whomever God grants a good outcome, let him have it. For it is far better to die in good faith and with honor than to live in shame, lose everything, and then die dishonored."

"For the love of God," said King Tradelmant, "what are you saying? We know very well that there are so many of them that for every one of us they number thirty. And you can be sure that what you advise us to do will not work. Nevertheless,* as for myself, I am ready to do whatever you and the other barons are willing to undertake."

"Indeed," said the King of the Hundred Knights, "I will send out my messengers right away, and I will tell the barons in my own name just what I have said to you, and they are to let me know whether or not they are willing to do it."

"Then may it be as God wills," said King Tradelmant. "As for me, I will do what you and the others want. I am but a single man, no less than you, but you cannot suffer any harm that I do not share in."

With that, they took to the road and went straight toward Arundel, to the spot where the first battle had been. There they found a very great wealth of everything a man needs for his well-being, and each one took his fill of what he wanted, for they did not need to split the booty into shares. So the wealth and the foodstuffs were enough for everyone. And the two kings parted company and did nothing more at that time.

King Tradelmant went straight to North Wales, his stronghold, with seven thousand armed men who were left from the fighting. And the King of the Hundred

---

* Sommer's text appears to be garbled. The sentence begins *& por ce ne le di iou mie que* (163, ll. 28-29): "And I am not saying this so that …"; but it continues as follows.

Knights went to Malehaut with eight thousand men. Then he chose his messengers and sent them to the [164] barons, of whom there were ten by count, and he relayed to them the words he had spoken to King Tradelmant.

But here the story falls silent about him and his messengers and begins speaking again about Aguisant of Scotland, who had come straight to his own lands when he left Sorhaut.

19. KING URIEN'S SONS AND NEPHEW; KING NEUTRES AGAINST THE SAXONS.[*]

Here the story says that when King Aguisant had come to his citadel at Coranges, he brought together knights, men-at-arms, and crossbowmen, on foot and on horseback, until he had at least fifteen thousand under arms. And it happened on a Monday morning that the Saxons had more than fifteen thousand men on horseback, and they were riding between Coranges and Lanvemis, and King Aguisant was going after the plunder that Oriel, Meliaduc, Sorbares, Maglory, Braidon, Pignoras, Pincenar, and Salebrun were taking away in their army that was before the city of Vambieres. As they came, they laid waste all the land, and they leveled villages, towns, and castles, and set fire to everything, for they meant to reduce the whole countryside to nothing; as they took plunder, they carried it off with their army. And they committed such dreadful slaughter throughout the land that, no matter how hard or wicked your heart, you would have been moved to pity for the ladies and young women whose children they so grievously and wrongfully killed in their arms. And when the common folk hid in caves or any other place of refuge, they threw firebrands inside and burned them up. So the news ran so fast throughout the countryside that King Aguisant heard it, and he ordered all his barons to take up arms. And so they did.

They got on their horses and rode two leagues before daybreak. They went at a slow gait until after the hour of prime, when they looked down the road toward Lanvemis. They saw the air billowing and thick with dust and red with the fire the Saxons had set to the countryside, and they heard the uproar, the howls and screams the common folk uttered over their losses, the harm that had come to them, and their friends, whom they saw going to their doom. King Aguisant and his men were filled with sorrow and agony, and they began riding faster. They were a good fourteen thousand strong, and King Aguisant put himself in the vanguard with eight thousand men, and Waldin of the Fearsome Vale[†] led the rearguard with seven thousand knights who were all young men, worthy and skilled at arms, and they rode good, strong, swift horses.

This Waldin was King Aguisant's cousin on his father's side, and he later did many beautiful feats of arms before the stronghold for love of the maiden Lady of

---

[*]   Corresponds to Sommer, 164-171.
[†]   In Sommer's text, *gaudins de val esfroi* (164, l. 29).

Branlang, whom he wanted to take by force to be his wife, and before the wealthy town of the Narrow Wood, which was so praiseworthy until Waldin won it by his prowess, just as the story will yet set forth, if there is anyone who can tell it to you, but it is not yet time or place. For now it is right to tell you about King Aguisant of Scotland, who rode with his companions until they came upon the wagon train and the plunderers, about which nothing more was said or done.

But as soon as they saw each other, each side struck out against the other as fast as their horses could take them. There was a very great slaughter of men and horses there, and right from the start the Saxons took very great losses in men because they were not ready to fight, for they had spread [165] throughout the land, some here, others there, and King Aguisant and his men killed more than six thousand of them. But when the king of the Saxons got to the place where the battle was being fought, King Aguisant and Waldin suffered great losses, for he had more than forty thousand men on horseback and ready to defend themselves, while they were only fourteen thousand strong, and they did not believe they could keep up the fight

And they could not hold out for long, for the Saxons only grew in number, and there were only ten Scottish leagues between them and the main Saxon army, and the ten kings* I have told you about were all riding back and had their armor on, and they had so many men that the whole countryside was covered with them everywhere, and they had sent them on their way, willing or not. And King Aguisant suffered there very great losses in men-at-arms and knights, for before the hour of nones had gone by the Saxons struck hard at them and harried them, for the Saxons could see on two sides just the fourteen thousand men, riding good horses and able to fight, whom King Aguisant had with him; in the end, there were left not six thousand of them whom he could gather together who were not killed or wounded.

And you should know in truth that, if it had not been for a stroke of luck that happily befell them, not one of them, however many they might have been, would have got away, for they would all have been killed or taken prisoner. But King Urien had come out that morning to the fields along with his nephew Bademagu, who was a good knight, skillful and bold, and they had left behind in the city Yvonet,† who was a good and worthy lad, and another one; he had fathered Yvonet‡ with Brimesent, King Arthur's sister, who was a very good lady.

With Yvonet was Meleagant, who on that day was a very young boy, and he was the son of King Bademagu with his first wife. Those boys guarded the city very well, but they were not yet knights, for they were too young. And with them was Yvain the Bastard, who was also the son of King Urien with his seneschal's wife, who was so beautiful that he cast his own wife aside for more than five whole years and kept her in his castle against his seneschal's will, and with her he had a son. When the boy was born, such a great interdict was raised against the land that he

---

*   Only eight are named in Sommer's text (164, ll. 9-11).
†   The name Yvonet is a diminutive of Yvain. In the immediate context, the forms are used interchangeably.
‡   The syntax in Sommer's text (165, ll. 20-21) makes it ambiguous as to whether Yvonet or the "other one" (i.e., either Meleagant, who is mentioned next, or the other Yvonet/Yvain, the Bastard) is the son of Brimesent.

had to let her go, like it or not, but he had the boy taken away with him, and he reared him until he was big and handsome and could ride a horse. And the king, who loved him very much, gave him a share of his lands so that he could have an income to keep up his household.

That Yvain, who was called the Bastard, was handsome and skilled at arms, courtly and bold, and for the great love the king bore him, he made his companion his son Yvain the Great. And because he was sired in adultery, he was called Yvain the Bastard.* And the other Yvain, who was the king's son and was to be the rightful heir to the land through his mother, they called him Yvain the Great when they used his right name. This Yvain was wondrously handsome; he was worthy and bold. But never, after they had heard tell of King Arthur, did either Yvain want his father to make him a knight; rather, they often said to each other when they were alone together—for they greatly loved each other—that they would never be knights before King Arthur made them so. And Yvain the Bastard was younger than his brother Yvain the Great. [166]

Those young men I have told you about were in the town to protect it, and King Urien and Bademagu had managed to come straight to the battle in which King Aguisant was routed, and he and his army were fleeing to Coranges the citadel. When King Urien saw that King Aguisant had been so put to flight, he was wondrously sorrowful, and he looked it very much indeed. As soon as he came upon the pursuit, he struck the Saxons harder than anyone else could. He was riding a horse worthy of such a man, and he had ten thousand men with him, fully armed and all on good horses. And they ran into the Saxons so hard that many were killed or wounded. There the fighting was fierce and awesome, for the household of King Urien was most valiant. They fought all day long, and they underwent such hardship that no one could have suffered more. And King Urien himself did wonders.

King Aguisant had turned back because of the help that had come to him, and there was a great slaughter of men and horses, but King Urien could not have held out any longer if night had not fallen and put a stop to the fighting, for there were too many Saxons against him. So he went back into the city of Sorhaut, tired and weary from the blows he had given and taken, but the Saxons stayed behind in the plot of land that had been the battleground, and they lay there that night still wearing their armor.

But there befell King Urien a beautiful stroke of good luck that should not be forgotten in the story, for he and his army met a company of Saxons in a heath, and they had rich stocks of food, arms, and other supplies.† A good three thousand of them were driving this wealth in a train, and they had stopped and were sitting down to take food, of which they had a great plenty. They did not think they needed to be on guard against anyone, since they knew about the withdrawal of King Urien and the rout of King Aguisant's army, so they split off from the main army in order to come more quickly to the army that stood before the city of Vambieres, as you have heard earlier in the story, and they believed they were safe in the place where they were.

---

* In Sommer's text, *yvains ti auoutres* (165, etc.): "Yvain, the offspring of adultery."

† Sommer's text abbreviates *sesnes & harnois* (166, ll. 20): "Saxons and armor." Sommer provides the fuller reading from the Harley manuscript, 166, n. 2.

When King Urien and his nephew Bademagu saw the Saxons stopped as they were, and the tents and pavilions they had had set up, and the bright light burning inside the pavilions, they sent to ask who those people were. And those inside the pavilions answered right away that they belonged to King Brandegorre* of Saxony. When King Urien and Bademagu heard that they were Saxons, they shouted to their men that they would now see who was worthy. And they rode headlong into the midst of them, and they found them utterly unarmed, so they could hardly defend themselves. So the Christians began to bring the tents and pavilions down on their heads. There you would have seen a filthy jumble of tables overturned, cups and goblets spilled, and what they had held strewn about and trampled under the horses' hooves! There was a great slaughter of the Saxons there, for our men hated them with deadly hatred!

And the Christians numbered eight thousand, and they were fully armed, riding strong, swift horses, and there were only forty† thousand Saxons, and they were unarmed because they had been sitting at supper and did not believe they had to be on guard against anyone. And the night was beautiful and bright, and it was very clear, for the month of April had just begun, so the story says. And the Saxons were so badly slaughtered that no more than six thousand out of forty thousand of them were left who had not been [167] killed or cut up. And the ones who got away fled into the great, deep woods and forests, and they felt the greatest sorrow that anyone could conceive.

And King Urien and his nephew took all the wealth they had won from the Saxons, who were so well supplied, and they rode straight to Sorhaut, and they were bothered by nothing else. And the city was again fully stocked with every kind of goods, and they took their ease, happy and gladdened by the good fortune that had befallen them in that land.

After King Urien and his nephew Bademagu had left the battle, just as you have heard, news came to the city of Sorhaut about King Lot's sons and Galescalain, how they had left their fathers without their permission and gone off to be given their arms by King Arthur. They had not found him, for he was away in the kingdom of Carmelide, but they had stayed in Logres and were doing very well protecting the borderland; they were waiting for King Arthur to come back to his country, and they had taken the most wealth in booty that anyone had ever won.

So the news spread, and at length Yvonet, the son of King Arthur's sister, heard it. And when he had heard it relayed, he spoke to his mother privately and said to her, "Dear mother, my cousins have gone to King Arthur's court to serve him and to be given their armor by him, and they know him as their uncle. We could not be in worse straits than we are right now, yet I am happy with my lot so long as you are willing that it be so. Now tell me what you want, what you would like for me to do, for I would never do anything to hurt you. You are well aware that my father has given his land over to his nephew Bademagu, but there is nothing else he can take away from me except my life, which I hold from him, for your lands, which come

---

*   Sommer's text has *brangoire* (166, l. 30).

†   Sommer's text has *.iiij.* with a superscript *m* (166, l. 38): "four thousand"; however, a few lines later, the text speaks of forty thousand (*.xl.* with superscript *m*), of whom six thousand survive (166, l. 42).

to me from you alone, I can never lose, unless it is your will. But I would sooner lose it all than not go after my cousins to serve my uncle. Now get my things ready so that I can leave in a way befitting my honor! Come what may, I mean to go, for I would rather die in honor than live in shame in this prison where we are."

When the lady heard Yvonet talking that way, she could not keep from weeping, for she was fully aware that his heart bore the traits of high nobility, from which he had come. So she answered him, "Dear son Yvonet, where does the feeling that you must leave your father and go serve someone else come from?"

And he said, "Lady, for God's sake, everyone can vouch for the fact that King Arthur is your brother and my uncle, and my heart tells me this is so. My cousins have already gone to his lands, and I would be very cowardly indeed if I stayed behind where I couldn't do anything worthwhile and help him keep his lands as my cousins are doing. And you can be very sure that if you do not give me your leave, I will go just the same. Now do what you must, if you do not want to lose me, so that I can go to court in a way befitting my honor."

"Dear, sweet son," said his mother, "bear with me, and I will put your gear together so stealthily that your father will not know anything about it, for if he did, you would lose him utterly. You must seek out the companions you can and wish to take with you, and I will get the clothing, arms, and horses you will need."

"Lady," he said, "thank you very much!"

Then Yvonet stirred himself and came straight to his brother, whose name was Yvonet the Bastard, [168] and he disclosed to him what was on his mind. When he had told him everything, his brother answered that never, God willing, would he go into a strange land without him, and he was ready to leave whenever he wanted. "I want us to set out," said Yvonet, "in a week's time."

They put their gear together, and Yvonet the Bastard sought out companions befitting one so worthy and keen until he had a hundred, and Yvonet the Great found two hundred, and his mother got robes, money, and armor in great plenty. So they went, with the lady's leave, one night after supper, in the middle of the night after bedtime, and Fragient, a noble youth who knew all the byways of the country, led them all the way to Logres.

But with that the story falls silent about all of them and King Urien, and it does not talk about them anymore right now, but it begins speaking again about King Neutres of Garlot.

Here the story says that when King Neutres saw that he had lost his son Galescalain, he was very sorrowful and upset, and he said wicked things to his wife and blamed her very harshly; he was so angry that he did not want to speak to her for another month. Then, one Thursday evening in April, it happened that a messenger came to tell him the great disaster that had befallen King Aguisant, how the Saxons had routed him, and how he would have been killed or taken prisoner had it not been for King Urien, who came to the rescue in time to halt the pursuit of King Aguisant. After him came another messenger, who told about the defeat of the Saxons that King Tradelmant and the King of the Hundred Knights had brought about between Saxon Rock and Arundel, where they won a great deal of wealth.

When King Neutres heard this news, he was sorely grieved for King Aguisant, and he resolved in his heart to go patrol the borderland near the Welsh Causeway between North Wales and Sorelois, where the strait was wondrously far across. But he had hardly made up his mind to lead the mounted patrol when he heard such an uproar raised throughout the countryside that you would have thought the land had sunk into a bottomless pit, and he saw the common folk running in flight on every side, so he asked the fleeing people what was wrong. They told him that all the Saxons in the world had invaded the country and were burning, tearing down, or killing everything they met with. They were coming in by every way in such great numbers that so large an army had never been seen. And they had dug in before the stronghold of Broceliande,* on the river Severn,† in the midst of the meadows, where they were awaiting the great wagon train that was coming with their foodstuffs. And their leaders, they said, were King Maragond, who was Hengist the Saxon's cousin, King Braolant, and King Pignoras. "And the plunderers come to more than twenty thousand. They have spread out through the midst of our land, which they are burning and pillaging, and they kill everything in their path. And if you don't believe me, you can hear it and see it for yourself."

When King Neutres heard this speech, he made up his mind that he could not stay there without great hardship.

Then he shouted in a loud voice, "Noble knights, now to arms! Now we'll see who's worthy! For there is no knight who does not defend his land against his mortal foes!"

Then a great many knights and men-at-arms ran to put on their armor, [169] and when they were fully armed there were at least twelve thousand of them. King Neutres took seven thousand of them and gave them to Dorilas to lead, and he entreated him to fight boldly. He was a very good knight, a kinsman of the king. He went in the direction from where he saw the common folk fleeing, and he rode until he came to the place where people were being killed and maimed. The Saxon advance force was a good five thousand strong, but they were not together in a formation, but spread out up and down the river, burning and plundering.

When Dorilas saw them wreaking such harm, not believing in God, His religion, or His commandments, he let his men run on them as fast as their horses could go, and they struck them with sharp lances that cut them through; a great many Saxons were brought down and slaughtered, for they had been taken unawares and had not seen them before they were running them through. They had killed more than two thousand of them before King Neutres got there, and those who were left turned in flight toward the castle of Broceliande, where the four kings were encamped, but King Neutres and his men followed hard on them, brought them down, and killed them, and they pursued them until they had driven them into the tents and pavilions. It was past the hour of nones, and when the Saxons saw them rushing in, they hurried to get their arms. But they could not run to them before five hundred of the tents had been brought down about their heads and more than a thousand of their men slain.

Then the Saxons blew a horn at the tent of King Maragond, and he gathered together such a great number of men that they came to more than thirty thousand.

---

*   Sommer's text has *briolande* (168, l. 33).

†   Sommer's text has *riuiere daisurne* here (168, l. 33), but elsewhere *riuiere de surne* (172, ll. 5-6), *riuiere de sauerne* (175, l. 11), and even *riuiere darsoune* (173, l. 8).

And then the four kings rode out, and King Galescin came stealthily to meet them with a thousand men; then they all stood against Dorilas, King Neutres's nephew, who was doing all he could to harm the Saxons, and he had fought very well throughout the whole day; then Mahaglant the Saxon came in. As soon as the enemies took note of each other, they rode against each other, their lances lowered, and they hit so hard that their shields flew into splinters, but their coats of mail were so strong that not one link broke. They shattered their lances as they made their passes, but they had struck so hard that they were all brought to the ground. Men on both sides ran to their rescue, and a great, wild fray broke out; the fighting was so fierce and so awesome that many were slain on both sides, but the Saxons lost more than the Christians.

And King Neutres had ridden toward the pavilions on the other side, between the woods and the river, and he and his men brought down a great many pavilions and tents. The Saxons lost a great deal there, for they lacked somewhat for supplies, and there were many killed and wounded before they could get to their gear and tack. And they would have lost a good deal more, when King Falsabre attacked King Neutres with seven thousand Saxons, and they fought very hard.

When King Neutres saw the huge number of Saxons who were coming against him, he rode to meet them like the good, skilled knight he was. He ran in among them and fought so well, along with all his men, that he put the seven thousand to flight in a rout. He drove them, despite their resistance, into King Pignoras's company, [170] with eight thousand Saxons, which gave them help and comfort. And King Pignoras struck hard among King Neutres's men, and with the sheer strength of his numbers, he threw them back more than a crossbow's shot, beyond the tents between the woods and the river.

And when King Neutres saw his men being driven back, he let out his battlecry and shouted to them, "Noble knights, where are you going? Please turn around and fight back for as long as you are alive, for you will never have a better chance! You must remember who you are, for it is better to die fighting than fleeing shamefully! We are still as good as dead, I think, wherever we might run."

And when they heard their lord's speech, they turned about and drew together in a body so thick and tight that not another man would have fit in, and they held their ground without moving, and they bore up and withstood the attack until the others had broken their lances on them and rested beneath their shields to catch their breath. And then they bore the blows they gave them and withstood the attack until they rested for a while and stopped raining blows down on them. And when they saw that the Saxons were somewhat tired, they let their horses run against them and began to fight so well that the Saxons were amazed by the wonders they saw them doing against them.

Meanwhile, Dorilas was fighting Mahaglant's men and put them to flight in a rout, and he drove them, despite their resistance, into Falsabre's company and that of Pignoras, who was fighting very hard against King Neutres's men. So they all ran into each other in the fray. There was wondrous fighting there and fearsome combat, and each side held out as long as the other until it was near the hour of vespers.

At once King Maragond moved out, and he had more than fifteen thousand Saxons with him. He was very bitter that so few men had stood their ground against so many Saxons, for he saw clearly that there were less than half as many Christians as Saxons. Then he shouted to his men and ordered them to fall upon them so hard that not one would be left in his saddle, and they did so, for it seemed to them that they could utterly defeat them just as they were coming at them. But when King Neutres saw such a great number of Saxons coming, he drew his men in around himself thick and tight and withdrew little by little toward the woods. The Saxons rushed on him and drove hard after him, for they believed they could take them, and they hit them so hard that their lances flew into bits.

King Neutres and his men struggled backward to reach the woods, which were very deep, by a narrow way where a path was. And the woods were high on both sides of the path and so thick that nothing could get in but wild beasts. And through the middle the path went deep into the woods, but it was so narrow that it would be a wonder if you could throw a stone any way down the path.* King Neutres and Dorilas backed down the path until all their men had got into the woods. Then they put the hilts of their weapons into the ground and turned the tips upwards; they began to wait for their enemy, and they were ready to defend themselves. And the enemy came upon them full of wrath and sorrow for the harm they had done them, and they attacked. The Christians defended themselves mightily, and they kept fighting until one man could hardly see the other because of the darkness, for night had fallen. Then the Saxons withdrew. They lost there more than they won.

When King Neutres saw that the Saxons were leaving, he and his men set out, [171] and they rode until they came to Wissant. And it was plain by the look of their armor that they had not had a restful trip, for their shields were full of holes, their mail was undone and the links broken, their helmets were bashed in and the nose-plates filthy with blood and gore. And the people throughout the town looked at them in wonder, and they said to one another, "Those men have not had a lot of rest!" So they went to their lodgings, took off their armor, and took their rest, for they had toiled for a very long time.

But now the story falls silent about them and begins speaking again about King Brandegorre.

20. DODINEL THE WILDMAN.†

Here the story says that when King Brandegorre had left Sorhaut and come to his citadel Estrangorre, he stocked it with food and knights and men-at-arms, until there were some fifteen thousand men fully armed, and for a long time he held the borderland fast against the Saxons, who did them hardly any harm. At length, it

---

* In Sommer's text, the sentence ends abruptly with *a merveille* (170, l. 36): "it would be a wonder." The translation adapts the text from the Harley manuscript supplied by Sommer in a note.

† Corresponds to Sommer, 171-174.

happened one day that the Saxons had invaded his land and the borderland of South Wales, where King Belinant was lord, the brother of King Tradelmant of Wales. That Belinant had a fair, rich land, and his wife was beautiful, wealthy, and young; her name was Eglantine, and she was the daughter of King Machen of the Lost Island. And Belinant had a son with his niece, who was of very great beauty, and he was fourteen years old. He was rightly named Dodinel the Wildman, and I will tell you why they called him that:* it was because he sought to do nothing but hunt boars, deer, and bucks with bow and arrow through those great, wild forests, and it was because he liked to be there so much that they called him Dodinel the Wildman. And King Neutres was Eglantine's brother on their mother's side, so Dodinel the Wildman was the cousin of Galescalain, and afterwards, in the household of King Arthur, he† won great renown, and he was so skillful at feats of arms that he became one of the most highly esteemed knights of the Round Table.

But here the story does not speak of him, but of King Brandegorre and the Saxons who had come into his land sorrowful and stirred up because of their friends whom they had lost between the Rock and the stronghold of Arundel. And the Saxons took to the road that led beneath the Castle of the Narrow Way. There were a great many of them, and they burned the whole countryside and plundered as they went along; they harmed the Lord of the Narrow Borderland, the castellan of Lindesores, King Belinant of South Wales, and King Brandegorre more than all the others. And when King Brandegorre found out about them, he summoned all his liegemen, and after they had gathered, fully armed, they set out to avenge the damage and hurt that were theirs. The Saxons came so numerous and so thick that the whole land was covered with them, and they set fire throughout the whole countryside. Meanwhile, King Belinant had raised a very great army, and they rode until they saw the Saxons who were bringing shame and ruin to the country; they were leading such a great slaughter that their wails and screams could be heard two leagues away, and the air was red and billowing with the dust, so that the whole sky was blackened with it, and the sun had lost its brightness and its light.

When King Brandegorre saw the ruin and the slaughter, he was sorely stricken with grief, and tears streamed from his eyes. Then he entreated his liegemen to set their minds to fighting hard and defending Holy Christendom.

And the Saxons rode [172] hard and fast, their standard raised, and they were more than fifty thousand strong, and they were led by Baramal, Caroman, Lidras, Hardiant, and Kinkenart. Those five kings were wealthy and powerful, and each one had with him ten thousand men well armed one and all; and all five of them were kinsmen of Hengist, whom Uther Pendragon killed. And King Brandegorre was waiting for them to cross a bridge over the river Severn, which was very wide and deep, and as soon as they drew near, they let their horses run against them, and they hit them so hard it was a wonder to behold. There was a great shattering of lances there, a dreadful slaughter of men and horses, a loud hammering together of cudgels and swords, and the fighting was great and mighty; men from both sides

---

* Sommer's text has only *dodynel* (171, l. 18), but the comments explain only the surname "Wildman," not the Christian name, which recalls *dodin* ("deceiving").

† Sommer's text has the relative *qui* (171, l. 22), which appears to refer to Galescalain, but the sense of the passage seems to require continued reference to Dodinel.

fell into the water, which swept them downstream, for it flowed swiftly, and it was not yet the hour of prime.

That river flowed before the city of Estrangort, which King Caradoc held in his sway. And he was leaning out of one of the windows of his great hall, gazing at the meadows and river, and he looked into the water, which was clear but turbulent, for the river ran fast, and he saw shields and lances floating downstream in great numbers. And he looked toward where they were coming from and saw the sky red and burning with the fire the Saxons had set in the borderland of Estrangorre, and he saw coming down through the water the gear of knights and the trapping of horses that had drowned. Now it dawned on him that King Brandegorre was fighting with the Saxons.

Then he quickly jumped to his feet and shouted to his men, "Now to arms, worthy men! For any knight would be valiant and bold in this time of need!"

There was a highborn youth there who was valiant and bold. He brought the king his armor, and his name was Kay of Estral. King Caradoc had called him many times to become a knight, but he answered that he did not yet want to be one, and he said this because he yearned to be made a knight by the hand of King Arthur. And when the king was armed, he asked whether the other knights were ready, and he was told that they were all on their horses waiting for him before the gate. The king mounted his horse and led his men out of the city, and they rode hard and fast until they came to the battle, and it was right at the hour of nones.

And as they drew nearer, they heard the uproar and the sword fight going on at the bridge crossing, which King Brandegorre was very fiercely contesting with fifteen thousand men against the Saxons. The Saxons were so many, and so thick, that by their sheer numbers they drew them away from the bridge into the open field, and King Brandegorre would have suffered great hardship, but King Caradoc came along, his banner raised, with ten thousand men, and they rushed headlong into the fray as fast as they could spur their horses. The fighting grew dreadfully more fierce, and there was a great slaughter of Saxons, for their armor was not so strong as they needed it to be; and they struck blows and kept cutting until well past the hour of nones. Then the Christians began to waver, for there was a great horde of Saxons, and the shouts and the uproar grew so loud that people could hear the sound half a league away.

Now look! King Belinant of South Wales came up with four thousand men who had good horses worth a great deal and good, strong lances with sharp tips, and they were well stocked with all kinds of armor. They rushed into the fray so hard that they drove everyone back. Then the fighting was fierce and awesome, [173] for King Belinant's companions were very worthy men, for he was the lord of Lindesores and lord of the Narrow Borderland. And the lord of Glocedon was there, and the castellan of Galenice, and those of the Marshlands, Roestoc, Camugnes, and Blakestan; so too were Caradoc, lord of the Dolorous Tower, and Drian the Merry of the Perilous Forest. Each one had two hundred knights with him, the worthiest anyone could find, and they killed as many as they came to, and the slaughter was such that the great stream of blood flowing from the bodies made the river Severn, which had been clear, run red. And if night had not fallen, which, against all their wills, broke up the battle, not one of the Saxons, who had been at least fifty thousand strong, would have got away; yet the Christians did not number more than thirty thousand.

But night fell, which broke up the battle, and one side drew away from the other, until morning, when they meant to start fighting again. But the five kings of Saxony took counsel and ordered the Saxons to go all night and take the straightest way they could back to Saxon Rock, but they lost a good deal of their armor, for they hurried to leave the country and did not carry with them half of their equipment. So it was until day broke the next morning.

When it was light, King Caradoc, King Belinant, King Brandegorre, and all the barons of their lands got themselves ready and mounted their horses, for they were very much afraid that, for lack of prowess, they might lose their advantage and Holy Christendom would be brought down and shamed. So they gathered their battalions together, got their men into formation, and their companies in order, and went where they thought they would find the Saxons. But when they saw that their enemies had left, they were very distraught that they had got away from them, for it was clear to them that they had gone toward the Castle of the Rock.

And when they saw that there was nothing else they could do, they turned back. The barons began to make merry together, and they split up the equipment the Saxons had left behind in such a way that each one got what he wanted, for there was so much that it made every man wealthy. And when the time came to leave, each of the kings* offered his service to the others: whenever anyone needed it, he should let them all know. Then they parted company. King Caradoc went to one of his cities, and King Brandegorre went to Estrangorre, which was filled with all kinds of goods.

Then word spread that King Lot's sons had gone off and left their father, as had the sons of King Neutres and King Urien. And when Dodinel heard the news, he said he would do likewise, and he told his father that he would go to court, but he got his gear together in secret. And he sent word to Kay of Estral at the stronghold of his uncle, King Caradoc, and he entreated him to come confer with him at the Castle of the Thorn and please not to fail to come for any reason; and he should bring with him his little nephew Kehedin. And the messenger rode until he came to Estrangort,† and he spoke to Kay and told him in private what Dodinel had sent him to say, that he should come confer with him at the Castle of the Thorn and that he should come ready to travel. And Kay sent word back that he would be there within three days' time, but he told Dodinel that *he himself* should make ready to leave, for he had already got his things together. [174]

With that, the messenger took leave of Kay of Estral and went back to Dodinel the Wildman and told him Kay's answer. When he heard it, he knew very well what Kay had in mind, so he got himself ready and summoned his companions; and when they had gathered, there were a good seventy of them, all young squires from twenty-two to twenty-four years old. Dodinel and his companions went straight to the Castle of the Thorn with rich clothing and very valuable housewares of gold

---

*   The word is not in Sommer's text (173, l. 29), but it seems reasonable, as Sommer suggests in a margin note, that the promises of mutual service should be made by the kings alone rather than all of the barons.

†   Sommer's text has *estrangoire* (173, l. 39).

and silver, and they waited there until Kay of Estral came with his companions, forty worthy young men with their first growth of beard. When the young men saw one another, they rejoiced mightily, for they had not been together for a long time.

And after they had celebrated a good deal, Dodinel the Wildman spoke and said to Kay, "Dear fair friend, I sent for you and you have come, and I thank you very much; now it is only right that I should tell you why. A short time ago news came to me that King Lot's sons, along with Galescalain and Yvonet, have gone to court to be given their arms; and because they have gone there, I want to go too. And I love, and have loved, you so much that I don't wish to do anything without your leave. I strongly desire to follow my cousins. Now tell me whether you will go with me. I would in no way go back to my father's household, for I have gathered my belongings together and I am on my way!"

"Sir," said Kay of Estral, "that is why I have come to you, for I knew just about what you had in mind, and I too have all my gear and everything I need, and I have forty highborn youths with me, all worthy and bold, and this one is Kehedin,* my nephew. Now let us set out when you will."

"You speak very well," said Dodinel. "We'll move out tomorrow morning."

So the young men stayed the night there, and in the morning they took to the road and set out for Logres.

But now the story falls silent about all of them and begins speaking again about King Clarion of Northumberland.

21. The Plight of the Saxons; King Clarion Opposes the Saxons.[†]

Here the story says that when King Clarion had left Sorhaut,[‡] he called up as many knights and men-at-arms as he could find, and he garrisoned the city of Northumberland and stocked it with foodstuffs. Then he sent word throughout his land and ordered those who owned cattle, sheep, or any other livestock to lead them into the great forests, wild, deep, and very old, until they found safe pasture. Then he sent orders for all men who could bear arms, until there were at least fourteen thousand. And King Clarion also thought about how to protect the countryside. He lay down to sleep only in the woods,[§] in a tent or pavilion, or on the wayside, and he found no spy whom he did not hang or take away a prisoner.

At length it happened one night that the Saxons were gathered at the tents of King Bramangue[¶] and King Mahaglant, the wealthy king of Ireland who was first

---

*   Sommer's text has *hedins* (174, l. 21), but this is Kehedin the Small (cf. 178, l. 27).
†   Corresponds to Sommer, 174-178.
‡   From ch. 11 (Sommer, 131).
§   Sommer's text has *son fores non* (174, l. 34), which may be read as *s'en fores non* ("except in forests").
¶   *Banaigue* (175, l. 8), but *bonegue* here (174, l. 37), *bauaigne* (for *banaigue?*) (175, l. 3), *bermagne* (198, l. 30), *bramangue* (175, l. 15), *brangue* (175, l. 41) *bramague* (176, ll. 21, 28; 340, l. 12), *branmague* (395, l. 4). The form chosen is the one of the variants preferred by G.D.West (47a).

cousin to the king of Denmark and brother of King Ammaduc, the wealthy king of Hoselice; and Bramangue was lord of part of Denmark and Ireland. And he sadly mourned his losses at the Castle of the Rock and the great harm the men from the countryside were doing him every day. At the same time, he was deeply worried about the stocks of food, which grew smaller and smaller in [175] the army and had become very scarce. Then a young knight, who was very worthy and bold, sprang to his feet. He spoke loudly enough for all to hear him, and he said to Bramangue, "Dear uncle, if you will let me go plundering in a land I know of, I will bring back food enough, for the land is wealthy and full of all kinds of goods. Entrust me with as many of your men as I may choose, if Minaduc, my father, is willing for me to go, for I would not without his leave. You should know in truth that if anyone is to strive for such a deed, it should be I."

"Dear nephew," said King Bramangue, "I have nothing but good things to say about what you mean to undertake. But tell me first, what land are you bent on going to?"

"I will tell you truly," said Oriel, "I want to go to Northumberland, following the river Severn, and then to come back by the river Humber before a castle named the Dolorous Tower, and you can know for a fact that it is the most bountiful land in the whole world. If we should ever need provisions, send to that land for them, and we will have them plentifully."

"I grant you what you ask, dear nephew," said Bramangue. "Go pick out the men you want and take them."

"Sir," said Oriel, "many thanks!"

Then Oriel left and chose the men he wanted, until they were a good sixty thousand strong, not counting the foot soldiers who went along after them for the booty. They took to the road and went straight to Norhaut, and they plundered and burned the whole countryside.

And King Mahaglant, who had stayed with the army before Vambieres, called his nephew Soriondes forward and said to him, "Dear nephew, what are you doing that you don't go anywhere? Take my men, as many as you want, and go to the land of King Yder. Take as much plunder as you find. If you find him fighting you for it, take care to have enough men with you to help you avenge yourself."

When he heard his uncle saying this, he sprang to his feet happy and gladdened, for he was of very great prowess, and he said to him, "Sir, many thanks!"

Then he left him and chose as many men as he wanted, until he had a good forty thousand all on horseback, and they set out for Cornwall, and they plundered the countryside wherever they went, laid it waste, and burned it.

But the story does not say any more about them at this time; rather we will tell you more about the Saxons' meeting.

Now the story says that Soriondes, nephew of King Mahaglant, had left the army, just as you have heard, and King Minaduc called his nephew Arrant* and said to him, "Dear nephew, you must go to Loonois and Orkney, the lands of King Lot

---

*   The form here (175, ll. 33, 42) is *hertant;* elsewhere in the *Merlin* (340, l. 12) occurs the form *airant.*

Take as many of my men as you want. And take care to see this through in such a way that I may be thankful to you."

He sprang to his feet and said, "Many thanks, sir!"

And he left and took such companions as he wished, and when they had got on their horses, there were at least forty thousand of them. So they left and rode until they came into the lands of King Lot, and they began to pillage in the worst way they could.

But here the story falls silent about them for a while, and we will tell you about Bramangue and Mahaglant, for when Soriondes, Oriel, and Arrant, those three cousins, had left the main army, [176] all the kings in the army held a meeting to decide how they could take the city of Vambieres, for it was wondrously strong.

And the story says that Vambieres stood on flat ground, and there was no hill or mountain within two leagues on all sides. All around the town were great moats, wide and full of very deep water, and a* great marsh stretching as far as an arrow could be shot. Beyond the water and the moats were the walls and fortified stone turrets one after the other, only four yards apart. There were only two ways into the town, and each of the gates had two portcullises; the gates were shut with two iron locks and great, stout bars held crosswise. Why should I go on laying out the town for you and telling you how strong it was? For not only was it strong, but above all it was a town of rivers, for flowing water beat against the walls on two sides. Dry land and wetlands were all around everywhere else, so that no one could mount a siege except on one side, where there were two pairs of great moats, wide and deep, and beyond that was a great marsh wide as an arrow could be shot from a crossbow and a good four leagues long.

So the kings went to see how they might go about taking the town, and they held a great meeting, and they asked each other what they could do, for they saw clearly that it could taken only by starving the people out. There was a king there named Maragond. He came to his feet and said to King Bramangue, "Sir, I think that we must stay in this land long enough to starve the city out. And while we are before this town, we could starve out and take another, so we would have two at the same time."

"By my head," said King Mahaglant, "you do not lie! And if you want my advice, we should send a third of our men before the city of Clarence, and any others who come from our land will go to the siege with them. For there are not so many people in this country that we can't throw them out with a fourth of our forces."

"Dear sir," said King Bramangue, "Which ones would you agree to let go there?"

"I will certainly tell you that," said Aminaduc. "King Hargadabran will go there, and King Sinaglorre, King Sorbares, King Maragond, King Mysenes, King Pignoras, King Sapharin, King Thoas, King Satiphus, King Plantamor, King Sornegrieu, and King Mathamas. And let each one have twenty thousand men at his banner, and they should besiege the city so harshly that none may go in or come out without being killed or maimed!"

---

*   Sommer's text has the definite article (176, l. 5).

So they ended their meeting, and all agreed that they should go straight to the city of Clarence. They did so, and encamped all around the city and stayed there for a very long time. But now the story falls silent about the siege, and we will tell you about the Saxons who invaded the land of King Clarion of Northumberland.

When King Clarion saw that the Saxons were laying waste his land, he was highly distraught, so he chose a spy and sent him out to learn whether it was a big force. When the spy had seen them, he came back to the king very frightened and told him that there were forty thousand or more of them, and they were stripping [177] the countryside. When King Clarion heard what he said, he picked a messenger to send to Duke Escant of Cambenic, and he told him to meet with him at the narrows of Margot Rock on the river Severn with as many men as he could muster, for the Saxons had invaded his land and were laying it waste.

When the duke heard this news, he ordered up all his men and brought them together in a force of twelve thousand, then he rode off with them to the Rock. And when they got there, they found King Clarion with thirteen thousand armed men, and as soon as they saw one another they began to rejoice mightily. They had been there for just a short time when they saw the smoke and fire rising up throughout the land and the dust flying so thick that the air quivered with it. And when the king and the duke saw it, one need not ask whether they were sorrowful or upset about it. Then they set out toward where they saw the fire billowing up, and they met the people fleeing from it wailing and moaning over their losses and the harm that had come to them, so that the king was overcome with great pity for them.

So they rode until they met those they wanted to meet; they tarried no longer, but rode against them very fast. There they led a great slaughter of men and horses, and the Saxons lost very many of their men because they were spread out down the river and were bringing plunder back to the main army. There were more than fifteen thousand plunderers, and King Clarion and Duke Escant gave them a great fight; they fought from the hour of prime until midday, and the story says that they killed at least ten thousand of the foot soldiers. But when the body of knights came in, our men were very frightened, for it was a large force with many good knights, although with our men was the lord of the Dolorous Tower with a hundred worthy knights, valiant and bold. And Christopher was there, along with Sansadoine, a castellan from Norhaut, and a thousand men wearing full armor (Sansadoine held his stronghold in the deep woods of Northumberland). Brun the Ruthless of Salerno was there, and Sanebron was there with Duke Escant and three thousand knights riding good horses, and so was Mares, lord of Roestoc, who led a fair, rich company of two thousand all wearing good armor, and the lord of Camengues with three thousand companions worthy and bold. And there was the lord of the White Tower, who was very worthy and bold, with six hundred knights, and Waldin, King Arthur's nephew, who was wearing very costly armor, with three hundred companions. And Gravadain of the Strong Castle was there with four hundred knights all riding strong, swift warhorses.

When they came together, there were more than thirty-five thousand of them all told, and they stood beside a wooded spot near the narrows made by a great rock in the river Severn. And the Saxons came upon them in such forces that they would not have withstood for long if it had not been for the narrows where they found themselves. The fray was dreadful, for those on the Saxons' side were proud, wealthy, and powerful, among the best knights in the whole army. With this, they were so strong and they came in such great numbers that they feared nothing, and when they saw the Christians, they fell upon them very hard. But the Christians defended themselves so well that they could do nothing to throw them out of the place where they were, and they could not get at them except with weapons that could be hurled. So they threw [178] spears and sharpened pikes at them, and the men on both sides inflicted very fearful wounds on one another. The fray lasted this way for three whole days, from morning until night, and no one took off his hauberk or his helmet until nighttime, when they all ate what little there was to eat.

But now the story falls silent about them, until it is time and place to tell more about them, and it begins speaking again about King Arthur and his companions, who were in the city of Carhaix in Carmelide, taking their ease and highly honored by King Leodagan.

22. KING CLARION OF NORTHUMBERLAND AND DUKE ESCANT; SAGREMOR'S ARRIVAL IN BRITAIN.*

In this part the story says that they celebrated and feasted in the city of Carhaix because of the victory they had won over their enemies and the booty they had taken from them.† They brought their people together from far and wide, and King Arthur was greatly honored and handsomely served by King Leodagan and his daughter, who was eager to do as her father bade her.

It happened one day that Merlin took the three kings aside and said to them, "My lords, I must go to the kingdom of Logres, for there they are in dire need of help and advice, not because the country is still worried about being rescued from outlaws, which is not true, but because, as you should know, the barons are being grievously harassed by the Saxons, for there are very many of them in the land, and they have, in their great pride, burned two cities in the land, one being Vambieres and the other Clarence. They have gathered together men from more than forty kingdoms, and their numbers are growing every day."

Next he told them how the Saxons had spread throughout the land, with one part going against King Yder in Cornwall, the second against King Lot in Orkney and Loonois, and the third against King Clarion of Northumberland and the duke of Cambenic. Afterwards he told about the harassment and all the battles there had been, what had happened between the Saxons and their kings, the great meeting they had held that led them to besiege the two cities, how Yvonet the Great and Yvonet the Bastard had left the castle of their father King Urien, and how Dodinel, Kay of Estral, and Kehedin the Small‡ had left their country and gone to Logres,

---

*   Corresponds to Sommer, 178-180.
†   From ch. 17 (Sommer, 156-159.).
‡   Called Kehedin the Fair, 148, ll. 17-18, and 198, l. 38.

with Gawainet, and they would not let themselves be made knights until Arthur had girded their swords at their sides. "And you should know that they cannot succeed on their own, and this is the true reason why I am going there. Now, be careful to take your ease and get your rest, and don't go anywhere until you see me again; it will take me only a short while, and this I say in truth."

"Ah, Merlin!" said King Ban, "don't be gone for long! We would soon be dead or in dreadful trouble if you left us on our own! And we would say that you had forsaken us—or betrayed us."

"What?" said Merlin. "Dear lords, do you then believe that I won't be back? Take care never to think of such a thing, or you will lose my love."

"Sir," said King Ban, "I do not think that at all, except for your companionship, which I hold so dear."

"Then let it be," said Merlin. "You will have me back with you in time, before there is a battle in this kingdom. And I commend you to God, [179] for I cannot tarry."

Then he left them so quickly that they did not know what had become of him. And that same evening he went straight to Blaise, his master, in Northumberland, who was very glad to see him because he loved being with him. And Merlin told him all the adventures that had happened in the kingdom of Carmelide since he had left him, and afterwards he told him everything that had happened in the kingdom of Logres, until there was nothing left to be told. He put it all in writing, word for word, and it is through him that we still know what we do know about those things. When he had written this all down, Merlin told him why he needed to leave the three kings in the kingdom of Carmelide. And on the very evening that Merlin spoke to Blaise, Oriel's company encamped on the river Humber, for they had just invaded the land.

But now the story stops talking about Merlin and Blaise and the Saxons, and we will tell about Sagremor, who had left Constantinople with three hundred companions and gone to King Arthur's court to be newly made a knight.[*]

Here the story says that Sagremor made his way, after he had left the wealthy city of Constantinople, until he came to the port of Wissant. There they took to the sea and sailed with a good, light wind, until they came ashore at the port of Dover. After they had crossed over, they were very glad. Then they packed up their gear, climbed on their horses, and started out on their way to Camelot. And they wandered about because they did not know the roads, nor did they find anyone they could ask for news of King Arthur, for they found the countryside burned and laid waste, since the Saxons had wreaked destruction there, but those youths knew nothing about that.

At length they came upon the great company of Saxons that Oriel had broken off from the main army, and they were a good twenty thousand strong. They were posting lookouts around Norhaut, lest someone should steal any of the plunder they had taken. As the young men drew within a league of the Saxons, they met the people running from them. The youths asked them what was wrong, and they

---

[*]   From ch. 11 (Sommer, 132).

told them that they were fleeing because of the Saxons, who were laying waste the whole countryside. And Sagremor asked them, "Where, then, is King Arthur?"

And they said that he was in the kingdom of Carmelide.

"And who, then, is watching out for this country?" asked Sagremor.

And they answered, the sons of King Lot of Orkney, who had come to serve the king so that he would give them their arms.

"And where are they?" asked Sagremor.

They are in Camelot," they said. "But for God's sake, young lords, don't go on, for you will all be killed or wounded."

"Now tell me," said Sagremor, "which way to Camelot?"

"In truth, dear friend," they said, 'you are on the right road, if only it weren't for the outlaws who are coming this way. But get away from here, or you are all dead!"

"And how far is it to Camelot?" said Sagremor.

"Sir," said one of them, "at least ten Scottish leagues."

When Sagremor heard that it was only ten leagues, he shouted to his companions, "Noble men, now to arms! Now we'll see who is worthy! Make sure that those heathens, who are laying waste this country, take nothing of ours that they do not pay for dearly. If we can fight our way through them, [180] we can put ourselves between them and Camelot, then we'll be well away thanks to our horses' strength if we must."

Then the squires dismounted and dressed in their armor. They put their hauberks on their backs, fine and bright, and they shone like polished silver. They were handsomely armed and ready for the fight, for they were worthy, bold, and stouthearted. They had good steel war hats, and they tied them on their heads over their iron coifs, and they got on their horses, which were covered with iron armor that was so strong that none better could be found in any land. Then they formed their ranks and drew tightly together like a flock of starlings, and they rode out to meet the Saxons, whom they saw coming.

But now the story stops talking about them and begins speaking again about Merlin, who was in Northumberland with his master Blaise.

23. MERLIN AND THE YOUNG HEROES AGAINST THE SAXONS.[*]

Here the story says that when Merlin had told Blaise all the adventures of the land, just as they had happened after he had left him, he got up in the morning and departed, and he came straight to the city of Camelot. And he took on the likeness of an old man, and he was wrapped in a tattered, old burlap cloak with its hem ripped off. Before, he had been tall and brawny; now he was short, stooped, and old, and his hair was unkempt and his beard long and stringy. He was holding a club at his neck, and he was driving a great herd of cattle. And when he was before the

[*]   Corresponds to Sommer, 180-186.

city, he began to moan and wail so loudly that all the people atop the walls heard him clearly, and they heard him saying, "Dear Lord God, what a great shame about such handsome young men who will be killed and hacked up so wrongfully! Ah, King Arthur, sir! What fast friends you will lose today! They would have helped you, if they could have reached the right age, in winning your lands back from your enemies. Ah, Sagremor, highborn squire, noble and courteous man who has borne the agony of death for us, may God keep your body from death and maiming! And if you have died, may He keep your soul in His holy paradise and let it not be tormented in the trials of Hell. Just as truly as He is true God and all-powerful, may he watch over you and your companions!"

Merlin uttered these words, and Gawainet and his brothers heard them. They had gone up on the wall of the town, fully armed, and they were watching the red from the fires the Saxons had set round about the land, for they had come to Camelot to protect the town as soon as they knew the Saxons had invaded the country, and they had climbed up to see whether the Saxons were coming to storm Camelot. And Gawainet called to the peasant, "Farmer, come here and speak to us. Tell us what's wrong with you and why you are wailing so. And tell us who he is whom you are mourning so deeply."

And he turned a deaf ear to him, and he beat the ground with his club as if he were out of his mind and his heart heavy with sorrow. Then he leaned on his club and began to wail again very loudly, and after he had let out his sorrow, he began to drive his cattle back around, as if he meant to rush into the woods. Then he said in a loud voice, "Ah, knighthood of Logres! what has become of you? It was already being said less than [181] a week ago that the wonder of the whole world had come into this land, and our salvation! They said that King Arthur's nephew was protecting this country, but he seems to be doing very badly indeed, since he* is allowing the wonder of the whole world to be slain!"

When Gawainet heard this speech, he was most eager to find out why the peasant had said these things and why he was so sorrowful. He called to him again and again, three or four times, very forcefully: "Countryman, countryman! Speak to me, tell me what is wrong with you!" But he turned his face away and looked as if he had not heard him. He called to him once more, and the man raised his head, which was very ugly, with hair shooting out all over, and looked at him with one eye open and the other shut, and he gritted his teeth like a man looking into the sun, and answered, "What do you want?"

"I want you to speak with me for a while," said Gawainet. "Come over this way."

And he drew nearer, until he came to the edge of the moat, at the foot of the wall, outside the city. "Now you can say to me what you will," he said.

"I want you to tell me," said Gawainet, "why you are weeping and who it is you are mourning. And why have you cast blame on the knights of this country?"

And the peasant said to him, "If you were willing to strive to free him, I would tell you."

---

*   Sommer's text has a generalized third plural (181, l. 3).

"I promise you faithfully as a squire," said Gawainet, "that I will try as hard as I can."

When the countryman heard that Gawainet was so eager to know why he had come there, he said to him, "Dear sir, who are you?"

"My name is Gawainet," he answered, "and I am King Arthur's nephew."

"Then I will tell you," he said. "Indeed, I am full of sorrow because of a company of young men of high birth who are fighting against the Saxons at the borders of this land. They are fighting harder than such a small band has ever fought, for there are only three hundred of them against more than three thousand Saxons."

"Who are they," asked Gawainet, "and what are they looking for?"

"They say," said the peasant, "that their leader is named Sagremor. He is the grandson of the emperor of Constantinople, and he has come into this country to take his arms from King Arthur. Now I have told you all I know about him. But if I told you that you should go to rescue him, I would be wasting my words, for I know very well that you do not have the heart or the boldness to go. Nevertheless, if you did go, you could rescue him, and you could brag that you won booty worth a great deal."

When Gawainet heard the words of the peasant who was calling him a coward, he was very deeply shamed, so he shouted, "Now to arms, noble companions! Get on your horses and follow me, for I am going there!"

As soon as he had said this, he mounted his horse, followed by all his companions, and they rode out of the city. And when they were outside the city, there were at least four thousand of them. Gawainet rode out in front of them, and he came to the peasant and told him to get on a horse and lead him to where the youths were fighting; and he did what he was ordered, for he sought nothing else, and he rode out in front to where they were fighting.

As they drew near the battle, they found that the youths were fighting very hard, and they had slain more than three hundred Saxons, but there were so many of them that they could not break through. And Sagremor was fighting with greater prowess than any had ever seen, for he was holding an axe in both hands and was out in front of his companions on a warhorse that was wondrously strong [182] and swift, and when he went into the fray, he struck so hard that he became lost among the Saxons, as if he had fallen into a bottomless pit and his companions along with him. And they closed in about them on all sides, for they thought they could take them prisoner.

But they were so worthy and quick that none was so bold as to put his hand out to take them prisoner, for Sagremor, who had his axe, was in front of all his companions, and he was striving to break through the throng, so he landed such uncommonly hard blows left and right that he killed in one swing as many as came within his reach. All who had seen his blows fled to every side, and there was none so bold as to dare face up to him. So they began hurling sharpened swords at him, until Sagremor and his companions could hardly hold out any longer, and they were all close to being killed or taken prisoner, when Gawainet arrived with all his men.

When Gawainet came into the fray, the youths were in dire straits, and he and his men rushed in so hard that they brought down more than two thousand Saxons on their first attack. And Oriel was greatly distraught by this, for never had he seen, he said, so few men hold up so well. He took a stout, sharp lance, and rode into the heat of the fray, and he said that he would like to pit himself against a man whom he would mightily upset. And Gawainet and his companions fought their way in until they found the young men, who were shaken and weary, and he saw Sagremor, who was at the very front wielding a Danish axe with both hands, with which he struck uncommonly mighty blows. He was tall and big, one of the sturdiest youths anyone could ever hope to find, and as many as came within his reach, nothing could keep them from being split open or having an arm or a leg cut off. He could only do wonders all around. And when Gawainet saw him, he asked the peasant who he was, and he told him that it was Sagremor the Unruly, grandson of the emperor of Constantinople, "but spur your horse right now, and run help him, for he needs it sorely."

Then Gawainet and all his companions broke ranks and rode headlong into the Saxons so hard that they brought down two thousand or more, dead and wounded, and there was a wondrous fight and a great hue and cry.

But the young men were holding out at a very great cost, for on Gawainet's side there were only four thousand, along with the three hundred the young men had brought with them, while the Saxons were more than twenty thousand strong, not counting the ones spread up and down the countryside who were burning and plundering, who brought the number to at least forty thousand.

When Oriel saw that so few men were doing them such harm, he grew very bitter, and he said and swore that they would never get away. He picked up a lance and rode toward Agravain, who had struck down his nephew and killed him, which had greatly upset him, and he let his horse run and struck Agravain on his shield so hard that he drove his weapon beneath his armpit and cut through the two layers of his hauberk, so that the tip showed through on the other side; he hit him so hard that he bore him to the ground over his horse's backside.

When Gawainet saw his brother fall, he was afraid that he had been killed. He took up a sharp axe and came toward the Saxon who had brought his brother down, and he meant to strike him through the helmet. When Oriel saw the stroke coming, he grew wary and thrust his shield out to fend it off, but the blow was so strong that the shield split in two. It was a mighty blow! Oriel kicked his horse forward, and Gawainet's axe glanced down off his helmet so that it sliced off a [183] fourth of the helmet and cut through the mail on his back. And Gaheriet struck Solunant through the head so hard with a cudgel that he brought him down dead to the ground, and Guerrehet struck Malubre through the helmet and split him down to the teeth, and Galescalain hit Swiados so that he sent his head flying into the middle of the field.

When the Saxons saw Oriel lying on the ground, they were afraid that he had been killed, so they spurred their horses to where he was to rescue him, and they came from every side and gathered all around him. He was merely dazed from the blow he had been given so that he could not get to his feet or move any part of his body, but his face looked so ghastly and he was laid out in such an unsightly way that all who saw him thought he must be dead. And they mourned him so sorrowfully that all the fighting stopped.

Meanwhile, the young men had got Agravain up, on the spot where he had been struck down, and put him back on his horse. And the peasant who had brought Gawainet had taken the shape of an armed knight, and he came to Gawainet and his companions and said to them, "For God's sake, my lords, if you were to take my advice, you would get yourselves on the road back to Camelot while the Saxons have their minds on their mourning."

When Gawainet heard his speech, he understood that his advice was right and just. So he rode straight to Sagremor and told him that he and his companions were indeed welcome, and Sagremor returned his greeting like the highborn, courteous, and noble knight he was. Then Gawainet said to him, "Sir, if you like, it might well be time now for us to go and take with us our men who are left, for we have won a great deal as long as we get back safe and sound."

Then Gawainet asked Sagremor who he was, for he had spoken to him so courteously; yet he did not know him.

And he told him that his name was Sagremoret,* and he was the emperor of Constantinople's grandson. "And you, sir," he said, "who are you who have helped me when I needed it so much?"

"Sir," he said, "my name is Gawainet, and I am the nephew of King Arthur and son of King Lot of Orkney. My brothers and I are protecting my uncle's land until he comes back from Carmelide, and the only reason I have come here is to help you, for this very morning I was told that you and your companions were being attacked by the Saxons."

Just then the knight who had spoken to Gawainet came forward and shouted to him, "Ah, Gawainet, dear brother! What are you waiting for? Why don't you get on the road? Don't you see all those men riding hard toward you? They won't be willing to let you get away if you wait for them."

When Gawainet heard him giving him a lesson and trying to get back to safety, he looked around and saw the Saxons coming in such great numbers that the whole field was covered with them, and they were wearing good iron armor. They were riding headlong, hard and fast, and they were raising such an uproar that people could have heard them a league away. And when Gawainet saw them bearing down so wildly and in such numbers, he said to Sagremoret, "Sir, let us go, please! Look at all those Saxons riding this way, may God damn them!"

And Sagremor answered, "Sir, very willingly!"

They immediately took to the road straight to Camelot, and they rode together in such a tight formation that you could have thrown a glove onto their heads, and it would not have hit the ground before they had ridden a whole league.

The Saxons turned their thoughts back to their mourning, but after a while Oriel came to his senses; he looked around and saw them all about him [184] mourning very sorrowfully, and he asked them for a shield, lance, and helmet. He was most stouthearted, a good, bold knight, and he said that if he could meet the man who had given him such a hard blow that knocked him senseless, he would reward him handsomely!

---

*   Sommer's text has the diminutive form here (183, l. 24) and elsewhere (186, l. 27) that compares with Yvain/Yvonet and Gawain/Gawainet (see p. 110n; p.182n).

Then he got on a strong, swift charger and rode to where he thought he would find the Christians, but by then they were more than a league off. Then Oriel let out his battlecry and said that they were cursed if they got away, and the Saxons spurred their horses and raised their screams and shouts in such a loud uproar that people could have heard them for more than a league. And the dust rose from the horses' hooves so dark and thick that the air, which had been clean and clear, billowed with it. Then the Saxons came so near to them that they almost caught up with them.

When the knight who had advised the Christians to ride away saw that the Saxons had come so near, he began to urge the young men to get going and ride faster, and before they came to Camelot, they were at a very great speed. But the worthy Gawainet, Gaheriet, Guerrehet, Agravain, Galescalain, and Sagremoret were riding last, and the six of them were driving their men and equipment just like the old man who drove his cattle to market from behind; they allowed the Saxons to break their lances on them, and when they saw their companions overwhelmed with blows, they did all they could to allow them to break free, for they could withstand a great deal. And they fought so fiercely that no Saxon was bold enough to face up to them.

Then Oriel rode out before the others brandishing the great standard, and he had his sharp, well-honed sword; he saw the one who had struck him down and recognized him, and he swore to his god that he would avenge himself. Then he struck his horse with his spurs, and the young man saw him coming, but he did not look worried. When he got near enough to strike, Gawainet avoided the blow and let him go by, for Oriel could not hold his horse back. And Gawainet, who was very valiant and nimble, brought his horse around, ran upon him, and hit him right on top of the helmet, but it was with the flat of his sword, for he had been in such a hurry to strike that he could not take aim. Nevertheless, it was such a mighty blow that sparks flew into the sky, and it stunned Oriel and sent him sprawling to the ground.

Sagremor struck another one and sliced off his arm at the shoulder, and Galescalain struck Placides and sent his head flying. Agravain, Gaheriet, and Guerrehet had each taken a sharp, stout spear; the first struck Guinebal, the second Taurus, and the third Favel, and each one knocked his man dead to the ground; on the same pass, they brought down three others. Gawainet, Galescalain, and Sagremor had stopped near Oriel, and they were doing their best to take him prisoner, but the Saxons would not let them; they bunched together and ran upon the three companions. These three killed so many of them that their arms and legs and the heads and manes of their horses were dripping with blood and gore, and they fought so well that none was brave enough to face them.

But so many Saxons had swarmed in around them that they had to leave Oriel. Then they trampled him under the feet of their [185] horses until they had utterly crushed him; after trampling and beating him, they still had not killed him, so they rode off down the road after their companions, who they thought would already be near Camelot, for after the three had stayed behind, the others were not pursued, but rode away freely.

When the three companions saw that their army had made its way into the city, they were very happy and joyful, so they took to the road at a slow gait. The Saxons stayed where they were for the sake of their lord, whom they found badly beaten and broken, and they were woefully sorry for him. And when he came to his senses, he was so upset that the three had got away that he nearly went crazy; and he swore that if he could get his hands on one of them, he would have him skinned alive or ripped apart by horses. "Sir," said his men, "the one who brought you down twice today is a wicked coward."

"That is true," said Oriel, "but if 1 can get hold of him, no one can keep him from being maimed!"

Thus did Oriel threaten Gawainet, who rode along with his companions until they reached Camelot, where they stopped. When those who had ridden ahead did not see the three companions, they wondered what had become of them, and no one knew what to say. When Guerrehet, Agravain, and Gaheriet heard that their three young lords had got lost, they said they would not stop looking for them until they had found them. Then they set out at a fast gallop the same way they had come.

They had not gone far when they met the peasant, sitting on the warhorse Gawainet had given him; he was the very one who had told the news about Sagremor. And when he saw the three brothers, he asked them where they were going, and they said they were looking for their brother Gawainet, their cousin Galescalain, and the emperor's grandson, for they did not know what had become of them.

"Then you have not been looking hard enough," said the peasant. "Those worthies are in plain sight right where they are. Look, here they come! And they don't have you to thank for their lives, for you left them behind like cowards, and they stayed for your sake and for the sake of the others who are safe and sound. Then they did many a beautiful deed of knighthood and struck many a handsome blow, for which everyone should hold them in high esteem—and take you for what you are! And you showed clearly that you would forsake any companion of yours, as if he meant nothing to you, when you left your brother in a time of need; yet he would not forsake you even if he were risking his life! And so all worthy men who hear stories about you should rightly and justly blame you and forevermore mistrust you in times of need, and you can be sure that you will be most rudely taken to task for it."

With that, the peasant left, for he was unwilling to say anything more to them, and they went on their way, shamed and upset by the harsh words the peasant had spoken to them. And they had not ridden far when they met the three companions, who, by the look of their armor, seemed to have come from a most evil place. When they had met, rejoiced, and were gladdened, the companions asked the whereabouts of their other friends, and the three brothers told them that they had left them outside Camelot, where they were waiting for them. With that, the six young noblemen rode away together, rejoicing in their new companions, [186] who had come to help them, and happy that they had rescued them safe and sound.

They had not gone far before they met the peasant's horse, very frightened, which came running toward them, and they saw that his saddle was covered with blood. When the companions whom the peasant had upbraided saw him, they looked at one another and began to smile. Galescalain caught sight of this and asked them why they were smiling, but they were loath to speak. He entreated them a second time, and Gaheriet told them everything the countryman had said to them. When they heard this, they were amazed and wondered who he could be. Then Gawainet rode over to the horse, took hold of him, and saw that the saddle was covered with blood, and thought that the peasant had been killed. Then he asked Agravain if they had met with any Saxons after they left Camelot, and they all said that they had not seen anyone, man or woman, "except the peasant, who was sitting on that horse."

"You can see," said Gawainet, "that he is dead or very badly wounded. Let's go look for him and not stop until we have found him. If he is alive, we will take him to Camelot, for it would be a great shame for him to die comfortless out in the open."

With that, they got down from their horses and began looking for him up and down, in fields and woods, but they would have looked for a long time before they found him, for he had already come into their army in the likeness of a foot soldier, carrying the stump of a lance. And when the young men saw that they could not find him, they went back to Camelot, where they found their companions still waiting for them at the head of the bridge, and they were very gladdened to see them coming safe and sound. Then they all went into the city.

After the bridges were raised and the gates shut, they climbed high on the walls to see whether or not the Saxons were coming to storm the city, but the Saxons did not have the will, and they were not eager to tarry there. Then the young men took off their armor, went to their lodgings, and delighted in everything befitting a man. And they rejoiced in Sagremoret and merrily sang his praises when they knew who he was and he had told them why he had come from Constantinople to King Arthur to be given his arms, and they held him in high esteem. In the two days' time they rested there, no news came to them from anywhere, except that the Saxons had gone on to Northumberland and the duke of Cambenic's land, and they had been left in peace.

So the story now stops talking about the young men who were in the city of Camelot, and it begins speaking again about King Clarion of Northumberland and Duke Escant of Cambenic, who were still fighting Oriel's men very fiercely at the narrows of Margot Rock on the river Severn.

24. THE VICTORY OF KING CLARION AND DUKE ESCANT; BYLAS ATTACKS URIEN'S SONS.*

Here the story says that King Clarion's and Duke Escant's armies suffered great harm when Oriel came into the fray. He tried to hurt them as badly as he could, for he was quite distraught over the treatment Gawainet had given him in the meadows beneath Camelot, and he would very gladly wreak his vengeance, if he could, on those he had found. He called his men together and swore that not one would get away. Then the fighting grew hard [187] and awesome. Spears were hurled and arrows shot, and many were wounded and maimed, but never could the Saxons,

---

*   Corresponds to Sommer, 187-191.

try as they might, drive the Christians from the crossing at the narrows; and when they saw that they could not break through, they withdrew and dug in by the river Severn, saying that they would post guards near the crossing and keep them from getting out to forage in the countryside. "By God," said Oriel, "if we can keep them hemmed in, they won't hold out against us."

Then the Saxons' foragers spread throughout the countryside, set fire to everything and took a great deal of livestock and other plunder, for the land was very wealthy and the people thereabout had only just begun to lock up their livestock for safe keeping; many were taken unawares before they could put anything away, and the Saxons came down on them, took everything they had, killed or put to flight as many as they found, and set fire to the whole countryside, so that King Clarion and Duke Escant clearly saw the fire from where they were at the narrows.

And Duke Escant said to King Clarion, "Sir, I don't think we will win a great victory if we stay here, for the Saxons are laying waste all the land hereabouts. To give you faithful counsel, I would advise that we go out to them and fight them and hurt them as much as we can."

King Clarion answered, "And what if we lost this crossing? From here they would get through to the whole land and lay all of it waste!"

"I will tell you what we'll do," said the duke. "We will leave some of our men at the crossing to protect it. You and I will go over to Breckham Forest, and we will hide there in the woods until we see that the men we mean to fall upon have gone by, then we will fight with them. And the lord of Palerne, who knows the narrows very well, will take the booty we'll have won to a safe place and then come back to help us with the fighting, so we will do as much damage to them as we can."

"God's mercy!" said King Clarion. "Why do you say that we should go fight them? There are so many of them that we wouldn't even have enough men to give them communion!"

"Don't you see, then," said the duke, "that they are spread throughout the whole land? They are in disorder, and they lack supplies. Their greatest strength lies right here in front of us by the river, and they have come here only to guard the crossing. They all wander safely throughout the land and are not afraid to go anywhere."

"I did not say that for anything having to do with me," said King Clarion, "but only for the sake of the good men who are with us, for I would not want to lead them madly anywhere they might be harmed."

When those worthy men heard King Clarion's speech, they held him in great esteem, for they knew he had said that only for the sake of the common folk, for he would very much have liked to keep them safe. So they said to him, "Noble king, have no fears for that. But let's go take vengeance for our shame and our suffering, for we can see what they are doing to us before our very eyes! Furthermore, we would by rights be in far worse straits if what has befallen us happens to you, for, but for your crown and your sovereignty, we are what you have at stake in this."

When King Clarion heard what his men said, he began to weep with feeling beneath his helmet, and his men saw this and said to him, [188] "Ah, sir! do not weep, but let's go fight them! For it would be a great deal better for you to die honorably than to live bereft of what belongs to you."

"Let us go, then, in the name of God!" he said. "I am ready to go right now, but first we must choose the ones we want to leave here."

And they chose the lord of Norhaut, the lord of the Dolorous Tower, and Brun the Ruthless, and they had with them many fully armed men. These would protect the crossing, and the others left that night after midnight and rode toward Breckham Forest. And when they had come there, they found a very beautiful heath. It was a beautiful, lovely-smelling morning, such that no one would have wished to leave because of the sweetness of the birds' songs. They tarried there until after the hour of tierce. Then they saw cattle, swine, and sheep coming, and horses heavy-laden with salt meat, wheat, and every kind of food, and the herd lasted for a whole league and more.

After King Clarion and Duke Escant saw that the herd had gone by, they set out to storm the ones who were leading it away, and they and their men numbered at least five thousand; they all wore armor and were riding horses. And after the lord of Palerne saw that the livestock had gone by, he left where he had been waiting with seven thousand knights; they also fell upon the men leading the drove. King Clarion, Duke Escant, the lord of Palerne, and their companions* killed all of them, and not one got away. The lord of Palerne rounded up the wagons and livestock and took everything to Cambenic, which was two leagues away, and after he had put them in a safe place, he rode back with his companions.

When the Saxons saw that the drove had been snatched away from them, they were upset and angry, and they rode out to attack the enemy, and they struck their shields very hard with their lances. So a fierce and wondrous fight began, and there was a frightful slaughter of men and horses. The fray lasted from the hour of tierce until the hour of nones. Then the Saxons wavered and turned tail in flight toward their main army. There the Christians killed more than seven thousand, and they pursued the fleeing men, but they very nearly lost everything, for they had not the least inkling that they were riding into the huge mounted guard that Oriel had left at the crossing of Margot Rock.

The Saxons flew headlong into the cavalry. When Oriel saw them he asked them why they were running so hard, and they told him about the great harm the Christians had done them. When he heard that they were so near, he ordered the Saxons to ride after them, and no sooner had he uttered his command than they struck out very wildly after them. The Christians had withdrawn toward the woods, but they needed to ride hard and fast before they could get there. In a very short while the Saxons had caught up with them and attacked them with their lances, which they broke on them.

The Christians withstood the onslaught and then went on toward the woods, where they would be protected. They had drawn together so tightly that the Saxons could not break through them, and when they saw that they had got near the forest, they turned their horses around and attacked the Saxons with their sharp spears,

---

*   According to the letter of Sommer's text, the two sorties—the one led by King Clarion and Duke Escant, the other led by the lord of Palerne—are entirely separate actions; the lord of Palerne alone is credited with the attack in which the Saxons are killed and the drove liberated. Not only do the other two leaders figure in the plan for the attack, however, but King Clarion, Duke Escant, and their men are also included in the victorious contingent that later spends the night at Cambenic.

and they left many dead and mortally wounded. The fighting was ruthless and deadly, and there was a great slaughter on both sides. Our men would have lost more than they did if they had not been backed up against the Forest of Breckham, but the Saxons could not boast of [189] winning anything there, for more than ten thousand of them died there. Our men were also in dreadful trouble, for they had been forced to fall back into the forest when King Oriel came, and he bore down on them so hard that they would all have been killed or cut to bits if nightfall and the woods had not separated the two armies.

When King Oriel saw that the Christians had got away, and that they had done him so much damage, he was most angry and upset; nevertheless, he drew back a little way from the forest. And the Christians rode much of the night and did not want to take off their armor, and they came very late to Cambenic Castle and lay there for the night. The next day King Clarion left, and the lord of Cambenic promised to send him his share of the booty as soon as the Saxons had gone away. So they parted company, and no more harm came to them at that time.

The next morning, as soon as it was light, the Saxons got on their horses and went looking throughout the countryside to see where the Christians had gone. The messengers came straight back to Oriel and told him that the Christians had gone to the castle of Cambenic, and when he heard this, he was very sorry. He had his horns blown and his timbrels and drums beaten, and set out for Cambenic. The Saxons had sent out before them three thousand plunderers to set fires throughout the countryside, to burn and lay waste the whole land. In the vanguard, there were many wagons in the train and a great many cattle, with ten thousand Saxons to drive them. So they rode until they came to Cambenic, and the plundering men-at-arms were setting fire everywhere.

When Duke Escant saw the destruction of his land, he was filled with sorrow. He ordered his men to put on their armor; they did so straightway and got on their horses lined up in formation, and they were a good two thousand strong. They came upon the plundering men-at-arms who were setting fires, and they followed them into a dell, where they ruthlessly rode down on them. When they saw them coming, they turned in flight, but they had taken them unawares very close at hand, because their horses were strong and fresh; they put them to the slaughter and killed so many that of the three thousand there had been at first, not even forty got away with their lives.

These fled into the vanguard and screamed, "Filthy sons of whores! What are you waiting for? Can't you see we have been slaughtered? Shame on Oriel if he does not hang you like any other thieves, for you have brought shame to him! Have all these men maimed or killed!"

"Be still," said Nabin. "You are talking rashly. I would rather you were brought to this than that all of us had gone into such a place to be beaten so badly that we could not get away, try as we might. But all that aside, where are the ones who have done this to you?"

"By God," said the plunderers, "they've already gone." And they were telling the truth, for as soon as they had routed them, they went back to Cambenic without lingering.

And the Saxons went on by and left that place, and they never again did them harm. And they rode until they came to the city of Clarence, which Hargodabran had laid siege to, along with twenty other kings. And when Oriel came into the army, Hargodabran bade him welcome, and they all greeted him joyfully, for Oriel resupplied the army with foodstuffs he had brought in, and for this he was held in great esteem.

Meanwhile, as soon as Duke Escant saw that the Saxons had gone by, he sent King Clarion, by the lord of Palerne, his share of the booty [190] they had won from the Saxons before Breckham Forest.

But now the story falls silent about them and says no more about them, but begins speaking again about Yvonet the Great and his brother Yvonet the Bastard, the two sons of King Urien who had left Sorhaut.

Now the story says that when the two brothers had left Sorhaut, they rode through woods and across open lands until they came to Arundel. And they heard it said that Soriondes, son of Maglahant,* was encamped in the meadows of Bredigan and was resting there with his army, for he was tired and weary from burning King Yder's lands. And the young men heard the news that they would have to go into the midst of the Saxons' host, but it was not an easy thing to do, so they withdrew into Arundel.

The Saxons ran hard straight through the land of Bredigan, and came very near to Carduel. And Gawainet and his companions heard the news that the Saxons were encamped in the fields below Bredigan and were laying waste the land all about. Then Gawainet sent out messengers and summoned men and supplies from everywhere throughout the kingdom, and he gathered together thirty thousand men, for they all loved Gawainet's companionship. And they rode until they came to Carduel, where they stayed two whole days. And the youths were most distressed that they had not come in time, for otherwise they would have fought the Saxons who had gone through. After two days they left Carduel and rode until they came to Bredigan, where they were welcomed joyfully.

The Saxons had spread out throughout King Yder's land and burned and plundered it, and they came back along the river and through the woods and meadows below the stronghold of Arundel, and they numbered, so the story says, more than forty thousand, all on horseback, and there were more than ten thousand men-at-arms plundering and setting fire everywhere they went, for they meant to do as much harm to the land as they could. When King Yder saw the harm they were doing to him, he was greatly upset, so he mounted with as many men as he had, and there were a good fourteen thousand, all on horseback, and he began to pursue the hordes until he reached them going across a causeway. King Yder fought with them very hard, for he was a good knight, skilled and bold, and that day he did many a wondrous feat, for he had many other good knights with him who helped him; and they fought all day with the end of the army, where there were a good twenty thousand men. And the others, in the main body, rode all day until they came to within a half-league of Arundel, and they were at least forty thousand strong, while

---

*   Not to be confused with King Mahaglant of Ireland, whose nephew Soriondes is (175, ll. 20-21). Maglahant is reintroduced below (197, ll. 15-16), where, however, he does not seem to address Soriondes as a father might his son.

a good ten thousand made up the vanguard, for the Saxons had heard that a great many fighting men had come to the castle of Bredigan, and they were afraid of being taken unawares.

When those within the castle found out that the Saxons had gone into the land of King Yder of Cornwall, they did not think that any would be left between the castle of Arundel and Bredigan. And when the two sons of King Urien heard it said that the Saxons had all gone through, they did not believe they had anything to worry about, so they fully armed themselves and left the castle of Arundel, at least four hundred [191] of them by count, all on good horses. They rode until they came to the bridge that was four leagues away from Bredigan. After they had crossed over, Bylas took them unawares and stormed them with fourteen thousand armed men, and this was Soriondes's vanguard that was keeping watch at the crossing so that no one might come out of Bredigan to harm the rearguard when they went to plunder.

When the young men saw them coming, they were very frightened. Nevertheless, they made a stand at the head of the bridge and fought hard to defend themselves. Meanwhile, King Yder also attacked them, and he succeeded in putting twenty thousand of them to rout. None would have got away, but Soriondes came back around with his huge army, and if he had not happened to fall back upon King Yder, King Urien's sons and their companions would have held the day, and no Saxon would have got away from them.

But now the story stops talking about all of them, so we will tell you about Merlin, who had gone to Camelot in the likeness of a foot soldier when Sagremoret was rescued.

25. MERLIN AS MESSENGER BOY; KING YDER AND THE EXPLOITS OF ARTHUR'S NEPHEWS.*

Here the story says that when Merlin saw that Gawainet and his companions had gone to Bredigan, he was very glad, for he was well aware that the two brothers Yvonet the Bastard† and Yvonet the Great had left the castle of Arundel, and he knew that they were in grave danger of being killed or taken prisoner. Then he took on the likeness of a young man who was running,‡ and he bore sealed letters in a shield painted with the arms of King Urien. He kept running until he got to

---

* Corresponds to Sommer, 191-195.

† Sommer's text does not have the epithet (191, l. 17).

‡ Here Sommer's text reads *garchon a pie courant* (191, l. 19). Previously, Merlin had appeared in the army near Camelot as a *garchon a piet* (186, l. 18), properly understood as a common foot soldier, all the more so since he was carrying a broken weapon. The reference just above to Merlin *en guise de garchon* (191, l. 13) seems to be meant to recall that earlier transformation. The same pejorative expression recurs here; yet the long description that follows is hardly that of an ordinary infantryman; however, the term *garchon* recurs later in the same context (192, l. 13). The following note marks an apparent truncation in Sommer's text where a second transformation may have occurred in an original.

Bredigan, and he was weary from the race. He had* a garland of flowers on his head and held a long staff in his hand. He wore low buckled shoes and black silk† hose and was dressed in a cotton robe,‡ black with gold threads and gold bindings that were on the hood and sleeves, too, and at his waist was a white belt worked with iron and brass. He was tall and swarthy and had no beard, and between his shoulders a felt hat was hanging from his neck. He went straight to the great hall and climbed the steps that went up to it. And when he had gone up, he asked for Gawainet, and they showed Gawainet to him. He went straight to him, fell to his knees, and greeted him on behalf of his cousin, the son of King Urien. Gawainet raised him up, and the youth gave him a letter and told him that his cousin Yvonet had sent it.

As soon as Gawainet heard him speak of his cousin, he sprang up and read the letter; it was not hard for him to do this, for he had learned to read when he was a child, so he found what the letter said: "I, Yvonet, son of King Urien, send greetings to Sir Gawainet, my cousin, and to my other friends. Next, I want you to know that I am gone from Sorhaut without my father's leave, but my brother Yvonet the Bastard and I did take leave of my mother, and we have made our own way. We have just left Arundel and come to the bridge over Lake Diana, where we have found ten thousand Saxons who are now fighting us above the bridge, and there are only three hundred of us. At the same time, King Yder is also fighting them, but he has only fourteen thousand men, while the Saxons on the road below Arundel are at least forty thousand strong. As soon as King Yder [192] leaves the fight, those Saxons will fall upon us, and they will take us, if God and you do not find a way to help us. If we are slaughtered or taken prisoner, the shame will be yours, though we will be the ones who are hurt; all the days of your life you will be called to task for it, for everyone who hears about it will say, 'Look, there goes Gawainet, who through his cravenness lost his cousin, although it was in his power to rescue him!' For God's sake, turn your mind to mercy, nobility, and courtesy!"

When Gawainet had grasped what the letter said, he shouted in a loud voice, "My lords! Now to arms faster than ever before! Never will he be praised who is not worthy!"

When the squires heard Gawainet, they ran to get their armor, happy and gladdened, for they wanted very dearly to be in a place where they could strike a mighty blow, for which they would be praised, in order to win higher esteem. As soon as they had their armor on and were on their horses, they rode out of the town; they were led by the same youth who had brought the letter, and they were a good twenty thousand strong. They split their men into six companies. Agravain led the first, and he had three thousand men; Guerrehet led the second, and he too had three thousand men; Gaheriet led the third, and he also had three thousand men well fitted out, and they rode after the others at a slow gait, all drawn tightly together—and each leader carried a banner around which his men would rally when they fought the

---

*   Sommer's text lacks the verb and reads *fu en cors escorcies .j. chapelet* (191, l. 21): "he was tired from the race a crown." The text seems to be truncated (see preceding note).

†   The word in Sommer's text is *sinbrun* (?) (191, l. 23).

‡   The word in Sommer's text, *fustane* (191, l. 23), names only the cloth from which the garment is made: a cotton fabric that could have metal threads.

Saxons. Sagremor led the fourth, and he too had three thousand men;[*] Galescalain, Gawainet's cousin,[†] led the fifth, and Gawainet strongly urged him to fight well and to go carefully, and there were also three thousand with him following after the others; and Gawainet himself led the sixth company, and he knew well how to put things in order. He carried a blue standard of fine silk, with a diagonal band bearing a silver lion, and he had five thousand men with him all wearing armor, and he rode after the others at a slow gait with his men tightly drawn together.

But now the story falls silent about the Saxons who were riding toward the Diana bridge and begins speaking again about King Yder, who was fighting very hard.

In this part the story says that King Yder fought the twenty thousand Saxons so hard that he put all of them to flight. There was a fearsome rout with dreadful bloodshed; men and horses fell to the ground dead or wounded. And when Soriondes saw fleeing Saxons, he asked them what was wrong with them, and they told him that King Yder had done them great harm in the rearguard, "for he has routed us all."

Then Soriondes turned back angry and upset, and he rode with his army until he caught up with his enemies on the road to the bridge. There they were still fighting the followers of Margalant, a most awesome and wicked Saxon who sorely hated the Christians; and he was feared so much that no one dared come a step closer to him or get onto the road, but they hurled well-honed spears that hailed down on him. Soriondes came up with his great army and put himself on the other side of the roadway; then they ran upon them as hard as their horses would go. There they waged a fearsome, deadly fight, and King Yder's men had a very hard time of it; they lost a great deal in this onslaught, but the Saxons paid dearly for each one of them. You do not [193] have to ask whether King Yder was sorry and upset. He cursed the hour and the day that he ever grew angry with King Arthur, "for through the sin we have on us because of that," he said, "'all these mishaps have befallen us. But things have gone on for so long that it is too late for us to repent."

So King Yder withdrew, for he had lost too much. And Soriondes went back to fetch his booty, which lay in abundance on the roadway; then the Saxons went on freely and made their way until they came to the Diana bridge. He put sixteen thousand men in his vanguard and twenty thousand in the main body to take his booty, and he was in the rearguard with fifteen thousand men. And they rode on until those in the vanguard saw the young men at the bridge fighting against ten thousand Saxons who had been guarding the crossing. And as soon as they had seen them, they did their utmost to ride as fast as they could, for they were very eager to take them.

And when the youths saw them coming, they were sorely frightened. But then Yvonet looked toward Bredigan and saw Agravain coming to bring him help, and he went to his companions and told them to take heart, for he had seen Christians riding their way. And his companions answered, "Sir, how can we take heart? Look

---

[*]   Sommer's text does not mention the fourth division, but skips from the third (192, ll. 17-19) to the fifth (ll. 19-21). Later Sagremor leads a company into battle following Gaheriet (195, l. 32).

[†]   Sommer's text has *son cousin* ("his cousin") (192, l. 20), which appropriately follows Gaheriet, but not the inserted reference to Sagremor; however, the subsequent elaboration suggests Gawain might more properly entreat him to fight well.

here! Saxons are coming at us front and back, and there is no way for us to get away without being killed or taken prisoner!"

"I'll tell you what we'll do," said Yvonet the Bastard. "We will all draw tightly together; we will look as if we wanted to take them on in a fight, but then we will spur our horses down along the river, and the Christians will still be coming. If we wait for them to come to us here, the Saxons will have killed us or taken us before help has got to us."

All the companions agreed to the trick that Yvonet the Bastard had set forth, so they squeezed together; but before they could line up in formation, the Saxons had come so near that you could have shot an arrow from one side to the other. The Christians spurred their horses and set out across the bridge straight through the ten thousand Saxons, and they brought down more than two hundred as they came. But when the Saxons thought they could hem them in, they veered to the side down along the river where they saw Agravain coming. And King Soriondes's vanguard flew after them because they were getting away; they were more than fifteen thousand strong, and they spurred across the bridge, then drew so tightly together that they came close to knocking one another to the ground or into the water. And the ten thousand who had been guarding the crossing rode after the youths until they caught up with them in a meadow between two rivers.

Such harm would have been done there, and such woe come to the kingdom of Logres, that things could never have been put aright, had not Agravain come riding hard; he had seen the pursuit begin as soon as they had got off the bridge. And Agravain led his men against them as fast as their horses would go, and they ran headlong into the midst of the Saxons so hard that the whole river and the woods all about resounded with the blows. After they had broken their lances, they drew their swords from their scabbards, and the fierce and deadly slaughter began. Never have so few men gained the upper hand so fast. They drew the Saxons to themselves, and at length they drove them back farther than an arrow shot. The youths sorely needed this, for Yvonet the Great and his brother Yvonet [194] had been brought to the ground most dreadfully. They were fighting hard on foot, and more than a hundred of their companions had also been struck down and were very gravely wounded.* But the two brothers were soon back on their horses, and they struck out at the Saxons most fiercely.

And the company of fifteen thousand Saxons came to help the ten thousand as soon as they had crossed the bridge, and they spread out down along the river and rushed into the fray. Our men could not have held out for long, and they would all have been killed, if Guerrehet had not come to rescue them with three thousand men in armor. And they ran into the fight so hard that they sent all the ranks reeling, for not a single one in Guerrehet's company failed to bring his man to the ground when they met. Then all the Saxons staggered back toward the bridge, and the Christians did not stop until they had driven them back into the king's vanguard, which was by the river at the head of the bridge.

---

*   This sentence is not in Sommer's text and is supplied from an extensive variant (194, n. 1).

And when Yvonet the Great and Yvonet the Bastard saw the Saxons falling back, each one said to the other, "Good Lord God! who can they be that have come to help us? I would very much like to know them."

A young nobleman was there whose name was Aces of Beaumont. He came to them and said to them, "Dear lords, did you come into this land to look at tournaments and skillful blows traded by knights? If you want to know who they are, ride over to them and fight so well that they ask you who you are! For it is by their valiant feats of arms that people know who the worthies are. Here, you are whiling away all your time in foolishness. But ride over there and help them put these heathens to flight, for whoever they are, they are worthy men (and I am amazed at where so many Saxons can have come from!). Now the best warriors will show who they are, and I entreat you to fight against your enemies who have so badly hurt your friends and your forebears. If we die in this effort, we cannot die more honorably than in raising up the love of Jesus Christ and upholding His religion."

When the young men heard Aces speaking as he did, they were greatly ashamed and said that no one would ever take them for cowards. And Aces spurred to the front and said, "Now the best warrior will show who he is!" And they broke ranks all together and rushed in headlong among the Saxons. They began to strike them down, and they fought so boldly that word of their praiseworthy deeds reached Agravain and Guerrehet, who were fighting very fiercely. And when these heard the news, they knew very well that those were King Urien's sons. And they drew to the side and did such wonders and caused such a slaughter that it was a wonder to behold, and they had to fight hard, for the fifteen thousand had come to help out the ten thousand.

Agravain asked [195] Aces who those youths were, and he told him that they were King Urien's sons, "who have come to this land to serve King Arthur so that he will make them knights, and here you see all their household."

"Which ones are they?" asked Agravain.

"Sir," said Aces, "there they are with those shields half white and half red. And who are you who want to know such things about them?"

"Indeed," said Agravain, "we are King Arthur's nephews, the sons of King Lot of Orkney and Loonois. My name is Agravain, and that other young man over there is my brother; his name is Guerrehet. God be praised that we have found each other safe and sound!"

Then they greeted each other with great gladness. But they had not been thus for long when they saw Gaheriet coming with three thousand companions; they then fell upon the Saxons, and the slaughter was so great that they brought down more than four thousand of them as they came in. They killed and wounded so many that* they held them at a standstill for a very long time, but at length the Saxons gained ground over them.

So the story falls silent for a while about them and will talk about Soriondes.

---

* The adjective phrase and conjunction are not in Sommer's text (195, l. 12).

26. ASCENDANCY OF THE YOUNG HEROES; GROWTH OF THE HEROIC CIRCLE.[*]

Now the story says that they fought at the head of the bridge for so long that the wagon train with the booty and supplies got there, and those who drove it were a good twenty thousand strong or more. And the chief leaders were Margalant and Pignoras. And when they reached the bridge, they said that they would not cross until they knew what the outcome of the battle would be, "for on this side we needn't worry that a great force of men will fall upon us, and if any come against us from the other side, we can make our stand at the head of the bridge and defend ourselves so well that they won't have anything of ours."

So they pitched their tents, set up their pavilions, and camped there. And Soriondes rode until he came to the bridge, and he asked them why they were encamped there, and they said that they were safer there than on the other side of the river, "for we don't know who is over there."

"Now take care," said Soriondes, "to be fully at the ready, so that you can help our men if need be."

And they said that they would.

And Gaheriet was fighting with nine thousand three hundred men against the Saxons, who numbered twenty thousand and more; both sides lost a great many, and the Saxons more than the Christians. But our men could not hold out for long, because the youths were very young and untried, so they had to fall back. And they were about to lose a great deal, when Sagremoret came spurring with three thousand armed men who were most eager to come into the battle. They rushed in so hard that they stopped the pursuit by their sheer strength. Then the fray grew more fearsome, and there was a great shattering of lances and a hard beating of swords against helmets and hauberks, and Sagremoret and his men fought so fiercely that many Saxons were struck down there.

But for all the great deeds Sagremoret and his [196] men did there, it could not last, for the Saxons had so invaded the roadway that his and the others' feats of arms availed them little. Then came Galescalain with three thousand fully armed men, and they rode upon the Saxons so hard that none stood before their lances. They shouted "Clarence!" very loudly—that was King Arthur's battlecry—and they met the Saxons[†] so fiercely that they made them all stagger backwards, and the shouting and the uproar rose loud above them. With their blows they drove them back without stopping to the Diana bridge, and there was such a great slaughter of men and horses that of the twenty thousand Saxons they had numbered, our men killed more than seven thousand before they could reach the bridge, and if help had not been so nearby, not one of them would have got away alive.

But Margalant and Pignoras came to rescue them with twenty thousand men in armor, and as soon as they had ridden across the bridge, they ran headlong into the fray, letting their reins loose, and struck down many as they came. There

---

[*]   Corresponds to Sommer, 195-202.

[†]   Sommer's text has *li sesne les encontrerent* (196, l. 3): "the Saxons met them."

they fought wondrously, and the Christians were indeed in dire straits, and they lost a great deal, for the Saxons still numbered thirty thousand or more and the Christians only fifteen thousand, all told. So they were forced to fall back as far as a crossbow could shoot, and Galescalain, Guerrehet, Gaheriet, Agravain, Sagremor, Yvonet the Great, his brother Yvonet the Bastard, Aces of Quimper-Corentin,* and their companions underwent great trials, and they performed great feats of prowess against the whole horde, but in the end they could not long hold out.

Then, behold Gawainet who came to help them with five thousand men in armor! Great was the fighting there when they rode hard into the fray, for as soon as Gawainet got there, he began to fight so well that he made all the Saxons fall back and yield ground. He struck down and slaughtered men and horses with blows from his lance and from his sword, then he brought out a very well-made axe and put his sword back into its scabbard, which hung from his saddle, grasped the axe with both hands, and began striking and wounding all who came within his reach, and no iron or wood or armor of any kind could save them. By himself he kept the battle going, for the Saxons were fleeing from him on every side, and none dared stand up to him, and he bore down upon them so hard that, by the time it was just after the hour of nones, his strength had doubled three times. It was not wise to stand up against them one by one, for they were too bloodthirsty, so he kept bearing so hard against them that in the end he threw them back across the Diana bridge, where they crowded so thickly against one another that more than a thousand fell into the water and could not get out, and so they drowned and went floating downstream.

When Soriondes saw the frightful harm they were doing him, he was so distraught that he almost went mad. He wanted very much to get across the bridge, if he could, to fight, but the crowds were so thick on the bridge and down the river that no one could get through. Even if the bridge had been open, it would not have been easy to go across, for he was very much afraid of Gawainet, Galescalain, [197] Sagremoret, Agravain, Guerrehet, Gaheriet, Yvonet the Great, Yvonet the Bastard, and their companions, who were standing against them on the other side and keeping them away, for none was so bold that he dared go across. They were slaughtering so many Saxons that great heaps of them built up, so that one could not get to the other.

The fighting lasted all that day until nightfall, when both sides withdrew. And Gawainet and his men went off to Bredigan, happy about the young men they had rescued when they were in trouble. They celebrated all that evening and enjoyed everything befitting a man. Afterwards they went to bed and rested, for they were tired, and they slept until daybreak.

And at nightfall, as soon as they had left the bridge where the fighting had been, Soriondes sent for the highest-ranking men in all his army to seek their advice as to what he could do. When he saw that the barons had gathered together, he asked them how he could go on, for he had found the Christians to be very bloodthirsty and wicked, and he was very much afraid of them, for they had done him dreadful harm. And then Maglahant rose to his feet, a great, wicked giant who had a very keen mind indeed, and he spoke loudly enough for everyone to hear him.

---

* Called Aces of Beaumont, 194, l. 14.

"King Soriondes," he said, "if you accepted my advice, the wagon train would set out right now, and it wouldn't stop until it had met our main army. Our knights should ride out first, and Pignoras should lead the vanguard with ten thousand men, and we should be in the rear with as many men as we can put together. And even if the Christians did pursue us, they could not prevent the wagons from getting through. This is the best advice I know how to give."

Then all who were there shouted that his advice was good. And Soriondes ordered all their equipment to be loaded into the wagons at once, and he had the vanguard cross the bridge with ten thousand Saxons or more. And when the train had crossed over, he himself followed it with thirty thousand Saxons riding at a slow gait in the rearguard. They rode day and night, and nothing bothered them, until they came to the valley of Vambieres, where the siege was very harsh. They were welcomed with great gladness; they had been eagerly awaited for their food, for the besiegers were in dire want. They had brought enough to supply the whole army again.

But the story stops talking about them here and starts speaking again about the youths who were in the city of Bredigan celebrating and resting.

Now the story says that the youths were happy and gladdened when King Urien's sons came, and they celebrated and feasted until they went to take their rest. And when it was light the next morning, Gawainet sent out a spy to find out how the Saxons were behaving whom they had left at the Diana bridge. When he got there, he found that they had left the night before, so he went back and told Gawainet what he had seen, and Gawainet was most unhappy that they had got away. But [198] since he could not do otherwise, he let it go, and they all rested there and waited for news to come to them from somewhere.

One day, before time to eat, the youths happened to be in pavilions by the river. And Gawainet came to Yvonet the Great and said to him, "Dear cousin, how did you find out that we were gathered here? Who advised you to send me a letter the other night?"

"What letter?" asked Yvonet. "Indeed, I have never sent you a letter in my life, nor did I have any news at all about you before God Our Lord sent you to me in the state you saw me in, for we would all have been killed or taken and held prisoner if you had not come as soon as you did."

"What, dear cousin?" said Gawainet "Are you indeed telling me that you never sent me a letter?"

"Sir," he answered, "I am telling you the truth, and not a word of it is a lie."

When Gawainet understood that Yvonet had never sent him a letter or any other message, he was struck with amazement, and all those who heard it wondered where the letter could have come from. Then they sent people out to find the boy who had brought the letter and see if he was still in the city, but they could not find him or anyone who knew anything about him, and they wondered what might have become of him.

So they stayed in the city for a full week, until news came to them, and it was said that the young men who were in the garrison at Arundel were having a very hard time of it, for the Saxons were fiercely storming the stronghold every day, and they knew that sooner or later they would be taken. And when Gawainet had heard the need that those in the stronghold of Arundel were in, he was most distraught.

Then he called his companions and told them that they would do well to go into the borderland of Scotland to the castle of Arundel to rescue the young men, who needed help, "and all the sooner we will hear news about my father King Lot and how he is faring."

And they said that they would do as he wished.

Then the young men busied themselves getting ready, and they set out on the road. There were ten thousand of them, without all the best-equipped men in the land, for they did not want to strip the countryside of men. So they rode through the most out-of-the-way places until they came within a half-league of Arundel. There they heard a great uproar, for Haram, the son of Bramangue, had invaded the land of Loonois and laid waste everything as he came in. He was attacking the stronghold of Arundel very fiercely, and he had burned down the whole town outside.

And then a troop of highborn young men happened to come nearby from the land of Estrangorre, and there could have been a good seven thousand of them; but they had taken no heed of King Haram, who had spent all day storming the stronghold of Arundel. But those within had defended themselves so well that they lost nothing but the town the Saxons had set fire to. Then the Saxons pulled back in disorder, and as they withdrew, they met the seven thousand squires, whom Kay of Estral and Kehedin the Fair* were leading together. And as soon as the Saxons saw them coming, they let out their yell and overran them from this way and that, for they recognized at once that they were Christians; and the Christians defended themselves so well that never have so few men done better. And when those within the castle of Arundel saw the fight begin in the meadows by the river, they recognized at once that they were Christians, and they watched them [199] for a long time. But there were so few of them that they barely stood out among the Saxons, though they fought very hard. They could not last for long, however, for they had too many men against them. And those who had been in the stronghold rode out, and there were still four hundred who were very worthy and bold, for they had taken pity on the youths because they were Christians.

And they ran headlong into the fray and rode so hard that they broke through the Saxons as far as the place where they were squeezed together so thickly that they could not go beyond. And when the Christians came together, they recognized one another or found out who the other was. Then the fighting grew stronger and became very bitter; many a blow was given and taken, which made the Saxons distraught and upset, and this showed plainly when they began to blow their horns and trumpets and beat their drums, which meant they needed help. So the Saxons began to come together from all sides, for they had spread out up and down the river Aran,† and those from Saxon Rock‡ were going toward the city of Clarence

---

*   Called Kehedin the Small, 178, l. 27.

†   Sommer's text has *riuiere darsone* (199, l. 12).

‡   Sommer's text has *cil du chastel misme qui estoient issu hors* (199, ll. 12-13): "those from the castle itself who had come out."; however, it cannot be a question either of the Christians from the stronghold who have just left to come to the aid of their friends, to be sure, nor of the Saxons who have left the siege and are already engaged in battle. The convoy is later mentioned as originating at the Rock, 200, l. 2.

with a great wagon train with supplies that had been sent to them from Saxony, and the ones who had brought them over were driving the train, and there were a great many of them, all fully armed. And the story says that they were more than forty thousand strong, not counting those who had spread out through the countryside to plunder; and these had so laid waste the land in four days' time that you would not have found a cottage or a house where a man could shelter himself or his horse, nor could you have found enough to eat to feed anyone one meal.

But now we will leave them and tell you about the young men in the meadow below Arundel who were in great distress and fearsome danger, for there were only seven score of them along with the four hundred who had come out of the castle of Arundel. They were all worthies, for out of the stronghold had ridden Yvonet of the White Hands, Yvonet of Lionel, Yvonet the Shining, and Gaswain of Estrangort, and they had stayed there to await King Arthur, for they were not willing to be dubbed knights by any but the hand of King Arthur. They were all men of high birth and very powerful, for they were the sons of kings, earls, and dukes, and they were close kinsmen of King Lot of Orkney and King Brandegorre, and they had all left their homelands as stealthily as they knew how. They had come in groups of twenty, and they had all stopped there as hirelings to win booty, for they had brought very little wealth from their homelands, and they had many times been quite successful in taking their winnings from the Saxons.

When the youths came into the battle, the uproar and the shouts grew stronger, for they were four hundred worthy, very bold young men who had ridden out of the stronghold, and when they came up to the seven score, Yvonet of the White Hands, who was the most eloquent, asked who they were. And Kay of Estral told them that they were squires who were going to ask King Arthur for their arms, and they were close kinsmen of the two kings of Estrangort. When the youths heard that they were squires, they told them that if they wanted to come with them, they would always be faithful to them, and they would all wait for King Arthur until he came: "then we will all go together to ask for our arms, for we have also come to be given our arms by him."

And they answered that they were very glad about that. [200]

While they were talking together, the wagon train from the Rock drew near; there were twenty thousand men out in front who were leading the train and twenty thousand in the rear. And as they came closer to Arundel, they saw the battle between the youths and the Saxons. When they found out that it was King Haram's vanguard, they rushed in at breakneck speed, surrounded the young men, and gave them a very tough fight. The young men struggled hard to turn back toward the stronghold, but the Saxons swarmed so thick that they could not break through.

It would not have taken long for them all to be killed or taken prisoner, and for the castle to have been taken along with them, when Gawainet and his companions got there with ten thousand men in armor, and as soon as they got to the fray, they ran in headlong. There the fighting was fierce, wondrous, and hard, and many a hauberk was cut through or broken apart, so that the fields were covered with the dead and wounded. There the Saxons suffered very great losses, about which they were sorely distraught, for they killed so many that they hurled them back toward the wagon train they had been leading.

And when Gawainet saw the youths, he asked them who they were. Yvonet of the White Hands told him that they were King Arthur's men, "and we had come out of the stronghold to rescue those young men," and he showed them the ones the Saxons had fallen upon.

"And who are you, dear friend, who ask about them and were so helpful to us in our need?"

Yvonet gave him his name and said that he had come there with his companions to help him out. And when Gawain heard that, he was happier than anyone could be, and praised God and thanked Him for the help that had come to them. Then they all spurred their horses together and called out King Arthur's battlecry; they overran the Saxons and wounded and slaughtered so many that the fields were strewn with them, for they tried to harm them as much as they could. There Gawainet did wondrous fighting, as did his three brothers, and Galescalain, Sagremor, and Yvonet the Great and his brother, and King Urien's two sons. They worked wonders, and over here, Dodinel the Wildman, Yvonet of the White Hands, Yvonet of Lionel, Gaswain of Estrangort, Kay of Estral, and Kehedin the Small fought very well too. These fourteen* were out in front of everyone, and they wreaked such havoc that no one dared stand up to them, and all the other companions fought so well that they put them all to rout, and they threw them back onto the twenty thousand who were driving the supplies in the wagon train.

Then an old man came riding a horse, unarmed, and he called Gawainet, who wanted to storm the Saxons again, and said to him, "Gawainet, Gawainet, if you will take my advice, you ought to turn about. Take your companions back to Arundel. Look at the Saxons riding here. You will not hold out for long, there are too many of them."

When Gawainet heard the worthy man's words, he looked at him. He looked so old and so feeble that Gawainet was amazed that he could keep himself on the horse. He saw that his beard was so long that it came down to the knot of his girdle, and it was all white. He had a garland of flowers on his head and wore a black robe. He grasped the saddlebow with his hand and said to Gawainet, "Dear friend, you would be wise to believe me, for your companions do not all have your strength and skill. You should love their welfare [201] and their lives as much as your own. You would commit a deadly sin if they were brought to ruin by your foolishness, for they can yet come into their full strength and do great good, and they will be of very great help to your uncle King Arthur in his need, when he has come back from Carmelide."

When the worthy old man had had his say, he took to the road for Loonois in Orkney as fast as his horse could carry him. And Gawainet stopped and called his companions around him and held them back, for he readily believed the advice the worthy had given him. So they left the pursuit and rode back toward Arundel at a slow gait. When they came to the stronghold, they went inside and climbed up to the top of the walls. They watched the Saxons gather in formation and ride toward Arundel, but they were going after King Haram, who had laid waste all of King Lot's land. They were a great horde, and nothing could hold them back. King

---

* Sommer's text has *xvij*. (200, l. 28).

Lot fought against them many times, and he lost many of his men. He was most distraught over this, and in the end he had to take his wife to the castle of Glocedon because it was strong.

When the king saw that the Saxons had laid waste his land and utterly ruined it, and had killed and wounded so many of his liegemen that he could no longer stand up to them, he was sorely distressed and worried. And he cursed the hour and the day he had run afoul of King Arthur, "for because of him," he said, "I have lost all my people and my children, and my city is so weakened that those within are doomed to be taken!"

For the walls had been broken down in many places, and King Haram was encamped all around, and King Lot did not have enough men with him to hold out for very long. King Haram meant to rest awhile before he attacked. He could have starved them out quite soon, but he did not wish to; instead, he waited for his men, who were burning and laying waste the land.

When King Lot saw himself in such a state, he sought advice from such counselors as he had. And this is what was decided: late that night, he would ride out, along with his wife and little son Mordred, who was not yet two years old, and take them to Glocedon, and bring along five hundred knights all in armor, while the others, still six thousand worthy, bold men, stayed behind; and they promised him faithfully that they would defend the city, for it would not be lost as long as they were alive.

That night, the king and his knights mounted their horses at midnight, along with his little son Mordred, whom King Arthur had begotten, just as the story has recounted it (a squire took him in a cradle which he carried in front of him); and the lady mounted a palfrey, very strong and easy-going. And they all rode out through a little gate hidden by the garden, took to the trail, and rode all night and the next day until after the hour of nones. Nothing had bothered them until then, but right at that time King Lot became very frightened because he met King Taurus with three thousand men. He was coming back from Arundel and was bringing plunder to King Haram.

As soon as he and his men had seen King Lot, they ran over to fight him, but the match was not even. There the fighting was hard and fierce, and King Lot and the five hundred knights who were with him fought very well. But skillful fighting did them little good, for they were put to flight and routed from their encampment, and King Lot's wife [202] was taken and held prisoner. And one of the knights flew toward Arundel as fast as his horse could carry him.

But now the story stops speaking about King Lot and goes back to Gawainet, who was happy and joyful in the stronghold of Arundel.

27. HELP FROM A MYSTERIOUS KNIGHT.*

Here the story says that the youths were very happy that night in Arundel when they had got to know one another. And as they were celebrating so heartily, a knight in well-made armor came riding a great dappled warhorse that was soaked in sweat. His shield was dented and full of holes, and his hauberk was broken through and the links had come undone in many places. He came galloping up before the castle, brandishing his lance, and when he got to the gate, he stopped and saw the youths high up on the walls having such a very good time together. When he caught sight of them, he began to shout: was there any squire there so bold as to follow him wherever he went and to swear that he would give heed to no man but him? And when Gawainet heard him, he asked him where he would take him.

"And you," asked the knight, "who are you who have spoken to me?"

"I am," he answered, "Gawainet, son of King Lot."

"Then I'll tell you," he said, "for the adventure has to do with you more than any of the others. In this forest there happens to be such an adventure! It is one of the most honored adventures in the whole world! And you will be better thought of if you can achieve it. But you don't have the heart; you aren't bold enough to dare go through with it. And you can know for a fact that if you don't go there, I will."

When Gawainet heard him call him a coward, he was very upset, and he said that even if he should die, he would go with him. And the knight, who knew Gawainet's heart and mind so well, turned to go, but Gawainet called him back and said to him, "Sir knight, wait for me! Look here, I'm all ready to go with you. But you ought to swear to me that you don't mean to lead me into any danger and that you'll do all you can to help me against all who might wish to hurt me."

When the knight heard this, he stopped and a sneer began to spread on his lips, and he said that nothing could keep him from swearing such an oath. And Gawainet asked for his armor and put it on forthwith, and the knight waited for him, but tried to hurry him.

And his companions came to Gawainet and asked him, "What is this? Where do you mean to go? Don't go with that knight unless we go too, for you don't know whether it's for good or ill."

And Gawainet answered that he was willing for them to go along, if it suited the knight. "We will ask him," said Galescalain.

Then Sagremor came straight to the knight and said to him, "Sir knight, there are men in there who would very gladly go with you, if you are willing, as long as you don't think you'll lose anything by their company. They entreat you to let them be your companions."

And he said that he would be glad for all to go who wanted to, "for the adventure is such that no one who undertakes it will fail."

When Sagremor heard this, he was very happy. So all who were there made much ado about putting on their armor. There were at least eight thousand, for they did not want to take more; but they were all the most noteworthy, and they had the best

---

*   Corresponds to Sommer, 202-206.

horses. And when they rode out of the castle, [203] Gawainet took the knight's oath that he had not come seeking him to do him any harm and that they had no one else to fear, and he swore it.

Then they left and rode all one day and the next night until daybreak. All at once they heard at the edge of a heath very loud shouting and a great uproar, and it seemed to them that a great many people were there. Then they saw a squire riding away at breakneck speed on a big, strong horse, and he was carrying in front of him a child in a cradle. Gawainet asked him why he was fleeing and where he had come from. He looked at them and saw that they were Christians, so he said that he served King Lot, whom the Saxons had routed at the edge of that heath by the woods as he was going to Glocedon. He was taking his wife with him, but they snatched her away from him and drove him from the field, "and I fled just as you see, and I won't stop until I have brought this child safely out of the Saxons' reach, for he is the youngest of the five sons King Lot had with his wife. For God's sake, my lords, don't go on, for you will find there such a great horde that you can't hold out!"

"I'll tell you what to do," said Gawainet. "Go hide in those woods until you see how we have fared in this battle. Afterwards, come away with us, and we will take you to a place where you and the little boy need not be afraid."

And the man agreed to do so, since Gawainet had asked him to.

With that, the squire went his way. And the knight begged Gawainet to hurry and follow him without tarrying. He went first, and Gawainet and his companions rode until they had gone through the forest. They saw that the pursuit of King Lot had already begun; he was flying toward Glocedon with as many people as were left after the battle. Elsewhere, Gawainet saw in the meadows a most comely lady; she would have been of very great beauty were it not for the great sadness that had overcome her. Her hair was undone and all unruly; indeed, two Saxons on horseback were holding her by the hair and dragging her behind them, and the long dress she had on kept making her stumble, so that she could not stand upright. And she wept and wailed and cried aloud, "Holy Mary, Our Lady, Mother of God, help me!"

Every time she called on Our Lady, Taurus slapped her full in the face with his hand gloved in iron. At length, he knocked her senseless to the ground, and when he saw her lying there, he picked her up and put her in front of him on his horse. But she fell to the ground again, and she howled and wailed like a woman under torture. She said that she would rather they had killed her; never, for as long as she lived, would she swear faith to Taurus, however strong he might be. When he saw that he could not hold sway over her, he took her by her locks and led her alongside his horse, beating her and dragging her along until the blood flowed down all over her. And he had beaten her and jerked her about so much that she could not help but howl, and she was so badly hurt that she could not keep herself on her feet.

When the knight saw the lady being so maltreated, he said to Gawainet, "Do you know this lady? If you ever loved her at any time, set your mind to avenging her."

And as soon as Gawainet had seen her, he recognized her at once, and he was so [204] filled with anguish that he nearly lost his mind. He did not think he could catch up with her in time, but he spurred his horse and took a stout and sturdy spear with a sharp tip. It was after midday, and the sun was high; the iron on the spear sparkled in the sunlight and shone very brightly indeed. And Gawainet shouted, "You son of a Saxon whore, you thieving heathen, let go of that lady! You will rue the beatings you have given her, and you can be sure that you'll never have paid so dearly for any foolishness you have done before!"

When Taurus saw him coming at him so fast, yelling at him so harshly and threatening him, he dropped the lady in the middle of the field, fitted himself out with armor, and took a stout and sturdy lance with a sharp, well-honed tip. He let his horse run toward Gawainet and rode upon him so hard that he was screaming like an eagle. When they came together, the shock was so great that their weapons flew into bits, but Gawainet's aim had been so good that he put his iron tip into Taurus's chest and right out the back, and he brought him to the ground so hard that he broke his neck clear through. Agravain, Guerrehet, and Gaheriet got off their horses: one cut off Taurus's head,* the second ran his body through with his sword, and the third sliced off both his arms, for what Gawainet had done to him was not yet enough for them, so they cut him into small bits.

Then Gawainet and his companions ran headlong into the Saxons and brought about such a slaughter that they killed more than ten thousand of them before they left them alone. Gawainet killed so many that he was befouled with blood.

When the Saxons saw the great havoc that had been wreaked against them, those who could get away took to their heels and fled through woods and across open land. And Gawainet rode back to where he had seen his mother lying. He got down from his horse, took her in his arms, and began to weep most tenderly; then he wailed and wrung his hands, and he was so deeply sorrowful that his companions gathered about him, and they felt so sorry for him that there was not one of them who did not weep hot tears for him. And when Gawainet's brothers got there, the wailing began all over again, more deeply felt than anyone could say or describe.

At length the lady heard the youths weeping and wailing all about her, and she opened her eyes and saw Gawainet, who was holding her in his arms, and she recognized him at once. She raised her hands to Heaven and thanked Our Lord for the help He had sent her. Then she began to speak as best she could and said, "Dear son Gawainet, do not weep, for I have no wounds I'll die of, though I am very badly hurt."

Then she asked him where his brothers were, and they came before her, wailing so sorrowfully that it was a great pity to see, and they said to her, "Lady, here we are."

And when she saw them, she thanked Our Lord. But after a while she said, "Alas, I have lost my son Mordred and my husband, your father, who tried so hard to rescue me today. After he had lost all his men, I saw him fighting five hundred Saxons, and he held out longer than it would take someone to walk half a league, but I am sorely afraid that he is wounded and will die, for I saw knives and javelins being thrown at him as thick as rain. He would not leave my side until I myself

---

* Sommer's text has the plural (204, l. 14), but the subsequent construction seems to demand this introduction.

entreated him, for the sake of the thing he loved most in the world, to get away, and he was yet as sorrowful as any man could be."

"Lady," said Gawainet, "I can tell you what has happened to my brother Mordred. You can be sure that he has not been hurt in any way, [205] for the squire who was carrying him has taken care of him like the keen and worthy man he is;* he is waiting for us in the forest over there. But we know nothing whatsoever about the king our father."

When the lady heard what he had said, she heaved a sigh from her heart, then she fainted in Gawainet's arms. He kissed her over and over again and wept bitterly. And when she came to her senses, she heaved a sigh, then the coloring came back into her face. Gawainet asked for water so that he could wash her face, which was filthy with blood, and they brought it to him in great plenty, so he washed her face as gently as he could. Afterwards, they made a litter tied to two palfreys and put on it a great deal of fresh grass, then they laid her there as gently as they could. After that, they gathered up their booty and took to the road for Arundel drawn up in tight formation. They had ridden but a little way when the squire came to meet them with the little boy. When Gawainet saw him, he was most glad indeed. They rode until they came to Arundel, where they rested for a whole week, until the lady had been restored to health. Then they left there and headed for Logres, King Arthur's chief city. They† had left two hundred men-at-arms at Arundel to safeguard the town and had taken the lady and her little son Mordred along with them. And the four brothers swore that King Lot would never have his wife back before he had made peace with King Arthur.

What the young men said made the lady very happy. And when they got to Logres, they were very warmly welcomed by one and all. Then Gawainet sent people everywhere to see if anyone knew the knight who had taken them to rescue their mother, but they found no one who could say anything about him. The news spread near and far, and Doon of Carduel, who was a most worthy and clever man, heard all about it, and he thought deeply about who that knight might be. At once he went straight to Gawainet and said to him, "Dear friend, did you ever find out who the man was who first brought you news about Sagremoret?" And he said he had not.

"And did you ever know," he said, "who brought to you in Bredigan the letter from your cousin Yvonet?"

"I never found out who he was," said Gawainet.

"Did you ever learn who the man was who told you about your mother?"

"No," said Gawainet.

Then Doon began to think about who it could have been, and he started to smile. And when Gawainet saw him, he wondered why he had asked him, and he begged him, in the name of his lord the king, to tell him why he had smiled and why he had asked him those things. And Doon said to him, "Gawainet, Gawainet, you have asked me repeatedly, I must tell you. But be careful to tell no one else what I am about to say to you."

* Sommer's text has the redundant *comme sages & sages* (205, l. 1): "like a wise and wise [man]." Sommer provides the Harley variant in n. 1, as translated: *comme saige et preux.*

† Sommer's text has the conjunction *mes que* (205, l. 15): "except that," "although," etc.

And Gawainet said that he would sooner have his tongue cut out.

"Now you can know," said Doon, "that the man who brought you the news is called Merlin, and he is the best seer* there ever was or ever will be." [206]

"What, Sir Doon?" said Gawainet. "Are you talking about that Merlin who was such a good friend of King Uther Pendragon? who was conceived in a woman by a devil?"

"He is the very one without a doubt," said Doon.

"By God's mercy," said Gawainet, "how can it be that I have seen him look so many ways? For I have seen him in three likenesses!"

"You can be sure," answered Doon, "that however you may have seen him, it is he. For he knows so much about the arts that he can change into whatever likenesses he wants."

Then Gawainet crossed himself in great wonder, and he said that he would very much like to be his friend, if he could. "For now I am sure," he said, "that he indeed loves us, since he is willingly drawn into our doings."

"You can be sure," said Doon, "that if he wishes it, you will be friends, for we can say or do nothing that he doesn't know about."

So they stayed in Logres, happy that Our Lord had brought them together, and they kept such a close watch over the countryside round about that the Saxons lost more than they won.

But now the story falls silent about them, and it will say no more about them at this time; rather, it begins to speak again about the knight who brought Gawainet to rescue his mother.

28. MERLIN WARNS LEONCE OF PALERNE, THEN MEETS VIVIANE AND TEACHES HER HIS MAGIC.[†]

In this part the story says that after Gawainet and his companions had taken on Taurus in battle, and Merlin saw that Gawainet had rescued his mother, Merlin left so fast that they did not know what had happened to him. He went into Northumberland, to Blaise his master, and he told him all the adventures that had happened in the kingdom of Logres, and Blaise wrote it all down; and thanks to his book, we still know it. And when he had stayed there as long as he wanted, he said that he wished to go off to the kingdom of Benoic, for the two kings might have trouble there, "King Ban and King Bors, who are in Carmelide, and it would be a deadly sin, for they are both very worthy men. For King Claudas of the Land Laid Waste[‡] has sworn faith to the king of Gaul and has given his land over to him. And King Claudas has provided for himself in other ways as well, for he has gone to Rome, and both he and the king of Gaul have sworn faith to the Emperor and

---

*   The word is not in Sommer's text (205, l. S9).

†   Corresponds to Sommer, 207-212.

‡   Sommer's text omits *terre* (206, ll. 24-25) "land."

become his vassals. The emperor Julius Caesar has sworn to send them help, for he wishes to seize the two kingdoms of Gaunes and Benoic. So they have got together and sent for men far and wide, and the Romans have already moved out in a great army. The leader is Pontius Anthony, a senator* of Rome who is very wealthy and powerful. For love of them, Frollo, emperor of Germany, is coming back there. He is a man of very high standing, powerful in lands, holdings, and friends, and he is Pontius Anthony's first cousin. He is leading twenty thousand men under his banner. And the people of the kingdom of Benoic know nothing about this. They would be utterly destroyed before they knew it, and it would be a very bad thing if they did not find out, for great harm would come from it."

When Blaise heard him, he began to weep, and he told him for God's sake to keep Christendom from shame and destruction. And Merlin said that as long as he lived he would put his whole mind to it as best he could. "But this is the country," said Merlin, "that I should hate the most, for the wolf† has already come into the land who is to bind the lion with rings that are not of iron or wood or silver or gold or lead, [207] and the lion will be bound so tightly that he cannot move."

"For the love of God," said Blaise, "what are you saying? Is not a lion stronger than a wolf and more to be feared?"

"You speak the truth," answered Merlin.

"Now tell me, then," said Blaise, "how can a wolf overpower a lion?"

"You will learn no more right now," answered Merlin, "but I'll tell you this much: this prophecy befalls me, and I know very well that I cannot keep myself from it."

Blaise crossed himself because of the wonder he felt, and he started to say to Merlin,‡ "Now tell me this much: if you go to Gaul, what will become of this land, which the Saxons are so bent on laying waste?"

"Don't worry about that," answered Merlin. "King Arthur will not yet have come to the head of his nobles before the Saxons are soundly beaten, and you can be sure that very soon they will be driven out. I would not go away were it not for the love of the wondrous leopard that will come out of the kingdom of Benoic so great, so strong, and so fearsome that he will overcome all the beasts in his land—and out of Great Britain will come a great lion to whom all the other beasts will bow down and at whose glance the heavens will open. But it would be a sin for me to avoid what Our Lord has given me such wisdom and such insight for—to help in fulfilling the adventures of the Holy Grail, which must be accomplished and brought to an end in the time of King Arthur. But don't bother asking me any more, for you will yet know how that can come to pass; you will see it yourself with your own eyes before you die, and that's the truth."

After Merlin had spoken, thus hiding his meaning, and Blaise had heard what he had to say, he thought long and hard about his words; anyway, he wrote them down just as Merlin had spoken them.

Then Merlin left and went to the kingdom of Benoic. He came straight to Leonce of Payerne, drew him aside, and told him enough about himself that he knew who

---

* *Conseilliers de romme* (206, ll. 30-31, cf. 208, l. 4).

† The word is omitted in Sommer's text, which implies "the one" (206, l. 40). The context suggests that a female wolf is intended (cf. 207, l. 3).

‡ According to Sommer's text, *merlins* is the subject (207, l. 7).

he was, for he had seen him before. Leonce was very glad, for he was a very worthy man, a cousin of King Ban and King Bors. And Merlin spoke to him in the likeness in which Leonce had seen him the other times with the three kings, but it was so stealthily that no one knew a word that was being said, and Leonce believed everything he told him.

After they had recognized each other, Leonce said to Merlin,* "I am greatly bothered by something I want to ask you about, but don't get upset."

"I know what you are thinking," Merlin answered, "and I don't mind at all. But say to me whatever you wish."

"Tell me yourself," said Leonce, "since you know it already."

And Merlin very gladly said to him, "All for your sake whom I love so much. You want to ask me why I left the three kings and why I have come here."

"Yes indeed," said Leonce, "you are speaking the truth! And I would truly like to know, if you will."

"Of course," said Merlin. "I'll be glad to tell you everything right now, for you can be sure that I have no reason to tarry here. Leonce, it is the truth, and prophecy says so, that the serpent will drive out of the old Wild Forest the leopard who once was so strong, so fierce, and so awesome that all the beasts round about bowed down to him and lowered their heads to the ground. You have a most evil neighbor, named Claudas of the Land Laid Waste, who has sworn faith to the king of Gaul and given his lands over to him, in return for the king's oath [208] to keep up his lands and uphold him in warfare. They have sworn an alliance together, and now they both hold their kingdoms from the Emperor of Rome. And Claudas himself has gone to Rome and arranged for Pontius Anthony, one of the senators of Rome, to lay waste this countryside. He is coming to this land with Frollo, his first cousin, a leader from Germany, who is very wealthy and powerful and outstanding in battle; and they mean to lay waste this countryside; but it will not be as they think. For I have come here to this land to tell you to call together, from far and wide, friends, kinsmen, and foot soldiers; send for as many as you can. Stock your castles and towns and bring together all the game you have and all the grain and put them where no one can get at them. Get ready so that when they overrun the land—and they will run over you very harshly— they will find nothing to take; and if they fall upon castles or towns, defend yourself so stoutly that you cannot be blamed. But as you love yourself and the honor of the two kings, hold yourself back from going out to do battle with them, or the loss will be great. You should know that you will have all the help you need on the Wednesday before St. John's Day, when there will be a battle before the castle of Trebe, between the Loire and the Arsonne, before daylight, two leagues from where the Romans, the Gauls, and the Germans will be encamped. You will withdraw to that side with as much armor as you can carry, and you will hide in the forest near Darnantes. Watch out where you go, and be careful to move so stealthily that none of your companions will know it, however much they may be your friends, but for Gratian and Farien: tell these two in private, for they are very worthy, noble men. And have the roadways so well watched by your

---

*   According to Sommer's text, it is Merlin who speaks to Leonce: *si li dist merlins* (207, ll. 29-30).

knights that no spy may take to them to go tell those on the other side anything about your doings, for you would soon come to harm."

And he said that, when it came time to leave, he would do that so well that Merlin would praise him for it.

"I don't know what else to tell you," said Merlin, "but I'm leaving, for I've much to do elsewhere."

"Where will you be going?" asked Leonce.

And Merlin said to him, "When I leave this country I will go to Carhaix in Carmelide, where the three kings are. And I'll tell them how the giants and the Saxons will be hiding outside the country, and the battle on the Thursday after Whitsunday will be so great and so wondrous that none such has ever been seen in the land of Carmelide."

"Sir," said Leonce, "greet my uncles and my cousin King Arthur on my behalf."

"I will do so very gladly," said Merlin. "Now set your mind on doing good, and I commend you to God."

And he answered, "God bless you and bring you salvation."*

And as soon as Merlin had left Leonce, he went straight to a maiden of very great beauty who lived in a very beautiful and rich castle that sat beneath a round mountain at the edge of the Forest of Briosque, which was most delightful, good for hunting, and full of all kinds of deer.

The maiden I am telling you about was the daughter of a vavasor of very high birth named Dyonas. When he was young,† quite often Diana, goddess of the wood, came to talk with him and spent many a day with him, for he was her godson. Once,‡ as she [209] left, she gave him a gift that proved to be of great worth to him. And she said to him, "Dyonas, I trust you. And may the God of the moon and stars grant that, after my death, when Vortigern of Great Britain begins to reign, your first girl-child be sought after by the wisest, most learned man on earth, that he may show her the greatest part of his learning, and that he may teach her everything she asks—all through the power of necromancy, so that he might be so much under her sway from the moment he sees her that he lacks the power to do anything against her will."

Thus Diana gave her gift to Dyonas, and as soon as she had given it, it was granted. And when Dyonas was grown up, he became a very good knight, handsome and full of all manly traits. He was large and strong and for a long time served a duke of Burgundy who gave him one of his nieces as his wife, a fair and well-bred maiden. Dyonas had loved the delights of wood and river in the time of his youth, and the duke of Burgundy owned a share of the Forest of Briosque, so that one half of it belonged to him outright and the other to King Ban. So when the duke wed his niece, he granted to Dyonas his share of the forest and a great deal of land he owned round about.

---

* In indirect discourse in Sommer's text: *& si li dist que diex le conduie et maint a saluete* (208, l. 36).

† Not in Sommer's text, but required for clarity; cf. *Et quant Dyonas fu grans*, "And when Dyonas was grown up" (209, ll. 8-9).

‡ Not in Sommer's text, but the switch from the iterative (*si vint maintes fois a lui parler* [208, l. 42]) to the definite (*si li douna .j. doun* [209, l. 1]) implies such an emphasis.

When Dyonas went to see it, he was so greatly pleased and taken with everything about it that he had one of his dwellings built there, which was quite beautiful and rich, beside a pond that was also quite rich and beautiful. And when it was built, he came to live there for the hunting and fishing in the woods and on the river that were nearby. He stayed there a long time and often went to the court of King Ban. He served him many times, as was his duty as a knight,* and he helped him in many a time of need against King Claudas, to whom he did great harm. At last King Ban and King Bors welcomed him with great love because they knew him to be a worthy man and a faithful and brave knight. King Ban granted his own part of the forest to him and his heirs forevermore, and he gave him lands and endowments in great plenty in exchange for the knightly faithfulness he found in him. And Dyonas was so likable that all who came around him treated him as a friend.

Thus Dyonas dwelt in that land for a very long time, and at last he fathered with his wife a daughter, who was most lovely. She was baptized Viviane, a name in Welsh that sounds in French as if she said, "I will do nothing"; and hardship befell Merlin, as the story will tell later. That maiden grew in body and mind until she reached the age of twelve.

When Merlin left Leonce of Payerne, he made his way until he came to the Forest of Briosque. He took on the shape of a most handsome youth and drew near a spring that fed a pond, very beautiful and very clear, with sand that shone so brightly that it seemed to be of fine silver. Viviane often came to this spring to play and enjoy herself, and she was there on the very day that Merlin came. And when Merlin saw her, he looked at her for a long time before he said a word. And he said to himself† that he would be most unwise to fall asleep in sin and lose his mind and his knowledge just to know the delights of a young lady, to shame her and to lose God. [210]

After Merlin had long been deep in thought, he went forward and greeted her nevertheless. And when she saw him, she answered, like the well-bred girl she was, "May the Lord who knows all thoughts bestow on you the will and the heart to treat me well, and may He bestow on me as well the worth and honor that are my due."‡

When Merlin heard the maiden speak, he sat down at the edge of the spring and asked her who she was. She told him that she had been born in that country, the daughter of a vavasor there, "a noble man," she said, "who lives in this manor. And who are you, fair, dear friend?" asked the maiden.

"Lady," he said, "I am a wandering apprentice, seeking my master; he used to teach me my trade, which is most praiseworthy."

"And what trade is that?" she asked.

"In truth, lady,"§ he said, "he has taught me so well that I could raise a castle right here and have a great many people take refuge inside and others fall upon it from

---

*   Sommer's text has *lui* (?) *disime de chevaliers* ("the knight's 'tithe'") (209, l. 21), which suggests service owed as to an overlord.
†   Not in Sommer's text (209, l. 39).
‡   In indirect discourse in Sommer's text (210, ll. 2-4).
§   The word here is *dame* ("married lady") (210, l. 10), not the usual (and expected) *damoisele* (cf. 210, l. 8). *Dame* occurs elsewhere in 9,12,17, etc.

without. And I could do something else just as well: I could walk across that pond without getting my feet wet. And I could make a river flow over there where no water has ever run before."

"Indeed," said the maiden, "this is a worthy trade! I would give a great deal to learn to do such fine tricks."

"To be sure, lady" he answered, "I know many others that are even better than these are and more delightful for entertaining highborn men. For no one could suggest any kind of trick that I couldn't do or continue doing as long as I like."

"In truth," said the young lady, "if you don't mind, I'd like to find out about your tricks, and I would swear to be your lady love and your friend forever, without any wrongdoing or baseness, for as long as I live."

"Indeed, lady," he said, "you seem to me so gentle and of such noble bearing that for your love I would show you a few of my tricks, on your oath that your love will be mine, for I ask you for nothing else."

She granted his wish without seeing or understanding his cunning. And Merlin went off and drew with a staff a ring in the middle of a heath; then he came back to the maiden and sat down again at the spring. But it was not long before the maiden looked and saw ladies, knights, maidens, and squires in great number coming out of the Forest of Briosque. They were holding hands and came singing and making merry as no one had ever seen, and tumblers, dancers, and musicians passed before the maiden and gathered all around the ring that Merlin had drawn. And after they had gone inside, there began such wonderful singing and dancing that no one could tell a fourth of the merriment there. And Merlin raised up a castle fair and strong, and beneath it an orchard with all the good smells in the world; the blossoms and fruit gave off such a sweet smell that it is wonderful to tell about. The maiden, who heard and saw all of this, was so astounded by the wonder she beheld and so happy looking at it that she was speechless; and she was so bewildered that she did not know what song they were singing unless they sang it again.* Truly, love begins in happiness and ends in grief! Their merrymaking went on thus from the ninth hour until vespers; people heard the noise far away, and it was [211] loud and clear and delightful to listen to.

There seemed to be a great many people, so all who were in Dyonas's manor came out, men and women in very great numbers, and they looked and saw what they thought was the beautiful orchard, the castle, the ladies, and the dancing outside that was so mirthful that they had never seen fairer merrymaking, and they looked in wonder at the castle and orchard they saw there, which were more beautiful than any they had ever seen. Moreover, they wondered where so many ladies and maidens, so finely arrayed in dresses and jewels, had come from. After the dancing had gone on for a long while, the ladies and maidens sat down on the cool green grass. The squires set up a target dummy† in the middle of the orchard, where the young knights began jousting, while elsewhere noble young men went jousting against the squires; they did not stop tilting until vespers.

---

* Sommer's text reads *fors que tant quil dient au refrait de lor chant* (210, l. 41): "except until they told [it] in the repetition of their song."

† *La quintaine* (211, l. 10), a dummy used for target practice with the lance.

Then Merlin went to the maiden, took her by the hand, and said to her, "Lady, what to you think of this?"

"Dear friend," answered the maiden, "you have done enough to make me yours!"

"Lady," he said, "keep the promise you have made me."

"Of course I will, gladly," she said, "but you haven't yet taught me anything."

"So I'll tell you about my tricks," said Merlin, "and you'll write it all down, for you know your letters well enough, and I will teach you more wonders than any woman has ever known."

"What?" said the maiden. "How do you know that I can read and write?"

"Lady," he answered, "I know it for a fact, for my master has taught me so well that I know everything that everyone does."

"In truth," said the maiden, "this is by far the fairest learning I've heard about, and the most useful anywhere, and I would know it most gladly. And things that are yet to come," the maiden went on, "do you know anything about that?"

"Yes, of course, my fair friend," he said, "a great deal."

"For God's sake," said the maiden, "what do you go on looking for? In truth, you would put up with a great deal if you got some pleasure out of it!"

While the maiden and Merlin were talking together, the ladies and maidens gathered together and went off dancing toward the wood, along with the knights and squires. And when they got to the edge, they rushed in so fast that they did not know what might become of them. Indeed, the castle and everything had all faded into nothing, but the orchard stayed some time afterwards because of the maiden, who sweetly entreated Merlin. And the orchard was called "The Haven for Joy and Happiness." And when Merlin and the maiden had been together for a long time, Merlin said to her, "Fair maiden, I am going away, for I have much to do elsewhere."

"What?" said the maiden. "Fair dear friend, won't you teach me anything about your tricks?"

"Lady," said Merlin, "now don't get into a hurry, for you will know everything soon enough, and you will need a great deal of time and a long stay in the same place. Meanwhile, you have not yet given me any pledge of your love."

"Sir," she said, "What pledge would you have me give you? Tell me and I will do it."

"I want you to swear," he said, "that your love will be mine, and you along with it, to do whatever I wish whenever I will."

And the maiden thought awhile and then said, "Sir, I will do this if, afterwards, you swear to teach me everything I ask you, so that I will know how to do it."

He [212] told her that that suited him. And the maiden pledged that she would keep her oath just as she had sworn, and he took her pledge. Then he taught her a trick that she worked many times afterwards, for* he taught her how to make a river appear wherever she wished, and it stayed there as long as she wanted, and many other tricks the words of which she wrote down on parchment just as he told them, and she knew how to bring about many things. And after he had stayed

---

*   Sommer's text has *ear* for *car* (212, l. 3).

until vespers, he commended her to God, and she him. But first, the maiden asked him when he would come back, and he told her the eve of St. John's Day. Then they parted company. Merlin went to Carmelide, where the three kings made him feel very welcome when they saw him. But here the story stops talking about him and goes back to the King of the Hundred Knights, who had sent his messenger to speak with the princes on the advice of King Tradelmant of North Wales.

29. ARTHUR BETROTHED TO GUENEVERE; BATTLE AGAINST RION.*

Now the story says that the messengers of the King of the Hundred Knights rode fast until they had given to all the kings the summons entrusted to them. The kings answered that they would talk together on Whitsunday at Lancaster,† where they would gather as secretly as they could, and there they would take counsel as to what they should do; and so they would inform one to another. Time and the seasons went by until Whitsuntide came, when the barons came together at Lancaster, each with only three companions. Everyone was most glad to see the others, and they told one another about their anger, their troubles, and the harm the Saxons had done them. They found out that King Aguisant had lost more than all the others, and King Lot mourned his wife and children whom he had lost, and said that he would rather die than live.

Then spoke the King of the Hundred Knights, on whose advice they were gathered together, and he said to them, "Dear lords, would we not all do better to go forth and gladly die for Our Lord, to avenge our deaths and those of our friends and kindred, than to go on living wretchedly and cravenly and in such grief as we are every day? For the Saxons are pressing us so hard that we cannot find food unless it is what they bring in from their own country and their own lands. And when we have bought it we have paid dearly for it, for we are losing a great deal, our kin and our friends, and every day we weaken and become fewer while our enemies only grow in numbers and strength. Thus they will strike us down and drive us little by little from our land, and we will do very little indeed to hurt them. But now let us go out and fight them all together, and let us do to them the worst harm we can, so that forevermore people will talk about it after our deaths!"

When the barons heard the king, they held him in high esteem and praised what he had said, for they knew that he spoke only out of the great prowess there was in him, and they talked about it among themselves and said that they heartily agreed to [213] what he had told them. Among themselves they then set a day for gathering together with as many men as they could muster: a week before the Feast of Mary Magdalene‡ in the meadows by Suret, a castle belonging to the duke of Cambenic

---

*   Corresponds to Sommer, 212-222.
†   In Sommer's text, *lincestre* (212, ll. 16, 19). Earlier, the King of the Hundred Knights summons the council at Lindesores in Broceliande (163, l. 21).
‡   July 22, so the assembly is set for the 15th.

which had bountiful goods and was very rich. With that they parted and went straight back to their lands. They called for and brought together all the men they could gather, friends and kinsmen close and distant, some convoked by entreaty and others by force, and they made their way until they came to the meadows by Suret. They set up their tents and pavilions between two branches of a very great river that sprang from the sea and flowed back into the sea, and the story calls it the Severn, beside a forest called Breckham, which is very bounteous and rich with every kind of game. There they awaited one another, working on their armor and getting it ready; so they had their hauberks reworked with mail, their helmets and swords cleaned, and their lances fitted with sharp tips. But the story falls silent about them and says no more about them right here; rather it goes back to talking about Merlin and how he left Viviane.

Here the story says that when Merlin had left the maiden who had granted him her love, he came in the evening to Carhaix in Carmelide, where the three kings were very glad when they saw him, for they had wished for him a great deal. And King Leodagan had bestirred himself until all his men had come, and they could hardly wait for the armies to gather and make their way to drive King Rion from where he was at the siege of Aneblayse. Then the three kings drew Merlin aside to talk, and they said to Merlin, "What shall we do, for the armies will move out very soon?"

"I will tell you what you will do," said Merlin. "Go tell King Leodagan to get his men ready for battle and to group them into echelons. Be on your way the day after Whitsunday, one echelon after the other. Be so wise as to have ten knights all on horseback always going before the main body, and they will scout the countryside as they go along. They should take all the spies from thereabouts, of whom there will be many throughout the countryside, in order to learn how the people are faring, and they should kill them straightway or take them prisoner, so that they might say nothing to the people of the country. Always ride at night through the most out-of-the-way places you know. And I myself will lead you to the front lines, for you and your companions, along with the knights of the Round Table, will be in one echelon with no other men."

After they had talked thus for a long time. King Arthur asked Merlin for news from his lands and how his men had fared since he had last heard.[*] He told[†] all the adventures that had happened in the kingdom of Logres after he had left it, how King Lot's sons had rescued their mother and how they had sworn that never would King Lot count them[‡] among his companions, and never would he be their friend, "until he has made peace with you."

When King Arthur heard these words, he was so happy that he smiled from joy, and he thanked him heartily for his service. Afterwards Merlin went straight to King Ban and King Bors, and he said to them, "Dear lords, how shall we do what

---

[*]   Sommer's text reads *& comment si homme lauoient puis fait* (213, l. 35): "and how him men had done since."

[†]   Not in Sommer's text (213, l. 35).

[‡]   Sommer's text bears the singular *ne laura* (213, l. 38).

we have to do?"* For you are faced with a growing threat from which you will have much grief and hardship." [214]

Then he told them everything that Claudas of the Land Laid Waste had done and how Frollo and Pontius Anthony were coming with an army they had called together to take the kings' lands and strip them bare. "I have since spoken," he went on, "with the earl of Payerne, your cousin, who sends you greetings by me, and I have told him what those who are heading toward the kings' lands have done."

When the two kings heard Merlin speak, they were so astounded and so bewildered that they did not know what to do or say. When King Arthur saw them so stricken, tears began to fall from his eyes and he said to Merlin, "Dear friend, take pity on them and their lands. Talk with them and tell them what you know they need to do. For I am convinced that if you fail them, they have lost everything, and I would never know happiness as long as I live."

"In truth," said Merlin, "they need not worry about being defeated or driven from their lands as long as I have my powers. But you may well know that hardship is growing every day for you and for them. For the great dragon, thus says the prophecy, will come to drive the great crowned lion out of Great Britain utterly, with help from twenty-nine serpents who are wonderfully big and strong, unless the great leopard, so big and strong, stops him in part by the love he has for the crowned serpent,† to whom all the beasts of Great Britain and the kingdom of Carmelide will bow down, and in part by his great fierceness and prowess. But the great leopard is not yet born by whom that great lion will be so upheld that the great dragon will not have the power to drive him out of his habitat."

When the three kings heard Merlin speaking this way, they were greatly astounded, for they had never heard him use such shadowy language, so they asked him what it meant. He told them that they would not know any more about it at that time, "But King Arthur should know now that the great undertaking rests on his shoulders." And so they dropped the subject.

Then King Ban asked Merlin what advice he would give him to save his land. And he answered that as soon as they had helped drive the invaders‡ out of the countryside, "you must set out with as many men as you can muster out of this kingdom. We will go past the great city of Logres and the castle of Bredigan, and we will take the great treasure that lies in the forest, where there are twelve of the best swords in the whole world. And King Arthur will knight his nephews who, to serve him, have left their fathers, their mothers, their kinsmen and their friends, and we will lead them into the kingdom of Benoic, for the men from there will make a wondrously great horde. And when the battle is over, and during our stay in the land, the great leopard will be fathered who will be so fierce and full of pride, and for fear of whom the Great Dragon from the Distant Isles will draw back from the Great Crowned Lion of Great Britain so that he cannot harm him, although he will have the strength to do so; but in the end the leopard will overcome him and make him kneel before the lion to beg his mercy."

---

*   Sommer's text has *quel le ferons nos* (213, ll. 41-42), "what will we do?" but the Harley manuscript reads *comment le ferons nous* (213, n. 2): "how will we do it?"
†   In the feminine: *la serpente coronee* (214, l. 16).
‡   Sommer's text has only *cels* (214, l. 26): "them."

"Sir," said King Ban, "do you know the outcome of the thing we have come here to do?"

"Have no fear," answered Merlin, "for before you leave, the whole kingdom will be in King Arthur's hands, God willing."

"Sir," said King Ban, "will you tell us anything about those murky words which, as you remind us, we cannot understand?"

"No," answered Merlin, "but King Arthur should know that all of this will happen in his [215] lifetime."

With that a messenger came in and asked the host where the men-at-arms were and whether* the meeting had ended, and he came straight in. He was very well-bred, worthy, a fine speaker, and a great knight; he was a cousin of King Leodagan, his name was Guiomar, and he was twenty-six years old. He was the one on whose behalf the knights of the Round Table went through such hardship for the harm Queen Guenevere did him because of the great love Morgan, King Arthur's sister, had for him; she loved him so much that Guenevere cast much blame on her, just as the story will tell you later. But now we will stop talking about that until another time, when the story takes us there, and we will tell you how Guiomar came into the room where the three kings and Merlin were.

Here the story says that Guiomar went straight to the three kings and greeted them on behalf of King Leodagan, and he said to them, "My lord asks that you come meet with him." And they answered that they would very willingly do so.

Then they called for their horses, mounted, and rode straight to court. And as soon as they had got there and climbed down the steps of the great hall, King Leodagan came forward to meet them and took their hands, so that they went into the hall hand in hand. They went into a room to take counsel together. Then King Leodagan spoke like the wise and learned man he was, and there were just the five of them.

And he said to them, "Dear lords, I hold you to be most worthy men and most faithful, and you should know that I love you with greater love than you think; indeed I should, for you have saved my lands, my honor, and my life. But I do not know who you are, and this bothers me; there is nothing in the world that I long so much to know; yet I'll know it only when you want me to and when the time is right. Now I would like to ask you what we will do. You know that King Rion has come into my lands and has besieged one of my best cities with the strength of twenty crowned kings, each one of whom has twenty thousand† men in his company. My men have gathered on the other side, but there are so few of them that they cannot take them on. So I ask you, for the sake of God, to advise me as to what we can do, for in everything I seek to work with you and your counsel."

Then Merlin spoke forcefully and said to the king, "Sir, don't be dismayed. For by the faith I owe you, before King Rion gets away from you, he would rather be in his own country utterly naked, even had he lost the best city he has! You are not yet in such dire need that you do not have forty thousand men-at-arms and more, and I'll tell you what to do. You will send ten of the best knights you have to scour

---

*   Sommer's text has *ou* (215, l. 2): "where."

†   Sommer's text has *.xx. hommes* (215, l. 26).

the countryside* so that there is no spy left or scout who is not laid hold of, brought before you, and put into prison; this way, those on the other side cannot find out what you are up to. And then you will divide your men into echelons, and you will make ten of them, no more, and put eight thousand men into each one. Monday morning we will march two leagues before daybreak, one echelon after the other, without disorder, so that we can be there on Wednesday, a little before light. And you may know for a fact that we'll find them all asleep, for their army has got a great deal of grain, meat, and other [216] goods, and they are drinking and eating so much each evening that they forget themselves and do not post guards around the army. But they have succeeded in raising up a defensive wall toward the flatlands with wagons and carts, so that little harm can be done to them on that side. And toward the woods, they have set up walls of sharpened stakes from trees they have cut down, so that no one could do them any harm from that side. So we must make our way very craftily, for I know a spot that they do not worry about, and that is where they will be found all asleep, and, if God wills, we can do with them what we want. And we will put them to rout so soundly that they will never have the heart to take this land or the strength to lay it waste."

When King Leodagan heard Merlin say this, he was deeply puzzled as to who he could be, and he looked at him so fixedly that his eyes never left him. And then he looked at his companions, who were so still that they said not a word, for they were watching the man who had spoken. After looking at them for a while, he heaved a great sigh, and he thought that they were men of even higher and nobler stock than he had believed. And then his heart was struck with such tenderness that his whole face was flooded with tears that welled up from his heart to his eyes, and his heart was so full of feeling that he could not utter a word. He fell down at their feet as though he were dead, and he cried out to them to have mercy and, for God's sake, to take pity on him and his land, "for I know for a fact," he said, "and my heart tells me, that I'll lose everything unless God and you stand behind me."

When King Arthur saw him down on his knees before him, he was moved to great pity, as were the other two kings, so they took him into their arms, lifted him up, and soothed him as best they could. Then all five of them went over to a couch and sat down together like the good and faithful companions they were.

Then Merlin began his speech and said to King Leodagan, "Sir, you would very gladly know who we are and our kindred."

And he said that there was nothing he would rather know.

"I will first tell you," said Merlin, "what we have come looking for. See here one of our young lords, a young man, and a very good knight, as you know. And you may know for a fact that he is a man of higher birth than you and higher in any other way, although you are crowned a king. But he does not have a wife betrothed to him, so we go about through the countryside seeking adventures until we find a highborn man who would give him his daughter as a wife."

"Oh, God have mercy!" said King Leodagan. "Why go on looking? I have the most beautiful daughter in this land, the most nobly behaved and the best taught anywhere! She could lack nothing in breeding or good lands. If it is to your liking,

---

*   Sommer's text has *la contre* (215, l. 35) for *la contree*.

and his, I would give her to you. Take her as your mate and wife. I have no other heirs to bequeath my lands to but her."

And Merlin said that he would not turn him down, God willing, and the four companions thanked him heartily.

Then the king himself went to find his daughter, and he had her dressed and adorned the most beautifully and the most richly he could, and he led her by the hand into the room where the four companions were waiting for her. A great crowd of knights [217] followed him in. All the knights of the Round Table were there, and the forty about whom the story has told you earlier, and other highborn men who had come to the army to help King Leodagan. And when the king and his daughter came into the hall, which was large and beautiful, the four companions came to meet him.

Then King Leodagan spoke so loudly that he was heard and understood by all, and he said, "Noble young lord, I do not know what name to call you by. Come forward and take my daughter as your betrothed, who is so lovely, wise, and courtly, and all the honor that she brings with her after my death, for I could not give her to one more worthy, as all the nobles here well know."

He stepped forward and gave Leodagan his thanks, and the king gave her to him with his right hand, and each pledged his assent to the other with very noble bearing. And the bishop of Carhaix, who had been sent for, blessed them with his right hand. Then the joy and merrymaking were as great as they could be.

Then Merlin came forward and spoke, and he said to the king, within hearing of all who were there, "Sir, wouldn't you very much like to know who we are and to whom you have given your daughter?"

And the king, who longed so much to know that he never thought he would find out very soon, answered that he would very much like to know.

"Now, may all who will hear it," said Merlin, "know that you have given your daughter to King Arthur of Britain, the son of Uther Pendragon, and you must swear faith to him, and all those of this kingdom who wish to do him honor must do so as well without delay. And then we will go all the more gladly and all the more confidently to fight the bearded king* who means to take and hold this land, but it will go otherwise than he thinks. And you should know that these two worthy men here are brothers, and both have been crowned king. One is named King Ban of Benoic and the other King Bors of Gaunes, and they were born of the highest stock anyone knows. And the other companions are sons of kings and queens or earls or castellans."

When King Leodagan and the other barons heard that he was King Arthur, they were happier than they ever had been. The companions of the Round Table were the first to come before him, and they swore faith to him, for they had long wished to do so, and afterwards came King Leodagan and then all his companions all together. Then the betrothal was celebrated, so grand that none had seen better, and more than anyone else, Guenevere was happy with her betrothed.

And that evening Merlin made himself known to the companions of the Round Table, but no others. When King Leodagan saw who he was, he said that God had

---

* The Harley manuscript has *le Roy Rion* (217, n. 1; cf. 1. 21): "King Rion."

granted him good fortune in this world to have given him the love and friendship of such a worthy man. "And above all else, dear Lord God," he said, "it does not bother me that you have made me your agent, since my daughter and my land are bound over to the worthiest man in the world."

Thus spoke King Leodagan, and they all went to sleep and rest. And in the morning the king sent ten knights to the places Merlin told him about where King Rion's men were to gather. They then made up their echelons, so that there were ten of them, just as Merlin had ordered. [218]

King Arthur, King Ban, and King Bors led the first echelon,* where the dragon banner† was, with‡ the forty-two companions, the knights of the Round Table, and enough others to bring the count to eight thousand. In the second echelon was Guiomar, nephew of King Leodagan, who knew well how to lead a company with eight thousand well-armed men. Elinadas, a young lord and nephew of the wise Lady of the Forest of No Return, led the third echelon; he had eight thousand men with him. Blias, lord of Bleodas, a wonderful castle, led the fourth echelon, and there were eight thousand armed men on horseback. Audolus, a knight of great renown, led the fifth echelon, and there were also eight thousand in it. Beleis the Blond, who was very wealthy and powerful, led the sixth echelon, and there were seven thousand men on good horses. Yder of the Land of the Northmen led the seventh echelon; in King Arthur's court he had the wonderful adventure of the five rings which he took from the finger of the dead knight who asked to be avenged, for no knight in King Arthur's court could pull them off,§ just as the story will tell you later. And I tell you truly that there were seven thousand men with him. Landreas, nephew of the seneschal of Carmelide, led the eighth echelon; he was a wondrously good, stout-hearted knight, and he had with him the seven thousand men he had brought there. Sir Pearmuzzle¶ led the ninth; he was a good knight, but his nose was no bigger than a cat's; he had seven thousand men, and he could trust them. King Leodagan and Cleodalis his seneschal led the tenth, which they knew how to put to good use; and there were a good ten thousand men, each as worthy and as stout-hearted as the other, and they would not fail him for loss of life or limb.

When the ten echelons had broken off each from the others, each one was lined up off by itself, and the leaders** talked about when they would move out. They agreed in the end that they would set out early in the night on the Monday after Whitsunday, so they rested all that day and the next. On Whitsunday King Leodagan held court

---

*   Sommer's text has *bataille* (218, l. 1; cf. 228, l. 8), which could mean "battle" or "battalion, muster." Elsewhere in this passage the word *esc(h)iele* ("echelon") is used (cf. 218, ll. 4,5, etc.).

†   Not in Sommer's text (218, l. 1).

‡   Not in Sommer's text (218, l. 3), which, unlike the parallel descriptions, makes no distinction between the leaders and the men constituting the echelon.

§   Sommer's text has *nel pot traire ne auoir* (218, l. 15): "could not pull it off or get possession of it."

¶   Sommer's text has *groing poire mele* (218, l. 19), and he notes a variant in the Harley manuscript, *groin poire molle* (218, n. 5). Both *groin* ("snout.") and *poire* ("pear") occur in Modern French as slang or familiar terms for face; *poire mele* (for *poire melee* ["*honeyed pear*"]?) and *poire molle* ("soft pear") may be varieties of pears (cf. *poire de mollart* and *molard* in Cotgrave). In any case, as the text continues by noting the abnormally small size of this knight's nose, the term "pear" may denote an unusually rounded or featureless face; the humor in the name is of course stressed by the opposite trait suggested by the term "snout."

**   Not in Sommer's text (218, l. 25).

for the sake of the barons who had gathered there. The three kings and Merlin sat all together at the head of the high table. In front of them sat the two Gueneveres, each of whom looked very much like the other, except that King Arthur's betrothed was a little taller and darker than the other Guenevere; she was better-spoken, for of all the ladies in the world, she was the best trained in eloquence and speech, and her hair grew much thicker, but in every other way they were so much alike that people could hardly tell one from the other, unless it was a lucky guess.

Next were seated the knights the king had brought along with the knights of the Round Table; he did this out of friendship and love, for Merlin and Guinebal the clerk wished it. And when they had eaten, they went to bed to rest, but they slept only a short while, for they had to get up early in the night and put on their armor. King Arthur's armor was brought in, and Guenevere was very deft at helping him put it on, for she knew very well how to go about it, and she herself girded on his sword at his side. And when the king was armed except [219] for his helmet, she herself brought his spurs and, kneeling, fastened them on his feet. And Merlin, who was watching this, began to smile, and he showed the two kings how she endeavored to serve the king. The two kings held her in high esteem, and in the end she had a rich reward, when she lost the king through her mishap because of the traitor Bretelai, just as the story will tell you later.

While Merlin was looking at the young lady serving her betrothed, he began to smile. He said to the king laughing, as he wanted to poke fun at him, "Sir, you have never been so fit a knight as you are now, but you need just one thing to make you a new knight again, and you will have a right to say that the daughter of a king and queen has made you a new knight!"

"Sir," said the king, "now tell me what is the thing I need, and I will have her do it, unless it is so unseemly that she would be ashamed to do it."

"In truth," the well-bred, well-taught young lady said to Merlin, "I could never find shame or dishonor in anything I might do for you, for I know that you are so worthy and so courtly that, for the best castle you might have, you would not ask me to do anything that might turn out to be disgraceful or blameworthy and make people rebuke me in my lifetime or in yours."

"Lady," said Merlin, "you speak wisely, and you will never be ashamed because of anything I have said, nor will anyone cast blame on you that you might find shameful."

"And what is it, sir," said Arthur, "that I need? Tell me, if you will."

"It is, sir," answered Merlin, "a kiss, if the lady wishes it and would like it."

"Indeed," said the king, "I'll never let that keep me from becoming a new knight!"

"In God's name," said the maiden, "then, God willing, it will not be long before you are mine and I yours. Why should I make you beg me? It pleases me as much as you."

When the king heard what the maiden said to him, he ran to her and took her in his arms, and she put her arms around him too, and they embraced and kissed each other sweetly, holding each other tightly, for they were youthful and very much in love. And after they had kissed for some time, the horses were made ready and the men* mounted. The maiden gave her betrothed a very wonderful helmet and put it on his head; then they parted and each commended the other to God.

Then the echelons set out on the road one after the other, their banners folded and their lances lowered. They were riding at a slow gait, just as Merlin led them; he rode out ahead because he knew all the ways and byways. And the ten knights who had ridden out before had taken forty outlaws who were all King Rion's spies; they had been tied up and taken prisoner. And the way was so well guarded that no one in King Rion's army ever had any news about what they were doing.

Why should I go on telling about it? Merlin, who was leading the first echelon, made his way until, early Wednesday night, they came upon King Rion's army. The night was still and quiet, and the moon shone somewhat weakly, so the men in the army went to sleep very sure of themselves, because it was so still, and it had been quite hot during the day and they had eaten and drunk well.

Merlin went between the wood and the river and ordered that no one should ride into the army before hearing a horn blow. And just as the echelons came by one after the other, each one lined up off by itself far from the others; [220] and Merlin waited for them all to come and then linked them all up.

Then Merlin rode out with the banner and blew a horn so loudly that the whole forest resounded, and the horn's blast was heard very far away. Then Merlin shouted, "Holy Mary! Lady, entreat your dear Son to help us! Spur your horses, noble knights!" he went on. "Now we'll see who the knights are! It is the truth that you are all in this for life or death, and there is not a man alive here who will not have to defend his head!"

When they heard the horn blowing, they gave their horses free rein and struck them with their spurs, and they went flying in as fast as they could make their horses run. There you would have seen tents and pavilions overturned and falling to the ground. And Merlin raised such a great whirlwind that not a tent was left standing, but every one fell on the heads of the men lying inside. And they stormed into the army from every side and killed or maimed as many as they came to. There was a very great slaughter before the men in the army knew who was overrunning them, but at last they heard the dreadful screams and wailing when men were being killed or wounded. Then the highborn men ordered their squires to round up the army's horses, which they did; then the knights ran to their arms and hurried to put on their armor as fast as they could. As soon as they were armed, they gathered at King Rion's tent, and they blew horns and sounded trumpets very loudly. But the others had stormed in so many times, striking up and down, that more than twenty thousand of the enemy would never be able to go back to their homeland, and they drove the survivors to King Rion's tent, where they stood their ground. There they gave battle, for the men were very strong and powerful, and those who were not already armed had time to get their armor on. Then daylight came fair and bright, and the other echelons drew up and one and all were made ready. Then Merlin raised up his ensign again and rode into the giants so hard that he left them shaking. And the sun, which had risen, beat down on the helmets and made them shine, so that one league away people could have seen them sparkling like stars.

---

*   Not specified in Sommer's text, where the subject could still be Arthur and Guenevere (219, l. 27).

When King Rion saw the harm that they had done to him, he was very angry, and he almost went mad from the sorrow he felt. He was seated on a wonderfully strong and fast horse, and he held in his hand a heavy bludgeon that was so big that a peasant would have been loaded down with it, and he went about telling which men would ride before him and which after him.

Then he called Solinas, a most worthy and bold knight who was his nephew, and he said to him, "Solinas, come forward! You will lead the first echelon with a hundred thousand men of your choice, and we will avenge the shame and harm done to us."

And he said that he would do it in such a way that he should not be blamed for anything. Then Solinas, who was so worthy and sturdy, rode away. And as soon as Merlin saw him coming, he rode against him with the dragon in his hand, and he changed shape so that no one but the three kings could see who was bearing the dragon.

When Merlin saw* him drawing nearer, he said to King Arthur, "Arthur, now we'll see what you can do here today. See to it that the kiss that your lady gave you is dearly paid for, so that it will be talked about all the days of your life."

He answered that he would be quick to do so, and then said no more to him.

Then the two echelons [221] drew so close to one another that everyone could recognize everyone else. Then they all broke ranks, holding their lances straight, and when they came together, they struck one another so hard, with the sharp tips splitting through their shields, that men everywhere were wounded and borne to the ground. There King Arthur did a feat that many a one witnessed. For when he saw the giants getting close to his echelon,† he struck his horse with his spurs and met Jonap, a wondrously large and strong giant. When Jonap saw him coming, he feared him very little because he looked like a child to him. And they rode hard and fast toward each other. And King Jonap struck King Arthur so hard on his shield that his lance, which was stout, went through an arm's length. And King Arthur struck him so hard that he drove the sharp tip of his lance through his shield and hauberk and into his shoulder and out the other side. But he was a Saxon of great pride and of such great strength that he never showed that he had anything wrong with him. Rather, their horses and they themselves clashed so hard that they brought their horses down on top of themselves, and they lay there for a long time so stunned that they neither saw nor heard each other. Then knights from both sides rode to their rescue; there was a great shattering of lances and a great rain of blows on helmets and shields, and there the giants lost more than the Christians. Nevertheless, they struggled so hard on both sides that the two kings got back up, and the battle started over again mighty and fearsome.

There the knights of the Round Table and the forty-two companions did wonders. No company of men could bear up against them, so close did they stand together; in fact, they drove them back into the town that was their stronghold,‡ and Solinas's household was so utterly frightened that they thought only of fleeing. And those

---

* Sommer's text has *vint* ("came") for *vit* ("saw") (220, l. 39).

† Sommer's text has *si pres lesz vns des autres* (221, l. 6): "so close to each other."

‡ The Old French word is *estandart* (221, l. 22), a wooden fortification that serves as a rallying point. His *estandart* is so large, however, that it has streets (I. 24).

who were on their heels struck so hard in their midst that they made all the streets shake. Then the fighting began to be so fierce that deadlier has never been seen or heard of. There the companions of the Round Table and King Arthur's companions fought very well indeed.

But above all others stood out a young lord about whom the story must in truth speak, for he should not be skipped over, but it must indeed be brought to mind where he came from and what his name was. For as long as he was able to follow knighthood, he was one of the best knights there were in the time of King Uther Pendragon or in King Arthur's time. The stories taken from the histories[*] say that he was the first cousin of Perceval the Welshman, on his mother's side, about whom the story will speak later, for now is not the place. For he was the son of Havingues, sister of Joseph, and she was the wife of Bron, who had seventeen sons with whom the land of Britain shone. He was a close kinsman of Celidoine, son of Duke Nascien of Betica, who first saw the great wonder of the Grail, and he was a kinsman of King Pelles of Listenois and his brothers; his name was Nascien. This Nascien later had Lancelot of the Lake, son of King Ban of Benoic, in his service—the story will tell you their histories one after the other just as they happened from day to day. This Nascien about whom I am telling you was named after Duke Nascien, who was such a worthy man, and he lived such a good life that, after he had forsworn knighthood, he became a hermit. And Our Lord endowed him with such grace that he later became a priest who could sing Mass. [222] And he was a virgin and was chaste for as long as he lived. Then the Holy Ghost took this Nascien and brought him away to the Third Heaven, where he openly beheld the Father, the Son, and the Holy Ghost. Afterwards he was entrusted with the Holy Story, and he wrote it down at the behest of the Holy Master. And he wrote until he fit it to the book of Blaise, who did what he did for Merlin's sake. He later gave fruitful advice to King Arthur when he was in danger of losing his lands at the time when Galehaut, lord of the Distant Isles, was waging war against him with the strength of thirty kings, all of whom he had defeated. But now the story stops telling about these things and goes back to telling word for word what happened in the battle against King Rion.

30. VICTORY OF LEODAGAN AND ARTHUR OVER RION.[†]

The story says here that the battle was heated, and, on the Thursday after Whitsunday, the fighting between the army of King Rion of Ireland and the army of King Leodagan of Carmelide was rough. The knights of the Round Table performed great feats of arms, but above all the others Nascien and Adragain the Dark shone.

[*]   The text has *li conte des estoires* (221, ll. 31-32); *conte* ("account," "story") is the term used to describe the Merlin text; explicitly, here, the (Latin?) *estoires* ("histories") are texts from which *contes* are made. See also 230, l. 33 (below, p.248n.).
[†]   Corresponds to Sommer, 222-236.

They did wonders, and they tore their swordbelts apart from the strain,* and King Arthur was there with them. These three fought so hard that they left all their companions behind; wherever they went King Arthur's ensign showed them the way. Their companions tried hard to follow the banner, but they fell so far behind, and the fighting was so thick, that they could not break their way through and they had to give up, like it or not. And the three companions tried as hard as they could to get to the stronghold where King Rion's banner, borne by four elephants, waved in the wind.

Meantime, King Ban and King Bors saw that they had lost King Arthur and that the giants had closed them out, so they spurred their horses, left their companions behind, and flew into the press with their swords drawn, and they killed and cut down as many as they reached, nor did they stop driving through before they came to Merlin, who was holding the dragon before King Arthur. And when the five companions came together, they had their standard-bearer who showed them the way, and the fighting began so fierce and so fearsome, and it was a wonder to behold. And King Rion happened to come to that side with his bludgeon in his hand, and he was the largest and brawniest man in the world, as far as anyone knew. As it happened, he met first King Bors, who was pursuing King Falsaron, holding his sword drawn. This was following a wonderful blow to the shield he had dealt him with his lance, so that he had nearly brought him down, for he had bent him over his saddlebow and would doubtless have unhorsed him if his lance had not broken; and when his lance broke, King Bors stood upright and fixed himself in his stirrups so fiercely that the iron bent. He wielded his naked sword and held his shield tight against his chest, and he rode hard after the giant had dealt him the wonderful blow. When the giant saw him coming, he turned in flight, for he did not dare stand against him. And King Bors rode after him burning to avenge the blow he had dealt him. But it was very unwise for him to do, for he had left his companions an arrow-shot behind him, and they† could not reach him. It was then that he happened to meet King Rion, who was wondrously riding fast with the strength of eighteen crowned kings, and he urged his men to do [223] their utmost. King Rion went straight out ahead of his army as far as a small stone can be thrown; he was gripping his great bludgeon, made of heavy copper, and was astride a strong, swift warhorse; and he met King Bors, who had been hard on the heels of King Falsaron and was putting so much pressure on him. He struck him such a hard blow on the helmet that he sent him crashing forward over his saddlebow. He wanted to carry through with the other blow to cut off his head, and when the horse he was riding had taken the bit in its teeth, it took him farther along on this pass than he wanted to go, but King Bors had already begun the stroke and could not hold it back, and it fell where he did not mean to strike, for it cut off the head of King Falsaron's horse even with the ears, and it stumbled to the ground in a heap. Then he rode right on top of him, and he would have liked very much to get down from his horse if he could have, but King Rion, who was riding an arrow-shot ahead of his men, shouted to him, "Sir knight, you have gone so far afield that it is too late for you to change your mind. For this

*   Implicit in Sommer's text (222, l. 14).
†   In Sommer's text the verb is in the singular (222, l. 41).

man belongs to me, and I have come to challenge you for him, and you will soon know whether there is any love between him and me."

Then he spurred his horse so hard that blood spurted out from both its flanks in great gushes, and he ran upon him so unbelievably fast that the whole field, which was strewn with tiny stones, resounded from it, and sparks flew so thickly from the rocks that the horses' shoes were being chipped away.

King Bors looked, and it seemed as if a devil were riding his way. He had got so close to him that he could not get away from him, and he saw such a great number of men coming behind him that the whole field was clothed with them, and he saw clearly that if he stood his ground against him, he would put himself in great danger of being killed. Nevertheless, he said, "Dear Lord God, if I leave here, I will never have honor in my lifetime, for I would always be rebuked and called a coward. I would much rather die with honor than live in shame. Now may the Lord God do with me as He will, for I will take a stand against him."

Then he made the sign of the True Cross and grasped his sword, which was of very great worth, and stood against the one who was riding toward him with his bludgeon* held ready. And when King Rion got to King Bors, he dealt him a blow that was so grievous and so remarkable that he very nearly killed him, but he took the blow on his shield, which flew into splinters, so hard did Rion hit it; and King Bors struck him a blow on his helmet, as he was going by, that was so hard that it sent him forward over his saddlebow.

When the giant saw that he had missed him, he grew deeply angry, and he turned around with his bludgeon raised high. And King Bors, who saw the great throng of men coming, thought to himself that he would be most unwise to take a stand against them, so he stood up again in his stirrups and flew back into the press. And he saw that King Aroans of Betinia was holding Hervi of Rivel down with his foot on his helmet, and that he and his men had beaten Hervi so badly that blood was pouring out of his mouth and nose. And he would have cut off his head a long time before had it not been for Adragain the Dark, who was shielding him against more than forty knights who were craving only to cut off his head (that would have been a great shame); and they were about to kill him when King Bors rode up. And when he saw Hervi in such dire straits, he was deeply grieved, so he spurred his horse [224] toward Aroans and hit him so hard on the helmet with his sword that he struck him from his horse to the ground so dazed that he could not hear or see. And when Hervi saw that he was thus freed, he took the king's horse and readily jumped on, and he let it run into the fray, which was growing ever rougher, for all of King Leodagan's echelons had thrown themselves against King Rion's stronghold.†

And King Rion‡ rode after King Bors until he caught up with him where he had brought down King Aroans, and as soon as he saw him he ran upon him with his

---

*   Sommer's text has here *hache* (223, l. 29): "battle-axe."

†   Sommer's text has *al estandart que ti rois rions conduisoit* (224, ll. 5-6): "against the *estandart* that King Rion was leading." The sense of the word *estandart* may have shifted from that of fortification (above, p243, n.; see also 222, ll. 20-21, where it is a place where a banner waves) to that of a group of men, in whose midst the standard is borne, whom the king leads (cf. also 227, l. 25).

‡   Sommer's text has *il* (224, l. 6): "he."

bludgeon* in his hand. He meant to strike him on the head, but when he saw the blow coming—and he did not have a shield—he spurred his horse, and King Rion missed him and hit the horse so hard between the back saddlebow and its rump that he broke its spine and brought the king and his horse to the ground all in a heap. When King Bors saw that his horse had fallen, he sprang back to his feet, for he was very strong and tough and brawny, and daring above all knights. And the press was so great all around him that he could hardly turn around, for so many men were following King Rion that no one could have told the number. And the ones rushed in so hard that they drove the others back into the middle of the field as far as an arrow could be shot. There King Bors was very badly wounded, for King Rion was doing all he could to kill him. And when Hervi of Rivel saw the worthy man in such straits, for he had seen him fall to his hands and knees four times and get back up, he spurred over to help him out. And he took a strong, straight lance which he had taken out of a giant's hands, and he struck King Rion right on the shield so hard that he broke through it and cut through his hauberk on the left side, but not as far as his flesh, nor by any blow that he dealt him did the king come to harm in any way, but he kept wielding the bludgeon with which he had killed many a Christian. He was bent on smashing Hervi on the head, but he threw up his shield against the blow, and it landed so hard that it knocked a fourth of the shield to the ground. The king was about to strike again, for he was a man of great strength, but Hervi had drawn his sword and meant to hit him right on the head. The king threw up his shield against the blow, but Hervi landed such a great blow that it split his shield down to the boss. And the king raised his bludgeon again and was bent on striking him on his helmet. And Hervi drew on his reins in order to fall back, for he was very much afraid of the blow, and the giant missed him, but struck his horse on the breast and broke its neck crosswise, and the horse stumbled to the ground and took the knight with him. When Adragain saw his companion down, no one had to ask whether he was sorrowful. He rode over gripping his sword, and he struck King Rion with it so hard on his helmet that he sent him spilling over his horse's neck, and if he had not grasped it, he would have fallen sprawling to the ground. And if Adragain had had time to strike again, he would have taken his vengeance without stopping.

When the giants saw King Rion in such danger, they grew very angry, and there was a most proud king who was King Rion's cousin; his name was Celinas, and he was quite saddened in his heart when he saw King Rion being so badly mishandled. He was holding a lance in his hand, and he struck his horse with his spurs and hit Adragain so hard between his shoulders that he bore him down sprawling to the ground, but Adragain sprang back to his feet right away. When the three companions saw that they were being dealt with so roughly, [225] they drew closer together and began defending themselves so hard that no one dared get near them to take them, but their foes threw spears and feathered halberds at them, and they wounded them in many places; but they were men of such great heart that they cared nothing for what the others did, but killed and brought down as many as they got to. But King Rion bore in on them so close that they would have been hemmed in there and taken prisoner, but Nascien came in holding a bloody spear in his hand.

---

*   Sommer's text has *hache* (224, ll. 7-8): "battle-axe".

When Nascien saw King Bors in such dire straits, along with the two companions he loved so much, and King Rion so eager to do them harm, he spurred his horse over to them so fast that he sent everyone he met sprawling to the ground, and he wielded his sword and struck King Rion so hard right on his hauberk, close to his right side, that he threw him to the ground head over heels and so dazed that he did not know where he was, and Nascien rode back and forth past him two or three times. When King Rion's men saw him they spurred to his rescue. Knights were fighting thickly crowded together, and there was a great clanging of swords. Nascien's horse was killed under him, and the four knights were hard-pressed.

Very soon there might have such woeful harm that it could never be undone, but Merlin, who knew all these things, called King Arthur, King Ban, and all the other companions of the Round Table, and said to them, "Now follow me, for King Bors is fighting along with three companions of the Round Table, and they are in very great danger. For King Rion is bearing down on them so hard that they could be killed at any moment."

When King Ban heard Merlin's speech, his heart trembled with fear, and he said to Merlin, "Oh, sir! Tell me where this is, for if my brother dies there I will never be happy for as long as I live."

"Follow me, then," said Merlin, "for we cannot be slow."

Then Merlin cast a most wonderful spell. He raised up a great dust storm with winds so strong that all the dust rained over the giants in such a way that they could hardly tell themselves one from the other, and the hue and cry rose so loud that you could not have heard God thundering. Then Merlin turned about, waving the dragon, which was breathing fire out of its mouth, so that the air glowed red, for never had it thrown so much fire. And the fire fell onto the giants' banners, which caught fire and burned brightly. All who saw this dreadful wonder were stricken with fright.

While Merlin worked to break up the press and get through, King Rion's companions rode up, and there was such a big crowd of them that no one could tell how many there were; but from the other side King Leodagan's echelons came back around, and they ran headlong into one another. There the fighting was wondrous and rough, and very many of the Christians would have come to a bad end, and they could not have held out for long had it not been for Merlin's knowledge, which is all that saved them. For every man King Leodagan had there were three belonging to King Rion; even so, the Christians were more worthy, better armed, and more orderly, and they fought and struck down as many as they found before them to fight against. [226]

The uproar was very loud, and the fighting was deadly before the city of Aneblayse,* for all on one side were doing their utmost to bring harm to those on the other. There the companions of the Round Table made great efforts to follow Merlin's banner wherever they saw it go, even though the crowd of men was so great that they could hardly get through. There King Ban did wonders all by himself, for he was deeply afraid for his brother. And wherever Merlin went, King Arthur,

---

*   Sommer's text reads *la cite de danebloise* (226, l. 1); cf. *la cite de daneblaise* (226, l. 32; 300, l. 16).

the forty companions, and the companions of the Round Table were always there also. There no body of men could hold them back before they found King Bors on his feet, and his companions were in such bad shape that their helmets were split open or cut into pieces or falling down over their eyes so that they were blinded, and their hauberks were broken and torn, but as yet none had been wounded so badly that it hurt them to bear their arms. And they wielded their swords with both hands and defended themselves wonderfully, for they had killed many men and horses, and the heaps were so high all about them that the giants could reach them only with their lances.* And King Rion did his very best to take them and hold them prisoner, for he thought, judging from their great skill at defending themselves, that they were highborn and powerful men. Then he thrust at them, so that they could well have been lost if help had not come to them.

When King Ban saw his brother in such a plight, he well understood that, unless he and the companions with him came in fast, he could not come out of it hale and hardy. Then he gave free rein to his horse and struck King Minap† through the head so hard that he split him down to the chest, and King Arthur hit a Saxon so that he sent his head flying right before King Rion; the other companions rushed in headlong among them so hard that each one bore his man to the ground dead. And when King Bors saw the help they were getting, the men who were with him put their feet together and jumped over the heaps of dead men and horses they had slaughtered. All of them took horses, put their helmets back on as fast as they could, and outfitted themselves with shields, and when they were ready, they struck out into the fray again with their swords drawn. There the fighting grew fiercer, and the echelons‡ were broken apart and split into pieces everywhere. The men on one side took after those on the other, hitting them, killing them, and cutting them down, and the fighting lasted all day until the hour of low vespers. Then the Christians pulled back toward the city of Aneblayse,§ and the weeping and wailing grew so loud that the people in the city climbed up to the battlements and saw that the Christians had had by far the worst of it.

Then Sadoine the Castellan saw his uncle in such a plight, for he and his men would have been driven from the battlefield had it not been for King Arthur and his companions, who numbered almost three hundred; these men were upholding the whole battle, for they always won wherever they went in the battle.

And when Sadoine saw the danger that had befallen his uncle and his companions, he shouted out, "Noble knights, now run quickly to arms! For this has to be done, I see it very well, for today we must lose everything or win everything back. So let us defend our lives and our birthright against the enemies of Jesus Christ. And those who will die defending holy Christendom will be safe and sound. We will never need greater honor than we must find [227] right now. Look over there at King Arthur, our rightful earthly lord, with that dragon! He is the best knight in the world, and in order to help us he has put himself in danger of being killed. And

---

* Sommer's text reads *com ne pot mais a aus auenir sen lanchant non* (226, ll. 14-15): "that no one could ever get to them except by using a lance [or throwing something]."

† Sommer, 226, l. 22; for Jonap (above)?

‡ Somraer's text has *bataille* (226, l. 30): "battalions."

§ Sommer's text has *la cite de daneblaise* (226, l. 32); see above, p. 248n.

when he puts himself at risk for our sakes, we should risk ourselves for him. We should feel great pity for him and his men, for they are suffering a great deal and have undergone much; we should be frightened that they have been driven back so. And we who are so many do nothing to help them! For there are more than ten thousand of us in here, and we see plainly that there are only three hundred of them who are holding out so strongly that they will not be driven back farther* or yield their ground, but all day long they have suffered and endured fighting and beating that have not let up. For God's sake, noble knights, let us strike out to help them, and you can be sure that if the Saxons are hit hard in the first onslaught,† then we can send them on their way. Whatever happens, it is better for us to die with honor than to be shamed and stripped of our lands through cowardice. Furthermore, we should be greatly cheered because we are defending our birthright and holy Christendom, which our Lord God has newly founded among us!"

Then the men in the castle readied themselves and mounted their horses and rode out of the city.

And when King Leodagan saw them, he shouted very loudly, "Now to them, highborn knights! Here comes the help that my nephew Sadoine brings us. In the name of God, spur your horses and uphold your honor and ours!"

"Sir," said Guiomar, "why do you preach to us when every one of us is ready to defend our lives? For we have gone so far that we will all die or we will win the victory, and each one of us is as good as a king in fighting for his life. But let us ride all together against our enemies,‡ and let them be struck so hard that they will be utterly overwhelmed!"

Then they drew tightly together and rode toward the stronghold§ where King Arthur, King Ban, King Bors, and the companions of the Round Table were doing such wonders that never had greater been seen. And when King Leodagan and his men drew nearer the stronghold, they ran into the crowd so hard that they were all rocked and shaken. There the fighting was so wondrous and so deadly that the giants lost many of their men, and King Leodagan's men were so greatly heartened that they made the giants yield their ground and drove them back to where their army was encamped, and there they gave them a very rough and most wondrous fight.

Merlin had withdrawn from the fray, and he gathered the companions of the Round Table about him and made them saddle and harness their horses anew and give out shields and helmets to those who needed new ones, and he put back together as many as he could of those who had been in the echelon, and there were more than six thousand of them; each one took a strong, sturdy lance with a sharp tip. And after they had taken the fresh air, and had been there for a while, they saw their friends being dreadfully driven back, for the Saxons had recovered as soon as the companions of the Round Table had withdrawn from the fighting.

---

*   Not in Sommer's text (227, ll. 8-9), but implicit in that Sadoine has just pointed out (ll. 5-6) that they have been pushed back.

†   Sommer's text has *sil sont bien encontre* (227, l. 11): "if they are well met." The idiom recurs 227, ll. 41-42.

‡   Sommer's text has *a els* (227, l. 23): "to/against them."

§   Sommer's text has *lestandart* (227, l. 25; also l. 28); see above, p. 246, n.

And when Merlin saw the Saxons rallying, he shouted, "Noble knights! Now at them! We'll see who can fight the best! For if you hit the enemy* hard, we will send them on their way!"

Then he said to King Arthur that he must have forgotten the kiss his ladylove had given him, for he had done poorly in the first [228] fighting. And when Arthur heard this, he blushed all over from shame, and he hung his helmeted head and said not a word; but he stood so hard on his stirrups that the iron bent. And King Ban began to smile within his helmet and pointed him out to King Bors, his brother; then all the knights of the Round Table looked at him, and they found him very worthy and held him in high esteem because they saw his look of noble pride. Indeed they said that if he lived long, never would there be such a king, and with great feeling they entreated God to keep him from danger.

When Merlin drew near the echelon,† he shouted to the men, "Now at them!" And he drove so hard into their midst with the dragon banner that he struck to the ground everyone he ran after, so that nothing was left standing before him. And King Arthur, who held a wonderful lance,‡ struck King Clariel so hard that it went right through his side, and he knocked him from his horse to the ground so hard that he had no need of a doctor. Then he caught sight of King Rion, whose clothing and armor§ were decorated with sheaves of grain and crowns, and he drew his sword and rode toward him as fast as his horse could go, and he drove straight through the press with his good horse, so that nothing held him back, but he knocked to the ground as many as he came to. And when he got to King Rion, he struck him hard with his sword, which went through his shield and hauberk, and if it had not been for the snake skin shirt he was wearing beneath his hauberk, he would have killed him; the snake skin was so hard that he could not break it or cut through it, but he still kept hitting him so forcefully that he sent him spilling head over heels to the ground.

When the giants and Saxons saw their lord fall, every one of them began to quake, because they were afraid that he would be killed, so they ran King Arthur down and fell upon him and struck him from all sides, so that they bore him and his horse to the ground in a heap. When Merlin saw King Arthur fall, he had the six thousand fly to his rescue. There they fought fiercely, the ones striving to rescue King Arthur; and the others, to avenge King Rion, whom he had struck down so dreadfully. King Ban began working wonders, for with main force he got King Arthur back up in the midst of his enemies, and he slaughtered so many giants that none dared take a stand against him. Meanwhile, the six thousand fought as well as they did thanks to the endeavors of those of the Round Table, for there were few of them who did not bring their adversaries down to the ground dead, and they made them yield their ground despite themselves. There King Rion was much kicked about and trodden under foot before he could get back on horseback, but when he

---

* Sommer's text has *se vous bien les encontres* (227, ll. 41-42): "if you meet them well"; for another version of the idiom (227, l. 11), see above, p. 250, n..

† Sommer's text has *bataille* (228, l. 8): "battle" or "battalion, muster."

‡ The word here is *espiel* (228, l. 11).

§ Sommer's text has *le roy rion qui estoit couers de couertures* (228, ll. 15-14): "King Rion who was covered with coverings."

saw that he was being beaten and that, like it or not, he should take flight, he said that it would be better to die than not to avenge his shame in part or to soothe his heart a little for the hurt he had suffered. Then he sprang to his feet, grasped his bludgeon with both hands, and began striking blows right and left that were so rough and unduly strong that he struck down as many as he came to, and those who saw him work those wonders fled to every side, for they did not dare stand their ground against him.

Meanwhile, King Arthur, King Ban, King Bors, Nascien, Hervi, Ulfin, Kay the Seneschal, and all the other companions kept fighting until they came to King Rion and his banner, which the elephants bore. There the fighting was most dreadful, and the slaughter and death were so great that the [229] blood ran in streams through the field and into the River Thames, which ran on the far side. There King Rion's stronghold was brought down and the ensign overthrown. Then the din grew so loud over the giants that they all turned in flight, for they understood that they had been put to rout. They brought King Rion his horse and made him get on quickly, like it or not, for they were greatly frightened for him; and he was full of such sorrow that he nearly went mad. And before he left, he wreaked great damage on King Leodagan, for of his men he left twenty dead ones for him before he left the field. But when he saw that his own men were giving up, he did not dare stay behind any longer, but took to the road as full of wrath as anyone could be, and he went away, fleeing through a wood all alone with none of the barons who belonged to him.

When King Leodagan saw that King Rion and the giants were in flight, he ran after them with Sinados, Cleodalis, and Guiomar, and they brought many of them to the ground. Meanwhile, the knights of the Round Table slaughtered so many of them that heaps of them lay all along the low side of the fields like sheep throttled by wolves. For the palisade hindered them dreadfully, so that they could not get away quickly, and the Christians ran them down so hard that they could find no way to defend themselves, and they slaughtered so many of them that the whole field and the stronghold were strewn with the dead and wounded; and the chase lasted all day until nightfall.

When King Rion left the battle so full of sorrow and wrath, as you have heard, he was seen by no one who knew who he was except King Arthur. Arthur said to himself that he would rather die than have him get away, so he spurred his horse and left his companions behind, so that none knew where he had gone. Meanwhile, King Ban was in hot pursuit of Gloriant, Minados, and Calufer, those three kings so full of pride, and he rode after them all alone through the wood; and the other companions had ridden away, twenty here, ten there, thirty elsewhere, and the chase lasted until they felt they would have to give it up or postpone it until daylight. And they had killed and wounded so many of them that of the two hundred thousand there had been at the beginning, not twenty thousand got away. But right here the story now falls silent and does not speak of them at this time; rather it goes back to telling about King Arthur, who was riding after King Rion.

Right here the story says that King Arthur rode after King Rion of Ireland until he caught up with him in a great, deep valley between a little wood and a meadow; he was crossing a stream that flowed from two springs on a nearby mountainside;

the sun was sinking so low that all its brightness was blocked by the mountains and woods that hid it, and there King Arthur caught up with King Rion.

And when he had got close to him, he shouted, "Lowborn giant, turn about or you are dead! You can see that there is no man here but you and me."

When the giant saw the young man who was thus threatening him, he grew very scornful, for he looked so small to him that, beside him, he seemed to be a little child. Then he turned about to face him with his great bludgeon in his hand, and he held out in front of himself his shield that was of elephant bone. [230] King Arthur gripped his strong, stout lance* with a sharp tip of steel, and they rode straight for each other full of wrath and ill will, the one eager to win honor and renown and the other craving to avenge his shame and hurt. And King Arthur rode in fast, for he had come from far away, while the other one waited for him holding his bludgeon; and King Arthur struck him so hard that the sharp tip of his lance went right through his shield and hauberk and broke apart the two panels of his hauberk on his left side, so that his blood spurted everywhere. But for all the battering Arthur did, he did not budge him from his saddle one bit, and his lance flew into splinters. And when King Rion felt that he was wounded, he gritted his teeth and rolled his eyes in his anger, and he raised his bludgeon to strike. He was large and wondrously strong, more than any man anyone knew about. The story says that he was fourteen feet tall, in the feet they counted then, and there was more than a span's length between his two eyes; he was thin and sinewy, and powerfully built all over, so that he was fearsome to behold.

When King Arthur saw the giant raise his bludgeon, he feared him mightily. He urged his horse with his spurs, and man and horse flew against him so hard and fast that they were all hurled to the ground, the horses atop the men, but soon they had sprung back to their feet. But before King Arthur had picked up his arms, King Rion was back up and ready, for he was much quicker and more nimble; King Arthur was still only twenty-eight years old, but King Rion was at least forty-two and was bigger and stronger than he by a third. As soon as they had got up again, they ran at each other; King Arthur drew Excalibur out of its scabbard, his good sword that he had pulled out of the stone and with which he had that day dealt many a fine blow. And as soon as he had drawn it from its scabbard, it cast a very bright light, as if it were a blaze of fire, and he covered himself with his shield and struck a blow on the giant, before he could shield himself, right on the head. And when he saw the blow coming, he threw his shield up against it, for he mightily feared a blow from the sword he had seen glowing and throwing off fire; he well knew that it was of very great worth. He raised his bludgeon against it, and King Arthur hit it so hard with both hands that it flew into pieces, although it was bound in iron. The blow was strong and powerfully struck, and it fell on his shield and split it as far as the boss,† and thrusting the sword back away from himself he sent King Rion staggering; he was upset for having lost his bludgeon. Then he grasped his sword, which was one of the good ones in the world, for it was, so says the story drawn

---

*   The word here (230, l. 1) and elsewhere (cf. 230, l. 9) is *espiel.*

†   The word here is *blouque* (230, l. 31); elsewhere (224, l. 29), *boucle* ("boss") occurs in the formula.

from the histories,[*] the sword of Hercules, who led Jason to the island of Colchis to search for the Golden Fleece. And with this sword Hercules killed many a giant in the land where Jason brought Medea, who loved him so much, but afterwards Jason failed him at the very time that Hercules helped him, in his great nobility of spirit, because he had taken pity on him. And the story says that Vulcan forged the sword; he reigned in the time of Adrastus, king of Greece, who kept it in his treasure house for many a day. Tydeus, son of the king of Calcydon, had this sword the day he brought his message to King Eteocles of Thebes, who afterwards had much strife because of Polynices, his stepbrother. And then the sword went from hand to hand, and from heir to heir, until it now belonged to King Rion, who was of the bloodline of Hercules, who was so worthy and bold. [231]

When King Rion saw that his bludgeon had been cut to bits, he drew his sword, which was of such great goodness. And as soon as he had brought it out of its scabbard, it gave off such a great brightness that it seemed as if the whole countryside had been lit up; and its name was Marmiadoise. And when King Arthur saw the sword blazing with light, he deemed it most worthy, and he drew up a little to look at it, and he began to yearn for it a great deal, and he said that anyone would be lucky if he could win it.

And when King Rion saw him keeping so still, he stopped and spoke to him as you can hear. "Sir knight," said King Rion, "I do not know who you are, but you are very bold to dare follow me and run after me all alone. But because I see that you are so worthy, I will grant you such a boon as I would give to no man. Hand that sword and those arms over to me, then tell me your name, and then you will be free to go, for I have taken pity on you because you look so young to me."

When King Arthur heard King Rion's speech, he held him in great scorn and answered him very harshly: "How else, then, do you think you might have me so close, unless I surrendered to you like a coward because you are so big and strong? Rather, put your sword and your arms away and throw yourself on my mercy to do with you what I will. You can be sure that all I can warrant you is death."

The giant laughed aloud at this, turned his head aside, and asked him who he was and what his name was, and he entreated him on his faith to tell the truth. And King Arthur said to him that he would tell the truth and swore to tell him who he was, and he agreed.

"Now you should know," he went on, "that I am the son of King Uther Pendragon and my name is Arthur, and I have come to challenge you for this kingdom, which is mine free and clear, for King Leodagan has betrothed his daughter to me. And all the barons of the kingdom have already sworn fealty to me, as has King Leodagan himself. Now tell me who you are and what your name is, for I have told you the truth about myself."

"What?" answered the giant. "Are you telling me as a truth that you are King Arthur and that you were the son of Uther Pendragon, the one who killed Algis the Saxon before Saxon Rock?"

---

[*]   The text has *li contes des estoires*; unlike the occurrence in 221, ll. 31-32, however, it may not here be a question specifically of the supposed Merlin source, but generally of ancient authoritative texts that transmit the story of Jason, such as Valerius Flaccus's *Argonautica*, the Theban material, such as Statius's *Thebais*, etc.

"I am talking about that very man," said the youth.

"I swore to you," said King Rion, "that I would tell you my name. You may know for a fact that my name is Rion and I am king of Ireland. I hold all lands as far as the Land of the Grazing-Grounds, and the land beyond would be mine as well if people could get in there, but no one will go in until its ugly appearance is taken away; this is a blessing that Judas bestowed, and it betokened that he had won all the land up to there. And the ancients say that just as soon as that appearance is taken away, the adventures of the kingdom of Logres will begin to draw to an end. Now I have told you who I am and what my name is. But I will never eat again as long as I know that you are alive. For I was defeated by you and driven from the field, and I will avenge my sorrow on you if I can."

"God help me," said the young man, "you'll be fasting for a long time, then, for I will never die by your hand. And this my sword defies you to the death! And if you are so bold, you may take vengeance upon the man who threatens to chop off your head!"

When the giant heard the youth speaking thus, he became most frightfully angry. He put his shield on his arm and ran upon him [232] holding his sword high, and he meant to strike Arthur on the head, but Arthur thrust his shield against the blow and jumped aside toward the middle of the field, and King Rion hit his shield so hard that a piece of it flew to the ground. Arthur sprang forward and gave him such a blow beside his right eye that he wounded him deeply, and if his sword had not slipped in his hand, he would have put an end to him forever.

When the giant felt his blood flowing from his left cheek, he grew so angry that he nearly went mad. He ran against Arthur, for he meant to take him and crush him in his arms, but Arthur avoided him because he did not dare take such a stand against him, and, as he withdrew, he struck many hard blows that hurt him dreadfully. Even so, the giant ran against him waving his sword in his hand, but he could not hold the giant back.

And while they were behaving in this way, Nascien, Adragain, and Hervi de Rivel happened to come upon them while fiercely pursuing six Saxons, and all six were kings; one was named Kahanin,* the second Misshapen,† the third Frenicas, the fourth Coward, the fifth Baufumes,‡ and the sixth was the strong King Minadap.§ Those six kings were riding out very hard just down from the great rock, and they were running their horses, which were strong and fast, at breakneck speed. When the two kings who were fighting each other heard the uproar made by those who were charging so hard in their direction, they looked and saw the six who were fleeing and the three running after them, and King Rion was filled with dread, because he knew that they were most worthy and bold, and he was sure that if he stayed any longer where he was, he could not get away without being killed or put in great danger. Then he went straight for his horse and swiftly mounted, but as he was doing so, King Arthur struck him so hard that he cut off better than a fourth

---

* Here *kahamus* (232, l. 13), a misreading of *kahanin(s)* found elsewhere (e.g., 232, ll. 37, 41; 409, l. 27), or *cahanin(s)* (e.g., 232, l. 42; 233, l. 3).

† Sommer's text reads *maltaillies* (232, l. 13).

‡ Sommer's text reads *baitrames* here (232, l. 14), but *baufumes* elsewhere (234, l. 27; 235, l. 1).

§ Sommer's text reads *maidrap* here (232, l. 14), but *minadap* elsewhere (234, l. 27; 235, l. 2).

of his helmet, so that the links in the mail beneath shone through all white, and he dazed him so much that he bent forward over his saddlebow; and if he could have recovered to wield another blow, he would have sent him sprawling from his horse to the ground. But the horse, which was of very great strength, was frightened by the stroke it heard falling, and it ran away with the king up toward the great rock.

When King Arthur saw him thus on horseback, he jumped on his horse quickly and began to run him down, spurring his horse to run as fast as it could. And after King Rion had straightened up in the saddle, he looked behind him and saw King Arthur coming up fast and riding him down, and Arthur was unwilling to let him get away. With that he picked up speed to race toward the forest. And the six kings whom the three companions were pursuing were flying so swiftly that they caught up with King Arthur, who kept fast on the giant's heels and with his sword dealt him, from time to time, heavy blows that fell on the shield he held over his head to take the blows from the good sword he felt to be one of the best in the world.

And while the giant was setting his mind to fleeing and King Arthur his to riding him down, Kahanin shouted to Arthur, "Serf, you are making a mistake to run after him, for I'll fight you for him. You'll be sorry you left your companions."

When King Arthur heard him thundering at him so loudly, his sword slipped in his hand, and King Rion got away and flew off into the forest. And King Arthur went straight for Kahanin, his sword in his hand, and Kahanin, who was not afraid of him, rode toward him, and they began trading blows on their helmets. And King Kahanin struck King Arthur so hard that he sent him down onto the neck of his horse, [233] and King Arthur hit him back so hard that he cut off a great chunk of his helmet; this mighty blow fell between his shoulder and his shield, and it cut off his left arm where the shield's straps were held on. And when Kahanin saw that he had been wounded in this way, he ran upon him to grab him and bear him down over his horse's neck, for he was of very great strength. But King Arthur saw him coming and struck him with his sword between the wrist and the elbow, so that he sent his fist flying still grasping his sword. And when he saw what had become of him, he began to yell and roar like a bull, and his horse bore him away where it wanted. And when the five others saw what had happened to Kahanin, they were filled with great sorrow, so they rode King Arthur down with their swords drawn; he covered himself with his shield, for it would have been unworthy of him to run away from them. They hit him high and low, wherever they thought they could do him the most harm. They cut up his shield in many places, but they did not wound his flesh; but one of them* did hit him so roundly on the shield that he cut him in the thigh, and he sent him falling head over heels from his horse.

Now behold the three companions spurring to rescue him: Nascien, Adragain, and Hervi of Rivel. And when the other kings saw them coming, they turned in flight, galloping at full speed after King Rion, where they saw him going, and the three companions rode after them because they did not want to let them get away. But now the story falls silent about King Arthur and his companions and goes back to speaking about King Ban and how he was running after the three kings.

---

*   Sommer's text shifts to the singular: *il fier[t]* [sic], *quil li colpe la cuisse si le porte* (233, l. 12).

Now the story says that King Ban rode after the three kings until he came upon them in a great heath in the midst of a forest where they took their stand, for they had caught up with ten of their knights; and they rode against King Ban as soon as they saw him. He hit the first one he came to* so hard that he split his head into two halves, then he struck the second on the shoulder and sliced his arm off, and he struck the third and sent his head flying. They all began to hit him on the helmet and shield, but they did not wound him in the flesh, for the hauberk he was wearing was of great worth.

And while he was fighting them, the four kings whom King Bors was pursuing came up and saw that King Ban was bearing in so close to the ten knights that they did not have room to turn about. And the four kings rushed into the battle to help those whom King Ban was fighting. When they came into the battle, they turned their horses' heads against the one who had followed them,† and King Bors rode headlong into their midst and hit so hard and with such speed that he sent Margot and his horse down to the ground in a heap; then he struck King Gaidou so hard that he sank his sword into his brains. Then King Bors took stock and saw his brother, who was fighting with ten knights, and he spurred his horse and flew into the fray so hard that he bore a Saxon to the ground with his horse falling on top of him, and then he struck another so hard that he hurled him to the ground dead. And the kings he had been following rode toward him and [234] caught up with him in the crowd. They hit him so hard on the helmet that they sent him down onto his horse's neck, but he was not slow to get back up, and he turned his horse's head against them and stood facing them, grasping his sword. And the two brothers began striking such mighty blows against those who had attacked them that they did them much harm with their weapons. But they had not been at it for long there before King Rion happened along; he was holding his sword, but was dreadfully wounded and woefully frightened, and he was bleeding quite heavily from two wounds he had, one in the side and the other on the head. And when he saw the fight of the thirteen against the two brothers, he turned to face their way, holding his sword in his hand, for he was most willing to take vengeance for his pain and suffering.

When King Rion came to the battle, he rushed in so hard that he sent them scattering, like it or not, and in the onslaught he bore King Bors to the ground with his horse on top of him. Then he raised his sword high to strike King Ban through the head, but Ban threw his shield and struck his horse with his spurs to ward off the blow, which still cut and sliced through as much of him as it reached. And King Ban dealt him a great blow with his sword Wrathful;‡ he threw his shield out against it, but the blow struck there so hard that it cut through down to the strap by which it hung from his neck, and he sent the shield flying to the ground in two halves.

Meanwhile, as soon as the giants saw King Bors thrown onto the ground, they ran against him and hit him very hard and wounded him in many places, and his horse, which was tall and thick, lay on his left thigh and held him fast to the ground so

* The text is ambiguous (233, l. 22): *quil ataint* for *qu'il ataint* ("whom he comes to") or *qui l'ataint* ("who gets to him").

† Not in Sommer's text, but supplied from the variant in manuscript 105 (233, n. 3).

‡ Sommer's text has *couroucese* (234, ll. 16-17).

that he could not get back up. And the king entreated God to keep him from being killed or wounded. Then King Ban spurred to that side and struck King Margoras so hard that he sent his head flying, and then he struck again and hit another, whom he sliced in two crosswise right through the backbone, and he stopped beside his brother, who was trying to get back up.

And while he was fighting, King Baufumes, King Misshapen, and King Minadap* happened to come there, for King Arthur and his three companions were riding very hard after them; one of the companions was Nascien, the second Adragain, and the third Hervi de Rivel. And as soon as the three kings saw King Rion fighting, one of ten who were against one knight alone, they turned to that side and ran headlong into the press, and they tried to help King Ban and his brother as best they could. And King Bors pulled and jerked, for he was a man of very great strength, until he could get up with some distress, and he saw his brother in great danger and defending himself. And as soon as he had got back up, he struck Misshapen, who had come in just before, so hard that he sliced his arm off at the shoulder and cut so deeply that his liver and lungs showed, and he fell to the ground. Then King Bors took his horse and put himself into the saddle, for he was very strong and bold, and when he was mounted, he flew into the press and struck King Rion so hard through his helmet that he cut it into two halves. And King Rion paid him back with such a mighty blow that he cut off half of his shield.

Thus began the fighting there that was wild and fierce, and the four others who had just come to the rescue rode into the fighting so fast and each one hit his man so hard that they all bore them dead to the ground. [235] There were slain Minadap, Baufumes, Glorians, and Madolas, for whom King Rion was most sorrowful, for they were his near kinsmen.

When King Rion saw such dreadful ill luck turning against him, he was so filled with wrath that he nearly went out of his head. He grabbed his naked sword and ran down King Arthur, and he meant to strike him on the head, but King Arthur turned aside, for he greatly feared the giant's blow, which fell on his shield so hard that it was split in two down to the boss. King Rion started to pull his sword back out, but King Arthur hit him across the arm so hard that he wounded him dreadfully, and King Rion left his sword in his shield. And when he felt that he was so badly wounded, he grew as angry as any could be. And King Arthur† cast aside his shield with the sword, for it did nothing but hinder him. And when the giant saw that he had lost his sword, he became so angry that he almost lost his mind. He ran King Arthur down on horseback and grabbed him by the shoulders; he meant to take him down by raw strength, and he would have done so if he could have, for he was very strong.

When King Arthur felt the giant on him, he threw his sword to the ground, because he was afraid that he might take it away from him by force. Then he put both arms around his horse's neck, while the giant jerked and pulled, but he could not take him out of the saddle. And King Ban looked around and saw the bout

---

*   These kings are named, along with two others, 232, ll. 13-14. Here the first is called *baufumes* and the third *minadap* (234, l. 27); for Misshapen, see above, p. 255n.

†   Sommer corrects his manuscript, which bears *artus*, to read *rion* (235, l. 9 and n. 1); he appears to have lost track of the direction the combat is taking.

between King Arthur and King Rion, so he spurred to that side because he was very much afraid for King Arthur. The giant looked and saw him coming, and he greatly dreaded King Ban, so he ran at him with his fists, which were big and thick. But King Ban struck him so hard with his sword Wrathful that he broke his hauberk open, cut through him beneath the shoulder, and wounded him very deeply. And when King Rion felt himself so dreadfully wounded and saw his companions lying dead on the ground, he was taken by a mighty fear, for he did not know what to defend himself with, so he turned his horse, which was of very great worth, and fled away as fast as he could go. The companions let him go, for night had fallen, and he went away so full of wrath that he nearly went mad, and he cursed his religion and his beliefs, and swore that he would never in his life give up until he had taken his revenge, and, as soon as he came into his country, he would call together such a great force of men that no land could stand against it, and he said that he would destroy all Britain, bring all of King Arthur's vassals to harm, and skin alive the king and all his helpers. Thus King Rion went away filled with wrath, and he made his way for days upon end until he came to his country.

And King Ban came to King Arthur and asked him whether he was hurt, and King Arthur told him that he was hale and hardy.

"And your sword," said King Ban, "where is it?"

He answered that he had thrown it to the ground as the giant came running to take hold of him with his bare hands, "and I tell you that I have won the richest prize today, one that I love better than the best city there is in the world."

"And what is that?" asked King Ban.

"You will see it very soon," said King Arthur, "if you wish."

Then he dismounted and first went straight to his sword Excalibur, and he wiped it clean of the blood that befouled it, then put it back into its scabbard. Then he went to his shield, drew King Rion's sword out of it, hung the shield around his neck, and got on his horse. He showed the sword to King Ban, and it cast such a great light that it was a wonder to behold. King Ban held it in high esteem, and they entreated Our Lord soon to grant that they might find some adventure [236] where they might try it out and see whether it was as worthy as it was fair.

They were much nearer Aneblayse than they thought, but before they could get there, there befell them an adventure such that the worthiest and bravest would have been hard pressed to come to terms with it. But right now the story falls silent about all of them and goes back to speaking about King Leodagan of Carmelide.

31. ARTHUR FIGHTS THE SAXONS.*

Here the story says that when King Leodagan saw that the giants had been put to rout, he rode very hard after them until dark night had closed in, and he and his men had slain many. Then it happened that King Leodagan and Cleodalis his seneschal were cut off from their men because of the forest, which was quite dark, and no one belonging to them knew what had become of them. And when King Leodagan's army saw that night had fallen, they began to turn back, but the companions of the Round Table did not turn about, nor did King Arthur's companions; rather they kept on riding the Saxons down with all their might and killed many of them. And the story says that King Leodagan and Cleodalis ran after Zidras and Caulas the Chieftain,† Collocaulus,‡ and Dorilas until they had fled far from their men in the forest, and when they had gone a long way, they fell in behind a good two hundred eighty other men of theirs who were sorrowing and angry about their losses.

When the four who were in flight were safe, they shouted to their men, and when these took stock, they saw that there were only two who were riding after the four, so they ran upon them with all their might. King Leodagan and Cleodalis withdrew under an oak tree which was most fair and leafy, and their backs were to it. There King Leodagan was struck down and his horse beneath him. And when Cleodalis saw him, he got down from his horse and put him on his own horse, and he told him to ride away and he would stay behind there. When King Leodagan saw his seneschal's faithfulness, he sighed deeply inside his helmet and sorrowed in his heart that he had wronged him so much, and he said in his heart that he wished to repay him for this good deed and reward him for it, if he should live so long. Meanwhile, he was defending himself very hard, for their enemies had fallen on them fiercely, and the oak that was at their backs was a great help to them. So the story stops speaking about them and goes back to Guiomar and Sinados, who were first cousins, and they had fought very well in the battle.

Now the story says that Guiomar and Sinados had ridden so hard after the Saxons in the forest that they left their men far behind and never heard or saw them, and they were hot on the heels of twelve giants. And when the twelve had been long in flight, they caught up with a good fifty of their companions who had fled in fear. Guiomar and Sinados knew not a word about this until they had, just the two of them,§ rushed headlong into their midst; and each one struck his man down dead. And when the Saxons saw that there were only two of them, they drew their swords and fell very hard upon them; thus a great fight was begun, for the two knights were worthy and bold. But they had been there for only a short while when a knight rode in very daringly to help them. There the fighting was rough and lasted [237] a very long time. But now the story falls silent for a while about that, and we will tell you about another adventure.

---

* Corresponds to Sommer, 236–243.
† The word is *laumacour* (236, l. 16), for *l'almaçor* (from the Arabic).
‡ Here Sommer's text reads *caulus* (236, l. 16). Later he is called Collocaulus (241, l. 13; 242, l. 14).
§ The text reads *si abreue com il estoient* (236, l. 37): "as reduced in number as they were."

In this part the story says that when the giants were put to flight, Antor,[*] who brought King Arthur up, Kay the Seneschal, Girflet, Lucan the Wine Steward, Meralgis,[†] Gornain Cadrus,[‡] Gales the Bald,[§] who had been put in with them, Blioberis, Galesconde, the Ugly Worthy,[¶] Calogrenant,[**] and Kehedin[††] the Fair—these twelve were riding very hard through the thick forest after the Saxons, and they killed and wounded many of them on the run.[‡‡] The Saxons fled very fast before them, and they rode after them until they cut them down, at the heels of King Alipansin, who had with him two hundred Saxons, on very good horses, who were most angry for the harm done to King Rion and because they did not know what had become of him. And when the twelve companions caught sight of them, they rode headlong into the midst of them, and they began a most wondrous battle, for the companions were most worthy and bold. The fighting there was fierce, and it lasted until midnight, when[§§] they broke apart and began fighting in three clusters: in the first were King Leodagan and Cleodalis his seneschal, in the second were Sinados and Guiomar, and in the third were King Arthur's twelve companions.

Elsewhere were King Arthur, King Ban, King Bors his brother, and three of the companions of the Round Table, as the story has told you before, and all the others had gone back toward the city of Aneblayse.[¶¶] And when they came into the meadows outside Aneblayse and did not find any of their companions, they thought that they had been killed, and when the saw that neither King Arthur nor King Ban nor King Bors nor King Leodagan had been found, they mourned most sorrowfully, for they truly thought that they were dead. Even so, they waited to hear any news that might come, so they camped in the open meadows, for they did not want to go into the city, but kept watch over the city very well until daybreak. So the story stops speaking about them for a while and goes back to speak about Merlin.

The story says here that when the Saxons and the giants were put to rout and driven from the fields, and the chase began, Merlin rode after a company of a good ten thousand men until he ran them down on a wide heath. Galahad, lord of the

---

[*] The following companions are first listed among the forty-two knights who ride to rescue Cleodalis (148, ll. 3-23). Here many of the names appear garbled, as subsequent notes demonstrate.

[†] Earlier *meraugis de port le gues* (148, l. 18): Meralgis of Portford; here *ameraugis* (237, l. 5).

[‡] Earlier *gornains cadrus* (148, ll. 18-19); here *agornain & cadrus son compaignon* (237, l. 5): "Agornain and Cadrus his companion." The latter is to be rejected not only because Cadrus does not appear separately in the earlier list, but more especially because, with the independent Cadrus, the knights total thirteen, not twelve, as the text specifies (237, l. 7). Gornain Cadrus is named later (239, l. 37).

[§] Sommer's text has *ablechin le uoir* (237, l. 6): Ablecin the Right One (?). Such a name does not appear in the earlier list; however, Gales the Bald, which is found there (148, l. 22), recurs later in the same group (e.g., 239, l. 38).

[¶] Sommer's text has *alait hardi* (237, l. 7); the earlier has *li lais hardis* (148, ll. 19-20), which recurs later (239, l. 38).

[**] The text has *atalogrenant* (237, l. 7). Sommer conjectures that this should read Calogrenant (237, n. 3), which is consistent with the earlier list (148, l. 15).

[††] Here *akehedin* (237, l. 7); Sommer conjectures Kehedin (n. 4), which is consistent with the earlier list (148, l.17).

[‡‡] Sommer's text reads *en la cache* ("in the chase") and continues *quil font parmi la grant forest* (237, l. 9): "through the great forest."

[§§] Sommer's text has *anchois que* (237, l. 16): "before."

[¶¶] Sommer's text reads *cyte de daneblaise* (237, l. 22), cf. *defors daneblaise* (ll. 22-23), etc.

Land of the Grazing-Grounds, led that company, and as soon as they had come into the heath, Merlin cast a wondrous spell. He made a wide, roaring river well up before them in the way they had to go, and it fell so swiftly from the mountainsides that even the boldest among them took fright; and when they tried to turn back, they saw a fog coming in so thick and so fearsome that they did not know where to go, so they stayed there all night and did not go back or forward. And why Merlin cast this spell, the story will surely tell you, for it is right that it should tell you the truth about it in just the way the truth must run. [238]

Now the story says, and it was true, that in the borderlands of Carmelide and Bredigan, and toward the lands of King Rion, that is toward the west, there was a most wealthy kingdom where King Amant was lord. King Uther Pendragon had waged war against that kingdom for a very long time, while he was alive, because King Amant would not become his liegeman, and his lands were so strong that he was not afraid of Uther. Even so, King Uther Pendragon bore down on him* until he won from him a very rich castle that was called Charroie. This castle had five hundred knights in fee, each of whom owed the garrison a full three months every year whenever they might be called to serve, and the domain stretched for twenty leagues on every side. King Uther Pendragon gave that castle and the whole domain to King Bors of Gaunes and his heirs, for he held King Uther Pendragon in high esteem for as long as he was alive and helped him fight his enemies. And as soon as King Bors became lord of the castle, he gave it to his brother Guinebal to keep. Guinebal was a very good clerk, wise, skilled in fighting, bold, and he was his teacher. And King Amant was most unhappy about that. And when he heard it said that King Arthur was in King Leodagan's land and that, meanwhile, the Saxons had fallen upon Britain, King Amant brooded and then thought that he would never, for a long while, have a better time than right then to win back his castle he had lost so long before, so he called his men and brought them together, and soon there were a good seven thousand and more. So he set out and rode until he came to the valley where King Galahad had stopped with his men, who were a good ten thousand strong, and they had stopped there for fear of the water that Merlin had brought forth.

And on the Friday morning after Whitsunday, it was still and the weather was fair and mild, and the water had gone away and the spell was broken, so the Saxons got on their horses and took to the road. But they had not gone far before they met King Amant, who had set out toward the castle of Charroie. When King Galahad saw King Amant and his men,† he thought that they belonged to King Leodagan, who had ridden after them. On both sides they were all riding good horses. King Amant's men rode hard and fast against King Galahad's, who welcomed them very warmly with the tips of their lances, for many of them were good, strong knights, and harsh, fierce fighting began that lasted the whole day. But right now the story falls silent and does not say any more about them; rather it goes back to speaking about King Arthur, the two brother kings, and the three companions of the Round Table, Nascien, Adragain, and Hervi of Rivel.

---

*   Sommer's text has *les greua* (238, l. 6): "harmed them."
†   "And his men" not in Sommer's text (238, l. 27), but implicit in the plurals that follow immediately.

Here the story says that when King Arthur had pulled his sword out of the shield, he showed it to his companions, and they were all very glad; they esteemed it highly and praised it. Then they set out on the way back to Aneblayse.* They thought they were keeping to the right road, but they went astray when they turned to the left onto an old, grassy trail where it was very dark because of woods that were deep and high and leafed out as in the month of May; the moon, which had been full three days before, had not yet risen. And after [239] they had ridden a little while, they began to hear blows in a far-off battle resounding through the forest, so they went toward those parts, as the trail was taking them there. And as they drew nearer, they knew from the voices that it was their men who were still fighting the giants whom they had ridden after, so they hurried along toward the voices they had heard. The moon began to rise, and as they came still closer they could see a great battle, in which three knights were fighting against more than fifty Saxons; and after they were near enough to make them out, King Arthur recognized Guiomar and Sinados, but they could not make out who the third one was, although they did see that he was worthy, bold, and skilled, and the six companions who came upon the fight praised and esteemed him highly. They let their horses run and rode headlong into their midst so hard that they left them shaking, and they struck to the right and left, and they killed or brought down as many as they met. There King Arthur skillfully tried out Marmiadoise, the worthy sword that had belonged to King Rion, for the story bears witness to his having slain more than ten all by himself. And when the three knights saw that they had got such a wealth of help, they gave their horses free rein to run against them, and caused such a great slaughter that each one sent his man sprawling to the ground dead, and they dealt with them in such a way that in very little time they had slain or wounded all but seven of them, who fled away into the woods with the others, who wanted very much to kill them if they could catch up with them, hot on their heels. But they had not been riding after the seven for long when they heard wondrously hard beating on helmets and shields, so that the great woods resounded with it.

Then King Ban spoke and said to King Bors that they would have to delight in fighting all night, and King Arthur† said that he would not mind because he had not thoroughly tested the good sword he had won.

"What?" said King Ban. "Haven't you already tried it out and tested it in this first fight?"

"Not at all, sir," said King Arthur, "for there were too few men. What's more, you and the others brought so many of them down that I could not test it as I would wish."

Then the barons smiled at what he had said, and they found him all the worthier, and they praised him because they had beheld his valorous deeds, so they said that he would be a worthy man if he lived long enough. While they were thus talking, they drew close to the combat, which was heavy and deadly, and when they were near they saw a good hundred Saxons who were fighting hard against twelve knights, of whom four were on foot and eight on horseback, and they were all holding their

---

*   Sommer's text has *daneblayse* (238, l. 39).

†   Sommer's text has *il* (239, l. 23), but the Harley manuscript specifies, as the context requires, that it is King Arthur (n. 1).

own. And when they came closer still, they saw that it was their companions who had come with them to Carmelide, twelve of them by their reckoning; the four who were on foot were first Antor, second Gornain Cadrus, third Gales the Bald, and fourth Blioberis, and a fifth, the Ugly Worthy, was brought down from his horse* right before their eyes, but he was defending himself with great strength.

When King Arthur saw Antor on foot, no one had to ask whether he was sorrowful, for he showed it plainly, and as he was coming nearer to the fighting, he spurred his horse, his naked sword in his hand, and struck the first man he met so hard that he split him down to the waist; then he struck the second so that he sent his head flying, [240] and then the third and the fourth, and he began such an onslaught among them that it was a wonder to behold. And King Arthur fought so well with his good sword that he cut everyone he fell upon, and he said that King Rion was not wrong to love that sword, for Excalibur would never be worth anything beside this one, and he could work with it any way he wanted. Then the blows started up again even harder and more wondrous, for the twelve companions were very worthy and bold, and the six who came to their rescue were so skillful that they got the five who were on foot back on their horses; and then they rode against the Saxons in such a fierce and wondrous onslaught that they put them all to the rout and drove them from the field, and they dealt with them so harshly that no more than sixteen of them got away. And they went back gladdened and happy by the adventure that Our Lord had sent them.

When King Arthur and his companions had helped rescue the twelve companions, as you have heard, and as they were riding back, they happened to meet Merlin, holding the dragon standard, who was riding their way. And as soon as he saw them coming, he said, "Ah! King Arthur, why aren't you and your companions riding faster? For you don't know the great harm that awaits you up here, unless God puts His mind to it. King Leodagan and Cleodalis his seneschal are fighting against more than fifteen giants, and they have already been brought down from their horses. They will soon be lost if you do not help them out. Now follow me, for I am going straight there!"

And when they heard what Merlin had to tell them, they spurred after him, and the dragon that Merlin bore threw out from its mouth such a bright light and such great billows of fire that the twenty-one companions could see clearly where to go even though the night was darker than any in winter. And they rode, Merlin leading and the others behind him, until they came to two oak trees, where the two knights were still fighting very hard, for they had great courage and much strength. But they were woefully beleaguered, for they were both on foot and had fallen many times to their knees.

When Merlin and his companions came upon the two worthies fighting, as they had been doing so long, King Leodagan had fallen to the ground, for he was so tired and he had been worn down so hard by the blows he had given and taken that he could no longer stand on his feet, so he went sprawling to the ground. Anyone who saw him in such a plight would feel deeply sorry for him. And the giants thought then that they would take him prisoner, [241] but Cleodalis leapt forward with his

---

*   "From his horse" not in Sommer's text, but implicit from the context (239, ll. 38-39).

sword, and he defended him so well that none was bold enough to dare lay a hand on him.

Then Merlin and his companions came up, and when they drew near enough to recognize them, Merlin shouted, "Now at them, noble knights! Now we'll see who is a knight! Here you can show your skill and your boldness. Don't worry if there are more of them than you, for more of your companions will come to your aid."

Then they flew headlong into their midst as fast as their horses could run, and they hit them and struck them down and broke the press, and at last they came to the two worthy knights who were beneath the oaks and still fighting as best they could. For King Leodagan had got up and was defending himself with all his might, and they quickly put him back on his horse.* And the twenty-three knights were so worthy and so handy that they killed and wounded many of them.

But when Zidras, Caulas,† and Collocaulus saw the great damage they were doing to them, even though there were so few of them, each shouted to his knights, "Now at them! Shouldn't we be ashamed that so few men have outfought us? There are a good seven score of us fighting against no more than a handful of them! Now avenge the harm and the hardship they have inflicted on us."

When the Saxons heard the will of their lord, they gave their horses free rein and charged, and they fell hard upon them, but they defended themselves fiercely. There‡ King Arthur, King Ban, King Bors, and Nascien, those four, did wonders of strength, as did the nineteen others, and when Merlin saw that the fighting was going thus, he left them and went into the forest. He did not tarry long before he brought back with him twelve knights, and they rushed in among the giants. Then Nascien, Adragain, and Hervi of Rivel looked and knew that they were beside their companions of the Round Table.

Then the fighting grew heavy and wondrous, and Merlin went back into the forest, wherever he wanted to go, and he stayed there a very long while. And when he came back he brought twenty knights with him, and they drove headlong into the fighting with great strength. It was plain from the look of their armor that they had not been taking their ease! And they killed and brought down as many as they met on their way, and the ones who had come before them looked and saw that they were some of King Arthur's companions. And they drew into formation, one after the other, for [242] they were very bold and skilled in knighthood, and Merlin still carried the dragon before them.

Then he went to the three kings and said to them, "Do you want to know," he said, "how those giants will be put to rout?"

And they said that they could hardly wait.

"You must know," said Merlin, "that there are but four men in this place who are keeping them going."

"And where are they?" asked King Ban.

---

* Sommer's text adds *qui quen pesast* (241.1. 11): "whomever it might worry/whether they liked it or not."

† Here Sommer's text reads *callas*, but elsewhere the name is *caulus* (236, l. 16; 242, l. 16).

‡ Sommer's text adds an elliptical *fist merlin &* (241, l. 20): "did Merlin and"; but *icil .iiij. fisent meruilles* ("these four did wonders") in the next line (l. 21) and the subsequent mention of the nineteen others (l. 22) suggest that the introductory statement should be eliminated.

"Follow me now," said Merlin, "and I'll soon show them to you if you dare to see them."

Then he spurred his horse and charged so hard that he knocked down as many as met his horse's chest, and he held up the dragon, which gave off such a bright light that they could see each other clearly.

When Merlin saw the four kings, he showed them to King Arthur and said, "Now you can put that good sword you have won to the test."

And he looked at them and wanted very much to have at them, for he was sure that they were the ones Merlin had told him about. But he was not so quick that he could fall upon them before Nascien was there, his sword in his hand, riding to meet King Collocaulus; he struck him with his sword right on his helmet and cut through down to his teeth, and Collocaulus fell to the ground dead.

"Now there is one fewer!" said Merlin, and he said to King Arthur, "Now we'll see whom you'll hit!"

And King Arthur struck Caulas and sent his head flying. And King Ban struck the third one so hard that he sliced his arm off at the shoulder and cut so deeply that his liver and lungs showed. And King Bors hit Dorilas, an emir, on his helmet and cut him down to the shoulders. And when the other companions saw that they had fought so well, they rode against the Saxons so hard that there was not one of the enemy who was not brought down bleeding and dying, and when the giants saw that those who had been their leaders and lords had been slain, and that the Christians were doing them such harm, they said that anyone would be a fool who waited to be killed. So they turned and fled through the forest, each man for himself, and the Christians wanted to ride after them, but Merlin held them back and told them not to worry about giving chase, for in time men about whom stories would be told would mete out grief and sorrow to them.

They then left at a slow gait and rode until they came out of the forest, and dawn was beginning to break when they got to the tents where the Christians were camped. And the guards recognized them and came out to meet them. They were very glad to see them, for they thought that they had all been killed, and the news was spread throughout the army that King Arthur had come back with King Leodagan, King Ban and his brother, and all their other companions. And a great store of food was made ready for them, for they had had nothing to eat for a long time, but first they went to sleep and to take their ease.

When they had slept, the tablecloths were spread and they sat down, and they ate and drank a great deal, for they had rested well, and they certainly deserved it. After they had eaten and the tablecloths were taken away, they brought together all the great spoils they had won and put it into a heap, and King Arthur divided it following Merlin's advice. King Leodagan had no part in it, nor, after giving his daughter to King Arthur, when he knew who King Arthur and the worthy men with him were, did he undertake to do anything other than serve and honor him. And when King Arthur had given out the wealth, so that nothing was left, he let it be known throughout the army that if there were any young knights* [243] who

---

*   Sommer's text has *bacheler* (242, l. 43), technically a squire aspiring to knighthood (also 243, l. 24).

wanted to win booty and would go with him wherever he would lead them,* he would give them so much when they came back that they would never be poor another day in their lives. And so many of them came forward from here and there that it was nothing short of a wonder, for many wished always to be in his company because of his openhandedness, and they swore and pledged that they would never fail him. He retained twenty thousand, and he could have taken more if he had wished, but he said he did not want to strip the kingdom of men, for fear that they could not defend themselves if anyone came into the land to do wrong. And he told them that if the need arose, King Leodagan† should send word to them to come to him, and they swore to do so, however far away‡ he might be.

With that King Arthur left the others and took away the twenty thousand troops along with King Ban, King Bors, King Leodagan, and the companions of the Round Table. And after King Bors had ridden with them awhile, he took his leave of them and went back toward the castle of Charroie, and he took with him forty champions who had come with King Arthur into the land of Carmelide and enough other knights to number five hundred, and they made their way until they came to the castle of Charroie, and they had no hindrance whatsoever. And when those in the stronghold saw them, they were very glad, because King Bors had not been there for a long time, and he stayed there a whole week.§ But with this the story falls silent about him for a while, and it goes back to talking about King Amant and King Galahad and how they fought.

32. BORS KILLS AMANT; GAWAIN AND HIS BROTHERS KNIGHTED.¶

Now the story says that it was a great battle and the fighting was deadly where King Amant and King Galahad were struggling against each other. For the giants were ten thousand strong, and there were many a good, bold knight among them, and King Amant had many young knights** who were very skilled at arms; and the battle lasted all day until the Saxons, of whom there were ten thousand, were about to be routed, and would have been had it not been for an adventure that happened to them. For the retinue of Zidras, which had fled King Arthur, happened upon them, and they certainly needed them because they had been dealt with so harshly that the ten thousand had been worn down to half. And King Amant had also lost half of the seven thousand he had brought with him; there the fighting was frightful and deadly, for King Amant's men were in great distress, but it was helpful to them that

* In Sommer's text, in the singular (243, l. 1), as is the antecedent (242, l. 43), but subsequently shifts to the plural.
† Sommer's text has only the singular pronoun (243, ll. 8-9). Although King Leodagan leaves with Arthur, he accompanies him only as far as Carhaix and then returns (244, ll. 24-28).
‡ Sommer's text has *en si estraigne lieu* (243, l. 9): "in however strange/foreign a place."
§ Sommer's text has only *.viij. tous plains* (243, l. 18): "eight whole."
¶ Corresponds to Sommer, 243-256.
** Sommer's text has *bachelers* (243, l. 24); see above p. 266n.

the others were tired and worn out because they had not stopped fighting the day before and had not slept all that night, and they were all the more harried and all the less fit because of it. And yet they went on fighting on every side until King Amant was utterly routed, and no more than three thousand of his men got away. There King Amant suffered a very great loss, and all those who remained alive were filled with great sorrow. They camped in a heath and were downcast, brooding about their kinsmen and friends whom they saw lying slain on the open heath, and they mourned so much that they did not eat or sleep all night.

The next morning, when it was light, they went looking for the dead bodies and buried them, for the Saxons had all left. Then the news came to King Amant that King Bors was in the castle of Charroie. When King Amant heard that he asked [244] how many men-at-arms he might have with him, and they said that he might have as many as five hundred knights. Then he told his council that he would not make a foray into the land because he had so few men left, but he would keep an eye on him until he could meet him in a place where he might easily fight him.

"For we have," he said, "more men that he does, and still he comes there; I mean to succeed in another way, unless he can stop me."*

Thus King Amant spelled out his wishes, and he could certainly allow himself to do that if he pleased, but some were thinking to avenge and so to renew their shame.† So the story falls silent right here about King Amant and King Bors of Gaunes, until another time when my matter brings me back to tell what happened to them; and it speaks about King Arthur and his companions, who were riding away toward the city of Carhaix.

Here the story says that King Arthur and his companions rode until they came to the wealthy city of Carhaix, where they were welcomed very happily. There they stayed for two full days, and on the third King Leodagan came to King Arthur and asked him to wed his daughter Guenevere, but Merlin told him that first he would have to accomplish a hard task: "But first he must go to the kingdom of Benoic."

And he told him the reason, but it was in secret because he did not want it to be known to anyone who was to go there. And when King Leodagan had heard about the task, he asked him to think about coming back as soon as he could. Merlin said that it would do no good to ask, but that all should get themselves ready, "for in the morning they will have to ride out."

Then King Arthur asked him, "Sir, shall we not wait for King Bors, who is in the castle of Charroie?"

"You will wait for him," answered Merlin, "at your castle of Bredigan."

And the king said, "As you wish."

They then made ready to go, got themselves dressed and armed, and in the morning set out on the road. So King Arthur left King Leodagan, and they kissed each other at their leave-taking, and Guenevere entreated him to come back soon.

---

*   Sommer's text seems somewhat obscure: *tout autrement en quide iou esploitier sen lui ne remaint* (244, ll. 5-6).

†   Sommer's text has *tels quide sa honte bien uengier qui lacroist* (244, l. 7): "He who believes he avenges well his shame increases it." The proverb is attested from the end of the thirteenth century (Morawski, no. 2351: "Teus cuide venchier sa honte qui la croist."). It is found in Cotgrave (see *Honte*): "Tel cuide vanger sa honte qui l'accroist."; the translation is Cotgrave's.

"For I will never rest," she said, "or be happy until I see you again."

And he said that he would like to have come back already. With that, they parted, and King Arthur left with King Ban, and Merlin rode before them and led them; and the three of them led the companions of the Round Table and the twenty thousand men-at-arms the king had engaged at Carmelide. And King Ban chose a messenger and sent him to the castle of Charroie to his brother King Bors, and he bade him come to Bredigan, as they had already set out, and there they would wait for him; and he should come as soon as he could. And the messenger made his way until he came to King Bors, and he told him what his brother had asked him to do. And when King Bors heard it, he took to the road toward Bredigan, and Guinebal his brother went along with him, and they made their way until they came to the Perilous Forest,* which was afterwards called the Forest of No Return. And why it was so named the story will spell out for you.

The story says here that King Bors and Guinebal his brother had gone into the forest, and they had no more than forty companions with them. As it happened, they took a path to the right, and they rode at a fast gait [245] until they had gone deep into the forest. Then they found a most wondrous adventure, for they found an open meadow enclosed all about by a hedge, and within was the most beautiful dancing by ladies, maidens, and knights they had ever seen in their lives. To one side sat a child, and it was the fairest young lady there ever was, and to the other side a knight, who was at least fifty years old, was also seated in a folding chair.

When King Bors saw the lady who was so beautiful, he dismounted, as did Guinebal his brother and all the others who saw her. And when the lady saw them coming, she rose to meet them, for she was noble, well-bred, and knowledgeable, and she took off her wimple, for she was fully aware that they had come to see her. And King Bors greeted her, and she returned his greeting in a most courtly way. They then sat down on the green grass and watched the merry-making. And Guinebal looked at the lady, and he yielded his heart and feelings to her, so that she stole into his heart and he could think of no one else but her. And then the young lady said that she would be very lucky if she could have such happiness all the days of her life. And Guinebal told her that she would indeed be so happy, if she wished and if she did not find him wanting. And she answered that she would never do that.†

"Now tell me," she said, "how can I have such happiness?"

"In truth," he answered, "if you granted me your love for all the days of your life, I would do everything, for your sake, to keep the dances going, so that all men and women who might come here and see the dancing would have to stay here. And this would go on until there came a knight who had never wronged Love in any way. Such a one is bound to be the best knight of his time."

And she answered that she would never refuse him, but he should hold to what he had told her.

---

* Sommer's text adds *entre lui & sa compaignie* (244, l. 37): "he [that is, King Bors?] along with his companions."

† This passage translates a difficult idiom, repeated in Sommer's text: *& sen fat ne remanoit. & ele dist que en lui ne remandroit il ia* (245, ll. 16-17); it recurs, translated somewhat differently, in 244, l. 6 (see p. 268n.).

"Now tell me," said Guinebal, "whether or not you have ever had a lover."*

She said she had not. Never had such a good girl as she come out of any mother's womb. "And yet," she said, "I am lady of a kingdom they call the Inhospitable Land Upheld."†

With that Guinebal told her that he was ready to fulfill his oath, and she gave herself wholly to him because he was most handsome. And the old knight said that he would put a chair there that would be all ready for the knight who was faithful to Love to sit in. And King Bors told him that, as this adventure had happened to him, he would set his golden crown out there, the one he had brought with him from the castle of Charroie, for the knight to wear because he deserved it so much. Then Guinebal and the maiden swore to each other their oaths, which they would keep willingly and faithfully for as long as they lived; and she pledged that, even if Guinebal died before she did, the dancing would not stop until the knight came who had never forsworn Love. Then Guinebal cast his spells and started the dance in the way you have heard, so that the dancers would not stop‡ at any time until the one came who had never wronged Love, except to take their meals and go rest and sleep, and two of them would be dancing at all times.

When the dance was started, the maiden told him that he should make another pastime that would go on forever and that everyone would talk about after his death. Then with his own hands Guinebal made a chessboard with two sets of men, the pawns [246] with the rest of the household, that were very beautiful: one was of gold and the other ivory, for he was very clever in the work he wished to undertake. When Guinebal had got the chessboard and chessmen ready, so that whoever wanted to play could use them, he so worked his spells and his magic that if anyone§ sat down at the chessboard to play and moved a pawn or bishop or knight or queen or rook or king, the chessboard would make a move against him. And no one would know how to play so well that the chessboard would not checkmate him in the corner, like it or not, nor would the chessboard ever lose a game until the best knight in the world put it into checkmate; and he would have to be so endowed with grace that he had never betrayed Love, and he would have to be the son of a king and queen. In the way you have heard Guinebal started the dance and set up the chessboard. Afterwards he made up other tricks and taught them to the lady, and later she worked them many times after he had died. For he made the castle spin around and the dances that Meralgis found afterward in the City Without a Name.

When Guinebal had accomplished all these things, King Bors took to the road. And King Amant found out from a spy that King Bors had left the castle of Charroie and was heading toward Bredigan, where King Arthur and King Ban were waiting for him. Then King Amant had his men mount their horses—as many as the five hundred who were left from the fighting—and they rode until they came to the Perilous Forest, to the way out on the road leading from the castle of Charroie

---

*   The word in Sommer's text is *segnor* (245, l. 25) ("lord"), which would normally be taken to mean "husband"; however, the context seems to call for a different kind of meaning.

†   In Sommer's text *la terre estrange sostenue* (245, l. 27).

‡   The verb is in the plural, with implicit reference to dancers (245, l.38).

§   In Sommer's text the subject and verb here are in the plural (246, l. 5), but the pronoun at the end of the independent clause is in the singular (246, l. 7).

that King Bors would be taking; and they camped* in tents and pavilions within the forest so that they would not be caught sight of† before King Bors rode out and left the dance that his brother Guinebal had set up so that all the knights who came there afterwards should stay and dance until Lancelot of the Lake came there, who undid it all, and he sent the chessboard that checkmated the players to Queen Guenevere, who was King Arthur's wife. And because all the people who came there stayed there to dance, the forest was named the Forest of No Return. And when King Bors had gone from there, he knew nothing about King Amant before he came upon the tents and pavilions and saw his men.

When King Bors beheld the pavilions, he sent to find out what men-at-arms they were, and they told him that it was King Amant, who had come there to spy on him. And when King Bors heard that, he ordered his men to arm and he withdrew to a stream that ran through the forest. And it was already pitch dark, and they kept their armor on all night; [247] and as soon as they saw the first light of day, they got on their horses and rode against the others. When they had got close to them, King Bors sent word to King Amant to come speak with him, and he went.

And as soon as they met, King Amant said to him, "Sir, it is true that you sent for me, and I have come here; and I tell you that you have done me a very great wrong with respect to a castle of mine that you have taken from me. This is why I would beseech you, on my pledge that I will be your faithful friend, to give it back to me before anything else is done."

"Sir," said King Bors, "the castle you are asking me for, it was not I who took from you, but the one from whom you held it as a fief, that is, King Uther Pendragon, may God rest his soul, whose liegeman you were to have been, but you were so full of pride that you never found it worthwhile to serve him as you ought and you did not swear fealty to him. And so he took away from you that which made you his vassal, and when he took it away from you, he entrusted it to me for safekeeping, because I had served him for a long time. But I have something much better to offer you. Come to Bredigan, where King Arthur is waiting for me, and swear fealty to him, as the barons will tell you you ought, and I will give the castle back to you free and clear."

"You will give me the castle in any case,"‡ said King Amant.

"Not at all, sir," answered King Bors, "for I owe you nothing;§ but become King Arthur's liegeman, and I will give back to you the castle I have in my charge."

"I'll do nothing of the sort," said King Amant, "for I'll never be his vassal as long as I live."

"Since you will not take my advice," answered King Bors, "I will hold my tongue, and you'll never hear me say any more about it."

"Sir," said King Amant, "you have brought but a few men with you, and I have brought few of my own. If we fought a battle against each other, great harm would surely be done on both sides, so let's do something else. You are here on behalf of

* Sommer's text has the singular *se loga* (246, l. 20).
† Sommer's text has the singular *quil ne fust aperceus* (246, l. 21).
‡ Sommer's text has *Nen feres vous autre cose* (247, ll. 16-17): "You will do nothing else about it."
§ Sommer's text has *de vous ne tieng ie riens* (247, ll. 17-18): "I hold nothing from you/I have no feudal obligation to you."

King Arthur, whom you hold as your overlord. Let us then fight in single combat, man to man, and agree that, if you defeat me, the castle will be yours free and clear and I will go off with you to Bredigan, where King Arthur is, and I will swear fealty to him for all my lands, I and all my barons. And if I should happen to defeat you, you will give the castle back to me and then go away a free man, for I ask nothing else of you. And thus we can bring to an end a thing that could be so hurtful."

"And if one of us dies," asked King Bors, "what will happen then?"

"If you kill me," answered King Amant, "my men will go off with you and will swear fealty to King Arthur. And if you should happen to be killed, my castle will be left to me and your men will be free to go wherever they will, and if they wish to become my liegemen, I'll willingly take them and with a glad heart."

Then they swore to keep this pledge, and they made all their men swear to hold to it without breaking their oath. With that they went onto a most beautiful heath, for they already had their armor on.

And Ulfin and Bretel came straight to King Bors, along with the forty companions, and they said to him, "Sir, what are you trying to do? You want to go against that king man to man, but you will not fight him on our advice! Rather let's all of us fight, for they won't hold out against us. Are you afraid that they cannot be put to rout because there are more of them than us? [248] Never think of us as knights if we do not make all of them come begging you for mercy or else are killed trying! We will not let you fight him man to man; we would be blamed for it by your brother and King Arthur."

"Hold your tongues!" said King Bors. "Since he has asked* me for single combat, I will not go back on my word to him, for I would be forever dishonored. Say no more about it, I beg you."

And when they saw that he would have it no other way, they let it go and spoke no more about it.

Meanwhile, Guinganbresil† and his lord Brandalis‡ came to King Amant and said to him, "Sir, what do you mean to do? A man as clever as you are ought not undertake combat and risk death out of greed for land or money."

"May God never help me," answered King Amant, "if I ever leave here before it is all mine or I have lost it all!"

"Now I'll tell you what to do," said Guiromelant. "You will pit the two best men from over there against two from this side, and you will not fight; we will be better assured of you and our lands, for we have no doubts that they will be defeated."

"No one will fight but him and me," said King Amant, "for that is what we have sworn to each other."

"You can then be sure," said Guiromelant, "that if harm befalls you—God keep you from it!—we will not swear fealty to King Arthur nor will any other man here with us who is a landholder!"

When King Bors heard the arguing, he called Girflet and Guiret of Lambale over and said to them, "Go to King Amant and tell him for me not to have any dispute or

---

*   Sommer's text has *ati* (?) (248, l. 4), with the variant from the Harley manuscript provided in a footnote: *requis* (248, n. 1): "requested."

†   Here *guigaubresil* (248, l. 8), but later the more familiar *ginganbresil* (e.g., 249, l. 35).

‡   Here *braudalis* (248, l. 9), but later *brandelis* (249, l. 35).

quarrel with any of his men over the fealty he has pledged to me he would swear, for if I should happen to win, his men will be free to leave and go wherever they will."

And they went and told him this. And when King Amant heard it, he found it most praiseworthy. He then rode to the middle of the heath, where King Bors was already ready and waiting. And as soon as King Amant got there, they withdrew each to his side and then rode against each other, holding their lances to their chests, and struck each other so hard that their lances drove through their shields and against their hauberks. Their double-mailed hauberks were strong and sturdy, and their lances flew into pieces with the shock of the blows each one dealt the other, for both worthy kings* were strong and bold. And they crashed together with their shields and bodies so hard that they were stunned, and each one thought that his eyes had spurted from his head. As it happened, King Amant fell from his horse so bewildered that he did not know whether it was day or night, and he lay on the ground for a long time in a daze from the hard jolt. But King Bors held himself on his horse and did not fall, for he was a very strong man, but he was still very dizzy. And when he had recovered from his dizziness, he drew his sword out of its scabbard—his was a sword of great merit, and afterwards Lionel his son struck many a fair blow with it, and he was most worthy and a good knight later on, just as the story will spell it out to you later.

As soon as King Bors had drawn his sword, he looked about him and saw King Amant, who was still lying on the ground in a daze. He drew up to him, got down from his horse, and gave it to a young squire to watch over—he was very [249] worthy and bold, and his name was Galesconde. And when he had dismounted, he went to the spot where King Amant still lay in a daze, and he brought the tip of his sword to rest on King Amant's chest and began to nudge him.

And he said to him, "King Amant, get up, for you have been asleep for a long time. The day is going by, and I have far to ride. It is not courtly of you to keep me waiting here."

After a while King Amant came out of his faint. He had heard King Bors call him, and he had understood what he said to him, and in his heart he held him in high esteem and blessed him for waiting so long without hitting him, for Bors was behaving toward him with greater courtliness and nobility than he would have shown Bors if he had had the opportunity. And he quickly leapt up and drew his sword, which was of great merit, out of its scabbard. He was deeply ashamed to have found himself lying on the ground, so he thrust his shield over his head, ran straight for King Bors, and dealt as heavy a blow as he could strike with his arm; King Bors† thrust his shield out, but the blow landed so hard that it split his shield down to the boss. And King Bors paid him back with a blow that split his shield into two halves and brought his helmet down to his shoulders, so that he could not see; and when he felt that he had been blinded, he jumped back, cut the straps off of his helmet, and threw it away; then he covered himself with his shield, for he was very much afraid for his head, where he had only his iron coif left to wear.

---

* The expression here is *li baron* (248, l. 30): "barons" or "worthy men."
† Sommer's text has only the personal pronoun *il* (249, l. 16).

When King Bors saw that King Amant had lost his helmet, he called over to him and said, "King Amant, now make peace with me, for you see plainly how it is with you. I beg you to come with me and swear fealty to King Arthur. It would be a great shame if you died here, for you still have a long life to live,* and I would be very sorry to kill you."

"No," answered King Amant, "you surrender and put yourself at my mercy! Do you truly think that you have beaten me just because I have taken my helmet off? You should know that I took it off only because it bothered me! Take heed of me, for I defy you!"

With that King Amant, full of wrath, ran upon him, and he meant to strike him on the head. King Bors, who was very skilled at swordsmanship, took the blow on his shield, but it hit so hard that it sent a big piece of it flying into the field. Then King Bors got ready to strike a blow, and he made it seem that he meant to hit him from below; King Amant thrust his shield down, but King Bors struck down from above and hit him squarely† on the head, splitting it through down to his shoulders, and he went sprawling dead to the ground.

When King Bors saw King Amant dead, he was filled with sorrow, and he said that he would rather have taken him alive to make peace between him and King Arthur. And when Guinganbresil, Brandalis, and Guiromelant saw that King Amant had been killed, they left with three hundred knights and said that they would never love King Arthur or anyone who was his liegeman. But two hundred knights stayed behind and said that they would go with King Bors to King Arthur and swear fealty to him, for they could not have a better overlord than he.

After King Amant had been killed, King Bors called his companions together and said that he would very gladly build a hospice there, where they would serve Our Lord thenceforth until the end of the world for the sake of King Amant's soul, [250] and where the Body of Jesus Christ would be consecrated and served for the victory that Our Lord had given him. There was a clerk who had served King Bors many a day; he came to King Bors and asked him a favor, and he said that he would very gladly dwell there if it pleased him. And King Bors very willingly granted him this, and he bestowed on him income fees and left behind a great deal of his own money to build the hospice. And the clerk thus lived there as long as it pleased and suited him, and he was afterwards a very worthy man who led a very holy life.

And after King Bors had had King Amant buried and had entrusted the clerk with the revenues, he left and made his way until he came to Bredigan, where he found King Arthur, King Ban his brother, and Merlin, who were very happy to see him.

And King Bors said to King Arthur, "Sir, here are part of King Amant's knights, who have come to you under my charge, and they say that they will swear fealty to you and hold their lands from you; and they are worthy and wealthy gentlemen, just as I have always been given to understand. Take their oaths and welcome them, as you ought."

And King Arthur told them that they were most welcome and asked them to believe that he would do only what was good for them, provided that they willingly

---

*   The text reads *encore estes vous de bel eage* (249, l. 22): "you are still at a fair age."
†   The text reads *a descouert* (249, l. 31): "openly."

acknowledge him as their overlord;* and they stepped forward and swore fealty to him.

And after they had sworn their fealty, he asked them what kind of man King Amant had been in his country. They began to weep with great feeling and said that he was dead, and they told him the whole adventure: how he had left his lands to go to the castle of Charroie, how they rode ahead on the road King Bors would take in order to do battle with him, how King Bors and King Amant† fought man to man in single combat, and how King Amant‡ had been killed. When King Arthur and King Ban heard about King Bors's deeds at arms, they were wondrously gladdened.

Then Merlin came to King Bors and said to him, "Sir, you have not told us about betrothing your brother Guinebal."

And King Arthur asked Merlin to tell how the betrothal was carried out. And Merlin told him about the tricks and spells that Guinebal had worked for the sake of his lady friend. Then King Ban asked Merlin if he knew who the knight was who would put an end to the dancing.

And Merlin told him that he had not yet been fathered. "And don't bother to ask any more, because we don't have the time right now."

And when everyone knew that King Bors had slain King Amant, they held him in high esteem and praised him for it, and they said outright that never had there been such worthy men as the two brothers were, and if it had not been for them, King Arthur would have lost everything.

And so they stayed there two full days. And King Arthur sent out for workers with picks and hoes, and there were a good five hundred of them. Then they went after the treasure in the forest that Merlin had told them about, and they dug and burrowed in the ground and found the greatest hoard that had ever been seen. They took it out of the ground and loaded it into wagons and carts in great numbers of [251] barrels, and when they had loaded it they sent it to Logres, King Arthur's chief city, where his nephews were waiting for it.

And beneath an oak tree Merlin had the earth dug out deep down until they found in a leather holder§ twelve swords, the most beautiful and the best that could be found in any ground. King Arthur brought this treasure back to Logres, and he kept them in his treasure-house until those came to court who might own them, and then they were put to good use.

As soon as Gawainet, his brothers, and the other companions heard it said that King Arthur was coming, they got on horseback and rode out to meet him all together, and not one of them was left there who did not go out happy and joyful, for never will anyone make such a show of gladness. And as they drew nearer, Merlin took King Arthur aside, along with the two brother kings, and he had them dismount in a quite beautiful bower to wait for the youths who were coming, and they commanded the army to keep to the road until they came to Logres and to take lodging and to spend their time resting. And when they heard the king's orders,

---

* The expression is *par tant quil le voelent amer* (250, l. 16): "as long as they are willing to love him."

† Sommer's text has the plural personal pronoun *il* (250, l. 21).

‡ Sommer's text has the singular personal pronoun *il* (250, l. 22).

§ The word is *vaissel* (251, l. 3): "vessel."

they left straightway and rode until they met the young men, who were coming at a gallop. When the young men* met them they asked where the king was, and they showed them the bower where he had dismounted, and the youths headed straight for it because they were in a great hurry. And Gawainet rode out before them, for they took him for their lord and master, and they were right, for he was the most knowledgeable man there ever was, the most courtly† and the most clever.

The story says that the young men rode until they came to the bower where the three kings and the companions of the Round Table had dismounted. And as soon as the young men saw them, they got down from their horses and ran to where the knights were seated on the green grass in the forest shade; they were taking the fresh air and cooling off, for it had been very hot all day and they had ridden with all their armor on, for they did not dare take it off because of the Saxons who had run into the land. And it was as warm as it should be at the end of May. The companions of the Round Table saw the young men coming closer—they had taken one another by the hand, and they were so delightfully dressed and adorned, and they were so handsome, that it seemed clear to those watching them that they had come from good stock,‡ and it was most fitting that they were holding one another by the hand, and they took it as a mark of their high birth that they got along together so flawlessly.

And when the knights saw them coming, they got up to meet them, and as they drew closer Gawainet spoke and greeted them, and asked them which one was King Arthur: "Please show him to us, if you would be so kind."§

Nascien, whose behavior was that of a highborn man, answered him: "My boy, there he is over there with those worthy gentlemen, and he is the youngest of them all."

And he pointed Arthur out to him.

When Gawainet heard that, he moved by him and answered, "Sir, many thanks!"

And he went straight to where King Arthur and his companions were, and they stood up as soon as they saw him coming. When Gawainet saw his uncle and his companions, [252] all the youths fell to their knees and greeted the king and his companions.

"Sir," said Gawainet, "I have come to you with my brothers and our cousins and kinsmen because you are our earthly liege lord, and these others have come as well, in part for the good they have heard about you and also because they wish to have from you the order of knighthood; and they will serve you most willingly and with a glad heart, just as we must serve you if our service pleases you. That is not to say that they have not already served you as though they were yours while you were away from this country, for they helped safeguard your lands against your enemies just as if it had been their own, and they have come to the aid of those who have kept your lands for you. And since they have come here, they have undergone great

---

* 	Sommer's text has the plural personal pronoun *il* (251, l. 16).
† 	Sommer's text expresses this negatively as *qui mains auoit uilounie* (251, l. 20): "who had the least villainy/lowborn behavior."
‡ 	The expression in Sommer's text is *de boine lieu* (251, l. 32): "from a good place."
§ 	The expression in Sommer's text is *par uostre merci* (251, l. 37): "by your mercy."

hardship, and I would like you to know it, for we should bring before* the worthy gentleman the good things we have done for him, but hide them from the evil man because he will not be troubled to reward them, and his eyes do not have the strength to behold a worthy man."

When King Arthur heard the young man speaking with such wisdom, he took him by the hand, and he ordered everyone to stand up, and they did. And King Arthur began speaking to them, and he asked Gawainet who they were.

"Sir," said Gawainet, "before you learn that from us, we wish to know what you want to do, whether you mean to retain us, so tell us what you want and then, after that, ask us what you will and we'll tell you very gladly whatever we know."

When the three kings heard the young man's speech, they held him to be very clever, and King Ban told King Arthur that he was right.

Then King Arthur said to him, "Dear, fair friend, I'll very gladly retain you, and with my own hand I will make you and your companions knights, and you will all be welcome. And I want you all to be my friends and companions of my own household."

And when the brothers heard what the king had to tell them, they all thanked him and fell to their knees, but the king bade them stand up, and he took Gawainet by the hand and said to him, "Dear friend, now tell me who you and your companions are, for I am very eager to know."

"Sir," said the youth, "by my right name they call me Gawainet, and I am the son of King Lot of Loonois and of Orkney, and over here these three young lords I'm holding by the hand are my brothers. The eldest after me is named Agravain, and the second is Guerrehet and the third Gaheriet. And our mother has led us to understand that she is sister to King Arthur on his mother's side. And those young lords over here are our first cousins, for they are our aunts' sons. This stout young man is named Galescalain,† and he is the son of King Neutres of Garlot. And this other young squire is the son of King Urien, and his name is Yvonet, and the other young lord whom Yvonet‡ is holding by the hand is his brother by his father, and his name is Yvonet too. The other young lords you see there standing with us§ are very highborn men. This tall, brawny one is the son of King Belinant of North Wales, and he is Galescalain's cousin. Those other two have come from the king of Estrangort; one is named Kay of Estral and the other Kehedin the Small. And those other two young lords standing together are first cousins, and they belong to King Lot, my father, and they are sons of earls; one is named Yvonet of the White Hands and the other is Yvonet the Buck.¶ And this other one is Yvain of [253] Rivel, and this one is Yvain of Lionel. And this other young lord, so brawny with the smiling

---

*   The word is *reprocier* (252, l. 11): "to bring out, bring to the attention of," specifically in order to cast blame, "to reproach." Gawain definitely means to suggest revealing good things to the noble man as opposed to hiding them from the unworthy man; perhaps he also intends an elegant play on "approach"/ "reproach."

†   Sommer's text has *galescins* (252, l. 33).

‡   The name here in Sommer's text contains another diminutive ending: *yuoniaus* (252, l. 35), rather than the expected *yuones* (cf. l. 35).

§   The verb *entretenir* (252, l. 37) suggests standing together in a group.

¶   Here Sommer's text has *clains* (?) (252, l. 42) for the usual *dains* ("buck"); in the same vicinity is found *lesclains* (254, l. 2).

face, whose limbs and body are so well built, is the grandson of the emperor of Constantinople, and his name is Sagremor of Constantinople, and he has come with us in a spirit of the highest nobility* to take his arms from you as you make him a knight, and he will serve you gladly; and I would wish that he and I were companions in arms as long as it pleases him to stay in this country. And these other young lords whom you see all about us, of whom there are a great number, are all men of high birth, and they are our friends and kinsmen; they have left behind their honors and their lands to come serve you, because of their love for you."

When King Arthur heard the youth speak of these things, he threw his arms around his neck and told him that he was indeed welcome, and he kissed him and embraced him and showed him how glad he was to see him.

And after they had made merry for a long while, he said to Gawainet, "Dear nephew, here! I bestow upon you the post of high constable of my household and, after me, lordship over all my lands. Henceforth you will be commander over all who live in my lands, and this is my will."

Gawainet fell to his knees and said, "Sir, I thank you!"

And the king bestowed this office with his right glove, and then he made him stand up. Afterwards they went to their horses and mounted, and they rode until they came to Logres.

When King Arthur went into the city, his sister, mother of Gawainet, came to meet him, and with her came Morgan, who was his other sister, and she was endowed with great learning.† And when the king recognized them, he was very glad to see them, and they rejoiced with great gladness, because they had not been together for some time. And they kissed one another like brothers and sisters, and then they went up to the high hall which was hung all over with silk cloth, with fresh and tender, sweet-smelling green grass strewn all about, and everyone through the whole city made merry with such great rejoicing all day long that it cannot be told. That same day the king ordered the young men to go to the main church to keep watch until morning, and the story says that it was the second Sunday after Whitsunday,‡ and King Ban, King Bors, and the companions of the Round Table were there, and they kept watch with the brothers, for they did not want to leave them for any reason since they had got to know them.

Next morning after Mass, King Arthur took his good sword, the one he pulled from the stone on Merlin's advice, and he girded it on his nephew Gawainet's side, and then he put his right spur on him and King Ban the left, then King Arthur embraced him§ and besought God to make him a worthy man. He then dubbed¶ the three brothers and gave each one a sword from among those found in the hoard that

---

*   Sommer's text reads *par sa deboinarete & par sa francise* (253, l. 4).

†   Sommer's text reads *qui moult estoit boine clergesse* (253, ll. 19-20): "who was a very good woman clerk."

‡   The text reads *la quinzaine apres la pentecouste* (253, ll. 26-27).

§   That is, gave him the ceremonial *collee* (253, l. 33) which may also have involved a tap on the neck with a sword, similar to the modern notion of dubbing.

¶   Here *adouba* (253, l. 34), meaning literally that he conferred arms on them; confused in English with *to dub* ("to hit, tap") with respect to *la collee*, also part of the investiture ceremony (see preceding note). Henceforth, *adouba* is translated "dubbed" in this passage, except in the case of Sagremor, where the context requires the primary meaning (253, ll. 37-40).

Merlin had shown him. Then he dubbed the two sons of King Urien and Galescalain, Dodinel, Kay of Estral, and Kehedin, and he gave each one a sword from the hoard. And after them he bestowed on Sagremor arms such as those he had brought with him from Constantinople, for he had been outfitted very well with everything a new knight needs, and the king girded him with a very good sword he had brought from Constantinople, where his forebear King Hadrian had given it to him, and he then put on his right spur and King Bors the left, and then King Arthur hugged him [254] about the neck. Then King Arthur dubbed the four cousins Yvonet of the White Hands, Yvonet the Buck,* Yvonet of Lionel, and Yvonet of Rivel, and Alles and Aces, who were their kinsmen, and he gave each one a sword from the hoard. But the story says that Dodinel never had one of those, but he got the sword that had belonged to King Amant, and King Bors gave it to him because his kinsmen were from far away.

After the brothers had been dubbed, each one of them dubbed those they had brought with them as companions. And when they had all been dubbed, they went to the church to hear Mass, which the archbishop of Brice sang; and after Mass had been sung, they went up to the great hall and sat down to eat. King Arthur held court most grandly and gave quite a great feast; it is not fitting to speak of the foods they were served that day, for it would be tiresome to put it all down, and it would be a waste of words.

After the meal, when the tablecloths had been taken away, the young men wanted the target dummy to be set up out in the meadows, but the king forbade them to do so, on Merlin's advice, for the country was too upset and full of too much warfare, and Christendom was being harrowed by the Saxons who had forayed into the countryside. Thus they left aside the games and merrymaking of the young lords who were new knights, and they stayed inside the city for three full days.

And King Arthur gave out great shares of goods to the young men he had engaged, and they came there from everywhere in huge numbers, from here and from there, until there were at least sixty thousand, some on foot, others on horseback, not counting those he had brought with him from the kingdom of Logres and from Carmelide. And while they were staying in the city, Morgan and Merlin became friends; she was endowed with great learning,† and she grew so close to him and came around him so much that she found out who he was. He taught her many wonders in astrology and necromancy, and she kept them all in her mind. And when the third day came, Merlin spoke to the king and told him that they should get ready, for they had to leave and could not stay, for Pontius Anthony and Frollo, with the men of the king of Gaul and Claudas of the Land Laid Waste, had already come into the land and the kingdom of Benoic. And the king answered that he would leave whenever it pleased Merlin,‡ and that he awaited only his orders.

"Go," said Merlin, "and order all your men to keep their armor on tonight and to mount their horses in the early hours. But you will lead only twenty thousand men out of this land along with the twenty thousand you brought out of Carmelide who

---

* Here Sommer's text has *lesclains* (?) for the more usual *dains*, see above, p. 278, first n..
† The expression is *boine clergesse* (254, l. 22); cf. 253, l. 20, and above, p. 278n.
‡ The text reads *il li plairoit* (254, l. 28): "when it pleased him." As the context indicates, Arthur refers not to his own, but to Merlin's pleasure.

belong to King Leodagan's kingdom. And you will leave twenty thousand behind in this city, for this city must not be bereft of men-at-arms, so you will leave Doon of Carduel here to safeguard the city." With that their counsel ended, and the king ordered Gawainet to do what Merlin had entrusted to him, and he got their baggage together, divided everyone up, and had all the ones they were to take with them ride out of Logres. And when he had done this, he went straight to the king and Merlin, and he found them taking counsel together and told them that he had got everything ready.

When Merlin saw him coming, he told the king to ask him who the knight was who brought him to rescue his mother. And the king called him over and said to him, "Gawainet, dear nephew, who was the knight who took you to rescue your mother in the meadowlands of Glocedon?"

And Gawainet asked him what he knew about it and who told him about it.

"You may know for a fact," said the king, "that the one who told me about it knows the truth."

"God help me," said Sir Gawainet, "I never [255] saw him well enough to know him again."

"Now ask him," said Merlin, "whether he knows the one who brought him the letter from his cousin Yvonet, son of King Urien."

And Sir Gawainet looked and saw the one who was sitting beside the king, and he wondered why he was having him ask him those things. He then began thinking, for he was quite clever and sharp-witted, and he recalled the words Doon of Carduel had spoken to him.

And the king asked him if he knew the man with him, and he told him that he did not; "however, I have been led to believe that it was Merlin, but in truth I don't know him, and I'm sorry for that, for he has done me many other kindnesses and services. He had Sagremor, the grandson of the emperor of Constantinople, brought back to me from the danger of death he was in, as well as Yvain my cousin, and me he saved beneath the castle of Arundel. He is the one man in the world I would like best to know right now."

"You will know him very soon," said Merlin.

Then the king began to laugh out loud, and he said to him, "Gawainet, dear nephew, sit down beside me now and I will tell you what I know about it."

And he sat down on the bed, and there were three of them, no more. Then he said to him, "Dear nephew, look, here is the gentleman because of whom you went to Arundel when you fought against the Saxons, the day Dodinel the Wildman and Kay of Estral came from their countries. Now thank him for the services he has done for you, for you should thank him, love him, and serve him if need be, because he has served you very well.

"Sir," said Gawainet, "I don't know what to offer him or give him, but I say this much nevertheless, that I am his man and will do what he orders. He is so wise, I am sure of this, that he already knows the feelings I have for him in my heart."

And he answered that he was his friend and that he did know very well what was in his heart, and he wished him to be his friend, his intimate friend. But he asked him not to tell anyone else what he had told him, however close a friend that might be. "And you will see me in so many shapes," he said, "that you will be astonished.

I do not wish to be recognized by anyone, for envy and jealousy are strong in this world."

And he told him that he would not speak to anyone about that.

That is how Gawainet came to know Merlin in the presence of his uncle King Arthur. And after they had spoken together for a while, Merlin said to him, "Dear friend, go take leave of your mother, then get to the army and have your men mount in the early night hours. Take to the road and head straight for the port of Dover. Get boats and bring them together on the shore, so that your uncle will have only to go aboard when he gets there, as well as the two kings who are very worthy gentlemen, and for God's sake, do them their due honor: they are King Arthur's men, and they come from the noblest stock there is. Be careful not to let anyone know where you are going."

And he said that everything would be done as he had ordered.

With that Sir Gawainet left, and he took leave of his mother, who was a very well-bred lady, and she loved him a great deal with a great love, and she commended him to God and besought Him to keep him from harm. And he left and went straight to the army, he and his brothers, Sir Yvain whom he greatly loved, Galescalain, Dodinel, Sagremor, Yvain the Bastard and his four cousins who were all named Yvain, Kay of Estral, and Kehedin his nephew. These men were never foot soldiers, but the army [256] was under their leadership,* just as Gawainet had taught them, and they were all ready to go. When early night came, Sir Gawainet had all their equipment bound up, put into trunks, and loaded onto pack horses, and he set up a watch all around the army so that no spy could get in, and the ones the story has named for you were in the watch. Then they set out on the road at a slow gait, and they made their way until they came to the port of Dover. But King Arthur stayed behind in Logres with Merlin, the two brother kings, and the forty knights from the kingdom of Carmelide who were the companions of the Round Table.

And when Sir Gawainet had come to the port of Dover, he sent messengers throughout all the harbors and landing places to look for boats, and he had them taken and brought together until he had gathered a very great fleet. When Merlin found out that everything was ready, he had the three kings mount their horses at night, and he commended them to God and told them to have themselves taken straight to La Rochelle, "and when you go ashore there," he said, "you will not set out until you see me."

"What?" said King Arthur. "Won't you come with us?"

"No indeed," said Merlin, "but you will have been there only one evening before I come."

With that, they went their own ways and commended one another to God. Merlin went to Blaise, his teacher in Northumberland, who was very glad when he saw him, because he loved him with a great love. And Blaise besought him to tell him what he had done since the last time he had been there, and he told him everything just as you have heard it in the story after he left him, and Blaise put it all down in writing, and this is how we still know it. And when Merlin came to the part about

---

* The sentence (255, l. 43-266, l. 1) is constructed on a pun: *oste* ("tenant," a freeman of higher status than a serf, but who does not own his farm)/ *ost* ("army"). Sommer's text reads: *icil ne furent onques oste cil orent lost en lor Baillie.*

the young lady whom he loved with his whole heart,[*] Blaise was deeply sorry, for he feared that she might betray him and that he might lose his great knowledge, so he began to give him warnings.[†] He told him about the prophecies that had already been fulfilled and others that came about in the land afterwards, just as the story will recount for you later. And Blaise put it all down in writing just as Merlin told it to him. But with that the story falls silent right here about him and goes back to speaking about King Arthur and his companions.

33. ARTHUR'S FORCES BATTLE CLAUDAS'S AT TREBES.[‡]

In this part the story says that on the very first day of June King Arthur left Logres, his chief city. Mild weather had come back with the pleasant season when the orchards and woodlands are in leaf, when the birds sing sweetly and softly and the blossoming, leafy forests ring with their singing, when the meadows are thick with grass and the gentle waters go back into their beds—and when it is better to make war than any other time of the year. In this season King Arthur rode out with King Ban, King Bors, and their companions, and they did not stop until they came to the sea at the port of Dover. And when they got there, they boarded the boats without tarrying. They had a good, soft wind and sailors who steered them so well that they lost nothing, and at last they came to La Rochelle. Then they got off the boats and camped in tents and pavilions outside the city, and there they awaited Merlin. He came the next day at the noon hour, just as he had told King Arthur. And they were very glad to see him—the three kings and Sir [257] Gawainet, who loved Merlin with a very great love, as Merlin loved him because of the great faithfulness he found in him. And they stayed there and rested, and they put watchmen along all the roads and byways so that no one might come and go who could take news to their enemies. But now the story falls silent for a while about them, and speaks no more of them right here, but it goes back to Leonce, the lord of Payerne, and Pharian of Trebe, who were most faithful and worthy toward their liege lord.

Here the story says that when Merlin left Leonce, lord of Payerne, after he had told him about Pontius Anthony and Frollo of Germany, who were coming with forty thousand well-equipped men, and about Claudas of the Land Laid Waste, who had twenty thousand men from the kingdom of the Land Laid Waste, Leonce sent out and called his men together from near and far, his kinsmen, men-at-arms for hire, and his friends, until he had a good ten thousand from the kingdom of Benoic, all with good horses and well armed, not reckoning the foot soldiers he garrisoned in the strongholds. Meanwhile, for his part, Pharian sent word throughout the kingdom of Gaunes and called together a good ten thousand men on horseback

---

[*]   Sommer's text has *quil ama par amor* (256, l. 21), which implies that he is in love with her, by contrast with the deep affection Blaise feels for Merlin: *moult lama de grant amor* (256, l. 18).

[†]   Sommer's text has *castoier* (256, l. 23), which suggests forewarning by means of moral lessons.

[‡]   Corresponds to Sommer, 256-268.

as well as foot soldiers he garrisoned in the castles and strongholds, where they brought in food from everywhere to store it for safekeeping. And when they had done these things, Pharian went to Benoic with his army, as did Leonce, and they waited until news came to them that their enemy was overrunning their land and setting fire wherever they thought they could do the most harm. But they found little to take in the countryside or anywhere else in the land, because it had all been stored away, and Claudas of the Land Laid Waste was upset and angry because of that, and he was right to think that the enemy had been warned by someone of their coming. That is why the foragers did not stop running throughout the land, but they found little to take.

After they had run up and down, they went back into the great army and talked about what they could do. Then they agreed that they would lay siege to the castle of Trebe, so they rode there and encamped in the meadowlands beneath, but it was far away, for the castle was built very high up, and at the bottom was a deep marsh all around; there was but one way in, across a long, narrow causeway that went on for nearly half a league. In those meadowlands, Pontius Anthony was camped on one side, Frollo of Germany on another, and Claudas of the Land Laid Waste on another, while on yet another were the king of Gaul's men, who were led by Randol* the Saxon, his seneschal, who was very bold and skilled at fighting; and each one had twenty thousand under his banner. Thus the castle of Trebe was besieged on four sides, and the besiegers were so thick that no one could go in or out without being taken and held prisoner, for they thought that they could take the castle by force. But no assault would work,† for no one could get to the castle because of the marsh that went all the way around, so they were at siege there for a very long time.

And Queen Elaine, who was within, and her sister were most distressed, and they were afraid they might be taken prisoner by force or through a betrayal, so they wept long and hard for their husbands, who had been away for so long, and from whom they had had [258] no news. And Gratian comforted them and told them not to be frightened of anything, for it would not be very long before they would be helped in a grand way, and they were sure to see their husbands very soon.

Thus did Gratian comfort the two ladies who were sisters. And he had a son whose name was Banin of Trebe; he was King Ban's godson. This Banin was a young lord, a worthy lad, and he was a kinsman of Leonce of Payerne, who was a kinsman of the brother kings. When he saw that the castle was under siege, he sent word to Anselm the Seneschal to come speak to him, and he came straightway. And when he had come, he told him to get his gear together, "for tonight you must ride out. And be careful to move so stealthily that no one will know where you are going, and wait for our men in the forest of Briosque at the spring in the middle of the clearing. And make sure that the army is so well guarded that no one can get away who might give news to our enemies."

And he said that he would do that so well that there would be nothing to set right.

---

*   Here *raudoul* (257, l. 33), but elsewhere *randol* (261, l. 16.)

†   Sommer notes that the Harley manuscript contains a phrase apparently omitted in his base text: *ny avoit mestier* (257, n. 3): "was of any use to them."

With that Anselm the Seneschal left, and he did everything as Leonce ordered him to. And Leonce took one of his nephews and sent him to Gaunes to Pharian, and he asked Pharian to come to the forest, to the place he had spelled out, and to be outfitted as he knew he should be. And his nephew made his way as he had been asked and gave his message just as he was ordered to do. And when Pharian heard that Leonce had set out and was already on the road, he got himself ready quickly and gathered around him as many men as he knew would be needed, and he took to the road through the narrowest places he knew of, and they were a good ten thousand strong by count. And Leonce was on the road with Anselm, and they rode until they came to a great valley, enclosed all about by a thick growth of trees, in the forest of Briosque, just as Merlin had told him. And the army was so well guarded that no one got out, and they stayed until Pharian came there with his men; and they were all there until the Monday before St. John's Day, which was to fall on the next Sunday.

And when Merlin found out that they were all ready and waiting only for the help he had promised them, he said to Sir Gawainet, "Sir, take ten thousand of your men, and no more, and put yourself on one side of the field. Be sure that Ulfin bears your standard, for he is worthy and faithful. Now do all this right away."

When Sir Gawainet* heard Merlin's order, he left with Ulfin and his men, and they put themselves on one side of the field with ten thousand men. Afterwards Merlin called King Ban over and said to him, "Come forward, noble knight. You will lead the second echelon, and there will be ten thousand men with you, and we will see how you defend your lands and how you take revenge† against King Claudas for the harm he has done you, and he still beleaguers you every day as much as he can."

"Sir," said King [259] Ban, "it will be as it pleases God, and if I ever have happiness, it will be from God and from you and King Arthur."

"Go," said Merlin, "and take your men over to one side, and have them put their armor on forthwith to ride against your enemies."

With that, King Ban left and took ten thousand knights from the army and led them to one side; they were young, untried knights,‡ but they were most worthy and very skilled at arms, and he had them get ready.

Afterwards Merlin called King Bors of Gaunes over and said to him, "My lord king, come forward. You will lead the third echelon, and you will have in your company the three hundred knights from King Amant's land, and you will take enough others who came from the kingdom of Carmelide so that you will be ten thousand strong, and you will get them ready to defend themselves. Take swiftly to the road. And take care that knighthood is not brought low by you. And we will see how you fight and how you defend your land against your enemies!"

"Sir," said King Bors, "we will do what pleases God, and we will do our very best."

Then King Bors left, took his men away from the main army, and had them mount their horses.

*   Sommer's text has *au roy artu* (258, l. 29).

†   Sommer's text repeats *desfendres* (258, l. 36), "defend."

‡   Sommer's text has *iouenes bachelers* (259, l. 5).

Afterwards Merlin spoke to King Arthur: "Sir," he said, "you will lead the fourth echelon, and the companions of the Round Table will be with you; they will not let you down even if it means their death."

Then the king ordered Nascien, Adragain, and Hervi to get them armed and ready, and they did so well that nothing was left to do but mount their horses. Then Merlin took the dragon and called Kay the Seneschal: "Sir, come forward. Carry King Arthur's ensign, for that is your right. And take care that knighthood is not brought low by you. You know what you will do when you come upon your enemies: you will keep riding and holding the banner up!"

And Kay said that he would do so.

By the time the echelons had thus been made up, it was the noon hour; they prepared to eat, and they sat down. And after they had eaten, the barons gathered together to ask what they would do.

"I will tell you what to do," said Merlin. "Tonight, in the early hours, you will set out, so that tomorrow evening you will be at Trebe, for your enemies have besieged it on all four sides, and each of the princes has laid siege to one side, and each one has twenty thousand men with him. And each of our echelons will go fall on one of the armies, so that there will be onslaughts on all four sides. Now, they have set up very good watches, and we'll have to move very craftily."

"What?" asked King Arthur. "Do they then have more men than we do?"

"Yes," said Merlin, "we have half as many. But help will come to us in a grand way, for twenty thousand more men will come there on time, and they have camped in the forest of Briosque."

"How will they know that we have got there?"

"Sir," he said, "I'll go and fetch them. Blioberis will lead the army, and he will ride out ahead, for he knows the ways and byways I'll show him. And when you see that day has broken, spur your horses all together and ride very fast to where you'll hear a horn blowing. There you will see a great fire burning high up in the air: you will look over that way, for there the help I'll bring you will be made ready."

"Sir," said King Arthur, "when will you take to the road?"

"Right away," answered Merlin, "for we mustn't tarry. I commend you to God." [260]

Then Merlin left the king, and when he was away from the army he disappeared so thoroughly that no one knew what had happened to him. Before the hour of nones he appeared in the army of Leonce of Payerne, who was not expecting any news of him. Merlin came there with Pharian, Anselm, and Gratian; and he said, "Leonce, why are you and your men not mounting your horses? You will find King Arthur as soon as you come to the army."

And when Leonce heard it, he was very joyful. And when they had rejoiced, they asked him news of their lords, and he told them that they would see them in due course, because they were riding at full speed, "but now form your echelons, and I'll lead you to the army."

"Sir," said Leonce, "many thanks. Now I know that we will prevail, since you will be with us."

Then the four companions divided their men into four groups. The seneschal took five thousand and separated them from the others; and Gratian also took five thousand, as did Pharian. And Leonce stayed with the rest, and his men, who were well armed, numbered five thousand or more. But now the story falls silent about Merlin and Leonce the lord of Payerne and their companions and returns to King Arthur.

Here the story says that when Merlin left King Arthur, King Arthur had all his men mount their horses, and one echelon moved out after the other, and Blioberis rode ahead of Sir Gawainet's echelon, for he was the one who knew the ways through better than any in the land. There could be seen many an ensign of gold and silver and silk waving in the wind. The weather was mild and still, and the countryside was delightful, for there were many forests and meadowlands where birds were singing in the many ways that gladden those who are deeply in love. They rode that night until it was daylight before they knew it, for they had listened so closely to the bird songs that they forgot what they were doing.

Suddenly they came to a very fair heath that was filled with shrubs in bloom, and it was beside the Loire River. The grass was so high that the horses stood up to their bellies in it. There King Arthur's men rested all day until the hour of vespers, and they ate and drank as they needed to, and they slept, for it was a pleasant and delightful spot.

When it was past the hour of vespers on Tuesday, all of them put on their armor, big and small, and they mounted their horses, for they had only seven leagues to ride to come to King Claudas's army. There you would have seen many a faithful warrior* with rich clothing, many a thick hand-held lance with a sharp iron tip, many a dazzling helmet and shield; and they rode drawn tightly together, one after the other, and Blioberis the first in line. They rode at a slow gait without shifting the shields they held before their chests, for they yearned to strike hard and fight well.† The echelons rode nearly a half-league apart, and King Arthur was in the lead, where Kay bore the dragon. And the four‡ echelons went thus one after the other all night until day broke, when they came out of the forest of Briosque. They rode along the Loire River and then [261] stopped there to watch for Merlin's sign, for he had told them about the fire that was to burn up in the air, and he had said to listen for the sound of a horn blowing. They had drawn so close to the enemy army that they were five arrow-shots away. They saw clearly that there were a great many fires burning and a great many men, and they heard the horses neighing, and as they drew closer still the men guarding the army could hear the great din. They sent men out on horseback to spy on them and find out whose men they were, and they rode out and looked at their armor.

When those in the enemy army heard the news about King Arthur's men, they ran to put on their armor, broke away from the main body, and drew up in ranks, each one under his banner, in the middle of the field, and they all said one to another that they did not know what army had come riding against them in such numbers. And Pontius Anthony, who knew a great deal about warfare, rode out from the main body wearing all his armor, and he went into the forest of Briosque toward the way

---

*   The text reads *maint vassal* (260, ll. 34-35): *vassal* can simply designate a warrior or indicate the quality of his fighting.
†   The text reads *& de lor cuors desfendre* (260, l. 38): "and defend themselves."
‡   Sommer's text has *.iij.* (260, l. 40).

they were coming in, and he ordered his men to follow him, which they did as soon as they put their armor on. And Frollo, the duke of Germany, rode out after him, and he set his path toward a little river called the Arroux. And Randol, the king of Gaul's seneschal, went toward the orchards, while Claudas of the Land Laid Waste set out toward the causeway. And they all rode away from the tents and pavilions in great strength, in troops, and they all went under their banners.

While Arthur's men* were listening to them putting their armor on and making ready, Merlin came out of his hiding place in the woods, for he was well aware of all their comings and goings; then he took a horn and blew it so loudly that the river and the whole woods resounded with it. After that he cast a strong and wondrous spell, for he made a great fire appear up in the air redder than a lightning bolt, and it was right above the tents of the enemies' army. When King Arthur's men saw the great fire burning in the sky and heard the horn blowing, they crossed themselves for the wonder they felt; then they let their horses run as fast as they could. And Sir Gawainet flew headlong into the camp of Duke Frollo of Germany, King Ban of Benoic overran the tents of Claudas of the Land Laid Waste, King Bors rode in among Pontius Anthony's pavilions, and King Arthur among the tents of Randol the Seneschal. There tents and pavilions were brought crashing down, and the uproar and the yelling rose so loud on every side that the hearts of the boldest shuddered. There they lost many of those who were still in the camps, for they were not yet fully armed, and many were killed and wounded, and the wounded wailed and screamed, for they were beset by death. Then it was broad daylight and the sun began to rise. The sun shone on the armor, which flashed in the light, and it was so beautiful and pleasing to look at that it was a delight and a melody to watch.

When Claudas, Frollo, Pontius Anthony, and Randol saw the great harm the attackers had done to them, they were filled with sorrow, for they believed that they had lost more than ten thousand men all told from their ranks. And when Randol the Seneschal saw the harm the men who ambushed him had done to him, he was so full of wrath that he nearly went out of his mind. He then rode back toward [262] the tents he had left, in order to rally his men around him. And when Sir Gawainet looked and saw Frollo coming, he boldly rode to meet him. Frollo had many bold knights with him, and they were a good fifteen thousand men strong, but he had lost a good six thousand of them, killed and cut into pieces. And as they drew closer, they ran upon one another as fast as their horses could go.

As the armies crashed together, Sagremor was the first one in, and Frollo, who was full of anger, rode out to meet him; he was tall and wondrously strong. He and Sagremor struck each other so hard with their lances that each brought the other to the ground with his horse falling on top, but both sprang back up on their feet, for they were both skillful, strong, bold, and nimble. They drew their swords from their scabbards and thrust their shields over their heads and ran against each other, and they began such a great fight, rough and fierce, that both of them were in great danger of being killed, unless they got help, for they were wonderfully good knights, and their swords were so good that they did not need to look for better ones; and they fought for a long time before they stopped.

---

*   Sommer's text has non-specific *cil* (261, l. 20): "they."

When Sir Gawainet saw Sagremor on the ground, he and Ulfin, who bore the ensign, spurred their horses to his rescue, while those on the other side rushed to free the duke. And they hit one another on their shields with their lances, and they struck down and killed one another, and there began a great and dreadful battle that lasted a long time. And there was such clanging and crashing together that Sagremor and Frollo* were put back on their horses while the fighting was heavy and fierce and wondrous. There the twelve companions, who were new knights, did wonders, as did the forty companions who were with them. But after the noon hour had passed, there was none who fought better than Sir Gawainet: he did wonders, and he struck down and killed men and horses, as did in their turns Sir Yvain, son of King Urien, his brother Yvain the Bastard, and Galescalain, son of King Neutres of Garlot; and Gaheriet fought so well that he was held to be the best of them all after Sir Gawainet. And elsewhere Agravain, Guerrehet, and Sagremor fought very well, as did all the companions together.

On the other side King Ban was fighting King Claudas's men, and it happened that King Ban and Claudas met in the midst of the ranks, which were big and dangerous. As soon as they had caught sight of each other, they ran against each other with their drawn swords held high. Claudas was a very good knight, strong and sure of himself, but he was envious of those who were set above him. He struck King Ban so hard on his helmet that burning sparks flew into the air, and he ran against him so hard that he made him hunch over his horse's neck. But with great bearing King Ban sat back up straight, and he gave him a heavy blow on the helmet; he hit him with a glancing blow, for he was leaning over, and it fell on his horse's neck, and he cut his horse through the backbone and brought it to the ground with Claudas astride. Claudas sprang up very quickly, but before he was upright, King Ban dealt him three blows on the helmet such that [263] he nearly made him fall in a faint; he made his blood spurt from his mouth and nose, but Claudas was so strong that he kept himself from falling. He threw his shield over his head and came straight for King Ban, and the fight began, and the war would have been ended forever for King Claudas if they could have kept together for just a little longer, but his men, of whom he had half again as many as King Ban, very forcefully rescued him. King Ban's men numbered only ten thousand, and the others were a good eighteen thousand strong. Nevertheless, each side fought as hard as the other, until Claudas got back on his horse and King Ban's men had to withdraw, and if King Ban himself had not been the help they needed, they would have been driven from the field and put to rout; but he kept the battle going all by himself, and no one could run him off the field, any more than if he had been a castle keep, and he held his ground there in that way until after the noon hour.

Elsewhere King Bors was fighting against the men of Pontius Anthony at the tents and pavilions, where they lost many of the ones who had stayed behind there. And when Pontius Anthony saw the great harm that had befallen them so suddenly, he was wondrously angry and upset. And when he had got his men in order beside the forest where he had taken them, he went back toward the tents, where he saw the great slaughter. When King Bors saw them coming, he went to meet them with

---

*   The text reads *li doi* (262, l. 21): "the two."

his shield about his neck and his lance very boldly clenched in his fist. And when Pontius Anthony saw him coming, he went to meet him and struck his horse with his spurs as hard as he could, for he was in a great hurry to get to him, and, riding their horses very fast, they struck each other on the shield with all their strength and drove through and shattered them; and Pontius Anthony broke his lance on King Bors. But King Bors struck him so hard that he drove his shield against his arm and his arm against his body, and he thrust the tip of his lance through him above the trappings of his sword and opened a great wound on his left side. Red blood ran down over his thigh to his heel, and King Bors jolted him so hard that he sent him sprawling, so that the ground shook all around with a thud. Pontius Anthony lay there in a daze for so long that no one knew whether he was dead or alive, and when his men saw him thrown down they were very much afraid that he would be killed, so they spurred to his rescue. And King Bors's men rode against them and welcomed them with the tips of their lances, and they put many of them to death.

There the battle was wondrous and the jousting* deadly, for there were twenty thousand on one side and ten thousand on the other. Pontius Anthony was rescued and put back on his horse, and his men found that he had been wounded a little on the left side, but he had no wound that would not heal harmlessly; even so, he was quite a bit worse off from his fall than from his wounds, for he had never before been brought down from his saddle by a blow from a knight, and he would gladly take revenge for his shame and distress if he ever got the chance. So he drew his sword and entered the jousting, which lasted a long time, and then Pontius happened to meet King Bors, who was doing wonders all by himself. And as soon as Pontius Anthony saw him, he recalled that it was he who had struck him down, so he ran against him with his sword drawn and dealt him such a blow on his helmet that he split it and made him hunch forward over his saddlebow. [264] And as Pontius Anthony was recovering to strike the second blow, King Bors hit his horse with his spurs and flew into the midst of the fighting. Then he reined his horse around and came back clenching his sword, and Pontius Anthony came against him as well, and they hit each other on the helmet with such hard blows that they were both stunned. But in striking they were not equals, for King Bors struck Pontius Anthony so hard on the side of his head that he made his blood come spurting from his nose and mouth, and he stunned him so much that he sent him sprawling to the ground in such a daze that he never knew where he lay. And King Bors jumped atop him and trampled his body until it was utterly broken. Pontius Anthony fainted from the agony he felt, and King Bors would have gladly got down from his horse to cut off his head, but he did not have his way, for the Romans came that way spurring their horses to rescue Pontius Anthony, and they flew headlong right into the middle of King Bors's men and so hard that they drove them back an arrow-shot, for there were a very great many of them. And they kept the battle going that way until after the noon hour.

Elsewhere King Arthur was fighting very fiercely against the men of Randol, the king of Gaul's seneschal. They had found more than seven thousand of their men killed and maimed among the pavilions, and when Randol saw the very great

---

* The word here (263, l. 35) and elsewhere (e.g., l. 40) is *tournoiement*, "tourneying."

damage and losses, he was filled with great sorrow. He came out against King Arthur and his men* with the fourteen thousand armed men he had left; they were skilled at warfare, bold, and heartened to avenge the deaths of their friends and kinsmen whom they had seen slaughtered before their eyes, so they rode against them, with their lances under their arms, full of wrath and eager to do them great harm. So they, who were so learned† in warfare, came against them, and they were good leaders, but Arthur's men held them in very low esteem, for they saw that they would be taken,‡ so they welcomed them with the tips of their lances, and many of them were left dead and wounded. There many worthy knights§ were killed and maimed, which brought great sorrow and losses to their friends. There the knights of the Round Table did wonders, for they killed knights and horses, and with them was King Arthur, who made all the ranks shine forth wherever he went,¶ and they fought so skillfully that they broke through them and cast them aside by sheer force, like it or not, and they did not once stop until they came upon Pontius Anthony's men, who were sorely beleaguering King Bors and his men.

And when they got to them, there was such a great din that no one could have heard God thundering, and they raised so much dust that the sun, which was high in the sky, was dimmed. And Kay the Seneschal followed them, holding the dragon that Merlin had entrusted him to bear, and it gave off from time to time such great bursts of fire that they rose up in the air and were so huge and dreadful that the hearts of all who had never seen it before shook with fear. And they all said one to another, "What will become of us?"

For all that, the dragon had great meaning in and of itself. For thus were meant King Arthur and his power, and the flames that shot from its mouth stood for the great suffering that people underwent [265] and the great slaughter that happened in the time of King Arthur. And its tail, which was all twisted, was a sign of the great betrayal of his people, by whom he was himself betrayed afterwards, who were stirred up against him by Mordred, his son, whom he fathered with his sister, King Lot's wife, when he went across to take the land of Benoic because of the wrath of Lancelot of the Lake. He had laid siege there because of the ill will that had grown up between the two of them over his wife, Queen Guenevere, whom Lancelot loved, just as the story will recount later. But here the story speaks no more about that, for it is not yet the place; rather, we will tell you about the battle that was in the meadowland below Trebe, between King Arthur's men and the men of Randol the Seneschal. He had yielded the field and run helter-skelter into the

---

*   Sommer's text has *lor* ("them") without an explicit antecedent (264, l.19),

†   Sommer's text has *ditit* (264, l. 23), which he marks as a curiosity (n. 2) without offering a variant. It seems appropriate to connect the form with *doit* (<*doctus*) ("learned") or the verbs *ditier* (<*dictare*) ("to dictate, teach") or *doitier/ditier* (<*digitare*) ("to point out, teach").

‡   Sommer's text has *si les prisierent moult petit car il uirent quil furent pris* (264, l. 24): "and they prized them very little for they saw that they were taken." The meaning, somewhat obscure, seems to depend in part on the association of the words *prisierent* and *pris* (which as a noun can mean "price," "value," etc.).

§   The word here is *vassal* (264, l. 26): "worthy men."

¶   Sommer's text has *par tout lo il aloit* (264, ll. 28-29), perhaps for *par tout l'o* [for *ost*] [*ou*] *il aloit*: "throughout the whole army where he went."?

men of Pontius Anthony, who were keeping King Bors's men at close range, and King Bors was in very great need of help.

When Pontius Anthony saw the runaways coming, he rode out to meet them and shouted his battlecry; then he rushed against his enemies. King Bors was quite overwhelmed, and he would have been thrown from the field if Kay the Seneschal had not come up with his echelon.* There the fighting was quite wondrous and very heavy, and many fell on both sides; yet the two sides were about equal. Elsewhere Sir Gawainet and his companions had fought so hard against the men of Duke Frollo of Germany that they made them shift about and overrun the echelon of Claudas of the Land Laid Waste. He was fighting against King Ban of Benoic, who was in very dire straits. And when the four echelons came together, they all upheld one another, and the din and the fracas grew loud and the fighting grew very heavy. There Sir Gawainet did wonders all by himself, and never thereafter did anyone see a man work such wonders as he did that day. And the story says that it was after noon when Sir Gawainet happened to meet Claudas, who was fighting with about thirty men against King Ban, who had only about twenty, and King Ban was in very dire straits. And Sir Gawainet rushed headlong into them, his sword held high, to strike Claudas on the head. And Claudas thrust his shield against the blow, and Sir Gawainet hit him so hard that he sent his shield flying in two halves, and his sword fell upon his saddlebow and sliced his horse between the shoulders so that it stumbled to the ground in a heap. Gawainet rushed right by and did not stop, for he did not know who it was, and he met another one and struck him and split him down to the teeth; this was a very skilled and very bold knight from the house of King Claudas. And afterwards he struck Antorilas so hard that he sent his head flying. He struck right and left until he killed twenty of their men, who were all lying at the feet of the king, and he fought so well that none who saw or felt his blows dared take a stand against him.

When King Ban saw the wonders that the young man was doing, he thanked God for him and worshipped Him, and he came to him and said, "Gawainet, you are most welcome, and you are doing much good for me. God help me, King Arthur has not misplaced the authority he gave you to lead his army, for he could not have entrusted it to anyone better than you. And I beg you for God's sake to grant me your company all day today."

"Sir," said [266] Sir Gawainet, "I very gladly grant it to you today and any other time, and thank you very much for asking. But I must go looking for my brothers and cousins, for I do not know what has become of them. As soon as I have found them, I'll come back to you."

"Sir," said King Ban, "I would gladly go with you, but I would very much like to know how I can take revenge on my deadly enemy, whom you have brought down, for this war would be brought to an end if he could be killed."

"What?" said Sir Gawainet. "Which one is it? Show him to me."

"Look, there he is!" said King Ban. "See his armor painted with silver blossoms and his parted shield, half white and half red, with the lion rampant. He has got back on his horse as you and I are speaking!"

* The word here is *bataille* (265, l.16): "battalion."

"Sir," said Gawainet, "we can yet bring this to an end today. Let us overrun them, for you see that I'm all ready!"

"Indeed," said King Ban, "I wish nothing so much as to harm him, for it is because of him that I have had so much harm done to me."

"What is his name?" asked Sir Gawainet.

"His name is Claudas of the Land Laid Waste," answered King Ban.

"What?" said Sir Gawainet "Is it thanks to him that all these men have come here?"

"In truth, yes." answered King Ban.

"Then let's ride to him together," said Sir Gawainet, "for we mustn't tarry."

With that they spurred their horses to where they had seen King Claudas, and as soon as he saw them coming, he very boldly came out to meet them, and the clanging and fighting began. And Sir Gawainet and King Ban fought with help from their companions until they sent Claudas's men on their way. And when King Claudas saw that it was his turn to have losses, he rushed headlong into the press where it was thickest, for he greatly feared the ones who threatened to cut off his head—he was sure of this—if they could lay their hands on him. And when Sir Gawainet and King Ban saw him ride away, they set out, spurring their horses after him; and when Claudas saw them coming, he turned in flight and rode hither and thither through the battlefield, and after him were Gawainet and King Ban, who did not want to let him go. And had it not been for something that happened to them* on the battlefield, he would never have escaped from them.

While King Ban and Sir Gawainet were giving chase through the battlefield, Gawainet looked and saw his brother Agravain lying on the ground with his horse on top of him, and Guerrehet was also down with his sword in his hand, and elsewhere he saw his cousin Galescalain, whom Duke Frollo of Germany was holding by the helmet; and Duke Frollo had more than two thousand men who were helping him, and they would have killed them† had it not been for Sagremor, Gaheriet, Sir Yvain and his brother; and Yvonet of Lionel, Dodinel the Wildman, Kay of Estral, and Kehedin the Small were also there, along with the forty companions who were with King Arthur in the kingdom of Carmelide—these kept the battle going against the two thousand, but they could not bring out the three who had been struck down.

And when Sir Gawainet saw the trouble his brother was in, he said to King Ban, "Sir, I am sorry. I am going to help those men over there whom I am bound not to forsake."

He then showed the ones who were in dire straits.

And when King Ban saw them, he said to him, "Spur your horse on; we can't lose any time!"

And they quickly spurred to that side and rode [267] as fast as their horses could carry them, and they flew into the fray so fast that all the ranks shook, and they went straight to where Agravain and Guerrehet had been brought down, and they hit and slaughtered and struck down right and left as many as they met, so that none dared stand up to them; even the boldest and strongest gave way to them, for

* Sommer's text has *se ne fust vne auenture quil trouerent en la bataille* (266, ll. 27-28): "if it were not for an adventure they found in the battle."
† Sommer's text has the singular personal pronoun *l'* (266, l. 33).

in very little time they knew them to be the worthy gentlemen and good knights they were. And when Agravain and Guerrehet saw help coming, each one jumped on a horse, with his shield about his neck, for there were many of them all around them. And when they were back on horseback, the fighting began to be wondrously heavy; but Galescalain was not at all well off, for he was still under the horses' hooves. When Sir Gawainet saw the danger he was in, he rushed into the fighting so hard that he brought down more than seven men before he could get to him. As he drew closer, he struck Duke Frollo so hard with a lance that he went through his whole shield, but his hauberk was strong and so sturdy that he broke not one link, but Sir Gawainet had hit him so hard that he bore him sprawling to the ground; then he took his horse by the rein and had Galescalain get on. Galescalain had the heart to avenge his shame, if he ever could, and indeed he did, and he lost very little time in doing it. After he had got back on a horse, he saw that Duke Frollo had also remounted in the midst of his own men, but Galescalain hit him so hard that he knocked him back down to the ground most shamefully, and he had ridden back and forth over him more than seven times without stopping before any of his men came to help him; and when, after the seventh time, Duke Frollo happened to get back up, he again sent him sprawling back down to the ground so shamefully that his men expected his death.

In this way Galescalain brought Duke Frollo down, and he rode his horse over him seven or eight times before his men could get to him to take him away or even move him, so angry was he about the harm he had done him and his distress, and he broke him and crushed him against the ground; and Duke Frollo was so distraught and so full of agony that he was very much afraid that he would die.

Sir Gawainet saw everything Galescalain did to Duke Frollo, and he showed it to King Ban and said to him, "Sir, look there and see my cousin Galescalain, how daringly and how boldly he behaves toward his enemies!"

"Indeed," said King Ban, "anyone who has Galescalain as a companion can boast that he is with one of the best knights in the world."

With these words that King Ban spoke, he came to where the fighting was going on,* and they were all running one another down helter-skelter, burning to hurt one another as best they could, for King Arthur, King Bors, and the knights of the Round Table were striking and hitting right and left, until at last with main force they drove Pontius Anthony's men and Randol the Seneschal's into Frollo's men and Claudas's. These welcomed them warmly because they were worthy gentlemen and good knights. There was a great heaping up of bodies, and the dust rose so thick that out on the battlefield as well as in the meadows, you should know this for a fact, no one could see anything. And after the four echelons had come together, just as you have heard, there was such a profusion of horses and men that it was a wonder to behold; [268] they were drawn tightly together, so close one to another that if anyone had taken a glove and thrown it on their helmets, he could have ridden a half league at a slow gait before it fell to the ground, so thickly were they crowded together. But all of King Claudas's men were very much afraid, and they dreaded the dangers they were up against. When King Arthur saw that the men he

---

*   Sommer's text has *uindrent les batailles* (267, l. 33): "the battles (or battalions) came."

had been fighting* had thus got away and run headlong into the others, he spurred after them with very great vigor, and he and his companions rode helter-skelter into the press. There the fighting grew heavy again, hard and wondrous. So the story now falls silent about them for a while, and we will tell you about the two queens who were in the castle of Trebe.

34. VICTORY OF ARTHUR'S FORCES; ELAINE'S DREAM.[†]

The story says here that when those in the castle of Trebe heard the hue and cry raised by the people outside, they wondered in amazement what it could be, and the uproar grew so loud that the two sisters climbed up to the highest windows of their tower and looked down into the meadows, and they saw the biggest crowd of people they had ever seen. And they saw the dragon Kay bore that threw such great bursts of fire out of its mouth that the air grew red from it, and the dust that had risen also glowed red wherever the dragon had gone. And when the ladies and those of the city saw the ensign,[‡] which they had never before seen, they crossed themselves for the wonder they felt. Then they sent someone to find out who those men were who were fighting against the men from the army and whose ensign that was, and they sent a messenger outside the castle. And when he came to the battlefield, he met a knight from the kingdom of Logres who was laying aside his helmet and putting another on that was strong and whole, for his own was worth nothing anymore. And the knight's name was Bretel, and the boy came over to him and greeted him, and he returned the greeting most courteously.

"Sir," said the boy, "I would like to entreat you with all courtesy to tell me what people you are who are fighting against those from this army."

"Dear friend," said Bretel, "you can tell those in the castle yonder who have sent you here that it is King Ban of Benoic and King Bors of Gaunes who have brought King Arthur from Great Britain to rescue their lands and country from their enemies, who have wrongly and sinfully overrun them; but now the time is drawing near when they will have their reward and win their renown, if God keeps King Arthur safe. There you see his banner with the dragon which the seneschal is bearing."

When the boy heard this, he commended him to God and thanked him very much for what he had told him. With that the boy went away happy and gladdened by the news he had heard, and he could hardly wait to tell it to the two sister queens, and so he came straight back to the castle. And he would say nothing to anyone who asked him about those on the outside, but told them that anyone who wanted to find out should "follow me to the great hall."

---

*   Sommer's text has the ambiguous pronoun *cil* (268, l. 5): "they/those."

†   Corresponds to Sommer, 268-279.

‡   Instead of *enseigne* ("ensign, banner"), Sommer's text has *le signe* (268, l. 18): "the sign." Farther down (273, l. 1), it is clearer that *signe* means both "ensign" and "sign."

And when the ladies saw him coming back, they went out to meet him because of the great number [269] of people they saw coming after him. And when he had come before them, he told them, loudly enough so that all who had come there to hear the news understood it, everything just as Bretel had told it to him.

When the ladies heard the news the boy told them, the joy they felt was not slight, and they went back up to see the fighting, which was the worst they had ever seen in their lives. And on both sides they fought on until they were utterly weary. But those inside had been watching those on the outside fighting for just a short time when they saw coming out of the forest of Briosque four banners, which were going unhurriedly one before the other. And when the banners drew closer, they recognized the banner of Anselm, seneschal of Benoic, and the second belonged to Gratian of Trebe, the third to Pharian of Gaunes, and the fourth to Leonce of Payerne. And when those within saw them, they were very greatly gladdened, and they would very willingly have gone out if someone had let them, for they had been shut in for too long a time and there were many good knights whose kinfolk and friends were there, but they could not go out because it was forbidden on pain of death. And Anselm was drawing nearer all the while.

And then King Arthur looked and saw the banners; he recognized them and showed them to Sir Gawainet, and he said to him, "Sir Gawainet, you can be sure that soon our enemies will be put to rout, for I see four banners over there bringing us very able help that will strike fear in them."

And then Sir Gawainet said, "Let's withdraw awhile and go look for our friends and kinsmen until we find them and bring them all together, for before long our enemies are bound to ride away in flight;* and after we are gathered together, we will go out first and put ourselves where we think they will be heading. Do you know why† I am telling you this? So that, after they have seen, in the place where we'll have lain hidden in the woods, that they have been thoroughly punished, those who are left alive will go into their country and can say and bear witness to the fact that they did not come across stable-boys or hired hands, and that next time they will keep themselves from coming into your lands or the fiefs of King Arthur of Great Britain. And you can be certain that in the end they will not be happy!"

"Sir," said King Ban, "I wish it all to be as you want and would like it to be."

With that they drew to one side of the battlefield, first the companions of the Round Table, King Arthur, and King Bors, and then afterwards the forty knights who were engaged in the land of Carmelide, and after them the sixteen young lords who had become new knights. And when they were gathered together, there were three hundred knights, all very worthy men, and they were the flower of the army. Then Pontius Anthony rode headlong into the battlefield as fast as he could make his horse run. There was much splintering of lances there and much clanging of swords. There King Ban of Benoic's battlecry was loudly shouted and that of King Bors of Gaunes, and there was a great slaughter of men and horses. And when Gratian came, he flew into the fray so hard that they all yielded ground to him,

---

* Sommer's text reads *il ne puet remanoir que grant defoulemmt ni ait* (269, ll. 22-23): "there cannot fail to be a great stampede." The text does not specify, although the context makes it implicit, who will be in the stampede and where it will be heading.

† Sommer's text has *coi* ("what.") rather than *por coi* ("why") (269, l. 24).

the meadows and the stream, and the companions spread out down through the meadows, and the fighting grew so heavy and deadly that many a knight there was killed or bleeding wrongfully and sinfully, for they never deserved it. Thereby Holy Church was brought low so [270] shamefully that more than twenty thousand of them died on both sides, and all was due to the faithlessness of Claudas of the Land Laid Waste, who afterwards had his evil reward, for he died bereft of his earthly birthright, as the story bears witness of it to us. But with this the story falls silent about that right now, and we will tell you about the two armies that were fighting in the open fields before the castle of Trebe.*

In this part the story says that the fighting was fierce and the combat deadly where the echelons had come together, that is, those from the kingdom of Benoic had become jumbled together with Duke Frollo of Germany's men and those of Pontius Anthony with King Arthur's, and they fought very hard on all sides, and after they had spread down through the fields, no one knew which ones had the upper hand, for on the side that had been Claudas's there were yet some thirty-five thousand, and they all fought about equally well. And the three hundred companions had withdrawn to one side, and King Arthur had a good thousand companions as well. The three hundred were repairing their armor and fixing their helmets. Meanwhile, King Claudas's men thrust forward and drove back those from Little Britain and the kingdom of Logres; these got the worst of it, whereas they had had the best, and they wondered at what had become of their prowess. But these were not the ones who had done wonders fighting that day, and they were most distressed at not hearing news of those who had; nevertheless, each one tried to defend himself as best he could, for they knew very well that they were as good as dead if they had lost the three hundred who had helped them when they needed it and who had done wonders fighting.

While they were in such distress, Pharian of Gaunes, holding his ensign, came with five thousand men in iron armor; and when Claudas saw him coming, he knew very well who he was, and he grew very frightened because Pharian had often done him harm in less weighty times. He then told Pontius Anthony and Frollo to set their minds to fighting well and cutting down his enemies, "and I'll ride against them, for there I see new forces coming. If I could send them along their way, we would quickly be rid of the others. You should know for a fact that he is one of the men in the world who have done me the worst harm."

With that, Claudas left with ten thousand armed men, and they rode against Pharian. And when Pharian saw them coming, he boldly went out to meet them, for he was a worthy, bold, and skilled warrior, the most reasonable in the country. And after they had moved closer together, they spurred against each other as fast as their horses could run, gripping their lances, and many fell on both sides. But Pharian's men were hurt worse, for it was two men against one of his, but Pharian's men were newcomers and Claudas's were tired and worn down, so Claudas lost more men than Pharian, and if there had not been [271] so many of them, they would have been routed, but in the end Pharian's men had to withdraw toward the forest where they had come from.

---

*   Sommer's text adds *en mi la praerie* (270, l. 5): "out in the meadow."

When Claudas saw that they were leaving, he thought they had been beaten, so he drove against them so hard that they had no relief and could not recover, and Pharian was so upset that he nearly went mad. And he shouted "Gaunes!" time and again, but it was not worth his while, for skillful fighting by him or anyone else would not have kept them all from being killed and crushed to bits until Leonce of Payerne came with five thousand men in iron armor, and he flew into them so hard that he sent more than a thousand to the ground never to get up again.

Then the fighting grew fierce and deadly, for each side hated the other, and they fought equally well and neither side gave the least bit of ground. Meanwhile, those from the kingdom of Logres were fighting and getting the worst of it. At last Merlin, who knew all these things, saw the men of Logres* so beleaguered, so he went to the place where King Ban, King Bors, and Sir Gawainet were hiding in the woods. And when he got to them, he said, "What, my lords? Have you come to this country to watch the jousting and all the skillful fighting the men from here know how to do? You should know that you have behaved badly with respect to one thing, for many of our men have been lost since you rode away, and they are frightened because they do not see you. Now get going and ride against your enemies, and you will turn against them the rest you have taken here, so that any who slip out of your hands can say that they did not find hired hands or stableboys in the kingdom of Logres, but worthy men and good knights. And you, sir," he said to King Arthur, "this is the reward King Ban and his brother King Bors deserve! They have so often put themselves in danger of death to help you out in times of less need when all others failed you, and now you have come here to hide like a coward! You can be sure that this is something you will be upbraided for many times by many people—and by your lady friend when she finds out how you have behaved, and she will rebuke you for it."

When King Arthur heard Merlin's speech, he hung his head in shame, and he was so upset that he was awash in sweat from the shame and distress; at the same time, he dreaded that Merlin might be angry with him. After that Merlin went to Sir Gawainet and his companions and said to them, "Young men!† Where are the knightly skills you used to brag about? You said that you were coming to fight against your enemies in Little Britain and that you would see whether they could bear arms! Now you have shown what good knights they are by the fright they gave you. Did you come here to hide? And you don't have the heart or the boldness to let them see how afraid of them they have made you!"

Then he said to King Ban and King Bors, "And you, my lords, what did you come looking for in this country? You were supposed to be good knights, worthy and bold, but it has been proved now that you believed in those traitorous cowards who are so cravenly hidden away here! You ought to have put yourselves at risk to help and uphold those who have risked themselves and their lives to free your lands from your enemies. Now [272] they will have a right to say, when they go

---

*   Elsewhere Sommer's text has *cil del roialme de logres* "those of the kingdom of Logres", (271, ll. 11-12), but here reads *cil des loges* (271, l. 14).

†   The term is *vassal* (271, l. 33). Used as a term of address to young men, as the context of reproach suggests, the word does not necessarily imply knightly virtues, as it does in 260, l. 35 ("faithful warriors") and 264, l. 26 ("worthy knights").

back to their countries, that they were in the service of wicked men who left them in danger of death."

"In truth," said King Ban, "we have not done it out of wickedness or cowardice."

"Then," answered Merlin, "whatever your reasons,* you have behaved badly. Now see to it that the harm they have done you will cost them very dearly, so that they can boast of nothing if they get away from you."†

"Sir," said Gawainet, "let me tell you this. Whether or not I have behaved like a coward, before I eat again, I will make known whether or not I am worthy and valorous, even if I should be cut to bits, and I'll fight so well before I leave the battlefield that people great and small will know who I am, nor will any cowardice I may have done ever be held against me, God willing, or against my uncle King Arthur, as long as I am alive. And you," he went on, "my brothers, my cousins, my companions, if you wish to prove me blameless, follow me, for we'll soon show them that I did not steal away and hide out of cowardice!"

Then Merlin broke out in a smile, and he came straight to Kay the Seneschal and took the dragon out of his hand and told him he should not bear it, "for never should the ensign of a king be stolen away and hidden from the battlefield. No, it should be borne out in front!"

Then Merlin shouted, "Now we'll see who'll follow me, for soon it will be known who's a knight!"

And when Arthur saw him leaving, he said to King Bors that there was a very worthy gentleman in Merlin, and without a doubt he was full of knightly valor, and he was strong of body and limb, but he was dark-skinned and thin, more hairy than any other man, yet he was highborn on his mother's side. But of his father I will tell you nothing more, for you have earlier heard a great deal about the one who fathered him. But as we read, we do not find that he ever laid a hand on any man to hurt him, but it happened often that, when he was fighting in a press, he would strike down‡ both man and horse.

After Merlin had taken the dragon from Kay the Seneschal's hands, he set out on a great black horse that ran wondrously fast. And when he had drawn near the battlefield, he flew in so hard that the whole rank shook and shuddered until he got to where Frollo and Pontius Anthony were fighting. They were striving hard to put the men of Logres to rout. What did it matter that all their best men had been killed? They had already performed so well that their enemies were very nearly routed. The people within the castle of Trebe were grief-stricken, so more than five hundred squires ran to put on their armor, and they all went out on horseback. They were led by Banin, a young lord, son of Gratian of Trebe; he was King Ban's godson, and he was still no older than twenty, but he was very skilled at arms and quite bold. And they charged headlong into the battle, and they fought very well for squires and foot soldiers, for there was not one knight with them, and had it not been for them, the others would have been put to rout.

---

* The text reads *comment que uous laues fait* (272, l. 4): "however you may have done it."
† Sommer's text reads *quant il vous escaperont* (272, l. 6): "when they escape from you."
‡ Sommer's text adds *del pis del cheval* (272, l. 26): "from the horse's chest." (?).

With that, Merlin and his companions, who were more than a thousand strong by count, left the woods, and he was holding the dragon, which gave out from its mouth such brightly glowing fire that the air grew red because it. And those who had never seen it before said that Our Lord was dreadfully angry with them, [273] since He had made such a sign* appear to them. Then the way the battle was going changed for those who had had the better of it, for as soon as Merlin's companions had come rushing in among them, they all began doing such feats of battle that everyone who saw them was astonished, for they struck down so many men that in a very short time notice had been taken of them. There King Arthur did wonders all by himself, for he had his shield thrown behind on his back, and he wielded his sword, which was of such great worth, in both hands; he began to kill and maim everywhere he fought, and nothing could withstand him. And the story says that by himself alone he wounded more than two hundred of those who had wreaked such damage on Christendom, and all because of Merlin's sarcastic rebuke;† and he held the horse's reins in his right hand and let it run where it would. Meanwhile, Merlin was doing wonders as well as King Ban and King Bors, for they were doing their utmost to harm their enemies; they were very good, bold knights, and their knightly skill had always been wondrous and above that of all the knights of their time.

The story says that King Arthur had fought his way so deep into the battle that no one knew what had become of him, and they knew nothing of King Ban or King Bors. And when the companions of the Round Table became aware of this, they brought about such an outburst of fighting that no one stopped to wait for anyone else, and so did the forty companions, whom the story has sometimes named, as well as the eighteen young lords who were new knights. And there began such a great slaughter and such bitter fighting that they drew apart one from another, and no one knew where the others had gone; so it happened many times that day that they got separated and then found one another.‡ That day it happened over and over again that in that onslaught Sagremor did wonders, for the story says that he was one of the best in the whole army. And Galescalain was such an outstanding knight§ that many times he was pointed out. And Sir Yvonet, son of King Urien, began to fight so boldly that they needed none better than he, and the three brothers of Sir Gawainet stayed together all day long and did such feats of arms that they were praised many times. At the same time, the knights of the Round Table fought back very well, but¶ Sir Gawainet did better than any of the others. He drove in so deeply among the warriors that no one knew what he become of him, and people looked for him high and low.

---

* The word is *signe* (273, l. 1). Elsewhere (268, l. 18) the word seems to be more nearly equivalent to *enseigne* ("ensign, banner"), whereas here both meanings ("sign," "ensign") are appropriate.

† The word here is *ramprousne* (273, l. 10), "reproach" or "mockery" that is characteristic of the seneschal Kay, who is known for his ironic and sarcastic speech.

‡ Sommer's text is hard to understand here: *Si auint ... que le iour quil se partirent se trouverent* (273, l. 22): "So it happened. .. that the day they got separated they found each other." It is noteworthy that *Cel iour auint* occurs in the next sentence (l. 23), while *maintes fois* recurs in l. 25, which suggests the possibility of scribal anticipation in l. 22.

§ The text reads *i fist tant darmes* (273, l. 25): "executed there such feats of arms."

¶ The text repeats the formulaic structure *se recombatent tant ... que* (273, ll. 28-29): "fought back so well ... that."

After Sir Gawainet had gone into the fray, he looked high and low among the ranks until he found Randol, the King of Gaul's seneschal. As soon as he saw him, he fell upon him, for Randol was very worthy and bold. And Sir Gawainet struck him so hard in passing that he cut through his helmet right against the back of his neck, for the horse had taken him too far, and the sword went down right along his shoulders, cut through all the links in his hauberk it hit, and sliced off a good deal of flesh. As the sword slashed downwards, it cut through the saddle blanket, split the horse's backbone, and went into its bowels, and the horse stumbled to the ground in a heap. Then he happened to meet Dodinel the Wildman, Kay of Estral, and Kehedin, who had been knocked down off their horses, and it was a wonder how Pontius Anthony and his men were right on top of them. And when Sir Gawainet saw them in such dire straits, he turned to that side and [274] launched such an attack all about them that he drove them out and back and put them to rout, like it or not. And Dodinel, Kay, and Kehedin, who were very bold, jumped onto horses, for there were quite many of them all about. Then the fighting grew very heavy again, and most wondrous, and they tried their best to stay close to Sir Gawainet, but it was not long before he was so far away from them that they did not know what had become of him.

Very heavy was the fighting in the meadows beneath Trebe, and the knights of the Round Table did wonders.* They looked for King Arthur all throughout the army, but they could not find him because he had ridden so far away from them. He had gone so far that he had fallen upon Frollo and Pontius Anthony, who had seven hundred knights with them, the best in their whole army. And King Arthur fought hard against them, and there was none who dared stand up to him right away; he was without a shield and wielded his sword with both hands, and all he met were hit so hard with his flawless blows that no armor could keep them from death.

And when Pontius Anthony saw him, he and his men rode against him. Then Sir Gawainet happened along with his sword drawn, and they fled from him too on all sides, for no one, no matter how skilled and bold he was, dared take a stand against him right then. And when he saw his uncle King Arthur—for Pontius Anthony and Frollo of Germany had struck him from in front and behind and had made him hunch forward over his horse's neck—he was so filled with wrath that he nearly went out of his mind. Then he put his sword back into its scabbard, and he hurled himself against the others with his bare hands, and he snatched a lance out of a knight's hands so fiercely that he brought him to the ground. Then he held the lance straight and went right for Frollo. And when Frollo saw him coming, he rode off to one side, for he did not dare stand up to him right then. Rather, he went straight into the thickest press he could find. Gawainet kept hot on his heels, but Frollo's knights moved in between them, and when Gawainet saw that he could not get to him, he threw the lance so hard that it drove through his shield and into the hauberk right on the left shoulder; in fact, he sent the tip and the shaft in so deeply that the tip stuck out the other side, and Frollo fainted because of the anguish he felt. And when his men saw this, they were sorely distressed, for they truly thought that he had been killed. A little while after that, Frollo came out of his faint, and he had

---

*   The text adds *de lors cors* (274, l. 7): "all by themselves."

his armor taken off and his wound bound, for it was bleeding a great deal. And Sir Gawainet went straight to his uncle, who was fighting very hard. Pontius Anthony and Randol had got back on horseback, and they endeavored to avenge the blow Sir Gawainet had dealt Frollo. Then Sir Gawainet went flying headlong in among them, striking right and left, and he fought long enough to free his uncle.

Then Sir Gawainet met Pontius Anthony, and, in passing, he struck him so hard on the shoulder that he drove his sword into the bone, and he went flying from his horse to the ground, and he was badly hurt from his fall. Gawainet then struck Randol the Seneschal through his helmet, and he cut through his iron coif down to his skull; he bore him bleeding to the ground, and all who saw it thought that he was dead. Then it happened that the enemy began to withdraw their echelons,* and they led them as far as the echelon of Claudas, who was fighting against Leonce of Payerne and Pharian. After all those echelons had been linked together, they fell back against King Arthur's men. [275] There was a great crush of men and horses then, for those who were retreating were crowding in on King Claudas.†

When King Arthur saw that they were riding away, he called Sir Gawainet over and said to him, "Dear nephew, come closer to me, for it seems to me that they are going away. Don't leave me now, but stand by me here."

"Sir," said Sir Gawainet, "they are right to leave, for staying behind is very harmful for them. But let's ride after them! Let's help them run away in defeat!"

"After them right now!" shouted King Arthur. "For it does us no good to stay behind."

While the king and Sir Gawainet were talking, behold King Ban and King Bors striking out among them with their swords drawn, and they killed and brought down as many as they met. And it was very lucky for Pontius Anthony and Randol the Seneschal, for they had fled before the pursuit began. And when the four friends saw one another, they were filled with great joy. They began the chase anew and rode after those who had turned in flight. They then met the three knights of the Round Table who had fought very well all day: one was Nascien, the second Adragain, and the third Hervi of Rivel. They were all seven of them worthy, bold knights.

After the chase had begun, the seneschal Kay found King Arthur's shield lying on the ground, and when he saw it, he was very much afraid that he had been killed or taken prisoner. He had a squire pick it up, and he told him to come after him; he said that he would go looking for King Arthur until he found him.

Then he joined the chase after the others; it lasted a long time, for they did not stop before they got to Claudas's echelon.‡ They were held up there for quite a while, for there was a great plenty of people; and Kay followed the pursuit until he found the companions I have named for you. He was very glad that he had found King Arthur, and he went to hang his shield about his neck.

---

* The word here, as frequently elsewhere, is *bataille* (274, l. 41, cf. l.42): "battalions."

† Sommer's text reads *li fuiant se retiennent le roy Claudas* (275, l. 1): "the retreaters hold King Claudas back," perhaps, but *se* (intended as the reflexive pronoun?) is ungrammatical as a second direct complement. The possibility adopted is *li fuiant sere tiennent le roy Claudas* for *li fuiant tiennent le roy Claudas sere* ("the retreaters hold King Claudas squeezed in").

‡ The word here is *lesschiele* (275, l. 22).

Then Merlin came along holding the dragon, and he shouted to them, "Now at them, noble knights, and they will soon be put to rout."

And Sir Gawainet took a lance and was the very first to break ranks. He struck King Claudas on his shield, which he went through as well as his hauberk, and he drove it all the way through his left side. He hit him so hard that he sent him sprawling to the ground. He then trampled him with his horse, and Claudas fainted from the agony. Then Sir Gawainet drew his sword and flew in where the press was the thickest he could find, and he broke in so hard that he went all the way through. All of the companions were talking about the bold deeds they saw him doing. And the others rode in to rescue their lord King Claudas; it was very hard for them to bring him out of the press and put him back on his horse.

With that Agravain, Guerrehet, and Gaheriet came spurring their horses. And when they saw the men gathered about Claudas, they flew headlong in among them so hard that they drove them all away. There King Claudas was brought to the ground again, and he was wounded very painfully in three places, not counting the wound that Sir Gawainet [276] had given him; so badly hurt was he that he nearly died. Even so, his men struggled hard until they had rescued him, but they lost many before they got him away. Then it happened that their echelons* swung about wildly and rode away in flight one after the other, but Pontius Anthony, Frollo of Germany, Randol the Seneschal, and King Claudas pulled aside. King Claudas was so badly wounded that he could hardly ride, and the others were not so well off themselves. When they saw their losses and the harm that had come to them, they grew most sorrowful, and they asked one another where they should go.

"Sir," said King Claudas, "it is my advice that we should go into the Land Laid Waste,† for that is the best refuge we could have, and it is the strongest and the closest. And we should go through the Humber Forest along an old trail I know about. But I am so badly hurt that I can barely ride my horse."

While they were talking thus, they saw their echelons break up and fall back one upon the other. Then the pursuit grew so fast and so wondrous that they did not know where they were going, but King Ban's men‡ struck down and killed so many of them that the place was heaped up with the dead and wounded. As soon as King Bors's men saw the tide turning against them, they posted themselves at a narrow pass they knew about, and King Arthur struck out among them with his men scattered all about, for they longed only to kill and maim them, and they took and killed as many as they wanted. And when those who had been put to flight came up against King Bors's men, who had gone to the pass, so many of them were killed that the field was heaped up with them. The pursuit lasted all day until nightfall, and a very great many prisoners were taken. King Claudas, Pontius

---

*   The word here is *batailles* (276, l. 3): "battalions."
†   The word here is *le deserte* (276, l. 9), that is, King Claudas's homeland.
‡   The noun phrase *les gens au roy ban* (276, ll. 14-15) is in the oblique rather than the nominative. In fact, the grammatical and syntactical relationships with each other of expressions representing the two sides are confused throughout. For example, in the next sentence (ll. 15-17), King Bors's men are depicted as moving out when they saw that they were being routed: *si tost comme il virent la descomfiture sor aus tourner* ("as soon as they saw the rout turning against them"); but *sor aus* surely must refer to the enemy. Indeed, in the following sentence Arthur's men are hot on their heels and strive to kill and maim any and all.

Anthony, Duke Frollo of Germany, and Randol, the seneschal of Gaul, defended themselves as well as they could, but very few of their men were left, for the story says that of the eighty thousand they had numbered at the beginning, not half got away, nor even did ten thousand go back home with them, for they had run in flight through the wild forests to save themselves and to stave off death.

Thus were the four princes put to rout, just as you have heard, on the advice of Merlin, and after the three kings* had run after them until nightfall, they turned back with a great many prisoners, and went straight to the castle of Trebe. And they took lodging in tents and pavilions, which they had got set up, and they were very happy and made merry all night long, for they found the places where they stayed to be very well stocked with everything a man needs, and nothing lacked, nor did they have to use up any of their own food at all. The next evening, when they had settled in through the whole army, Gratian and Pharian stood watch so that they would not be taken by surprise by anyone.

And King Ban and King Bors took Sir Gawainet straight to the king and his companions of the Round Table, the forty knights the story has named for you, and the new knights in the castle of Trebe, where everyone was glad to see them. There were at least three hundred knights from the countryside by count, so they were indeed well served that evening with everything that befitted them. However joyful they may have been, it came to nothing beside the great rejoicing the two sister queens did when they saw their husbands they had longed for, and no wonder, [277] for they had not seen them for a very long time, and they were young ladies of very great beauty. And everyone sought to serve and honor King Arthur and his companions.

Why should I go on telling you about their merrymaking and the happiness they felt? For they were richly served as befitted gentlemen as worthy as they were. And after they had eaten they went to bed, for they needed very much to lie down, because they were tired and worn out from the hardships they had undergone all day. And King Arthur, Sir Gawainet, Sir Yvain, Sagremor, Didoine, and Kay all slept in a quiet room off by themselves. And after King Ban and King Bors had seen to their comfort, the knights of the Round Table and the newly-dubbed knights were made comfortable in another room by themselves. And then King Bors and King Ban went to bed with their wives, and they left the tapers burning where the barons were.

That night the two kings showed their wives their great love, for they loved them very much. And that night, so says the story, Queen Elaine, King Ban's wife, conceived a child. And when they had lain together enough, they went to sleep. And the queen fell into a wonderful dream† that lasted a long time, and she was very much frightened by it as she slept, for she thought that she was on a high mountain, and she saw all about her a great many wild beasts of various kinds that were feeding on the grass that grew fair and thick. After they had fed for a while, there welled up among them such a loud uproar that they began to run into one another and tried to run one another away from the feeding-ground. And they broke

---

*   The text has only the ambiguous personal pronoun *il* (276, l. 29): "they."
†   The word here is *pense* (277, l.17), a state of brooding.

up into two herds, and one went one way and the other another, and each was led by a wonderful lion. On one side were fewer than half of them, and a lion wearing a crown was their leader, but he was smaller than the other one by more than a foot.

This crowned lion had with him eighteen cubs, all wearing crowns, each one of which had lordship over part of the beasts that were turned toward the lion. And the other lion, which was not crowned, had thirty cubs in his company; they were all crowned, and each one had lordship over a part of the beasts that had turned toward the big, uncrowned lion. After the beasts had been broken up and divided into herds, she looked toward the one belonging to the crowned lion and saw four hundred bulls that were tied together about the neck and gathered in a circle eating tender sulks from a haystack.* And because it seemed to the crowned lion that the feeding-ground was better around the crownless lion, he was beset by envy and ran against him to take it away from him. And the uncrowned lion took part of his beasts and put them into three great flocks, and they went out to fight against the crowned lion, which had his beasts gathered into eighteen flocks each with a cub that had lordship over the others and led them. And the four hundred bulls, which were fearsome and full of pride, and three of the eighteen flocks† that were with the crowned lion undertook together such hard fighting that you have never heard tell of any harder, but in the end the crowned lion's beasts had to fall back, even though the other lion had been very much frightened that he might lose his feeding-ground.

While the beasts were fighting, it seemed to the lady that a great leopard, [278] the lordliest‡ there had ever been, was running through a deep valley, but it seemed to her that a thick fog was keeping her from seeing what was happening to it. After she had lost sight of it, she turned back toward the wild beasts, which were still fighting, and she saw that the crowned lion was getting the worst of it by far. Then§ a great leopard came out of the forest and watched the beasts' battle for quite a long time; and when he saw that the crowned lion was losing, he went to help him and fell upon the crownless lion and fought his beasts so fiercely that he drove them back, and as long as he was against them the uncrowned lion could not win.

When the uncrowned lion saw that he could not win as long as the leopard was against him, he left the fray and befriended the leopard so that he finally took him away with him. And on the third day the battle among the beasts started all over again just as it had been before, but the leopard was on the side of the lion that was not crowned, and the beasts fought hard together until the crowned lion was put to rout thanks to the leopard, which was against him. When the leopard saw that the crowned lion was being put to flight, he made a sign toward the crownless lion that the crowned lion¶ should go to him and beg his mercy. He did so, and peace

---

*   The text has *dun rasterlier lerbe menue* (277, l. 33).
†   The word here is *monchiaus* (277, l. 39): "heaps."
‡   The expression is *li plus orguillous* (277, l. 43-288, l. 1): "the proudest," with pride taken as a sign of lordly power; cf. *autresi comme le lupars est orguilleus sor toutes autres bestes, autresi sera il li mieudres* (280, ll. 10-11): "just as the leopard has lordship over all beasts, so will he [an unknown knight] be the best there will be in that time."
§   The text has *Quant* (278, l. 5): "When."
¶   The text has only *quil* (278, l.16): "that he."

was made between the two lions, so that never thereafter did they get angry with each other.

And then the lady looked carefully at the leopard to see whether she could find out who he was, and it seemed to her at last that it was he who had sprung from her loins and had grown so tall and strong and made such efforts that all the beasts of Great Britain, and all those of Gaunes and Benoic, were bowing down to him. And after he had won lordship over these beasts, the lion went away; she did not know where or what had become of him.

The lady was wrapped in this dream all night long, and she did not come out of it until daylight, when she awoke and crossed herself because of the great wonder she had seen in her sleep. And when the king saw her so frightened, he asked her what was wrong with her, and she told him the dream just as she had seen it in her sleep. And after she had told him everything, the king said that, God willing, it could only be something good. King Ban and his wife then got up as early as they could and went straight to the first Mass; they did not want to awaken King Arthur or his companions, who were still asleep, for they had been sorely worn down the day before. And King Ban prayed Our Lord to give him death when he should ask Him for it; he was a most worthy man in his faith and belief, and he uttered this prayer many times afterwards, until it happened one night while he was asleep that a voice told him that his prayer had been heard. He would have death the first time he asked for it, but first he would have to commit the deadly sin of adultery one time before he would die, and it would not be before long; he should not fear, for he would be reconciled with Our Lord.

In the dream King Ban was having, it seemed to him that the voice that had told him those things was withdrawing, when it let out such a loud scream that it sounded like the most deafening thunder and the most wondrous he had ever heard. And the king, who was holding the queen in his arms, began shaking so hard that he almost fell out of the bed, [279] which was big and wide, on top of her. The queen was so frightened that she could not utter a word for a long time, and her husband was so upset that he did not know where he was. And when he regained his memory, he got up and went straight to church, where he made his confession and heard Our Lord's service. Thereafter he always confessed every week and took the Holy Sacrament from the altar, and King Bors, who was a most worthy man and led a good life, did likewise.

Thus was King Arthur in the kingdom of Benoic, and he stayed there a whole month. And they overran King Claudas's land every day and plundered it and laid it waste so that it would be a long time before he would overrun King Ban. But afterwards he did, thanks to the forces of Pontius Anthony and the king of Gaul, as the story will reveal it to you later, and hurt the two brothers so badly that they had not one acre of their lands left, and they were so stripped of their wealth that they died poverty-stricken, and their wives were so poor and distraught that they became nuns in the royal convent out of fear of king Claudas.* For afterwards they could not get help from King Arthur, who had so much to do in his own country

---

* Sommer's manuscript has *roy cler* (279, l. 15) but he notes (n. 1) that in the *Lancelot* it is once again a question of King Claudas.

that he could not give them heed; the heirs the two kings fathered were for a long time without their birthrights, but later King Arthur won their lands back for them, and he gave them the kingdom of Gaul, as the story will reveal it to you later. I will stop telling you of these things until it is the time and place for it; instead, we will tell you about Merlin and King Ban and how Merlin told King Ban and his wife about the dreams they had had.

35. MERLIN AND THE EMPEROR OF ROME.[*]

Here the story says that one day King Ban came to Merlin and said to him, "Sir, I am filled with dread about a dream that came to me in my sleep and one my wife had, too. I am in great need of counsel, and you are the most learned man now alive, so I beg you to tell me, if you will, what this dream means."

"In truth," answered Merlin, "there is great meaning in these two dreams, and it is no wonder if you are afraid."

Then King Arthur asked what the dreams were, and Merlin related them just as King Ban and his wife had dreamed them as they slept, so that the king himself knew that he spoke the truth. When King Arthur, King Bors, and Sir Gawainet heard the dreadful words Merlin had spoken, they were greatly amazed as to what they could mean, and they brooded on them long and hard.

And after they had thought awhile, King Arthur said to Merlin, "Sir, you have told us what the dreams were, now tell us the meaning, if you please, for I would very much like to know it."

"Sir," said Merlin, "I mustn't explain everything to you from beginning to end, for I don't wish to; even so, I'll tell you something about them, as much as it is fitting for me to do."

Then he began to tell about the lady's dream.

"King Ban," said Merlin, "it is the truth that the great lion that is not crowned stands for a prince, a very wealthy man in goods and in friends, who will conquer thirty kingdoms,[†] and he will bring all thirty kings together as his companions. And the other lion, the crowned one, which came with eighteen cubs, [280] signifies a most powerful king who will have eighteen kings under him who will all be his liegemen. And the four hundred bulls she saw in her sleep stand for four hundred knights who will have sworn oaths to one another to help them to the death, and they will all be that king's men. And the prince I told you about before will fall upon that king to take his lands, but he will defend himself as best he can. And when, as it will happen, that prince begins to defeat that king, there will come an unknown knight who has been lost for a long time, and he will help the king until the prince cannot drive him from the field or put him to rout. And the leopard stands for that knight, for just as the leopard is lordly above all beasts, so will he be the

---

*   Corresponds to Sommer, 279-291.
†   The text adds *j. mains* (279, l. 41): "one less" or "one morning"?

best knight in that time. And by that knight will peace be made between those two princes, who'll have hated each other so much. Now you have heard about the dream and its meaning," Merlin went on, "so I will go away right now, for I have much to do elsewhere."

And when they had heard the wonder of the dream Merlin told them about, they fell more deeply into thought than they had before. Then the king asked him if he would enlighten them any more, and he said that he would not.

With that Merlin left the three kings and went straight to his lady love, who was waiting for him. And it was on a St. John's Day that she was waiting for him, according to the oath she had sworn to him. And when she saw him, she was very glad to see him, and she took him with her to her rooms so stealthily that no one ever took note of it. She asked him many things she sought to know about, and he taught her quite a lot, for he loved her so deeply that he nearly went mad. And when she saw that he had welcomed her greeting* with such great love, she begged him to teach her how to put a man to sleep as deeply as she would like without his waking up. Merlin knew very well what she was thinking, so he asked her why she wanted to know this.

"Because," she said, "every time I wanted to talk to you, I would like to put my father—his name is Dyonas—and my mother to sleep so that they might never take note of you and me. You can be sure that they would kill me if they found out anything about what we're doing."

She very often said such things to Merlin. One day they happened to have gone into a garden, beside a spring, and the maiden had him lie down with his head in her lap,† and she drew him to her from time to time, so that Merlin was burning with love for her.‡ Then the young lady begged him to teach her how to put a lady to sleep. He knew what she was thinking, but even so he taught her this and other things besides. For God our Lord wished it so, and he taught her three names that she should write down, and every time he wanted to lie with her, they would have such great power that, for as long as she had them on her person, no man could know her carnally. And from that time on, she worked on Merlin in such a way that every time he wanted to speak with her he did not have the power to lie with her. And this is why they say that women have one more wile than the devil.

So Merlin stayed there with the maiden a full week, but we do not find, when we read, that Merlin ever sought anything unworthy§ of her or any other woman, but she was very frightened of him while she knew him, and she had found out how he was sired, and so she armed herself against him. And he taught her everything the human heart could think of, and she put it all down in writing. And [281] then Merlin left her and came straight to Benoic, where King Arthur and his companions were, and they were very happy when they saw him. And Sir Gawainet had overrun King Claudas's lands, and he had taken a great many knights with him, and they

---

* The text has *quil lauoit cueilli[e]* (280, ll. 21-22): "that he had welcomed her," that is, that he had accepted her welcome of him.

† The text reads *le mist couchier en son giron* (280, ll. 29-30): "laid him down in her lap."

‡ The text reads *que merlins lamoit a meruieilles* (280, l. 30): "so that Merlin loved her wondrously."

§ The word here is *vilounie* (280, l. 39): "lowborn behavior, uncourtliness."

had plundered the whole land and laid it waste. Nor was Claudas ever so bold as to stand up to him. And as soon as Sir Gawainet and his companions had gone back from Claudas's lands, Pontius Anthony left Claudas, as did Frollo of Germany and Randol the seneschal of the land of Gaul, and they were sorrowful and angry about the harm that had been done them. So they swore an oath that never would King Ban or King Bors ever be served by them, and just as soon as they could avenge themselves, they would give due rewards for service done on their behalf. Thus was Claudas left poor and distraught. But he got all of his land back, as the story will reveal it to you later, with the help of the king of Gaul and Pontius Anthony. Pontius Anthony came back from Rome with a very great horde, but this was ill-timed for his own good, for afterwards he was put to death by the hand of King Ban of Benoic in the meadowlands before Trebe. But Claudas had such a great horde that he besieged the castle, as you will hear later in the story when it will be the place to tell it.* But now the story falls silent about all of them and goes back to talking about Sir Gawainet, who came back from Benoic happy and lively.

When Gawainet had plundered Claudas's land and laid it waste, he went back to Benoic, to the three kings who were there, and Merlin with them, for he had come back from his lady love. And when they saw the great wealth that Sir Gawainet was bringing back, they showed how very glad they were. And the next morning they took to the road to go to Gaunes, a wealthy city and full of all kinds of goods. There they were made most welcome, for King Bors served the greatest feast that could be brought together. They stayed there for three days, and on the fourth they set out toward La Rochelle, where they put to sea. But before that, Merlin had drawn the three kings and Gawainet aside and told them that, as soon as they could, they had to go to the kingdom of Carmelide, and they should take only three thousand men-at-arms with them, the best in the whole army.

"What?" said King Arthur. "Merlin, dear friend, will you not come to my wedding?"

"Sir," answered Merlin, "I have hard work to do that I must see through to the end. But you will not have been in the kingdom of Carmelide long before you see me there."

With that, they set out and went their own ways. King Arthur put to sea with his companions. But here the story falls silent from talking about them, and it will tell you about Merlin.

Now the story says that when Merlin had left King Arthur, he went to dwell in the wide and deep forests of the country about Rome.† At that time Julius Caesar was emperor, and that is why he went there, and it is right that I should tell you why he went there. In truth, so says the story, Julius Caesar had a wife who was of the highest birth and of very great beauty, but she was lustful above all women, though by the emperor she had but one daughter, who was also most beautiful.‡

---

*   Text from "with the help of the King" to here is not in Sommer's base text, supplied by him from other manuscripts (281n.).

†   The expression is *es fores de romenie* (281, l. 32).

‡   The emperor's daughter is named Foldace (292, l. 36).

That lady kept with her twelve noble youths dressed as girls* with whom she went to bed every night the emperor was not with her, for [282] she was most lustful, more than any of the other women in the land of Rome. And because she was afraid that beards would grow on her twelve boys,† she had their chins smeared with lime and yellow arsenic‡ steeped and boiled in stale urine, and they were dressed in big, flowing gowns and wrapped in wimples, and their hair was long and grown out, and cut in the manner of maidens, so that they looked very much like girls.§ They were with the empress for a long time without being found out.

At that time it happened that a maiden came to the emperor's court. She was the daughter of a prince whose name was Mathem, and he was a duke in Germany.¶ And that maiden came to court dressed as a squire. Now Frollo had stolen that Mathem's birthright from him and driven him from his land, so his daughter came in great distress, because she did not know what had become of her father and mother. And she was tall, straight, and strong, and in every way she behaved as a squire behaves without unseemliness,** nor was she ever taken to be a woman. She stayed with the emperor and was most skilled at arms, and she sought to serve the emperor better than all the men. Indeed, she was so outstanding in serving him that he made her a knight on St. John's Day, along with the other young lords, of whom there were more than two hundred, and afterwards she was seneschal of the whole land. She had herself called Grisandoles, but in baptism her name was Lovely.†† And the emperor had made her seneschal of all his land because she was most worthy.

It happened one evening that the emperor lay beside his wife, and he went to sleep. A dream came to him in which he saw a great sow right in the middle of his court before his great hall, and it was bigger and more wonderful than any he had ever seen. The bristles on its back were so long that they trailed more than a yard behind, and on its head was a circle that seemed to be of gold. And it seemed to him that he had seen it other times and that he had bred it, but in no way did he dare say that it belonged to him. And while he was looking at that sow, he saw twelve wolf cubs coming out of his bedchamber, and they made straight for the sow and lay with it,‡‡ and all twelve went out one after the other.

---

* The text reads *damoisiaus atorne a guise de damoiseles* (281, l. 38): "young lords dressed as young ladies."

† Here the word is *serians* (282, l. 2): "hirelings."

‡ The word is *orpiement* (282, l. 3): "orpiment." (<*auripigmentum*), tri-sulfide of arsenic.

§ Here the word is *puceles* (282, l. 6): "maidens."

¶ The text reads *dus dalemaigne* (282, l. 8): "duke of Germany." This would seem to be an appropriation of Frollo's title. Later Merlin refers to him as *duc Mathem de Soane* (291, l. 10): "Duke Mathem of Soane."

** The word is *uilonie* (282, l. 12): "lowborn behavior, boorishness, uncourtliness."

†† Old French *auenable* (282, l. 17).

‡‡ Sommer's text reads & *estoient a planije* (282, l.26): "and they were combed" (taking *a planije* as *aplanoié* ["smoothed, planed, caressed"]. Sornmer notes a variant from the Harley manuscript: *et huy estoient plaisans* (282, l. 1): "and they were pleasant/loving to it." Just below, the action is more clearly summed up as *la truie a qui li louel auoient ieu* (282, ll. 28-29): "the sow with which the wolf cubs had lain," which squares with Merlin's subsequent account (288, l. 1). Significantly, Merlin's account, which is fuller, refers to the sow as *aplanoie* (287, l. 36) and to the cubs as *aplanoies* (287, l. 41). In fact, the lines *.xij. louiaus biaus & aplanoies & venoient tot par mi la sale a la truie si gisoient tout .xij. a li lun apres lautre* ("twelve beautiful wolf cubs and they all came through the hall to the sow and all

When the emperor saw the wonder, he asked what should be done to the sow with which the wolf cubs had lain. And someone told him that it was not worthy to be around people and that no one should eat anything that was born of it, and it and the wolf cubs were condemned to be burned; and it seemed to him that they were all burned up in a heap. Then the emperor awoke very frightened and deeply worried about that dream; and he did not wish to talk about it with his wife, for he was a very wise man. In the morning he got out of bed as soon as he could and went to hear Mass in the church; and when he had got back, he found that his barons had come back and gathered in the high hall, for they had already heard Mass. They spoke about one thing and another until the meal was ready and the tables set up, then they sat down to eat and were very well served. Then it happened that the emperor fell into deep thought, brooding about the dream he had seen in his sleep, and when the barons saw him stewing they grew very worried and stopped talking all at once. And there was not a single one of them who dared utter a word, for they sorely dreaded making the emperor angry. But now the story stops speaking awhile about that, and we will tell you about Merlin, who was in the forests around Rome.* [283]

Here the story says that while the emperor sat brooding so at the meal, as you have heard, Merlin knew very well about it, so he came all the way to the gate leading into Rome, and then he cast a spell and took on a wonderful new shape. He became a stag, the biggest and most wonderful that anyone had ever seen; he had one white forefoot and five-branched antlers on his head, the biggest that anyone had ever seen on a stag. Then he struck out running throughout Rome and made as great an uproar as if a thousand men were after him. And when the common folk saw him running all about, there arose from every side such a great hue and cry that no one could have heard God thundering there. And they all ran after him, big and small, with fire and sticks and all kinds of arms, and for a very long time they ran after him through the whole city until they came to the great hall where the emperor was sitting at his meal.

And when the serving men heard the people, they sprang to the windows of the hall, and when they found out what it was, they went outside. And the stag came running at full speed, with the common folk after him, and he came to the great hall and stormed headlong through the main gate. Then he dashed in among the tables and spilled food and wine and meat everywhere, and there began such a great breaking of pots and dishes that it was a wonder!

And when the stag had had enough in that part of the hall, he came right up to the emperor, knelt, and said to him, "Julius Caesar, what are you brooding about? Stop stewing, for it is not worthwhile. You will not find anyone to tell you about your dream until the Wildman vouches for its meaning, and you would be wasting your time to worry about it any more."

Then the stag stood up and saw that the doors of the hall were closed, and he then cast a spell so that the doors opened† so fast that they flew into bits.

---

twelve lay with her one after the other" [287, ll. 41; 288, l. 1]) suggest that here a scribe garbled the text by telescoping.

* Again, *es fores de rommenie* (282, l. 42); see p. 309n.

† In this clause *li huis del palais ouri* (283, l. 23) is in the singular.

After the doors had opened, the stag sprang out and went running down through the city, and the chase after him began again and lasted for a long time, until at last he ran out into the open field, and he disappeared so that no one knew what had become of him. And when the folk had lost him, they turned around and went back. And when the emperor saw that the stag had not been held back, he grew very angry and had it cried out throughout the city that he would give his daughter and half his kingdom to anyone who could take the Wildman or the stag, so long as he was a man of noble birth, and after his death he would have all the kingdom. Then many a wealthy young lord of great worth got on his horse and looked for the Wildman through the forest and great stretches of countryside, but it was all for nothing, for no one could find out anything about him, so they turned back. But whoever else may have gone back, Grisandoles did not, but rode back and forth through a great forest, one hour each way, and he* was there for a full week. Then it happened that, one day, he got down from his horse to pray Our Lord to give him counsel as to what he was looking for.

And while he was praying, it happened that the stag that had been in Rome came up before him and said to him, "Lovely, you are running after madness, for you cannot succeed in your quest in any way unless you go after pork stewed in pepper, milk, and honey, and hot bread. And bring four companions with you and a serving boy who will turn the meat on a spit until it is cooked. And come into this forest, to the thickest part you can find, and set up a table beside the fire and put out the bread, the milk, and the honey, [284] and you will hide some distance from the fire. Do not be afraid, for the Wildman will come without fail."

And after the stag had said this, he went away galloping through the forest, and Grisandoles climbed on his horse and began brooding about what the stag had told him, and he said in his heart that it was a spiritual thing, for it had called him by his right name, and he said that only something very meaningful could come from such an event.

These were the things Grisandoles thought about and worked out in his heart while he was riding. At last he came to a city near the forest, and he got there everything he needed. Then he went back into the forest to where the stag had spoken to him, and he took four men and a boy with him. When they came to the depths of the forest, they found a great, leafy oak tree, and they got down from their horses, because Grisandoles and his companions found it to be a cheerful spot. They let their horses graze and lit a great and wonderful fire, where they started roasting meat. And the odor of the meat on the spit spread throughout the forest, and people smelled it quite far away. Then they set up their table next to the fire, and when everything was ready they hid themselves and crouched by a bush. And Merlin, who knew all these things and had worked out a disguise so that no one would know him, came by there one morning, batting cabbages from oak tree to oak tree. He was black-skinned, wild-haired, bearded, and shoeless, and he was wearing a ragged tunic. He came straight to the fire where the meat was cooking. And when the boy saw him coming toward them, he was nearly frightened out of

---

* The masculine is affirmed in the next sentence: *quil fu ... descendus* (283, l. 36): "he had ... got down."

his wits. And Merlin came up to the fire and began to warm himself and rub his hands over the heat, and he kept looking at the meat. He began to smack his lips like someone who was starved, then he looked and saw that the food was done to his liking and made ready just as you have heard. And when he saw that the meat had been cooked long enough, he went over to the boy and snatched the spit out of his hands like a madman, and he ate until nothing was left of the meat; then he ate some of the warm bread and honey. And after he had eaten all that and was so stuffed that he almost burst, he warmed himself by the fire and fell asleep.

And when Grisandoles saw that he was asleep, he and his companions went straight to him as stealthily as they could, and when they reached him they wrapped an iron chain around his waist, and they tied one of their companions to the other end of the chain. After they had tied him up, he awoke, jumped up, and started to pick up his cudgel like a madman, but Grisandoles grabbed him around the waist so hard that he held him still. And when he saw that he had been taken prisoner and bound, he was ashamed and downcast. Then the horses were brought and he was raised onto one of them, and they bound him fast to the saddle with two tethers, and the one who was tied to him climbed up behind him and rode with his arms around his waist. Then they took to the road, and the Wildman looked and saw Grisandoles, and he broke into a broad smile. And when Grisandoles saw him smiling, he came alongside him and began to ask him about many things, but he did not want to say a thing.

And he asked him why he had smiled just then, but he answered nothing but, "Unnatural creature who have gone from one shape [285] into another, deceitful trickster worse than any other thing, more stinging than a horsefly, deadlier than a snake's poison, be still! I will say no more to you until we go before the emperor, where we are headed."

With that the Wildman fell silent and said no more to him. And they rode together for a very long time, and Grisandoles was thunderstruck by what the Wildman had said to him and talked to his companions about it. They thought that he was a very smart man and said that because of him wonders would come to the land. So they rode along together talking about many things until, one day, they went by an abbey where they saw a great many poor folk before the gate waiting for alms. And when the Wildman saw them he began to smile. And when Grisandoles saw him smiling, he came to him and asked him most courteously, for God's sake, to tell him why he had smiled.

Then the Wildman looked at him sideways and said to him, "Unnatural, reworked image, do not ask me anything anymore, for I will tell you nothing until we come before the emperor."

When Grisandoles heard this, he let him be and did not ask him any more for the time being, but they all talked about this and that and rode the whole day until evening and the next morning until the hour of prime. And it so happened that they were about to pass a chapel where Mass was about to be sung, when Grisandoles and his companions alighted from their horses and went inside the church to hear Mass. There they found a knight and a squire who were listening to the service. When the knight saw the man wrapped in chains, he wondered who it might be. While he was looking at the Wildman, his squire, who was standing in a corner of the chapel, came toward his master, raised his hand, and slapped him so hard that it resounded through the whole chapel; then he went back to where he had come from, filled with shame that he had struck him. But by the time he had got back to his place, he was not bothered about it any more, for the feeling of shame lasted only as long as it took him to walk back.

And when the Wildman saw that, he burst out laughing, and the knight who had been struck was all bewildered, so that he did not know anything to say or do except take it. And Grisandoles and his companions wondered what this could be. And they had not been there for long before the knight was slapped even harder by his squire, who went back to his place. And the Wildman burst out laughing very hard. If the knight was thunderstruck before, he was even more so the second time. And after the squire had gone back to his place, he was not bothered by it. And Grisandoles and his companions were struck with wonder, but they still went on listening to the service. And as they were listening to it, the squire went back a third time and slapped his master still harder than he had done before, and when the Wildman saw it he started to laugh again.

Then Mass had been sung and was over, and Grisandoles and his companions left the church. And the knight whom the squire had struck went out after them, and he asked Grisandoles who he was and what kind of man he was taking with him all tied up.

And he said that they belonged to Julius Caesar, the emperor of Rome, "and we are taking him a wildman we caught in that forest; he is to tell the meaning of a dream he had. But tell me now, fair [286] lord," said Grisandoles, "why this squire has slapped you three times and you didn't say a word about it? Is this a custom you have?"

And the knight answered him that he would know that soon if he was willing to wait a little while. Then the knight called his squire over to Grisandoles and asked him why he had struck him.

He was so ashamed and downcast that he answered that he would rather be dead, "but an urge came over me."

The knight asked him whether he had any urge to hit him then.

And he said that he would rather die, "but such an urge came over me that I couldn't hold back."

And Grisandoles crossed himself in wonder. Then the knight told him that he would go to court to hear the things the Wildman had to say.

With that they set out on the road, and Grisandoles rode side by side with the Wildman and asked him why he had laughed in the church when the squire struck his master.

He looked at him askance and said to him, "Reworked, deceitful image, sharp as a sting,* likeness of a creature by which many a man is killed and maimed, razor more fit for slashing and sharper than any weapon,† be still! And don't ask me anything until we go before the emperor, for I'll tell you nothing."

---

* The text reads *comme a lesne* for *comme alesne* (286, l. 13).
† The text continues *fontaine sourians ki ia niert espuchie* (286, ll. 12-13): "smiling fountain that will never dry up."

When he heard his strong words, he was astonished, and he never dared ask him anything thereafter, so they rode for many days until at last they came to Rome. And when they went into the city, the people caught sight of them and came running to meet them to see the Wildman. The news spread throughout the city, and they gathered about him to see what he looked like, and they took him along with them until they reached the great hall. And the emperor came out to the hall's doors to meet them, for they had managed to climb to the top of the steps.

And then Grisandoles came to the emperor and said to him, "Sir, look. You see here the Wildman, whom I give you as a gift. Guard him well from now on, for I am handing him over to you. You can be sure that I have had a great deal of trouble with him."

And the emperor said that he would reward him very handsomely and that he would have the Wildman very well guarded. Then the emperor sent for an ironsmith to put him in bonds, but the Wildman told him that he need not bother with that, for he would not go away without his leave. The emperor asked him how he could be sure of that, and he answered that he would swear it to him on the Christian faith he held to.

"What?" said the emperor. "Are you then a Christian?"

"Sir, I am," he answered, "without a doubt."

"And how did you come to be baptized?" asked the emperor.

"I will be glad to tell you that," he said. "The truth is that my mother was coming back one day from the market in a town and it was getting late. She went into the Forest of Broceliande but strayed from her path, so that she had to spend the night in the forest. And when she saw that she was all alone and lost, she lay down under a tree and went to sleep. Then a wildman of the forest came along and sat down beside her. And when he saw that she was alone, he lay with her, and she did not dare defend herself, and that night I was fathered in my mother. And when she got back home, she worried for a long time. And after she saw that she was with child, she carried me until I was born and baptized in a font. And she raised me until I was grown, and as soon as I could get along without her, I went away to live in the deep forests. Because of my father's nature I had to go back there, and it is because he was wild that I am. [287] Now you have heard how I was baptized and became a Christian."

"May God never help me," said the emperor, "if ever you are bound and chained on my account, as long as you pledge to me that you will not go away without my leave."

Then Grisandoles told the emperor how he had laughed when he caught him and when they were before the abbey and in the chapel, and he told him the various things he had said to him. "So ask him why he laughed that way so many times."

And the emperor asked him, and he answered that he would know everything in a short while. "But send for your barons and then I'll tell you this and something else."

With that the emperor took the Wildman and went straight to his rooms, and they spoke together about many things. The next day the emperor sent for his barons, who he thought would gather quickly. And they did come very gladly from everywhere.

On the fourth day after the Wildman had come, the barons were gathered in the great hall. And the emperor brought the Wildman in and had him sit beside him, and everyone stared at him long and hard. Then they asked the emperor* to tell them why he had sent for them.

And he answered that it was because of a dream that had come to him in his sleep, "and I want it to be explained before you."

They said that they would gladly hear its meaning. Then the emperor ordered the Wildman to tell him, but he answered that he would say nothing until the empress and her twelve maidens had come there. She was called for, and she came in with a cheerful face, because she did not worry about anything he might say. When the empress and her twelve maidens came in, the barons rose to greet her. But as soon as the Wildman saw her, he burst out laughing scornfully. He stopped laughing after awhile and then stared fixedly at the empress, the emperor, Grisandoles, and the twelve maidens. Then he turned toward the barons and began to laugh loud and hard as though to mock them. When the emperor saw him laughing thus, he entreated him to have the kindness to tell him what he had sworn he would and why he had laughed then and just before.

"My lord, my lord," said the Wildman, "if you will swear to me before all your barons gathered here that you will not hold it against me, that no harm will come to me from it, and that you will give me leave to go as soon as I have interpreted your dream, I will tell you."

And the emperor granted him this and swore that he would do everything he wanted. Then the Wildman said that he would tell him.

So he began to speak: "Sir," said the Wildman, "one evening you happened to go to bed with your wife, who is over there. And after you had fallen asleep, a dream came to you in which you saw a sow before you that was fair and well-groomed. And the bristles on its back were so long that they trailed more than a yard behind it. And it had on its head a circle of shining gold. It seemed to you that it had been bred in your household, but you could not recognize it, although it seemed to you that you had seen it before. And after you had wondered at this thing for a time, you saw twelve beautiful, well-groomed wolf cubs come out of your bedroom and go to the sow into the middle of the hall. [288] All twelve lay with it one after the other, and when they had done to it as they wished, they went back into the bedroom. Then you went straight to your barons and asked them what should be done with that sow you had seen behaving in such a way, and the barons answered that it was unworthy and unfaithful, and they condemned it to be burned along with the cubs. Then a great and wonderful fire was set in this courtyard, and the sow and the cubs were burned. Now you have heard the dream just as it came to you in your sleep, and if I am mistaken in anything, say so before your barons."

And the emperor said that he was not mistaken in even one word.

"My lord emperor," said the barons, "since he has told you what your dream was, we can believe him as to its meaning, if he will tell you what it is. And this is something we would very much like to hear."

---

* The text has the ambiguous singular personal pronoun *li* that could refer to the emperor or to the Wildman (287, l. 14).

"Indeed," said the Wildman, "I will explain it to you so plainly that you will see clearly that I am telling the truth."

"Then tell us," said the emperor, "for I would very much like to hear it."

"Sir," said the Wildman, "the great sow you saw stands for your wife the empress, who is over there; its bristles that were so long stand for the robe in which she is dressed; and the golden circle it was wearing on its head stands for the great crown with which you had her crowned. And for the sake of your feelings, I would stop talking now and say no more."

"Indeed," said the emperor, "you must speak if you wish to fulfill your pledge."

"Sir," said the Wildman, "then I'll tell you. The twelve wolf cubs you saw coming out of your bedroom stand for the twelve maidens who are with your wife. I swear to you that they are not women, but men, every one of them. Have them undressed and you will see whether or not this is true. And you should know that every time you leave the city, your wife has herself served by them in her rooms. Now you have heard the meaning of your dream, and you can find out whether it is true or not."

When the emperor heard that his wife had broken faith with him, he was so astounded that he could not utter a word for a time. Then, full of wrath, he spoke and said, "We will soon see."

Then he called to Grisandoles, his seneschal, and said, "I want these maidens stripped right now, for I want my barons to see the truth."

And Grisandoles sprang up* and had them strip before the emperor, and they all found that they were formed in every part of their bodies just as other men are. When the emperor saw them, he was so deeply shamed that he did not know what to say. Then he swore an oath that he would have justice done straightway as it was meet. Some of the barons judged that, since the empress† had been so unfaithful to her husband, she should be burned and the wanton boys hanged. There were others who judged that they should be skinned alive. But in the end they agreed that they should be burned up in a fire. Then they told the emperor that they all deserved to be burned. As soon as the emperor heard the barons' judgment, he ordered the fire to be set in the courtyard,‡ and as soon as he had given his orders it was done. Then he had their hands bound, the empress's as well, and had them all thrown into the fire. They were very quickly burned up, for it was a wondrously huge fire. [289]

Thus did the emperor take vengeance on his wife, and the news was widespread throughout the whole country. And after justice had been done to the empress and her twelve whoremongers, everyone said that the Wildman was very wise and a great seer, "and he will yet tell us about a very great wonder that will happen to us and to the whole world."

Thus did the emperor learn, thanks to the Wildman, about the life his wife had been living for quite some time. And the emperor asked him if he would tell them anything more, and he answered that he would indeed tell him anything he asked.

---

*   Sommer's text adds *li tiers* (288, l. 30).

†   The text has the personal pronoun *ele* (288, l. 35).

‡   The word here is *la plache* (288, l. 40).

"I want you to tell me," said the emperor, "why you laughed when you saw Grisandoles, when you rode before an abbey, and when he took you to* the chapel where the squire hit his master with his hand, and I want to know what words you spoke to my seneschal when he asked you why you had laughed. And please tell me why you burst out laughing when you saw the queen come into the great hall."

"Sir," said the Wildman, "I will gladly tell you these things. The first time I laughed was because a woman had taken me prisoner, thanks to her powers and her wiles, as no man could do even with all the power you have. And you should also know that Grisandoles is the most beautiful woman and the best in all your land, and he is a maiden. And that is why I laughed at him. As for my laughter before the abbey, I laughed because there is to be found the greatest treasure in the world, before the gate buried in the ground, and I laughed because the treasure was under the feet of the ones who were waiting for alms. And they had greater wealth under their feet than the whole abbey and all that was dependent upon it were worth, and I laughed because of the treasure that was within their grasp and they did not know how to take it.

"And when Lovely, your seneschal who had herself called Grisandoles, asked me why I was laughing, the words with hidden meanings I spoke to her were because she had taken on the form of a man and was wearing clothing other than her own. Yet all the words I spoke to her are true, for through woman is many a worthy man shamed and cast down, many a city burned and laid waste, and many a land plundered. I do not say these things out of any spitefulness, for you can see on your own that by woman many a man is brought to shame. But now you needn't worry about your wife, whom you have destroyed, for she deserved it fully. And don't be angry at other women, and do not scorn them because of what she did. For there are many of them scattered here and there who have not done wrong to their husbands. But for as long as the world will last, they cannot help but sink lower, and this will happen to them through the sin of lust, which dwells and smolders within them. For woman is of such a nature that, when she has the best husband in the world, she believes she has the worst. This comes from their great weakness. But do not bother yourself with that, for there are many faithful ones in the world. And if you have been betrayed by your wife, you will yet have one who is worthy of becoming empress and being given such a mighty empire as this is. If you will believe it, you will win much more than you lose.

"But the prophecy says that the great dragon will fly out of the Roman country.† It will see the kingdom of Britain brought down and the crowned lion put under its lordship despite being forbidden by the dove that the dragon had fed under its [290] wings. And as soon as the dragon stirs to fly against Great Britain, the lion will go out to meet it and will fight until a fearsome and proud bull, which the lion will have brought, comes into the battle. And the bull will strike the lion with one of its horns and will hurl it down dead. In this way the great lion will be saved. But I will not tell you the great meaning of these words, for I mustn't, but it will happen in your time. Do not believe evil counsel, for there is much of it all about you.

---

* The text repeats *deuant* (289, l. 9): "before."
† The text has *rommenie* (289, l. 40); cf. 281, l. 32).

"The second time I laughed in the chapel," said the Wildman, "was not because the squire slapped his master, but because of the great meanings there are in it. Do you know what they are? In that very spot where the boy stood is a wonderful treasure heaped up under the ground. The slap means that because of wealth man grows so proud that he finds no one worthy and does not love or fear God, any more than the squire feared his master. Rather the wealthy seek to trample upon the poor. And this makes the rich unfaithful when anything bad happens to them, for they curse God and wrong Him, and they say that He will have a hard time getting what He has given them. Do you know that it is pride in the wealth they have that makes them say that?

"The second slap stands for the rich usurer who bathes in his treasure. He goes about mocking and poking fun at his poor neighbor and the man who comes to him in need to borrow a few pennies from him. He watches* him and waits to see how he can hurt him, and he weighs him down little by little until he must sell his land, like it or not, to the man who has hankered so much after it and because of whom he has lost† so much of his wealth. So you can see that this one is a wicked slap.

"The third slap stands for wicked lawyers who wrongly buy and sell‡ their neighbors out of hatred, for they see them thriving without being under their sway. And when lawyers see that their neighbors do not serve them as underlings, then they bring suit against them in order to take away what belongs to them. This is why they still say that he who has a bad neighbor gets only curses.§ Now you have heard why those slaps were given, but the boy did not have that in mind when he dealt the blows. Rather, Almighty God, who knows all and sees all, willed it thus in order to bring out the meaning¶ that He did not wish mankind to become proud because of wealth. For ever since** wealth came into the world, riches have meant only death to those who fall asleep in sin and forget God to do the works of the devil, who leads them to everlasting death†† through the delights they find in great wealth.

"But I still must tell you why I laughed this morning when the empress came in with her lechers. You should know that it was only because of her sinfulness and I did it scornfully, for she had as her husband the worthiest man known of your youthful age, yet she gave herself over to twelve whoremongers; she meant to keep up her unfaithfulness for the rest of her days, and so underhandedly that she would not be found out. But I was greatly distressed by it for love of you and of your

---

*   Beginning here pronouns referring to the usurer and verbs are in the plural (290, ll. 19-21).
†   The verb is *presente* (290, l. 22): "given away."
‡   The text reads *ki uendent & enpruntent* (290, ll. 34-35): "who sell and lend (to)."
§   The proverb *qui a mal uoisin il a mal matin* (290, l. 28) is recorded by Morawski (no. 1809). The positive antithesis (Morawski no. 1785) is cited by Cotgrave as "Qui a bon voisin a bon matin," who translates "bon matin" as the greeting: "He that hath a good neighbor gets good words" (under *Voisin*), "hath a good morrow" (under *Matin*). Cotgrave also gives a proverb, not found in Morawski, referring to lawyers as neighbors: "Bon advocat mauvais voisin," translated as "The best lawyer is the worst neighbor" (under *Voisin*) and as "A good lawyer is an evil neighbor" (under *Advocat*).
¶   The text reads *por prendre exsample* (290, l. 30): "to take/serve as an exemplum."
**   The text reads *Car ausi comme* (290, l. 31): "For just as"; however, the sense is unclear.
††   The text reads *a la pardurable fin* (290, l. 34): "to the everlasting end."

daughter. For there is no doubt that she is your daughter, and you can be sure that she will not be like her mother.

"Now you have heard why I laughed. Now I will leave, if you will permit."

"Please stay awhile," said the emperor, "and we will see the truth about Grisandoles, and we will send someone to dig up the treasure, for I'll want to know whether or not it is true." [291]

And he agreed.

With that the emperor ordered Grisandoles to be undressed, and it was done; and they found that it was one of the fairest maidens that anyone had ever seen in any land.

When the emperor found out that she was a woman, he crossed himself many times in wonder. Then he asked the Wildman what advice he had to give him about his having granted her his daughter and half of his kingdom, for he did not want to break his oath.

"I will gladly tell you," said the Wildman, "if you are willing to take my advice, and it will be good."

"Tell me then," said the emperor, "and I will love you for it."

The Wildman said, "You will wed Lovely. And do you know whose daughter she is? She is the daughter of Duke Mathem of Soane, whom Duke Frollo drove from his lands, and he fled with his wife and a son, who is a most faithful youth, and they are in Provence, in a wealthy town called Montpellier. Send for them and give them back their birthright, which they have lost wrongfully. And wed your daughter to Lovely's brother, for he is most handsome and worthy, and his name is Patrick. Rest assured that you could not do any better."

When the barons heard what the Wildman had said, they took counsel among themselves and said that the emperor could do nothing better. Then the emperor asked the Wildman what his name was and who the stag was that had come to speak to him.

And he answered, "Sir, don't say anything more about it, for the more you saw and heard, the less you would know who he was."

"Won't you say anything more?" asked the emperor.

"Yes, sir," he said, "about the crowned lion I was telling about a while ago and the flying dragon. I want you to remember this, so I'll tell you in another way. It is true," the Wildman went on, "and the prophecy has said so, that the great wild boar of Rome, which is meant by the dragon, will go toward the crowned lion of Great Britain against the forbiddance of the dove with the golden head that will have been the boar's* friend for many a day, but the boar will be filled with such great pride that he will not believe the dove, rather it will go off with all its offspring to the faraway parts of Gaul to fight the crowned lion, which will have come there to meet him with beasts from everywhere. Then it will come to pass that one of the crowned lion's offspring will slay the great dragon. And this is why I beg you, if you will do anything for my sake before I go, to do nothing against your wife's forbiddance from the day you are betrothed to her. If you will do as I say, you will profit greatly.

---

* The text has the ambivalent *samie* (291, ll. 25): "its friend."

"With that, I am leaving now, for I have nothing more to do."

And the emperor bade him farewell and commended him to God.

And on his way out of the hall, he wrote letters above the door* that were all black, and they said, "May all who read these letters know that the Wildman who interpreted the emperor's dream to him was Merlin of Northumberland; and the antlered stag that spoke to him in full sight of his barons, which had been chased through the city of Rome and had spoken to Lovely in the forest, that was Merlin, chief counsellor of King Arthur of Great Britain."

Then he left without stopping again.

So with that the story falls silent about Merlin and tells about the Emperor of Rome. [292]

36. THE SAXONS DEFEAT THE REBELLIOUS PRINCES.†

Here the story says that when the Wildman had left the emperor of Rome, the emperor sent men to find the father and mother of Lovely and Patrick, their son, in Montpellier, where they had taken refuge, and they came back happy and cheered by the good fortune God had bestowed on them. When they got back to Rome, they were greeted joyfully, and the daughter was very glad to see her father, mother, and brother, as they were to see her, for they did not think they would ever see her again. They stayed with the emperor, but they had not been with him long before he gave them back their lands, which Frollo had taken from them. Frollo contested this as well as he could, and the war lasted a long time because he was quite powerful, but at last the emperor made peace. And when he did so, he gave his daughter to Patrick, while he himself took Lovely as his wife. And the joy and merrymaking were great that the barons did, for the lady had made herself loved by every man and woman.

While the emperor was rejoicing and making merry, a messenger came to the emperor from Greece to tell about a dispute that had arisen between the barons of Greece and the Emperor Hadrian. For the Emperor Hadrian, who was their rightful lord, could no longer ride on horseback, except for a short while, because he was very weak and quite old. And after the messenger had told what he had to say, he started out on his way back, and he happened to look up above the door to the great hall, and his eyes fell upon the letters that Merlin had written there. As soon as he had seen them, he read them easily because he knew his letters, and after he had read them he began to laugh out loud.

Then he went back to the emperor and said to him, "My lord, my lord, is it then true what the letters say?"

---

*   The text says *es listes del huis* (291, ll. 34-35): "at the edges of the door." The translation "all around the door" would be satisfactory here, but later the text specifies that they are above the door and the reader looks up to see them (292, ll. 18-19).

†   Corresponds to Sommer, 292-298.

"What do they say?" asked the emperor. "Do you know?"

"The one who wrote them down," he answered, "interpreted your dream about your wife, and he has let you know that he spoke to you in the likeness of a stag, and it was Merlin, chief counsellor of King Arthur of Great Britain, because of whom you have wed Lovely, your wife."

When the emperor heard these words, he crossed himself for the astonishment he felt. And then a great wonder happened in full view of all who were there. For as soon as the emperor heard what the letters said, they all disappeared and faded from sight, so that no one knew what became of them. And when they saw this, they were struck with amazement, and afterwards the news was spread far and wide throughout the countryside.

But with that the story falls silent about the emperor, who dwelt happily and joyfully in his country with his wife Lovely, and they lived a good life for a long time, for they were quite young. The story says that at that time he was no more than twenty-eight years old, and Lovely was only twenty-two, so they lived a good life for a long time, and Patrick and Foldace were even happier. But the story falls silent about them, and we will tell you about Merlin.

In this part the story says that as soon as Merlin had left Julius Caesar, he took to the road back toward Great Britain, to Blaise, his master, who welcomed him warmly and gladly. The trip did not bother him much, for he came from Rome in one day and one night, for he was endowed with powerful art. [293] Then he told Blaise all the things that had happened in the Roman country, and then he told him about how ten kings and one duke had banded together to go fight the Saxons before the city of Clarence; he told him about the battle that had been fought before Trebe in the kingdom of Benoic with King Arthur against the Germans, against the Romans, and against the Gauls, and about Claudas of the Land Laid Waste and how he was put to rout, and about how King Ban had fathered a child by his wife who would rise above all the knights of his time. And after he had told Blaise everything, Blaise set it down in writing, and it is because of him that we still know it. But now the story falls silent about Merlin and Blaise, and we will tell about the ten kings and one duke who had gathered together with their armies.

Now the story says that when the ten kings and the duke had gathered in the fields of Cambenic, and they took counsel as to how they would arrange their echelons, and then they would move out at night so that no one would catch sight of them. So the King of the Hundred Knights led the first echelon,* and he had eight thousand men with him. And Tradelmant of North Wales led the second with seven thousand men wearing armor. King Belinant of South Wales led the third echelon with seven thousand men wearing armor. King Caradoc Shortarm led the fourth echelon with seven thousand men. King Brandegorre led the fifth echelon with seven thousand armed men. King Clarion of Northumberland led the sixth with seven thousand armed men. King Yder led the seventh echelon with eight thousand men. King Urien led the eighth echelon with eight thousand men. King Aguisant led the ninth echelon with five thousand men, for he had lost more in the war than all the others.

---

* The word here and elsewhere is *batailles* "battalions" (293, l. 15, cf. l. 19), as opposed to *echieles* (293, l. 14), *echiele* (l. 17, etc.).

The king of Orkney led the tenth echelon—he had lost everything, wife, children, and all his fair household, and he was so full of grief that he would rather die than live; he had been so stricken as to have but few left of the fourteen thousand men he had before the war, but those he did have were very worthy, very bold, and the best in the whole army at bearing up under distress and hardship. King Neutres of Garlot led the eleventh echelon; he was deeply worried about his son Galescalain, for he had with him but two thousand men, so many he had lost in the war against the Saxons. And Duke Escant of Cambenic led the twelfth echelon with seven thousand knights in armor.

After their men had gone their way, the barons asked how they should wage the campaign. In the end they agreed that they would go fight before the city of Clarence, and they would ride only at night; they would be very watchful throughout the whole army, and they would fall upon their enemies by surprise. For they said that they would rather die with honor than live in shame.

With that the baron's council was over, and each one went into his pavilion. And when they had eaten their evening meal, they ordered their men to put on their armor and get ready to take to the road, so they armed themselves and set out. There was a spy from King Hargadabran there who had heard what the barons meant to do. That spy left [294] so stealthily that no one took note of him, and he made his way until he came to the city of Clarence, which was under an awesomely heavy siege. The spy came straight to King Hargadabran and told him everything he had seen and how the Christians were coming; he said that there were at least forty thousand of them. When the Saxons heard this, they scorned them, and they did not think it worthwhile to arm even a fourth of their men; even so, they set up a watch to look for the army night and day. Meanwhile, there were twenty kings who were unwilling to get their armor ready after they had heard the news about the Christians.

But with that the story falls silent about them, and I will tell you about the Christians.

In this part the story says that the Christians' armies rode from nightfall until they came near the Saxons' encampment a little before daybreak. There was a heavy fog, and a thick, misty rain began to fall, so that the men in the Saxon army were all the drowsier and slept all the more soundly. Nor did the Christians worry that anyone would attack them in such weather. When the Christians saw the encampment, and no one went out to meet them, they took up their arms. And when they were ready, they split into three battalions.* In one were King Lot of Orkney, the King of the Hundred Knights, Duke Escant of Cambenic, and King Clarion of Northumberland. In the second battalion were King Neutres of Garlot, King Caradoc, King Brandegorre, and King Yder. In the third battalion were King Belinant, King Tradelmant, King Aguisant, and King Urien. And after they had been divided and split up, they rode on at a slow gait with their heads down under their helmets, holding their lances, wearing armor all over, and armed with every weapon. And when they came to the encampment, they let their horses run as fast

---

*   The word here and afterward is *parties* (294, l. 17, cf. ll. 18, 20, 21): "parts" or "divisions."

as they could go, and they cut the ropes and strings that held up the tents,* and they brought down tents, pavilions, and everything else that was in their way, and the hue and cry rose so loud that the whole forest resounded with it. There was much bloodshed there and a great slaughter of the Saxons before those who were to safeguard the army could get on their horses.

When they saw that they had been taken by surprise, they jumped on their horses and went to tell King Hargadabran. Horns and trumpets blew everywhere, and the men, armed and unarmed, gathered. Then the twenty kings mounted—each one had twenty thousand men with him. As soon as the two sides laid eyes on each other, they let their horses run, and with their lances they struck one another and pierced shields and hauberks so that the tips came out the other side; they traded blows and slew one another most wondrously. There the fighting was heavy and hard, and the slaughter was dreadful on both sides. The Christians lost many, but the twelve princes bore up under the fighting, for they were very good knights; and Segurade, Adrian, the Lord of Salegne, Dorilias, Brandilias, the Lord of the Dolorous Tower, and Brun† the Ruthless put themselves forward as well. No man has ever fought better than they did. And King Caradoc, his brother the Lord of the Narrow Borderland, the Castellan of Gazel, the Lord of Blaskestan, the Lord of the [295] Marshlands, the Lord of Windsor, Galien, and King Urien's nephew Bademagu‡— these are not to be forgotten either, for no armor had withstood their blows,§ no matter how strong and hard. These twelve knights had put themselves in the twelve princes' ranks as soon as they had seen them in the encampment where they had begun the battle. There the fighting was hard and wondrous, and the Christians killed so many that the horses were up to their fetlocks in blood. But there were so many Saxons that because of their sheer strength the Christians had to withdraw away from the tents. Yet their withdrawal was not unbecoming, for the worthy men and the good knights saw that they had been driven back, and they were deeply shamed and very bitter. The Christians shouted their battlecry, gathered together, and turned back to face them, and the fighting was wondrous. Every man displayed his boldness, and they said that there should never be a knight who did not put himself forward in this time of need, so that he might be spoken about all the days of his life and, after his death, for as long as the world lasts.

Then they struck their horses with their spurs and yelled their battlecries, and they ran headlong in among them so fast that they left dead and wounded lying on the ground. But the Saxons were coming out of their tents in such numbers that they could not be counted. King Hargadabran went straight out before the others, and the story says that he stood fifteen feet tall (in the feet they had then), yet he was not more than twenty-eight years old. He sat on a big, gray warhorse,

---

* *cordes & lices dont li os estoit logie* (294, ll. 25-26): "ropes and strings with which the army was sheltered."

† The text reads *brehu* (294, l. 40); elsewhere, however, his name is *bruns* (177, l. 27; 297, l. 32).

‡ The text reads *gaudins li nies le roy vrien* (295, l. 1). Elsewhere, Urien's nephew is named Bademagu (e.g., 165, ll. 18-19), as is true later in this same episode (296, l. 23), while *gaudins* (Waldin) is Arthur's nephew (177, l. 32) or King Aguisant's nephew (297, ll. 34-35),

§ The text reads *caus* (295, l. 2): "lime" (?). Based on a (rather weak) reading in the Harley manuscript (*encontre leur corps* ["against their persons"]), Sommer suggests that an exemplar may have read *cops* ("blows") (295, n. 1), perhaps, one might add, with a variant spelling such as *cous*.

with his shield about his neck and holding his lance, and he had a cudgel hanging from his saddlebow with which he gave many a man cause for grief and worry that day. When the Christians saw that great devil coming and were most fearful about him, the very best and worthiest knights in their army made way for him. Then Caradoc of the Doleful Prison happened to meet him, for he was the biggest and the brawniest in the whole Christian army, and he rode the best horse, and yet he was not yet thirty years old. And as soon as he saw that great devil coming, he let his horse run toward him and held his lance straight out, and the other one, who feared him not at all, came toward him, and they hit each other on their shields so hard that their lances flew into pieces against their chests, and as they passed, they hit each other so hard, body and shield, that they took each other down with their horses under them. When the Christians and the Saxons saw those two spill to the ground, men from both sides spurred to the rescue. There the Christians suffered much strife and great hardship before Caradoc was on horseback again; the rain also bothered them a great deal, for it did not stop raining until after midday, and their ensigns were so wet that they could barely recognize one another except by their speech. There the Christians showed their worth, for despite all their enemies they got Caradoc back on his feet, and Brios of the Emplacement brought him a horse from which he had struck down King Graelent. And Mathans and Aliborc kept up fighting so well that they could not be found blameworthy.

Then the weather [296] began to clear, for it was after midday, and the sun shone very hot and dried their armor, so the Christians were very glad, for they could fight all the better. But there were so many Saxons that the Christians had to withdraw from the battlefield, and they were driven back to a hedgerow. There they stood their ground for a long time, for the King of the Hundred Knights was the first to take a stand: he shouted the battlecry many times, and he said to the barons, "My lords, what is this? Where are you going? We are holding very poorly to what we have worked out, for we are all hale and hardy, yet we have been routed so badly that none of us knows what he is worth when put to the test! This should be held against us for the rest of our lives, and we must also remember that, after we go our own ways, we have not come out of this strife any the better for it."

When the barons heard the King of the Hundred Knights, they turned about and began fighting. They flew into the midst of the Saxons, and each one hit the first man he met and struck him down dead. And when the Saxons saw them taking a stand, they ran upon them giving their horses free rein, and the fray grew so dreadful and so deadly that one could barely tell about it. There the King of the Hundred Knights did wonders all by himself, for he withstood the onslaughts so well before he left the field that all the barons were awestruck. For his shield was cut to pieces, and he had only a third of it left, and his hauberk was broken through and the links were coming undone, while his helmet was all bashed in. His arms were filthy with blood, and his forward saddlebow and the neck of his horse were smeared with blood and brains, so that no man could know who he was but for his speech. Meanwhile, Urien, his nephew Bademagu, King Yder, King Lot, King Neutres, and King Belinant—they were unwilling to give up the fight for as long as they could last in that place. So they did very great harm to the Saxons, for they killed more of them there than they had all day before then.

When the Saxons saw the harm they were doing to them, they blasted on their horns and trumpets, and they blew so loudly that people heard them four leagues away. Then a king came in with four thousand men in armor, who were fresh and rested, and they rode into the fray so hard that they made all the Christians give ground. And the uproar grew louder and the pursuit harder, and it lasted for the rest of the day until nightfall. The Christians could not have recovered and taken a stand, rather they would have been put to rout; if night had not fallen quickly, they would have got the worst of it. And when the Saxons had lost their daylight, they came back to their tents, took off their armor, and went to eat, for they had indeed had an easy time! And after eating, they rested and slept as though they had nothing to fear, although they were quite angry about the harm the Christians had done them that day. But they yearned to take vengeance. And the history* says that the Saxons lost twenty thousand and the Christians ten thousand.

But with that the story falls silent for a while about them, and it goes back to the twelve princes who were distraught over the rout, and they said that it would not be thus for long and that they would not leave in such a state. [297]

After the Christians had been beaten, they rode a short distance from the Saxons' tents. They alighted from their horses and tied them up, then they repaired their armor. And they were all so filthy with blood and brains that the color of their armor did not show through. When they were ready again, they mounted and rode at a slow gait drawn tightly together, and so stealthily that no one could hear them utter a single word. They rode until they came to the tents, and then they stormed in fast. They were better than five thousand strong, all on horseback, and they struck down tents and pavilions, and they killed and maimed as many men as they met. Nothing that fell into their hands got away.

And the Saxons, who were asleep, leapt from their beds and ran about the tents screaming, "We've been betrayed! Now to arms!"

Then they gathered at Hargadabran's tent, where horns and trumpets were blowing so loud that the ground shook, and the Saxons tried as hard as they could to run where they heard the trumpets and drums. There they got dressed as quickly as they could, and they lit lanterns, tapers, and torches in great numbers, so that the light could be seen from four leagues away.

But the Christians did not stop slaughtering and striking down as many as they came to, and they were over their ankles in blood, which flowed in streams as though from a spring. The bloodshed and killing lasted that way until daylight. And when the Saxons saw the loss they had suffered and the harm that had come to them, they were so distraught that they nearly went out of their minds; filled with wrath, they ran upon the Christians and meant to destroy them. The latter defended themselves as well as anyone could wish, but still the Saxons drove them from the tents. Then the Christians' horses began to slow down, for they had not been fed for two days and they began to weaken, and the barons saw that they were in danger of dying. Then, as it pleased God, the feeling came into their hearts, and those of the

---

*   Here the word is *estoire* (296, l. 39), rather than *conte*.

young men* whose names I have told you, that they should go joust with the Saxons in order to win horses to ride, or else, if they did not, they would be killed.

Then each of the barons took a straight, strong lance, and up to forty knights of worth put themselves into rows. And it is fitting and right that I should give the names of some of them. There were the eleven kings I have named to you before, and the Duke of Cambenic was the twelfth. Then there were the Lord of the Deep Valley; the Lord of the Dolorous Tower; Brim the Ruthless; Domas, the King of North Wales's nephew; King Aguisant's nephew, whose name was Waldin; the Lord of Salergne;† Bademagu, King Urien's nephew; Caradoc the Great—and so many other knights who were most worthy and bold. These rode out front, in the first row, and they held their lances in the felt holders ready to joust, for they sorely needed horses. And each one struck his man so hard that he brought him down dead to the ground; they took the horses by the reins and rode away with them, then dismounted from theirs and climbed on the new ones. And as soon as they had come into the ranks, the fighting and hitting became heavy and was so awesome that they killed and wounded everyone they met. [298] They began to knock horses down; they took the best ones and let their own go, and thereafter they and their new horses never wanted to be apart.

But the Saxons grew in numbers, and they made the Christians empty the field, like it or not, but it was a great struggle, for the Christians did their best to avenge the harm that the Saxons had done them; but they wanted to avenge the deaths of their friends whom the Christians had slain, and in the end they put them to rout and drove them from the field. There the forty knights underwent great hardship, for they put themselves behind the others who were fleeing to defend them because their horses were so slow they could barely walk, and the forty companions understood that if they left them behind they would be killed or taken prisoner, so they kept the battle going as long as they could. By their sheer strength they kept fighting until the others had got away; then they set out after them and, after they had followed them for a while, they stopped and fought the Saxons very hard once more. Whenever one of their companions happened to fall, the others did not yield before he was back on his horse. Nevertheless, they lost many men in the end, for many were killed or taken prisoner.

Thus were the Christians put to rout, and the Saxons ran after them until they had driven them into a forest; this is how they lost them—and because night fell. And the Saxons went back with a great many prisoners. But from that time on, the Saxons were never as secure as they had been before, and they set up forty thousand men to guard their army so that no one would harm them.

And the Christians sought refuge in the forest, and they rode until they came to a very beautiful heath, where they dismounted. They bewailed their losses long and

---

*   The text reads, ambiguously, *lor vint en corage comme a dieu plot & as iouenchaus* (297, ll. 26-27): (1) "it came into their hearts, as it pleased God and the youths" or (2), as translated, "it came into their hearts, as it pleased God, and the youths' [hearts]." The former is the clearer syntactically; the latter, while syntactically quite plausible but more complicated, has the advantage of putting the youths on a level with the barons (*lor/iouenchaus*) rather than with God (*a dieu/as iouenchaus*).

†   The text reads *li sires de salergne* (297, l. 35). Elsewhere, Brun the Ruthless is referred to as the Lord of Salerno (177, l. 27).

hard, and they were so distraught that they no longer knew what to do or where to go. But in the end they agreed that each one should go back to where he lived, and if the Saxons came to attack any of them, he should defend himself as best he could. With that, they got on their horses and went their own ways, weeping and bemoaning their loss. And when every one of them had got to his country, he supplied himself as best he could with men and food. But after the Saxons had defeated them, they were no longer afraid of them in any way, so they rode among their tents, and, as many as they met, they took them prisoner. There was none so bold as to stand up to them, and no one dared ride out from his stronghold to fight them.

But with that the story falls silent about them and goes back to King Arthur, who is at sea on his way back from Brittany and the land of King Ban of Benoic.

37. The Tournament at Carhaix; the False Guenevere.[*]

Here the story says that when King Arthur and the high barons had boarded the boats, they sailed until they came to Great Britain. And as soon as they had come ashore, they got on their horses and rode until they came to Logres in Britain, where they were welcomed richly and joyfully; and they stayed there for three days [299] feasting and playing. And on the fourth day, King Arthur and Gawainet his nephew and King Ban and Bors of Gaunes moved out with no more than three thousand men in iron armor, and they rode for as many days at it took them to come to the kingdom of Carmelide, three leagues from Carhaix, where King Leodagan was staying. And when he heard the news that King Arthur was coming, he went out to meet him with his whole household. And when they met, they were very glad to see each other, and they embraced and kissed each other because they were very fond of one another, and they went back to Carhaix.

They found Carhaix covered with wall hangings and the floors strewn with sweet-smelling grass, and they saw ladies and maidens dancing, the fairest ever seen. Elsewhere the young men were jousting and breaking lances with each other. It was like that all the way to the hall, where Guenevere, King Leodagan's daughter was. She came out to greet them, and she was happier to see them than the others had been, for as soon as she saw King Arthur she ran to meet him with open arms, and she told him that he and his companions were most welcome. She kissed him very softly on the mouth in plain sight of everyone who wanted to see it, then they took each other by the hand and went up into the great hall. After they had rested, they went to eat a most plentiful evening meal, for they had the time for it, and when they had eaten, they went to sleep, for they were tired and exhausted from the riding they had done. In the morning King Arthur, King Ban, and King Bors got up—they liked more than anyone to rise early—along with Sir Gawainet and Sir Yvonet, and they went to the church to hear Mass. And after they had heard

---

[*]   Corresponds to Sommer, 298-312.

Mass, they went back up to the great hall, where they found King Leodagan out of bed, for he had already heard Mass in his chapel. Then they all got their horses ready and mounted, just the six of them and no more, and they went out to enjoy themselves riding through the fields to see the meadows and the river, which was beautiful.

After they had ridden about for a long while, King Leodagan spoke to King Arthur and asked him when he would wed his daughter, for it was the right time. King Arthur answered that it would be whenever King Leodagan wished, for he was ready. "But I need the best friend I have, and I will not be wed without him."

When King Leodagan heard this, he asked him who that friend was.

He said that it was Merlin, for it was through him that he had won all the wealth and honor he had.

When Sir Gawainet heard this, he said that he was right. "Indeed, every one of us should want to have him too. Rest assured that he will soon come, since you wish for him, and may God bring him to you quickly."

"In truth," said the king, "he told me that he would be here soon."

"Then there is no reason not to name the day for the gathering," said Sir Gawainet.

Then they set the gathering for one week from that day. They went on talking of such things until they got to the great hall. The food was ready and the tables set, so they sat down and were served as kings and worthy gentlemen should be. After they had eaten, they went out again to enjoy themselves. And this is how their stay was for the whole eight days.

But now the story falls silent about them and goes back to the twelve princes from the Kingdom of Logres who had been routed before the city of Clarence. [300]

Now the story says that after the twelve princes had been put to rout, no sooner had each one gone back to his abode than the news came to them that King Arthur had crossed the sea and that he had knighted King Lot's young men; King Urien's two sons; Galescalain, son of King Neutres of Garlot; Dodinel, son of King Balinant of South Wales; Kay of Estral, King Caradoc's nephew; and Sagremor, grandson of the Emperor of Constantinople, and the companions he had brought with him. And they also heard that King Lot's wife was in Logres, where her children had brought her, but the youths had sworn that King Lot would not have her back with him until he had sworn fealty to King Arthur, and he could be sure that he could never have worse enemies than they would be to him. And how King Arthur had fought against King Claudas of the Land Laid Waste before the city of Trebe and against Pontius Anthony, a counsellor of Rome, Frollo, a duke of Germany, and Randol, seneschal of Gaul, and he had put them to rout and driven them from the field; and he had given the two brother kings back their land. And how he had betrothed himself to the daughter of King Leodagan of Carmelide. And how he had routed King Rion before the city of Aneblayse.* And how he had gone to Carmelide to take a wife. The princes said among themselves that it was a great sin that filled them with anger against King Arthur, and such a hurtful thing could come only

---

*   The text reads *cite de daneblaise* (300, l. 16).

from sin. So they prayed God most tenderly that He make peace between them for their happiness and for their honor.

And the news spread until King Lot heard it all, and he learned that his wife was at Logres and his little son Mordred as well, and he was very happy in one way and sad in another—happy because she was not in the hands of the Saxons, who had taken her from him, and sad because the youths had her so that she would not be with him. Nor would he have their love, until he swore fealty to King Arthur. But he did not see how he could honorably make peace with him, unless Our Lord God helped. Then he brooded and thought of a very clever trick. He thought that King Arthur would send his wife to Logres, his chief city. And as soon as he could find out when she was coming, he would go to meet her with as many men as he could find, and he would fight until he had taken Arthur's wife from him. For through her he would get his own wife back.

This is what the king thought, but he could plot as much as he wanted, for things would go otherwise than what he believed, if God safeguarded King Arthur and Sir Gawainet. With that, King Lot sent his spies out far and wide to find out when King Arthur was coming from Carmelide to wed his wife and how many men would be with him. And he made ready to leave when he had to.

But with that the story falls silent about him, and it speaks about Merlin, who was in the hermitage with Blaise, his master, and who told him all the things you have heard before now, and Blaise put everything into writing. And the story says that as soon as King Arthur had told Leodagan that he was waiting only for Merlin, Merlin knew it. And he knew King Lot's thoughts and how he had sent his spies along all the roads, and he told it word for word to Blaise, who wrote it down. And after Merlin had told Blaise everything, he came straight to Carhaix, where the barons were waiting for him; it was the evening before the king was to wed his wife.* [301] And when the barons saw him, they were joyful.

But with that the story falls silent about them, and we will tell about Guenevere, stepdaughter of Cleodalis, seneschal of Carmelide, and about her kinsmen, who hated King Leodagan a great deal.

Now the story says that Guenevere, Cleodalis's stepdaughter, had very wealthy kinsmen on her mother's side, and they were very good knights. They hated King Leodagan for the great shame he had brought to Cleodalis because of his wife, whom he had kept for so long in spite of them all. As it happened, they were gathered together on the same evening Merlin came, and there were sixteen of them in all, and they were talking together of many things; but Cleodalis was not at this meeting, and he knew nothing about it. And they asked one another what they could do to hurt the king more and annoy him. They agreed at last that they would speak to the nurse of King Arthur's betrothed, and they would be so generous toward her that, on the night when Guenevere† was to lie down with her husband,

---

* Sommer suggests, doubtless because *espouser* normally has a complement, that the text must have dropped *sa feme* (300, n. 2).

† Sommer's text, which does not mention the serving woman, reads *ele* (301, l. 11): "she." See the following note.

the old woman would put the seneschal's daughter with the king instead of her;* and she would take Guenevere to play in the garden that evening,† and "then we will seize her and take her to such a place that he will never hear news of her, nor will she be recognized, wherever she goes. Now let's go and talk the nurse‡ into doing this, and when it is over we will be lords of the king and his kingdom."

Then they decided that seven of them would undertake the kidnapping, and they would have a boat ready where they would take her. After this planning, the traitors went their ways happy and cheerful because they thought that they had done very well, and they bought the boat and everything they needed. And they made the nurse such promises that she agreed to do what they wanted.

But as soon as they had reached their agreement, Merlin knew it. He went straight to Ulfin and Bretel and drew them aside by themselves, and he explained to them the treachery word for word just as they had plotted it; and when they heard it, they crossed themselves in wonder. Then they asked Merlin what they should do about it.

"I will gladly tell you this," said Merlin. "Tomorrow evening, after you have eaten your meal, put your armor on over your clothing, and go hide under an apple tree in the garden. They will come unarmed but for their swords, and they'll go to their lookout where they'll hide until it is time for the nurse to bring the queen to play. And be careful that you are ready to rescue her as soon as they have taken hold of her, for you will lose her very fast if they can get her into the boat."

"Sir," said the barons, "God willing, we will not lose her, since we know so much about it."

"Take care," said Merlin, "not to tell anyone that I have said this to you, for I would never love you."

"In truth," said the worthy gentlemen, "we would rather lose our birthright than say anything about it."

With that, the three friends went back into the hall, and they found that the knights wanted to leave, and they went straight to their lodgings to rest and sleep until daybreak the next morning. Then the barons and the knights got out of bed and gathered in the hall. And King Leodagan had his daughter dressed more richly than any king's daughter ever was, and she was of such great beauty that everyone stared at her in wonder. And King Ban took her [302] on one side and King Bors on the other, and they led her to the church of St. Stephen. There was a great gathering of nobles there to walk along with her, and they all held hands and walked two by two. The first two were King Arthur and King Leodagan,§ the second two Sir Gawainet and Sir Yvain, and after them went Galescalain and Agravain, and next Dodinel and Guerrehet, and next Sagremor and Gaheriet, and next Kay the

---

*   Sommer gives the variant reading, found in two manuscripts, about the plan to bribe the old woman and substitute the other Guenevere (301, n. 3). Because the nurse is not mentioned in Sommer's text, it appears at first that Guenevere was to be the agent of her own kidnapping.

†   When the plot is executed, the old woman takes Guenevere into the garden to make water (308, l. 27).

‡   Where the variant lesson is *maistresse* (301, n. 4), Sommer's text has *marastre* (301, l. 15): "stepmother." The text repeats *marastre* in l. 20, but *maistresse* occurs in l. 28 and thereafter.

§   The text reads *bohors* (302, l. 4); however, Bors and Ban accompany Guenevere. As Sommer notes (302, n. 1), the Harley manuscript has Leodagan.

Seneschal and Kay of Estral, and after them came King Ban and King Bors, who were leading the young lady. She wore flowing robes,* she had the richest cap that anyone had ever seen on her golden head, and she was dressed in a robe of beaten gold so long that it trailed more than a half-yard behind her, and it fit her so well that everyone was astounded by her great beauty. Next came Guenevere the stepdaughter of Cleodalis, who was wonderfully beautiful and comely, and she held Girflet and Lucan the Wine Steward by their hands. Next came the newly knighted two by two, and after them the companions of the Round Table, then the barons of the Kingdom of Carmelide, then the noble ladies of the country and the burghers. This is how they came to the church.

When they got there they found the archbishop of Brice, in the land of Logres, and Sir Amustan, Leodagan's good chaplain, and it is he who married King Arthur and Guenevere and blessed them. And the archbishop sang Mass, and great were the offerings of kings and high princes. And when the service was over, they went back to the great hall, where there was a great crowd of all kinds of singers.† Why should I go on telling you about it? All the joyful merrymaking that could be done was done there. After this the tables were set and they went to eat, and they were served as befits a king's wedding. And there is no man alive who could talk about the presents that were given. After eating, when the tablecloths were taken away, the barons got up and went into the meadows before the great hall. There the jousting dummy was set up, and the new knights went to tilt along with the forty knights that King Arthur had engaged to come with him to Carhaix. As it happened, the knights of the Round Table came out too, and they began hitting roughly, although they were playing, because they were good knights. At length the news about that reached Sir Gawainet, who was still sitting at table eating with his companions. When Sir Gawainet heard that his friends were jousting so hard, he asked for his arms, his shield, and his lance, as did all his companions, and they got on their horses not wearing armor, except that Sir Yvain had on a short hauberk with double mail. That was always his custom—not because he would ever think of cheating or wrongdoing, but he dreaded that a fight might break out among his companions through the fault of some thoughtless or evil fellow, of whom there are many on the earth. But when Sir Gawainet and his companions came into the tourney, the newly knighted were being badly beaten, for the companions of the Round Table were doing with them what they would. When Sir Gawainet saw them getting the worst of it, he was not happy about it, so he and his companions went to their side. When they saw that they were being helped, they gathered about Sir Gawainet and his companions and asked them if they were on their side, and they said that they were. [303]

When Sir Gawainet went in on the side of the knights Arthur had engaged, they were very glad and the others angry. Then they swore that they would never fail one another in life or death, and this showed clearly that day, for they fought so

---

* The text reads *si fu toute desafublee* (302, l. 7): "and she was all undressed," which is clearly not the case. As the Merlin narrator does not characteristically engage in ironic descriptions, the meaning here must partake of conventional associations of *desafublee* with open, loose-fitting, or flowing dress.

† The word is *menestreus* (302, l. 21), which could apply to servants and artisans as well as singers and musicians.

well that the knights of the Round Table bore them a grudge that was to prove most costly in the quarrel that arose at the tournament in Logres where Sir Gawainet was hailed lord and master for his valiant deeds there, as the story will reveal it to you later, after he had become the knight of Queen Guenevere.

When Sir Gawainet had taken his companions' oaths, they turned out in rank order; it was Sir Gawainet who set them in order, for he was a wise knight, the courtliest and the best taught there ever was in Great Britain. After he had set his companions in order, they rode out two by two, one after the other. King Arthur, Merlin, and many of the others were standing at the windows of the great hall to look at the tournament, and there were a great number of ladies and young women with them, and they all saw that they were turned out so well that they were sure to win the tournament together. And the companions of the Round Table were on the other side, a hundred and fifty all told, and Sir Gawainet sent forty jousters out against them: Sagremor was the very first, and Nascien was on the other side.

They all let their horses run against each other, but Sir Gawainet rushed in between them and separated them, and he called the companions of the Round Table and said to them, "My lords, you are all worthy gentlemen and the best knights anyone knows about. Now let us do the right thing. You go get your armor, and we'll do likewise, and then let us behave the same way on both sides and swear that if we take one of yours, it will count against you, and if your take one of ours, it will count in your favor and against us. And when we have caught one of yours, put another in his place, and we will do the same if you catch one of ours."

Then they swore to follow these rules and sent for their armor, and as soon as it was brought to them, they quickly put it on.

The news had reached the city about how Sir Gawainet had undertaken the tournament against the companions of the Round Table, and they esteemed him and praised him, and more than any of the others King Bors esteemed him, and he said that never again would such a knight be seen in his lifetime, "and if he lives long, he will be the best knight there ever was and the one I would most like to be like."

This is what King Bors said about Sir Gawainet.

When they were on their horses and ready, they rode against each other. The first to break ranks with the knights of the Round Table was Adragain the Dark, and Dodinel the Wildman came to meet him. They rode as fast as their horses could run and hit their shields with their lances so hard that they drove through the boards and broke them into pieces with the strength of their arms—and of the horses that carried them; the tips of the lances stopped against their hauberks, which were so strong that not a link was broken, but the lances could only shatter. Then they ran into each other so hard, shield against shield and body against body, that they took [304] each other to the ground. As soon as they had knocked each other down, they came running to the rescue from both sides, and they struck one another so stoutly on their shields that their lances flew into bits; some bore each other to the ground while others went by without falling. Then they drew their swords and began the fray on foot and on horseback.

Then, as it happened, Sir Gawainet and Nascien met and struck each other with their lances on their shields with all their might. Nascien's lance flew into bits, and

Sir Gawainet hit him so hard that he drove his shield against his arm and his arm against his body, and he bore him from his saddle to the ground with his legs in the air. But he sprang back to his feet, for he was quick, as he was worthy and bold, and he drew his sword from its scabbard, covered himself with his shield, and prepared to defend himself.

Sir Gawainet went through with his pass, then he turned back around, drew his sword, and came straight toward Nascien. And when Nascien saw him coming, he was hardly afraid of him at all, so he hurried to strike him. And he hit Sir Gawainet beneath his shield so that his blood began to flow down, but Sir Gawainet gave him back such a great blow on his helmet that the sparks flew up, and he sent him flying to the ground on his hands, but he was soon up again and made straight for Sir Gawainet with his sword raised high, and he dealt him such a strong blow on his helmet that he made him lean over. When Sir Gawainet saw that Nascien was so worthy and such a good fighter against him, he loved him very well for it. Then he struck him so hard through the helmet that he made him stumble and fall to his knees. He who was of such great strength sprang back to his feet, but as he was getting up, Sir Gawainet took hold of him by the helmet and tore it from his head so hard that his nose and forehead hurt, and he threw it as far as he could into the press.

Then he yelled to him, "Sir knight, surrender!"

And he answered him that he had not reached the point where he should surrender for any man whom he could see. Then he covered himself with his shield, and Sir Gawainet struck his shield so hard that a great piece of it went flying into the field. Then he ran at him and hit him so stoutly with the hilt of his sword that he sent him sprawling to the ground. Then he came down from his horse and jumped on him, took his coif off of him. and told him to surrender to him or else he was dead. He answered that he could go ahead and kill him, but never, as long as he lived, would he be thought of as a coward.

"What?" said Sir Gawainet "Sir knight, is it then true that you would rather die than surrender or admit that you have been bested?"

And he said yes.

"I do not want to kill you," said Sir Gawainet. "That would truly be a shame, for you are most worthy. But I'll have you stripped naked so that you won't be getting on a horse for a while."

"I do not know what you'll do with me, but as long as I am alive I will not admit that I have been beaten."

When Sir Gawainet saw that he could get nothing more from him, he was convinced that he was of great heart. Then a most noble thought came to him that any other man would have been wary of, and he came straight to him and said, "Sir knight, take my sword, for I know that I have been bested."

And when Nascien saw such great nobility in him, he bowed low and said, "Ah! For God's sake, sir knight, do not say that, but take my sword instead, for I hand it over to you. Many have seen how it is with me, and you should know that I could never pay back or deserve such a favor."

Then they embraced each other, and each was very happy with the [305] other, and after they had enjoyed each other for a while, they took up their arms and rode fast to the tourney, which had already begun, and Nascien took Sir Gawainet's side, for that was right and just.

When Sir Gawainet and Nascien came to the tournament, Dodinel was already back on his horse and had taken Adragain prisoner by main force, and the fighting, which was underway again, was most wondrous. Sagremor had already struck down Hervi of Rivel and was holding onto his helmet with both hands trying to make him swear to become his prisoner; and Gaheriet, Sir Gawainet's brother, had also taken Migloras. And when Sir Gawainet saw that, he began to fight so well that he made every one of them fall back and yield ground; and twelve of Sir Gawainet's companions fought so well that they took by force twelve of the companions of the Round Table, who were so sorrowful over it that they nearly went out of their minds. Then forty companions from each side came in, and the fighting in the tournament grew heavy and awesome, for the companions of the Round Table had said that from then on everyone should take care, if he knew how, to do as much harm as he could: "For we cannot hold ourselves in very high esteem when such boys drive us back, and they have never fought in a tournament before. People will think we are cowards, and we would indeed be blameworthy."

Then they let their horses run together, and they rode in hard and fast, for they were grief-stricken about the companions who had been taken prisoner. But the others came out to meet them, and they very boldly welcomed them with the tips of their lances. There the fighting was fierce and hard, and it went on without letting up until after midday. Then Sir Gawainet left the tournament to change helmets, for his had been so badly treated that it was useless to anyone, for it had been dented and broken into pieces, so that it hung down over his shoulders. And while he was coming back, and he was putting another helmet on, he saw his men withdrawing on every side. Then he struck headlong into the fighting. He held a strong, stout lance, and he took down the first man he came to and sent him sprawling. And Sir Gawainet fought so well that his side won their ground back.

And then, as it happened, he found Sir Yvonet on foot, along with Kay, Griffonet, Lucan, Blioberis, Girflet, Oswain the Stouthearted, Lanval, and Agravain, and the whole tournament was around the nine of them,* for all the companions of the Round Table were striving to take them. When Sir Gawainet saw them, he headed toward them holding his lance, and he rode in so hard among them that he made them all shudder, and he sent the first man he came to sprawling to the ground. Then he lowered his lance and broke it, and with the stub he struck down another one so mercilessly that he did not know where he was.

After this, Sir Gawainet drew his sword and began to fight so skillfully that everyone was struck dumb, for he cut up their shields and hauberks so that none of them dared make a stand against him, but even the best of them gave ground to him, and so he scattered them hither and thither. Meanwhile, his companions had got back on their horses, and they had the strength of heart to avenge the shame the others had brought them. And Sir Yvain began to fight so boldly that one and all held him in great esteem, and all the companions fought so well that everyone who

---

*   The text has "eight." *ces .viij.* (305, l. 30), resulting either from an error (for *.viiij.*) or from an attempt to distinguish the last eight from Yvain.

saw the tournament praised them highly. And the three kings* spoke about them a great deal; they were standing at the windows, and they said that the young men would be [306] most worthy gentlemen if they lived long. The deeds of prowess they did matched those of Sir Gawainet, for it was thanks to his prowess alone that the other side was driven back and chased as far as the town. There the companions of the Round Table stopped, for they were filled with sorrow and anger, and they said that they would be cowards to let themselves be treated in such a way, so they turned their horses around again to make a stand against the ones running after them. Then the hitting began, and it was wondrous, for none had been harder or more bitter all day.

The fighting was very heavy and the battle was hard, before the gate to the city of Carhaix, between those of the Round Table and the newly knighted. Then Sir Gawainet began a brawl that was so great that it was spoken of for a long time afterwards. He had fought hard the whole day long, and when he saw that his companions had been stopped and that the companions of the Round Table were defending the gate against them so that they could not break through, he was so filled with wrath and anguish that he hardly knew what to do. Then he withdrew and put his sword back into its scabbard. This was not Excalibur, but a very hard sword made for tourneys. He went to a staff of oak and took it in his hands, and he threw his shield on the ground in order to move more freely; then he made straight for the press where he saw that the fighting was roughest. As he came in, he dealt one knight a heavy blow on top of his helmet; it was so hard that he sent him sprawling to the ground and almost knocked him senseless. Then he struck another one down all in a daze, so that blood flowed from his nose and mouth. He struck left and right and brought down as many as he met in his path, and he wounded and maimed many of them.

And when the companions of the Round Table saw that he was trying only to hurt them, they ran upon him and his men with more than enough vigor, and they said that from that time on they would do the worst harm they could, for they no longer cared just for tourneying. So the fighting grew so heavy and so awesome that there would have been great losses on both sides if it had not been for Merlin, who called King Ban, King Bors his brother, and King Arthur and told them to go break it up, for it was high time to make peace between them. When the barons understood Merlin's meaning, they asked for their armor and their horses, and the serving boys went out and brought armor and horses to them. They donned their armor, and when they were mounted, they rode out to the fray. And Merlin went along and rode ahead of everyone.† And the others were fighting very hard, one side hot with anger against the other. Sir Gawainet was hitting very hard with the staff he was wielding, but his foes‡ defended themselves with all their might because they would not yield ground regardless of what was done to them.

---

* The text has *li .iiij. roy* (305, l. 43): "the four kings."

† Sommer's text reads *& merlins uait auoec deuant tous les autres. Et chil se combatent* ... (306, ll. 31-32): "and Merlin went along before all the others. And those were fighting ... " Sommer cites the variant in the Harley manuscript: *Et merlins vint deuant tout premier a ceulx qui se combatent* ... (306, n. 1): "And Merlin came out front, the very first, to those who were fighting ..."

‡ The text has *cil* (306, l. 34): "those/the [other] ones."

When Sir Gawainet saw that they were holding their own so well, he flew headlong into their midst, angry as a wild boar, and he worked until he broke through the whole of them, like it or not. Then he began to harm them in the worst way, for he meant to hurt them all if he could. As Merlin and the three kings rode up to separate them, Merlin, as it happened, was facing Minodales, who had struck him on the chest with a lance and almost brought him down with his horse,* and he was very sore from the blow Minodales had given him. Sir Gawainet [307] made straight for him and raised his sword to strike him on the helmet, but when the latter saw him coming, he leaned forward to ward off the blow, but the staff landed lengthwise across his shoulders and knocked him head over heels to the ground.

Then came King Arthur, who had clearly seen the young man's stroke, and he shouted to him, "Dear nephew, put your staff down, for you have done enough with it."

But he was hot with anger and bent on inflicting pain. Merlin rode over to him and grabbed him with one of his hands and with the other took his staff away, and he said to him, smiling, "Hold still, sir knight, for you have been caught. Surrender to me, if you please, for you have done enough fighting."

When Sir Gawainet saw that it was Merlin, he told him with great courtesy that he was indeed his prisoner, since it pleased Merlin.

With these words, King Arthur came to him and said, "Dear nephew, let the tournament be, for you have done enough fighting, and it would be a good thing to let it go with that."

And Sir Gawainet told him that it suited him, since that was his pleasure. With that the five of them rode away, and as soon as Sir Gawainet had left the tournament, the others stopped fighting, and they all went to their lodgings to take off their armor. But the companions of the Round Table were most distressed, because they had got the worse of the tournament, but they were quite sure that they would avenge themselves so that the newly knighted could not boast about it.

These words were overheard by a young man who was riding near them, and he went to tell Sir Gawainet, whom the three kings and Merlin were leading away, along with Sir Yvain and Galescalain. And the boy came up to them and told them what the companions of the Round Table had said. And when Sir Gawainet heard their threat, he regarded it with great scorn, but he did not let the others see this, except to say that they could have their tourneying without stopping for as long as they wanted, "until I am at the point of sending† ten unskilled knights‡ out against them!"

Sir Gawainet kept to the words he spoke, for it was very clear who the best knights were on the day they won together the tournament in the meadowlands

---

*   The text adds the formulaic *en .j. mont* (306, ll. 41-42): "all in a heap."

†   The conjunction *por .j. peu que* (307, ll. 24-25) normally refers to a present or past action (modern French *peu s'en faut que je* ["I almost..."]) rather than, as here, to the future.

‡   The term is *chevaliers daide* (307, l. 25), which can refer to knights whose duty it is to ride to others' rescue (but *laisse coure* ["I let run/send out."] suggests an attack, mock or serious), to knights who are to be used only in cases of urgency (auxiliary in one sense), or to knights who aid other knights (auxiliary in another sense). In any case, the term implies second-rate knights and, appropriately for Gawain's scorn, a sarcastic tone of voice.

outside Logres, when the new knights fought against those of the Round Table. There were many wounded and maimed then, just as the story will recount it for you later. And it will tell you how oaths were sworn on one and the other side.

But right now the story stops speaking about this thing until it is the proper time and place, and it goes back to speaking about the knights of the Round Table, who went to their lodgings to take off their armor, just as I have told it earlier.

Here the story says that as King Arthur was taking Sir Gawainet to the great hall, the common folk said to one another, about Sir Gawainet, "Look at the good knight here!"

They asked Merlin who he was and what his name was, and he told them that he was named Gawainet and that he was the son of King Lot of Orkney. And when they heard this, they said, because they were most happy to hear it, that he was very bold and that he was indeed a man to imitate. Thus the townsfolk talked as they would. And after the companions of the Round Table had taken off their armor, they dressed themselves in their best robes and came straight to court. And as soon as they saw [308] Sir Gawainet, they drew to one side and grumbled to themselves about him loudly enough for him to hear, and they said that he had hurt them dreadfully in that first tournament; now he was certain to be lord and master of them all and a companion of the Round Table as well. Sir Gawainet indeed heard them, but he answered them not a word. And from that day on he could indeed be lord and master and a companion of the Round Table whenever he wanted,* and it was right, for there was in him the worthiness of a great gentleman; he was a good knight and faithful for as long as he lived and full of other good qualities, and he was more courtly than any other.

Straightway the cloths were laid on the tables, and the knights within washed their hands. There were three halls full of knights, and they were very well served with all the good and fitting things a man's body needs. When, after the meal, the tablecloths were taken away, the knights began to make merry and to play games with one another, which was the right thing to do. Then the vesper bells were rung at my lord St. Stephen's Church, and all those knights went to hear vespers. Afterwards King Arthur's bed was blessed, and the knights left and went to rest and sleep in their lodgings.

And Guenevere stayed behind in her room alone with her nurse. And that day the treachery was brought into play whereby she was to be taken prisoner and betrayed by the kinsmen of Guenevere, stepdaughter of Cleodalis the Seneschal; they had convinced the old woman, who was the nurse of Guenevere, King Arthur's wife, to grant them what they wanted. They said that they would wait for her in the garden beneath the great hall, and they would have the other Guenevere with them. After they had made their case, they went into the garden and hid under the trees; there were ten of them, but they were armed only with swords. They had the false Guenevere with them, and they stayed there for a long time until the barons had left and gone to their lodgings.

---

* The text, which is not so forthrightly conditional, reads *fu il sires & maistres & compains de la table roonde sil le vaut estre* (308, ll. 5-6): "he was lord and master and a companion of the Round Table if he wanted to be."

And the queen was undressed as though to go to bed. Then the old woman took her into the garden to make water.* The traitors were lying in wait in the garden hidden beneath a grafted pear tree;† when they saw her coming, they kept very still and crept toward the wall little by little. But Bretel and Ulfin had not forgotten what Merlin had told them. They were well armed beneath their clothing, and they had hidden crouched under the steps the queen was to take to go outside. They kept very still and were seen by no roan or woman, and they likewise had their ears cocked to listen. After they had been there quite a long time, they saw the old woman who held the queen by the hand and was going straight to where the traitors were on the lookout. And when they saw that the queen‡ had gone far from her room, they laid hands on her from all sides and handed the other Guenevere over to the old woman. And when the queen§ saw her, she understood clearly that she had been betrayed, and she prepared to scream, but they told her that if she uttered a single word, they would kill her—even if she made any sound at all. Then they drew their bare swords and left along the river that ran below the garden, where a boat they had come in was tied up. The garden was quite high above the river, and the only way they could get there was by a little path which was very hard to go up and down because of the rocks that were heavily strewn all over it. And if they could [309] only have got into the boat, the queen would have been lost without hope of recovery.

When Ulfin and Bretel saw the ones they were yearning so much to see, they jumped out of their hiding-place and shouted at them. They called them traitors and said that they would be sorry for what they had done, for they would die because of it. And when the traitors heard them yelling, they looked about and saw that there were only two of them, and they held them to be of little worth. So they took the queen and gave her over to five of their companions, and the other five stayed behind to fight the men who were coming for them with their swords drawn.

When the queen saw how they were treating her, she became greatly frightened and let herself fall to the ground, onto the green grass, but they picked her up and carried her, whether she liked it or not. And when she saw the two men coming to rescue her, she twisted out of their hands so forcefully that she got away from them, and she turned in flight down through the garden until she came to a fruit tree, and she flung both arms around it and held on tight. They came right to her and tried to pull her away, but they could not move her from it; however much they pulled and tugged, they could do no more with her. They were so angry they could have killed her.

And Ulfin and Bretel ran until they came to the five who were waiting for them holding their naked swords. Bretel struck the first man he met so hard that he split him open down to his teeth, and Ulfin hit the second one and sent his head flying.

---

*   In the exposition of the plot, the old woman was to take her to *esbatre* (301, l. 13): "frolic."

†   The text reads *une ente de sainrieule* (308, l. 28). The word *ente* is common for a grafted fruit tree. The *Französiches Etymologisches Wörterbuch* records the regional term *sans-règle* ("ruleless"), cf. Old French *rieule*, attested since the fourteenth century, for "a kind of hardy pear tree" and its fruit (10: 224, col. 2), probably so named because the tree bears erratically (10: 224, col. l,n. 28).

‡   The text has the ambiguous personal pronoun *ele* (3: 308, l. 36): "she."

§   Again, the ambiguous personal pronoun (308, l. 37).

The other three fell on them, but they could not harm them because they were wearing good armor; they lost heart and wanted to flee, but the two stayed right on them until they had killed all three. Then they went straight for the five others, who were trying so hard to get the queen away, but they could not pull her from the tree, and it was a wonder that they had not torn her arms from her body.

When Ulfin and Bretel saw the distress the queen was in, they ran toward her and yelled at them, and they came out to meet them. They began hitting one another with their swords, and Ulfin and Bretel killed two of the five. And when the others saw that there were only three of them left, they turned in flight straight to the path that led down to the boat. And when the two companions saw them running away, they did not want to chase them. Instead, they came back to the spot where the dead men lay, picked them up, and threw them down the cliff, and the old woman along with them—they went rolling from rock to rock and did not stop until they came to the river. Then Ulfin and Bretel took the queen and led her away very frightened to her bedroom, and they told her not to be afraid anymore. Afterwards they took the false Guenevere and led her off to their lodging, for they did not want anyone to find out about their secret.

Just as you have heard, the traitors were dealt with according to Merlin's advice, and the queen was rescued by the two worthy men. And as soon as they had left, Merlin knew it, and he came straight to King Leodagan and told him to send three of his young ladies to the queen's room to put her to bed. And the king asked him, "Why? Can't her nurse do it?"

And Merlin told him the whole truth just as it had happened. When the king heard it, he was deeply amazed [310] about it, and he said that he could never rest until he had spoken to her. Then King Leodagan left and came straight to the bedroom where his daughter Guenevere was, and he took three young ladies with him to get her ready for bed. When she saw him, she began to weep mightily, and the king took her by the hand, drew her to one side, and spoke to her all alone. And she told him the truth just as it had happened, from beginning to end, and the king told her that she had nothing to fear, for she need worry no more. And the king ordered the three ladies to get her ready for bed, and they did as they were told; nor did King Leodagan want to leave the room before they had put her to bed. After that, he came to his daughter's bed, raised the cover, and turned it down until he saw the mark of the crown on her back. Then he knew indeed that she was his daughter, whom he had had by his wife. After that, he put the cover back over her and went out of the room without saying a word, and the ladies wondered why he had done that.

Just then King Arthur came back from reveling with his companions. When he came into the hall, Merlin and King Leodagan came to meet him, and they told him to go to bed with his wife, for it was high time; he said that he would do so very gladly. So he went into the room where the three maidens were who had helped her get ready for bed, and as soon as the king was in bed, the ladies left the room. No one was left there but the king and queen, and all night they spent a most happy time together,* for they loved each other deeply, and they did not stop until daybreak, when they fell asleep arm in arm.

Thus was Queen Guenevere to have been deceived by the traitors—by the ones because of whom she later had very great sorrow, which happened a long time afterwards, just as the story will relate it to you, if there is anyone to tell it to you.† For the king lost‡ her for a good three years, when he never had her with him. Galehaut, a wealthy prince in the kingdom of Sorelois, took her away for love of Lancelot. And the king kept the false Guenevere as his concubine§ until one day when, as it happened, he was taken ill. And this was because of Bertelay,¶ a traitor who brought it about that King Arthur was unwilling to give her up for anyone's sake; in the end, everything on earth rotted. And the land and kingdom were under interdict for nearly three years, when no man's or woman's body was buried in consecrated ground except secretly and under threat of excommunication. And Our Lord allowed such hardship to befall them for the breech of faith in their sins, and they were sinful indeed. And all of this happened through a knight who afterwards died a dreadful death because of it, as the story will tell you later. But it is right and fitting that the story should tell you why this happened, for this is the place for it, and reason accords with this.

It was true that King Leodagan, who was a good ruler and lawgiver, had a knight who was most worthy and shrewd; he was a good knight who had served him well, and he was of noble stock. This knight's name was Bertelay, and he hated another knight with deadly hatred because the latter had slain one of his first cousins to have his wife because he loved her. When Bertelay found out that he [311] had killed his cousin, and knew that his wife had shamed him, he never bothered to complain to the king. Rather, he went to him, broke faith with him, and threatened him with death, and he kept watching him many a day and many a night. At last, on the night that King Arthur wed his wife, when the knights left the court and went to their lodgings to rest, Bertelay happened to see his enemy. He ran him down and killed him with a short sword he had with him. As soon as he had killed him, he went straight to his lodging, and the two squires who had been with the slain knight raised the cry, and people came pouring out everywhere with lanterns and torches aflame and found the slain knight. They asked the two squires, who were mourning sorrowfully, who had killed him, and they said that it was Bertelay the Red. After the squires had wept and wailed over their lord for a long time, they picked him up and carried him to his lodging, and they did to him what was fitting for a dead

---

*   The text reads *menerent ... moult boine ui ensamble* (310, ll. 20-21): "let a very good life together." The expression recurs (313, ll. 26-27).

†   Sommer's text has *sil est qui le vous die* (310, l. 25), as translated. However, he also provides a variant from the Harley manuscript, *sil est que ie le vous dye* (310, n. 1): "if I have a mind to tell it to you."

‡   Sommer's text has *causa* (310, l. 26): "blamed, contested with." He provides the variant from the Harley manuscript in a note (310, n. 2).

§   Thus reads Sommer's text, *en soignantage* (310, l. 28): "in concubinage." He also provides a variant from the Harley manuscript, *en lieu* (310, n. 3): "in [her] place."

¶   In Sommer's text, the reference to Arthur's illness is followed by *& a bertolai* (310, l. 29), with no apparent syntactical link with the preceding.

knight. They watched over him until daybreak and carried him to the church, and they had the service said* and then buried him.

And in the morning, Ulfin and Bretel together sent for Cleodalis the Seneschal, and they ordered him to come speak to them at their lodging. He came there very willingly, for he was well-bred and noble. When they saw him, they drew him aside and told him what had happened just as it had occurred and how his daughter had behaved.

And when he heard the high treason† she had done, he said that she could never be his daughter, "for if she were my daughter, she would never have done it no matter who might have begged her to."

While the three of them were talking in this way, King Leodagan had arisen very early, for he was very frightened by the strange things that had happened to his daughter that night. And Merlin was already out of bed, and he went straight to the king‡ and bade him good day, and when the king saw him he turned a cheerful face to him and said God bless him. Then they took each other by the hand and came out of the hall talking of several things, and they walked until they came before the lodging of Ulfin and Bretel. Then went inside so stealthily that those within did not know they were there until they were almost on top of them, but when they caught sight of them they sprang up to greet them, for they were not awkward at honoring worthy gentlemen. Then all five of them§ went into a room by themselves, and Ulfin left and brought Guenevere in, and he told them what she and the traitors had done, although they already knew about it because Merlin had told the king.

Then King Leodagan spoke and said, "Seneschal, sir seneschal, I love you very much indeed, and I would gladly do anything for the sake of your honor; I would willingly increase that honor, and so I shall, if I live long enough, for you have served me faithfully and well. And I would do nothing or strive for nothing that could bring you shame or dishonor if I could shield you from them. Do you know why I say this? Look, this is your daughter, who has surely deserved to be condemned by the law. But you have been so faithful to me that, for love of you, I would have to forgive her for an even greater misdeed than this. But, as it would nevertheless be fitting for me to take vengeance in some way, you must take her out of this kingdom so that no man or woman who sees her will know who she is; for that is my pleasure and my will."

But the seneschal answered that she was never his daughter, "but [312] because it is your will, I will do it. And God help me," he went on, "I would rather she were burned, or buried alive, in sight of all the townsfolk, for she does not belong to me in any way."

"Now, right now," said the king, "let it lie! Take care that everything is done so that I may never again hear tell of her—and take as much of what is mine as you will."

* The text says, without reference to how the service was conducted, *fisent le seruice faire* (311, l.14): "had the service done."
† The text has *la grant desloiaute* (311, l. 19): "the great faithless/illegal/criminal act."
‡ The text has the ambiguous personal pronoun *lui* (311, l. 23): "him."
§ That is, including Cleodalis.

This is what the barons decided, and right away, without a break, Cleodalis got himself and his stepdaughter ready to ride, and they took to the road and made their way until in time they came into another kingdom,* to an abbey that was in a wild, lonely place, where he put her. And there she stayed, so says the story, until Bertelay the Red found her; through his craft and trickery he set her free. Then many times he had his way with her and lay with her openly.

But with that, the story falls silent from talking about them right here, and it will tell you about Cleodalis the Seneschal, who came back to Carhaix, where King Arthur was.

38. BERTELAY CONDEMNED; ARTHUR TO HOLD COURT.[†]

Here the story says that after King Leodagan had ordered his seneschal to take his daughter out of the kingdom of Carmelide, he left Ulfin's and Bretel's lodging with Merlin, and they came back to his hall hand in hand. There they found the barons all out of bed and dressed; the bells had already been rung for Mass, and they were going to the church. When Mass had been sung, they came back to the hall. There the kinsmen of the knight whom Bertelay had slain came to bring their suit to the king. King Leodagan sent for him at his lodging, and he came right away, wearing armor beneath his clothing and carrying hidden weapons. And he had with him a great many knights, for he was full of great courtliness; he had always had a good tongue in his head, and he was always beautifully dressed.

And when King Leodagan saw him, he asked him why he had slain the knight unlawfully.

He answered that he would indeed defend himself against anyone who called him a criminal: "I do not say that I did not kill him, but I did break faith with him first. And I did not kill him without reason, for many know for a fact that he had slain a first cousin of mine to have his wife, whom he was shaming. So, as I see it, a man should harm his deadly enemy in all the ways he can—after he has broken faith with him."

And the king answered that he was mistaken, "but if you had come to me and brought suit against him, I would not have ruled against you; then you could have taken vengeance. But you did not find me worthy enough to seek justice from me."

"Sir," he said, "say what you will, but I have never done you any wrong, nor will I ever, God willing."

"It is my will," said the king, "that a rightful judgment will be pronounced."

"Sir," said Bertelay the Red, "I see clearly that it must be as you will."

Then the king ordered the decision to be reached in full sight of his barons.

---

*   The text says "into the kingdom of Carmelide," but this is clearly an error, since Cleodalis has been ordered to remove the false Guenevere from Carmelide.

†   Corresponds to Sommer, 312-315.

At that trial were King Arthur, King Ban, King Bors, Sir Gawainet, Sir Yvain, Sagremor, Nascien, Adragain, [313] Hervi of Rivel, and Guiomar. These ten were to make the judgment, so they talked together about many things until at last they agreed that Bertelay should be stripped of his holdings and put out of King Leodagan's land forever. And King Ban made the speech, for he was wonderfully well-spoken, just as it had been entrusted to him:

"Sir, these barons gathered here have judged that Bertelay the Red should be stripped of all the land he holds from you as his overlord, and then he must forsake the kingdom forever. The reason is that he took it upon himself to judge the knight he killed, and at night, but justice was not his to mete out. Moreover, you hold high court, which should guarantee that all who have ever been there may come and go freely."

With that, King Ban sat down and said no more. And when Bertelay saw that it could not be otherwise, that he had been forsaken, he turned around without saying a word. He did not dare argue against the judgment, for the highest men in the world—and the mightiest—had made it; but if any others had made it, he would have done all he could to dispute it.

So Bertelay left, but he took along a most handsome following of knights to whom he had many times given fine gifts, for he had been a good and strong knight. And he made his way, little by little, hour by hour, until at last he came to the place where the false Guenevere was. There he lingered for quite a long time, and he brooded very darkly, like a man who had known every sorrow, about how he could take vengeance against King Leodagan and King Arthur, who had forsaken him. From this such great ordeals befell King Arthur, and such great strife arose between him and his wife, that he cast her aside for a long time, just as the story will relate it to you later.

But now the story falls silent about them and talks no more about them, and it goes back to good King Arthur of Britain, who was with his wife in the city of Carhaix in Carmelide with King Leodagan.

In this part the story says that King Arthur spent a most happy time together with his wife* for a week—eight days after he had wed her. On the ninth day, he called his barons aside and told them to prepare to ride, for he very much wanted to go to the kingdom of Logres, and they said that they were all ready.

And King Arthur drew Sir Gawainet aside and said to him, "Dear nephew, take enough of your companions with you so that no more than five hundred knights are left behind with me, for I want to ride as quietly as I can. And you will go straight to Logres, my chief city, and gather together as much food as you can find, and see to it that nothing is lacking. And send the word out far and wide, for I will hold court this mid-August as grandly as I can."

"Sir," said Gawainet, "I am afraid that you may be fallen upon by some attackers."

"I'm not worried about that," answered King Arthur. "But go quickly!"

---

* The text reads *moult demena li rois artus boine vie il & sa feme* (313, ll. 26-27): "King Arthur led a very good life together with his wife." Cf. 310, ll. 20-21.

And Sir Gawainet left his uncle right then and went straight to his companions. He told them to go get ready, for they had to ride. They went to their lodgings and put their armor on, but before that, they had taken leave of King Leodagan and the barons of Carmelide, and they had very tenderly commended one another to God. [314]

So Sir Gawainet left court along with his companions. And King Arthur stayed behind with five hundred men, for that was his pleasure; of them two hundred fifty were knights of the Round Table. And Sir Gawainet and his companions made their way and at last came to Logres. But Sir Gawainet's heart was heavy for his uncle the king, whom he had left in the kingdom of Carmelide, lest something should happen to him on his way, for he had to go through a great land that bordered on his enemies, before he came into his own land. So he hurried to do what his uncle had ordered, and he sent word far and wide to all those who loved King Arthur that they should come to his court, which was to be as splendid as they could make it, and they were to be there at mid-August. And Sir Gawainet had foodstuffs brought in from everywhere in wagons and carts and on pack horses, and he stocked the court so well with all the things a man or woman needed that nothing was lacking. For he was, as the story says, the shrewdest knight in the world, the most learned, one of the most courtly, one of the least slanderous, and the least boastful. And when he had got everything ready, he set out to meet his uncle, for he was very much afraid that Arthur might be harmed along the way.

But right now the story falls silent about him and his companions, who were riding hard, and we will tell you about King Arthur and those who were with him.

Now the story says that on the third day after Sir Gawainet had left his uncle King Arthur, the latter, along with his wife, took to the road straight toward Bredigan, and with him were King Ban of Benoic and King Bors of Gaunes—they were brothers and the two best knights one would have hoped to find in any land—and the two hundred fifty companions of the Round Table, who were liegemen to King Leodagan. And the queen had begged Sir Amustan, who had been the chaplain of her father King Leodagan, to come with her to the kingdom of Logres; indeed, he was chaplain there for a long time thereafter. And she brought Guiomar, her cousin, who was a handsome, well-bred knight, and Sadoine, his elder brother, who was castellan of the good city Aneblayse. As soon as King Arthur had left the kingdom of Carmelide, King Lot found out about it from his spies, and he took to the road with his knights and hid in the Forest of Sapinoie, and he said that he would wait for King Arthur there and take his wife from him if he ever could.

But here we will stop talking to you about him for a while, and we will tell you about King Arthur, who had left the kingdom of Carmelide. And the story says that King Leodagan rode with him for three full days, and on the fourth he went back into his kingdom. And then Merlin came to King Arthur and took his leave, and he said that he would go to Blaise, his master, for he had not seen him for some time.

"What?" said King Arthur. "Won't you be at my court in Logres?"

"Yes, indeed," answered Merlin, "I'll be there before it is over."

He then commended him to God and left. But he had not gone far at all before they did not know what had become of him. [315] And Merlin came straight to Blaise that very evening, and Blaise welcomed him most joyfully when he saw him. And Merlin told him all the adventures that had happened since he had left him, just as you have heard, and he told him how King Lot was hiding in the Forest of Sapinoie. He also told him many other things that happened afterwards in the kingdom of Logres. And Blaise put everything into writing, and thanks to him we still know it.

But with that the story falls silent now about Merlin and Blaise, and we will tell you about King Arthur.

39. LOT SURRENDERS TO ARTHUR, AND GAWAIN BECOMES THE QUEEN'S KNIGHT; NEWS OF THE GRAIL.*

The story says here that after King Arthur had left King Leodagan and Merlin, just as you have heard, he rode with five hundred well-armed men wearing iron mail, and he was taking Queen Guenevere his wife along with him. They rode in short stretches until they came within two leagues of the Forest of Sapinoie, where King Lot lay hidden with seven hundred men wearing iron mail. And the youths who were leading the packhorses knew nothing about them until they were right on top of them. As soon as they saw that they were men-at-arms, they knew that they were not there to help them; they stopped and did not go a step farther, but sent word to King Arthur that a great many men-at-arms were lying in wait in the woods.

When King Arthur heard that he was about to fall into a trap, he dismounted and gathered his men about him and put them in order to fight. He put the queen in the care of forty knights and told them to take her to safety if they saw it was needed. Then he and his men climbed on their horses and rode hunched down beneath their helmets, burning to defend themselves and to attack others if they found anyone who wanted to block their way. So they rode until they came upon the place where King Lot's men were lying in wait. King Arthur was riding out ahead with King Ban, King Bors, and the companions of the Round Table. And King Lot sprang out of his hiding place with his men in armor, seven hundred by count, and they met them with raised lances under their arms, their shields before their chests, giving their horses free rein and riding as fast as their horses could run; and they screamed at them so loudly that the whole forest resounded with their yells. When King Arthur's men saw them coming, they went out to meet them very boldly, and they welcomed them with the iron tips of their lances. They struck one another on their shields so that they drove through and split them; some there were who knocked one another from their horses, and others broke their lances and passed by without falling. And when their lances were gone, they drew their swords and began an uproar that was loud and awesome; no one had ever seen a greater one from so few men, for they were very good knights on both sides. And it lasted long enough for King Arthur and King Lot to run against each other with raised lances, and they let go at each other with as much speed as they could get from their horses and hit each

---

*   Corresponds to Sommer, 315-335.

other on their shields so hard with their lances that they broke through and split them, but the tips of their lances stopped against their finely mailed hauberks. They thrust at each other with all their might. King Lot broke his lance, and King Arthur struck him so hard that he bore him to the ground over his horse's backside [316] with his legs flying, but he was quickly back on his feet, for he was very skillful. He drew his sword from its scabbard and covered himself with his shield, but it hurt him so much that he had been struck down by a single knight that he nearly went out of his mind, for he was not used to falling very often.

King Arthur had turned about and was coming back toward King Lot. And when Lot saw him coming, he moved out of the way so that he missed him and passed by. And when he saw him going by, he struck King Arthur's horse so hard in the gut underneath that he split it open from one end to the other. King Arthur went sprawling down in such a way that his thigh was pinned between his horse and the ground, and his horse held him fast so that he could not get up. King Lot jumped on top of him, grabbed him by his helmet, and twisted and pulled as hard as he could. He was trying his best to cut off his head, and he would soon have hurt him so badly that he could have never recovered, had not King Ban, King Bors, and the companions of the Round Table come spurring to his rescue. Meanwhile, King Lot's men came riding in, and they flew into each other just as they had met before, and the fighting began all over again, very fierce and very heavy, and there was none so skilled that he did not feel the worse for it. Even so, they fought long enough on both sides that the two kings got back on horseback. And after they were back on, the fighting began again heavier and more awesome, but King Arthur's men had suffered great harm, for King Lot had two hundred more knights than King Arthur.

Just then, behold Sir Gawainet with eighty well-armed companions and Kay the Seneschal, who eagerly yearned to join the fighting—he was very skilled at arms, for he was a good knight, strong and bold, in his own right, but for a single flaw he had, which is that he wept too readily because of his great love of laughter. He was also a jokester, one of the greatest there ever was because he liked to poke fun, and many knights hated him for it—they had been shamed by things he said; and so he was unwelcome in many a place, for the knights he had laughed at gave him a great deal of trouble. But he was a faithful knight toward his overlord and toward the queen until his death. Nor in his life did he ever do but one unlawful thing, that is, against Loholt, King Arthur's son, whom he killed in the Perilous Forest, and he was accused in court by Perceval the Welshman, who had been told about it by a hermit who saw him slay him.

When King Arthur saw his nephew coming so fiercely, his whole heart rose within his chest from the joy he felt. Then he came to King Ban and said to him, "See what splendid help is coming to us. Do you know who the first man is riding that black warhorse? The one holding that ash lance with the shield of gold and blue with the lion rampant, its face turned sideways, with those silver crowns?"

And King Ban stood upright and said, "Sir, who is it? Tell me, for I do not know him, except that to me it looks like your nephew Gawainet."

"Indeed," he said, "it is he in truth! And beginning right now, I can say that those who have fallen upon us will be sorry they came. For if God keeps him and his companions from harm, they would not last until the noon hour even if there were as many more of them!" [317]

"In God's name," said King Ban, "it would be unwise of them to wait and fight them."

While they were talking there, Sir Gawainet and his companions rode up, and he was out ahead holding the thick lance. And as he drew near, he recognized his uncle and saw clearly that he needed help. So he charged headlong among them, crashing in hard, his banner flying, and it so happened that Gawainet met King Lot, his father, who had just got back on his horse, and he was holding a stout lance. He came upon him as fast as his horse could go, and they struck each other on their shields with all their might. King Lot broke his lance on the shield of Sir Gawainet, and Sir Gawainet hit him so hard that he drove through his shield and his hauberk and wounded him a little in the side, so that his blood spurted out, and ruthlessly he sent him spilling from his horse to the ground, so that he did not know whether it was night or day; and Gawainet passed by so fast that his armor made a great noise.

And when he came back, he found his father still lying sprawled on the ground, and he rode over him three or four times with his horse and crushed and maimed him so dreadfully that Lot nearly went mad. Then Sir Gawainet dismounted, stuck his lance into the ground, and drew his sword Excalibur, which threw off a very bright light, and made straight for King Lot, who was still lying sprawled on the ground. And he grabbed him by his helmet and tore it off his head so hard that his nose and forehead hurt, and he badly wounded him. Then he pulled the coif of his hauberk down to his shoulders and told him that he was a dead man if he did not swear to become his prisoner.

And he was so distraught and in such great pain that he could answer very little, but he tried with all his might and said at last, "Ah! noble knight, do not kill me, for in truth I have done you no wrong that you should kill me for."

"Yes, you have," he answered. "You wronged me and everyone in this place when you attacked my uncle and blocked his way."

"What?" said King Lot. "Who are you that call him uncle?"

"What does it matter to you who I am?" he answered. "I won't tell you. But do quickly what I tell you or you are dead and your men as well."

"Tell me," said the king, "by the faith you owe to the thing you love most in the world, what is your name?"

And he answered, "First I will know the name of you who ask me."

"In truth," he said, "I am King Lot, the wretched king of Orkney and Loonois. Nothing but bad things happen to me, and this has been so for a long time. Now tell me your name and who you are."

When Sir Gawainet heard that it was his father, he named himself and said that he was Gawainet and that he was King Arthur's nephew.

And when King Lot heard him, he sprang to his feet and tried to throw his arms around him, saying, "Dear son, you are welcome indeed! I am your sorrowful, wretched father, whom you have struck down so improperly."

But Sir Gawainet told him to get away, for he would not be his father or his good friend until he had made peace with King Arthur and begged his forgiveness for his unlawful deeds, and then he would have to swear fealty to him openly and in full sight of all his barons: "Otherwise, you cannot trust me to do anything for you but kill you, and the only pledge you'll leave is your head!"

When King Lot [318] heard him, he fainted and fell to the ground, and when he came out of his swoon he begged for his mercy and said to him, "Dear son, I'll do whatever you like. Take my sword, which I hand over to you."

And Sir Gawainet, who pitied him, took it, happy and joyful; tears fell from his eyes beneath his helmet, and he wept tenderly, for his heart was heavy with sorrow that he had wounded his father so badly, but he did his utmost to resist going to him.

Then they both went back to their horses and mounted, and they came to their men and broke up the fighting. But King Lot's companions were in a very bad way, for Sir Gawainet's companions had done them such harm on their first strike that more than forty of them had been sent sprawling to the ground from their horses and did not have the strength to get back on horseback. And Sir Gawainet came in: he split them up and pulled them off one another. Then Sir Gawainet went straight to King Arthur, his uncle.

As soon as King Arthur saw him coming, he came out to meet him and said to him, "Dear nephew, you are welcome indeed! How did you come here? Did you know anything about the ambush that was set up here?"

And he said that the only reason he came was because his heart always yearned for him, "and I would never had been at ease until I had seen you." And Sir Gawainet went on to say, "May the Lord God be praised for the battle that has befallen you today, for it is my father, King Lot, you have fought with. Now, thank God, it has happened that he comes to beg you for your forgiveness as his earthly lord for the wrong and misdeeds he has done to you. So take his oath of fealty, as you should, for he is all ready to swear it."

When King Arthur heard this, he raised his hands to heaven and thanked God for the honor He had given him. Thereupon King Lot and his knights came down through the meadowlands on foot; they had taken their helmets from their heads and lowered their coifs down to their shoulders, and they came very meekly.

And when Sir Gawainet saw his father walking out ahead, he said to his uncle, "Sir, look, here comes my father to swear fealty to you."

As soon as the king saw him, he got down from his horse, and all the barons did the same. And King Lot came forward and knelt before King Arthur. He held out to him his sword, fully bared as were his misdeeds, and he said, "Sir, take this. I surrender to you as one who has wronged you and should have served and exalted you and yours, yet I did nothing but give you trouble and sorrow. Now do with me and my land what you will."

There King Lot became King Arthur's liegeman in sight of all his barons, and he swore to him his oath to do as he ought whatever King Arthur willed.*

Then King Arthur took him by the right hand, raised him up, and said to him, "Sir, stand up. You have too long been on your knees, for you are such a worthy gentleman that I would forgive you a greater misdeed than this. But even if I hated

* The text has the ambiguous personal pronoun *il* (318, l. 35): "he."

you to the death, you have children like these who have given me such service that I could not wish to do you harm. And so I entrust to you myself and everything I have, high and low, to do with as you will for the love of your dear son Gawainet, whom I love more than any other knight in the world. Yet there are two knights here whom I must love as much, and they are kings, for they have loved me [319] and helped me in all times of need."

And King Lot stood up and said, "My deepest thanks, sir."

Thus was peace made between King Lot and King Arthur. Then they climbed on their horses, happy and joyful over what had happened to them, and they rode for as long as it took them to come to Logres, where everyone welcomed them joyfully. There were a great many people there, and the number was growing daily, for all the peasants were coming there because of the Saxons, who were laying waste the land all around, and there were so many people that they had to be encamped on the meadowlands. And when King Arthur saw the gathering, he was very glad, and he said that he would hold high court, so he sent word by his marshals that all should quickly come to court on the next day.

As soon as the news had spread throughout the country, all came to court straightway, and the next morning King Lot swore his oath to King Arthur in the chief church in sight of the great crowd of people who were there. And King Arthur endowed him again with all the land he had held in his lifetime, and if anyone ever meant to do him wrong, he would safeguard him with all his might. King Lot accepted this happily and joyfully like a worthy gentleman, and from that time forth they were good friends for the rest of their lives.

After Mass had been sung, they all came to the high hall, where the meal was all ready and the tablecloths had been laid, and they all sat down to eat and were served most handsomely. After eating, the knights went to see the meadows and streams as well as the tents and pavilions that were set up outside the town, for there were very many rich and beautiful ones. And this is how they disported themselves for eight full days in comfort and delight. And the crowd of people kept growing, for the king had sent word to them that he and his wife would hold plenary court, where they would wear the crown, at mid-August. And when the day before the feast came, and they had all gathered, King Arthur bestowed gifts of his belongings— horses, armor, palfreys, gold, silver, and coins, for he had a great plenty of everything. And the queen gave out clothing and other gifts; she was well provided with them, for she knew all things fitting and honorable. All the knights welcomed her with very great love, and they said that they had won the lady of all ladies; and if the knights esteemed her, the ladies old and young, near and far, spoke even more highly of her. And as renown flies everywhere, hers ran through all lands and spread so far that the princes who were King Arthur's enemies heard about the peace that had been made between King Arthur and King Lot, how he was to hold a lavish court at mid-August, and that all people were gathering there. And some said in their heart of hearts that they would very gladly have behaved as King Lot had done, and others prayed in their hearts that God not let them die before they had made peace with him, and still others said that all the troubles that had befallen them had happened only because of their sin against him.

Thus spoke one and another of them. And King Arthur was in Logres, filled with joy and delight, just as you have heard. And when the day of mid-August came, all of the knights came to court dressed in their richest clothing, and the queen and her ladies were arrayed as handsomely as [320] befitted such a feast. And when the bells had rung for the high Mass, they went to the church and heard the service, which the archbishop of Brice sang for them. That day King Arthur and his wife, Queen Guenevere, wore crowns, and King Ban and King Bors wore crowns for love of them. And after Mass they came back to the hall, where tables had been set up and cloths laid, and the barons sat down as they should there, each at his own place. That day Sir Gawainet served at the high table, where the four kings sat with Kay the Seneschal, Lucan the Wine Steward, Sir Yvain the Tall (son of King Urien), Girflet, Yvain the Bastard, Sagremor, Dodinel the Wildman, and enough others so that there were twenty-one at the high table. And forty young apprentices to knights served at the other tables there, and all were served as handsomely as anyone could be.

And when the end of the meal came and all the food had been set out, King Arthur spoke loudly enough for all to hear up and down the hall, and he said, "Listen to me, my lords and all who have come to my court to gladden me. I thank you and God above all for the joy and honor you have given me. And you should know that I wish to found a custom in my court to gladden me every time I will wear my crown: I swear to God that I will not sit down to eat before news of some adventure comes from wherever it may have happened, provided that it is a fair adventure and one to make the knights of my court go after it—knights who would win glory and honor and be my friends, my companions, and my kinsmen."

And when the knights of the Round Table heard the oath King Arthur swore, they began to talk among themselves, and they said that, since the king had sworn an oath at court, it was fitting that they should swear an oath of their own. At last they agreed on one thing, and they chose Nascien to speak about it before the king, so that all the barons could hear.

Then the companions of the Round Table went straight to the king, and Nascien began his speech, and he spoke loudly enough for all those in there could hear him.

"Sir," said Nascien, "the companions of the Round Table, who are here, swear to God, before you and all the barons who are here, that, as you have sworn an oath, they will swear another oath—that, henceforth, whenever a maiden in need comes to your court seeking help or assistance that can be carried out by one single knight fighting against another, one of them* will willingly go to help her out of trouble wherever she may wish to take him, and he will strive until he has righted all the wrongs that have been done to her."

And when King Arthur heard him, he asked his companions if they had agreed to what Nascien had said, and they answered yes, and they swore to him that they would keep their oath to the death. Then there was even greater rejoicing than there had been before. And when Sir Gawainet heard and saw the delight and gladness

---

* The verb *aillent* (320, l. 35) is in the plural, but other pronouns and verbs referring to the rescuer are in the singular.

they were feeling in the hall because of the customs they had founded with their oaths, he came to his companions, [321] for he knew everything that was fitting, and said that if each one of them was willing to grant what he was about to say, he would offer them something from which great honor would come to them all the days of their lives. And they said that they would grant anything that came out of his mouth.

"Then promise me," he said, "that you will keep us all together."

They all promised, and there were eighty companions by count.

When Sir Gawainet had taken his companions' oath, he came straight to the queen and said to her, "My lady, my companions and I come to you and beseech you to retain us as your knights and members of your household so that, when we are in faraway countries to win glory and honor, and anyone asks us whom we belong to and what land we are from, we can say that we are from the land of Logres and we are knights of Queen Guenevere, King Arthur's wife."

When the queen heard him, she stood up and said to him, "Dear nephew, many thanks to you and them, for I do retain you most gladly as my lords and friends. And just as you give yourselves to me, so do I give myself to you with a good and faithful heart. God give me the strength, and may He let me live so long, that I may reward you for the honor and the courtesy you have promised to bring me."

"My lady," said Sir Gawainet, "thus we are your knights and you have retained us, and we thank you. Now we all swear an oath to you: that all who come among us seeking help or assistance in fighting against a knight will have it, one knight against another, man to man, and they will take him wherever they wish, no matter how far away. And if it should happen that he does not come back within the month, then we will all go looking for him, each one by himself, and the quest should last a year and a day without coming back to court, unless he brings back the truthful news that he is alive or dead. And when they are all back in court, they will each tell, one after the other, about the adventures that have happened to them, whether they are good or bad, and they will swear on the saints that they will lie about nothing in their going out or coming back. And this is the will of all of us."

When the queen heard the oath that Sir Gawainet swore, she was filled with gladness, and the king was happier than all the knights who were in his court. And because the king wanted the queen to be even more glad, he said to her, "My lady, since God has given you such fair company, yours must be even better than mine! And for love of them and yourself, do you know what I am going to bestow on you? I endow you with all my treasure, so that you are lady over it and have the power to hand it out to all you please."

And when the queen heard him, she knelt before the king and said to him, "Sir, many thanks!"

Then the queen called Sir Gawainet over and said to him, "Dear nephew, I wish to set up four clerks here who will undertake to do nothing but put into writing all the adventures that happen to you and your companions, so that after our deaths the deeds of prowess by the worthy gentlemen from here will be remembered."

"My lady," said Sir Gawainet, "I agree."

And then four clerks were chosen who put into writing all the stories of adventures* from then on. And afterwards Sir Gawainet said that he would never hear of an adventure [322] without going out to seek it, and he and his companions would strive to bring the right news about them to court, and his companions and the companions of the Round Table said the same. And from that time forth were Sir Gawainet and his companions called the knights of Queen Guenevere.

With that, the tablecloths were taken away, as were the tables, and the happy reveling began here and there. But above all those who were there was heard Danguenes of Caerleon. He was having an amazingly good time, and he behaved so that they were all looking at him, but he was a fool by nature and the most cowardly piece of flesh there ever was. He began to stamp his feet and to dance about, and he shouted in a loud voice that in the morning he would go seeking adventures:

"And you, Sir Gawainet, you will come, too. You are such a big, handsome knight! And you, my lord companions of the Round Table, in truth I do not believe that you have the heart or the boldness to dare follow me where I'm going tomorrow!"

Thus spoke Danguenes the Craven, and the knights there laughed at him. Indeed, many times he put on his armor and rode into the woods. He would hang his shield from an oak tree and then hit it until all the paint had fallen off and the shield was split in several places. Then he would come back and say that he had slain a knight or two. And when he did happen to meet a knight in armor, he would turn in flight even if he had just shouted to him. And many times he happened to come upon a knight who was making his way lost in thought and saying not a word; he would take him by the bridle and lead him away as his prisoner. That is the way that Danguenes was; that is how he behaved. Yet he was quite a handsome knight from good stock; he did not seem a fool from the look of him, but when the words came out of his mouth, then people took note.

Great were the joy and the merrymaking on that day of mid-August in Logres when the oaths were sworn. And when the serving men had eaten, Kay the Seneschal came and said, "What is this, sir knights? Shouldn't we be tilting to begin the revels at such a high feast as today?"

When Sagremor heard him, he sprang forward and said that it would be cowardly of him if he did not go tilting. And when the knights heard themselves being challenged, they went straight to put on their armor. And when Sir Gawainet heard this, he asked how they would tourney, and Minoras answered that they would fight against the knights of Queen Guenevere, and they would take as many knights on one side as the other. Then Sir Gawainet asked how many knights they wanted to fight; Adragain answered that there would be five thousand on their side, and Sir Gawainet said that his side would also be five thousand strong.

---

* In this context particularly, the word *aventure* applies without clear distinction to an adventure as event and the account of the adventure. See esp. *deuant que aucune auenture i sera auenue de quel part ke che soit* (320, ll. 17-18): "before [news of] some adventure happens to come from wherever it may be"; *si dira chascuns ... toutes les auentures qui auenues li seront* (321, ll. 25-26): "and each one will tell ... [the story of] all the adventures that have happened to him"; and *qui mistrent en escrit toutes les auentures si com elles uenoient a court* (321, l. 42): "who put into writing [the stories of] all the adventures just as they came to court."

"Now there's no reason to stay here," said Pinados, "except to go put on our armor, for the day is going by."

Then they went to their lodgings and very quickly put on their armor, and they rode straight to the meadowlands outside the town; they kept coming until there were ten thousand of them from both sides. Then the order was shouted that each one should go where he belonged, so they parted and each went straight to his banner. Then Sir Gawainet came and took away his contingent, so that there were five thousand on each side.

And the heralds began to cry, "This is for the honor of arms. Now we'll see who fights best!"

And when it was time to gather the men in order, [323] a messenger came to Sir Gawainet and said to him, "Sir, King Arthur your uncle sends for you to come speak to him at those windows, where he awaits you."

And Sir Gawainet went there, and he took his cousin Yvain with him and Sagremor and Girflet, and the contingents were so close to each other that they were waiting only to spur their horses.

The very first to break ranks was Pinados, one of the knights of the Round Table. And from the other side came one of the queen's knights, who was Sir Gawainet's brother; his name was Agravain the Proud. They were both riding wonderfully good horses, and they struck each other on their shields with their lances, and they both broke through them so that the tips of their lances stopped against their hauberks. They were both strong and proud, and their hauberks were strong and fast, so that not one link broke, but they made the lances fly into splinters. And as they passed by, they knocked against each other with their shields and horses so hard that they sent each other spilling to the ground with their horses coming down on top of them. Knights from both sides spurred to the rescue, and they hit one another with the sharp, cutting tips of their lances.

And Sir Gawainet rode until he came to the moat near the windows where King Arthur, Queen Guenevere, King Ban, King Bors, and a great many ladies and maidens were leaning out to watch the tournament. And when the king saw him coming, he said, "Dear nephew, I beseech you, by the faith you owe me, to watch over those men-at-arms so that no wrath or anger will rise among them and no wrong will be done."

"Sir," he answered, "there will never be any wrongdoing because of me, but I cannot keep every one of them from their madness. But as for you, if you see that it is turning bad, you should try to break it up. For you should know that I could not bear for your companions, who are troublesome, to mistreat mine in front of me, and I would help them out with all my might."

"Sir," said King Ban, "Sir Gawainet has spoken like a worthy man. What you need to do is take a part of your men and arm them well, so that, if they are needed, all they have to do is get on their horses."

"In God's name," said King Arthur, "it will be as you say."

Then King Arthur ordered three thousand soldiers and squires to put on their armor, and he himself did likewise, as did the three kings who were with him.

And Sir Gawainet went back to the tournament, which was already growing hot around the two men who had fallen, and they succeeded in getting back on horseback. Then the fighting began to get heavier, and the knights of the Round Table, who were two hundred fifty strong, did their best to defeat the eight companions of Sir Gawainet, who were in dire straits and were getting much the worst of it. They bore up very well because they willingly helped one another, but no good deed would have been useful to them if it had not been for King Lot's knights, who supported them with great vigor. Many a joust was fought there, and many a knight was struck down whose horse fled through the fields. There the companions of the Round Table would have been mistreated had not a company of seven hundred knights come to help them, and then the knights of the Round Table had the best of it. For there were more of them, and they drove the others from the field, despite their efforts. And then the hue and cry rose so loud around them that no one could have heard God thundering. [324]

When Sir Yvain heard the din and the uproar around his companions, he looked that way and saw that they were in trouble, and he was filled with sorrow. And he said to Sir Gawainet, "Look! Dear cousin, we are tarrying here too long, for our companions are being routed!"

"In God's name," said Sagremor, "may he never be called a knight who does not help them in this time of need!"

"I don't care a whit," said Girflet, "for words without deeds! Now we'll see who fights best!"

At once they spurred their horses and rode away as noisily as the sparrow-hawk that means to catch prey when it is starving. And when they came into the tourney, they rushed headlong among them holding their lances straight out, and they bore to the ground the first four they met. Then the four companions began to fight so skillfully that they stopped the rout. They were recognized in little time even by those who had never seen them before. And when the queen's knights saw Sir Gawainet, they drew up around him, and so did King Lot's knights, who were very good and brave knights.

And Sagremor began to fight so well that those who were at the windows of the great hall pointed their fingers at him and said, "That is Sir Sagremor. In truth he does not bear treason in him, for if he is a handsome knight in body and limb, he is yet a better knight in spirit. And she who has him can well boast that she has one of the best knights in the court; likewise, she would be uncourtly and unwise who refused the love of such a knight."

Meanwhile, Girflet was fighting very well in his own right, and so was Galescalain, who was highly esteemed by one and all. And these three were joined by the brothers of Sir Gawainet, who were very skilled and bold. These knights fought wondrously well, and Sir Yvain began to do so well again that none better than he was needed for the fighting. And when the companions of the Round Table saw that the pursuit had been stopped, they began to work all the harder to drive their opponents from the field, and they did many feats of arms. But whoever did well and who not, above all the others Sir Gawainet fought hard, for there was no company he came upon, no matter how tightly drawn together or how thick, that he did not get through by sheer strength, and he struck down knights and horses, he tore helmets from heads and shields from necks; and if the companions of the Round Table had the better of it before, now they had the worse, for Sir Gawainet and his companions kept fighting so close to them that they drove them back in a rout as far as the moat, and there they stopped.

And the story says that their hardship was such that ten of their best were struck down to the ground: one was named Minoras, the second Mataly, the third Pinados, the fourth Blaharis, the fifth Carismal, the sixth Partreus, and Grandome, Ladinel, Ladinus, and Traelus. These ten were forcibly taken prisoner, and this was done by Sir Gawainet, Sir Yvain, Sagremor, and Kay the Seneschal; they sent them to the queen on behalf of Sir Gawainet, whom they took as their leader, and they were right to do so, for he was a most worthy gentlemen, and he was most helpful to them in every time of need. And the ten companions who had been taken came straight to the queen and handed themselves over to her [325] on behalf of Sir Gawainet, and she welcomed them most joyfully, and she gave each one of them some of her jewels. Then they went to lean out of the windows of the great hall to see the tournament, which was wondrously beautiful and fierce.

When the knights of the Round Table saw that they had lost ten of their companions, no one could have been sorrier than they, for never before had they been driven from a field by force even if those against them were twice as strong. And then their opponents' great battalion came from near the bridge, and they brought them vigorous help and succeeded in putting them back into the middle of the field. And the company that kept itself about Sir Gawainet came back against the ones who had come in fresh. They ran headlong upon one another, and they began such a wonderful combat that they all grew weary, and it was already near the hour of nones when Sir Gawainet and his companions began to fight so boldly that they drove the others to the edge of the moat.

When the knights of the Round Table saw that they had been turned to rout, they said that from that time on they would try to fight as wickedly as they could. Then they took up their stout, straight lances, and put them into their holders. That was the most evil thing they could do, for tournaments ought to be fought without treachery. So they made ready to strike their opponents as if it were a deadly war. As soon as they had picked up their lances, they flew in among the queen's knights, whom they greatly hated. On the first onslaught they struck down twenty of the worthiest; they were quickly back on their feet and drew their swords, but the others were on top of them to take them prisoner, and the clanging on them was loud and wondrous. They could have lost very quickly, but Sir Yvain caught sight of them—he was in the thickest fighting along with Sir Gawainet and Sagremor.

And when they saw the wicked things the others were doing to their companions, Sir Yvain said, "My lords, look at that fine game the other side has started against us!"

And when Sir Gawainet saw it, he said that they were not behaving like worthy knights and he would not stand for it. Then he called to Cuiret of Lambal and Guiomar and said to them, "My lords, go to the knights of the Round Table on my behalf and tell them that my companions and I send them word that they have wronged us at this time, and we beg them please to stop the mad things they have begun. We strongly protest what they have done to us, and we call them to judgment for it before the king; and if here on our side there is anyone who has done them any wrong whatsoever, we will make it up to them in any way they like."

When they heard Sir Gawainet's order, they turned about without saying a thing and went straight to the companions of the Round Table and gave them their message just as it had been entrusted to them. And the knights of the Round Table answered that they cared nothing for any word they might send them; they would continue doing as they were, "and if anyone wants to be angry over it, let him be angry, and we'll do even more than we have done! And you can tell Gawainet and his companions that soon people will see who is the most skilled and who hits hardest in the fighting."

When they heard such shocking insolence, they turned around and came straight to Sir Gawainet, [326] who had already got his companions back on their horses, and they told him what they had found out And when Sir Gawainet heard it, he was filled with wrath.

"What?" he said. "Is it certain that they will not do otherwise? Then let them know that, since we have come to defiance, we will soon know, in the onslaught, who the most skilled knights are."

Then Sir Gawainet left the tournament, along with Sagremor, his three brothers, Sir Yvain, Galescalain, Dodinel, Kay the Seneschal, Girflet, and Lucan, and he took them aside and said to them, "My lords, the companions of the Round Table have given us a most wicked challenge out of pride and treachery because it seems to them that they have been wronged by our people, and they think that they can win it all by showing their cruelty and wickedness. I want each one of us to go get his hauberk and the strongest armor he has and leave nothing out!"

They did as he said, and they sent for their armor, went to the tourney, which was going strong, and put it on; they were most eager to get in where the fighting was heavy, for all ten thousand had thrown themselves into the battle. When Sir Gawainet and his companions were ready, they were eighty strong by count; they got on their horses and, drawn up tight together, they rode at a slow pace to their companions, who were already keeping up the fighting and running up and down looking for the companions of the Round Table, and they were so distraught that they could not find them that they nearly went out of their minds, for the companions of the Round Table were very badly mistreating them.

Then came Sir Gawainet and his companions, and they rushed headlong in among them so hard that they struck down almost forty of the others in the onslaught. When Nascien and Adragain saw this, they stopped and said to their companions, "Dear lords, we have made a very bad mistake in the challenge we have undertaken against the queen's knights out of envy, and it would avail us nothing to ask for the fighting to stop before anything worse happened. For King Arthur's nephew and their companions will do us great harm, you can count on it, and it cannot end without great loss; perhaps there will be deaths, so it would be best if it stopped right now. You should know that there are twenty on their front line who will soon have sent forty of ours on their way, and they are highborn men and among the strongest in the kingdom of Logres."

And they answered that they had spoken too late: "Every man look out for himself, for now it cannot be otherwise."

Then they struck out into the fray, and the eighty companions came to meet them. Then they drew their swords, and the fighting on foot and on horseback grew fierce and wicked and treacherous. And when King Lot's seven hundred knights recognized the folly and disorderliness the companions of the Round Table had started, they drew to one side, fitted on their armor very well, and came straight to Sir Gawainet and said to him, "Sir, now you can ride safely against the jealous ones. From now on we will never forsake you, neither you nor your companions, for any distress we may find ourselves in. We recognize very well the kind of fighting that is going on between us and the companions of the Round Table, but they have too few men to carry out what they have undertaken. We see clearly that they are two hundred fifty strong, and you [327] have only eighty, so it is no wonder that they have the best of it. But they have a right to boast that today they have made two hundred enemies who will show them whether or not they are wise to have undertaken such madness!"

And Sir Gawainet thanked them most heartily, and he set them in order around him, for he was a man who knew how to get things done.

Then Sir Gawainet called a young lord, a highborn man, whose right name was Galesconde, and he said to him, "Go quickly to my uncle, King Arthur, and tell him not to be sorry if my companions and I defend ourselves against those of the Round Table, who have begun doing mad things to us. And tell him how this has happened from beginning to end."

When Galesconde heard Sir Gawainet's order, he turned about and left to deliver the message just as it had been entrusted to him. While Sir Gawainet was tending to this business, the queen's knights were being beaten. The knights of the Round Table had rescued their companions and got them on horseback, and they drove the others from the field with their sheer strength. And when Sir Gawainet saw this, he rushed in against them so hard that everything around them shook and shuddered. And Sir Gawainet shouted, "Now at them, noble knights! They'll be sorry they began such madness!"

When the queen's knights heard Sir Gawainet saying that, and when they saw the handsome company of knights who were following right behind him, they turned about and were most grateful for the help, for now they could see plainly that they would not get the worst of it, and they knew it. Then they gathered tightly together, holding their shields in front of their chests, and Sir Gawainet rode before them in the front with his sword drawn, since he had broken his lance, and he struck Douglas so hard on his helmet that he cut through it and his iron coif too, and he made a great wound in his head and stunned him so badly that he sent him head over heels to the ground. Douglas's* companions shouted that he was dead, and they ran upon Sir Gawainet† from every side, and he hit the first one he met, as he passed by, on his nose-guard and gave him a great wound, and he fell to the ground bleeding. Then he struck another one on the shield so hard that he maimed him dreadfully and sent him sprawling to the ground. Then he came to Nascien and meant to strike him on the helmet, but Nascien saw the blow coming and pulled back on his reins, and the blow fell in front on his saddlebow and cut all the way through the horse, and he brought horse and knight to the ground all in a heap. And

---

* The text has the ambiguous possessive *si* (327, l. 27): "his."
† The text has *li courent sus* (327, l. 27): "ran upon him."

when Nascien found himself on the ground, he leapt to his feet very swiftly, for he was a very good knight, and he drew his sword and thrust his shield over his head, because he was afraid that Sir Gawainet might deal him another blow before he was ready. And when Sir Gawainet saw that he was indeed ready, he turned the sword he was holding toward him.

And Nascien looked at him and said to him, "Look, Sir Gawainet! You are not so courtly or so worthy a gentleman as they say. You are bearing arms as if you were fighting a deadly war, for you have brought along your good sword. And you can be sure that you will yet be rebuked for that elsewhere more than here."

"I do not know what people will do," said Sir Gawainet, "but [328] I know of no knight against whom I would not defend myself if he dared call me faithless—or against two such, if need be, one after the other. But you and your companions behaved faithlessly when you began your treachery; we sent messengers to you, and you would not hear them."

"Sir," said Nascien, "things have gone madly up to now, and it is high time to stop, if you will, for the one who first talked about it and started it has won nothing from it, for I believe that he is dying from his wounds. But for God's sake, I beg you to separate the two sides at once—that would be a good and courtly thing to do—before more harm comes from it."

"I do not know what harm will come from it," said Sir Gawainet, "but they will never be separated by me. If the companions of the Round Table ever undertake treachery against us, I will gladly start fighting them with my lance held high, and I'll be the very first in! That is why I want you to tell them, 'Shouldn't you beware of me now?' And you'll also tell them that the king and queen may not interfere. For we companions will gladly meet them in battle, and sooner or later they won't be able to help themselves."

"Sir," said Nascien, "once before you behaved lovingly to me and did me a good deed, and I could never pay you back, nor did you need it. When you say that we have fought among ourselves enough, you are telling the truth, for you are a high and mighty man, and they are lower knights than your companions; they cannot overwhelm you when you seek to do them harm and injury."

Suddenly Sir Gawainet rode off and left Nascien standing there. He and his companions rushed headlong into the battle, and they crashed and hammered on helmets and shields, they cut apart and struck down knights and horses, and they handled them so fiercely that they drove them all from the field in a rout as far as the river, which was deep and wide; and many of them could not keep from being knocked down into the water. You would have seen lances and shields floating downstream in great numbers, and you would have seen horses without their masters, reins dragging behind them, drowning from one bank to the other.

When Sir Gawainet saw that they were gone and did not have the strength to recover, and he saw it clearly, he wiped off Excalibur, his good sword, and put it back into its scabbard, because he was afraid for it, and as he was fastening it, he saw some of the companions of the Round Table sitting on horseback, blocking the road. He grabbed a piece of an appletree limb and threw his shield down to the ground; he held the stick in both hands and said that he would make them give way. Then he ran headlong upon them as fast as his horse could carry him, and he hit the first one he came to on the shoulders and sent him sprawling to the ground, and then the second and the third, and every man he struck, no matter how strong he was, he hurled to the ground. And when they saw that he was treating them so badly, they grew very angry and rode after him with their swords drawn, for they bitterly hated him. They fell upon him from every side and struck where they could get at him, and they succeeded in killing his horse under him. So he sprang to his feet very swiftly, for he was skilled and nimble, and used his stick as a shield. He drew Excalibur from its scabbard [329] and damned to hell anyone who would think that they were the best knights in the world, for they had not shown themselves to be good knights when they had slain his horse. So he ran them down very swiftly and split their shields, their helmets, and their hauberks on their shoulders and arms, and he cut their legs and their horses' heads with such great strength that he brought to the ground as many as he met. In a short time he had struck down more than twenty, they lay on the ground battered and wounded so badly that they needed a doctor if they wanted to get well, for otherwise they would die.

With that, ninety companions and the seven hundred knights of King Lot came into the battle. They had been following it all day, and they charged in as roughly and as fast as they could go. They found Sir Gawainet on foot, holding his sword that was bloody from the horses he had killed. There they got Sir Gawainet back on his horse, and he put his sword back in its scabbard and picked up his stick again in both hands. He swiftly ran them down, and he struck out hither and thither, he did not care where, and he put them to rout in no time and sent them on their way through the town gates. And the other five thousand, who had stayed behind on the river bank, fought against all who were on the other side, those whom King Lot's knights had left for them, and the queen's ninety knights drove them utterly from the field.

Then the tournament began all over again: it was wonderful, and there were many handsome jousts which the ladies and maidens, who stood on the town walls, were glad to watch. The tourney lasted for quite a long time, for the men were skilled on both sides, and they fought like good knights. But in the end the knights who were with Sir Gawainet could not hold out, for there were fewer of them than on the other side, and they began to drive forward one moment and fall back the next. Meanwhile, news about the fighting came to Sir Yvain, who had stopped outside the town gate, and the twenty-four companions who were with him. And when he heard that his friends were having the worst of it, he called his companions together and set out to help them. As soon as he came to where they were, they all began to fight very well, better than they had done all day long, and, thanks to their skilled fighting, three or four times they broke through their opponents' lines clear to the other side, and they routed them and sent them on their way, driving them back through the gates and into the streets of the town. There they brought them down and trampled them under their horses' hooves, for they were unwilling to take any of them prisoner, so angry were they about the outrageous deeds the companions of the Round Table had undertaken to do in their pride.

Elsewhere were Sir Gawainet and the knights of Orkney, who had ridden hard and run fast after the knights of the Round Table; at last they came to the Church of St. Stephen. There the companions stopped, for they had kept pace as long as they could. But there were soon to be dead and wounded, when at last King Arthur, King Bors, and King Ban came there. As soon as Galesconde had given them his message, the squires, who were a good four thousand armed men strong,* and the three kings rode toward St. Stephen's, while some of the squires, a good three hundred of them, were riding down the high street. There [330] they met the knights of Orkney following Sir Gawainet, who was badly beating the companions of the Round Table, just as you have heard. And as soon as they saw the squires, they thought it was an ambush, so they fell upon them, and wondrous fighting broke out. Sir Gawainet's companions were in great trouble, above all those fighting the squires in the narrowest part of the street, for there were many who had been struck down and wounded. Soon word came to Sir Gawainet that his companions were being badly taken to task: "I do not know who has attacked them in the gateway," but they had beaten them senseless.

As soon as Sir Gawainet heard the news that his companions had been attacked from the rear, he left the fighting to the companions where he was and came straight to where the others were. But beforehand he had set up good lookouts to guard the river bank, lest those of the Round Table should turn back around. Then he came to where they were fighting, and as soon as he saw who was there,† he swore that they would be sorry that they had come. And when the squires‡ saw him coming, they shouted to him to surrender, for otherwise his men would be killed. When Sir Gawainet heard them threatening him with death, he became very angry, and he called them whores' sons, cowardly traitors, wicked oath-breakers, "for you set up an ambush. And you should know that if you get away from me, even the boldest would want no part of it for all of this kingdom!"

Then he drew his bloody sword, and they ran hard at him with axes and swords, and he dived in among them and hit the first one he met and sent his head flying, then the second, the third, and the fourth, and he struck right and left and cut open feet, arms, heads, and sides, and he fought so hard that in a short time none dared make a stand against him, but they turned in flight, wailing and moaning, and they said, "Let's flee, let's flee. Look here, this is a devil that has come unleashed from hell!"

After Sir Gawainet had freed his companions, he went back and took forty knights and sent them on the way to the river bank so that no one might fall upon them.

"And if you are attacked," he said, "come back and find me."

Then he went the other way, toward St. Stephen's, where the knights of the Round Table were, and they were fighting against the knights of Orkney. And when Sir Gawainet got there, he rushed in hard among them and called them traitors, for he was truly convinced that they had set up the ambush. And when they saw that they were hated so much, they did not know what to say, for they believed he was calling them that because they had been the first to behave defiantly when they were all tilting with lances. They would very gladly have set that right, if they could, for now

---

*   Earlier the soldiers and squires together are said to number three thousand (323, l. 29).

†   The text reads *il les uit uenir* (330, l. 14): "he saw them coming"; note that the next sentence begins *cil le uoent uenir* (330, ll. 14-15): "they see him coming." Logically Gawain cannot "see them coming," for he is riding toward them.

‡   The text has the ambiguous demonstrative *cil* (330, l.14): "those/they."

their shame had doubled; thus the wise man says in a proverb that some thinking to revenge renew their shame,* and this is why they were ashamed and downcast. And Sir Gawainet rode in headlong among them and struck Adragain so hard on his helmet that he cut through his iron coif and into his flesh, and he bore him to the ground so dazed that he did not know whether it was day or night. Then he struck Pindolus across his shoulders and cut the strap on which his shield hung and cut through his hauberk into his flesh, and he ran his sword through the shoulder bone so deeply that he nearly killed him, and the shield flew to the ground on one side and the knight on the other. Next he struck Ydonas above the cheekbone, and his sword went down to his teeth, and Ydonas fell to the ground in a faint. [331]

When the companions of the Round Table saw that he was wreaking such havoc on them and that no weapon could stop him, they all rode back to the church together. And he and his men ran after them, for they did not want to let them go so soon. Then, as it happened, Sir Gawainet was on the heels of Hervi of Rivel, and he struck him on the head.

And as he raised his sword again, the other one thrust his sword to meet the blow and said to him, "Sir knight, you have fought enough, and you should be glad to stop at once, for you truly deserve to be blamed for the cruelty there is in you. They used to say every good thing about you, and now they will say only bad things. For you should have helped them and safeguarded them against all in the world who would harm them; yet you have killed them and wounded them with all your might, although they have done you no wrong."

"Hervi," answered Sir Gawainet, "did they not do wrong when they began this madness and this treachery against my companions to whom I must bear faith? And they were not satisfied with that, so they set up an ambush against us."

"Sir," said Hervi, "if, in their foolishness, they did wrong this one time, they will make it up to you as grandly as you wish—not for anyone else's sake, but for love of you, whom they will henceforth take as their friend and companion."

"They will not make amends to me," said Sir Gawainet, "for I will never love them. And tell them indeed that whenever they treat my companions with hatred and envy, they do the same to me. Whenever they want to challenge the ninety of us to a tournament, we'll always fight them, if they are willing to undertake it with one hundred twenty of the best knights among them. They should know also that wherever I may be, in this country or in a foreign land, if I am ever challenged, and they have anything to do with it, I will do all I can to hurt them."

"Sir," said Hervi, "what you are saying is wrong and a sin. Such may be your wish, but it will not soon be fulfilled, for it would be a dreadful shame if so many worthy knights were to come to grief for such little foolishness. And besides, they would utterly forsake your uncle's court."

"I do not know what they'll do," said Sir Gawainet, "but they won't leave it on my account, and if they do, whatever land they go to, they'll be found, for I and mine will go anywhere we hear it said that they are."

---

* The proverb is attested by Morawski (#2351) and Cotgrave (under *Honte*), whose translation this is. The proverb occurs elsewhere (244, l. 7); see also p. 262n.

"Sir," he answered, "cool your anger, calm your wrath, for, God help me, if they began the madness, they have paid dearly for it, for many of them are wounded and badly maimed; there are a good thirty of them who will never carry a shield, so I believe, and it is a great sorrow and a great shame, for they were very worthy gentlemen and good knights."

While they were talking thus, King Arthur rode up, and he heard some of the words they spoke, and he said to Sir Gawainet, "Dear nephew, is this what I bade you do this morning? In truth, you have shown clearly that you do not hold me dear, for against my will and against my orders, and to spite me, you have killed and wounded my men, and you have done the worst things you know how. And you should know that I am grieved by what you have done."

"Sir," said Sir Gawainet, "the one who began the madness should pay dearly for it. I have done nothing to spite you, and if anyone accused me of such a thing, there is no man against whom I would not defend myself, all the more so because, just as soon as the madness began to grow, I sent you word of it by Galesconde, one of our companions. And [332] they had very badly hurt us long before we stirred to move against them."

And King Lot, his father, came to him and took hold of his horse's bridle, and he said, "Gawainet, dear son, stop this madness at once, for you have fought long enough; let the king say what he will. In due time the anger between you two will be healed, for we have seen clearly a part of what has happened."

And King Ban and King Bors came to him and spoke to him of many things, until at last they calmed him.

This is how the fight was broken up between Sir Gawainet, and his companions, and those of the Round Table. And the four kings took him away with them, and they went to Galesconde, to the wondrous fighting within the gate to the town, where Sagremor, Sir Yvain, and their companions were giving them the worst of it. And Galesconde broke them up, although it was very hard to do, for they were struggling hard with one another. Then each and every one went to his lodging; they took off their armor and washed in warm water; then they dressed in their tunics. As many as could went to the court, but the maimed and wounded stayed behind in their lodgings to have their wounds tended and taken care of. Meanwhile, Sir Gawainet and his companions went to take off their armor in one of the queen's rooms that had been set aside to house them. And when they had taken off their armor and bathed, they dressed most handsomely, and they were so well served that they could not ask for more, for none served them but maidens, of whom there were a great many. There Sagremor was often looked at and stolen sight of by many of them, for he was a most handsome, strong knight, and Dodinel too, for both of them were very handsome knights, and they were highly esteemed and praised by everyone who saw them.

As soon as they were dressed, they came straight to the high hall two by two, holding one another by the hand, one pair after the other. Thus went the ninety knights, with Sir Gawainet and Sir Yvain leading the way to the high hall before the king, who was very glad to see them. And when he saw them he rose to greet them; he took Sir Gawainet by one hand and the queen took him by the other, and they all three went to sit on a couch. And the other knights sat down and played and joked with one another; then they all began to engage one another in conversation, for they had a great deal to talk about. But above all those who were there, the queen was most joyful and happiest because of her knights, who had won the tourney. Little did it matter how happy she was, for the companions of the Round Table were not joyful or happy or cheerful; rather they were ashamed, downcast, and full of wrath because of their companions, many of whom were wounded. And they spoke of many things, until at last they talked about how they could become reconciled with Sir Gawainet and his companions, and they agreed to send Hervi of Rivel, who was a most worthy and learned gentleman, and Nascien, for no other two could serve as messengers better than they, and Minados as well, who was a most worthy knight and moderate in his speech. When these three companions saw that it was up to them to deliver the message, they took one another by the hand and came straight before King Arthur. And when the king saw them coming, he rose to meet them, for he knew better than any other how to honor worthy gentlemen. [333] He told them that they were very welcome. And Sir Gawainet rose as well.

Then Hervi spoke to the king and said, "Sir, the companions of the Round Table have sent us to speak to Sir Gawainet, to my lady the queen, from whom he has a part of his holdings, and no less to you, who are our overlord. And they would like you to know, and they beg you that, if they have wronged Sir Gawainet in any way or his companions, however they may have done so, they are ready and willing to make up for it as you and my lady see fit, provided that all wrath and ill will are forgiven on both sides."

And the king looked at the queen and said, "Lady, they won't ever refuse that."

And the queen answered that she would be very glad if Sir Gawainet did not. And Sir Gawainet kept quiet and did not say a word, but he fell into deep thought.

When the king saw him brooding, he took him by the hand and said, "Gawainet, dear nephew, what are you brooding about? Try not to think about anything sad or distressful. For, as the worthiest men in the world bow down to you, only honor can come to you, and they offer to make up to you all their misdeeds."

"Worthy men, sir?" said Sir Gawainet.

"In truth, dear nephew," answered the king, "they are indeed worthy."

"Then they must be," said Sir Gawainet.

At once he fell silent. And the king, who saw clearly that he was angry at them, looked at the queen and said to her, "Appeal to him, my lady, I beseech you, and it is my will."

"Gladly, sir," she answered.

Then the queen took him by the hand and said to him, "Dear nephew, do not be angry, for anger has blinded many a man and has made the wise seem foolish for as long as the wrath lasts. Now believe me and do as I beseech you, and the king as well, for it is for the sake of your honor and worth. How well you know that this land is in sorrow and has been scourged by the Saxons! Here there are but few of you, but I'll tell you what you should think about doing: you should be faithful and love one another and help one another against all others, and if your enemies come to fall upon you, you should be hard and fierce against them, but not against those who tomorrow might give themselves to be maimed or slain for the sake of my lord, who is here, and myself. And all for one mad thing they have done in their folly, would you deprive me of them? So forgive them, dear nephew, I beg you, as does the king your uncle, who is deeply distressed by it."

And Sir Gawainet looked at her and began to smile because of the speech she had given him, and he answered, "My lady, my lady, anyone who will learn from you can learn a great deal. And blessed be God for making such as you and for granting us the company of such a good and noble lady. And my lord the king may well boast that, if you live a full life, you will be the wisest lady alive—indeed, you already are, I believe! And do you know what you have won in this? You may do with me whatever you will, unless it bring shame to me or my lord the king."

"In truth," said the queen, "any lady who sought that of you would be neither worthy nor wise, and I do not ask such a thing, nor will I ever, God willing."

This is how the queen soothed Sir Gawainet, and so peace was made. [334] And then Nascien, Hervi, and Minados went to fetch the companions of the Round Table, and they told them how they had done. Then they all came straight back to the king. And the queen had called Sir Yvain, Sagremor, and some others aside, and she told them how peace had been sought with the companions of the Round Table. Sir Yvain said that only good could come of it and that one should rather delight in love than in hatred.

With that, the companions of the Round Table came before the king; and as soon as they had gathered there, they knelt before Sir Gawainet and folded back the hems on their cloaks;* and Hervi of Rivel spoke and said, "Sir, we make amends to you, on behalf of ourselves and all our companions, for all the wrong, without saying more, we have done you. Forgive us everything, if you please."

And Sir Gawainet leapt to his feet and said that he forgave them everything, and he raised them up by their arms, and Sir Yvain, Sagremor, and Sir Gawainet's three brothers raised the men nearest them,† and they got all the others to their feet, and they all hugged and kissed one another, and each forgave the other their wrath and anger. And from that time forth Sir Gawainet was lord and master and a companion of the Round Table. And the queen freed the knights taken prisoner whom her own knights had sent her, and she gave new clothing to every one. Thus the knights of the Round Table and Queen Guenevere's knights were reconciled, and they swore that they would never again turn against one another, except when knights by themselves wished to be tested and were in disguise and did not want to be recognized for who they were before they had won renown for deeds of great knightly skill and the knights of the Round Table let them into their company. And the story says that the queen's knights that day were only ninety strong,‡ but their numbers grew afterwards until, as the story will relate it to you, there were four hundred of them before the quest for the Holy Grail had ended. That is why they suffered much bitter hardship in order to achieve the quest, which lasted for a very long time. And many a day they tried hard to undertake many other quests, and I will tell you why they did it.

---

*　As a sign of their desire to make amends (Cotgrave, *ployer*).

†　The text reads *chascuns le sien* (334, l. 14: "each his own [man]").

‡　Sommer's text has *.lxxx.* (334, l. 25), but this number is inconsistent with the count in the immediate context; in fact, other manuscripts give the number as ninety (334, n. 2).

It was true that news spread throughout the kingdom of Logres about the most holy Grail, in which Joseph of Arimathea had caught the blood that flowed from the side of Jesus Christ when he and Nicodemus took Him down from the glorious Cross; about the most holy vessel that came down from heaven onto the ark in the city of Sarras, in which He first sacrificed His holy body and His flesh through His bishop Josephus, whom He consecrated with His own hand; and about the most holy Lance with which Jesus Christ was wounded in His side. They had come to be kept in the land of Logres, for Joseph had brought them there, but no one knew where they were, [335] and they would never be found or seen, so the prophecy said, by anyone, nor would the wonders of the Holy Grail and the Lance that bled from its iron tip, until the best knight in the world came there. And by him would the wonders of the Holy Grail be discovered. This news had spread everywhere, but no one ever found out where it had come from or who was the first to utter it.

And when the companions of the Round Table heard that all of these things would be brought to an end by the best knight in the world, they undertook a quest that lasted many a day in order to find out who the best knight was, and they looked for many a long day in many a land, and everyone sought to be thought of as the best. Whenever they heard it said that there was a good knight in a country, they undertook the quest for a year and a day without lying down in the same town more than one night. Whenever they happened to find him, they did what they could to bring him back to court, and when there were witnesses that he was worthy and skilled, they welcomed him into their company, and then his name was written down with the other companions'. And as soon as each one came back from his quest at the end of the year, he told about the adventures that had happened to him that year, and the clerks took them down in writing word for word just as he told them.

Now you have heard why and how the quests were begun in the kingdom of Logres, and now, with that, the story falls silent about them, and it goes back to the matter it left off in order to tell about these things. I did not want to forget it because it belongs right here.

40. ARTHUR TO PROPOSE A TRUCE WITH THE REMAINING REBELLIOUS PRINCES.*

Now the story says that the companions of the Round Table were very glad that they had been reconciled with Sir Gawainet, and they highly esteemed the prowess they had seen him display at the tournament. They said among themselves there in the hall that the ten best knights there could not have outlasted him fighting man to man. So spoke the knights there, and they said what they would, but the ladies and maidens, who were in the rooms, said even more about him. Soon the horn was blown for washing their hands, and the cloths were put on the tables, and the

---

* Corresponds to Sommer, 335-339.

knights all sat down right where they ought. The queen's knights sat next to the knights of the Round Table, just as they should have. And King Arthur, King Ban, King Bors, and King Lot sat at their own table, and no one else sat with them. That day Sir Gawainet served, along with Sir Yvain, Lucan the Wine Steward, Girflet, and up to forty others. And they were all served better than anyone could describe: I do not know how to tell you about the food they ate or the many kinds of drink.

After eating, when the tablecloths had been taken off, the knights went here and there in the meadows and along the river bank, and the weather was fair and still. But although others went out to enjoy themselves, the four kings lingered. They went into a room by themselves to one of the windows through which they could see the meadows and river, and the view was wondrously beautiful and health-giving. The air was soft and sweet that blew in through the windows, and the ones who had stayed behind were more comfortable, for it was still very hot in the land. And they talked together about many things that came to their minds. [336]

After they had been there for some time, King Ban spoke to King Arthur and said to him, "Sir, if you wanted to do something that I would praise highly, and I have thought about it in my heart, it seems to me that it would be good for you, and your land and your hospitality would be worth more because of it; you would be feared more by friends and strangers alike, and the knights in your court would love you more."

"Tell me then," said the king, "what this thing is, for, if I can do it without shame and dishonor, I will do it."

"Sir," said King Ban, "you will not ever be ashamed of this, God willing, nor will you be rebuked for it. Take care—for as long as you wish to hold your lands—that your knights never fight against one another in a tournament, for much anger could come from it out of envy, for they are all good knights. But every time they want to tourney, send them to tilt with the noble men in your borderlands, for there are many of them who are wealthy and powerful."

And the king said that what King Ban had said was a good thing and that he would indeed do it. Then the queen, who had heard him talking, came in and said that he had spoken well and that he should be blessed by God for having said it, "for there are many throughout the countryside who would never have bothered to say that, and he wouldn't have either, if he didn't love you."

Afterwards King Lot spoke and said, "Sir, it would benefit Holy Christendom if the faithless Saxons were driven out. They have come into this country and, in their pride, have besieged two cities at the same time; but they have so many men that it will be very hard to drive them out if Our Lord is not mindful of it, and you know very well that we do not have enough men under our sway to drive them out of the land or to take a stand against them on the battlefield. But if only there were someone who could succeed in making a truce between you and the princes who still hate you, so that we might go all together against the Saxons and help one another until they have been run out of the country! It seems to me that would be the greatest good deed, and the most worthwhile, that anyone could do for this country! The truce should last as long as a year, and when the Saxons have been driven out, we can make peace between ourselves and the barons, if such is to be, or, if not, let each one do the best he can."

"In truth," said King Arthur, "I would like that very much indeed, if only I had anyone to send there, for people would be needed whom the barons could believe in, for they are fearsome and full of pride."

"Sir," said King Lot, "the Saxons have done them such dreadful harm that, when they hear about the truce and know that they'll have your help, I don't believe they'll thwart you."

"I don't know what to say to you," said King Arthur. "You know very well that I am needed in this land to do what I must do, and I am but one single man, just as all of you are. But look to yourselves and choose the one among you who could fulfill this mission."

"Sir," said King Ban, "if I didn't think that King Lot would hold it against me, I would say that he would be better for it than anyone else you could send, and he would tell them better than we what they want to hear, for he is friendly with them and behaves kindly toward them."

"In truth," said King Arthur, "he is better suited for the undertaking than anyone we could send."

The queen said that no one would be more fit for the mission but for the Saxons, who would strip him of his belongings and [337] hold him prisoner, "but it would be less harmful if, instead of him, we lost a poor but well-spoken knight."

"My lady," said King Arthur, "I know all of the princes to be so proud that they would not listen to any knight I might send to them."

When King Lot heard that they agreed he should go on that mission, he knew that they were right, so he said that he would go and take his four sons with him.

"Truly," said King Bors, "if you take them, you needn't worry about any man born of a woman."

When King Arthur heard that they had agreed for King Lot to take his four sons with him, he heaved a great sigh, for he was afraid for Sir Gawainet, in whom he had wholeheartedly put his love, for there was not anyone or anything else in the world he loved so much.

And when the queen saw him, she knew part of what he was thinking, so, wise and keen-witted as she was, she said, "Sir, grant King Lot leave to take his sons with him boldly (and he has nothing to fear, God willing), for, as they are your fastest friends, they will conclude peace all the more earnestly, and they will put their hearts into it more than others whose hearts are not touched by it."

"My lady," said the king, "I will agree, since the barons have worked it out."

And then he told King Lot to get ready for the trip so quietly that no one would find out where he was going. Sir Gawainet and his brothers, who were reveling in the great hall with the others, were called straightway, and they came at once to meet King Arthur.* He told them that they were most welcome, and they returned his greeting most courteously. Then King Arthur told them, just as they had worked it out, that they had to go on the mission, and they answered that it was all to the good.

Afterwards King Lot said to Sir Gawainet, "Dear son, you and your brothers, go get ready so that you'll have everything you need when we leave."

---

* The text has the ambivalent personal pronoun *li* (337, l. 19): "him."

"What?" said Sir Gawainet. "What do we need besides our armor and our horses? We won't be taking packhorses or trunks or anything else but the good, swift, eager warhorses we'll be riding—they'll carry us to safety when the need arises! And we should not tarry here, for, if you'll believe me, we should leave shortly after nightfall and ride in as long stretches as we can. No one should put off a mission such as this!"

"Dear nephew," said King Arthur, "you speak the truth. Now go rest and sleep a little."

Then Sir Gawainet turned toward the queen and said to her, "My lady, I beg you to think about my companions, who are yours forever, for my uncle's companions do not love them wholeheartedly, but envy them, as you know yourself. And it may well happen, after my brothers and I have gone, that they'll want to do some jousting in order to build up a tournament among themselves. And I beseech you, for you are my lady, not to allow there to be a challenge."

"And I warrant you," she said, "that there will not be. And if my husband the king believed me, no tournament would be planned for as long as they are in this country."

And the king answered that, by the faith he bore her, there would not be, if they wished to have his love. [338]

At once they left and went to their rooms to rest and sleep. And those who had been left in the hall broke up and went to their lodgings. But whoever else may have left, Guiomar, the queen's nephew, did not. Instead, he stayed behind talking to Morgan, King Arthur's sister, in a bedroom under the great hall where she spun golden thread, for she wished to make a headpiece for her sister, the wife of King Lot. This Morgan was a young lady, very cheerful and merry, but her face was somber; she had a rounded build, not too thin and not too plump. She was quite clever and comely in body and in features; she stood straight and was wonderfully pleasing and a good singer. But she was the most lustful woman in all Great Britain and the lewdest. Yet she was a woman of wondrous learning, and she knew much about astrology,* which Merlin had taught her. And later he taught her a great deal more about it, just as the story will recount it to you later, and she put her whole mind to it; and she learned it so well that afterwards she was called Morgan the Fay, sister of King Arthur, because of the wonders she worked throughout the country. She was the best worker with her hands that anyone knew about in any land, and she had the fairest head of any suited for a woman, the most beautiful hands, and wondrously well-made shoulders, and she was the cleverest of all. Her skin was softer than millet† And she had yet another quality that must not be skipped over, for she had a sweet, soft way of talking, and she was well spoken. And as long as she was in her right mind, she was more courteous than any, but when she was angry with anyone, there was no need in trying to reconcile them. This showed very clearly when to the man she ought to have loved best she brought the worst harm and such great guilt that people talked about it afterwards for as long as she

---

*   As before (e.g., 23, l. 15; 75, l. 26; 102, l. 28), the Old French word is *astrenomie* (338, l. 11). Here especially the meaning appears to spread into magic and necromancy.

†   The word is *millart* (338, l. 18).

lived. This had to do with the noble Guenevere, just as the story will later explain to you how and why.

When Guiomar went into the room where Morgan was, he greeted her most kindly and bade her a good day from God, and she returned his greeting most courteously, for she was not mute, and he came straight to her and sat down beside her. He began to handle the golden thread she was working with and asked her what she meant to make. He was a handsome knight, slender, and well built; his hair was curly and blond, he was handsome, delightful to look at, smiling, and courteous above all other knights. He spoke to the maiden about many things, and she was glad to watch him, for she found him handsome, and she liked everything he did and said. They spoke and at last he asked for her love. The more she looked at him the more pleasing she found him until she welcomed him with such great love that she refused him nothing he asked of her. And when he understood and saw that she would willingly grant him what he was begging for, he took her in his arms and began to kiss her most sweetly until they began to heat up as hot as Nature demands, and they threw themselves onto a large, beautiful bed; they played the game everyone plays, as they yearned to do, and they were joined in very great love, for he loved her and she loved him more. So they stayed together all evening long and made love for quite a while, and no one [339] knew it. But Queen Guenevere found out about it later, just as the story will explain it to you later, which is why they were separated; Morgan began to hate her for it and afterwards did many troublesome things to her, and she cast such blame on her that it was not forgotten for as long as she lived.

But now the story falls silent about them, for it no longer speaks about that right here, but it goes back to talking about King Lot and his sons, who had gone to their lodgings to sleep.

41. GAWAIN AND HIS BROTHERS BATTLE THE SAXONS.[*]

Right here the story says that shortly after nightfall King Lot and his four sons got up and got themselves ready with their armor. They had chosen five of the best horses they could find in the whole court; they took them with them and five serving boys on foot, and they had five very good palfreys that they rode as they went. And when everything was ready, they mounted their horses by the Bricoune Gate, and the five boys who were leading the horses, all covered with iron, went out ahead, and they all went as stealthily as they could, for they wanted no one to catch sight of them and raise a warning. And when they had ridden enough to be half a Welsh league away, Sir Gawainet asked where they were going.

And King Lot told him that he did not know, "for warfare," he went on, "is so widespread in the countryside."

---

[*]   Corresponds to Sommer, 339-346.

"Now I'll tell you what we are about to do. We are riding toward Arestel in Scotland. That's the closest land, and it is the most densely shaded by trees of any in this country, and that makes for the best hunting* anywhere!"

And King Lot answered, "Dear son, since that is what you want to do, I am most willing, for what you say is best. And we'll go by way of the Castle of the Fir Forest, through the Plains of Roestoc and the Forest of Brambles beneath Caranges, and we'll go along the river Severn through the meadowlands of Cambenic. From there we'll skirt the wealthy city of North Wales, which belongs to King Tradelmant, and from there on to Arestel, which is four leagues away from the Saxons."

And the young men all agreed to this.

So the messengers rode along talking about this and that until dawn, and from the next day on they made their way through the most out-of-the-way places they knew of; they slept in forests and in hermitages, and they rode thus for eight full days. And they were never bothered until they came to the Plains of Roestoc. Then, at midday, they happened upon at least seven thousand Saxons who were taking away a great deal of plunder and a good seven hundred prisoners whose feet they had tied under their horses' bellies, and they were driving them by beating them ruthlessly with sticks. Sorbares, Monaclin, Salibrun, Ysores, and Clarion were leading them, and Clarion was riding Gringalet, a horse so named because of its great worth, for the story says that it could run for ten leagues without heaving or panting, nor would there be any sweat on one hair of its rump or shoulder.

When the Saxons saw them coming on horseback, they knew by their armor that they were not any of their own, so they stopped and waited. And when Sir Gawainet saw that, he stopped and ordered his father and brothers to get on their warhorses, and they did so. And [340] the boys went to the palfreys, mounted, and set off into the forest where the road had turned, but the knights went straight for the Saxons, because they did not want to meet them at the angle the road would have made them take. It was after midday and drawing near the hour of nones. King Lot rode out ahead and Sir Gawainet after him with his brothers alongside him, and they were going at a slow pace without breaking out of line. When they had gone far enough to be quite close to the Saxons, Gawainet said to his father that he yearned for nothing but to ride into them, and for his brothers to be with him, until they had gone through all of them.

Then the Saxons shouted, "Knights, surrender and tell us who you are and what you are looking for."

And King Lot answered, "We are five messengers from King Arthur, who has sent us on a mission, and we will not tell you more."

"Stand still and don't go on," they ordered. "We are guarding the roads for King Hargadabran, for Orient, son of Bramangue, and for Arrant,† son of Magaat.‡ We are taking this plunder and these prisoners to them, and we'll make them a gift of you as well."

"Indeed," said King Lot, "when you can do so."

---

*   The word is *traire* (339, l. 20): "shooting."
†   The form here is *airant* (340, l. 12); elsewhere in the *Merlin* occurs the form *hertant* (174, ll. 33, 42).
‡   The form here (340, l. 12) is *maagart*.

They said that it would not be long, "so surrender, and you'll be doing the wise thing, before something worse happens to you."

And they answered that that would never happen. Then they let their horses run as fast as they could go, and the Saxons did likewise, for they feared them very little. But King Lot and his sons stormed in among them with their lances under their arms, and each one hit his man so that he knocked him down dead; then they struck five others and brought them down dead, and they did the same in four drives they made all the way through them, but they were not hurt. And then they began galloping away holding their bloody lances, and when the others saw them riding off, the shouting and the uproar grew loud after them, and they undertook a wondrous pursuit. The dust rose so thick that they could barely recognize one another.

Right then the five* kings, who had heard the news, came spurring their horses. They shouted to their men, "Now after them! You'll be sorry if they get away."

And they themselves took to the road after them. They were riding good horses, and they gave them a frenzied chase. The runaways rode at a full gallop, and they went until they came to a mill, where they had to cross a very wide and dreadful ford that was full of filth and mud, so they had to stop and go on at a slow gait. And the five kings, who were not afraid of the bad crossing, caught up with them there, and more than five hundred Saxons were behind them. They broke their lances on them as they came in, and King Ysores, who was riding out ahead, struck King Lot's horse with his lance and brought it down dead under him.

When King Lot saw that his horse had been killed, he sprang to his feet and drew his sword. He stood his ground beside a clump of rushes because of the mire, which was wide and deep. The Saxons ran upon him and attacked hard, but he defended himself so well that they did not have the strength to take him. Then Gawainet looked about and saw his father on foot, and he was so worried about him that he nearly went out of his mind. He struck his horse with his spurs so hard that the blood poured out of its sides, and he struck Monaclin so hard that he drove through his shield and hauberk, into his side, through his ribs, and out the other side, and he sent him to the ground dead. When he fell, Gawainet's lance broke, so he drew his sword, which was named Excalibur, and looked at his father, who was defending himself against more than forty Saxons. [341] He ran upon them with his sword in his hand and struck right and left, and he cut off their heads, arms, and legs, and he did such wonders that they scattered everywhere, for they did not dare make a stand against him. And Sir Gawainet struck one Saxon who was striving to hold King Lot down, and he split him down to the chest; then he caught his horse and took it to his father. And a hue and cry rose for the man who had been slain.

Meanwhile, King Lot got on the horse despite all those he was fighting with. Then Sir Gawainet's three brothers came; they had been in such a slaughter that all of their armor was filthy with blood and brains. And when they had all drawn together, they began such hard fighting and such a slaughter that it was a wonder to see. And the Saxons came in from everywhere because they believed, for the great slaughter the brothers had done, that they were a huge army.

---

*   The text reads .*vj*. (340, 1. 24): "six."

When King Lot saw the great numbers that were coming against them from all sides, he called to his sons and told them it was high time to go, for it did not make sense to stay there any longer and take forty blows for every one they gave. "But let's go," he said, "and if they run after us, then we'll rout them when it is the right time and place for us."

With that, they went their way, and they rode right across the ford without any hindrance, and when they were on the other side, they took to the road. When the three kings saw them going off, they shouted after them, "We'll not let the traitors get away!"

Then they crossed the ford and ran after them for quite a long time. King Clarion, who was sitting on Gringalet, went out ahead all the others more than an arrow-shot. And Sir Gawainet was behind his companions, holding his bloody sword, when the Saxon, who was striving hard to catch up with him, yelled out, "You worthless dog, surrender now, for all of you are dead!"

And Sir Gawainet looked about and saw the horse hugging the ground and bursting to go, and he began very much to yearn for him in his heart, and he said that if he had such a horse, he would not give him away for the best city that King Arthur had. Then he began to slow his pace and run at an easy gallop. King Clarion was still giving him chase and would not let him get away. And when Sir Gawainet saw how close he was to him, he turned his shield against him. King Clarion struck him so hard that his lance flew into bits, and Sir Gawainet hit him so hard on his helmet that he split it down to his iron coif and cut to the bone; he dazed him so badly that he flew over his saddlebow onto the ground, and he hit so hard that he fainted from the agony he felt.

And Sir Gawainet took Gringalet by the bridle and led him toward a stand of trees almost half a league away. His father was still going out ahead with his three sons, and he was thinking of nothing but riding and thought that all his sons were along with him (the dust had risen so thick on the road that no one could see very far); yet they had left Sir Gawainet two arrow-shots behind. And when Sir Gawainet came to the trees, he saw the five boys coming out of the forest, and they were riding the five palfreys. When he saw them he was wondrously happy, and he praised them and held them in high esteem because they had struggled so to keep up with them. Then he got down and mounted Gringalet, and he gave one of the boys his horse to lead [342] beside the one he was riding, and he ordered them to go after his brothers, who had ridden out ahead, "and tell them to keep their minds on making their way, and I will follow. But first I want to see what has become of those men."

But he stayed behind for nothing, for they had stopped running after them when they found King Clarion; instead, they gathered all around him, because they believed that he was dead, and they were weeping and wailing so loudly that Sir Gawainet heard the screams from where he was.

So Sir Gawainet lingered for a long time in the trees to find out whether anyone was coming. Meanwhile, King Lot and his three sons rode until they came to a small woods. And after they had gone inside, King Lot looked about and did not see Sir Gawainet. Straightway he said, "Something dreadful has happened! I have lost everything!"

The others looked about and said, "Sir, what is wrong with you?"

And he answered, "My children, your brother is missing! In truth, if he is dead I'll kill myself, for I would not seek to live a single day after him."

"Sir," said Agravain, "do not worry. God willing, he won't have anything to bother him."

While King Lot was wailing, the five serving boys came up. They were bringing along the five palfreys, and one of them was leading Sir Gawainet's horse on the right side. When King Lot saw them, he knew well who they were.

Very quickly they were drawing near, and Guerrehet yelled to them, "Where did you leave my brother?"

"Sir," they said, "in that stand of trees, where he is atop the best horse in the world, and he struck a king down from him. Those who were weeping and mourning for the king said that his name was King Clarion and the horse was called Gringalet. And he gave us this horse and sent us to tell you to keep riding and he will catch up with you when he wants to."

When King Lot heard that he was safe and sound, he was very gladdened and looked toward the trees. And when Sir Gawainet saw that they were no longer giving them chase, he said that he would show them the good horse before he left. Then he rode out from the trees and headed to where he saw the greatest number of men, who were still in the throes of their great sorrow. He saw one Saxon who was holding a wonderful spear with a short, thick shaft and an iron tip that was a foot and a half long, and it was bright and sharp. Then he put Excalibur back into its scabbard and dashed toward the Saxon as fast as the horse could run, and he tore the spear out of his hands so ruthlessly that he sent him to the ground; and on this same pass he ran the spear through another one's body and hurled him down dead. He drove all the way through them and came back so fast that he was all flushed. But before he got all the way out, his shield knew it well, for it was split into pieces. But what did that matter to him? He had so badly hurt fourteen of them that never again, for their own well-being, did they get back on a horse. Then he rode away without slowing down. The hue and cry rose loud after him, and the chase was so hard that it was a wonder. When he saw that he had ridden some distance from them, he turned about holding his sword, and he struck the first one he met and sent him to the ground dead. Then he turned back and taunted them into following after him until they came to within less than an arrow-shot from the woods where King Lot and his three sons had stopped with the serving boys. [343]

When King Lot saw the Saxons coming so fast after his son, whom he loved and longed for more than anything, he shouted, "My sons, what are you doing? There is Gawainet, your brother, and those unbelieving whoresons are running after him!"

With that, King Lot tied his helmet back on and spurred his horse and rode out against the Saxons; his sons did likewise. And King Lot met Sir Gawainet and said to him, "Gawainet, dear son, you were wrong to leave us! Why the devil did you stay back with those Saxons? Are you trying to defeat them all? Even if you killed twenty of them in one stroke, you would not be done in a month."

"Sir," said Sir Gawainet, "I have won such a horse that I would not give him away for the Castle of Glocedon. It was to try him out that I stayed behind, and I have found him to be such that no one need look for a better one in any land! Let's go now, and I won't leave you anymore, no matter what happens."

"As long as we are here," said Agravain, "damn anyone to hell who leaves before we have struck down and slain Saxons!"

"Indeed," said Sir Gawainet.

They did not have any lances, so they drew their bare swords. The Saxons ran upon them, thinking they could take them, and broke their lances on their shields, while King Lot and his sons struck them on their helmets wherever they met them. And the fighting grew so fierce that never has anyone seen harder fighting from five knights, and they killed more than forty before they could get away. But the number of Saxons kept growing.

When King Lot saw that it was time to go, he said to Gawainet, "Dear son, let's leave with your brothers, for you can see plainly that we can do nothing here and we're wasting time. We'll come back to the fight soon enough when we have the right armor."

And Sir Gawainet came up to his brothers and told them that it was time to go. With that, the five of them left, but first they tore five lances from Saxons' hands and put their swords back in their scabbards. As they were riding away, seven Saxons came down with lances held straight and fell upon Gaheriet. Two of them struck him between the shoulders, another two on his sides, and another two on the sleeve of his hauberk, while the seventh struck his horse right in the mid-section and killed it, bringing man and horse to the ground.

Then King Lot thought that Gaheriet had been killed. He turned around and said, "How dreadful! Now the four brothers are lost. Dear son Gawainet, this awful thing has happened because of you, for if you had come with us Gaheriet would not be in trouble now."

While King Lot was saying this, Gaheriet leapt to his feet, for he was very skilled and very bold, the best knight of all his brothers but Gawainet. He fixed his shield on his arm, drew his sword, and got ready to defend himself. The seven Saxons had turned about, and he ran them down. He struck the first one he met and sliced his right thigh all the way through beneath his saddle, and he fell to the ground. Next he struck another one on his helmet, but could not follow through; the sword came down by his shoulder and cut the strap of his shield and went through his right arm, and his shield flew to the ground with his arm. [344]

And Sir Gawainet struck the first man he came to and hurled him dead to the ground. Then he took his horse and led it to his brother and said to him, "Climb on, noble companion." And he got on straightway and took up his lance, which he did not want to leave behind. King Lot, Guerrehet, and Agravain had struck down three of them, and the seventh turned in flight. And when Gaheriet saw him leaving, he set out after him and followed him until they went down into a valley. There he struck him in the chest with his lance so hard that it went all the way through. Then he went galloping back to where he saw his brothers.

It was nearly the hour of vespers when they took to the road. The Saxons commended them to all the devils alive, and they said that they would not be run after by them any more. They also said that if the Christians had no more than ten thousand men in the countryside, King Hargadabran could be sure that the Saxons could not have held out against them no matter how many there were. With that, the Saxons went back to where King Clarion lay, and they found that his wound had already stopped bleeding. And when he saw them, he asked them if they had caught the scoundrels who had done them so much harm. They answered that they had not, and they told him about all the damage they had done and said that they could not take them prisoner do what they might. And when he heard that, he was stricken with sorrow. Then the Saxons went back to the siege, which was mighty, that they were holding before the city of Clarence.

And King Lot and his sons saw that the hour of vespers was drawing near, so they took to the road. But it would not have seemed to anyone who saw their armor that they had stayed to rest, for their shields were hacked up, their helmets smashed in, their armor broken, their horses filthy with blood and brains, and it was very plain that they had come out of a fearsome battle.* Right away they went into the woods where the serving boys were waiting for them. They dismounted from their warhorses and got on their palfreys, and the boys led their horses and carried their lances, their shields, and their helmets, and they went on at a walk through the thick woods; they rode quite far during the night, and the moon shone bright. They rode until they came to the house of a forester who was most worthy. He had four sons who were most handsome young men, and his wife was a most worthy lady.

The vavasor's house was well fortified with wide, deep moats all filled with water. Beyond these, it was surrounded by great, fully-grown oak trees, and the steep hillside† beyond grew so thick with brambles and thorn bushes that no one would have thought that there was a dwelling there. King Lot and his three sons came there at the cock's first crow, for the road happened to lead them to a postern, which was the way in. They had one of the serving boys call out and knock until someone opened the gate to them. One of the forester's sons asked them who they were, and they said that they were five knights errant "from this land, and we are going on a mission."

"Sir," said the youth, "you are most welcome."

And he led them into the courtyard. They dismounted from their horses, which were well provided with hay and oats, for there was a great deal to eat there, and the youth took them to have their armor taken off in a most handsome hall at ground level. The vavasor and his wife and their three other sons‡ and two daughters stood up to greet them. And they lit torches inside there and put water on to heat, and they washed their hands and faces and then dried them with beautiful, white cloths, and they brought to each one a cloak with a collar. [345]

And the vavasor had the tables set up and the cloths put on; and bread, a great abundance of wine, fresh venison, and salted meat, of which there was a great deal

---

* Sommer's text repeats *que de que de forte bataille* (344, ll. 20-21): "that from that from [a] great battle."

† The text has *li rubis* (344, l. 30). This rare word undoubtedly relates to Old French *robist* (from Latin *rupes* "rock, cliff"). Middle French *rubist*, "steep hillside" *FEW* 10:577), cf. the Old French derivative *desrubé* "steep."

‡ The text reads *.iiij. filg* (344, l. 40): "four sons." The woodsman is said earlier to have four sons (344, ll. 26, 31), one of whom is taking them into the hall and would not, therefore, get up to greet them.

there, were laid out. The knights sat down to the meal, and they ate heartily, for they needed food. The vavasor's two daughters looked hard at Sir Gawainet and his brothers, and they greatly wondered who they could be; and the vavasor's four sons waited on the knights, and the maidens served wine. The lady from there sat facing Sir Gawainet and the host Agravain; Gaheriet and Guerrehet sat facing each other, while King Lot was beside his host, but a little higher. They were quite well served for such a late hour, for it was almost midnight.

And when they had eaten and the tablecloths were taken away, the host asked King Lot, "Sir, if you and the others with you don't object, I would like very much to know who you are, where you are heading and why, unless these are things to bring you shame."

"In truth," said King Lot, "we will never be ashamed of it, God willing, but first tell us whose forest this is and the land all around."

"Indeed, sir," said the worthy man, "the forest belongs to King Clarion of Northumberland, and I keep it for him—I am his forester and his liegeman, and these young men here are my sons and those maidens my daughters."

"Indeed," said King Lot, "I know no worthier man of his age than King Clarion, and he could not better place the trust he has bestowed on you, it seems to me, for you have a most handsome, well-bred household."

"In God's name," said the forester, "if they are worthy, they are rightly so,* for they have kinsmen who are good knights, now among the most honored and best loved at King Arthur's court; I've been told that they have lately become knights of the queen and that this company has been founded by Sir Gawainet, King Lot's son. And I've also been told that King Lot is reconciled with King Arthur."

"And who are the knights your children are kin to?" asked King Lot.

"In truth," answered the forester, "this lady is the sister of Meralgis of Portford (I don't know if you know him), and she is first cousin, on her father's side, to Aiglin of the Vales and Kehedin the Small, and Yvain of Lionel is my cousin,† for he is the son of my uncle Grandalis, castellan of Crenefort. And I myself would hold a great deal of land, were it not for the Saxons who have laid waste everything."

"And what is your name?" King Lot asked the forester.

"Indeed," answered the forester, "my name is Minoras, lord of the New Castle in Northumberland."

"In God's name," said King Lot, "I know very well all the ones you have named to me. You can truly say that they are good knights in every way! And if God would only grant that King Clarion were sitting here beside me just as you are!"

"What?" said Minoras. "Are you then friends of his? Now I long all the more to know about you!"

"Truly," said King Lot, "I will not stop wandering until I have spoken to him. And I'll tell you," the king went on, "who I am. You can tell everyone who asks you that the guests you sheltered were King Lot of Orkney and his four sons."

"Ah, sir!" said the forester. "We could die [346] for not having served you better!"

---

*   The text reads *il ont bien a qui retraire* (345, ll. 22-23): "they have many to attribute [this] to."
†   The word is *nies* (345, l. 31), usually nephew or grandson.

Then he started to stand up beside him. "Keep your seat just as you are," said the king, "and don't move. For you have done so much for us that you have won us over, and you and yours will be rewarded."

"Ah, sir!" said Minoras. "What are you looking for in this country?"

"We seek," he answered, "to talk with the barons of this country, and we would gladly meet with all of them together on behalf of King Arthur, so that we might drive the Saxons out of this land and help one another like brothers."

"And where do you mean to have them gather?" "In Arestel, in Scotland," answered King Lot, "which is in the nearest borderland. We'll gather them there if we can."

"Sir," said Minoras, "I'll speak to my lord about it for you so that you will have less to do. When will he find you there?"

"In truth, you have spoken very well, and I am very grateful to you. Tell him that he will find me there on Our Lady's Day in September, and he must be sure to be there, for it is for his own good."

And Minoras told him that he would give him the message: "Now concern yourself with the others, for you needn't worry about him."

They spoke at length about many things until the beds were set up and they went to lie down and sleep, for they were worn out and weary, and much of the night had already gone by. And they slept until daybreak.

But now the story falls silent about them for a while and speaks about King Pelles of Listenois, the king's brother Pellinor, and King Alan, who were full brothers by the same father and mother.

42. THE CHILDREN OF PELLES; GALAHAD PREDICTED.[*]

Here the story says that King Pelles had a son who was not a knight, although he was a good twenty-five years old, but he was wondrously well built in body and limb, and he was wonderfully handsome. When his father asked him when he wanted to become a knight, he answered that he would never be a knight before the best knight known in the world should give him arms and hug him about the neck.[†]

"Indeed, dear son," said King Pelles, "you will then have to wait a long time."

"I don't know what I'll do," said the lad, "but I'll yet serve him three years before he makes me a knight, so that I can learn about arms and fighting while I am with him. And do you know why I want to get to know him and find out from which prince he comes?[‡] He could very well be one to whom I'll show the way to come to these parts in order to fulfill the adventures of this country that will soon begin, so I've been told. I have said this to you yourself many times, for I would

---

[*]   Corresponds to Sommer, 346-549.

[†]   That is, give him *la colee* (346, l. 25), the ceremonial embrace. See p. 272nn..

[‡]   The text reads *iou le voelle connoistre & veoir & de quel prinche il sera* (346, ll. 28-29).

be most distraught not to see my uncle healed from the wounds he has through his thighs.'"*

"Dear son," said King Pelles, "he would never succeed in this if you showed him the way, for he must be of such knighthood and so given to adventure that he will come here by himself to ask about the Holy Grail, which my fair daughter has in her keeping. She is still only seven years old, but a child is to be fathered on her by the best knight known to anyone, and there must be three to fulfill the adventures; two must be virgins and the third chaste."

"Sir," said the young man, "I very much want to go to King Arthur's court, for I have heard it said that the best knights in the world are there, and one of his nephews is there whose name is Gawainet, son of King Lot of Orkney in Loonois. He is the best knight in the world, the one I want to serve, and [347] I will be his squire, if he deigns to engage me; and he is such a knight, as people bear witness to him, that I will take arms and the embrace from him."

"Dear son," said King Pelles, "there are so many paths between here and there that it will not be an easy thing to go there, for the Saxons have spread out through the countryside, and they have laid waste the land; meanwhile, there is great strife between King Arthur and his barons throughout the land, and I could not rest easy until I knew that you were safe and sound."

"Dear father," said the youth, "we are all subject to adventure, and no one can die but of such a death as Our Lord has destined for him. And you should know that, as for me, I will never stop making my way until I am there, and I'll ride out tomorrow morning."

"Dear son," said the father, "I see clearly that you are bent on going and that nothing will keep you from it, for my sake or anyone else's. Indeed, I'm glad about it, because I see that you yearn for prowess and worthiness, and this comes to you from your great nobility of heart; at the same time I am very sad, for I do not believe that I'll see you again. Now tell me whom you'd like to take with you."

"Sir," he answered, "I'll go by myself and will take along only one squire to keep me company. But prepare whatever weapons and the kind of horse you know I need."

And the king said that he need not worry about a thing, for everything would be ready for him.

Thus ended the talk between son and father. And when the next morning came, his father had made ready a horse, weapons, and whatever else he needed, and he entrusted to him a worthy and righteous squire who had served him well, and the squire loaded armor, clothing, and plenty of money onto a pack horse. And when all was ready, the young man got on a palfrey that walked at an easy gait; he left without any more ado, and he commended his father and friends to God; and they did likewise, so that God might keep the young man and his squire from evil and harm. With that, the young man left with his squire, and they made their way many a day and found no one to give them any but good news. And they rode day in and day out until they came, on the plains of Roestoc at the midday hour, into a valley

---

*   The text reads *parmi ses cuisses* (346, l. 33): "in the midst of his thighs." The expression, which originates in Chrétien's *Li Contes del Graal* in speaking of Perceval's father and the Fisher King (ed. Hilka, ll. 436, 3513), doubtless indicates a sexual wound "between his thighs."

that was very wide and deep, where a beautiful stream flowed from the spring at the pine tree where Pignoras the Saxon and King Monaquin had stopped with five hundred men dressed in iron who were coming from the land of the Saxons and going to the wealthy city of Clarence, to the great siege that the thirty kings were maintaining. And they were leading forty pack horses loaded with meat and salt pork and plenty of other things, and they had taken them beneath the pine tree, in the shade, right by the spring. And they let their horses graze down through the prairie for as long as the heat lasted, for it was in the middle of the day.

Into that valley, which was wide and deep, came the young man and his squire, and they rode hard and did not stop making their way until they came to a high hill. And from there they could clearly see the Saxons who were eating beneath the pine tree. And when the young man saw them, he was struck with great dread. He asked for his weapons and fitted himself out quite fast. Then he fixed his sword to his saddlebow, mounted his horse, and ordered his squire, who was named Lidonas, to ride out ahead. He did as he was told, and he went straight down the road until they ran up against the Saxons. And when Pignoras saw them, he sent someone over to ask who they were. And they said that they were [348] from another land and that they were going about their business. And when Pignoras heard that, he ordered his men to put on their armor and get on their horses, and he had more than forty Saxons ride out after them and ordered them to stay back by force or for love of him. And the youth, who was making his way behind his squire, held a most strong lance, but he had no shield. And he had gone but a little way when he heard the men riding after him, shouting at him very loudly.

"Young men!" yelled the Saxons. "You must come back our way. Hand your horses and your weapons over to us and come to our lord, who is waiting for you under that pine tree."

The young man heard them very well and understood what they said, but he answered not a word, and he rode on after his squire at a little faster gait and then at a full gallop. And when the Saxons saw that he was riding away so fast, they spurred their horses after him and threatened him dreadfully. When the youth saw them coming, he turned his horse's head toward them. And one of the Saxons was coming out ahead of the others. He was holding a strong, stout lance, but he was rushing so fast and so hard that he missed hitting the youth. But the youth rode against him as fast as he could get his horse to go, and he struck him so hard that he pierced his shield and hauberk and drove his lance* through his breastbone; he threw him to the ground so badly wounded that no doctor would have done him any good. Then he drew his lance out and went back on his way, following Lidonas his squire, who rode ahead at full speed because he wanted to get as far away as he could from the Saxons.

And when the Saxons saw that the youth was riding off, they set out after him, because they did not want to let him get away. And the youth was going away at a full gallop, holding the lance, which had changed its color from white to red, for it was stained with the blood of the man he had killed. And as he rode he prayed God,

---

*   In this passage the words *espiel* (here, 348, 1.17), *lanche* (348, l. 28), and *glaive* (348, l. 30) are used interchangeably for Eliezar's lance. Elsewhere *espiel* is normally translated as spear and the other two as lance.

by His tender mercy, to keep him from being killed or taken prisoner. The Saxons were hot on his heels, riding as fast as their horses could go, and they followed him long enough that more than ten could strike him on the shoulders and sides. And he turned about and wielded his lance, and he struck the first one he met so hard that he drove the sharp tip, and a great deal of the shaft, into his body, and he hurled him down dead head over heels. Then he pulled his lance out and turned toward another one; he drove the lance through his throat and out the other side, and he knocked him from his horse into the middle of the road.

And the Saxons, more than ten of them, struck him with their lances all at the same time, and they threw him back over his saddlebow, but they did not send him down from his horse, for they broke their lances and the bits flew down to the ground. And the youth sat back up, wielded his lance, and hit one of those who had struck him and drove his lance through his body so hard that he knocked him down dead right before his companions, who were greatly saddened and distraught. But then he broke his lance, which had held up so well, and straightway he took hold of his sword, which hung from his saddlebow, and pulled it out of the scabbard. The Saxons were running upon him from every side, and he struck the first one he came to and cut off his whole right shoulder, and he had split his side open so wide that his liver and lungs let loose and spilled out through the wound, and he stumbled down dead to the ground. Then he struck the next one and sent his head flying with his helmet, [349] and then he ran after the others. He struck the third one crosswise and sliced him more than halfway through and cut his heart in two; next he struck the fourth one on his helmet so that he split him down to the teeth. But the ones who were coming after him hit him so hard that they wounded him, and when he saw that he could not last against so many men without being killed or taken prisoner, he left them; he spurred his horse and rode after Lidonas his squire at breakneck speed. And when the Saxons saw him riding away, the uproar and the shouts rose loud after him.

When the young man caught up with his squire, he rode up behind him and said that he would not take off his gear for as long as he could defend him. He was holding his sword in his right hand. And a Saxon fell upon him with his lance held out straight, and he struck the youth under his arm, twisted the mail of his hauberk, and made him hunch over his saddlebow; he would have brought him down, had he not held onto his horse's neck. And when he had straightened up, he looked at the man who had struck him and then hit him so hard on the helmet with his sword that he split him down to the teeth. Then the Saxons surrounded him on all sides, and he defended himself, because he was of great heart; he began to slay knights and horses and to send to the ground everyone he met. But his defense did him no good against the great crowd of Saxons that was about him, and in as much as Pignoras and Monaquin were on horseback, he could not help but be killed or captured, and he had been worn down by those who were about him. So he rode off at full speed when he could get away, his naked sword in his hand.

And Pignoras and Monaquin, who had not seen any of their men coming back, were on horseback, and they set out after the others at full speed down the road where the youth was going. They saw the dead men, whom the lad had slain, strewn all over the road, and asked who had done that. And the ones who were there answered that it was the young man who had just then come down the road. Then they asked which way he had gone, and they said that he had ridden down into a valley "where our men are fighting him but cannot take him."

And when Pignoras heard that, he shouted to his men, "Now after him fast. It will be a great shame if he gets away, for he has done us great harm."

And when they heard him, they ran down the paved road after the youth. Now may God lead him by His holy mercy, for if they could catch up with him, he would have no way of getting away without being killed. But He who helps in all times of need those who believe in Him, that is, Our Lord Jesus Christ, sent him a most fair adventure. And this is why the proverb says that whom God will help no one can harm.*

Now the story falls silent for a while about him and goes back to speaking about King Lot and his four sons who were with him.

43. AGRAVAIN AND GAHERIET DISCUSS LOVE; THE SAXONS ROUTED.†

In this part the story says that the night when King Lot and his four sons were lodged in the house of Minoras the Forester of Northumberland, they slept like men who that day had undergone great struggles and suffered great hardship, and they rested until the next morning. And when it was daylight, they got up and took their armor, which had been laid out in their room, put it on, and got dressed very quickly. Then they climbed on their horses, which had been brought into the hall for them. [350] The host, his children, and his wife were there, and King Lot and his sons most kindly commended them to God; they thanked them heartily for the good lodging and for the hospitality they had shown them, and they were keen to offer them their service if they should need it. They thanked their hosts and rode out through the gate, and the forester and his four sons got on their horses and rode with them for quite a way, while the five serving boys were ahead of them leading the five palfreys and carrying their shields and lances, for the forester had given them strong, stout lances with gleaming, sharp tips.

And after the forester had ridden with them for a while, King Lot asked him to turn back and not to fail to give his message to King Clarion just as he had promised. And he said that he would indeed do it, and there should be no doubt. So he took his leave forthwith and, with his sons, turned back toward his house. And as soon as they got there, he had two of his sons well fitted out and gave them two swift horses‡ to ride for fear of the Saxons, so that, should they happen to see them, they would be equipped to ride fast if they had to.

---

* This proverb, not mentioned by Cotgrave, is recorded in Morawski, no. 440 (cf. nos. 261, 252, etc).

† Corresponds to Sommer, 349-357.

‡ Despite the translation in Sommer's marginal note, adopted here, the word in the text is *ronchi[n]s* (350, l. 14; Sommer's emendation) "worthless nag," the opposite of the kind of horse described here.

When the two young men were on their horses and ready to go as quickly as they could, the forester said to them, "Dear children, you will go to King Clarion, who is our overlord, and you will tell him that King Lot of Orkney bids him, just as you have heard, meet with him in Arestel in Scotland on Our Lady's Day in September."

And they said that they would indeed deliver this message. So they rode away from the house straightway and set out on their way, and they rode until they came to King Clarion; they found him and his household in one of his strongholds. He was downcast and brooding about the Saxons, who were laying waste his lands and the whole countryside. And when he saw the two youths coming before him to tell him what King Lot was asking him to do, he was gladdened and joyful, and in his happiness he gave each of the youths a good horse, for he loved King Lot with all his heart. And he told them that he would be there without fail, if God kept him from mishap. And as soon as they had heard King Clarion's answer, they went back to their father's house very happy and joyful, and they handed over to him the horses the king had given them for the love of King Lot, to whom he had given shelter.

So now the story falls silent from speaking about them and goes back to speaking about King Lot and his children.

Now the story says that when King Lot and his children had left Minoras the Forester, they rode through the wild forest, which was very deep and high and quite delightful to ride in. The weather was quiet, and there had been much dew the night before. The birds were singing because of the softness of the sweet season, and they sang so sweetly and so forcefully in their language that the leafy woods rang with it; and they very gladly listened to them. And the king and his four sons, who were merry young men, rode along with their minds on the birds' songs. And Gaheriet, who was very much under love's sway, began to sing a new song, and he sang wonderfully well and pleasingly, and the woodlands resounded with it [351] for quite a way. And when the sun had risen, he looked about and saw that his brothers were far behind him, so he turned off the road to let his horse rest.

And he waited until they came, and he said to Guerrehet and Agravain, "Let's sing."

So all three of them began to sing, and after they had sung, Guerrehet asked Agravain and Gaheriet, "Now tell me, by the faith you owe our father King Lot, if you had one of our host's two daughters with you now, what would you do with her?"

And Gaheriet said that Agravain should answer first, for he was his elder.

"God help me," said Agravain, "if I felt like it, I would make love to her right now."*

"God help me," said Gaheriet, "I wouldn't do that, but I'd take her to safety. And you, Guerrehet, what would you do with her?"

---

*   The text reads *sil me seoit iou le feroie tout outreement* (351, ll. 8-9): "if it suited me, I would do it right now."

"I would," he answered, "make her my lady love, if she liked, and I would not do anything to her by force. For the game of love would not be sweet unless it pleased her as much as me."

As they were saying these things, they fell in with King Lot and Sir Gawainet, who had clearly heard everything they said, and they all laughed together and then asked which one had spoken best.

"Ask your brother Gawainet," said King Lot, "for I have chosen him to be the judge."

"And I'll tell you right away," said Sir Gawainet. "Gaheriet spoke best and Agravain worst. For if Agravain saw anyone hurting the women, he ought to help them, protect and defend them with all his strength. It seems to me that there need be no one other than he! Guerrehet spoke better still, for he said that he would not have wanted to do anything to them by force, and that can have come to him only from love and courtliness. But Gaheriet spoke like a worthy gentleman, and I would do what he said if it were up to me."

Then Agravain and King Lot himself laughed and joked about it more than any of the others, but King Lot attacked Agravain with his words when he said, smiling, "What, Agravain? Would you thus shame your host's daughter to satisfy your mad cravings? What a handsome reward you'd be giving him for the service he has done you! He truly put it to bad use."

"Sir," answered Agravain, "the daughters would lose neither life nor limb."

"No," said the king, "but they would lose their honor."

"I know of no man," answered Agravain, "who would spare a woman when he has her alone with him, for if he lets her go free, he will never have her love at any time."

"He should resist temptation," said the king, "for her honor and others' honor more than for himself."

"Truly," said Agravain, "even after he let her go free, he would just be the butt of jokes, and people would esteem him less because of it."

"I would not care a bit what people said to me," answered King Lot, "for as long as my honor was saved, I could not be vilely rebuked for it."

"Then there is no other way out," said Agravain, "than for my brother and me to become monks in a place where we do not see women."

"Ah, Agravain, dear son!" said King Lot. "If you behave as you are saying, you cannot fail to go wrong, and evil will befall you."

And it happened afterwards just as King Lot said, for there came a time when Agravain suffered a long time on this earth for his uncourtly behavior toward a maiden, who was riding with a sweetheart of hers against whom he fought until he wounded him in one of his arms. Then he wanted to lie with his lady love, but he found that one of her thighs was scabby; and he said such ugly, uncourtly things to her about it that she made one of his thighs and one of his arms [352] so that he would never have been healed if it had not been for the two best knights in the world, whom in the end she allowed to heal him, just as the story will recount it to you later—how he was healed by Sir Gawainet, his brother, and by Lancelot of the Lake, who was such a good knight, worthy and bold, and he was the best in the world.

But the story now falls silent from speaking about this until it is the right place for it, and it goes back to King Lot, who went along talking to his sons Gaheriet and Agravain, who were so wicked.

Now the story says that they made their way through the forest until after the hour of prime had passed. Then they left the forest and rode out onto a most beautiful heath that went along the edge of the forest as far as Roestoc. After they had ridden for a long time, they met Lidonas as they were coming down a hill. He was dreadfully afraid for his master, who was fighting in great distress, just as the story has told you. He was riding behind the packhorse that carried the clothing and was leading his master's palfrey; he was shedding hot tears, and he kept saying, "Holy Lady Mary, please help us!" And he kept beating one fist against the other.

King Lot and his four sons caught sight of him and felt deeply sorry for him. Agravain hurried to him as fast as his horse could go, and when he was near the boy he said to him, "Son, tell me why you are wailing so."

And the boy lifted his head and answered, weeping, "Sir, I mourn for a young lord, the most beautiful creature ever made on earth, whom the Saxons have attacked down in this valley. They have killed him by now, unless God looks out for him."

"And where did he mean to go?" asked Agravain.

"Sir," answered Lidonas, "he was going to King Arthur's court to serve Sir Gawainet, who is, we are told, so worthy. And we have heard so much about him that my master wants no one but Sir Gawainet to make him a knight."

Then he went on: "Ah, I am so wretched! I have lost him and will never see him again."

He then began to grieve so deeply that he nearly killed himself. And Agravain asked him where he was from.

"Sir," answered Lidonas, "from the Kingdom of Listenois. He is the son of the rich Fisher King."

And Agravain looked at Sir Gawainet and said to him, "Dear brother, now you hear what worthwhile things await you!"

And he answered that he had heard very well.

Then they tied on their helmets, took up their shields, and climbed on their horses. And Gaheriet said to Agravain, "Keep in mind those maidens you knew so well what to do with this morning and see to it that you are as good a knight with your arms when you fight against those Saxons!"

"Gaheriet," said Agravain, "I entreat you, please spare the Saxons as you did the maidens, for you would not dare attack them or even let anyone see the Saxons, I think."

"Sir," said Gaheriet, "you are my elder, so we'll see how well you fight!"

"God help me," said Agravain, "I would have very little strength, and I'd be quite craven, if I didn't fight better than you! The battle will not be put off because of your cowardice!"

"Sir," said Gaheriet, "it is not in the least courtly to brag about oneself, but when you come into the fray, just fight the best you can."

And when Agravain heard that, he became angry, and he said that he meant to go where Gaheriet [353] would not follow him even if he lost one of his limbs by not going. And Gaheriet began to laugh without getting angry, and he smiled and said, "Go on ahead. You can't go anywhere I won't follow you."

And Gawainet laughed at what they said, for he knew very well that Gaheriet was making fun and joking, and he told Guerrehet and his father the things they had said to each other. And the king said, "Dear son, let's go after them so they won't do anything foolish, for I am sure that Agravain is angry."

And when Lidonas saw them riding away, he asked them who they were, and they answered that they were of King Arthur's household, "and the man you are seeking is here with us."

"Ah, God!" said Lidonas. "Then I won't go any farther until I find out what this is all about."

"No," said the king, "but turn off the main road and ride until you see what happens, and then go to a hiding place in that forest."

And the young man said he would.

While they were speaking, they saw his master* come racing, holding his sword all dripping with blood, with a good two hundred Saxons after him as fast as their horses could run. Many times and very swiftly he turned about to face them, and he would strike anyone he met with such strength that his armor could not protect him; and after he delivered his blow, he started out again on his way. This is how the young man fought with them until he came upon the ones who were heading out to meet him. And when he saw that there were five of them, he shouted aloud, "For God's sake, noble knights, come help me! Take pity on me, for you see how much I need it!"

And Agravain said to him, "Hold on, friend, for you have nothing to worry about."

Then Agravain spurred his horse and wielded his lance with the sharp, cutting tip, and he struck the first man he met so hard that neither shield nor hauberk could keep him from driving the tip of his lance through his body, and he took him dead to the ground. And Gaheriet, who came after him, hit his man so hard that he sent the sharp tip through his shield and hauberk and into his chest and he bore him sprawling to the ground, where he died. He broke his lance then, so he put his hand on his sword straightway and drew it from its scabbard and said to Agravain, "Where are you now, dear brother? Now we'll see how you fight, for I'll strive on behalf of ladies and what is fitting for them, while you seek to do to them what is unseemly!"

Sir Gawainet and Guerrehet burst out laughing at those words, but when King Lot saw them idle and laughing, he said to them, "What are you doing, my sons? Don't you see your brothers in the midst of the enemy?"

When the youth heard that the three knights were brothers and this man's sons, and that he was warning them to behave well, he asked him who he was. And he answered that his name was King Lot of Orkney.

"And those knights," he said, "are my sons. Look there and you'll see the one you seek with the red shield."

And he showed him Sir Gawainet.

---

* The text repeats, somewhat ambiguously, *le vallet* (353, l. 12): "the youth."

When the young man heard what the king told him, he was filled with joy at the news, and he raised his hands to God and thanked Our Lord that he had found them so quickly. Then he said to the king, "Sir, how do you know that I am looking for him?"

"I know for a fact," he answered, "that you are seeking Gawainet. See him there!"

With that, they all charged headlong among the Saxons, and the youth was with them, and they struck down dead the first ones they met, then they spurred on and hit four others, so that they brought them down dead and their lances flew into pieces. Then they set [354] their hands to their swords, and they began to strike right and left. And the youth left the king and the others and rode after Sir Gawainet wherever he went. And Sir Gawainet had drawn Excalibur out of its scabbard, and he began a great slaughter of the Saxons, and there was such killing that all who saw him fled before him and did not dare take a stand against him. And he had gone so far ahead that he did not know what was happening to his father and brothers.

Agravain and Gaheriet* had pursued twenty Saxons until they ran into Pignoras, who had with him about a hundred Saxons. And when Pignoras saw who was giving chase and that there were only two of them, he shouted to his men, and they fell upon them. Agravain and Gaheriet struck two of them so hard that they brought them down dead, but then ten Saxons broke ranks and attacked Agravain so fiercely from all sides that they took him to the ground. Another ten attacked Gaheriet and bore him backwards over his saddlebow, but when his lance was broken, he quickly sat up straight again and flew back into the fray and did wonders on every side. And Agravain, who had fallen, sprang back to his feet with his sword in his right hand and held his shield against his chest. And they attacked him fiercely, but he defended himself as well as anyone could wish, for he had great heart and strength. And Gaheriet spurred his horse to where he saw his brother, and he put himself between him and the Saxons† who were attacking him most fiercely, and he defended himself with such strength that they did not dare get near him, so much did they fear the mighty blows he dealt them. They fought hard like this for quite a long while, for the Saxons yearned to take them prisoner, but they were fighting to stay alive.

King Lot and Guerrehet were fighting very hard elsewhere, and they went through the press looking for their companions. At last they saw Agravain on foot among the Saxons, wielding his naked sword with which he dealt them great blows, and Gaheriet was beside him striving his hardest to free him and get him back on horseback.

Then King Lot and Guerrehet charged headlong among them. The four of them gave them a good battle, and they fought hard against them, but they were worn out from killing and cutting up Saxons. Sir Gawainet fought his way to the top of a hill, holding his sword dripping with blood, and he looked back and saw that he had driven all the way through them, and the youth was still beside him at his spur.

---

*   Here the text reads *guerrehes* (354, l. 7).
†   The text reads *ou il vit ses freres & se met entre eus et les sesnes* (354, ll. 17-18): "where he saw his brothers and he put himself between them and the Saxons."

And he said to him, "Sir, I am following you so that, if my service pleases you, you will make me a knight when I ask you to."

And he answered that he was most welcome and said no more, but he kept him with him. Then he told him to stay close to him so that the Saxons would not wound him or strike him down. "I must," he went on, "look for my father and brothers, for I do not know what has become of them."

And the young man said to him, "Sir, I believe that they are in that crowd, for I see swords raised high and flashing."

Sir Gawainet looked and recognized his father by his helmet.

Then he said to the youth, "That is my father. Follow me."

With that Sir Gawainet spurred his horse on both sides, and he jumped a full eighteen feet, and he and the youth flew into the Saxons more fiercely than they had done before all that day, and they struck down before them as many as they came to. But the young man could not spur his horse fast enough to catch up with him, and he found his path strewn with the dead. [355]

Then the young man said, "Holy Lady Mary, I am afraid that I may lose him among these unbelievers! The man spoke the truth who told me that there wasn't such a knight in the world. Not one word he spoke was a lie, for he is even worthier than he said. The knight is good, and he has just the horse he needs. I truly believe that if he wanted to do his utmost, he could put as many as there are here to rout, for he cannot be taken out of his saddle, however many fall upon him. Now please God, who was born of the Virgin Mary, that the king my father could see him just one time, for I know in truth that he would hold him wondrously dear!"

Still he followed Sir Gawainet as closely as he could. And Sir Gawainet fought his way through until he found his brother Agravain, who was so tired and worn out that he was leaning on his shield holding his bloody sword, but he was so beleaguered that he could scarcely help himself. And they kept dealing him hard, weighty blows with lances and swords whenever they could get near him. He saw that, elsewhere, Guerrehet had been struck on each side from behind by two lances, and he went sprawling to the ground over his horse's neck; somewhere else Gawainet saw that twelve Saxons were holding King Lot his father by his helmet and beating him hard with the hilts of their swords. Gaheriet had thrown his shield to the ground and was holding his sword in both hands, and he was making his blows hurt deeply, for he was striking their shields so hard that he cut off arms, hands, and heads, and he split Saxons down to their teeth; he was fighting so well in his prowess that the Saxons did not dare make a stand against him, but yielded King Lot to him against their will.

And King Lot looked about and saw that it was his son Gaheriet who had rescued him, and he said to him, "Ah, dear son Gaheriet! If we had your brother Gawainet and the others with us, we could not lose any more."

"Where are they?" asked Gaheriet.

"Look, there they are under the feet of our enemies, who will soon kill them if God does not mind them."

With these words Sir Gawainet came storming in, bursting in like a shot from a crossbow, striking and wounding as many as he found before him, thanks to his horse's great strength. He wielded his sword and struck right and left such mighty and unworldly blows that he made the ground shake. And the youth was right there beside him, for he would not leave him, and he dealt many a fair blow with his hands, for which the brothers greatly loved him afterwards. And then, as it happened, Sir Gawainet met Monaquin, who was one of the best knights in the world, and he had ridden down Guerrehet to take him prisoner. And Sir Gawainet struck him so hard with Excalibur as he passed by him that he split him down to his saddle. And when the lad saw that, he crossed himself in wonder, and he blessed the arm that could strike such a blow.

Then Sir Gawainet took Monaquin's horse by the reins and led it to Agravain, and he said to him, "Brother, climb on this horse." And he did so, for he sorely needed a horse, and the youth held the stirrup until he had mounted. Agravain thanked him and told him that he had fought well.

When Pignoras saw that his brother was dead, he was greatly upset He held an axe in both hands, and he rode toward King Lot and struck him so hard [356] on his helmet that he knocked him to the ground; he was not hurt, but was dazed from the blow. Then Pignoras hit Gaheriet and sent him sprawling to the ground. And when Sir Gawainet saw that, he was filled with such sorrow that he nearly went out of his mind. He spurred Gringalet toward him, holding his naked sword, and when Pignoras saw him coming he covered himself with his shield and axe. But Sir Gawainet hit him so hard that he cut right through the handle of the axe, and the blow fell on his shield and across his right shoulder and split him down to the navel; and the youth took his horse and led it to Gaheriet, who climbed on straightway.

And when he had remounted, the young man took the horse Gaheriet's father had fallen from and led it to him by the bridle and had him get on. And when he was back on horseback, he rode against those who had pressed in around him, but the Saxons were so bewildered and frightened because of their two lords who had been killed that they fled and did not even try to defend themselves. And Vandalis, their seneschal, shouted to them, "Ah, you cowards, what are you doing? Avenge your two lords against the scum that have killed them! You can see that there are only six of them and you are four hundred strong! You should be ashamed that they have lasted so long!"

And they turned back against the six. Sir Gawainet went out ahead of the others and met them, for he knew their mettle. He was holding Excalibur, and he struck the first one and killed him, then the second and the third and the fourth. He then struck Vandalis the Seneschal so hard that he sent his head flying. And the youth took his horse and led it to Guerrehet and had him get on. And when the Saxons saw the seneschal slain, they took flight straightway, every man for himself. And the six rode after them, for they hated them above all things, and they killed and struck down as many as they came to.

Sir Gawainet sat on Gringalet, who bore him away swiftly, and he did wonders and slew many, and he stuck right to their heels so that none could get away anywhere, for no matter which way they turned, he was there to head them off. And when they saw that they could not get away, they ran for safety in the depths of the forest, and they rode off here and there, not waiting for friend or companion, and cursed the hour and the day they ever met the six, "for they are not men like any other, but ghosts and devils who have ridden out of hell. There are only six of them, and it has never happened that so few have beaten as many as we were. This is why we can say that they were not sired by mortal men, for no mortal man could do what they have done!"

This is what the Saxons were prone to say, but they were beaten and routed by the prowess of Sir Gawainet. And the survivors who got away did not stop until they had come to the horde before the city of Clarence, and they told King Hargadabran about the great harm the six had done them: "for they killed our two kings and also our seneschal Vandalis."

When Hargadabran heard this he was so upset that he nearly went out of his mind, for the two kings were his first cousins, and he cursed the hour when they ever invaded that land, for much evil had befallen them, and they had suffered great harm. [357]

But here the story now falls silent about the Saxons and speaks about King Lot and his children.

44. Agravain Quarrels with his Brothers; Gawain and Eliezer Rescue a Lady.[*]

In this part the story says that when the Saxons were routed in the Valley of Roestoc, King Lot was most happy, and his sons as well, about the adventure when they rescued the youth. Then they went to the place where they had left the packhorses, which they were to have taken to the siege of Clarence, and they gathered them up and tied them together. And when the horses were all together, they looked at them. Then Gaheriet made a speech that was well heeded: "Ah, dear Lord God, why are there so many poor young noblemen in this country who win nothing? In truth, they lose only out of laziness and cowardice. They ought never lie abed when they should be watching over the borderlands."

"Dear son," said King Lot, "there are indeed many cowards here. If anyone embraces something one time so that good will come to him alone, evil will befall him four times over."

"And then," said Gaheriet to his father, "dear sir, now ask my brother Agravain if he wouldn't long to befoul maidens if he had them here in these woods."

And Agravain gave him a sidelong glance full of great pride and said to him spitefully, "Gaheriet, it hasn't been such a long time since you wanted to boast, but just then that Saxon struck you down with his axe, and if it hadn't been for Sir Gawainet, my brother, you would have been very badly hurt."

"If I fell," answered Gaheriet, "I couldn't help it, but I was not so badly off that I couldn't defend myself against them. You could just as well have kept quiet about that, for I saw you today in such straits that, even if the fairest woman in the world

[*] Corresponds to Sommer, 357-364.

had begged for your love, you couldn't have said one word to her for the whole world. For a five-year-old child could have taken your sword away from you."

When Agravain heard that, he was filled with such wrath that he was a wonder to behold, for Gaheriet had called him a weakling; he turned red with anger and shame, and he stared at him straight on. If there had been only the two of them, they would have started fighting. But King Lot turned the talk to other matters, for he did not want them to quarrel, and he asked what they should do with the packhorses.

And Gaheriet answered, "Sir, ask Agravain."

Then Agravain grew angrier still, and he said that, as God was his helper, he would not take any more. He was holding the shaft of a lance, and he hit Gaheriet on his helmet with it so hard that it flew into pieces. And Gaheriet did not move, but forgave him most kindly. And Agravain recovered and hit and hit again until nothing was left of the shaft but the stub he held in his hand, and neither his brother Guerrehet nor his father could take it from him or stop him from running Gaheriet down when he could get away from them.

Just then Sir Gawainet came back from the pursuit and asked them what was happening. The king told him everything word for word, and when Sir Gawainet heard it, he went straight to Agravain and rebuked him harshly for what he had done. And Agravain swore that he would never forgive Gaheriet for it. When Sir Gawainet heard such wickedness, he told him that he could be sure that if Agravain laid a hand on him again, he would pay for it with life or limb, and he would put down no other wager.

"I will not abide that!" said Agravain. "Even if the worst were to befall me, [358] I would not stop for you!"

"Now we'll see," answered Sir Gawainet, "what you'll do about it."

Then Agravain kicked his horse with his spurs and ran upon Gaheriet with his sword drawn, and he dealt him such a blow on his helmet that fire and sparks flew out. But Gaheriet moved not a bit, whatever he did to him. And when Sir Gawainet saw that, he drew out Excalibur and sped toward him, and he swore on his father's soul that Agravain would be sorry for it. And when his father saw him going, he said to him, "Dear son, go kill that worthless scoundrel for me, for he is too wicked and too full of pride."

But Sir Gawainet knew what he meant. So he came to Agravain and gave him such a blow with the butt of his sword beside his ear that he knocked him from his horse to the ground, and he was so dazed that he did not know where he was. And Gaheriet ran over to him, for he saw how angry Sir Gawainet was, and he said to him, "Dear brother, don't be angry for anything he has done to me."

"Get out of here, you wicked traitor!" said Sir Gawainet "I will never love you if you ever spare him."

"Sir, he is my elder, and I must bear him honor. I was only joking when I said those things to him."

"You stirred all this up, and it was bound to come out badly!"

And Gaheriet answered, "In God's name, dear brother, if I could not play with you or with him, it would be bad if I played with someone I didn't know. But you can be sure," he went on, "that will be the first and the last time I will ever play with you or with him. And if we had not started out on this mission all together, I would go back right now and no longer be in your company."

And Guerrehet said in his turn, "May Agravain be damned if he does not pay you back for the blow he got because of you!"

"As God is my very helper," said Sir Gawainet, "if you or Agravain do anything to Gaheriet you shouldn't, I'll put both of you where you can't see your feet for seven whole months! And I forbid you, as you hold yourselves dear, ever to harm him, so take care!"

"Sir," said Guerrehet, "we will take care, since you command us to, for we would never want to go against your orders, but I am very sorry that you have got stirred up in this on his account and that you have hurt Agravain for nothing."

"It was not for nothing," said Sir Gawainet, "since he attacked Gaheriet against my orders and in spite of me right before our father's eyes. And Gaheriet did not get angry about any of the blows he dealt him. It is a great shame that he is so proud, and his pride will yet bring harm to you and to him."

"God help me," said King Lot to Guerrehet, "for a little I would take all the armor you have away from you and Agravain too, and I would leave you in these fields like worthless dogs."

"Sir," said Guerrehet, "you would not have the strength or the will to do what you say if others were not here."

"Ah, traitorous knave! You are now truly puffed up! Are you his brother? Then be kind to him now. And I order my son Gawainet, if you or Agravain should do anything to Gaheriet, to mete out justice to you as one ought to worthless, shiftless scoundrels."

When the youth saw that Sir Gawainet had struck Agravain to the ground and made his blood spurt out of his nose and mouth, he ran to catch his horse, and he brought it back to him by the reins and helped him get back on. Then Sir Gawainet came to Agravain and said to him, "Worthless good-for-nothing,* flee from here, for I'll have nothing to do with you, [359] and take care that I never see you again! Go wherever else you want, for you won't come any farther with me. And take with you all who love you more than me, and the ones who love me more than you will go with me."

With that, Sir Gawainet and Gaheriet took to the road, but King Lot asked what should be done with the packhorses.

"In God's name," answered Sir Gawainet, "send them to Minoras the Forester, if you'd like, the one who lodged us so well, for he served us handsomely in his house. They would be put to good use there, and it would be better for him to have them than for them to be lost here, for we cannot take them with us, and even if we could, we could still go where we might lose everything."

"Indeed," said King Lot, "you have spoken very well. And who will take them there?"

"Sir," he answered, "that young man's squire and one of our serving boys."

"Let them go with God's blessing," said the king.

---

* The text reads *biaus noiens* (358, l. 43): "dear/fair nothing."

They sent for the youth, and he was found at once. They told him about who the messenger would be and the gift he would give, and that he should then come back after them all the way to Roestoc. The lad's squire said that he would do it. He chose a serving boy to go with him, and they set out with the packhorses; they also took with them forty warhorses tied together by their reins. And they made their way straight to Minoras's stronghold. He was very glad to see them, and he served them as well and as handsomely as could be. And the next morning they took to the road again as soon as they saw daylight to go back after their masters just as they had been ordered.

But now the story falls silent about them and goes back to King Lot and his children.

Now the story says that after King Lot had sent the packhorses to Minoras the Forester, all six of them set out together on the road to Roestoc. They had stopped jibing at one another when they saw how angry Sir Gawainet was getting, and they no longer wanted to carry on with their bickering. King Lot, Sir Gawainet, and Gaheriet were then riding alongside one another, and they asked the youth where he came from and what his name was. And he said that his name was Eliezer, and he was the son of King Pelles of Listenois and nephew of King Alan of the Land Beyond and King Pellinor of the High Wild Forest; King Pellinor had eleven sons, all older than seventeen years of age, and another one, his twelfth, newly come to King Arthur's court to learn to be a knight, and their mother was pregnant with the thirteenth. "These are all my first cousins. And I was going away to King Arthur's court, to Sir Gawainet, to serve him. And thank God, I have found him close by, and he has taken me and will make me a knight when I ask him to."

"And so I grant you, dear sir," said Sir Gawainet, "and you are most welcome."

And they rode thus until nightfall, and they found no dwelling where they might take shelter. The forests were thick and shadowy, and the weather was warm and still. But after it was dark they happened upon a hermitage that was surrounded by moats and brambles. They knocked at the gate and shouted until it was opened to them. They dismounted from their horses, took off their harness and saddles, and gave them green grass, for there was nothing else there. [360] And they ate such food as the holy man gave them, which was bread and water; then they lay down on the green grass, of which they had a great plenty, for there was no other bed or pillow, and they slept quite happily.

But Sir Gawainet and Eliezer did not sleep, but stayed awake, for they were on the lookout for wicked people, of whom there were a great many thereabouts. And after midnight the young men* heard a lady and a knight wailing quite loudly as they went by there. Sir Gawainet heard them and felt deeply sorry for them. He ordered Gringalet to be saddled and bridled, and Eliezer jumped up at once and brought the horse to him all ready. Sir Gawainet took his weapons and very swiftly got on his horse and rode fast after the men who were taking the lady with them. And Eliezer also mounted, for he did not want to miss anything, and they rode until they came to a clearing in a deep valley that went on for a good half league.

* Here the word is *garchon* (360, l. 6), which normally designates boys, serving boys of low station, such as the servants who accompany King Lot and his sons.

Then Sir Gawainet listened and heard most pitiful wailing from time to time, and the lament went this way: "Oh, dear Lord God! What can I do? Have I deserved this hardship and the anguish they are giving me?" And he tenderly prayed God to give him a quick death, for he would rather die than suffer as he was doing.

It was a knight stripped to his breeches, whom five boorish fellows were beating with knotted whips, so that the blood was running down over his body.

Elsewhere Sir Gawainet heard the loud, pitiful screams of a woman, and it was plain that she was in great pain and needed help; and she said aloud, so that Sir Gawainet heard her clearly, "Holy Lady Mary, what is this woeful, wretched woman to do? For you can well kill me before I give in to you!"

When Sir Gawainet heard her voice, he was certain that she was in great need, but he wondered about where to go first, for he was deeply sorry for the highborn man whom he heard moaning so loudly, and he felt deeply for the woman who would be shamed if she did not get help soon. So he thought in his heart that it would be better if he left the knight in his agony than if the young lady were shamed. With that, he kicked his horse with his spurs and rode through the whole valley to where he heard the wailing, and he heard her screaming, "Holy Lady Mary, please help me!"

And when Sir Gawainet heard her voice, he looked under a tree and saw seven loutish oafs, one of whom was holding a young lady down on the ground and hitting her hard on the face with his mailed hand. She was twisting and turning, and she screamed, "You can kill me, but you will have nothing else from me!"

And as she was talking, he dragged her after him by her locks, which were so beautiful that they looked like fine gold. And when Sir Gawainet saw that, he spurred over there and shouted to the man who was holding the maiden, "Sir knight,* let the maiden go!"

And the fellow looked about in the moonlight and shouted to the ones who were with him to go out to meet Gawainet, and they did and asked him, "Sir knight, need we worry about you?"

And Sir Gawainet told them that he could assure them of nothing, "for I have come to help the lady whom that scoundrel is dragging about in such a loathsome way. Beware of me, I defy you all!"

With that, he kicked [361] Gringalet with his spurs and rode through the six whom he had met and came straight to the one who was still holding the young lady by her locks. He struck him so hard on the chest with his lance that he drove the tip through his body and out the other side, and he sent him sprawling dead to the ground. And the six others came toward him with their lances under their arms, and they hit him so hard from behind between his shoulders and on his shield that they sent him hunching over his horse's neck, and the shafts flew into bits. And after the lances had broken, Sir Gawainet sat up straight in his saddle and stood so tall in his stirrups that the iron bent. He drew his sword from its scabbard and struck the first one he came to so hard on his helmet that he sent him down dead. Then he hit the second one on the shoulder and cut it off from his body. Then he struck the

---

* Gawain uses the expression *dant chevaliers* (360, l. 38), where *dant* may be an ironic title of respect. The attackers address Gawain with the same words (360, l. 41).

third one so hard on the head that he sent it flying to the middle of the field. Then he struck the fourth and sliced him down to his teeth. And when the last two saw that their companions were dead and that he had slain one with each stroke, they turned in flight and did not dare make a stand against him. And Sir Gawainet came straight to the young lady and put her on his horse in front of him.

And the two knights who had fled came to their other companions who had dismounted beneath two olive trees to rest, and the latter had lain down on the green grass to sleep. And as soon as they were close to them, they shouted to them in a loud voice, "Noble knights, what are you doing here? A knight has just killed our Sortibran and four of our companions, and he has rescued the lady! Ride after him, for he is taking her away!"

And when they heard this, they were deeply upset, and they climbed on their horses and let them run at full speed after Sir Gawainet, who was taking the lady to safety.

But now the story falls silent for a while from speaking about them and goes back to speaking about the youth whose name was Eliezer.

The story says here that, as soon as Sir Gawainet had turned away to go help the young lady, Eliezer rode straight to where he heard the knight moaning. And when he came there, he saw that six boorish fellows were holding him prisoner, and they had beaten him so much that he could no longer stand up, but had fallen to the ground; he did not have the strength to say a single word, and he was barely holding out. And when Eliezer saw him in such a state, he felt deeply sorry for him.

Then the noble squire shouted out, "Ah, you wanton whoresons! What do you want of that worthy knight you are treating so badly? Has he done you such wrong that you should slaughter him like that?"

When they heard him speaking thus, they looked at him and asked, "What does it mean to you, sir vassal? We wouldn't stop what we're doing for anything you might say."

And when Eliezer heard that, he became very angry and said that they would have no more trouble that day "but from me!"

And he was holding a strong, straight lance with a sharp tip, and he rode at full speed straight for the ones who were holding the knight. He hit one of the six so hard that he struck him down dead, and he pulled a second to himself, hit him, and killed him; then he drew up, let his horse run, and came back at breakneck speed, and when the others saw him coming they gave way and scattered everywhere, but he struck one of them so stoutly in the ribs that he drove iron and wood through him. And when he turned about to face the others, [362] he did not know what had become of them, for they had set out into the thick of the forest to save their skins. It was well after midnight and he could not see far, but when he saw that he had lost them, he made straight for the knight and told him to climb on the horse behind him. And when he heard him, he forgot his anguish and got on behind him in very great distress.

Then Eliezer headed straight to where he thought he would find Sir Gawainet, but he had not gone far before he found him fighting against twenty knights, who were doing their utmost to hurt him. And he had put the young lady under a medlar tree at the edge of the wood. And when Eliezer saw this, he ordered the knight to get off the horse, and he did. And Eliezer took his lance, which was still whole, and he kicked his horse with his spurs and struck the first man he came to, knocked him out of his saddle, and sent him to the ground dead. And then he hit a second on the chest and drove the tip of his lance into him. Meanwhile, Sir Gawainet wielded Excalibur, his good sword, until he had struck down and killed seven of the twenty, not counting the five whom he had slain as he rescued the young lady.

But Eliezer had broken his lance, so he drew his sword, struck the first man he met, and split him down to the teeth. And when Sir Gawainet saw Eliezer helping him, he kicked his horse with his spurs, blessing the time when he had been brought into that country and the body that had sired him, "for he can't fail to be a worthy man if he lives."

With that, he rode to where Eliezer was fighting, and he struck heavy and wonderful blows in his attack, and he killed and wounded all of them but three, who fled into the forest to save themselves. And the night was so dark and the sky so cloudy that they did not know where they had fled.

Then Eliezer took two horses, for he was most worthy and bold in every time of need, and brought them to the knight and the young lady, and he had them get on. But first he had the knight dress in the clothing of one of the dead men, for he had lost his own. Then they put their swords back into their scabbards and set out all together on the road back to the hermitage that Sir Gawainet and Eliezer had left. Sir Gawainet rode alongside the young lady, and he asked her where she was from. And she said that she was the sister of the lady of Roestoc and that the knight was her first cousin.

"And how were you taken prisoner?" asked Sir Gawainet

"Sir," she answered, "last night my cousin and I were coming back from a forest we own near Taningues toward Roestoc. As it happened, our companions had ridden out ahead of us, and we turned down a path we shouldn't have taken, for my cousin and I were so intent on talking about our doings that we became lost and left the right road. And we went into a great woods, where those traitors had stopped to eat, and they fell upon us and took us prisoner; we couldn't hold out against them, for my cousin was not wearing his armor. Even so, he pulled off his horse's bridle and struck one of them on the head with it and killed him, and that is why they were about to beat him to death. And they took hold of him and stripped him, and they beat him until he was almost dead. And [363] when they wanted to rape me, he defended me and did not, for any fear of death, stop dealing them strong and wondrous blows with his fists wherever he could get to them, for he had no other weapons. Then six of the knaves grabbed him and took him away, beating him most dreadfully, as you have seen.

"Now I beg you, tell me who you are and why you have come here."

And Sir Gawainet told her that they were five knights from the kingdom of Logres, "and we are going on a mission that bears more heavily on our honor than we can say."

In this way they talked of these goings-on until they came to the hermitage, where they found their companions still sleeping. They dismounted from their horses, took off their harness, and gave them a great deal of green grass to eat

And they all lay down beside them and slept until morning, when King Lot got up. He called to Guerrehet and Gaheriet, who were beside him, and showed them Sir Gawainet, the maiden, the knight, and Eliezer, who were lying next to the horses; and Sir Gawainet was holding Gringalet with a halter, for he was unsettled around the other horses. And when the brothers saw the maiden lying there, they wondered where she could have come from.

So King Lot called Sir Gawainet and said to him, "Dear son, get up now, for you have slept long enough. See, it is broad daylight."

And the knight woke up; he was so badly wounded that he did not sleep soundly, nor did the young lady, so they sat up. And the king asked them what direction they had come from, and they answered that they did not know, but two worthy gentlemen, whom they prayed God to keep from harm, had brought them there. "One of them rescued this maiden," said the knight, "and the other rescued me: may God make him a worthy man and grant him honor and wealth."

"Which ones are these?" asked King Lot.

And he showed him Sir Gawainet and Eliezer.

When Agravain heard that, he was more distressed than ever, and he could not stop himself from saying that they had kept very bad company, since he had not gone with them.

And Gaheriet answered, for he was quite clever and was glad to poke fun at him, "He did not dare wake us up, because you were brooding about your girlfriend."

And the king asked the maiden how she had been taken prisoner, and she told him word for word how it had happened to them, and she left nothing out.

Then they got on their horses and set out on the road to go to Roestoc, and they did not stop riding from morning until the hour of vespers, and they found nothing all day to bother them or give them trouble until they got to Roestoc. They looked at the town, which was most fair and well laid out in a beautiful place, for all around, on every side, were woods and rivers, and the town's walls sparkled in the sun that shone down on them and seemed to set fire to them. And the town and its castle were wonderfully handsome, and King Lot and his sons esteemed them greatly when they saw them. And when they came to the gate, they found it shut and locked. And the knight who had been rescued called the gatekeeper in a loud voice, and the young lady did too. And the lady of Roestoc was standing on the walls and recognized them, and as soon as she had seen them, she ordered the gate to be opened straightway, and it was, so they rode in without lingering.

And when the maiden saw her sister, [364] she spoke to her privately, and the others did not know about what. But when their talk was over, the lady went out to the knights and welcomed them very joyfully. She had them dismount before the great hall, which was most handsome, and the castellan himself came out to greet them—he was the lady's husband* —and he had their armor taken off. Then they washed their faces and mouths with warm water, and after that they sat on a bed and spoke together of many things while the meal was being made ready. And

---

*   The text reads *sire ... a la damoiselle* (364, l. 4): "the young lady's [i.e., the maiden's] husband"; however, it is her sister who is the *dame de rohestoc* (362, l. 31): "the lady of Roestoc" Below the maiden is in fact referred to the castellan's *serorge* (364, l. 10): "sister-in-law."

when the food was ready, the tablecloths were laid, and they washed and sat down to eat, and they were well served with everything a man likes and needs.

And when it came time after the meal, the lord asked his sister-in-law where she was going and where she had come from in such a state, and she told him her whole adventure just as it had happened. And when the lord heard it, he was most gladdened and began to celebrate as he had never done before. And King Lot asked whom the castle belonged to, and the lord answered that it was a fief from King Arthur. Then the castellan asked him who he was, and he answered that his name was Lot, that he was king of Orkney, and that those four knights were his sons. And then the castellan jumped up and greeted him most joyfully, and he asked him what they were seeking. And the king answered that they were riding in search of adventures and truces with the princes and barons on behalf of King Arthur, so that at last the Saxons might be driven from the land. And when the castellan heard this, he gave thanks to Our Lord.

"And where will you go first?" he asked.

And the king said that he would like to be in Arestel in Scotland; then he said that he would be most grateful if the host would please send a messenger to the King of the Hundred Knights and tell him on his behalf to be in Arestel in Scotland on Our Lady's Day in September and not to miss it, for all the princes were to be there. And the castellan answered that he would send word to him no later than the next morning. "And I am very sure," the castellan went on, "that he is in the city of Malehaut."

That evening King Lot and the castellan of Roestoc spoke at length until the hour to go to bed. And Sir Gawainet did not want to make himself known that evening to anyone, because he was bent on seeking adventures in secret so that no one would know who he was wherever he went. And when it was time to go to bed, they went to sleep and took their ease for the whole night until the next day. And when it was daylight, they got themselves ready and took leave of the castellan, the lady, the maiden who had been rescued, and the knights from there, who rode along with them for a long way, then turned back to Roestoc.

And when the castellan saw that they had left, he chose a messenger and sent him to the King of the Hundred Knights on behalf of King Lot of Orkney, and the messenger delivered his message as he had been ordered to say it And the King of the Hundred Knights was filled with great joy for love of King Lot, whom he loved with his whole heart, and for love as well of the messenger, who was a good knight, and he gave him a strong, swift horse, as befitted a worthy gentleman.

But now the story falls silent about the King of the Hundred Knights and speaks of King Lot and his children. [365]

45. The Saxons Again Routed; The Rebellious Princes Agree to a Truce.*

Now the story says that after King Lot had left the castle of Roestoc, he headed straight to Cambenic by way of Leverserp, where he took shelter for one night, and afterwards he took to the road and made his way until he came to within two leagues of Cambenic. There he heard such loud screaming and shouting that he thought the whole countryside must have caught fire, and it was no wonder that there was a great uproar and that the people were frightened, for all around there ten thousand Saxons had taken plunder and stripped the land, and they were taking away a great crowd of prisoners. Duke Escant had ridden out of the city with three thousand men and fought for quite a long time, but in the end he was routed and driven from the field, and he was so upset that he nearly went mad. So the uproar and screaming were so loud that it was a wonder to hear: all were bewailing their losses and the harm done to them, all of which had been overwhelming that day.

When King Lot and his sons drew nearer to those people, they tied on their helmets, got down from their palfreys, and climbed on their great warhorses, with their helmets on tight and their shields about their necks, and they rode straight to the bridge where the fighting was—and it had been very heavy, but as they came in, the forces were beginning to withdraw toward the city. And Duke Escant was at the rear, going about stopping the withdrawal and defending his men most wonderfully; he tried hard and did his utmost, for he dreaded that he might lose his city in this attack. And King Lot, who was deeply sorry and most upset at seeing the duke and his men in such dire straits, drove forward and crossed the bridge to join with the duke, and his four sons were following him lustily. He went all the way across without being recognized, as did his sons, and he and his sons rode hunched down, their shields on their arms, holding their lances midway up the shaft,† their feet set in their stirrups. They spurred their horses to a full gallop, for they could hardly wait to take on the Saxons. And when the duke saw them coming, he stopped short, for he did not know who they were, and he said, as befitted a man beleaguered and at his wits' end: "Oh, dear Lord God, please show me what to do, for I am at a loss if You do not give me true guidance. What is worse, we have lost all the belongings we had left."

Then he looked at the five knights he saw coming and did not recognize them, for their shields were all chipped from the blows they had taken (if it had not been for that, he would indeed have known it was King Lot), but as they drew nearer he saw clearly that they were not from that country; still, he went straight to them and said, for he was very well raised, "Dear sirs, you are most welcome, wherever you mean to go. It seems to me that you are knights errant."

"Sir," said King Lot, "we wish to be in Arestel in Scotland."

"In truth," said the duke, "you have a hard way to go, for between here and there is a most treacherous pass. But if you would like to stay with us in this land, we

---

*   Corresponds to Sommer, 365-374.
†   That is, not fixed in the holders ready to attack.

would be most glad. You could go nowhere better for profit, for the Saxons have been fighting us for a few days."

"Sir," said King Lot, "how far can it be to Arestel?" [366]

"Sir," he answered, "it's a full two days."

"Who are you, sir," asked King Lot, "that you ask us to stay?"

"Sir," he answered, "that will not be hidden from you. I am the duke of Cambenic and lord of this land for as long as it pleases God. But those faithless people challenge me for it day in and day out, and just now I have ridden out against them. They are ruthless and proud, as you can see."

While the king and the duke were talking together, the duke looked and saw his men coming in flight and the Saxons after them riding hot on their heels.

And when King Lot saw them coming so, he said to the duke, "Sir, since we have happened upon you, and since you have invited us to stay, we will help you from now on with all our might."

"Many thanks, dear sir," said the duke.

And then Gaheriet said to Sir Gawainet, "Let's go out against them, for it is high time—here they come!"

At once the duke's men picked up new helmets, for theirs were all bashed in, and after they had put them on their heads and fastened them well with silk laces, they turned back toward the ones who were fleeing. And when these men saw the duke, their lord, coming, they stopped and made a stand, for they had great faith in him because he was a good and stalwart knight. And when the Saxons saw them stop, they ran upon them because they believed that they could take them and hold them prisoner. And Sir Gawainet, who saw them coming in broken ranks, went out against them, and he struck the first one he met so that he drove his lance through his body and knocked him down dead to the ground. And when Gaheriet saw his brother fighting the Saxons, he said that he would hold himself a coward if right then he did not do the same. Then he kicked his horse with his spurs and wielded his lance with a sharp tip, and he hit the first one he came to so hard that he drove through his shield and hauberk, and the tip of his lance and part of the shaft showed through his side; he was dead, and he sent him down sprawling. And the lance broke, because it could not bear the great weight, so he put his hand to his sword and set out after Sir Gawainet, in the tracks he made, and he did such wonders in his fighting that all who saw him were amazed. He hit no man whom he did not kill or cut down with his horse, and Sir Gawainet esteemed him greatly and praised him in his heart. He had never seen him fight so skillfully anywhere, and he was struck with wonder; he was glad in his heart, and he wondered at how he could stand up under so much fighting.

Elsewhere King Lot and Guerrehet were in the fray, and each one had struck down a Saxon so hard that he could only be dead. And when their lances had broken, they drew their swords and began wondrous fighting such as no one had ever seen even five knights do. And when the duke saw it, he went after them and began to fight as boldly, both to keep them near him and to behave as he ought in the undertaking, and he saw them fight so well before he left them that he was awestruck that any earthly man could give and take so much.

But when it was after midday, Sir Gawainet did all the wonders in the world. He was astride Gringalet, a horse that was so good and so handsome that he did not have to seek one fairer anywhere, and he who sat on it was wonderfully worthy [367] and quick. He held Excalibur in his hand all bare, and he cut up helmets, shields, knights, horses, and everything else he went after. He drove into the ranks roaring like a thunderstorm, and he left, slaughtering everything, as if it had been agreed to beforehand. And he was so furious, as the hour of tierce drew near, that nothing could stand against him. And it truly seemed that, when he raised his sword high to strike, it fell like a lightning bolt, so fast did it come down, for it sounded like thunder. And when the Saxons caught sight of him, they said, "Look at that devil that has just now come from hell. Let someone go tell Moydas, Brandalis, Oriance, and Dodalis!"* (Those four kings were the chief leaders of the army.)

When the four kings heard the wonders that the six companions were doing, they asked where they were. And the ones who had seen them pointed out the end of the bridge to them, just at the bank. At once the four kings bestirred themselves and came straight to where Sir Gawainet was, and he was doing the greatest wonders ever done by one man alone. Duke Escant had come to them with as many of his three thousand men as he could, and they were a good two thousand seven hundred strong. They had been dreadfully beaten, but King Lot and his sons joined them and quickly saved them from being taken by more than eight thousand men. These were led by Ydonas, a very proud Saxon who had inflicted great damage on Duke Escant's men with his army; nevertheless, the Christians drove them from the field and ran after them as far as the four kings, who were coming to help them.

And as soon as the four kings began fighting the Christians, the battle was very heavy and the damage fearful, for the Christians were only three thousand strong, but there were a good sixteen thousand Saxons who did with them as they pleased, despite the Christians' efforts.

And they would have been utterly routed if it had not been for the six knights, for they would not yield their ground. There Sir Gawainet did all the wonders any earthly man could do, and Gaheriet followed so close behind him that he could not get away from him, but had him at his side all day long, so that Sir Gawainet wondered in awe how he could stand up under so much, and he loved him in his heart all the more for it. Never was there another day all the rest of his life when he loved any of his brothers more, for they were all such good knights that none better could be found at that time.

The battle was very hard and the fighting deadly in the meadowlands of Cambenic, at the head of the Severn bridge, with two thousand seven hundred Christians against sixteen thousand Saxons, but the Christians would not have lasted long had it not been for the five knights from the kingdom of Logres, and Duke Escant of Cambenic fought very skillfully too, for he was a good and stalwart knight As they were striving to break the press and drive through, Dodalis, Moydas, Oriance, and Brandalis came, their shields about their necks, their lances in their hands, riding

---

*   The list appears as *a boydas & a mandalis & a oriance & a dorilas* (367, l. 11). Sommer notes other forms in the Harley manuscript: *moydas, brandalus, orientes, dodalis* (367, n. 1). In fact, forms closer to the latter occur later in Sommer's text (367, l. 39), and it is these that are adapted here when they differ from the ones given by Sommer.

swift, freshly-watered horses. They met Duke Escant in the ranks; he had fought boldly all day, and had undergone so much that he had to be tired and worn out, and indeed he was, for he had undergone such hardship all day long that it was a wonder how [368] he could keep sitting on horseback. As it happened, Moydas and Brandalis met him together, and they both hit him so hard on his shield that they sent him sprawling against his horse's neck, and Oriance and Dodalis struck his horse through the sides with their lances and killed it out from under him, and he and the horse fell to the ground in a heap. When the duke was on the ground, they stopped atop him, wielding their naked swords, and they were about to slay him right then, when his household knights came spurring to help him, while the Saxons came in from the other side to hinder his rescue. There the brawling came together from both sides, and many men were wounded, and the duke was in great agony, because his horse had fallen over on top of him. There were so many Saxons that the duke's men did not have the strength to get him back up, yet his enemies did not have the might to take him.

Even so, there were so many Saxons that the Christians could not withstand them, but they had to withdraw, like it or not, and the Saxons had indeed succeeded in taking the duke prisoner, and they led him away, beating him, despite all the Christians. When King Lot and his sons came spurring, wielding their bare swords, they came upon a great crowd of men taking him away. There many blows were given and taken, but if it had not been for Sir Gawainet's prowess, they could not have lasted, for he was out ahead of them all, and he held Excalibur bare in his right hand, and he struck to the right and left, and he slaughtered so many men and horses that all who saw him fled, and he did not stop breaking through the press until he came to Duke Escant, whom the Saxons were taking away. There the battle was harsh and the fighting ruthless, and Agravain and Guerrehet were struck down from their horses, and Sir Gawainet and Gaheriet did not realize it, for they were bent only on saving the duke from those taking him away; they did their utmost and at last rescued him and put him back on horseback.

When King Lot, who was fighting elsewhere, saw his two sons on the ground beneath the horses' hooves and in danger of losing their lives, he saw that he did not have the strength to rescue them or get them away from those who were attacking them. So he shouted in a loud voice, "Gawainet, dear son, where have you gone? Now your brother Agravain is on the ground and in very great trouble, and he will soon be killed if he does not get help!"

And when Sir Gawainet heard his father's voice, he turned his horse's head at once to that side, and he broke through the press with Excalibur, his good sword that no armor could withstand if hit in a deft stroke. He had not gone far when he found Agravain and Guerrehet on foot in the midst of the throng, defending themselves mightily, and King Lot was beside them, striving hard to defend them and get them away. And when Sir Gawainet saw their great distress, he threw to the ground what shield he had left and took Excalibur in both hands, and he charged into the press so hard that everyone who saw him thought it a wonder. He hit Moydas, whom he met first, on his helmet and split him open to the shoulders. With the second blow he dealt he cut off Brandalis's right arm and sent it flying into the middle of the field with his shield. And when the Saxon felt that he had been wounded, he turned

about and fled, [369] screaming and roaring like a bull. Gaheriet had hurled his
shield to the ground and was fighting with his sword in both hands, and he struck
Oriance on his helmet and knocked off a fourth of it, and the sword glanced off
and fell between his body and his shield, so that it cut the straps that held it on and
sent it flying out into the field, while the sword went down into his right thigh so
deeply that it cut entirely through it, and he fell down backwards. And Gaheriet
took his horse by the bridle and took it to Guerrehet, his brother, and he helped him
get on. Then he turned and hit a Saxon who was wearing wonderful armor, and he
struck him so hard that he sent his head flying; and he took his horse and led it to
Agravain, saying, "Climb up, dear brother." And he did so, for he had great need
of a horse.

And then they charged into the fray and drew toward where their father and Sir
Gawainet were, and Agravain, who burned with wrath against Dodalis, struck him
so hard that he sent his head flying.

When the Saxons saw that their noble men had been killed, they turned in flight
at once, for they had lost their leaders; they did not stop before they came to
Ydonas's banner, and the Christians rode after them that far without letting up. But
Sir Gawainet was out ahead of all the others with two hundred knights from the
household of the duke of Cambenic who were all bent on serving Sir Gawainet.
Eliezer was right beside him, and he was holding a cudgel covered with iron spikes,
and he saved his master from everything he needed to be saved from.

In that chase Duke Escant was knocked from his horse, for a Saxon had hit him
hard from behind, and he was badly hurt in the fall. King Lot, who was riding
on the right side with his son Guerrehet, saw that blow, and he was deeply sorry
about it. He was holding a strong, thick lance that he had taken from a Saxon, so
he spurred his horse and hit the Saxon who had struck Duke Escant down; he hit
him so hard on his side that he drove through his liver and lung, and he bore him
sprawling to the ground. Then he took his horse by its reins and gave it to the duke,
who got on and thanked him most dearly for the service he had done him.

And Sir Gawainet and Eliezer, who were hot on the Saxons' heels elsewhere,
pursued them* until they saw the banner of Ydonas. There the Saxons stopped and
made a stand for a while. And Sir Gawainet ran after them and rushed in among
them, wielding his sword, and he began to strike and cut down as many as he came
to. And when Ydonas saw him, he turned that way, and Sir Gawainet struck him so
hard on his helmet with Excalibur that he sliced him all the way down, so that his
liver and lungs could be clearly seen and recognized for what they were; and just
as soon as the Saxon had thus been laid open, he fell with his banner. And when
Duke Escant saw the banner falling down, he was sure that they had been routed.
Then in a loud voice he yelled his battlecry and gathered his men about him, and
he quickly fell upon the Saxons.

When the Saxons saw that their banner had fallen and that their enemies were
coming against them so fast, they did not dare stand against them, but yielded
the field and turned in flight, leaving all of their equipment. They did not wait for
one another, but fled over the flatlands disheartened and defeated. And the uproar

---

*   The text has the singular *le* for *les* (369, l. 29): "him" for "them."

rose so loud and the [370] dust so high that it was a wonder to hear and see. And the Christians ran after them and slaughtered so many it was astonishing. But Sir Gawainet was ahead of all those giving chase, for he was riding Gringalet and none could run with him, and Sir Gawainet killed so many Saxons in that pursuit that he was dripping with blood, as though he had been dragged through a river of blood, and his horse was too.

King Lot turned back, and so did all the others except Sir Gawainet and Eliezer, his squire, and this is why no one knew a word about what had become of them. But they had run after the Saxons until, with their sheer strength, they drove them into the ford of the river Severn, and there they cut down so many that the water ran red. And when they saw that those who were left had gone across to the other side, they turned back and rode at a slow gait. Duke Escant had stopped at the booty, which he had his men take back. And Sir Gawainet went by him and said nothing to him, but when King Lot saw him coming, he was wondrously glad to see him. He asked him how he had fought.

He answered, "Badly," since some had got away and he was coming back a coward for not daring to cross the ford the enemy had gone through. But King Lot said that that would not have been easy for a man to do by himself.

The duke of Cambenic heard what Sir Gawainet had said, and he told him that he had fought very boldly, for he and his companions had brought the battle to an end. But Sir Gawainet went right away and did not say a word to him. Yet, it was plain to see from his armor that he had not been sitting down all day, so King Lot asked him where he had left his shield. He said that the Saxons had cut it all to bits, and he needed to look for another one; and the duke said that he would have a good, strong one given to him, and he answered, "Many thanks, sir."

Then the duke went over to King Lot, because he had called him "my son" during the battle, and he entreated him most kindly to tell him his name. He answered that his name would be hidden from no one, and he would not hide it from him. So he said to him, "You ought to know me well, for we have been through much bad and much good together."

And he told him that he was King Lot of Orkney, and "those four knights," he went on, "are my sons."

And when the duke heard him, he told him that he was most welcome. "God help me," he went on, "for not recognizing you before, and blessed be God for bringing you here. For we would all have been killed and our land laid waste if it hadn't been for you. And you indeed speak the truth when you say that we have been through much bad and much good together."

And he asked him, "Sir, will you swear by God that these four knights are your sons?"

And he said that they truly were.

"God help me," said the duke, "they are very worthy men and good knights, and today they have showed it well indeed!"

So the six of them went on talking as far as the city of Cambenic. And they went straight to the high hall and dismounted from their horses. And Eliezer did his utmost to serve Sir Gawainet; he stabled Gringalet and helped Sir Gawainet and King Lot take off their armor. And while they were disarming, they saw Eliezer's squire coming and the serving boys who had taken the gift to Minoras the Forester. They greeted King Lot on behalf of Minoras, his wife, and all their children. Then Gaheriet looked at Agravain and burst out laughing, and he asked Lidonas how Minoras's daughters were doing. He answered that they sent them all their greetings, [371] and Gaheriet said that they were right to, "if they knew what my brother Agravain has in mind."

Sir Gawainet and Guerrehet laughed heartily at these words, but Agravain himself flushed and grew hot, although he did not say anything, because he knew that Gaheriet was joking. So they laughed and played until the meal was ready, when they sat down and ate and drank as much as they wished to. No one need ask if they were well served, for the duke and all the people there did their utmost.

After eating, the duke asked King Lot his children's names. And the king answered that the eldest was called Gawainet, the second Agravain, the third Guerrehet, and the fourth Gaheriet.

"And this handsome young man who is so worthy and gifted and well built in body and limb, who is he?"

And King Lot answered that he in no way belonged to him, but he was a king's son and a most noble man, "and in his high nobility he has come to serve Gawainet in order to learn to bear arms like a knight."

"God help me," said Duke Escant, "he has the heart of a highborn, well-bred man, and he bears himself like a noble gentleman. God grant him a better life, for he is worthy and bold, and he cannot fail to achieve the greatest prowess if he lives so long."

Then the duke asked the king what mission was taking him so fast to Arestel.

And the king answered, "You are well aware that the Saxons have overrun this land and have laid it waste and stripped it. For two years they have not stopped plundering our land, so, it seems to me, it would be of great profit to the country and to the whole land if we got together to decide how they can be driven out. You can see that they are four times stronger than we are, so I have called King Clarion of Northumberland and the King of a Hundred Knights for talks at Arestel, and King Arthur himself will be there on the Day of the Feast of Our Lady in September, and you and all the other noble worthies will be there. We will make a truce, and each will swear to assemble as mighty a force as he can, and all will gather on the appointed day, and then together we will go fight the Saxons."

And the duke responded that it was the greatest good that had ever been wrought; it would be good to make peace between King Arthur and the princes of the land, for it would be a hard thing to unseat him, since the people and the clergy had chosen him, "and we could not henceforth wage a war against him. So it would be good," the duke went on, "if peace were made between you and him."

"In truth, sir," said the king, "I know of no one who has made peace with him who has not also made peace with me."

"What?" said the duke. "Have you then come to terms with him?"

"Yes, without the slightest doubt," answered King Lot.

Then he told him how peace had been made, and he told him all his mistakes, just as they had been, and how his children had forsaken him. And King Lot and the duke talked together until at last the duke swore that he would be at Arestel on the appointed day, and he said that if peace failed to be made it would not be because of him. With that, they went to bed to rest, for they were tired and worn out from the hard fighting they had taken part in. And when morning came, the king got up to hear Mass at daybreak, and his sons and Duke Escant did likewise, and they heard Mass in a church. And when it had been sung, King Lot came to the duke and said to him, [372] "Sir, it would be a good thing if you chose four messengers, one to go to King Yder of Cornwall, the second to King Urien, the third to King Aguisant, and the fourth to King Neutres of Garlot And they should tell them on your behalf to be in Arestel on the Feast of Our Lady in September. And then send others* to King Tradelmant of North Wales, to his brother King Belinant, to King Caradoc, and to King Brandegorre, and have them tell them to be at the talks at Arestel on the appointed day."

And the duke said that it would be well taken care of. So they sent out the messengers, and they made their ways until they came to the princes, and they gave their messages just as they had been ordered to. And the princes got ready to travel as soon as they heard the order.

But with that the story falls silent now about all of them, and it goes back to King Lot and his children.

Here the story says that as soon as the messengers had left Cambenic to take their messages to the princes, King Lot and his sons set out on their way to Arestel. And Duke Escant rode a long way with them, and he gave to each one a painted shield just as they were used to carrying, weapons, and fresh, new helmets. And after the duke had ridden with them for quite a way, he turned back and got his baggage ready so that he could follow King Lot.

And King Lot and his sons kept to the road straight to North Wales, a city that belonged to King Tradelmant. And in the city they found the king, who was happy and pleased that they had come, for he loved King Lot very much. And he asked him where he was headed, and King Lot told him about the whole undertaking.

"A messenger coming on behalf of the duke of Cambenic told me the same thing," said King Tradelmant. "And I'll be there," he went on, "God willing, and if God grants me life and health."

And King Lot was filled with great happiness and joy.

That day he and his sons were most lavishly served. And the next morning, as soon as it was daylight, they set out on their way and rode until they came to Arestel in Scotland, where they stayed four days before any of the princes came. And they had quite a good life there for as long as they stayed. And they awaited the princes until King Clarion came, and he was the first to get there; he was one of the highest-born men in the world and a good knight. And King Lot was very happy when he came, and he was glad to greet him and Sir Gawainet and his brothers, for he had never seen them.

The next morning came the King of the Hundred Knights, because of whom everyone grew more joyful still. And afterwards came King Tradelmant of North Wales, then came his brother King Belinant, then came King Caradoc of

---

* The text reads *.j.* (372, l. 4): "one." But the plural is clearly intended, as the text substantiates in *& lor dient* (372, l. 6): "and have them tell them."

Estrangorre, then came King Urien and King Aguisant of Scotland, then came King Yder of Cornwall, then King Neutres of Garlot, and then came King Brandegorre and the Lord of the Narrow Borderland.

And when they had all gathered, King Lot began to speak to them, and he said that the next day he would tell them why they had gathered there. It was the eve of Our Lady's Day in September, and the kings were most glad to see one another; then they rested that night. The next morning the princes gathered along with Sir Gawainet and his three brothers, and after they had come together and sat down on a lush silken cloth that had been spread out on the green grass, [373] Sir Gawainet spoke to them on the orders of his father, King Lot, and he said to them, "Dear lords, we have come here to speak to you on behalf of my lord King Arthur, whose men we are. And my lord the king sends you word and beseeches you to make a truce with him, in faith and by oath, for safe conduct for him and for yourselves until Christmas, so that you may come and go freely where he holds sway and he may do likewise in your lands—and this in order, should it happen to please you, that we may all go together to fight the Saxons, who have overrun this land, until we have driven them out. And should God grant that they are defeated, then make a lasting peace among yourselves, if such can ever be. Forgiveness is granted to all who will join the battle against the Saxons, and they will be free from all sins just as they were on the day they were born."

When the princes heard the plea that Sir Gawainet brought before them, they asked King Lot straightway what his mind was, and he said that it would be the greatest good that had ever been said or done, "and you can indeed be sure that I do not say this just because I am his sworn liegeman, but rather because whenever you have been against him evil has befallen you. Those people, so it seems to me, would never have invaded this land if we had come to terms beforehand. I tell you, this has happened to us because of our sins."

"What?" said King Urien. "Have you then sworn fealty to him? You have not acted lawfully, and I'll tell you why. If for any reason we should happen to move against him or he against us after we drove the Saxons out, we would have to fight against you, and that would not be fitting."

"Yes, that is indeed the truth," said King Lot "And you may be sure," he went on, "that whoever wages war against him fights against me."

"By my faith," said King Urien, "that would not be lawful, for you are our sworn ally, and you could not forsake us."

"Sir," said King Lot, "I did it against my will and in spite of myself. I'll tell you for a fact that the day I thought I could harm him the most and hurt him the worst, I swore fealty to him. Gawainet, whom you see here, made me do it all."

And then he told them how it had happened to him, and not one word of it was a lie. And when the other princes heard it, they said that it could not be otherwise, since that is what had been done, and he should not be blamed, and there were some there, and many of the best, who would have given anything to have had that happen to them. And they spoke of many things, until at last they agreed to make the truce, and they swore to keep it on the hand of Sir Gawainet. And he set the day when they should do all within their power to gather on the Plain of Salisbury with as many men as they could find, but they all said openly that after the Saxons had been beaten, King Arthur should beware of them. And Sir Gawainet told them that, when the day came that they might want to harm him, they should agree to have no alliance or wish to do so, for anyone who threatened him might yet have his arms bound and his neck weighted down.

When the princes heard Sir Gawainet's speech, some smiled at it and others wagged their heads. But the King of the Hundred Knights, who was not given to boast or threaten others, said that he would be [374] on the Plain of Salisbury on All Saints' Day, if God kept him from death, and the others all said the same. And King Lot said that he would not move out until he had brought all of his forces together. Then they all took leave of one another and left at once, and each one went into his own country, and their lands were* absolved by the papal legate. They showed themselves in public and gathered as many men as they could, and they sent for their kinsmen and friends, and throughout all Christendom they spread the news about the pardon that would come from it. And those who had gathered their men the most quickly went straight to the Plain of Salisbury, and they took shelter in tents and pavilions, and in that way they waited for the others. And the story says that footsoldiers and crossbowmen came there both from the other side of King Clamadeu's land and from the land of King Aguigneron, a rich baron from the land of Sorelois, and King Brandegorre came there, and there were great armies from the land of King Lot of Orkney the Great, from the land of King Alan, from the land of Pellinor of Listenois, and from the land of the Duke of the Rocky Crags.

So now the story falls silent for a while about them and goes back to speaking about King Arthur and his wife, Queen Guenevere.

46. MERLIN VISITS BLAISE; THE QUEEN'S KNIGHTS BATTLE KNIGHTS OF THE ROUND TABLE.[†]

Now the story says that King Arthur led a most happy life with Queen Guenevere his wife after King Lot and his sons had left them. And King Lot sent word to King Arthur that the truce had been granted, and King Arthur was very happy, as were all the companions of the Round Table, the Queen's Knights, and the two brother kings. The next morning after the news had come, Sagremor, Galescalain, and Dodinel the Wildman got up very early, put on all their best armor, and went to romp in the forest, which was wide and deep. The evening before, they had decided to go play, and when they had come into the woods, they were delighted, for they heard the birds' songs, and then they said for the sport of it that they would go looking through the forest and countryside to see if they could find some adventure for which they might be esteemed and loved and praised.

---

* The text bears the singular: *& lor terre fu absause* (374, ll. 4-5): "and their land was absolved". Sommer suggests *la* ("the") for *lor* ("their"), but the Harley variant supports the adopted reading.

† Corresponds to Sommer, 374-383.

Meanwhile, three companions of the Round Table had left King Arthur's court, and they had taken armor that was not theirs, for they did not wish to be recognized, for they yearned to find any of the Queen's Knights to test themselves against them. One of these three knights was Agravadain, the brother of Belias, the Red Knight of Estremores who afterwards often waged war against King Arthur; the second was Moneval and the third Minoras the Wicked. All of them were good knights, and all of their armor was of the best. And when they were in the open fields, they let their horses run against one another without hitting. Then Minoras said to his companions, "Let's go wander through this forest to see if we can find adventure."

And his companions agreed and said that, some time before, they had heard it said that the forest was full of adventure, so at once they set out for the Forest of the Thornbush, for it offered greater adventure than all the others. They all three went straight into the forest and rode until they found three roadways that split them up, for each one went off by himself [375] as adventure led him.

So the story falls silent for a while about them and speaks awhile about Merlin.

Here the story says that at the time when Merlin left King Arthur at Carhaix in Carmelide, he went straight to Northumberland, to Blaise his master, who greeted him most joyfully when he saw him, for it had been a long time since he had seen him, and furthermore, he greatly loved to be with him. After Merlin had been there for a very long while, he told him how King Arthur had wed his wife, how she was to have been stolen from him, how Ulfin and Bretel had rescued her, how the false Guenevere and Bertelay, who killed the knight, had been banished, about the tournament the knights fought before Carhaix, how King Arthur had sent Sir Gawainet his cousin to Logres to call his court together, how King Lot tried to steal his wife from him, how Sir Gawainet came to help her and took his father and held him, how the knights tourneyed with one another and the wonders that Sir Gawainet did there, how King Ban advised King Arthur not to allow the companions to tilt together any longer, the advice to send messengers to the princes and what happened to King Lot and his sons along their way, how the princes had gathered at Arestel, and how the truce was made in order to fight the Saxons. And Blaise put it all down in writing in his book and left nothing out, and this is how we still know about it. And then Blaise asked him if there could be enough men to fight against the Saxons, and Merlin said not before the ones from Little Brittany had come or those from the kingdom of Logres and from Lambal, which had belonged to King Amant and which Gosengos had under his sway:

"And as soon as I leave here I'll go get the men of King Ban and King Bors in the two kingdoms, and I'll take them there. And you should know," he went on, "that people will come there from many lands to save their souls and to defend Holy Christendom. And there is not the slightest doubt that we greatly need Our Lord to help us in this fight, for never has there been such a battle as there will be, and the Saxons cannot be driven from this land before the princes have all made peace with King Arthur."

And Blaise told him that it seemed certain to him that King Arthur loved a lady, and the prophecy that had been foretold of her was about to be fulfilled. And so he entreated him most kindly and said:

"Merlin, dear friend, I beg you for God's sake to tell me who is to father the Lion of the Two Messengers and when that will be."

And Merlin told him that the time was very near when that would happen. Blaise said that it would be a very great shame, "and if I knew the place, I would gladly do my utmost to get him away from there."

Merlin said to him, "Write down for me what I tell you, and then you'll know how much help you can bring."

And he wrote it down, and this is what the story was:

This is the beginning. It is the story of the adventures in the country whereby the wondrous Lion, whom the son of a king and queen will hold, was taken prisoner. He must be chaste and the best knight in the world." [376]

And the things that Blaise wrote down Merlin scattered along the roads where the others were, and these things could not be brought about except by the ones who would fulfill them, and this is why the knights were all the more willing to ride out. And this was the only way the Great Lion would ever be destroyed.

Blaise said, "What? Can't I do anything else to help?"

And Merlin said no.

"Will I live long enough to know about it?" asked Blaise.

And Merlin answered, "Dear friend, don't worry. Yes, and you'll see many other wonders after that one."

Then Merlin had Blaise write down such things as he told him, and he took them where he wanted, then he went to Little Brittany. But before that, he most tenderly commended Blaise to God.

When he took leave, it was no later in the day than the hour of prime, and he came to Little Brittany on the hour of nones. And there he found the Lord of Payerne and Pharian, who greeted him very joyfully, and they took him in with them most courteously and had a good time for four full days. And when the fifth day came, they asked Merlin why he had come, "for we are certain that it was not for nothing."

And he told them that they had to cross the sea with as many men from the land as they could engage by oath.*

"Sir," said Leonce, "what place shall we go to?"

And Merlin answered, "To La Rochelle-in-the-Tidewater.† And from there to the Plain of Salisbury, where you will find men of many languages who'll have come for the same undertaking as you. And you will encamp to one side with your men, and do not move until you see me back there. Take care to make a white banner with a red cross and nothing more, and all the princes who come there will have the same. None of them will know a word about why they'll have done this, and yet it will have a great meaning."

And Leonce and Pharian said that it would be done as he said.

---

* The verb is *arembre* (376, l. 16), which Sommer apparently finds baffling (cf. n. 1). Perhaps it is to be connected with *aramir*. "to commit by oath, to swear an oath," etc.

† Sommer's text reads *a la roche flodemer* (376, l. 17), to which he compares the lesson in the Harley manuscript, which is adopted: *a la rochelle au flot de mer* (n. 2), the version approved by West (263, under "Roche Flodemer, la"). Elsewhere La Rochelle is taken to be a port in Brittany used for communication with Great Britain (256, ll. 13, 38; 281, l. 22).

"Now take care to take the most men you can with you," said Merlin, "for you should know that there will be a great many against us."

"And who'll keep this land?" asked Leonce.

"Don't worry about that," answered Merlin. "Leave behind here Lambegue, Pharian's nephew, and Banin, son of Gratian of Trebe, and the Lord of the High Wall.* You lead the armies of your two kingdoms and Gratian will lead the army of Orkney. The seneschal Alelme of Benoic will be with you, and Pharian and Dionas will lead the men from Gaul, but you must be careful not to give up leading the ones whom you'll have engaged to serve you."

And Leonce said that it would all be done just as he had said.

With that, Merlin commended them to God and entreated them to go quickly, for they could not linger.

"And I am leaving," he said.

"Sir," said Leonce, "Go then, for I would not beseech you to stay, for you know better than I what is needed."

Then Merlin went away, and he came to Viviane, his lady love, who greeted him most joyfully when she saw him. And his love for her grew and became stronger, so that he found it hard to leave her, so he taught her a great deal of what he knew.

But then he did go away to the kingdom of Lambal, which had been the land of King Amant, whose head King Bors cut off. And he told Gosengos not to fail for any reason to be, along with all his men, on the Plain of Salisbury at the Feast of [377] All Saints, and he said that he would be there without fail. Afterwards, Merlin went straight to the kingdom of Carmelide and delivered his message on behalf of King Arthur to the barons of the land, and they said that they would go very gladly; and they mustered some twenty thousand men who were bold† and skilled at fighting. And Leonce, Pharian, Gratian, and Dyonas fulfilled their mission so well that they gathered in little time forty thousand men in the flatlands below Gaunes, and when it was time to move out, the companions took to the road and made their way over land and sea until they came to the Plain of Salisbury. And when they had all got there, they found the twelve princes who had already come with as many men as they could gather, and each one had his army about him.

And Nabunal, who had been King Amant's seneschal, called his men together, and he entreated King Amant's sons to go with him, and they did so. They were most handsome young squires. And one of them had been in love with Queen Guenevere and would gladly have taken her as his wife if he had been a knight, but the fact that there had been warfare between their two fathers took her away from him. Queen Guenevere had always wanted him more than any other for as long as she was a maiden; they still very much longed to see each other, and they sent each other love messages.

When the youth came to Nabunal, who guarded the kingdom, he told him how King Arthur wanted to fight the Saxons. "And he sends me word," Nabunal went on, "to bring him all who can bear arms, big or small, and I would very much like to know whether you would be willing to come."

---

*   The variant here is *de la haute more* (376, l. 28): "of the High Heath."

†   Sommer inserts *[boin]* before *vassal* (377, l. 4), turning the adjective "courageous, bold" into the nominal expression "good vassals."

And he answered that he would indeed go. Nabunal was very happy about that and told him that he would come there with as many men as he could find, and he gathered them until he had twenty thousand. And they took to the road and made their way until they came to the Plain of Salisbury.

And Merlin came to King Bademagu as soon as he had left Nabunal, and he told him to send to the army as many men as he could, and King Bademagu sent word and called his men together, and he had at least twenty thousand. And they took to the road and made their way until the came to the Plain of Salisbury.

With that, Merlin went away, taking leave of King Bademagu, and came straight to Logres the very same day that the six knights went riding in the Forest of Adventures* to seek adventures.

When Merlin came to court, he found King Ban, King Bors, King Arthur, and the queen leaning out the windows of the great hall. They were watching the meadowlands and the three knights who had set out into the forest; these were the companions of the Round Table about whom the story has spoken before, but the barons did not know anything about them until Merlin happened upon them. And as soon as they saw him, they came straight to him and greeted him most joyfully. And after they had celebrated for a time, they sat down and spoke together of many things. Then Merlin came to King Arthur and told him to send for as many men as he had the power to summon, for there was no time to waste, and he should know for a fact that King Lot had fared very well, for people from various foreign parts were riding and coming together on foot from different countries to gather on the Plain of Salisbury. He asked what people were coming, and Merlin answered that King Lot was riding there as fast as he could. [378]

"You would be well advised," Merlin went on, "to accept the truce. And do you know what people are coming on your behalf? You have the men of King Ban of Benoic and those of King Bors of Gaunes, and they are a good forty thousand strong."

And when King Ban and King Bors heard that, they sprang to their feet and asked how that could be. Merlin answered at once that he had taken the message to them, "and they believed me, for which I am thankful."

And the two brothers said that he had done very well indeed and that nothing could have made them happier. Then Merlin resumed what he had been telling the king:

"Sir," he said to King Arthur, "do you know who is coming this way? Nabunal of Tharmandaise† is coming from the kingdom of King Amant, whom King Bors, who is here, killed in battle, and a young man who is his son and not yet a knight. And all the might of Carmelide is coming, and it is led by Cleodalis the Seneschal, but King Leodagan is not coming. I have achieved all this for you, so I should have my reward for it."

And the king said to him, "Merlin, I don't know what to offer you, but I make you lord of myself and my land, which I hold because of you."

---

* Here the text reads *forest auenturese* (377, ll. 30-31). Earlier it is called *la forest de lespine* (374, l. 38): "the Forest of the Thornbush," which was characterized as *auentureuse* (ll. 38-39).

† Here *camadaise* (378, ll. 9-10), but the reference is clearly to the character identified earlier as being from Tharmandaise.

"Sir," said Merlin, "when I happened in on you, what were you looking at so keenly over in the meadowlands?"

"We were watching three knights whom we had seen go into that forest."

"Don't you know who they are?" asked Merlin.

"No," said the king.

"You should know for a fact that they are knights of the Round Table who are very worthy and bold, but they are unwise, thoughtless, and envious, and I tell you truly that they have never needed help as badly as they will before they come back, and it will all be because of their madness."

"Merlin," said the king, "tell me who they are, if you will."

And Merlin said to him, "Sir, one is Agravadain of the Vales of Galore, the second Moneval, and the third Minoras the Wicked.* And I tell you that they won't have gone far before they find three of the Queen's Knights, with whom they will fight Please send someone after them, if you believe me, for there is no one to break up the fight. Men will be killed, and it will be a great shame."

"Ah, God!" said the king. "And who will go keep them apart?"

"Sir," said the queen, "Sir Yvain, Kay the Seneschal, and Girflet."

"Sir," said Merlin, "the queen has spoken very well. Send them out right away."

He did so. And Merlin told them where they would find them. But they did not come in time to keep blows from being dealt.

But now the story falls silent for a while about them, and we will tell you about the six knights and how they fared.

Here the story says that the three Queen's Knights made their way through the forest until they found a most beautiful heath, where they dismounted and rested. And Galescalain said to his companions, "Would to God that Sir Gawainet and his brothers had come here; if they were here, we would go see the Saxons."

And Dodinel the Wildman said that it would be a bad thing to go there because they would not find shelter in the forest, and their horses would starve to death.

While they were talking, the companions of the Round Table came upon them. Their arms were disguised, for they wanted very much to be pursued by Queen Guenevere's knights. And Sagremor asked his companions whether they knew who the others were, [379] and they said they did not. And they drew nearer all the while. Then Agravadain said to his companions, "I see over there three companions who would make me very sorry if they took their horses with them when they left."

"Yes, indeed," said Moneval. "There are only three of them, the same as we are."

While they were talking, the other three knights tied on their helmets, which they had taken off their heads to get some air. And they got on their horses, and they wanted to ride away to show that they meant no harm, since no one had asked anything of them. And when the companions of the Round Table saw them going, they shouted to them in loud voices, "You must joust or you will hand your horses over to us and then be free to go."

---

*   Sommer's manuscript reads *sienandes laigre* (378, l. 24 and n. 4): "Sienandes the Rough" (in his text Soramer corrected *laigre* to *lengres*); but elsewhere he is named *minoras* (374, l. 55) and *minoras li engres* (374, l. 33).

And when Sagremor heard them, he turned his horse's head and said, "What? Are you then robbers who make your living this way? You should know for a fact that when you go home tonight, you will have little to eat from the winnings you take from us, for we challenge you."

Just then the companions of the Round Table kicked their horses with their spurs so hard that their blood spattered down their sides, and they put their lances under their arms and their shields before their chests. And when Sagremor and his companions saw them, they did likewise and rode out to meet them.

As it happened, Sagremor and Agravadain hit each other on their shields with their lances so hard that they drove right through, and their hauberks split, and the links broke on their left sides. And Agravadain felt the iron of Sagremor's lance so deep in him that his blood gushed out in a great stream, and he broke his lance on Sagremor's hauberk. Sagremor had much heart and strength, and he thrust him so hard that he bore him and his horse to the ground in a heap. But Agravadain, who was quite skilled, nimble, and full of great boldness, sprang to his feet very fast, and he drew his sword from its scabbard and got ready to defend himself. And after Sagremor had made his pass, he came back a little way, jumped down, and tied his horse to his lance, but Agravadain's horse had fled into the woods at a gallop. And Sagremor put his shield on his arm, drew his sword out of its scabbard, and ran in great strides toward Agravadain, who was coming at him very strongly, and they dealt each other powerful, measured blows on their helmets wherever they could reach.

And the battering lasted for quite a long while, when Sagremor said to him, "Sir knight, you are dead if you do not surrender alive."

And Agravadain answered that he had not yet come to that Sagremor told him that he would, a great deal sooner than he thought. Agravadain said that he was not very frightened of him, and he asked him whether he was good at making threats. And Sagremor told him that it had been a threat made to a fool, "and this is why, even today, the proverb says that the fool is not afraid until he is slapped,* and this is just what has happened to you."

Then he ran upon him and they fought for a very long time, but Agravadain had the worst of it in the battle, for he was wounded dreadfully.

Elsewhere, Galescalain and Minoras came back, spurring toward each other, holding out their lances under their arms. As it happened, Minoras broke his lance on [380] Galescalain's shield, while Galescalain struck him with such strength under the bottom of his shield that he drove his lance through his thigh, so that the tip could be seen out the other side of his horse's flank, and both of them fell to the ground. Minoras's horse flew into them with all four hooves and dashed away, but Galescalain was quick to get to his feet, and Minoras got up as well. They drew their swords from their scabbards, and the two of them started to fight and dealt each other hard, dreadful blows with all their might.

---

* Agravadain's question is *manechieres est il moult boins* (379, ll. 34-35): "Is he a good threatener?" It is an implied reference to the idea in the proverb *Tel menace qui a grant poor* (Morawski, 2363): "The one who threatens is very much afraid." Sagremor replies with another proverb, *fols ne crient deuant quil prent la colee* (379, ll. 36-37): "The fool is not afraid until he takes the slap." The latter is recorded by Morawski (788) as *Fous ne crient devant qu'il prent.*

Elsewhere, Dodinel and Moneval let their horses run at each other, and they struck each other so hard with their sharp-tipped lances that their shields were driven through and splintered and the lance's tips stopped against their hauberks, but in such a way that the mail was not broken, for they were wondrously strong and tough, and there was no way to keep both of their lances from breaking. But as they passed by each other, Dodinel thrust against him with his body and his shield so hard that he knocked him sprawling to the ground; but Moneval was quickly back on his feet, for he was swift and nimble. And when Dodinel had finished his pass and come back with his sword drawn, he saw that he was all ready to defend himself: he then drew his sword and thrust his shield over his head, and the hard fighting began.

That is how the six knights fought very hard from the hour of prime until after midday, and the Queen's Knights began to take ground from the knights of the Round Table, and the Queen's Knights could do with them as they wished. And when they saw that the knights of the Round Table were flagging, they shouted to them, "Surrender!" But they answered that they would rather die. And when the Queen's Knights heard this—for they could not get another word out of them—and when Sagremor saw that they would not yield, they ran upon them very swiftly.

Sagremor* struck Agravadain on his helmet so hard that he split it in two as well as his coif, and he drove his sword into his scalp and wounded him dreadfully. And he was so dazed that he flew sprawling to the ground, but he did not stay there for long; he sprang to his feet, for he was very much afraid of taking another blow, and he covered his head as best he could. And Dodinel dealt Moneval a blow with his sword and hit him so hard on the arm holding his shield that the shield fell to the ground. And Galescalain struck Minoras on his helmet and knocked him to the ground head over heels so ruthlessly that blood spurted from his nose and mouth, and as he staggered to get back up Galescalain hit him with the hilt of his sword and sent him sprawling. Then he jumped at once onto his body and tore his coif from his head, and he threatened to cut his head off if he did not admit that he was beaten; but he said that he would not do it, and Galescalain answered that he would die without redemption.

While they were thus going on, there came Sir Yvain, Kay the Seneschal, and Girflet son of Doon, whom King Arthur had sent, but they had taken too much time. For Sagremor had so beaten Agravadain that he was all bathed in blood and was in great agony, and he staggered back and forth from one place to another. And Sagremor set out after him at once, for he wanted to land a sound blow. And Dodinel had so thrashed his man that he no longer had a shield about his neck or a helmet on his head, and it was all he could do to keep from dying. And Galescalain had drubbed Minoras so badly that he was holding him to the ground by his visor with one hand and had his sword raised in the other, [381] and Minoras would not have lasted for long, and all three of them would have met their end, had Sir Yvain

---

*   Sommer's text, apparently somewhat garbled, reads *Et quant il oent ce & que autre cose nen trairont si lor courent sus. & quant saigremor voit ce quil ne se uoelent rendre si lor courent sus mout uistement & feri* (380, ll. 21-23): "And when they hear this and that they will not drag anything else out of them, they run upon them. And when Sagremor sees that they do not want to surrender, they run upon them, and he struck. ..."

not come there riding very fast. And he shouted in a loud voice, "Enough, enough! I am coming to stand as their pledge. Please hand them over to me and those two other gentlemen who have come here, for we will guarantee whatever you ask of them."

And Sagremor turned toward them, looked at them, and knew at once who they were, so he answered Sir Yvain: "Very gladly, sir, and I would do more for you than this amounts to."

Galescalain and Dodinel said the same thing, and they handed them over at once. And they rode over to the Queen's Knights, got down from their horses, and began to rebuke them quite harshly for having begun such foolishness. And Sagremor answered straightway, "What, Sir Yvain? Did we do such wrong when we saved our horses from these three ruffians who meant to take them away from us? In God's name, we would have suffered worse shame if they had taken them by force without our defending them, and we would never again have had honor wherever we might have gone. Anyone who does not defend what is his own would badly defend what belongs to his companion."

"Ah, sir," said Sir Yvain. "They did not do it out of wickedness, for they meant it only as a game." "A game?" said Galescalain. "And so did we." And Sagremor began to smile behind his helmet, for he recognized from what Sir Yvain was saying that they were companions of the Round Table.

And Dodinel said, "Blessed be the game and the man who began it, for that way we can learn!"

"Leave these matters where they are," said Sir Yvain, "and let's get on our horses and go back, for there is no man so strong and mighty that he won't be fighting soon."

With that, the knights mounted, but three of them were very sad and downcast. Then Sagremor asked Sir Yvain who those three were.

"What?" said Sir Yvain. "Don't you know them? Then there could have been greater harm. You ought to know," he went on, "that the one you were fighting against is Agravadain of the Vales of Galore, a companion of the Round Table."

But Sagremor answered that he did not know him, but since things had happened as they did, "I can't do anything about it."

"Now let it lie," said Kay the Seneschal. "For the knights of the Round Table will go out one more time to avenge Forré!"*

Then they all began to laugh, except for the three who were wounded, but doubtless they did not feel like laughing, for they were ashamed and downcast from what had happened to them.

So they took to the road and rode together two by two until they came to the court at Logres. The three knights of the Round Table went to their lodgings to take off their armor, for all they needed was rest. And the other six went to court, and they found the three kings and the queen, who were still at the windows of the great hall, and Merlin along with them, and they spoke of many things because they had not seen him for a long time. Then the six knights went to take off their armor in a

---

* West notes (119b) that the expression was proverbial in Old French for making an empty boast. Forré is a pagan king mentioned in *chansons de geste*.

room, and when they had done so, Sir Yvain came to the king. And as soon as the queen had seen him, she said, "Sir, tell us your news."

"Lady," said Sir Yvain, "there is a great deal to say about it."

Then he began to tell them how he had found the six knights fighting. And the king asked him which ones had the worst of it, and he told them [382] about their ride back and the joking, and they laughed a great deal; but soon they stopped talking about it, because the king was upset. And Merlin came forward and said to them, "Do you know why there is strife between the knights of the Round Table and the Queen's Knights?"

"Not at all," answered the king.

"You should know," said Merlin, "that their jealousy has done that, and they want to test their prowess against one another."

And they asked Merlin which one could be the best knight among the Queen's Knights. (King Arthur had said that they belonged to the queen, for the Round Table was mainly his business.) Then King Ban said that he could indeed name the best, for it was Sir Gawainet, and the others said that he was right. And the king said that he would make him one of the companions of the Round Table just as soon as he came back, but Merlin said that it would not be before the Saxons had been driven from the country. So they stopped talking about it and went to eat. And as soon as they had eaten, the king chose his messengers and sent them throughout his land, and he called for all who were his men and could bear arms to come as if their lives depended upon it, and meet him in the Plain of Salisbury; they should not waste time or lag behind, but take to the road and hurry there.

Just as you have heard, King Arthur sent his messengers throughout his land, and as soon as they had left, King Arthur took King Ban, his brother King Bors, and Merlin aside, and said to them, "Let us go see our companions who are ill."

And they went to see them, along with many other knights. And when they heard that the king was coming, they wanted to get up to greet him, but the king did not let them. And he rebuked them harshly for the foolishness all three of them had done, but they answered that they could not resist it, and they did not know where the urge came from. Then the king gave them physicians to tend to their wounds, and one of the physicians told the king not to worry, for within a week's time he would bring them back to health, so that they could surely ride and bear arms. Then the king commended them to God and told them to follow him to the Plain of Salisbury as soon as they were healed, "for I am going there," he went on, "and there will be a great gathering of men."

With that, the king left them and commended them to God, and they went straight to the hall and found many knights who wanted to hold a tournament with the Queen's Knights, because Sir Gawainet was not there and they wished to avenge their companions. But the queen forbade them to and said that it would do them no good to speak of it, for never would they tilt against one another. "And I entreat you by the faith you owe to my husband the king and to me never to speak of it."

And they said that they would not ever speak of it, since that was her wish.

And when the hour of vespers came, King Arthur told everyone who would bear arms to get ready to go on foot and on horseback, for he wanted to ride out early the next morning for the Plain of Salisbury, where the common folk were to gather.

And as soon as the king had given his order, they went to work and made ready as best they could. And then there was such noise and such an uproar in the town that it could be heard half a league away. In the morning King Arthur set out with [383] King Ban, King Bors, the queen, and all who had come and gathered there, and they rode five whole days before they came to the Plain of Salisbury, for they did it in short stages. And after they had come there and encamped beneath the laurel trees, Kay the Seneschal brought out the great ensign with the red cross against a field that was whiter than snow, with the dragon under the cross, just as Merlin had ordered it. And when King Arthur was encamped, he was most glad and began to celebrate, and so did all who were with him. And there he awaited the princes and men who were coming from all parts.

Renown, who runs and flies everywhere, went out through the countryside until the Saxons at the siege of Clarence found out from the spies they had scattered about the country that men from all over the land were gathering in the Plain of Salisbury, but they did not know where they would be riding to get there. And Hargadabran sent for his nineteen kings, and they came to him. He told them that their spies had reported that the Christians had called for a gathering in the Plain of Salisbury, and he asked them what advice they had to give him. And they answered that the best thing would be to set up watches, so that they would not be surprised in their sleep, for in daylight they did not have to worry about any men in the land: "There are too many of us, and they could not hold out against us, but just the same, we advise our men to stay at the ready, and they should not go out foraging with fewer than thirty thousand men-at-arms with them, lest they meet someone who might harm them. But, as you well know, this land is not so big and wide that they have even a fourth of our strength."

In the end, they agreed that it behooved them to meet their enemy if they had to, so they parted company, and the nineteen kings went back to their lands to get ready. They ordered everyone under their sway, wherever they might be, to be armed and on the lookout at all times. And they sent word of this to the siege of Vambieres, which they made their men lift, and they all came back to the siege of Clarence. Their gathering was huge and fearsome, and their army stretched out from where the siege of the city was being mounted for five full leagues, and the encampments were spread out on all sides.

But now the story falls silent here from speaking about the Saxons and goes back to speaking about how the princes came to the Plain of Salisbury, one after the other.

47. Eliezer Knighted by Gawain; Further Battles Against the Saxons.[*]

Here the story says that, after the talks, the princes hurried to come to the Plain of Salisbury by the day that had been set, and they were equipped as befitted the wealthy, powerful men they were. The very first man and prince who came there was Duke Escant of Cambenic, and he had with him seven thousand men-at-arms who were lavishly equipped with all kinds of armor; they encamped in rich tents and pavilions squeezed tightly against one another. After him came King Tradelmant of North Wales with twelve thousand men wearing white hauberks with finely-linked mail, green helmets studded with gems, and strong, sturdy shields, and they encamped next to the Duke of Cambenic. [384] After him came the King of the Hundred Knights with ten thousand men in good armor and riding good horses, and they set up their encampment. Afterwards came King Clarion of Northumberland, who was a most handsome knight, worthy and smart, and he had eight thousand well-equipped men with him, and he led them beneath a banner white as snow with a red cross—such a banner everyone who came there had. After him came King Belinant, who was King Tradelmant's brother, with ten thousand men wearing iron armor, and he was most eager to see Dodinel the Wildman, his son whom he loved as much as any man's heart could love another, and he encamped behind King Clarion. After him came King Caradoc of Estrangorre, who was a companion of the Round Table from the time it was founded, but he never wanted to sit at the Round Table after the strife had broken out between the princes and King Arthur; he brought ten thousand men, and when he had come to the Plain of Salisbury, he encamped next to King Belinant, who was a most worthy gentleman. And King Arthur had not yet come, but there was no more room left to encamp.

After King Caradoc came King Brandegorre, whose holdings bordered on the land of Estrangorre, and he had with him ten thousand men wearing iron armor, and he encamped beside King Caradoc; he longed to see one of his wife's nephews who was in King Arthur's household, because he had heard much praise of his handsome looks and his worthiness, and his name was Sagremor of Constantinople. After King Brandegorre came Minoras, the seneschal of King Lac of Great India (whom King Lac had sent solely for love of Our Lord in order to have the pardon the bishop had granted), and he brought seven thousand mean wearing armor and riding good, worthy horses. After him came the seneschal of King Pellinor of the Land Laid Waste; he brought seven thousand men-at-arms whom King Pellinor sent for love of Jesus Christ. Afterwards came the seneschal of King Alan of the Land Beyond, who was King Pellinor's brother. Afterwards came Galehaut, son of the Fair Giantess, who was lord of the Distant Isles, and he brought with him ten thousand worthy and brave men-at-arms, and he came purely for love of Jesus Christ. After him came Anguingeron, a wonderful knight, and he was seneschal of King Clamadeus of the Isles; he brought with him six thousand knights, and he encamped next to Galehaut.

[*]   Corresponds to Sommer, 385-395.

Afterwards came King Cleolas, who was later called the King First Conquered, with seven thousand men riding very costly horses; he encamped next to Anguingeron, but he did not stay long, for he fell ill and returned home, and he entrusted his men to Guionce the Seneschal, who was a most worthy man and a good knight. Afterwards came Duke Belias of Doves, who came there for love of God; he brought seven thousand men and encamped next to Guionce. Afterwards came the seneschal of Sorelois, solely for love of God, with six thousand men wearing armor, and his name was [385] Margondes; the king of Sorelois sent him there, and he encamped next to Duke Belias.

And then came King Arthur, who encamped among the others. And Merlin came to him and said to him in private, "Sir, now see what Our Lord has done to safeguard you and your people! You ought to praise God to the heavens for this and heartily thank Him for bringing you such help in your time of need."

"Merlin," said the king, "you should know in truth that Our Lord does not forget His sinner, nor has He shown me up to now that He meant to forget me. And in His mercy He will yet do greater things for me than He has done, for I have great trust in Him, and I have such faith in Him and believe in Him so completely that I put myself utterly in His mercy and under His command, and I pray Him to watch over me in His holy pity and in His endless mercy."

"The trusting belief you have in Our Lord," said Merlin, strengthens you, has strengthened you, and will yet strengthen you—have no fears about that. And I advise you never to slacken in that resolve. For as long as you are steadfast in Our Lord and believe in Him, you will have victory over the enemies of Our Lord."

"Merlin," said the king, "may God never let me stray from His trust, but keep it so that at the end I may yield my soul to Him."

"May it be, sir, as you would have it," said Merlin. "But now you must look to what you can do to bring to bear the great nobility gathered here in defending Holy Church and driving the wicked people out of your land."

"Merlin," said King Arthur, "I will strive to do what you advise in everything, for without you I could undertake nothing. So I put myself in God's hands and in yours."

"Sir," said Merlin, "if you would like joyfully to greet the nobility gathered here to defend Holy Church and to do them honor, please go to their tents to see each one by himself, and thank them for the help that they have brought you, even those who hold no land from you and are not your liegemen. For the king has not yet been born who ever brought together such a fair company with so many worthy gentlemen and good knights, nor will there ever be such in this place until the day when the son slays the father and the father the son—that will be in this same place, and on that day the land of Great Britain will be left without its lords and without an heir."*

When King Arthur heard Merlin's words, he begged him and entreated him most kindly to tell him more plainly a part of these things. But Merlin said to him that it was not up to him to tell him, "but I will tell you this much: that after this day will

---

* A reference, obviously, to the deaths of Arthur and Mordred at each other's hand; see the end of the *Death of Arthur*.

come the uncrowned lion, and he will bring with him three lions, of whom two will be crowned. And these three will devour the wicked lineage of Logres. Don't ask any more of me," Merlin went on, "but let us go to the barons just as I told you."

"Very gladly," said the king.

With that, King Arthur got on his horse and took with him King Ban of Benoic, King Bors his brother, Sagremor of Constantinople, Kay the Seneschal, Yvain the Tall, son of King Urien, Guerrehet, Gaheriet, and Merlin; and these nine went straight to the barons in their tents. And when they learned that the king was coming, they went outside their tents to meet him. And King Arthur and his companions got down from their horses and the king greeted them all, for he was very well spoken, [386] and he thanked them for having come to help him in his need against the Saxons, "who through their pride and wickedness have stripped my land and despoiled it, and they mean to destroy Holy Christendom."

"Sir," said the barons, "God willing, they'll not have the forces or the strength, for we have gathered here to defend Holy Church and to help you, and we are willing to put our very lives in jeopardy to uphold our holy religion, and, before we leave you, we will strive, if it please God, until Holy Church has the victory and the Saxons are shamed and hurt. And we want you to know that we are not your liegemen and we have never held anything from you, but we have come solely for love of Jesus Christ and to defend Holy Church and defeat the Saxons."

"May God show you His thanks," said King Arthur, "in whose honor you do it, and may He grant that you go back to your lands safe and sound, which He truly has the might to do."

"May it be as you say," said the barons, "and as you would have it."

"May it truly be so," said Merlin.

So the story falls silent right here about King Arthur, Merlin, and the barons from far away who came to lend help, and we will tell you about the twelve princes who had come together to King Lot's tent.

In this part the story says that when the twelve princes had all come to the Plains of Salisbury, all twelve of them went to thank the foreign princes who had come to defend the land from the unbelievers for love of Jesus. And after they had done that, they gathered at King Lot's tent and sat down on a bed that was covered with a green silk cloth, and they talked for a long time about many things. And while they were sitting thus, Merlin came inside, and when they saw him coming, they jumped up to greet him, and they told him that he was most welcome. And he answered with the wish that God might grant them a happy outcome to their ventures and have them do what they needed for their souls' salvation and their bodies' well-being, so that through them Holy Christendom might be upheld and safeguarded from the hands of their enemies who by force had overrun her.

"It would never be we who failed," said the barons, "for we have come here to defend Holy Church."

"By my faith," said Merlin, "the harm they have done is very great, but it so happens that, friends and strangers, you have gathered here for a single quarrel, and it is right and reasonable that you might bring a great war to an end, but only if you are of one mind and one will, for otherwise you could not succeed. And it would be a good thing if you made peace with my lord King Arthur, who ought to be your overlord, and you would be all the more feared for it."

At those words King Lot of Orkney sprang up and said, "My lords, in truth Merlin has spoken very well, for it would turn out to be for the greater honor of God and the world at this time, and I have never believed that any one of you could achieve such honor as this would be if you did not reconcile with King Arthur straightway."

King Urien was greatly upset by this speech, and he sprang to his feet filled with dreadful wrath, and he said to the king, sweating with spitefulness, "What the devil is this? Didn't you have us come here under a truce [387] until we have destroyed the Saxons and driven them out of the land? And only then, if it was our pleasure and an honorable thing for us, would we do what our hearts might incline us to do. And now you want to talk about something else and put us on other paths! Now I ask you and beg you not to speak about it any more. As for me, I will do nothing about it I don't know what the others will do, but if they did otherwise, I would say that they had forsworn themselves against me."

"In God's name," said King Neutres, "I would take a false oath, for I would never make peace unless you ordered me to."

And the others said the same thing.

Then King Lot grew very angry, but it was best for him to take it in silence, so he kept his mouth shut and did not talk any more about it at that time. And Merlin began to smile and said to them, "Dear lords, do not get upset, for anger would not be a good thing right now."

While they were listening to these words, King Arthur, King Ban, King Bors, and the foreign princes with them came in and found the twelve princes in King Lot's tent. And as soon as King Lot saw them, he sprang to his feet and said, "Look! here comes my lord the king!"

And when the princes heard that, they stood up to greet him with honor and reverence, because he was a king. And King Arthur, who was most courtly and quite clever, knew very well what to do, and he greeted them before they had all risen and said that such companions were very welcome indeed. And they answered all together with the wish that God might grant him and all who were with him a good outcome to their ventures. Then they took hold of him on every side and had him sit down on King Lot's bed, and he had them all sit down, for he was the most courtly man in the world and the best bred.

Then he said to them, "Dear lords, you have come here, and I am most grateful to you for it, just as I have asked you, for the benefit of Holy Church and to defend the people and safeguard our lands against the wicked Saxons, who have already set a great part of those lands ablaze and killed and wounded our men. And because you have come here at my bidding, I thank you all together. And it would be good if we got ourselves ready, so that the Saxons could not say among themselves that they found us to be childish or cowardly."

"Sir," said King Lot, "getting us equipped and ready should be left to Merlin. He'll give the orders and we'll do what he says, for he knows better than we what we must do."

And the princes said that they would indeed agree to that, so they put the whole thing on Merlin's shoulders; with that they had no more to say about it, and King Arthur went back to his tent. The princes, friends and strangers alike, went with him, and then each one went back to his own pavilion. And King Ban, King Bors, Merlin, and Sir Gawainet went straight to King Arthur's room in his pavilion, and then Merlin said to them in private, "Dear lords, these men who have come here are tired and worn out from traveling, for some of them have come a very long way, and they need to rest and sleep; that is why I want them to rest for the rest of today and tomorrow. And Monday morning, with God's blessing, we'll take to the road straight to Clarence, where the Saxons are laying siege. And I'll let all the princes know that they are to get ready to ride out on that day to fall [388] upon their enemies.

The three kings, and Sir Gawainet along with them, agreed to that plan, and they said that it should be done for the honor of Jesus Christ and His sweet Mother. With that, they left the council and went at once to the chief pavilion. Then Eliezer, Sir Gawainet's squire and the son of King Pelles, came straight before Sir Gawainet, knelt down, and said, "Sir, I left Listenois and my father, King Pelles, to look for you, and I found you by the grace of Our Lord in a place where, if God had not sent you, I would have had to die. But your great prowess rescued me from the Saxons, who were running me down to slay me. And indeed I know that your great renown that runs throughout the world is truly deserved. It is clear to me, and I know it is true, that no worthier man than you could bestow arms on me, and so I beg you in the name of your nobility to make me a knight by your hand, so that I might test my new knighthood against that faithless people bent on destroying Holy Christendom; I will never be a knight for as long as I live unless I am made a knight by your hand. And you swore an oath to me the first day I ever saw you that you would give me arms when I asked you, and I ask you now before my lord the king, who is here, and before these gentlemen."

When Sir Gawainet saw his squire Eliezer on his knees before him, he raised him up in his arms and said to him most kindly, "Dear friend, I grant you what you ask, for you are indeed worthy of receiving the order of knighthood, and I'll do it just as you wish."

"Many thanks, sir," said the youth.

Then Sir Gawainet looked about and saw his brother Gaheriet behind him, and he said to him, "Dear brother, have armor fitted out for me that befits a king's son and one as worthy as this one is."

"Who is he, then, dear nephew?" asked King Arthur.

"Sir, he is the son of King Pelles of Listenois and nephew of King Pellinor and King Alan. And you can be certain that if he lives long, he will be one of the good knights of the world."

Then he told King Arthur about the great slaughter and the wonders he saw him do against the Saxons. And when the king heard this, he was amazed at how a man of his age could bear up under such heavy fighting, and the two kings wondered, too. And King Arthur ordered Gaheriet to have the most handsome armor he could find in his armory trunks brought in "and the best sword there is after my own."

"Sir," said Eliezer, "I have armor and a horse and everything else I need, for my father, King Pelles, gave me such as he knew would be useful to me."

Then he called Lidonas, his squire, and ordered him to bring his armor, which his father had entrusted to him, and Lidonas did as he was ordered, and was most happy to do so. And he brought it to him before the king and the other barons, who looked at it in wonder, for it was white except for a single diagonal stripe of fine gold on the shield, and the hauberk was of double mail sturdier and stronger than any other, yet so light that a child ten years old could wear it for a whole day without hurting himself; and King Arthur praised it highly, as did the other barons who saw it.

And Sir Gawainet armed Eliezer with Gaheriet's help, and after [389] they had put on his leg armor, they dressed him in his white hauberk, which was so well made that none in the whole army was its equal, then they fastened on his visor, which was white as snow. And when he was thus dressed, Sir Gawainet put on his spurs and fastened his sword at his side. And after he was fully arrayed, Sir Gawainet embraced him,* and he said to him most kindly, as he was the most courtly knight in the world, "Here, dear friend, receive the order of knighthood in the name of Jesus Christ our Savior, and may He grant that you uphold it so as to honor Holy Church and yourself."

"Sir," said Eliezer, "may Our Lord grant this by His grace and His mercy."

After Sir Gawainet had dubbed Eliezer, son of King Pelles of Listenois, Gaheriet and Guerrehet took him by the hand and led him to King Arthur's chapel to keep his vigil, and they stayed with him all night until the next morning, when Mass was sung. Then they went back to the tent of King Arthur, who did him a very great honor, for he ate that day at King Arthur's table with King Ban and King Bors, and they were very well served with great festiveness. And after the meal, they set up a target dummy in a meadowland that was below the Plain of Salisbury, and those nimble young men went out to test themselves, along with the knights of the Round Table and others, and there many a fair blow was struck that day, and they said that never in their lives had they seen such fair jousting with the lance. The knights of the Round Table would have liked very much to tourney with the foreign knights who had come into the army, but King Arthur was unwilling to allow it, for he was very much afraid that they would wound one another, so they put off the tournament and went back to their tents happy and joyful.

Then Merlin came to King Arthur and said to him, "Sir, now we must get ready, for you must ride out in the morning. Be careful to tell no one what part of the army you'll be riding in, but follow me wherever I go. And I'll tell all the other princes to be ready to set out at daybreak."

"Merlin," said King Arthur, "do what you will, for all my hope is in God and in you."

Then Merlin went straight to the princes' pavilions and told every one of them privately, one after the other, to be ready and equipped to ride out early the next morning. And they had their tents, pavilions, and other equipment stowed away in wagons and carts and packed on horses, and, wearing their full armor, they got on

---

* That is, *li douna ... la colee* (389, l. 5). See p. 279n.

their warhorses, ready to defend themselves and fall upon their enemies, except for their shields, lances, and helmets, which their squires were carrying ahead for them. And they had their white ensigns borne before them, and on each one there was a red cross in the middle, and this Merlin had ordered all the princes to do when they first set out. And Merlin was riding a dapple-gray charger, and he bore King Arthur's banner out ahead of the king and the whole army.

This is how they left the Plain of Salisbury, and with Merlin in the lead they went straight toward the city of Clarence, which King Hargadabran [390] and twenty other kings had besieged. They had surrounded the whole city and sent their foragers out into the land for twenty leagues on all sides, and they were laying waste the countryside and stripping it bare.

A part of the foragers came back by the city of Garlot, which was the chief stronghold of King Neutres, and four mighty kings were among them. They had with them a great horde of Saxons who had taken plunder by force, and they had wreaked havoc on the men from the city who rode out to fight them to recover their plunder. There had been a great slaughter on both sides, but in the end those from the city could not hold out against them, because there were so very many Saxons, and they had lost their belongings, their horses, and a great many of their knights. And the four kings had besieged the city and would not leave until they had taken it.

When the queen, who was within the city, saw that they were under siege, she was very much afraid that the Saxons would take her by force, so she took counsel with her seneschal as to what she should do. It was the seneschal's advice that the two of them alone should steal out of the city at night through a hidden gate that opened toward the river, and they would go to one of their nearby strongholds, which was six leagues away; it was called The Rescue,* because Vortigern had been rescued there when Hengist the Saxon was run down and killed in the same place.

The seneschal and the queen did just as they had planned, for they left about midnight and took only two squires with them. But the Saxons, who were very cunning, had put their spies everywhere, and so the seneschal and the queen were taken prisoner and the seneschal killed; the two squires were dreadfully wounded, for one was struck in his body with a lance and the other dealt a blow with a sword on his head. And they came, as adventure took them, straight to the army Merlin was leading, which had strenuously made its way to within four leagues of Garlot. And when the squires saw the army coming, they caught sight of the white banners with the red crosses, and they knew at once that they were Christians, so they headed their way in the greatest agony in the world. And when Merlin, who was ahead of everyone else, heard them moaning, he asked them what was wrong with them, and they told him everything just as it had happened to them and said that the Saxons had taken the queen.

"And which way are they going?" asked Merlin.

"Sir," they said, "she is still with the army, but the plunder is being taken away on the causeway."

---

* *La rescouse* (390, l. 17), not in West.

And Merlin shouted in a loud voice, "Follow me, for, God willing, they won't take the queen away!"

Then he kicked his charger with his spurs, and Sir Gawainet and Eliezer spurred after him, along with King Ban and King Bors, and each one had a good, strong, stout lance in his hand. And Leonce of Payerne led the men of Benoic, Dyonas those of Gaunes, Gratian those of Orkney, and Dorilas* King Neutres's men, and the other battalions came along all in order. And Merlin rode until he was about to go down a hill, and he saw the plunder being taken across a little bridge by four thousand Saxons. And when Sir Gawainet saw them, he said, "Let's not stay too far behind!"

And he kicked Gringalet with his spurs, and Eliezer said to him, "Sir, allow me [391] a favor and a service. Let me have the first blow of the battle, for I have not been in a fight since I've been a knight."

"And I grant it to you," said Sir Gawainet smiling, "for you are indeed worthy of it."

With that, Eliezer let his horse run, and he shouted to the Saxons, "Leave the plunder, for you will not take it with you any farther."

Then came Dyoglis, who was King Maglory's seneschal, and he turned his horse's head toward Eliezer, and they struck each other on their shields with their lances so hard that they cut beneath the bosses, and Dyoglis broke his lance. Eliezer hit him so hard that he drove his lance through his chest and hurled him dead to the ground, and his lance flew into splinters. Then he drew his sword out of its scabbard and rushed in among the others, who were in a great hurry to get the plunder across the bridge. He struck Antidolus, who was King Brandon's seneschal, and split him down to his teeth. Then Merlin said to Sir Gawainet that the new knight had started out well.

"In truth," said Sir Gawainet, "and he will fight even better."

With that, Merlin yelled King Arthur's battlecry, and Sir Gawainet and his companions let loose and charged headlong into the pillagers, and there were many dead and wounded, so that the Saxons had to give up the place and turned in flight toward Garlot, where King Maglory, King Brandon,† King Pincenar, and King Pignoras were. The kings were keeping up a vigorous assault in order to take the city, and they were quite upset to see the runaways coming, and they stopped their assault and ran toward them in disarray. And when the Saxons saw the Christians coming, they were quite amazed that there could be so many of them, but they rushed in among them, because the Saxons were numerous and very strong.

The Christians welcomed them most fiercely, but the Saxons pushed them back more than a lance's length in their first attack. And when the four Saxon kings saw Sir Gawainet and Eliezer and King Ban and King Bors fighting so boldly, they shouted to their men and struck out among them, and they began to slaughter knights and horses as if they were in an army gone mad, and it was indeed the strongest army in the world. And they drove King Ban's men and those of King Bors against King Neutre's men and the battalion of Duke Escant of Cambenic,

---

* Here the form is *doulas* (390, l. 38).
† The text reads *orandons* (391, l. 18).

and Sir Gawainet, King Ban, King Bors, and Eliezer received many a hard blow, and they were very badly hurt. But when these two battalions joined the fray, then could be seen wonders of fighting, and the Saxons were badly hurt in this surge, for many were killed or struck down. But King Brandon and King Pincenar did great wonders by themselves and with the knights of their households, who were most worthy and bold, for after they had struck, no one stayed in his saddle. And the men of Great Britain were stricken with fright, and they would have been put to rout if it had not been for the prowess of Sir Gawainet and Eliezer, King Ban and King Bors, King Neutres of Garlot, and Duke Escant of Cambenic; and nevertheless Pharian, Gratian, Leonce of Payerne, and Dorilas fought so boldly that no one could rebuke them. And Merlin, who flew from rank to rank without stopping, kept shouting, "Now forward!"

While they were in such great distress, King Pignoras called forty of his worthiest and boldest Saxons and ordered them to get the queen of Garlot and [392] take her away to the siege of Clarence and give her to King Hargadabran, and they answered that they would do as he wished. They left at once and set out for Clarence by the shortest way they could take, and they took away with them the queen, who bewailed the fateful things that were happening to her.

So King Pignoras charged once again into the fray, his sword in his hand, and he began fighting all over again, so boldly and so wondrously that no one could withstand his blows, for he did not meet a knight who could hurt him, and his skill was so great that the boldest made way for him. At last Sir Gawainet, who was ready at all times of need, caught sight of him and saw the great harm he was doing to their men; and he said to himself, "If that one lives long enough, we could lose a great deal."

Eliezer, who very gladly kept close to Sir Gawainet, heard what he said, and he spurred his horse to where he had seen Pignoras, whose arm and sword were filthy with the blood and brains of the Christians he had slain. And when Eliezer saw him, he said, "He would truly be a great harm to our cause if he lived any longer, and it's a misfortune that he's lived as long as he has."

With that, Eliezer drew nearer to him, and he left his horse's reins on the saddlebow in front, threw his shield behind his back, and fixed his feet in the stirrups. He lifted his sword in both hands and hit King Pignoras on his helmet with all his might, so hard that neither helmet nor iron coif could keep him from thrusting his sword into his brain; then with a twisting stroke he sent him sprawling dead to the ground. And when Merlin saw that, he said to Sir Gawainet, "He has given us time."

"Indeed," said Sir Gawainet "May Jesus Christ save for our sakes such a worthy companion as he!"

Then they rushed in among the Saxons, who were very angry and upset over Pignoras's death, and they began to strike right and left But more than any of the others, Sir Gawainet and Eliezer, King Ban and King Bors, Leonce of Payerne, Gratian of Trebe, and Pharian fought boldly. Only five of their battalions had gathered as yet, but the ones who were there did true wonders, for neither iron nor steel held up under their blows. And when King Pincenar, who was most worthy and bold, saw his men flagging and beaten, he was most upset, and he said that it would be better to die than fail to avenge Pignoras. He held his drawn sword in his right hand, and he flew into the crowd where he saw it was thickest, and he began hitting from side to side and striking down at once as many as he met. And right before King Ban, he killed a knight who was of his household and had fought hard that day, and King Ban went out of his mind and, filled with anger, went straight to where he saw the man who had slain his knight; he struck him so hard, in the great wrath he felt, that he split him open down to the teeth—and that was what brought him the most comfort all day.

And then the Christians closed in around the Saxons, and the fighting was heavy and most fearsome, for the Britons were all good knights. And when Merlin saw that the battalions had gathered [393] all about, he drew Sir Gawainet, Eliezer, King Ban, and King Bors aside and told them that forty Saxons were taking the queen of Garlot to the siege of Clarence, "and I think we should go after them."

"Ride ahead," said Sir Gawainet, "and we'll follow you."

So they took to the road, and there were a good one hundred companions.

And here the story falls silent about them and goes back to the knights who were taking away the queen of Garlot.

48. A Great Victory Over the Saxons.[*]

Now the story says that when the forty Saxons were two leagues away from the battle, they went into a wood where there was the most beautiful meadow with quite a lovely spring. And they turned that way to cool off and to drink from the spring, which was very clear. They helped the queen dismount beside the spring; she was filled with the greatest sorrow in the world, and nothing they said or did could comfort her. Instead she moaned aloud, "Ah, King Neutres! Today they will sever the love I have for you from the love you have for me, for I don't believe I'll ever see you again."

Then she fainted in the arms of the Saxons who were holding her. And when she came out of her faint, she clawed herself and showed such sorrow that the Saxons felt deep pity for her, and some of them would have been very glad if she were where she longed to be, and they tried to comfort her most kindly. But she did not want their comfort, but began to scream so loudly that Sir Gawainet and his companions heard her clearly. They turned to where they heard the screaming, and they rode until they saw the knights and the queen, who was calling in a loud voice, "Holy Lady Mary, please help this wretched, grieving woman!"

When Sir Gawainet saw his aunt, he spurred to where she was and said to the Saxons, "Dear lords, please leave the queen and go away, for I would be most grateful to you if you took pity on her. And I thank you very much for the courtliness you have shown her."

---

[*]   Corresponds to Sommer, 393-401.

When Margon, King Pignoras's wine steward, heard what Sir Gawainet said, he asked his companions what they would advise him to do. And they said that they would rather die than let the queen go.

"You have brought this on yourselves!" said Sir Gawainet.

Then he ran upon them, his sword drawn, and he struck the first one and sent his head flying to the feet of the queen. And the Saxons sprang up at once, and they suffered great harm as they got to their feet. Even so, they killed knights and horses, because they possessed great prowess. But in the end their defense did not keep them all from dying, and not one of them got away except Margon the Wine Steward, who stole away and hid in the woods. And Sir Gawainet and his companions came to the queen and comforted her most kindly, and she asked them who they were.

"Lady," said Sir Gawainet, "I am Gawainet, your nephew, the son of King Lot of Orkney. And this lord is King Ban of Benoic, and these other knights are our companions."

And when the lady heard this, she was filled with great gladness, and she thanked them over and over for the service they had done her.

Then they put her on a palfrey and went back toward the army where King Arthur and the other princes were fighting. And the Saxons lost a great many of their men, for King Arthur had killed Maglory, their king who was the mainstay of the Saxons, and [394] King Lot had chopped off the hand of Sinarus. And they had all turned in flight, when Sir Gawainet and his companions came back bringing the queen, whom they had rescued. They met King Brandon, who was fleeing and had to go through them; the Saxons were four thousand strong, and the whole army was close behind them and spurring ever faster. But Brandon turned back to face them many times, and his men did not hit any knight with a sound blow without killing him. And when Sir Gawainet saw what he was doing, and the great slaughter of his people, he was certain that he was a highborn man of mighty stock, and he showed by the way he fought that he was a king or a prince; Sir Gawainet highly esteemed him, and he would have been very glad if he had been a Christian.

And Sir Gawainet drew near him and said with great courtliness, "Knight you are worthy and very bold. Are you a king or a duke that you should have such strength and such heart?"

"By my faith," he answered, "my name is Brandon, and I am king of a part of Saxony. I am the nephew of the richest king in the world, that is, King Hargadabran, who has all of Saxony under his sway."

"Indeed," said Sir Gawainet, "that is quite plain to see, for you are a most worthy and skilled knight, and it is a great shame that you are not a Christian, and I wish very much that you were, so that I might give you a reprieve from death."

"Now you're telling me tales of wonders! Don't say any more to me about it, for I would rather die than be a Christian."

"You will come to that soon enough, and I am deeply sorry about it, for I would like very much to be your companion, if you're willing."

"I would never want that," said Brandon.

And when Sir Gawainet heard that, he ran upon him very fast and very angrily, and he struck him so hard with Excalibur that he sent his head flying.

And when the runaways saw their lord dead, they were so bewildered that they could no longer defend themselves, and the Christians fell upon them from all sides and killed them and cut them to shreds. And when they had done that, they thanked Our Lord profusely for the honor He had given them that day.

Then Sir Gawainet and King Ban came before King Arthur and all the nobility, and they gave his wife back to King Neutres, and they told, so that everyone could hear them, how they had rescued her. And the king very gladly and joyfully thanked them all, and the barons were all quite happy about it. Then they withdrew a little above the field where the battle had been, and King Arthur had his tent set up in the meadow, and all the others did the same; and they went to rest. And the next morning, when it was daylight, they set out on the road to Clarence.

But with that the story falls silent from speaking about King Arthur and his nobles and goes back to speaking about Margon, King Pignoras's wine steward.

Here the story says that Margon hid in the woods until Sir Gawainet, King Ban, and their companions had taken the queen away. Then Margon went back to the spring and found his horse, which he had tied to an olive tree, and got on. He rode until he came to the army before Clarence, and he told King Hargadabran that all the foragers he had sent out were dead or routed. And when King Hargadabran [395] heard him, he was quite sorry and upset. Then King Gundeflé jumped up and said to King Hargadabran, "Sir, if you please, I would like to go find out what has happened. And I would take with me Salebrun, Sorbares, Meliaduc, and King Bramangue; and we will have with us forty thousand men, for I could not believe that four such powerful men as your cousin King Brandon, King Pincenar, King Pignoras, and King Maglory could be brought to defeat by a force of no account."

And while they were saying these things, behold there came Sinarus, who had his hand cut off, and he told them the truth about what had happened to his arm.

When King Hargadabran saw Sinarus in such a state, his sorrow was wondrous, for he loved him greatly. And when he learned of the deaths of the four kings, it was as if he had gone out of his mind, for King Maglory and King Brandon were his nephews. Then he told King Gundeflé that he wanted to avenge his nephews, and he answered that he would very gladly do so. And so he set out on the way, and he took fifty thousand Saxons with him. And they broke their men up into five battalions, and each one had ten thousand Saxons. King Salebrun led the first one, Duke Lanor of Betingues the second, King Sorbares the third, King Brangor and Malakin* the Castellan the fourth, and King Gundeflé and his brother Transmaduk the fifth. They left the siege of Clarence, one battalion† after the other, and they took to the road toward the castle of Garlot, and they made their way all night and all day until they met Merlin in a most fair meadow that was a good league and a half long.

There Merlin had set up seven battalions with the first men to come. King Neutres, King Tradelmant, and Duke Escant led the first battalion with twenty thousand men. King Ban, King Bors, and the King of the Hundred Knights led the second with twenty thousand men. King Clarion of Northumberland, the king

---

* Thus 396, l. 21; here the text reads *machadins* (395, l. 18).
† Here the word is *eschiele* (395, l. 20): "echelon."

of South Wales, and Nabunal, the seneschal of Gosengos, led the third with thirty thousand men. Cleodalis, the seneschal of Carmelide, King Caradoc, and King Lot of Orkney led the fourth. Anguingeron, the seneschal of King Clamadeus, Flamus (the seneschal of King Evadain), and the seneschal of King Pelles of Listenois led the fifth with thirty thousand men. King Brandegorre led the sixth with thirty thousand men. And Sir Gawainet, his brothers, and the companions of the Round Table were with King Arthur in the seventh, where there were so many people that they could scarcely be counted.

In such a way did the hosts of the Christians and the hosts of the Saxons meet each other in the meadowlands half a Welsh league from Garlot. And as soon as King Salebrun saw the Christians, he let loose after them, and Margon the Wine Steward did the same. And when Duke Escant saw it, he went out to meet them. But Tromoret, who was castellan of Cambenic, went out ahead and struck Salebrun so hard on his shield that his lance flew into bits, and the Saxon hit him so hard that the tip of his lance* went through his body, and he sent him [396] sprawling dead to the ground. And when Duke Escant saw that, he grew very angry, and in his great wrath, he struck Salebrun so soundly that he drove his lance through his body. Then he said to him, "Lowborn traitor, now you are dead, but for all that, I won't have back my friend, who was my liegeman."

With that, the battalions gathered on both sides, and the clanging of swords and snapping of lances were very loud, and great numbers died on both sides. But as soon as King Ban, King Bors, and the King of the Hundred Knights, who were leading the second battalion, came in and saw the second Saxon battalion make its move, they rushed headlong into them, and great wonders of skilled fighting could be seen, with many knights tumbling and thrown down, many hauberks cut through and links undone, many helmets flying from heads and shields from necks; and the killing was fearsome on both sides.

And when Merlin saw that the Saxons were so mighty, he shouted to King Ban, "What are you doing? You should already have sent them all on their way a while ago, for you have half again as many men as they!"

When King Ban and the other princes heard Merlin shouting, they were deeply ashamed. Then they ran against the Saxons with great might, and the Saxons had to give ground, like it or not, and they were driven back into their third battalion, which King Meliaduc, Duke Frangiles, and Lanor of Betingues were leading,† and they came out to meet them. And the fighting was so heavy and wondrous, and the slaughter was so great on both sides, that it was a fearsome thing to behold. But then King Brangor‡ and Malakin the Castellan rejoined the fourth battalion, along with Galeguinant and King Cleolas, and the fighting was ruthless and wicked, so that in little time the field was covered with the dead and wounded. In that onslaught Margon the Wine Steward was slain; he was deeply mourned by the Saxons, and King Ban killed him with his lance. And when King Sorbares saw that, he was filled with sorrow, and he rode toward King Ban and meant to strike him on his helmet, but King Ban thrust his shield against the blow, and King Sorbares split

---

*   Here the word is *espiel* (395, l. 41), usually translated as "spear."
†   Above (395, l. 17) Lanor led the first Saxon battalion.
‡   Here the form is *mancors* (396, l. 21). See 395, l. 18.

it down to the boss; but then the blow glanced down to the neck of the warhorse, whose head went flying, and both the king and his horse fell in a heap. And King Sorbares stood over him with his sword drawn to strike him, but Pharian, who was very angry to see his lord on the ground, came over to meet him, and he struck King Sorbares so hard on the helmet that he split him open down to his teeth, and he fell sprawling dead to the ground. Then Pharian took his horse by the reins, led him to the king, and helped him get on.

And when King Ban was back on a horse, he flew into the fray filled with wrath, and he began to do wonders with his fighting. And Pharian, Gratian, Anselm, Dionas, King Bors, King Neutres, and all the other princes did wonders all by themselves, and there were so many Saxons dead and wounded that the field was all covered with them, and they could not get to one another except by going over the dead.

While this great slaughter was going on, all the battalions joined the fray except King Arthur's alone, and Merlin took this one around until they came up behind the others, and then they rushed in headlong without mercy. And as soon as Sir Gawainet and Eliezer, Yvain and his brothers, [397] and the companions of the Round Table had come in and gathered about the battalion, open displays of knightly prowess could be seen by all. They slaughtered knights and horses, they sent shields flying from necks and helmets from heads, they chopped off feet and hands, and they did such wonders that scarcely could anyone believe the great slaughter of the Saxons they did. And Kay the Seneschal, whom Merlin had entrusted to carry the great ensign, was always out ahead in the first rank, for he was very bold. There, above all, Sir Gawainet fought boldly, and King Arthur did as well, for he met no Saxon with a sound blow whom he did not kill. And the princes, who had come for the love of God, fought boldly too, and they did so well that they were sure to have the pardon. And the Queen's Knights fought so boldly that no one was left standing after they had hit, for they struck down as many as they met. And thus the fields were strewn with the dead and wounded, so that no one could move about without going over them.

When the Saxons saw that they were surrounded, they were so stricken with fright that they were put to rout. And without a doubt they were so dreadfully weakened that of five kings, one earl, one duke, and sixty-eight thousand Saxons, not four thousand of them got away, and all the rest were slain or maltreated. Even so, they gave themselves up at a fearsomely high price, for so many Christians were slain that the damage was bewailed for as long as King Arthur lived; many a lady was left a widow, and many a noble maiden was bereft of comfort.

When Duke Gundeflé and Duke Lanor of Betingues saw the great slaughter of their people by the Christians, and when they saw that they were shut off so that they could not get back to the army, they were deeply upset, for they saw plainly that they would be killed if they could not decide what was best to do. Then they looked to the side, over to the sea, where the Christians had left a little opening; they took flight that way, down through the meadowland, straight to the sea, which was nearby. And when King Arthur saw them heading there, he shouted, "Now, after them!" Then the Christians spurred after them all together, and many a blow was struck in the chase, for the Saxons were large and strong, skilled and bold, and full of great prowess, and many times they would turn about to face the ones who were following them. Many a Saxon was slain and many a Christian killed or wounded, and the chase went on, with the Saxons fleeing and then turning about until they came to the sea, where they found three of their galleys, which were led by Landalis, a Saxon who had stopped there to wait for foodstuffs from those who had gone to forage at the castle of Garlot. And when the runaways saw the galleys, they were greatly gladdened, and all those who could rushed aboard them, but they could not prevent more than two thousand on both sides from drowning, while those who had boarded the ships cut the anchor lines, hoisted the sails, and took to the sea as quickly as they could; and they went wherever they were taken by the wind, which had turned its wheel unfavorably.

And when King Arthur and his nobles saw that they had thus lost the Saxons, they turned back to their tents in the meadowlands of Garlot And after they had [398] taken off their armor, they rested and took their ease as best they could; they were in great need of it, for they were tired and worn out from giving and taking blows in the fighting, which had been very heavy. And then they went to eat, and after the meal, they looked to their sick and had them taken to the castle of Garlot. There were thirty-five knights wounded, five of them knights of the Round Table, about whom King Arthur was quite sad and upset; one of them was Hervi of Rivel, the second Males the Dark, the third Clamadeus, the fourth Aristobokis, and the fifth Landens of Carmelide. And the king entreated the physicians to take good care of them, and they answered that he should not be worried, for they would have them hale and hardy in a short time, with the help of God. And so they stayed there that night.

The next morning Merlin ordered the tents and pavilions to be taken down, and he said that everyone should come after him ready to fall on their foes and hurt them, and it was done just as he had ordered. And when they were ready, they took to the road straight to Clarence. And when they came near enough to King Hargadabran's army that they could clearly see their tents and pavilions, Merlin pointed them out to King Arthur and said to him, "Sir, look, there are the ones at whose orders your barons' lands have been laid waste and stripped. Now we'll see how they take their vengeance today. For now we have come to the point of winning or losing everything. Today we'll see who has prowess in him. Today we'll see who can fight boldly with sword and lance. Today the great and worthy knighthood of the Kingdom of Logres will be displayed. Today will be our time of great need and trial, for in this day the Kingdom of Logres will be destroyed or brought to honor. And I tell you and your barons together," he went on, "that you sorely need to pray to Our Lord to defend the Kingdom of Logres from shame and misfortune."

And they all answered, "So be it!"

And then they said, friends and foreigners alike, that they would do anything he wanted, and he advised them that, if they were willing to exert great effort, they need not worry, for victory would be theirs that day. And they answered that they were ready to do so.

"I want you to swear to me," said Merlin, "that you will do everything as I wish it."

And they answered that they would do so gladly.

"Even so," said Merlin to King Arthur, "you must swear it to me first."

And the king said that he could be sure that he was ready to do all his bidding, and he swore it straightway, and the others did as well.

Then Merlin said to them, "Dear lords, today has dawned the day of the destruction of Great Britain, if God does not help us. In no way can the destruction be avoided, nor can these people ever live in safety, until you have all made peace with King Arthur. And this is what you have sworn to me."

When the barons heard that, there were some of them who did not like it, but it could not be otherwise, so they agreed to everything Merlin wished, and they all swore fealty to King Arthur one after the other; and all who were not already his liegemen* received their lands and fiefs back from him. And there was great rejoicing throughout the army.

And then they set up their battalions and went out against the Saxons, who were at the siege before the wealthy city of Clarence, which they attacked every day. But it was so strong that they could not take any part of it, [399] for it was very well stocked inside with good men and food. All who could bear arms from ten leagues all around were in the city, knights and burghers, one and all; there were a good seventy-five thousand,† who were all skilled, bold, and good defensive fighters, and they strongly defended the city against the Saxons. They threw at them many a dart and many a big, sharp spike, with which they brought down many a Saxon, who would never get up again.

The city was quite large, and they were ruthlessly attacking it when Merlin and his companions came there. And when they were near the tents, Merlin sent in his men in four battalions against the four sides of the Saxon host, and they flew in among the tents and pavilions and began to cut the ropes and supports and overturn them. And the Saxons, who were not on the lookout for such an onslaught, heard the uproar and saw the pavilions falling down everywhere, and they were greatly frightened. They broke off their attack and ran to the encampment as fast as they could, and there was such an uproar and loud shouting of battlecries that they could be heard half a league away. Then bloodthirsty and wondrous fighting began, and they struck one another with swords and lances, and the slaughter was dreadful on both sides. But for every Christian who died, five Saxons were killed, although they were stronger and better armed, but the Christians were wonderfully swift and nimble and skilled at hard fighting and heavy warfare.

When the Christians had driven into the horde of Saxons, you could have seen the beginning of wondrous fighting. In the first assault many a Christian was struck down and many a Saxon put to death, and about this King Hargadabran was very sad and upset. He held a great shaft of oak with a big, sharp iron tip, and he rode as fast as he could make his horse run toward King Cleolas, who had come to the war for love of Our Lord with seven thousand men who were fighting quite well in the battle. And when King Cleolas saw him coming, he did not deign to move aside, for he was of great boldness, but he turned his horse's head toward him, his lance on

---

* Sommer's text is less specific, *qui le durent faire* (398, l. 41): "who ought to have done so/needed to do so."

† The text reads *.lx. & .xv. Mile* (399, ll. 3-4), that is, three score (thousand) and fifteen thousand.

its felt holder and his shield in front of his chest, and at full speed they struck each other on their shields so hard that they drove through them and cut their hauberks open, and the iron tips went right by their sides but did not break the skin. And they hit each other with their shields, for their horses had come in at great speed, and crashed into each other, chest to chest, so hard that they both spilled to the ground, taking their horses down on top of them, and their lances flew into pieces; and they lay on the ground in such a daze that neither of them could move. Their horses were lying on top of them as they had been killed, and the two kings lay beneath them in a faint. And the fight to get the two princes back on horseback was hard, for all the battalions of the Saxons had run to that side, as had those of the Christians, and many a blow was given and taken. At last the Saxons got King Hargadabran back on his horse, but before that, more than two thousand had been killed on both sides. At the same time, the Christians put King Cleolas on his horse, but they found that he had broken his left arm in falling, and his men were sorry and upset about it, and they had him carried at once to the baggage wagons. [400] And when they had laid him down and made him comfortable, he called his men together very kindly and entreated them to go straight back to the battle. He gave them his seneschal, Guionce, to lead them, and they granted him everything he wanted.

Then they charged back into the battle in great anger, burning to avenge their lord, and in the onslaught they killed two Saxon kings, one of whom was named King Brangor and the other King Margondes, the first cousin of Hengist the Saxon. And they began to fight so skillfully that they were praised, esteemed, and watched in great wonder by Saxons and the Christians. On the other side of the battlefield, King Ban, King Bors, King Neutres, and King Urien were doing their share of fighting. Elsewhere were King Tradelmant of North Wales, the King of the Hundred Knights, King Clarion of Northumberland, and Duke Escant of Cambenic. On yet another side, King Belinant, the king of Estrangorre, King Aguisant, King Yder, Minoras (King Lac's seneschal), and Claalant of Listenois were fighting in their turn. Somewhere else, Anguingeron, the seneschal of King Clamadeus; Flamus, King Evadain's seneschal; Galeguinant, the seneschal of Galehaut, son of the Fair Giantess; and Margondes, the seneschal of Sorelois, were doing their share, and they had all come there for love of Our Lord. Somewhere else still Gosengos, the son of King Amant, his seneschal, Nabunal, and Cleodalis, the seneschal of King Leodagan of Carmelide, were also fighting. And somewhere else yet again were King Arthur, King Lot of Orkney, Sir Gawainet, Agravain, Guerrehet, Gaheriet, Sir Yvain son of King Urien, Sagremor, and Kay the Seneschal, who bore the ensign. And the battle began in earnest on all sides, and it was a wonder to behold.

And Merlin went from one battalion to another, riding a huge charger, and he shouted in a loud voice, "Now we'll see, sir knights! The day has come when your prowess will be displayed!"

When the kings and princes heard him shouting these things, they sought, heedless of the danger, to show the utmost strength they could. And when those in the city saw that the fighting had grown so deadly, and they saw Christians and Saxons spill to the ground so thick that they were falling on top of one another, they were convinced that this was the help that Our Lord had sent them. So they had their gates opened and rode out all in armor, and they drove headlong into the battle with all their might and began to do wonders of fighting. But however boldly anyone may have fought that day, King Arthur outstripped them all, along with Sir Gawainet, his brothers, and King Bors, for no one could withstand their blows, and they fought so hard that the Saxons were routed. Of all the kings whom King Hargadabran had called together and brought there, he was one of six to get away, the others being King Orient, Sorbares, Cornicans, the fleet commander Napins, and Murgalant of Trebeham. These five got away with King Hargadabran; they had with them thirty thousand Saxons, and they all left, downcast and routed, [401] as fast as their horses could go, and they rushed straight to their fleet And those who were unwilling to let them go ran after them with all their might as far as the sea. They were on their heels as the Saxons boarded the ships they had, and a good half of them were slain or drowned. And the ones who did get aboard went away upset and bewailing the great loss they had suffered.

And they had not gone far before they met the ship of King Gundeflé and King Lanor, who were fleeing from their rout, and they recognized one another straightway. And thus they sailed out to sea.

But now the story falls silent about them and goes back to speaking about King Arthur and his companions.

49. THE CASTLE OF THE FENS.*

Now the story says that after King Arthur had routed the Saxons and they had boarded their ships, he and his nobles went back happy and gladdened. And they went out to the battlefield and thanked God most tenderly for the honor and the victory He had given them and for the lavish winnings they had in gold, silver, lush silk cloth, pavilions, warhorses, and good armor. With the permission of the princes, King Arthur had it divided among one and all according to their estate, and he kept none of it for himself, not a penny's worth. And then the princes went into the city happy and joyful. And they had the dead buried, and they stayed there five days.

And the news ran about the countryside that the Saxons had been driven away from the city of Clarence and killed or wounded. And even the Saxons who had not been in the rout left the country and went back to Saxony, sorrowing and upset about the friends they had lost.

And after King Arthur had stayed five days joyfully celebrating in the city, the princes left him and went back to their countries. They left in great love of Arthur, and they held their lands from him. And the foreign princes, who had come there out of love for Our Lord, also went back to their countries. And King Arthur, King Ban, King Bors, King Lot of Orkney, Sir Gawainet, and their companions came straight back to the city of Camelot. They were lavishly welcomed by Queen Guenevere and all the people.

*   Corresponds to Sommer, 401-407.

And then Merlin came to Arthur and said to him, "Sir, thanks be to God, this time you have freed the land from those wicked people, and you and all Christendom should have great gladness, for you are now in peace. Now King Ban and King Bors can go back to their countries, for it has been a long time since they have seen their wives and their lands; and in their countries they have a wicked neighbor who would willingly do them harm if he had the power, and that is King Claudas of the Land Laid Waste. So they'll cross the sea and take care of their lands and their business."

And when King Arthur heard this, he answered him most courteously and said, "Merlin, dear friend," said King Arthur, "the princes will do as they will, and you as you will, but I would rather that they and you should stay and not go away, for it should bother no prince to keep company with such worthy gentlemen as they and you are. Even so, since that is your pleasure and your will, I must accept it."

"Sir," said Merlin, "it must be so. Indeed, you do not need [402] them to stay behind."

So the two kings left and took to the road toward the sea amid great rejoicing. And Merlin, who loved them very much, went along with them because of that love. As it happened, the first night after they had left Camelot, they came upon a castle that sat in a marshland, and it was so well placed and so sturdy that it did not fear any attack. That castle was enclosed all around by two pairs of thick, high walls topped with battlements with narrow openings for easy defense. And within the bailey were five high, straight towers, all of them round, rising to the clouds; four of them were somewhat slender,* but the fifth was large, wondrous, and well fortified all about, and outside it was defended by a double moat full of water. And the tower in the middle was so high that one could hardly shoot to the top with a hand-held bow. And all around, beyond the outside walls, were marshes spreading out a good two leagues that were so full of mire† and water that no one could go in there without drowning. There was only one way into this castle, and it was so narrow that two horses could not pass if they met, and at the other end of the causeway was a quite lovely pine tree beside the water in a meadow a quarter acre in size, where the grass grew tall and fair; and the pine was full and beautiful. On one of the high limbs a horn of ivory whiter than snow hung on a silver chain, and those who sought shelter within or wanted to pass through blew it to ask for a joust. The horn that hung there served for the two things I have explained.

When King Ban, King Bors, and their companions came to the pine tree and saw the horn hanging there, they said to one another that it did not hang there for no reason, and they thought it must be for crossing the ford or asking for a joust, but they saw that the castle was so far away that they did not believe the sound of the horn could reach that far. Meanwhile, they found that the castle was handsome and rich and well placed, and they could not have had a better look at its great size than from where they were, and they also saw that the causeway and entry way were so strong and so narrow that they were struck with amazement.

---

*   The word here is *moienes* (402, l. 9): "medium."
†   The word is *rai* (402, l. 13), which Sommer did not understand. He suggests that it may be a scribal error for *tai* ("mud, mire") (402, n. 2). In addition to a kind of fish, also suggested by Sommer (n. 2), *rai* can mean a stream of water.

And the two kings asked Merlin if he knew the name of the castle that was so handsome and well placed that they would be happy to own it. And Merlin told them that it was the Castle of the Fens, and it belonged to a knight who was of great prowess and great renown, worthy and bold in fighting, and his name was Agravadain the Black.

"By my faith," said King Ban, "many times I've heard about Agravadain the Black. God help me, he must be a most worthy gentleman to have such a good dwelling, for this is the fairest of all the castles I've ever seen. I would be very glad to lie there tonight, if the lord who lives there is willing."

"That will indeed happen to you," said Merlin, "but no unknown knight may go to the castle, and no one dares [403] drink any of the water, without a fight, unless he has blown the horn."

"I will blow the horn," said King Ban, "if you allow me."

"By my faith," said Merlin, "there is no danger in blowing it, since you wish to ask for a joust or for leave to drink."

"By my faith," said King Ban, "it would be dangerous if I blew it and you had forbidden me to."

"I indeed advise you to do it," said Merlin, "for, God willing, no harm will come to you from it."

At once King Ban went to the pine tree where the horn was hanging; he put the horn to his lips and blew it loud and clear, for he was strong and had enough wind, and the marshland resounded with it And the sounds of the water and the marsh bore the sound of the horn into the castle, so that the lord who was the castellan heard it plainly. And he shouted, as was their custom, "Now to arms!" And the king started to blow another time, and he blew it three times very fast, for the castle was so far away that King Ban did not believe they could hear it there.

When the lord who was the castellan heard the horn being blown so hard and so many times, he took it as a great insult, so he mounted a big dapple-gray warhorse, his shield about his neck and his lance in his hand. The gate was opened, and he rode out at great speed and came straight to the ford. And when he saw the people on the other side, he shouted to them, "What people are you?"

And King Ban answered, "Sir, we are knights who ask you for shelter tonight in your castle. And, if you please, we would like to water our horses in this ford."

"Whose men are you?" asked Agravadain.

"Dear sir," answered Merlin, who was closest to the causeway, "they are from another land that is a part of Gaul."

"What part?"

"Sir, they hold their lands from King Arthur."

"In God's name, they have a good overlord. They cannot be dishonored by King Arthur, for he is a worthy man and a good knight, and he is my overlord. And for his sake you will have lodging to your liking."

"Thank you very much," said Merlin.

Agravadain turned about at once and told the knights to follow him, for they were most welcome. And they took off right away after the knight, one after the other, on the causeway. They rode as far as the castle gate and then went in behind the knight who was lord there, and they did not have room to turn their horses until they had gone through the gate. And then the lord himself led them up to the castle. Then serving boys and squires ran out to help them down. And the lord himself took the two kings by the hand, for they seemed to him to be worthy gentlemen and landed princes, and he led them into a room which was at the bottom of the tower, where he had their armor taken off, as was most fitting, and his own as well. And while he was being disarmed, three maidens endowed with great beauty came in; they brought in dark red cloaks lined with black ermine and put them over the shoulders of the two kings and their lord.

And King Ban, who was light-hearted and under love's sway, was glad to look at the maidens. He liked their company and the way they looked, for they were wondrously lovely and delightful to watch, and they were at a good age, for the eldest was not yet twenty-four years old. But the daughter of the castle was by far the most beautiful. Merlin looked at her [404] in great distress, and he thought to himself that anyone would be very lucky if he could sleep with such a maiden. "And if it weren't for the great love I have for Viviane, my lady love," he said, "I would be holding her in my arms tonight. But since I cannot have her for myself, I'll see that King Ban will have her."

Then he cast a spell with little ado, and as soon as he had done it, King Ban and Agravadain's daughter fell deeply in love with each other.

When the two kings had been dressed in the two cloaks that two of the maidens had put over their shoulders, Agravadain showed them how glad he was to welcome them. And when it was time to eat, the tables were set up in the middle of the hall, which was quite large and wide. And he had the two brother kings sit next to each other at the head of the high table, and Agravadain sat between them and his wife, who was most lovely and youthful, for she was not yet thirty years old; and the knights sat at tables throughout the hall. And the three maidens who were so appealing stood before the two kings and Agravadain—and before Merlin.

And Merlin had taken on the likeness of a youth fifteen years of age. He was wearing a somewhat short red and white tunic. About his waist was a silk belt two inches wide with gold rings here and there, and from this hung a purse of beaten gold. His hair was blond* and curly, and his eyes were wide-set and speckled gray. And he was on his knees carving before King Ban. People kept looking at him, for no one there knew who he was except the two brother kings, although the others with them thought that he belonged to the household of the lord of the castle.

And because of the great worth and beauty they saw in him, the maidens gazed at him from time to time. But Agravadain's daughter still had eyes to look at King Ban more than anything else because of Merlin's spell, and her color kept changing. She could hardly wait for the tablecloths to be taken away, for she very much would have liked to lie naked in his arms, yet she did not know where this yearning came from.

The maiden was brooding and suffering a great deal because of the spell Merlin had cast. At the same time, King Ban was in such distress that he shunned the laughter and games at table, and he did not know how that had happened to him. And he was in such great distress that his mind turned to brooding about it, for he

---

*   The text reads *si ot le chief blanc* (404, l. 18): "his head was white."

had a young lady for a wife, and she was of very great beauty, and he did not wish to wrong her; moreover, he thought that it might be treasonous, because the people of the castle had done them great honor there and had given them shelter, and it seemed to him that they could bring them no greater shame than to dishonor their host's daughter in such a way. He was so distraught that he did not know what to do, and all the time he said in his heart that he would not ask anything of her. And Merlin, who well knew what was happening to them, said to himself that it would not be as King Ban said, for it would be a very great shame if they did not get together, "for a fruit will be born of them, and the land of Britain will be honored by him because of his great prowess."

Thus spoke Merlin to himself. And after the tablecloths had been taken away and they had washed their hands, they went to stand at the windows and look up and down the marshes, and all around they could see the countryside that was so fair that [405] it was no wonder they forgot themselves until it was time to go to bed. Then they went into a room next to the great hall where the maidens had prepared two beds that befitted such princes as they, and they went to bed with great rejoicing. And when the two kings had lain down, Merlin began to cast another spell, and all who were there went to sleep except King Ban and the young lady. They were so overwhelmed by each other that they could not rest or sleep. And Merlin, who meant to bring to an end what he had begun, came into the room where the maiden lay, took her gently by the hand, and said to her, "Get up, fair one, and come to him who yearns so for you."

And she, who was so bewitched that she could hardly say no to what he wanted, at once jumped out of bed all naked but for her shift and underclothing, and Merlin led her by the hand past her father's bed and the beds of the other knights from there, but they were sleeping so soundly that they would not have awakened if the castle had been torn down on top of them. So Merlin and the maiden made their way until they came into the room where the two kings were lying, and they found King Ban and King Bors sleeping very deeply, because they were under Merlin's power.

They went directly to King Ban, who was very ill at ease, and Merlin said to him, "Sir, look, here is the good and lovely maiden who will bear the good and handsome son whose renown will be great throughout the kingdom of Logres."

When the king saw the maiden and heard what Merlin said to him, he stretched out his hands and, happy and joyful, took her to him, for he yearned deeply for her, and he did not have the strength to withstand temptation, because of the spell that had been cast; and if he had not been bewitched, he would not have done what he did for the whole kingdom of Logres, for he mightily feared Our Lord. But he sat up and welcomed the maiden into his arms, and she took off her underclothing and her shift and lay down beside him. And they were as merry and as loving as if they had been together for twenty years, for neither one was afraid or ashamed of the other, and this is the way that Merlin had ordained it. And this is how King Ban and the maiden were all night until daybreak. And then Merlin came in—he knew very well what time it was—and he made the young lady get up; and she put her shift and underclothing back on. And the king took a little ring off his finger and said to her, "Dear, you will keep this ring and my love."

And the young lady took it and put it on her finger; then she left straightway and commended him to God. And Merlin took her back to her own bed and made her lie down all naked. And she went to sleep at once, for she had conceived a son in whom Lancelot afterwards took great joy and great pride, because of the great good there was in him.

After Merlin had put the young lady back in the bed from which he had taken her, he went back to his own bed and lay down. Then he undid his spell and everyone in the castle awoke, and it was already quite late. So the squires and the serving men got up, put on their armor, saddled their horses, and packed up [406] chests and trunks. And Merlin came straight to King Ban, who was still asleep. The spell that made him fall in love with the young lady had been broken; he was well aware that he had lain with her, but he did not know how it had happened, although he did believe that it had been brought about by Merlin. And Merlin came to him and told him that it was time to ride. And when the two kings had got out of bed and dressed along with all the others, the lord of the castle and the three maidens came to the two kings and greeted them, and they returned their greetings. And when King Ban saw the young lady who had lain with him all that night, he looked at her very thoughtfully and she at him, lowering her face because she was deeply ashamed that she had been so intimate with him and had yielded herself to him. Yet, from that time forth there was not one hour when she did not love him more than any other man, and it was plain to see, for after that she never touched a man, but said to herself that a woman who had given herself to a king should not yield to a man of lower birth, nor did she ever want to take a husband.

And King Ban took her by the hand and said to her very kindly, "Lady, I must leave, but wherever I am, I am your knight and your friend. And I beg you to mind what you do and take care of yourself, for you are pregnant with a son who will bring you great gladness and joy, you can be sure of it."

Merlin had made him aware of this, and thanks to Merlin he knew some of the things that were to come.

And the young lady answered in a low voice, smiling, "Sir, if I am, then may God, by His holy will, grant me greater joy than I have in your behavior, for never have people in love been parted so quickly. But since it behooves you to go, I will be comforted as best I can, because I am left with child. And if I live long enough to see him, he will be for me a mirror and a reminder of you."

Hearing these words, King Ban put his arms about her neck and, smiling, commended her to God, and she went back into her room with her maidens. And the two kings and Merlin said farewell to the lady of the castle and the lord too, and thanked them most kindly for the courtesy they had shown them. Then they got on their horses and rode out of the castle across the causeway, one after the other. And Agravadain was a fourth member of their group and went along with his guests as far as the pine tree and then turned back.

And the two kings rode until they came to the sea, and they boarded boats and crossed over with great rejoicing and festivity. And when they had reached the shore in the port, they got out of the boats, got on their horses, and made their way until they came to the city of Benoic, where they were greeted with very great joy. But more than anyone else, the two queens were glad to see their husbands. The two kings stayed with their wives in the city of Benoic, and Merlin stayed there with them for a full eight days. And on the ninth, he took leave of the two kings and the two queens and the other barons and went straight to his lady love.

She was very glad to see him, for she loved him with a deep love, because of the great nobility she had found in him, and he loved nothing so much as her, for he taught her what he was unwilling to show anyone else. And he stayed a week with her and then left and came straight to Blaise, his master, who longed very much to see him. And Merlin [407] told him about the gathering on the Plain of Salisbury and how the queen of Garlot had been rescued, and he told him about all the things that had happened since he left him.

But with that, the story now falls silent about Blaise and Merlin and goes back to speaking about King Arthur and his companions.

50. ARTHUR'S MID-AUGUST COURT; KING RION'S CHALLENGE.[*]

Now the story says that when King Ban, King Bors, and Merlin had left King Arthur to go back to their countries, King Arthur stayed in Camelot, happy and joyful with Queen Guenevere, his wife, who loved him with great love and he her; and they spent a long time in love and pleasure until it was close to mid-August. And then King Arthur told Sir Gawainet that on that festival he wanted to hold a lavish court where all who held land from him would be.

"For at no celebration I have ever held," he went on, "have they been gathered all together."

And he wanted word to be sent to all of them near and far, friends and foreigners. "And I wish each one to bring his wife or his lady love with him," he went on, "to honor my celebration all the more."

And Sir Gawainet told him that he had spoken very well and that such a proposal had come from a noble heart. "So I beg you," he went on, "do your utmost, since you have talked so much about it, to bring honor to yourself then."

And the king said, "Of course, dear nephew, I long to hold such a court that it will be talked about forever."

Then King Arthur had charters and letters written, and he sent them to the barons and the knights, and he sent them word, if they held his love dear, to come to the city of Camelot on the eve of Our Lady's Day in mid-August, for then he wanted to hold a lavish high court, and everyone should bring along his wife or lady love. And the messengers went out to the princes and the barons; they showed them the letters and spread the message throughout the countryside. And the barons and princes adorned themselves the most handsomely and becomingly they knew how, and they came to court just as the king had ordered. And everyone who had a wife brought her with him, and the others, who were unwed, brought their lady loves. And so many came that it was a wonder to behold, for not a tenth of them could

[*]   Corresponds to Sommer, 407-413.

be lodged in the city of Camelot, and the others found shelter in the meadowland, which was wide and beautiful, in tents and pavilions.

The king joyfully welcomed them with great honor. And Queen Guenevere, who was the best-taught lady in the world, gladly welcomed the queens, the ladies, and the maidens, for she was more clever than any lady known in the world. She gave them lavish gifts of gold, silver, and costly silk cloth according to who each one was, and she did it so well that everyone said that there was no lady as worthy as she. Meanwhile, King Arthur gave out clothing, armor, and horses, and he did the gentlemen such honor and courtesy that they loved him for it for as long as they lived, and they showed it afterwards in many a battle and many a time of need, just as the story will reveal it to you later. [408]

King Arthur held a very great celebration the eve of mid-August for the wealthy nobility that had come. After the king and the barons had heard vespers in the High Church of St. Stephen, tables were set up everywhere, in tents and pavilions on the grass, which was green, for the king and all the barons ate in the meadows, because not all of them could do so in the city. Elsewhere were Queen Guenevere, the ladies wed and unwed, King Arthur's sisters, the wife of King Lot of Orkney, King Urien's wife, the queen of Garlot, the queens of Benoic and Gaunes, and the other countesses, queens, and ladies. And there was such joyful celebration that it was a wonder to behold, for in all the land of the king of Britain, everywhere King Arthur held sway, there was not a singer or musician who had not come to that festival. And everyone was served at that meal as befitted the court of such a powerful man as King Arthur was, and they all had a good time that evening until it was the hour to go to bed, when all who needed it rested until the next morning.

In the morning the king, the wealthy barons, and the queens got up and went to hear Mass at St. Stephen's, the high church of Camelot, and the service was celebrated in honor of the sweet Lady of Paradise, whose feast day it was, and the offerings were generous and lavish. King Arthur and the other kings wore crowns that day, as did all the queens, in honor of the high feast day, and there were twenty-six crowned heads, as many kings as queens, for King Arthur was the thirteenth among the kings and Queen Guenevere the thirteenth among the queens.

And when Mass had been said and the service ended, King Arthur went up to his great hall with all the other kings behind him, all wearing crowns, and Queen Guenevere did the same, with all the queens behind her, each one with a golden crown on her head. King Arthur sat at the high table and had the twelve other kings sit at his table from head to foot by rank, and in honor of the high Lady whose feast day it was, he had Queen Guenevere sit beside him wearing her crown, and all the other kings did likewise with their queens. At the other tables sat the dukes, the earls, and the other princes all in order, and the other knights were seated most richly in the meadowland in tents and pavilions, and they celebrated with great dignity and joy, and the knights and minstrels did so much singing that never had there been such rejoicing at any court.

While they were celebrating with such festivity, and as Kay the Seneschal brought the first dish before the king and queen, the most handsome form of a man they had ever seen came in. He wore a tunic of samite and was girded with a belt of silk with golden rings and precious stones that flashed with such brightness that all of the great hall shone with it. He had blond, curly hair and had a crown on his head like a king. He had on bright-colored stockings and shoes of white leather edged in golden embroidery, buckled with gold clasps. And he had about his neck a harp that was all of richly-worked silver with strings of fine gold, and it was studded with precious stones. And the man was so handsome of body, [409] of face, and of limb that a more beautiful creature had never been seen. But one thing was dreadfully wrong with him, for he could not see at all; even so, his eyes were clear and fair. A chain was hanging from his belt, and at the other end was tied a little dog whiter than snow; he wore about his neck a little collar of silk with gold rings. And this dog led him straight before King Arthur. He was playing a Breton lay so sweetly on his harp that it was good music to hear. And after the refrain of his lay, he greeted King Arthur and Queen Guenevere and all those gathered there. And Kay the Seneschal, who was carrying the first dish, lingered awhile before putting it down to listen to the harp, so keen was he to hear its sound.

But with that, the story falls silent here about all of them, and we will tell you about King Rion of the Isles.

In this part the story says that, when King Rion was routed by King Arthur and King Leodagan of Carmelide, he left the battle sad and upset and went back to his country gloomy and downcast, and he swore an oath that never in his life would he have joy and rest until he had King Leodagan stripped of everything that belonged to him and driven out of the land. And he sent out letters and called his men together from throughout his whole kingdom far and wide, and from the kingdoms of all the kings he had conquered, of whom there were nine by count, and so many came that it was a wonder to see. The first king who came at King Rion's summons was King Paladem, with fifteen thousand bold, skilled men. Next came King Safur with twelve thousand men dressed in iron. And King Sarmedon brought fourteen thousand, King Argant* eleven thousand, and King Taurus thirteen thousand who were stouthearted and burning to avenge King Rion's shame. Afterward came King Aride of Galore, who brought fifteen thousand with him. And King Solinas brought twenty thousand all riding good horses. And King Kahanin brought ten thousand, and they were all knights. And King Alipansin† of the Grazing Fields brought twenty thousand.

After they had come and joined together on the orders of King Rion, and he saw them before him, he lodged his complaint and made his plea for all to hear. And he told them quite frankly, "Sirs, you are all my men, and you hold your lands and fiefs from me, and by your oath you owe faith to me against all other men. And because I know your hearts to be noble and true, and you would not wish to wrong me in any way, I therefore beseech you to help me avenge my shame—not mine, but yours! For anyone who does a shameful or wrongful deed does it not to me alone, but to you all together. And so, on the oaths that you have sworn to me, I ask you to come two months from today before the city of Carhaix and move against King Leodagan of Carmelide, who by his might beat me and drove me from the field, and I ask that vengeance be taken."

---

*   Here the form is *agans* (409, l. 23); the form *argant* is found at 411, l. 13.

†   Here the form is *alipantis* (409, l. 27), but C.D. West (13a) identifies this *Alipantis des pastures* with another Saxon king, *Alipansis*, mentioned earlier (237, l. 11).

And they answered all of a voice that they did not need to be asked, for they would do it very willingly. With that, they went their own ways, and each one came back to his country. And they got themselves ready and [410] came back on the appointed day to the castle of Carhaix. At the same time King Rion came back with all his men. And they laid siege to the city all around and took in their plunder and whatever else came their way.

But Cleodalis, the seneschal of Carmelide who was a most valiant man and faithful to his lord, fiercely challenged them, for he was very worthy. He rode out with twenty thousand knights whom he had engaged there to guard the borderland, and he fought them very fiercely because they were pillaging what belonged to him. He won it back and brought it back into the castle and had the gates shut.

And King Rion and his men encamped around the castle and had tents and pavilions set up, and they rested all that night. The next morning they began an assault with shooting and hurling. And King Leodagan and Cleodalis left the town by a hidden gate that opened upon the river right at the tent of Solinas, who had gone to fight near a little gate. And King Leodagan and Cleodalis charged headlong in among the tents, and they threw to the ground as many as they came to, and they took gold, silver, dishes, and bolts of silk cloth, and they forced their way back to the castle with it.

Then those in the horde were most distraught and upset, but King Rion said that it would be worthless to them, for he would not leave the castle without taking it and having King Leodagan at his mercy. So they pulled back and stopped their assault, and they went on thus for five days, without shooting arrows or throwing spears. While King Rion was in this lull, a messenger came to him and told him that King Arthur had routed the Saxons and driven them from his land, and that on the day of mid-August he was to hold high court in the city of Camelot. And when King Rion heard this, he said, "Let's let him feast now, for as soon as I have King Leodagan in my power, I'll go see him with so many men that he can't hold out against them. Even so, if King Arthur came to me for mercy while I am still here, and before I go against him with my army, I would take pity on him, and I would let him rule if he held his land from me."

"Sir," said his men, "send him your messengers and let him know that, for he would be better off to become your man than to be stripped of his belongings and driven from his land."

"I'll do it," said King Rion.

Then he had a letter written and sealed with his seal, and he had all his barons put their seals on it. And when it had been sealed with ten royal seals, he called one of his knights whom he trusted very much and made him swear on holy relics that he would deliver the letter into the hands of King Arthur, and he swore that he would. Then King Rion gave him the letter, and he left him and set out on the road to Camelot with only one squire. And King Rion stayed behind at the castle of Carhaix and ordered his men to arm themselves to assault Carhaix, for it was quite bitter for him that this castle, which had so few people, meant to hold out against him as long as it could. He had, he thought,* more knights in his horde than there

*   Sommer's text misprints *anis* for *auis/avis* (410, l. 40): "opinion."

were men, women, and children all together in the castle, "and it is a great shame and a blow to our power that we ever laid siege here, for we ought to have taken the castle in one stroke when we came here. But now we will be less esteemed in all countries, and we'll be rebuked for weakness and cowardice, and [411] everyone else we'll want to overrun will say that we are so cowardly and so weak-hearted that we are worthless."

When the barons and princes heard King Rion saying these things, they were deeply shamed, for they were afraid that he would take them for cowards and weaklings. So they quickly ran to their weapons and began to assault the castle, shooting and hurling spears. And those within, who were most worthy men, threw great sharp stones down on them, and many of them were knocked down into the moats. And King Leodagan, Cleodalis, Guiomar, who was King Leodagan's cousin, Hervi de Rivel, and Malés the Dark rode out in full armor on their prize horses covered with iron, and they flew headlong into the army of King Rion. He had just stormed a gatehouse and was taking away fifteen foot soldiers, who were very worthy and bold, and they risked being very badly hurt and maltreated, when Cleodalis, holding his lance straight out, let his horse run against King Rion's men, and he struck King Argant so hard that neither shield nor hauberk could have kept him from harm or Cleodalis from driving the iron tip of his lance through his chest, and he killed him and sent him down sprawling.

When his men saw him on the ground, they left the ones they were taking away and ran to where he was. And when they found him dead, the wailing and the uproar about him grew so loud that the whole assault stopped, and Cleodalis and those with him rescued the fifteen companions, who were so worthy and bold, and took them to safety back in the castle, and they shut the gates. And those in the horde stayed outside and carried their king to the tent of King Rion, who was saddened and upset.

And so the story falls silent about them and goes back to speaking of King Rion's messenger, who was going to King Arthur.

Here the story says that, after the messenger had left his lord, he and his squire rode until they came to Camelot on the day of mid-August. They dismounted under an olive tree and went into the hall after Kay had put the first dish before King Arthur. He saw the kings and queens sitting about the high table, wearing crowns because of the day's great meaning, and he saw the harper playing, wearing a gold crown, and he was utterly amazed by the dog that led him throughout the hall. He asked Kay the Seneschal, who was serving at table, which one was King Arthur, and Kay pointed him out straightway.

And the knight, who was very mindful and quite well-spoken, came straight before the king and said to him loudly enough for all the men and women to hear, "King Arthur, I do not greet you, because I am not ordered to do so by the one who sends me to you; even so, I'll tell you what he means you to know. And when you have heard his message, you will do what your heart bids; if you do his will you'll have honor, but if you do not, you will have to leave your land in flight, poor and dispossessed."

When King Arthur heard him, he began to smile and said to him very kindly, "Friend, tell what your message is, for you can safely say what you will with no hindrance from me or anyone else."

And he said to him, [412] "King Arthur, the one who sends me here to you is the lord and master of all the Christians, that is, King Rion of the Isles, who is besieging the castle of Carhaix with nine other kings who are all his liegemen and hold lands, fiefs, and honors from him, for by his prowess he has made them all bow to him and by his boldness has beaten them all with his sword, and he has taken off the beards, along with the hide, of all the kings he has defeated, of whom there are nine by count. Now my lord bids you to come to him and become his liegeman, and this would be a great honor coming from such a mighty king as my lord is, for he is the lord of the West and of the whole earth."

When the knight had thus spoken, he drew out King Rion's letter, which was sealed with ten seals, and he said to King Arthur, "Sir, have this letter read that my lord sends you, and you will hear his will and his heart."

Then he handed it to him, and the king took it and handed it to the archbishop of Brice, who had come there to hear what the knight had to say. He quickly unfolded it and began to read it for all who were there to hear. And he read it just as you will hear:

"I, King Rion, who am lord and governor of all of the land of the West, make it known to all who will see and hear this letter, that I am laying siege to the castle of Carhaix in Carmelide, and I have nine kings with me and all the men belonging to them, as many as are fit to bear arms. And I have won all the swords of all these kings by my mighty prowess, and I have taken their beards along with the hide. And in remembrance of my victory, I have had a cloak of red samite made, and I have lined it with the kings' beards. This cloak is ready, and it is trimmed with clasps and all else that befits it but the fringe. But because the fringe is lacking, and I have heard stories* about the great goodness and worthiness of King Arthur, whose renown is so widespread through the whole world, I want him to be more highly honored than any of the other kings. So I bid you to send me your beard with the hide, and I'll put it on the edge of my cloak for love of you. Until my cloak has its fringe, it will never hang from my shoulders, and I want no other fringe than your beard, for at his hands and neck every prince should wear the noblest and most lordly things. And because you are lordly and a mightier king than all the others, as Renown bears witness, I order you to send me your beard by one or two of your best friends and then to come to me, and you will become my liegeman and hold your land from me. And if you will not do this, leave your land and go into exile, for as soon as I have defeated King Leodagan, I will put my whole army against you, and I will have your beard torn out against the grain, you can be sure of it!"

When the archbishop of Brice had read the letter before King Arthur and all the princes, he handed it back to King Arthur, who was very sorry and upset by the order.

And the messenger said, "King Arthur, do what my lord bids you and I'll go back."

* The text bears the synonyms *noueles & mention* (412, l. 24): "news and reference."

And the king told him that he could go back whenever he wanted, but he would not have his beard [413] as long as he lived, and he could be sure of that. So the knight left at once and came straight to his horse, mounted, and took to the road with his squire, and they made their way until they came to Carhaix in Carmelide, where they found King Rion, who was assaulting the castle with all his might, while those within defended themselves very forcefully, so that those outside were scattered time after time, and King Rion was quite distraught.

And when the messenger came before King Rion and told him King Arthur's answer, and he said that right after he had taken King Leodagan, he would fall upon Arthur with such a great number of men that he would not hold up against them.

So the story falls silent right here about King Rion and goes back to speaking about King Arthur and his barons.

51. THE BATTLE BEFORE CARHAIX.*

Now the story says that when King Rion's messenger left King Arthur, King Arthur stayed seated at his meal and took solace in festivity and rejoicing. And the harper went from one row to the next and played soothingly to everyone, and they all looked at him in wonder because they had never heard such harp-playing. And they found greater delight in the harper's playing than in anything the other minstrels did. And King Arthur himself wondered where such a man could have come from. Yet he ought to have known him well, for he had seen him many times in another shape or another likeness.

And after they had eaten and the tables had been taken down, the harper came to King Arthur and said to him, "Sir, if you please, I would like to have my reward for my service."

"Indeed, you will have your reward," answered the king, "and it is very right. Now say what you wish from me, and you won't lack for it if it's anything I can give short of my honor and my kingdom."

"Sir," said the harper, "you will have nothing but honor, God willing."

"Then say what you wish from me, for you can trust me."

"Sir," said the harper, "I ask to bear your ensign in the first battle you go to."

"Dear friend, would that be to my honor and my kingdom's honor? Our Lord has put you in His prison by making you blind. How would you see to bear the banner and lead us into battle? For my ensign must be the refuge and the safeguard of all other banners in the battle."

"Ah, sir," answered the harper, "God, who is the true Leader, will lead me, as He has led me through many a dangerous place; and it will be to your good."

And when the barons heard this, they were astonished. Then King Ban looked about and was reminded of Merlin, who, at the Castle of the Fens, served him in the likeness of a youth of fifteen years, and he thought that it might be he. So he said

*   Corresponds to Sommer, 413-419.

at once to King Arthur, "Sir, grant him his request, for he does not look to me like a man I'd refuse to give my warhorse to."

"What?" said King Arthur. "Do you believe that it would be to our good and honor to allow a minstrel who cannot lead himself to carry my banner into battle? And if I refused him, I do not see that it would be held against me, for this is not something that should be granted lightly if you don't fully trust the person you put into the battle to lead."

And as soon as he had said these words, the harper vanished from among them, and no one ever knew what became of him. Then King Arthur began brooding about Merlin, and he was most distressed [414] and upset that he had not granted him his wish. And all who were there were amazed that they had lost him so suddenly. And King Ban of Benoic, who saw clearly and knew that it had been Merlin, said to King Arthur, "Indeed you ought to have recognized him."

"You speak the truth," said King Arthur, "but I did not know who he was because he had a dog leading him."*

"Who is he then?" asked Sir Gawainet

"Dear nephew," answered King Arthur, "it is Merlin, our master."

"Indeed!" said Sir Gawainet. "God help me, I do believe you when you say that it is he, for many times he has disguised himself and changed likenesses before your nobles, and it is all to give us solace and to cheer us up."

While they were talking of these things, a little child eight years old came into the hall. All over his head his hair grew in patches, and he wore no breeches, but he carried a cudgel in his hand. He made straight for King Arthur and told him to get ready to move against King Rion in battle, and he bade him give him his standard to bear. And when those within the great hall saw him in such a state, they all burst out laughing. And King Arthur answered him laughing, for he believed that it was Merlin.

"God help me," said King Arthur, "you are indeed the one to carry it, and I heartily grant this to you."

"You have my thanks," said the lad, "for I'll put it to very good use indeed."

With that, he commended them all to God and left the great hall. Then he took on the likeness he bore most often and said to himself that it was time to call the king's armies together. So he made for the sea and crossed over, and he came straight to Gaunes, where Pharian and Leonce of Payerne were, and told them to gather their forces and any others they could muster in that land and come to the city of Camelot, and they said they would do as he ordered. Then Merlin went back toward the sea and crossed back into Great Britain, and he went throughout the lands of King Urien and King Lot and told the barons there to go to the city of Camelot two weeks after the feast of Our Lady in September, and they said that they would be there. Then he left them and came back to King Arthur's court, and Vespers had not yet been said in the church of my lord St. Stephen on that very same feast day.

---

*   The text is periphrastic: *ce quil se faisoit mener a .j. chien mauoit tolue la connaissance* (414, ll. 4-5): literally, "that he had himself led by a dog took away my recognition."

Then King Arthur asked him why he had disguised himself so many times, but he answered that he must surely have recognized him.

"You are right," said King Arthur, "to say that I might have known!"

And so they spent the rest of that day in joyful merrymaking.

The next morning King Arthur gathered all his princes together in his great hall, and Merlin was there too. And King Arthur told them that they had to call up as many men as they could in their lands, for they needed to help King Leodagan, Queen Guenevere's father. But Merlin told him that forces had already been summoned at Gaunes, at Benoic, and throughout the barons' and the princes' lands. King Arthur asked him when that had been done.

"Sir," answered Merlin, "I have been everywhere since the evening meal yesterday."

When King Arthur and the princes heard this, they were amazed, and so they feasted and made merry until their armies came to gather at Camelot. Then King Arthur and his barons rode out toward the kingdom of Carmelide, and Merlin bore the standard just as King Arthur had said he could. And they rode in stages until [415] they came to within a league of Carhaix, where King Rion had besieged King Leodagan.

And when they had drawn near the army, Merlin said to Sir Gawainet, Sir Yvain, and Sagremor, "Stay close to me."

And they answered that they would do whatever he liked.

"Then follow me right now, you and everyone in the army," Merlin said softly, "until we come to the battleground. Then you will strike out helter-skelter into the fighting, but always remember to come to my banner wherever you may see me go."

They answered that they would do so, and he said the same thing to King Arthur and the other princes. Then they set out and made their way until they rode into Rion's horde. And Merlin rushed out ahead of the others as fast as he could make his horse run, with the dragon raised on the tip of his lance and the banner's tails beating against his wrist. The dragon shot fire and flames from its throat and such great flares that everyone in King Rion's army was aghast. And Sir Gawainet, who followed it closely, holding his lance, crossed paths with King Pharaoh, who had started moving against them with his standard when he saw them coming nearer. And Sir Gawainet struck him so hard that neither shield nor hauberk could keep him from driving the tip of his lance through his body, and he brought him sprawling down dead to the ground. And he said in mockery, "This man has sworn peace, for King Arthur will never be bothered by him or lose one inch of his land!"

At once the two armies came together, one against the other, and great was the uproar and mighty the blows struck by King Rion's and King Arthur's men. And my lord Gawainet, my lord Yvain, Sagremor, Agravain, Guerrehet, Gaheriet, and the knights of the Round Table did wonders with their fighting.

When the two armies clashed, anyone could have seen a great slaughter of men and horses, for they were skilled and bold knights on both sides. And Merlin, who bore the dragon, drove headlong into the crowd, and Sir Gawainet and his companions came after him, holding their lances straight out, and they struck those they came against so hard that they bore them to the ground, and the splinters from their lances flew up into the sky. This was something that filled King Rion with dread, for his men all thought that devils had fallen upon their army, but they were so worthy and knightly that they were not disheartened for all that. Rather, they kept fighting wondrously hard against King Arthur's men; indeed, they drove them back after their first strike, so that Sir Gawainet and his companions were greatly distraught.

And Merlin shouted to them, "What can this be? My lords, have you stopped? Follow me, if you seek to grow in worthiness!"

Then the companions charged in headlong among the men of Ireland, who welcomed them most warmly with their swords. But Sir Gawainet and his companions fought so skillfully and so well that they drove right through King Rion's army, and by that time many a blow had been dealt and taken and many a knight struck down dead. And King Arthur, King Lot of Orkney, King Ban, and King Bors had ridden hard into the army elsewhere, and they did wonders, for no armor could withstand their blows. But King Rion's men struck back so hard that they brought down King Lot and King Bors in the middle of the field with their horses on top of them, and they might have been badly hurt, [416] had it not been for their great worth and skill, for they nimbly sprang to their feet, wielding their swords, and began striking down knights and horses with such strength that everyone who saw it took it for a great wonder. King Arthur and King Ban spurred to where they were in the worst of the fighting to help them back on their horses.

Merlin came there with the banner with the dragon that spewed fire and flame from its throat, and he had driven through where the press was heaviest. And when King Rion's men saw the fire and the great wonder of the dragon, they grew frightened and yielded their ground. The two kings whom they had run down stood quietly where they were, and Merlin came to them and gave each one a good, strong, and fast horse, for there were many strays in the thick of battle; they were eager to be mounted at once.

And when they were on horseback again, they flew into the battle and began to do wonders with their arms, as did all their companions. But the strength of King Rion's men was so great that those from the kingdom of Logres could not withstand them, and they would have been utterly routed if it had not been for Sir Gawainet, his brothers, and the other companions of the Round Table. They did wonders: they brought down knights and horses, and they struck to the ground as many as they stood against. It seemed to those who saw it that they were not men of flesh and blood, but devils from hell.

Elsewhere on the battlefield were King Neutres, King Tradelmant, King Urien, and the King of the Hundred Knights. They were fighting with great fierceness against the men of the Isles, who wonderfully held their ground against them, for in the Isles were great knighthood and great skill at arms; they had brought down the king of North Wales and were holding him by his helmet's nasal. And Merlin came to Sir Gawainet and said to him, "Now we'll see how well you can fight, for we have lost King Tradelmant unless someone helps him right away. So I beg you, follow me!"

Then Sir Gawainet and his companions started after him, and they fought their way through to King Tradelmant, who was in great danger of being killed. Then they fell upon the ones who were holding him and began to hit them so hard that all who saw it thought it a wonder, so that the ones holding King Tradelmant, who were most worthy and bold in battle, were overwhelmed and could scarcely hold onto him. The companions of the Round Table had a hard time rescuing him, but in the end they succeeded in getting him back on his horse, and the men of the Isles were filled with sorrow and heartache. Then the fighting and the hitting began again and grew hard and dreadful to see, for men fell down dead one on top of the other, and they lay in great heaps amid the ranks where the fighting was, for Sir Gawainet struck down so many with his sword that his arm and sword were all stained with blood and brains up to his shoulder.

When King Leodagan of Carmelide saw, from up above where he was leaning from a window, that the fighting was so hard and deadly, and he caught sight of the dragon that Merlin carried, spewing fire and flame from its throat so that the air was all red, he knew at once that it was the standard of King Arthur, for he had seen it many times before. And then King Leodagan shouted, [417] "Sir knights, now to arms. For my son King Arthur is fighting against our foes, and he has come to rescue us, for which I thank him!"

And when they heard him, they ran as one through the castle to put on their armor, and they rode out of the gate fully armed. There were a good ten thousand of them, all knights worthy and bold, and with great strength they charged in headlong among the men of Ireland and those of the Isles, who welcomed them heartily like men of great boldness. And Cleodalis the Seneschal, Hervi of Rivel, and their other companions began to do wonders of arms, and the fighting was so great throughout King Rion's army that it was a sheer wonder how many died on both sides.

When King Rion saw the dreadful killing and the great slaughter of his men, his heart softened and he took great pity on his people, and he said to himself that it was a great wrong and he could bear it no more. And then he took a sycamore bough and carried it in his hands before the armies to break up the fighting, and he rode until he found King Arthur. And when he had found him, he spoke loudly enough for all to hear and understand him, and this is what he said:

"King Arthur, why do you allow your men and mine to be slaughtered? Do what is right, if you are as worthy as the world has borne witness. Free your men from death and I'll free mine. Let us withdraw our armies; then let us fight each other, you and me, man to man, and this will be our pledge: if you can beat me, I'll go back into my country with my men who are left alive, and if I can win out over you, you will hold your land from me and become my underling, as all the kings are whom I have beaten, and I'll have your beard with your hide to make the fringe for my cloak."

"In God's name," said King Arthur, "You would have the better part of the wager, for you would go back to your country safe and sound if I defeated you, and you would not become my liegeman! But I'll fight you just as you have said if you will be my liegeman should I beat you, and I grant you the same if you defeat me."

"Sir," said King Rion, who was so strong and full of such prowess that he feared to fight no one man to man, and he had defeated nine kings who were all his liegemen, "I grant it just as you have said."

Then they swore between the two of them to hold to their oaths, and they broke up the fighting, which was so dreadful and dangerous that it was a wonder to behold, and they withdrew their barons, who were angry and upset by this agreement.

And Sir Gawainet, who was more distressed than any of the others, came straight to King Arthur and said to him, "Sir, please grant this fight to me, for you could well do so."

"Now don't ask me this again," said King Arthur, "for no one but I will put his hand to it, God willing."

Soon the armies were gathered on each side, and the two kings put on costly armor, whatever they needed, and each one took a strong, stout lance. They rode more than a furlong away from each other; then they struck their horses with their spurs and flew against each other like a storm, for their horses ran wonderfully fast. And the two [418] kings were of great strength, and, with their horses running as fast as they could, they dealt each other such hard blows on their shields, just above the bosses, with their lances, which were short and thick with sharp tips, that they drove through them, but their hauberks were so strong that not a link broke; and their horses were so powerful and the knights so skilled, and they had struck each other so hard, that their lances flew into pieces.

Then they took hold of their swords, which were very well made, and struck wondrous, heavy blows on each other's helmet, so that they broke the jewels' settings and knocked off the gems and stones, of which there were some that had great powers, and they cut through their shields and hauberks and struck so deeply into the flesh that the blood spurted out. Thus they had worked upon each other so thoroughly that they both needed a physician. And they had so sliced through their shields that neither had a piece big enough to cover his hand, so they threw what was left to the ground and took their swords in both hands, and they dealt each other such strong and heavy* blows that they cut open helmets and hauberks, so that their naked flesh showed through,† and they were both tired and worn out from the blows they had given and taken. This is what kept them going for such a long time, for if they had been fresh and rested after they had been left without shields, their hauberks had come unlinked, and their helmets had been split open and crushed, they could not have lasted without one or the other being killed; nevertheless, they were both very badly wounded.

When King Rion, who was most worthy and bold and a good knight above all others in his land, saw King Arthur holding his own against him with such liveliness, he was amazed, for he did not believe that he could outlast him. So he said to himself that never before had he found such a good knight. He grew deathly afraid of him and said to him, "King Arthur, it is indeed too bad for you, for you are the best knight I've ever fought. Yet I can see clearly, and I know in truth, that the great heart you have will be the death of you, for it will not let you come to me for mercy. And I know for a fact that you would rather die than be defeated, and that is a great shame! So I would beseech you, for the great knightly spirit you have in you, to have mercy on yourself. Acknowledge that you are bested so that you may

---

*   Sommer's text continues with *a descoue[rt]* [sic] (418, l. 14): "visible," "in full view," etc.

†   Sommer's text continues with a redundant *des cops quil sentredounent* (418, l. 15): "from the blows they gave each other." The phrase recurs in the next line.

save your life, according to the pledges we have made between us, so that my cloak may be finished while I am still alive. If you do not do this, you must know that you have come to your end."

When King Arthur heard the words King Rion spoke to him, he was deeply ashamed, because so many highborn men had heard him as well. Then he ran King Rion down, wielding his sword with both hands, for he was filled with wrath, and he meant to strike him over the head. But King Rion stepped aside, for he had seen the stroke coming at full speed; even so, King Arthur hit him on the helmet and cut him down across the nose, and, as the sword went downward, he struck his warhorse in front of the saddlebow and sliced all the way through its neck, and King Rion fell to the ground. And just as he thought he could get back up, King Arthur struck him on his right shoulder so hard that he sank the blade two finger-widths into his flesh. King Rion lurched and then went sprawling to the ground.

And when King Arthur saw him on the ground [419] again, he got down from his horse at once and ran upon him very fast. He grabbed him by his helmet and pulled him toward him with such great strength that he broke off the strings, tore his helmet from his head, and hurled it more than eight yards away. Then he raised his sword and told him that he was dead if he did not acknowledge that he had been beaten. But King Rion answered that he would never admit that he had been defeated by him, for he would rather die than live as a faithless coward. And when King Arthur saw that he could not succeed in making him acknowledge that he was beaten, he cut off his head in plain sight of all who were in the meadow.

Then the princes ran forward from every side and greeted him with great rejoicing, and they put him on his horse and led him into the castle of Carhaix. They took off his armor and looked after his wounds. And King Rion's men came to him at once and took their lands and fiefdoms from him; then they went back to their country and took King Rion's body back with them, and they buried him with weeping and sobbing.

And King Arthur stayed in Carhaix with his barons, glad and joyful because of the victory that God had sent them, and they stayed in the castle until King Arthur recovered from the wounds he had received in the battle. And when he was back in good health, he left Carhaix amid feasting and great rejoicing, and King Leodagan went with him a long way and then turned back after they had commended each other to God. And King Arthur and his companions made their way until they came to the city of Camelot, where Queen Guenevere and the other queens were—they were very glad to see them when they got there.

The princes lingered there for four days, and on the fifth they took their leave; each one went back into his own country, and those who had wives and friends there took them away with them. And King Arthur came back to the city of Logres and lived there for a long time with the queen, and Sir Gawainet and the companions of the Round Table were with them and Merlin, who had given them all great comfort as their companion.

Merlin came to King Arthur and told him that, from then on, he could get along without him, for he had brought a measure of peacefulness to his land, so now he could go seek pleasure elsewhere for a while.

When King Arthur understood that he wanted to go away, he was quite upset, for he loved him deeply, and he would have liked very much for him to stay. But when he saw that he could not keep him there, he begged him most kindly to come back. And Merlin told him that he would come back at once when he needed him.

"Indeed," said King Arthur, "I need you every day, for I can do nothing without your help. That is why I would like you never to leave me or my court at any time."

And Merlin answered, "I'll surely come back at once when you need me."

And the king fell silent for quite a while, and then he started to brood deeply, and after he had been lost in thought for a long time, he sighed and said, "Ah! Merlin, dear friend, please tell me in what time of need you are to help me!"

"Sir," said Merlin, "I'll tell you and then I'll take to the road. The lion, who is the son of the she-bear and was fathered by the leopard, will overrun the kingdom of Logres. That is the time of need."

With that, Merlin left.

So the story falls silent about the king and goes back to speaking about Merlin. [420]

52. KING FLUALIS'S DREAM AND ROMAN CLAIMS AGAINST BRITAIN.[*]

In this part the story says that, as soon as Merlin had left King Arthur, just as you have heard, he went out of the city of Logres and set out on the road so fast that no warhorse in the world could have kept up with him, so that those who saw him believed that he was truly out of his mind. And at once he rushed headlong into the forest, which was wide and deep, and made straight for the sea. He went across, as he did not wish to stop, and he made his way until he came to the region of Jerusalem, where there was a most powerful king whose name was Flualis. He was a worthy man of great renown in Islam,[†] for he was a Saracen.

He had brought together all the learned men of his land and others' lands, as many as there could be. And when they had all gathered before him in his great hall, he spoke to them, loudly enough for all to hear and understand him.

"My lords," he said, "I have sent word to you, and you have come at my behest, for which I thank you. And I'll tell you why I have sent for you. It is the truth that I was sleeping in my palace[‡] the other night, and I was holding the queen, who is right here, in my arms, or so it seemed to me. And while I was doing that, two flying serpents came to me. Each of them had two heads, and they were wondrously huge and ugly, and they were spewing fire and flames from their throats, so that they

---

[*]   Corresponds to Sommer, 420-427.

[†]   Sommer's text reads *de sa loy* (420, ll. 8-9): "with respect to his law, religion." The idea is to evoke a Saracen spiritual space opposed to Christendom.

[‡]   Exceptionally, in this passage the word *palais* (420, l. 14) is frequently translated as palace rather than great hall (cf. 420, l. 11). Doubtless the text means to evoke a building of Oriental splendor rather than the more utilitarian Western castle.

were setting fire to my whole palace. And one of the serpents grabbed me by the sides with its feet, and the other one took hold of the queen, who was lying in my arms, and they bore us up onto the highest roof of my palace, which is very tall. After they had carried us there, they tore our arms and legs from our bodies and hurled them down here and there, one by one. And when they had thus torn off our limbs, eight little serpents came straightway and each one took one limb and flew away high to the top of the temple of Diana, where my men had fled for safety,* and there they ripped our limbs into little pieces. And the two serpents that had taken our limbs from our bodies left us up on top of the palace, stirred up the fire inside the palace, burned our bodies, and reduced them to ash. And the wind picked up the ash and bore it throughout the land on this side of the sea. And there was not one good town left where a bit of it, or a little more, did not fall and lie. Such was the dream I had while I was asleep, and it weighs heavily on me.

"And this is why I have summoned you here. I beg you, I beseech you, mindful of all service and duty we owe one another,† if there is anyone among you who can interpret the dream for me, let him do it, and I swear faithfully to you that to the one who tells me the truth about it will I give my daughter as his wife and my whole kingdom after my death; or if he is wed, he will be lord over me and my land all the days of his life."

When the learned men heard King Flualis's promise after they had heard about the dream, they wondered greatly about what it might mean. One man said one thing, another something else, each one according to what seemed best to him. And after they had all spoken, Merlin, who had taken on such a shape that no one could recognize him or even see him, spoke loudly enough that everyone there could hear him plainly, and he said, "Listen to me, King Flualis. I'll tell you the meaning of your [421] dream."

When the king heard his words, he looked about him to see who had said this to him, and everyone in the hall did likewise, but they could not see him. But they heard the voice that was in the midst of them and said, "Listen, King Flualis, to the meaning of your dream. The two serpents you saw while asleep that had four heads and spat fire and flames stand for four Christian kings who border on your lands, and they are setting your country ablaze. And that the serpents carried you and the queen atop the highest roof of your palace means that they will have your whole land under their sway up to the gates of your stronghold. And that the serpents tore off your four limbs and your wife's means that you will forswear the evil religion you hold to in order to believe in Jesus Christ And that the eight little serpents picked up the limbs from your body and the queen's and bore them atop the temple of Diana, where your men had fled for safety, means that your children, who are your flesh and blood,‡ will be slain and cut up by weapons inside the temple of Diana. And that the serpents left you, and the queen with you, up atop the highest

---

* This clause is not in Sommer's text here (420, l. 25), but is mentioned by Merlin in his summary (421, ll. 12-13).

† Sommer's text reads *en tous seruices & en tous guerredons* (420, ll. 31-32): In [the name] of all services and all rewards."

‡ The text reads *ti membre & ta char* (421, l. 13): "your members and your flesh." The word *membre(s)* has been translated as "limb(s)" throughout the passage.

part of your palace means that you and she will be raised up in Christendom. And that the serpents burned the palace beneath you means that you will have nothing left worth a single penny of whatever you have under this evil religion. And that you and the queen were both burned and reduced to ash means that you* will be washed and cleansed of your sins by the water of holy baptism. That the ash from you flew through all the countries on this side of the sea means that you will have children under your good religion who will be knights worthy and bold, and they will be uplifted and honored throughout all the lands of the world. Now you have heard about the dream you had while you were asleep, and everything will happen to you just as I have told you."

With that Merlin went away and left the king bewildered by the voice he had heard and yet saw nothing. He made his way swiftly and did not stop until he came to the kingdom of Benoic. He went straight to Viviane, his lady friend, who was most eager to see him, for she as yet knew nothing that she wished to know of his art. And she greeted him the most joyfully she knew how, and they ate and drank and lay together in the same bed. She knew enough about his doings so that, when she understood that he wished to lie with her, she knew how to cast a spell and bring forth a pillow, which she put in his arms, and then Merlin went to sleep. This is not said to make the story relate that Merlin ever knew a woman carnally; but there was no woman in the world he loved so much as she, and this was shown to be true, for he gave himself so utterly to her, and from time to time he taught her so much of what he knew, that in the end he could count himself a fool.

He tarried with her for a long time, and she kept asking him about his knowledge and craft, so that he taught her a great deal. And she put down in writing everything he said to her, for she was well steeped in clerkly learning, so she remembered all the more easily what Merlin told her. And after he had been with her for quite a long while, he took leave of her and told her that he would be back at the end of the year. And each most sweetly commended the other to God.

And then Merlin went away to Blaise, his master, [422] who was most happy when he came. Blaise longed to see Merlin as Merlin longed to see him. And Merlin told him all the adventures that had happened to him after he left him, and he told him how he had been with Viviane and had taught her some of his spells. And Blaise put it all down in writing, and this is how we still know it

After Merlin had told his master all these things, just as they had happened one after the other, he took leave of him and went straight to the city of Logres, where King Arthur and his wife, the queen, were. And they welcomed Merlin most gladly. As soon as Merlin had arrived, a maiden went down before the hall riding a tawny mule, and she carried in front of her, on the other side of her saddlebow, the ugliest and most misshapen dwarf that had ever been seen. His nose was flat, he was skin and bones, his eyebrows were bushy and curly, his beard was red and grew so long that it hit his feet, his hair was coarse and black and unbecomingly disheveled, his shoulders were raised and twisted, he had one great hump in the middle of his back and another on his chest, his hands were fat and his fingers stubby, his legs were

---

*   From here to the end of Merlin's interpretation (421, ll. 19-24) the pronoun continues to be singular, and there is no further reference to the queen.

short, and his long backbone stuck out sharply. Yet the maiden was of very great beauty. And everyone stared at them.

And as soon as she had dismounted from her mule, she took the dwarf in her arms and helped him down quite gently, and she led him into the hall before the king, who was sitting at his meal. And when she saw the king, she greeted him most kindly, for she was filled with courtliness, and the king returned her greeting most courteously.

Then the maiden said, "Sir, I have come to you from very far away because of your great renown that runs through the world, and I would ask you a favor, for no maiden—so Renown bears witness of you—fails to have whatever she asks of you. So, inasmuch as everyone takes you for the worthiest man in the world, I have tried hard to come to your court to ask you just one favor. And be careful not to grant me anything you would not wish to give me or have done to me."

"Lady,"* said the king, "ask what you will, for it will not be in vain, so long as it is something that I can grant to my honor and my kingdom's honor."

"In what I wish to ask you," she answered, "you can have only honor."

"Lady," said the king, "say what you wish to say, for I am ready to do what you ask and more."

"Sir, I have come to entreat you to make a knight of this noble young lord whom I hold by the hand and who is my love. He indeed deserves to be a knight, and he ought to be one, for he is worthy and bold and of highborn stock. He should have become a knight quite some time ago, and he would have been made one, had he wanted, by the hand of King Pelles of Listenois, who is a most worthy and faithful man. But my love did not wish it so; rather, he swore an oath not to become a knight unless it is by your hand. This is why I ask you to make him a knight."

Then everyone in the hall burst out laughing, and Kay the Seneschal, who was most evil-tongued and full of bitter words, said to her, sneering, "Watch out for him and keep him close to you so that the queen's maidens will not take him from you! Soon they might steal him or snatch him away from you, for he is so handsome!" [423]

"Sir," she answered, "the king is such a worthy gentleman that, if it is God's pleasure and his, he would not allow any of them to wrong me."

"Indeed not, lady," said the king, "you can be sure of that, and I swear it to you."

"Sir," said the young lady, "I thank you. Now do what I ask of you."

"Lady," said the king, "I will do as you please." Upon these words, two squires rode into the courtyard on two strong, swift draft horses. One of them wore a shield about his neck with three golden leopards with azure crowns, and the field was as black as a mulberry; the handle was the work of a goldsmith, its parts of gold with inlay of little crosses. He had a sword hanging from his saddlebow. And with his right hand, the other one was leading a small warhorse handsomely shaped, with a golden bridle and a halter of silk. And the two squires had loaded† a pack horse with two lovely, well-made chests.

---

* The word here and later throughout the passage is *Damoisele* (422, l. 28): "Young lady."

† The verb is *cachoient* (423, l. 11): "were chasing, following, driving (out)" (*chacier*) or "were hiding" (*cachier*).

They dismounted at once beneath the pine tree and tethered their horses to it. Then they opened the chests and took out of one of them a double-mailed hauberk as white as snow, for it was of refined silver, and leg-armor made the same way, and then a helmet of gilded silver. Then they went into the hall where the king and his barons sat at their meal, and they went straight to the young lady.

And when she saw them coming, she said to the king, "Sir, I beg you to do what I ask, for I have tarried here too long. Here I have all the gear a knight needs, for you see the armor with which my love will be dubbed."

"Dear, fair friend," said the king, "I'll very gladly do what you wish, but come here and eat."

But she answered that she would never eat until he had become a knight.

Thus the lady stood in the hall before the king, and she kept holding her friend by the right hand. And after the king had eaten and the tablecloths were taken away, the lady drew from her purse golden spurs wrapped in silk. And she said to the king, "Sir, grant me what I ask, for I have stayed here too long."

With that, Kay the Seneschal jumped up and started to put the right spur on the dwarf's foot, but the lady grabbed his hand and said, "What is this, sir knight? What do you mean to do?"

"I wish to put the right spur on your friend, and so I'll make him a knight with my hand."

"That will never come about by your hand, God willing," she said, "For no one will put his hand to it but King Arthur, as he has sworn to me. I do not believe he will go back on his word if he can help it; otherwise he'll have betrayed me and hurt me to death! No one but a king should lay his hand on one so highborn as my friend."

"God help me," said the king. "Lady, you are in the right, and I'll do everything you wish."

Then the king took the spur from the young lady and fastened it to her friend's right foot, and the lady put the other one on him. And the king girded the sword about him after he had dressed him in the hauberk, for the lady wanted no one but the king to lay his hand on him. And when he was handsomely outfitted with everything a knight might need, the king hugged him about the neck* and said to him that he prayed God to make him a worthy knight, which it behoved him to say when he made a knight.

Then the young lady asked him if he would do anything more.

"Lady," answered the king, "I have done all I must do." [424]

"Sir," she said, "please ask him to be my knight."

So the king entreated him, and he answered that he would grant this, since it was the king's will.

Then they left the hall at once and came straight to the pine tree. And the young lady had her new knight get on the warhorse, which was more handsome than any other, all adorned in armor, and she herself hung about his neck the shield, which was just as the story has set forth. Then she climbed on her mule. She had the

---

*   That is, gave him the *colee* (423, l. 40), a ceremonial embrace; see p. 279n.

squires get on their horses and sent them back to her country. But she went the other way with her knight, and they rode into a deep and wonderful forest.

And King Arthur stayed behind in his great hall with Merlin and their companions, and they laughed a great deal about the young lady who had given her love to the dwarf.

"Indeed," said Queen Guenevere, "I wonder how such a thought could have come to her, for I never in my life saw such an ugly or hateful thing. Yet the young lady is full of such great beauty that no one could find the likes of her in four kingdoms! From what I can tell, I believe that devils or evil spirits have blinded or bewitched her."

"Lady," said Merlin, "she has not been blinded to anything but the dwarfs great ugliness. In all your life you have not seen such a wretched piece of flesh as the dwarf is; yet, he is the son of a king and queen."

"Dear sir," said the queen, "the young lady looks as if she comes from highborn stock, for she is beautiful beyond all others; yet her friend is so dreadfully ugly."

"Lady," answered Merlin, "the great good there is in him and his daring will do away with a great deal of the ugliness of which there's so very much in him, as you have seen. And you will learn of this quite soon."

"Dear friend," said King Arthur to Merlin, "who is the young lady? Do you know her?"

"Sir," he answered, "I'll tell you the truth. I never saw her before, but indeed I do know who she is and what her name is. But she will tell you herself in a very short while, and she will be better believed than I might be. And in the dwarf's own words you will find out who he is sooner than you think, and you will be both sorry and glad about it."

"How can I be sorry and glad?" asked King Arthur.

"Sir," answered Merlin, "I won't tell you now, for you have many things elsewhere to worry about. For Lucius, the emperor of Rome, has sent his messengers, and they have already dismounted in your courtyard beneath the pine tree before this hall."

While Merlin was saying these things to King Arthur, behold twelve princes very richly arrayed, dressed in costly silk cloth, and they came in two by two, holding hands, and each one carried in his hand a little olive bough, which meant that they were messengers. And they came thus before King Arthur, who was seated at the head of the high table in the great hall along with his barons. And they came before him, but did not greet him.

One, who was their leader and spokesman, said, "King Arthur, we are twelve princes from Rome who have been sent to you by Lucius, the emperor."

He then drew out a written document wrapped in silk cloth, handed it to King Arthur, and told him to have it read. And the king took the letter and gave it to the archbishop of Brice, who was beside him, and ordered him to read. The archbishop opened it and began in this way: [425]

"I, Lucius, emperor of Rome, who have power and lordship over the Romans, send word to my foe, King Arthur, that he has been faithless to me and to the power of Rome. I am amazed, and it comes to me as something most blameworthy, that he seeks, wrongfully and with haughty pride, to scorn Rome. And I wonder how and at what urging you would dare undertake warfare against Rome as long as you knew I was alive. This madness must have come to you from foolhardiness or melancholy, since you dared scorn Rome, which holds power and lordship over the whole world, as you have surely known all along and seen many times. And you will know again, more thoroughly than before, what a weighty thing it is to stir up the wrath of Rome.

"You have gone beyond your rights when you hold for yourself dues and lordship that are Rome's. You take our income and our lands, which you know belong to Rome. Know that if you keep this up any longer, the wolf will flee in fear of the lamb and the lion for the goat, and the rabbit will hunt the greyhound. You have no more power against us than the lamb against the wolf, and you are as much an underling to us as the lamb is to the shepherd, for Julius Caesar, our forebear, strongly and boldly undertook warfare in Britain. Lordship was granted him over it and all the islands round about, but, for the madness, pride, and great evil that are within you, you mean to snatch it from us!

"And so I summon you to come set it right, and, by the day of the Holy Nativity, you must be in Rome before me, ready to make amends for the wrong you have done. If you do not do this, I will take away from you Britain and all your lands you have under your sway, and I will come the next summer with such great forces that you won't dare make a stand against me, nor can you flee so far that I will not follow you and bring you back to Rome in bonds as my prisoner."

After the archbishop had read the letter just as you have heard, a great uproar broke out in the hall among the barons who had listened to it. They swore to bring dishonor to the messengers who had brought the letter, and they would have shamefully and wrongfully harmed them if it had not been for King Arthur, who said to them very kindly, "Dear lords, let them be. They are messengers and have been sent by their lord, and they must do and say everything that has been entrusted to them, and they should not be afraid of anyone."

Then King Arthur called his princes and barons together, and they went into a room to take counsel. Then spoke a most worthy and bold knight, whose name was Cador, and he said that they had wasted a very long time in idleness and games, "but, thank God, now the Romans have come to challenge us for our lands and holdings and have awakened us! And if they do what the letter sets forth, they, who have been at peace for such a long time, will have much bold, skillful fighting to do. I for one have never liked them!"

And my lord Gawainet said to him, "Sir, you surely know that peace after warfare is a good thing, for the land is all the better and stronger for it. And the games we play and the jesting we do with the ladies and young women are good things, too, for it is courtship and the love of ladies that make knights strive for boldness and skill in the fighting they do."

Then King Arthur ordered them all to sit down, [426] and they did. But he stayed on his feet and said to them, "My friends and companions, you have upheld my honor and welfare in the battles and wars I have fought since I came to hold this land, and I have led you in times of great trial over land and sea. You have helped me—and I am grateful to you for it—to conquer the lands all around which, thanks to your help, all bow down to me now. And now you have heard the summons the Romans, who have long worried us, have sent us. But, if God cares for you and me, they will take away with them, when they leave, nothing belonging to us that is not dearly sold to them. You see the emperor's messengers here. Now counsel me how to answer them as befits honor and reason. You see that the Romans mean to rise against us, and we must be ready for them when they come, so that they cannot harm us in any way. They want to have lordship over Britain and the other islands I hold, and they say that Caesar won them with his might, that the Britons could not stand against him, but granted him lordship and power over them. That is not right, and it comes from boundless pride. One does not rightly hold what one holds by force. And they have reproached us for the shameful things and the wrongs they have done us and our forebears. They boast that they defeated them and that our forebears granted them lordship over them. The more they have to give back to us, the more we should hate them and do them harm. We should hate the ones who hated our forebears and took their lordship from them and now wish to have it back by right of inheritance.* So we'll go challenge Rome, winner take all. As for me, I can do nothing other than what I have told you."

When the barons and princes heard the king saying these things, they answered all of a voice that he had spoken very well indeed. And they told him to send far and wide for his men and to gather his forces and to set out straight for Rome and move against the emperor who in his pride had so heavy-handedly and so wrongfully called him out: "So put the lordship of Rome under your power. And remember what Queen Sibyl foretold when she said that from three Britons would come those who would take Rome by force. Two of them have already conquered Rome. The first was Belinus, who was king and lord of the Britons. Constantine was the second. And you will be the third to take Rome by force, and in you will the prophesy be fulfilled. Now go forth and take the honor that God has granted you!"

Upon these words the king and the barons and knights left his room and came straight into the great hall, where the twelve messengers awaited them. And King Arthur told them to go back to their emperor and tell him on his behalf that his forebears had held Rome before him and had taken tribute from Rome, and that he meant to have it as well by right of succession and inheritance. As the Romans had not given him what they owed, he meant to have Rome as his own, for they had not dealt with him as they ought to have done to their overlord.

And they left. And the king gave them [427] lavish gifts as they went away, for he was the most courtly and most open-handed man in the world, and he did not want them to speak ill of him. And they came straight back into their country as quickly as they could, and they told the Emperor Lucius what they had heard from King Arthur. He was dreadfully upset. He sent for and gathered his forces. He crossed

---

* The preceding two sentences are supplied largely from additional text that Sommer provides from the Harley manuscript and others (426, n. 2). The additional text continues by attributing to Arthur material drawn from Geoffrey of Monmouth (e.g., Books 3, 5, and esp. 9) that recounts conquests of Rome by the British kings Belinus and his brother Brennius and later by Constantine the Great, thereby advancing a counterclaim that Rome belongs to Arthur by right of inheritance. The material derives from the "Mort Artu" section of the *Didot Perceval* (Didot manuscript only), where the story is told by King Lot (ed. Roach, pp. 258-61). It is referred to below in the barons' advice to Arthur (426, ll. 25-30); significantly, they speak as though they introduce the arguments for the first time.

the mountains of Montjoie* and came straight into Burgundy, near the city named Autun, and he seized the land far and wide.

But with that the story falls silent for a while from speaking about them and goes back to speaking about King Arthur.

53. THE EXPEDITION TO GAUL AND THE GIANT OF MONT-SAINT-MICHEL.†

Now the story says that after the twelve messengers had gone, King Arthur and his barons were left very badly upset by the summons the Emperor Lucius had sent. And Merlin said to him, "Sir, call your men together, for we mustn't tarry. The emperor has strongly equipped himself."

"Merlin, dear friend," said King Arthur, "I'll be upon him sooner than he wants. He'll be the worse off for attacking us."

"But now I bid you farewell, for I go to take your message to the barons."

At once Merlin vanished, and the king did not know what had become of him. And Merlin went straight to Orkney, first of all, and gave the message to King Lot to be in Logres within two weeks from that day with all his forces; he answered that he would gladly be there, and Merlin bade him farewell and left. Why should I go on telling you? He let all the princes who held land from King Arthur, but not King Ban and his brother King Bors, know that they were to be in Logres within two weeks.

Then he went back and found King Arthur in his rooms, and he said to him, "Sir, I have given your message to all your barons, and in fifteen days from today they'll be here ready to go!"

When King Arthur heard him, he was greatly gladdened. And he stayed at Logres until his nobles had come. King Lot of Orkney was the first to come, and he led five thousand men. And King Urien had four thousand, the King of the Hundred Knights four thousand, King Neutres four thousand, King Caradoc four thousand, King Tradelmant four thousand, and Duke Escant of Cambenic two thousand. And Gosengos and Nabunal the Seneschal led four thousand, King Yder four thousand, and King Aguisant four thousand. And after they had all gathered in the meadowlands of Logres, King Arthur was most glad, and he thanked them heartily. He told them about the emperor's proud and wrongful summons, and they told him to think of nothing but striving until the shame had been avenged.

Then the fleet was made ready and they went aboard the ships. And Merlin went out ahead and did not stop until he had come ashore at Gaunes. He found King Ban and King Bors, and he ordered them to get themselves ready, for King Arthur had set out on the sea to move against the Romans. And they said that they would be there for the fight. And Merlin turned about and went straight to the port before

---

* The text reads *les mons de mongieu* (427, ll. 5-6), that is, the Little St. Bernard Pass, the favored Alpine route between France and Italy.

† Corresponds to Sommer, 427-434.

King Arthur landed. And when the king saw him, he asked him where he had been, and he answered that he was coming from the city of Gaunes, where he had summoned the two kings "who will be there for the fight with mighty forces." And King Arthur thanked him heartily.

Then the barons left the ships and encamped for a while [428] along the shore in tents and pavilions, so that they could recover from the hard time they had had at sea. And so they went to sleep that night. And as King Arthur slept, he saw in a dream that came to him a great bear atop a mountain. And it seemed to him that a great dragon was coming toward it out of the eastern skies, and it spewed from its throat fire and flames so thick and awesome that they lit up the shores all about. Then the dragon fell upon the bear with all its might. The bear defended itself well, but the dragon took hold of the bear, sent it hurling to the ground, and killed it, so it seemed to King Arthur.

When King Arthur awoke, he was bewildered by the dream. He sent for Merlin, and he entreated him most kindly to tell him the meaning of his dream. Then he told him word for word what he had seen while he slept.

And then Merlin said to him, "Sir, I'll tell you the meaning. The bear you saw stands for a great monster, a huge giant that lives near here on a great mountain. He came to this country from the land of Spain, and he has stayed here. Every day he wreaks shame and harm on this land, but no man dares stand up to him for fear of his great strength. The dragon you saw in your dream that spewed fire and flames from its throat, so thick that the whole land was brightened by it, stands for you yourself, who burn with the fire of your bright boldness shining with divine grace. And that the dragon then struck with such might means that you will attack the giant, who will put up a good fight against you. And that the dragon took hold of the bear means that in the end you will kill him; have no fear about it."

Then they had the tents and pavilions taken down, and they set out on the road. But they had not gone far when news came to King Arthur about the giant, who was laying waste the land and countryside, and no man or woman was left, but they had all fled through the fields like dumb beasts for fear of the giant. And he had taken by force a maiden, Helaine,* a gentleman's niece, and had carried her off atop a mountain, where his lair was, that was surrounded by the sea. Now this mountain is called Mont-Saint-Michel, but at that time it had neither minister nor church. There was no man so bold or strong that he dared fight the giant, and when the men of the countryside got together, they could not hold out against him on sea or on land, for he killed them all with rocks and sank their ships. This is why the people of the country gave up their lands and homes to him.

When King Arthur heard the news about the giant who was laying waste the land, he called Kay the Seneschal and Bedivere, and he told them to get their armor ready while it was still dark, and they did as he ordered. And the three of them rode out with only two squires, and they rode until they came near the foot of a mountain, and they saw a great fire burning; beyond, they saw another mountain no less high than the first, and they saw a great and wondrous fire burning there as

---

* Her name, not given at this point in Sommer's text appears below (429, l. 14) in a context that seems to assume that the name has occurred previously.

well. And King Arthur did not know which mountain he should climb. So he called to Bedivere and told him to go find out on which mountain the giant was.

Bedivere then got into a boat, for the sea was at high tide. When he came to the nearer mountain, he climbed up the rocky cliff, [429] and he heard much weeping and wailing; and when he heard that, he grew fearful, for he believed that the giant was there. But he renewed his boldness within him, drew his sword, and went forth. It was his hope to yield to adventure and fight the giant, as he was not a man who wished, for any fear of death, to behave like a coward; and with this thought, he climbed to the top of the rock. When he was on top, he saw the fire, which burned very brightly, and he saw a grave nearby that had been newly dug. Beside the grave he saw an old woman sitting, her clothing all torn to shreds and her hair askew, and she was weeping and sighing in great sobs.

And when she saw the knight, she said to him, "Ah, noble knight! Who are you? What adventure has brought you here? For you life will come to an end most dreadfully if the giant finds you here! Run away from here as fast as you can, for you would be most unlucky to linger here until that devil from hell, ruthless to everyone, sees you. So go away quickly, if you want to stay alive!"

When Bedivere saw the woman weeping and mourning Helaine so tenderly, and she had told him to flee if he did not wish to die, he drew closer to her at once and said to her, "Good woman, stop weeping and tell me who you are and why you are mourning so beside this tomb."

"I am," she answered, "a sorrowful, wretched woman, and I weep and mourn for a maiden, a noble woman who was the niece of Lionel of Nanteuil. I nursed her and gave her the milk from my breasts. She lies here in this grave, and she was entrusted to me to nurse and keep safe! Now a devil has taken her away from me, a devil from hell that brought us here. He wanted to lie with the child, so young and tender, and she could not bear it, he is so ugly, so ghastly. And so he took her soul from her body, and he tore her away from me through his faithlessness. I have buried her here, and I weep over her and mourn her day and night."

"And why do you not go away?" asked Bedivere. "Why do you stay on here alone? You have lost her and cannot have her back."

"Sir," she answered, "I know very well that I cannot have her back, but, since I see that you are so noble and courtly, I do not want to hide anything from you. When my dear daughter was slain, for whom I thought I would die of sorrow, the giant made me stay here to satisfy his lust with me. He has defiled me by force, and I must submit to his will whether I want to or not. As Our Lord is my witness, it has been against my will, and the giant has very nearly killed me. And if he comes here to satisfy his lust with me, you are as good as dead. And he'll come soon, for he is on that mountain where you see the great fire. So I beg you, go away from here and leave me to mourn and weep over my daughter!"

Bedivere felt deeply sorry for the woman, and he comforted her with great kindness. Then he went back to the king and told him what he had seen and heard, and he told him that the giant was on the hill where he saw the great fire blazing. Then the king had his companions climb that hill. When they were on top, he made them stop. He told them that he would go by himself and fight the giant alone, "but, even so, watch out for me, and come help me if I need it."

And they answered that they would. [430]

They stopped there, and King Arthur went on toward the giant, who was sitting before the fire and roasting meat on a great spit; he was cutting off and eating the meat that had cooked the most. And the king, sword in hand, went toward him one step at a time, his shield strapped to his arm, for he meant to take him by surprise. But the giant, who was faithless and evil, looked about him and saw the king drawing near him. He sprang up, for the king had his naked sword in his hand, and he ran to get a cudgel that was nearby—it was so huge and so awesome that two men could scarcely carry it, and it was carved from oak wood. So he left his roast in the fire, and he swiftly lifted the cudgel as high as his neck, for he was quite lively and very strong, and he came at the king very fast and told him that it was unwise of him to have come there. He raised the cudgel and meant to hit the king on the head. But the king was very nimble and quick, and he jumped to the side so that the blow missed him. And as he jumped away, he thrust a blow at the giant, meaning to strike him on the head, but the giant, who was quite bold and quick, thrust his cudgel out—for otherwise the king would have killed him—and warded off the blow. Even so, the king followed through with his good sword, which he had won from King Rion, and aimed at his two eyebrows; he broke through his skin and flesh down to the bone, and the giant could see nothing, because of the blood that spilled down into his eyes, and so he could not see where to land his blows. So he began to strike out wildly all about him like a madman. The king began to bear down hard, but he could not reach him, for the giant was striking out so hard and fast that if one of the blows had hit him, it would have crushed him.

And so they fought for a long time. And when it dawned on the giant that he would not land a blow on the king, he threw his cudgel to the ground and reached out with his hands wherever he heard the king stepping, for he could not see him. The king was hitting him hard with his sword, and the awesome blows fell thick and fast, but the giant was wearing a leather jerkin made of snake skin, and it was so hard that the sword could not cut through, and the king was angry and upset. The giant kept thrashing out with his hands and jumping here and there, until at last he caught the king by his arms, and when he got hold of him, he was most happy, for he thought that he could soon kill him—and indeed he would have, had it not been for the great nimbleness of the king, who jumped about so much that the giant could hardly hold on to him, and he freed himself.

Then the king ran upon him wielding his sword, and he hit him so very hard on his left shoulder that his whole arm shook from the blow, but the leather jerkin was so strong that he could not cut through to his flesh. The giant still could not see him, as his eyes were too full of the blood that came down from his wound, so that he could not see heaven or earth; but at last he raised his hand to his eyes and wiped away the blood, and he could make out a shadow of the king. He ran to that side, but the king, who knew that the giant had great strength, did not dare let himself get caught in his arms. The giant ran about so much, here and there, that he stumbled against his cudgel. He grabbed it and, burning with hatred, ran upon the king, but the king stepped aside, for he did not dare make a stand against him, and that filled the giant's heart with even greater anger. He then threw his cudgel down and began reaching out again to take hold of the king with his hands. He kept wiping and rubbing his eyes, until he could see light as well as a shadow of the king. Then he leapt out and grabbed him by the hips with both hands, [431] and he squeezed him so hard that he nearly broke his backbone in two, and he began to feel for the king's arms because he wanted to take the sword out of his hand.

But the king, who saw clearly what was in his heart, dropped his sword, which fell to the ground and made such a loud noise that the giant heard it. He then held the king in one of his arms and leaned down to pick up the sword; but as he stooped, the king hit him with one of his knees and sent him to the ground in a faint. He then sprang to his sword, picked it up from the ground, and came back to where the giant lay. He raised up his leather jerkin and thrust the sword into his body. And this is how the giant died.

Then Kay the Seneschal and Bedivere came forward and greeted the king joyfully. They looked at the giant, who was wondrously huge, and they heartily praised God for the honor and victory He had given King Arthur, for they had never before seen such a great devil. And King Arthur told Bedivere to cut off the giant's head and to take it back so that the army could see the wonder of his great size, and he did as he was ordered. Then they climbed down the mountain and got on their horses. The tide had gone out and was already coming back in, and it was coming in very fast indeed, but they got across and rode straight to the army. The barons were quite troubled because the king had been away for such a long time, for they did not know where he had gone, but Merlin told them not to worry, for he would soon come back safe and sound.

While the princes and barons were so frightened for King Arthur, he dismounted at his tent, along with Kay the Seneschal and Bedivere, who had hung the giant's head on his saddlebow by its hair. The barons all came to the king as he was getting down from his horse, and they asked him where he was coming from, for he had given them a great fright. And he told them that he was coming back from fighting the giant who had laid waste the land and countryside all about them and that he had killed him, "thanks be to God." Then he showed them the head that Bedivere had brought back. And when the barons saw it, they crossed themselves in wonder and said that they had never seen such a huge head, and all who were in the army praised Our Lord. Then they took off King Arthur's armor with great rejoicing and merrymaking, and they stayed there resting the whole day.

And the next morning they took down the tents and pavilions and set out on the road straight for Burgundy, and they rode for as many days as it took until they came to the River Aube. And there news reached them that the Emperor Lucius had invaded that country and was laying it waste, and King Arthur was quite glad that he had found him so close by; however, he was sorry that he had stripped the countryside.

So he had his army encamp along the River Aube. And that very day King Ban and King Bors rode into the army with six thousand knights, but neither Pharian nor Gratian nor Leonce of Payerne had yet got there, for they had stayed behind to safeguard the land and defend it against King Claudas of the Land Laid Waste, should there be need to. As soon as the two kings had come into the army, they had their tents set up before the tent of King Lot, who was most glad to see them, for he truly loved them with great love. And they stayed there until King Arthur had a castle raised up there, where they could take refuge if they had to.

Then, following his barons' advice, King Arthur sent his messengers to the Emperor Lucius, and he told him [432] that he had most unwisely ridden over his land, and that, if he did not make amends for it, he would drive him out of Rome. He sent Sir Gawainet, Sir Yvain, and Sagremor on the mission, for they were courtly and well-bred, and they were worthy and bold.

And the king said to Sir Gawainet, "Dear nephew, you'll go to the emperor and, on my behalf, tell him to turn back and leave this land, which belongs to me. And if he does not mean to turn back, let him come prove in combat which one of us has rights to it, for I'll defend it to the end of my days against the Romans; I'll win it back in battle, and I'll prove against him man to man which of us will have it."

When King Arthur had spoken these words, the messengers rode out wearing their hauberks, their helmets fastened on, their shields about their necks, their swords girded, and holding their lances. And they talked together with Sir Gawainet, for they were young and light-hearted, and said that before they came back they would do something "that people will talk about forever, and it will be said that the war has begun."

So they rode until they came near the army. And when the Romans saw the messengers, they ran out of their tents everywhere to see them and to hear their news. They asked who they were and where they came from, but they would not stop or listen to anything they had to say until they reached the emperor's tent. They dismounted before his tent and had their horses tethered outside the doorway; then they came before the emperor and told him the message from King Arthur.

"My lord," said Sir Gawainet, "King Arthur sends you word to leave his land and this countryside, for it belongs to him by rights, and he forbids you ever to be so bold as to set foot in it again. But if you wish to challenge him in combat for any of it, I will defend King Arthur. Romans won it in battle in days gone by, and in battle it will be won back. Now let it be proved which one should have lordship and power over it. Come before dawn if you wish to challenge for lordship of the land—or go back, for you have nothing to do here. We have taken the land and you have lost it, so believe what I say and you will be wise."

When the emperor heard Sir Gawainet speaking in such a way, he answered him straightway, angry and upset, that he would not turn back, for the land and the countryside belonged to him; rather, he would go on ahead. He was very glad to hear such orders, for if he had lost his land, he would have it back when he could, and he truly believed that it would be soon.

A knight, whose name was Titilius, was sitting next to the emperor; he was the emperor's nephew, the son of his sister, and he was most evil and overweening, and he answered very wickedly and said, "Britons who make threats are good with words, but in deeds they are worth little."

And he would have gone on with his mockery, but Sir Gawainet drew his sword from its scabbard, stepped forward, and struck him so hard that he sent his head flying. Then he said to his companions, "Get on your horses."

They did so at once, and Sir Gawainet got on his horse, and they turned about without taking leave of the Romans or the emperor.

And then the whole army was in an uproar, for the emperor began shouting very loudly, "Take them! You'll be sorry if they get away!"

Then they all shouted, "To arms!" And you would have seen [433] men everywhere putting on armor, climbing on horses, and spurring after the messengers, who were riding away at great speed. They looked over at the Romans, who were coming at them from all sides, over the roads and across the fields, four here, four there, five over here, six over there.

But there was one of them who wore costly armor and was on a strong, fast horse, and he flew past all his companions and shouted to the messengers, "You are indeed taking your time, so I'll hand you over to the emperor!"

When Sir Gawainet heard him, he took his shield by the arm straps, turned his horse about, and hit him so hard that he sent him down dead to the ground. Then he said, "Sir knight, those are the tidbits I can give you to eat, you and my other foes. Wait for your companions who are following you and tell them that King Arthur's messengers have ridden by here!"

After him came a knight who had been born in Rome of very high stock, and the Romans called him Marcel. His horse was strong and swift, but he had no lance, for he had forgotten it in the haste of riding out. And he went alongside Sir Gawainet, for he had promised to take him back alive to the emperor. And when Sir Gawainet saw that he was riding alongside, he turned his reins, and Marcel rode into him as he was passing by. And Sir Gawainet hit him so hard that he drove his sword into his brain and all the way down to his teeth. Then he said to him in mockery, "You would have better luck if you were still with the emperor!"

Then all three messengers turned about and struck three Romans down dead.

There was a knight, who was Marcel's cousin, sitting astride a strong, fast horse, and he was very sorry about his kinsman* whom he saw lying on the ground, so be began to spur his horse across the fields. Sir Yvain caught sight of him, so he ran to where he was and hit him so hard that he could never get back up, for he had cut off his head. Then three† Romans struck him and broke their lances on him, but he cut one's head off and another's arm, and he hit the third so hard on the head that he struck him down dead and sent him sprawling from his horse. Then he rode after his companions, and the Romans ran after them until they came to a wood that was near the castle that King Arthur had had built.

But with that the story falls silent for a while about the messengers and those who were riding after them, and goes back to speaking about King Arthur and his barons.

Here the story says that at the time when the messengers left King Arthur to go on their mission to Lucius (the emperor of Rome), King Arthur, following Merlin's advice, sent after them seven thousand very well equipped knights to meet the messengers and rescue them if they needed. And they rode until they came to the woods, and there they waited for the messengers. At last they saw them coming, and after them the whole field was covered with knights who were giving them chase.

---

*   The word is *neueu* (433, l. 25): "nephew, grandson, progeny"; not the equivalent of *cousins* (433, l. 24): "cousin."

†   The text bears the definite article (433, l. 28).

And when they saw this, they rode out to meet them, and the Romans withdrew just as soon as they [434] saw them coming.

But many of the Romans were upset because they had run after them for so long, for the Britons had fallen upon them all too ruthlessly, and they had taken many and killed many. There was one quite renowned knight who was named Petrinus, and in Rome there was not his match in knightly skill or boldness. He had heard about the ambush the Britons had set up, and he set out at once to where they were with six thousand men in iron armor. And as soon as he got there, he pushed the Britons back by main force, for they could not hold out against him, nor could they stand their ground, so they made their way as far back as the woods, and there they defended themselves. And Petrinus fell upon them with all his might, but he lost very many of his men there, for the Britons slaughtered them, and there were many dead and wounded on both sides.

But now the story falls silent about them, and we will tell you about King Arthur and his companions.

54. BATTLES WITH THE ROMANS; ARTHUR'S VICTORY.[*]

When King Arthur saw that his messengers were long in coming back, he called Yder, son of Nut, to him and entrusted six thousand knights to him and ordered him to ride after the others until he found them. So they took to the road and made their way until they saw the two armies fighting against each other. Sir Gawainet was fighting with such wondrous skill, and Yder and his companions spurred to where he was and, with all their might, charged headlong into the Romans. Then the Britons came out of the woods and won back the field.

And Petrinus, who was a very good knight, worthy and bold, rallied his men around him. He knew how to fall back and turn about, and he knew how to storm in among his foes. (If anyone wants to meet a bold knight in battle, let him go against him, and the one who does must surely die!)

The barons spurred their horses all over the battlefield. They were unwilling to rest and wanted only to joust. They did not care how the fighting went, but only that the war had begun.

On the other side was Petrinus, very upset, and he kept his knights close by him. Sagremor of Constantinople was riding through the battlefield, striking down knights and horses, and he caught sight of Petrinus, who was turning about and then striking down Britons. He looked and understood from the wonders Petrinus did that there would be heavy losses if he did not kill him or take him alive, for the Romans were rallying, thanks to his skillful deeds alone.

He then took the best of his friends aside to talk and said to them, "We have begun this fight without King Arthur's order. If it happens to turn out well for us, he will be grateful to us, but if we come out badly, then we will have his wrath. This

---

[*]   Corresponds to Sommer, 434-441.

is why we must kill Petrinus or take him alive and hand him over to King Arthur, for otherwise, we cannot get out without losses. So I bid you, do what I do and spur your horses after me!"

And they answered that they would do so and follow him wherever he wanted to go. When he heard this, he was very happy.

And he had watched closely and seen where Petrinus was.

Then he started out at once to where he knew him to be, and his companions followed him all together, and they did not stop before they came to the spot where Petrinus was, where he was leading the knights of his household. And when Sagremor saw him, he spurred over to him and got close enough to him to put his arms about him, and Sagremor let himself fall with him like a man who had faith in his companions. And Petrinus lay on the ground in his arms, [435] for he was holding on to him very tightly. Petrinus was struggling hard to get up, and he began to twist and turn, but Sagremor held him so strongly that he could not move. And when the Romans saw Petrinus on the ground, they ran to his rescue, and there was hard and wicked fighting.

But Sir Gawainet rode straight into the press and cleared a way with the blade of his sword, with which he killed and struck down as many as he met right in front of him, and no one was so bold or so strong that he did not give way to him. And Yder, son of Nut, also slaughtered a great many of the Romans. And each one was so mightily strengthened by the other that they lifted Sagremor back astride his horse, and they took Petrinus and held him prisoner—he had been beaten hard and was badly hurt; they brought him out of the press by their sheer strength and handed him over to good guards, and they went back in to start the fray all over again.

And those who were left without a leader hardly put up a defense at all after they had lost the one who had led them; so the Britons kept killing them and striking them down in great heaps. They rode over the dead bodies to hold back the runaways, of whom they killed many and took many prisoner and gave them over to King Arthur.

They advised Arthur to send them into the land of Benoic and have them held in prison there until the Romans did what he wanted, for if he held them in the army, they could well have been lost. Then the king summoned Borel,* Richier, Cador, and Bedivere, who were good knights, worthy, bold, and highborn, and he ordered them to get up early the next morning and take the prisoners and lead them out of danger.

So the story falls silent here about King Arthur, the prisoners, and those who should lead them away, and goes back to speaking about the emperor.

Now the story says that when the emperor learned about the harm his men had suffered, he was grief-stricken and heartbroken. Then spies came to him and told him that the prisoners would be led away the next morning into the land of Benoic. When the emperor heard this, he had ten thousand knights take their horses and ride through the night, and he ordered them to ride until they were ahead of the prisoners and to rescue them if they could. Then the emperor called to him Sestor,†

---

*   Called *bretel* (435, l. 36) (see West 46, Bretel) and *bertelot* (436, l. 7).

†   The form here is *Gestoire* (435, l. 28). The form *sestor* (440, l. 31) is preferred by West (279).

who was lord of Libya; the king of Syria,* who was called Evander; Calidus of Rome; Matis; and Catenois—those five were well schooled in fighting and they knew a great deal about warfare. And the emperor ordered them to lead the ten thousand† armed knights. And they rode until they came to the road on which the prisoners were to go by, and they stopped‡ very quietly in a most delightful spot that they found near the road.

And early next morning King Arthur's household arose, just as they had been ordered, and they led the prisoners away. They rode in two clusters for fear of their foes. Borel, Richier, and Cador were leading one company where prisoners§ were, and the prisoners rode with their hands tied behind their backs and their feet tied under their horses. They were going ahead, and they fell upon the Romans' ambush. The Romans stormed out in front of them with such an uproar that the ground shook and quaked all about them, and they defended themselves like men of great strength. And when Bedivere and his companions, who were coming up from behind, heard the noise and the sound of blows ringing, they had their prisoners taken to a [436] safe place and ordered their squires to watch over them. Then they spurred their horses and were not willing to stop before they got to their companions, who were defending themselves with strength and daring. And the Romans spurred their horses here and there, but they did not mean to defeat the Britons so much as to look for the prisoners. And when the Britons saw them behaving in that way, they split into four battalions: Cador had with him the men of Cornwall, Bedivere and Richier had a great body of men each, and Borel had the men of Galloway.

When King Evander noted that his men were dwindling and that their strength was flagging, he drew them close to himself. And when they saw that they could not rescue the prisoners, they fell upon the Britons in good order and started a hard and wondrous fight. The Britons indeed had much the worse of it, for they lost a great many knights, and Yder, son of Nut, met King Evander, who struck him so hard that he sent him down dead to the ground. The Britons were greatly disheartened because they lost many of their men in the onslaught, and they would have all been killed or taken prisoner but for Cleodalis, the seneschal of Carmelide, when he came there with five thousand men whom King Arthur had sent on Merlin's advice.

And when Bedivere caught sight of them, he said to his companions, "Hold your ground and do not run away! See the help that is coming to us!"

And when they heard them, they shouted King Arthur's battlecry so loudly that Cleodalis heard them clearly. Then he and his men let their horses run. The Romans had their minds set on taking the Britons, and they took no heed of the men of Carmelide before they charged headlong in among them. In their first pass, they struck down a hundred Romans who never got up again. And when the Romans

---

* The form is *sur* (435, l. 28). West suggests Syria on the basis of readings in Wace (283, see *Sur²*).

† Here the text reads *.xiiiv.* (435, l. 31), whereas the original number is ten thousand (435, l. 25).

‡ Sommer's text adds *el chemin* (435, ll. 32-33): "on the road"; but this contradicts the later *pres del chemin* (435, ll. 33-34): "near the road," more suitable for an ambush.

§ The text reads *la compaignie ou li prison estoient* (435, ll. 36-37): "the company where the prisoners were"; but the other company also has prisoners (435, l. 42).

saw that, they were utterly dumbfounded, for they were sure that it was King Arthur with his whole army. They were so disheartened that they took to their heels and made for their encampment, for they did not believe they would be safe anywhere else. And the Britons followed hard behind them. And in the chase were killed King Evander, Catenois,* and more than two thousand others, and many were also taken and held prisoner. Then they went back to the battlefield, and they picked up Borel and the other dead who lay over the field and buried them. And then they carried the wounded away, and the men to whom King Arthur had entrusted the prisoners led them away and those who had been taken prisoner in that battle; they bound them tightly and took them where they had been ordered to lead them. And Cleodalis and his companions went back to King Arthur and told him how they had fared.

But with that the story falls silent for a while about them and goes back to speaking about the Emperor Lucius.

In this part the story says that the emperor was most saddened when he learned about the defeat and the great loss of his men, and he wept tenderly for King Evander and the others who had been killed and taken prisoner. And he saw clearly that it was going badly for him, and he was disheartened and afraid to fight against King Arthur or to wait for a second onslaught that was sure to come after him. So he laid his plans, got his men on horseback, and went straight to Langres with his army, and he encamped in the valleys below the city.

And when King Arthur learned this, he was certain that the emperor would not fight until he had gathered more men, but he was unwilling to let them encamp and stay [437] so near him. So he had his men get on their horses stealthily, and they took to the road toward the right-hand side of the castle between the town and the emperor's army. They made their way all through the night until the next morning, when they came into a valley that is called Suize,† which is on the road that goes straight from Autun to Langres. And King Arthur had his companions put on their armor so that, if the Romans fell upon them, he could welcome them quickly. And he had the lesser folk, who would not be needed in battle, stop beside a hill, and they looked like armed men wandering about, such that, if the Romans saw them, they would be disheartened by the great crowd. Then King Arthur hid himself in a wood with six thousand six hundred knights, and he ordered the earl of Gloucester to lead them: he was their head and leader. And the king ordered them not to move out from there for any reason until they could see that they were needed.

"And if I need you," he said, "I will come back for you, for if the Romans are put to rout, you would not spare them."

And they answered that they would do as he ordered.

Then the king took another company of knights, who were equipped most nobly, and led them to another spot, and he was their leader. They were from his own household, and he had raised them. And he had his dragon held up in their midst— the dragon that was always borne as his ensign. Then he split his men into eight battalions and put two thousand knights into each one; half were on foot and the other half on horseback. And he told each battalion how it was to behave. Then

---

*   The form here is *catelos* (436, l. 27).

†   The form is *ceroise* (437, l. 4). West identifies this as the Suize River which flows between Autun and Langres, though other suggestions are not implausible (West, 65-66, *Ceroise*).

he put enough other men into each battalion so that there were five thousand five hundred.

King Aguisant had the first battalion. Duke Escant of Cambenic led the second. Belcis, king of the Danes,* led another. And King Tradelmant and Sir Gawainet were with King Lot of Orkney, who led the fourth battalion like a king fit for great deeds.

After these first four there were four others, very well equipped. King Urien led the first, and Sir Yvain his son was with him, as were Yvain the Bastard, King Belinant, and King Neutres, and they had with them the men of their country. And the King of the Hundred Knights, King Clarion, and King Caradoc led the second battalion, and they had with them the men of their country. King Bors led the third, and he had with him the men of his country along with Cleodalis, the seneschal of Carmelide, and the ones he led from his country. King Ban of Benoic led the fourth battalion, and he had with him all the foot soldiers and crossbowmen and four thousand men on horseback all wearing good armor.

And after King Arthur had thus set up his men and worked out his battalions, he said to his barons and other men, "Now we'll see who fights boldly! For whatever deeds you may have done in your lives before now, everything is lost if you do not now fight well against these Romans."

And the princes answered him forthwith, and with one voice, that they would rather die on the battlefield than not have the honor and the victory.

And when King Arthur heard this he was most happy and gladdened.

But now the story falls silent for a while about King Arthur and speaks of the emperor. [438]

Here the story says that when the emperor, with his barons, who were very good, skilled knights, had encamped in the valley below Langres, he went to bed that night. And the next morning he left Langres and meant to ride to Autun. But then the news came to him that King Arthur had laid an ambush for him, and he saw clearly that he would have to fight or turn back. He said to himself that he would not go back for anything in the world, for he would be held a coward.

Then he called all his princes before him, and there were a good two hundred of them who made up his council, and he said to them, "Noble vassals, goodly conquerors, sons of goodly forebears who won great honors and great lands through their knightly prowess and deeds of boldness, Rome is head of the world, and if it weakens and falls in our time, the shame and dishonor will be ours to bear. For our forebears were worthy and noble, and by rights noble sons should spring from a noble father. Your fathers were worthy, and you ought to be worthy so that you can match them: each one of you must strive to be like his father. It would be a great shame if anyone lost his birthright—and whoever through his own cowardice gives it up and leaves behind what his father won through his prowess should be put to shame. I do not say that you are cowardly or that you have grown weak. Your fathers were worthy, and I hold you to be worthy and valorous and bold. And the Britons have closed the road to Autun to us, and we cannot go there or get by them

---

* The text adds here *& li rois loth dorcanie* (437, l. 24): "and King Lot of Orkney"; however, King Lot is leader of the fourth battalion, not co-leader of the third.

without a fight Take up your weapons and put on your armor. If they stand up to us, see to it that they are hit hard; and if they turn in flight run after them with all the strength you have. Let us strive to strike down their pride and cast asunder their might and their arrogance."

Then the Romans set up their battalions and lined up their forces, and many were the kings and dukes of pagandom who crossed swords with the Christians who had come to win the fiefs they held from Rome. There were many of them on foot and on horseback, and some they set on the hills and others in the valleys. Then you would have heard loud blasts from horns and trumpets on every side, and they rode tightly drawn together until they fell upon King Arthur's men. And then you would have seen arrows shooting and bolts flying so thickly that no one dared lower his shield from his face. After that, they turned to lances striking shields, and the clanging was dreadful. And when they had broken their lances, they turned to axes and swords, and they landed hard blows on helmets and hauberks, and the uproar was loud and awesome. And they fought together for a long time, and they struck and knocked against one another.

Yet the men of Rome never fell back the least bit, nor did the Britons win any ground from them, and no one could tell which ones were winning or getting the better of the others, before the echelon that King Urien, King Neutres, and King Belinant were leading drew closer. They charged into the Romans with their men where they saw the thickest fighting, and the three princes fought wondrously. And Kay the Seneschal, who was with them, hit them like a worthy knight so that the three princes said, "God, what a seneschal!"

And they said of Bedivere, "God, what a constable! Here are goodly ministers for a king's court!"

There many a blow was given and taken, and many a knight was killed and struck down. And Kay the Seneschal and Bedivere did wonders, for they trusted mightily in their prowess. [439] They kept together, but went too far forward, and they came upon a battalion that the king of Mede had brought; his name was Boclus, and he was a pagan of very great prowess. And Kay and Bedivere rode in against them and killed many of them.

When King Boclus saw the two companions who were doing his men such harm, he was filled with sorrow. He held onto his short, thick sword and rode Bedivere down and hit him so hard that he drove his blade right through his body and out the other side, and if he had struck him a little lower, he would have killed him. Even so, he bore him down senseless from his horse. And when Kay saw him fall, he was very sorrowful, for he thought that he was dead. He rode over to him with as many men as he could get together, and he made the men of Mede leave the field.

He came to Bedivere and took him in his arms; he meant to pick him up and carry him away from among the horses, for he loved him very much. And as he was taking him up, the king of Mede rode out of the fray and struck Kay the Seneschal on the helmet with his sword, and he gave him such a great wound on his head that he had to drop Bedivere, and he would have killed him had it not been for the men of Kay's household, who were showing their worth so well.

And one knight flew into the press: his name was Sebart, and he was Bedivere's nephew. And when he saw his uncle lying on the ground in a faint, he thought that he had been killed. He gathered his friends and kinsmen until there were a good two hundred of them or more, and he said to them, "Follow me, and we'll avenge my uncle's death!"

Then he drew near the Romans and caught sight of the king of Mede, and he turned to that side, shouting King Arthur's battlecry like a madman. He asked for nothing but to avenge his uncle. And his companions rode off after him, holding their lances down, and they slew many pagans there. And they rode until they came among the king of Mede's men, and when Segart saw King Boclus, who had brought his uncle down, he spurred to him and struck him so hard atop his helmet with his sword that he cut right through it and his iron coif as well, and he split him open down to his teeth and took him to the ground dead. Then he went over to him, pulled him up on his horse in front of him, took him to his uncle's side, and cut him up into little bits. Then he said to his men, "Let us slay those people who do not put their trust in God!"

Then he heard his uncle sigh, and he was filled with great joy. And he had him and Kay taken up and brought to where their equipment was. Then he went back to the fight, which was most dreadful.

And King Neutres met King Alipanton, who was king of Spain, and they traded blows as hard as they could. And King Neutres killed King Alipanton, but King Neutres had been wounded with a cut through his body. But the Romans were so strong that the Bretons had to withdraw, and when Sir Gawainet and Hoel of Little Brittany saw them turning about, they were filled with sorrow.

Then they rode headlong into the midst of the battle along with the men from little Brittany, who were following their lord Hoel, so that the crowd of men fighting could not keep them out, and they struck so hard that they made those who had come after them turn tail, and they sent many of them spilling to the ground. They rode hard on their heels until they came to the banner with the golden eagle. There were the emperor and the noblest men in the world, who had come from Rome. [440]

Then you would have seen great and wonderful fighting. And Herman, who was count of Triple, was riding with Sir Gawainet and Hoel, but a lowborn lad killed him with a javelin he had thrown. And the emperor's men struck out so hard against the Britons that they slew a good two thousand of them in that place, and the Britons suffered great harm, because there were many worthy gentlemen and good knights among them. And Sir Gawainet was so grief-stricken when he saw it that he nearly went out of his mind. So he charged into the Romans like a lion running among the beasts to make his catch. He fought with great skill, and he never tired of striking blows. He bit right and left until he came near the emperor.

When Sir Gawainet saw the emperor, he marked him well, as the emperor did him. And they let their horses run one against the other and struck each other with great might, but neither fell, for they were both very strong. The emperor was strong and sturdy, and he was very glad that he had withstood Sir Gawainet, for he knew well who he was by the blazons on his arms, which have been described before. And he said to himself that if he could hold out against him, he would boast about it in Rome. Then he raised his shield and lifted his arm, and he began fighting against Sir Gawainet with great fierceness. And Sir Gawainet hit him so hard with his good sword Excalibur that he split him open down to the teeth.

When the Romans saw the emperor dead, they ran upon the Britons and struck hard and deep into their midst, and they brought down more than three thousand in the onslaught. When King Arthur saw the Romans recovering and doing his men such harm, he was filled with sorrow. Then he shouted loudly to his men, "What are you doing? Ride after them and don't let anyone get away, for I am Arthur, who never fled from the battlefield for any man! Follow me and see to it that you do not behave like cowards. Remember all your knightly deeds and all the kingdoms you have won. For I will not leave this field alive if I do not win against the Romans. Today is the day when I'll die or have victory!"

With that he rode in among the Romans and began to strike down knights and horses, and everyone he reached was doomed to die. He did not strike one blow with his sword that did not kill the man he hit. Then he fell upon Sestor, king of Libya, in his way, and he sent his head flying, after which he said, "Be cursed, since you came here to do us harm."

Next he struck Poliplites, king of Mede, whom he found before him, and he cut off his head. When the barons saw that King Arthur was fighting so well, they rode against the Romans, but the Romans drove against them with such strength that they did the Britons very great harm. And if the emperor had not been killed, the Britons could not have lasted. Even so, they were greatly distressed by this, but they held out so well that no one could tell which side had the upper hand. When the six thousand six hundred knights whom King Arthur was to go back to fetch came down from the mountain, they rode into the crowd in such a way that the Romans saw none of them, and they struck them from behind so fiercely that they split the battle into two parts. They struck them down one atop the other and went about [441] trampling them under their horses' hooves and killing them with their swords. After they came in, the Romans could never have held out, so they turned in flight, for they were grief-stricken because of their emperor, who was dead. And the Romans and Saracens fled in a rout, and the Britons rode after them and killed as many as they wanted.

55. THE DEVIL CAT OF THE LAKE OF LAUSANNE; KING CLAUDAS'S MEN ROUTED.[*]

King Arthur was very happy with the Romans' defeat and the victory that God had granted him. Then he rode back into the field where the battle had been fought and had the dead buried in the churches and abbeys around the country, and he had the wounded carried away to be cared for. Then he had the emperor's body taken and sent it to Rome encased in stone, and his message to the Romans was that this was

---

[*]   Corresponds to Sommer, 441-445.

the tribute from Britain he was sending them, and if they demanded tribute from him another time, he would send them as much again.

And when he had done that, he took counsel as to whether he should still go on or turn back to Gaul, and the princes told him to seek Merlin's advice. Then the king called Merlin and said to him, "Dear friend, what do you wish me to do?"

"Sir," answered Merlin, "you won't go on to Rome, but you won't go back, either. You'll still go on, for there are people who need your help."

"What?" said King Arthur. "Then, is there a war in this land?"

"Yes, sir, on the other side of the Lake of Lausanne. For there a devil lives, such a devil that neither man nor woman dares dwell there, for he lays waste the countryside, and he kills and maims everyone he goes after."

"How can that be? Can no one stand against him? Isn't he a man like anyone else?"

"Not at all," answered Merlin. "It is a cat filled with devils, and it is so huge and frightening that it is a dreadful sight to see."

"God have mercy!" said King Arthur to Merlin. "Where can such a beast come from?"

"Sir," said Merlin, "I'll tell you in truth. It happened on the feast of the Ascension, four years ago, that a fisherman from that country came to the Lake of Lausanne with his tackle and nets to fish. And when he had got everything ready to cast his nets, he promised Our Lord the first fish he caught. And after he had cast his hook and line, he caught a pike that was worth at least thirty pence, and when he saw how beautiful and big the fish was, he said to himself, mumbling softly, for he was wily, 'God won't have this fish, but He'll have the next one I catch.'

"So he cast his line back into the water and caught a fish that was worth more than the first. And when he saw how big and beautiful it was, he wanted to keep it for himself, and he said that the Lord God would have to get along without that one, but He would indeed have the third.

Then he cast a third time and pulled out a kitten blacker than mulberry. And when the fisherman saw it, he said that he had a good use for it at home to rid his house of rats and mice. And so he raised it until it strangled him and his wife and children.

"And then it fled into a mountain that lies on the other side of the lake, as I have told you, and it has been there to this day. It kills and destroys whatever it touches, and it is wondrously large and frightening. And you will go that way, and from there your road goes straight to Rome. And, God willing, you will bring peace to the good people of the land, for they have fled to other countries." [442]

When the barons heard Merlin's words, they all began to cross themselves for the wonder they felt, and they said it was Our Lord's vengeance and a sign of the man's sin, for he did not keep the oath he had made to Our Lord. And they were convinced that Our Lord was angry at him because he had lied when he made his oath.

King Arthur ordered his men to turn aside and set out on the road, as they had been ordered, and they started toward the Lake of Lausanne. They found the land stripped and uninhabited, for no man or woman dared dwell there. And they made their way until they came to the hill where that devil lived. They set up camp in a valley that was within a league of the mountain where the beast was. And King Lot and Sir Gawainet took their arms, as did King Ban and Gaheriet, to go with

King Arthur and Merlin, for they said they wanted to see the devil that had done such harm in the countryside and throughout the land. They climbed the mountain, following the way Merlin led them, for he knew everything about the place, owing to the great knowledge he had.

When they had reached the top, Merlin said to King Arthur, "Sir, the cat lives inside that rock."

And he showed him a great cave in a meadowland that was wide and deep.

"And how will it come outside?" asked King Arthur.

"You'll soon see it come out," said Merlin, "and come out very fast. You be ready to defend yourself, for it will throw itself on you as soon as it sees you."

"Now all of you draw back," said King Arthur, "for I want to test its strength myself."

And they did as he ordered. And after they had drawn back a little, Merlin let out a very loud whistle. And as soon as the cat heard it, it sprang out of the cave at once, for it thought that a wild beast was there. It was starving and had gone without food for a long time, and, crazed with hunger, it ran straight for King Arthur. As soon as King Arthur saw it coming, he held out his lance to meet it. He meant to run it right through the beast's body, but it took the shaft in its teeth and began pulling on it so hard that the king staggered. The twisting and turning the king did with his lance made the shaft break off right at the iron tip, which stayed in the beast's mouth, and it began to roar as though it were mad.

The king threw down the broken shaft and drew his sword from its scabbard and held his shield up in front of his chest. The cat sprang at once, for it thought it could take him by the throat, but the king raised his shield so strongly against it that he sent the cat spilling to the ground. But at once it sprang back at the king very powerfully. King Arthur raised his sword and hit it right on top of the head so that he sliced the scalp, but its skull was too hard to cut through. Even so, he stunned it with his blow, so that it went sprawling to the ground.

But before the king could recover from wielding the blow, the cat leapt upon him and grabbed him fully by the shoulders, and it sank its claws right through his hauberk into his flesh. And it jerked him about so hard that it sent more than three hundred links flying from the mail hauberk, and his red blood flowed after the cat had withdrawn its claws, so that the king very nearly fell to the ground.

And when King Arthur saw his blood, he was very deeply [443] angered. Then he held his shield in front of his chest, took his sword in his right hand, and swiftly ran upon the cat, which was licking away the blood that had wet its claws. When it saw the king coming, it sprang to meet him. It thought it could take hold of him just as it had done before, but the king thrust out his shield, and the cat leapt on it with two of its feet and sank its claws right through. The cat jerked him about so hard that he bowed towards the ground. But the king held his shield so fast by the handles that the cat could not get away, nor could it pull its claws back out, but stayed hanging from the shield by its two forefeet.

And when King Arthur saw that it was hanging so fast from his shield, he raised his sword and hit it so hard between its legs that he cut right through them just below the knees. The cat fell to the ground, and the king threw his shield aside and ran upon the cat with his sword drawn. The cat sat back on its hind legs, bared its teeth, and opened its mouth wide. The king thrust at it and meant to strike it on the head, but the cat crouched on its hind legs and jumped onto his face, took hold of him with its hind claws and teeth, and tore at his flesh so that the blood spurted out from many gashes.

When the king felt the cat holding him so fast, he put the tip of his sword against its belly and started to thrust the sword through its body. When the cat felt the sword, it let go with its teeth and turned about to let itself go downward, for it thought it could drop to the ground, but the two feet it had fastened into his hauberk held so fast that it was left hanging there, its head down toward the ground.

And when the king saw it hanging as it was, he raised his sword and cut off the two feet it had fastened into his hauberk, and its body fell to the ground. As soon as it had fallen, it began to howl so loudly that all in King Arthur's army, which was in the encampment, heard it plainly. And after it had let out this howl, it began to hop about, for it had such great strength in its body, and it made for the cave it had come out of. But the king ran between the cat and its cave and then ran it down. The cat jumped at him, for it thought it could grab onto him with its teeth, but as it leapt, the king hit it with his sword above its forelegs and slit the cat open from end to end.

Then Merlin came running, and the others as well, to where he was, and they asked him how he was.

"I am well," he said, "thanks be to Our Lord, for I have killed the devil that did great harm to this country. You can be sure that I've never feared for myself any more than I did when I was entangled with that devil, except when I fought the giant the other day in the mountain that rises from the sea. And I praise Our Lord and thank Him for it."

"Sir," said the princes, "you are right to do that."

They looked and saw the cat's feet that were left in his shield and hauberk, and they said that they had never seen such paws. Gaheriet picked the shield up, and they went back to the army, rejoicing and merry.

And when the princes there saw the paws and claws that were so long, they were dumbfounded. They led the king to his tent and took off his armor, and they took notice of the scratches and bites the cat had given him, and they washed him and cleaned his wounds most tenderly; and physicians put on him what was needed to draw out the poison. And they took such good care of him that he did not have to stop drinking or eating or riding horseback.

They stayed there that day and [444] the next, when they took the road back to Gaul. And the king had his shield brought along—the shield where the cat's paws hung, and he had the paws from his hauberk put into a box, and he ordered that they should be well looked after.

And the king asked Merlin what that hill was called. And Merlin said the people in that country called it the Hill of the Lake* because of the lake that lapped at its feet.

"By my faith," said the king, "I want that name to be done away with, and I wish it to be called the Hill of the Cat because that is where the cat lived and where it was slain."

---

* Sommer's text has *le mont du lac* (444, l. 5)

And from the hour the king said this, the mountain has always been called by that name, and so will it be forever.

Here the story falls silent from speaking about King Arthur and his companions, and it goes back to telling about those who were taking the prisoners to France.

Here the story says that when the companions whom King Arthur had entrusted to take the Romans back to France took to the road, they rode from one town to the next and made their way day by day until they came to a castle, which belonged to Claudas of the Land Laid Waste, and there they met sixty-five knights from King Claudas's land. Through their spies these knights knew that King Arthur was sending to prison knights who were Romans, and they believed that if they handed those knights over to King Claudas, he would be grateful to them, for he dearly loved the emperor and his Romans.

King Claudas's knights were astride good horses, and they were well equipped, so they rode straight toward the ones leading the prisoners: they were a good two hundred strong, knights, squires, and men from that country who were riding with them; but of the two hundred no more than forty were knights, while King Claudas's knights numbered sixty-five,* and they were near their own castle, where there were many men-at-arms and foot soldiers whom they could rely on. So they hid themselves in a woods a little way from the road. And when they saw King Arthur's knights coming nearer, they let their horses run against them and fell upon them, and they almost took them by surprise.

But when King Arthur's knights saw them coming, they spurred their horses against them. They struck one another so hard on their shields that they went through them and tore open one another's hauberks; some were driven through with lances so that the tips stuck out the other side, and there were dead and wounded on both sides. When those who were leading the prisoners saw their knights spilling to the ground, they rode to where they were to help them and keep the others away. There was a mighty din and clanging of blows, and King Claudas's men suffered great harm, and they would have been worse off if the men from their castle, a good hundred and fifty strong, all on horseback, had not come out in strength to save them. Then the battle grew very hard and fierce. The Britons were strong and stalwart; King Claudas's men were strong and fierce, and they were in their own land—the way they defended themselves was a wonder.

Then fifty men-at-arms came out from the castle, each one with a bow in his hand and a quiver full of arrows, and they began to shoot at the Britons. They killed many of them in that onslaught, and the Britons were in great distress; they were forced to fall back as far as the prisoners, whom the foot soldiers were guarding. And the Britons would [445] have lost everything if something good had not happened them by God's will, for Pharian of Trebe and Leonce of Payerne were coming there in order to take the castle, and they had with them eight hundred knights, all on horseback and heavily armed. They happened upon the fighting and the rout of the Britons.

When those from the castle caught sight of them and recognized their flags, they were greatly distraught. They left the Britons and took flight toward their stronghold;

---

*   Here Sommer's text reads *.lxvi.* (444, l. 13).

they flew helter-skelter into the castle, every man looking out for himself. But they could not ride so fast that Leonce, Pharian, and their companions did not slay more than thirty of them while their mates were rushing to safety inside the castle. And those who were standing on the walls let the gates down after them, but a falling gate killed two of their horses.

Pharian, Leonce, and their men rode back toward the Britons who were guarding the prisoners. Pharian asked them who they were, and they answered that they belonged to King Arthur, who was sending the prisoners to France. And when they heard that, they said that they were well met. Then they took to the road all together and rode until they came to Benoic. There they got the prisoners down from their horses and locked them away, just as King Arthur had ordered. Then they all took off their armor and stayed there in joyful celebration.

Here the story falls silent from speaking about them and goes back to telling about the Lord of the Fens and his daughter.

56. The Birth of Hector; Flualis's Imprisonment.*

Now the story says that on the fifth day after King Ban, King Bors, and Merlin had left the marshes where they had lodged so happily, a powerful man from the country came to the castle at night. And the lord of the castle, who was a most worthy gentleman and wise, was very glad to have him as his guest, and in his honor he had his daughter serve him his cup, for she was most courteous, well-bred, and dutiful.

And the knight who had sought lodging there watched the young lady, and she pleased him so much that he asked her father for her hand and said that he would take her as his wife if he was willing. And when the father heard this, he thanked him most kindly, because he did him an honor in asking for her, and he was most happy, for this was the most powerful man in the whole country. And he said that he would speak to the young lady about it and then give him his answer.

After they had taken their meal, they went to bed. The next morning they rose early, and the gentleman spoke with his daughter about what the knight had asked him: he was such a powerful and highborn man that through him all their friends would be raised up and honored. And when the young lady heard this, she answered her father meekly and said to him, "Sir, it is not yet time for me to wed, for I am quite young. And so, I beg you, please say no more about it."

"My dear daughter, I see no use in refusing to talk about it. You ought to be glad in your heart that such a powerful and noble man stoops to ask for you as his wedded companion and friend, for you are a lowborn woman beside him, and you are scarcely worthy to take off his boots. So I beg you and command you to do what I wish."

---

* Corresponds to Sommer, 445-449.

"Sir," she said, "surely you can allow that, by the faith I owe you who are my father, [446] I am not of an age to wed."

"What is this, fair daughter?" the father answered. "Do you mean to go against my will?"

"Sir," said the maiden, "your will is not such that you wish to see me lost!"

"Lost? Dear daughter, rather I would win you!"

"No, lose me," she said. "For I would never have joy in my heart if I did not have as a husband the man to whom I have given and pledged myself. I know very well that I'll never have the one you wish me to wed; no, I'll keep myself for the man who has left me. He is a nobler, more handsome man, and a better knight than this man, and I know I would find greater happiness with him."

"My dear," said her father, "Whom are you talking to me about? Tell me plainly what is in your mind, so that I can hear from you something that will let me put this matter to rest."

"Sir," said the young lady, "I'll tell you, since you wish to know it, and not one word of what I'll say will be a lie."

Then she told him, in order, everything that had happened between her and King Ban of Benoic, that she was carrying his child, and that he had told her she would have a son through whom all her kindred would be honored and exalted, "to I beg you not to speak to me about marriage unless it is to the king, for by the faith I owe you, I'll have no husband but the king."

When the father heard his daughter, he was filled with sorrow and heartache, but he did not dare show it, so he answered her most meekly: "My dear daughter, since this is the way it is, I must abide it. Now don't worry about anything. I'll go speak to my lord, and I'll answer him according to your will, not mine."

He then went straight to the knight, who was already putting on his spurs, and he greeted him with great courtesy and said to him, "Sir, if you would wait two years, I would do what you wish." And he said this because he was convinced that he would not grant him the delay.

When the knight heard him, he answered not a word, but got on his horse—and his men did as well—and rode away without taking his leave. But he swore that, since he could not have the lady by love, he would take her by force; and after him, all others who wanted her could have her. So this is how he left, and he went into his country and called his men together until there were a good eight hundred knights, his own men and hirelings, and they rode as a body straight to the Castle of the Fens. There he had his tent pitched beneath a pine near the causeway, and he swore an oath that he would never leave before he had starved them all out.

And when the Lord of the Fens saw himself besieged, he was filled with sorrow—not because he was afraid of being taken by force or starved out, for all the men in the kingdom could not take him by force, and he would not be easily starved out, for he had food enough within for five whole years without having to go out through the gate, and there were sixty-two knights there, worthy and bold. For the Lord of the Fens was a most noble man.

And they stayed before the castle a full week, and nothing was shot or hurled. But it so happened that on the ninth day, about the hour of prime, a knight from the army whose name was Maduras went to the horn that hung there, put it to his mouth, and blew it three times with very great strength, so that the lord of the castle heard it plainly. Then he asked for his arms, put them on most nobly, and climbed on his strong, quick warhorse, his shield about his neck and his lance in his hand. [447] The gate was opened for him, and he rode out at great speed and rode the whole length of the causeway toward the army. And he shouted in a very loud voice that the man who blew his horn without his leave was very bold, and he would be sorry he thought of doing it if he were so foolhardy as to dare fight him.

When Maduras heard him, he said that he had blown the horn for no other reason, and he said he would joust with him if they swore an oath that the man who fell would hand himself over as a prisoner without further ado.

"And I agree to that," said Agravadain, "if Our Lord grants that I should worry about or be bothered by no one but you."

"In faith," answered Maduras, "you need fear no one, since you have come to that!"

Then Agravadain came down from the causeway, and they rode away from each other. The knights had gathered in rows all about to watch the joust. And the two knights rode toward each other as fast as they could make their horses run, their shields on their arms and their lances in their holders, and they struck each other on their shields so hard that they drove through them. Maduras broke his lance; and Agravadain broke his, but he had thrust his with such great strength that he knocked Maduras from his horse to the ground, and he struck so soundly that he broke his left arm between the wrist and the elbow.

Then he reached out his hand, took his horse by the bridle, and led it to the causeway; and he told Maduras to follow him and keep his oath. So he took to the causeway and rode off toward the castle, driving Maduras's horse before him. And he went through the gate and was greeted with great rejoicing.

And Leriador and his knights came to Maduras and found him in a faint, so that they thought he was dead. But after a while he opened his eyes and gave the order to be carried to the castle, so that he might fulfill his oath.

Then Leriador had a horse-drawn litter made of boughs and leaves. They laid Maduras inside and covered him with a rich silk cloth, and they raised him between two palfreys and took him inside the castle. And Agravadain took him in and had him put in a most lavish room, and they called for physicians to set his arm. And the ones who had brought him went back to their army and found Leriador full of sorrow and heartache, as were all the others.

The next morning yet another knight came to blow the horn, and Agravadain came out and jousted with him. He brought him down and made him swear himself a prisoner, and this one went away into the castle. And so Agravadain fought so boldly that he struck down eleven of them in all, and their lord was filled with sorrow. And he himself blew the horn on the twelfth day.

And when Agravadain came out, just as he always did, Leriador told him that with this joust the war would be over and the siege lifted. For if Agravadain could beat him, he would go back to his own country with his army, and never would he or his kin threaten anything that belonged to him.

"But if I defeat you," he said, "you will give me your daughter for my wife, for I ask no more of you."

So they swore on both sides. Then the two knights came together as fast as their horses could run, and they struck blows on each other's shields. They drove their lances through the bosses and ripped their hauberks open, and each one grazed the other's side with his lance, so that the blood spurted out from both of them. Then they bumped each other so hard with their shields and bodies that their horses stumbled and fell to the ground on top of them. Both of them [448] were knocked senseless, and they lay on the ground for a long time. But in time they both sprang back up, drew their swords, and ran each other down with great fierceness, and they traded hard blows on their hauberks, which had been ripped open, and they gave each other great and wonderful wounds. Both grew weary from the blood they had lost, but in the end it was Leriador who had to beg for mercy.

So the siege was lifted, and Leriador went back into his own country. And Agravadain went into his castle and had his wounds cared for. Then he sent the prisoners back to their countries, and he dwelt there happy and joyful until his daughter gave birth to a child who was afterwards of very great renown in the kingdom of Logres and in other lands. His right name was Hector,[*] and Agravadain was most happy with him and rejoiced in him, and he had him brought up in his own room. He gave him three nurses, and his mother[†] herself nursed him with her own milk, for there was nothing on earth she loved more than him. And he looked like King Ban, just as if he had been drawn from his likeness.

Right here the story falls silent from speaking about him, his mother, and Agravadain, who loved him very much, and it goes back to talking about King Flualis, about whom it has kept silent for a very long time.

Now the story says that when Merlin went away from King Flualis, whose dream he had interpreted,[‡] the king was left deeply distraught with what Merlin had said to him. And it was not long before everything Merlin had told him came true, for he saw his children at the temple of Diana, the temple torn down and violated, his land laid waste and impoverished, and his palace burned, and he himself was taken prisoner along with his wife.

But those who took them did not kill them; rather, they showed them the tenets of the Christian religion, and so much did they give them to understand day by day that they received the unction of holy baptism and were washed and cleansed from the filth of misbelief. They called the king by his own name, which was Flualis, but they changed the lady's name and called her Remissiane, whereas before she was called Subine. And they were husband and wife together for a long time, and in time they had four daughters who were later wed to four Christian princes, who were good and faithful men, and they had many children. For the eldest had ten sons, who all became knights, and seven daughters; the second had fourteen sons and three daughters; the third, twelve daughters and six sons; and the fourth twenty-five sons and one daughter. All of them were wed, and the sons all became knights in the lifetime of Queen Remissiane; they were filled with great joy and gladness, and they were thankful to Our Lord. When the king and the four princes saw that

---

[*]   The form of the name in Sommer's text is *hestor* (448, l. 9).

[†]   The word in Sommer's text is *meschine* (448, l. 11): "girl"— not what we would expect this noble lady to be called.

[‡]   Ch. 52.

they had fifty-five* sons and grandsons, all of whom were knights and brothers and first cousins to one another, they were much gladdened, and they said that Our Lord had given them to them to exalt Christendom; they also said that they would not die before they had put all of pagandom under Christianity and the law of God.

Then they summoned and gathered all the men under their sway, and they overran pagandom from every side and took towns and castles, and they killed many a pagan. They won lands and foreign countries, and they went over into Spain to Galicia and Compostela, and nothing could withstand against them. [449] At last King Flualis passed from this world in Spain, and the four princes and all his grandsons were filled with sorrow. He was buried in a city they called Nadres at the time.

Then they went back to the region about Jerusalem and took those lands into their hands; then they all scattered throughout various lands and conquered them and took all the honors. Some of them held Constantinople, others Greece, where there were four kingdoms, others Barbary and others Cyprus. Still others came into the kingdom of Logres to serve King Arthur, because of his great renown that ran throughout the world. With these came three knights who were most worthy and bold in fighting, but they lived for only a short time, and that was harmful to Christendom, for they were worthy and faithful gentlemen. Two of them died in a battle that Lancelot fought against King Claudas, and the other died in a battle that King Arthur fought against Mordred, just as the story will recount it later.

But with that the story falls silent about them all and goes back to speaking about King Arthur.

57. MERLIN'S IMPRISONMENT.†

In this part the story says that when King Arthur and his barons had defeated the Romans and the king had killed the cat, they began to make their way back. And they rode until they came to the castle that King Arthur had had built on the River Aube.‡ They spent one day there and then left and rode until they came to Benoic, where they were told that the prisoners were there. And Pharian and Leonce greeted them with very great rejoicing. Then they told them how they had rescued their men along with their prisoners, just as it had happened, for those from the castle had wanted to take them by force.

"By my head," said the king, "they'll be sorry they did that, for they will pay dearly for it."

Then he called Sir Gawainet and told him to go to the castle, which was called the Borderland, and to do what it took to tear it down to the ground so that those from other, nearby countries would not use it to attack his men or hinder him in any

---

*   The text reads *.liiij.* (448, l. 35).
†   Corresponds to Sommer, 449-453.
‡   Ch. 52.

way, and they would understand how mistaken they had been to wrong him. And Sir Gawainet ordered ten thousand knights to mount, and they took to the road.

They rode until they came there after nightfall, and they hid themselves in a wood five arrow-shots away from the castle. There they waited until the next morning, when those from the castle sent out men escorting the spoils from the battle. And as soon as the booty escort was all outside the castle, Sir Gawainet sent fourteen knights out and ordered them to ride past the escort and go toward the gate; he also sent with them five crossbowmen to shoot up toward the barbicans and crenels if they saw it was needed. They had to hold the gate until he could get there. It was still so early that they could scarcely see the gate. But as soon as the escort was outside, they started out toward the gate just as they had been ordered.

When Sir Gawainet saw the escort drawing nearer, he knew that the others were already beyond them. So he sent as many as twenty knights [450] against those who were taking the spoils. When those in the escort saw them coming, they left the spoils and started to ride as fast as they could back to the gates. But the knights and crossbowmen whom Sir Gawainet had sent there kept them from getting inside. Soon Sir Gawainet was there, and he and as many as five hundred knights struck out helter-skelter through the gates, and great were the shouts and the din. Those who were in the courtyard let down a portcullis that struck two horses on their rumps, and the knights fell to each side, but they were not hurt. Then the din and the yelling grew louder throughout the castle, and they ran to the barbicans and began throwing stones. But the five crossbowmen shot upward, while others began to cut down the gates and those who were outside rode in. And then those in the castle yielded to Sir Gawainet's will, and he took them prisoner and had them brought back to Benoic. Then he had the town's walls and gate torn down. And he went back to King Arthur, who was glad and happy about it.

And the king made the prisoners swear that they would never stand against King Ban or King Bors. Similarly, he made the Romans swear never to stand against the kingdom of Logres. And after the oaths were taken, he sent them all back to their countries. Then he stayed that day with King Ban, and he and his men left the next morning with great rejoicing and celebration.

Then a messenger brought news to King Arthur that King Leodagan of Carmelide had passed from this world— this is why he left King Ban. The next morning King Arthur left the two brother kings and never saw them afterwards, nor they him. It was a great shame that they left this life so soon, just as the story will recount it to you later in this history.

When King Arthur and his companions had left the two brother kings who had given him such honors, he made his way for as many days as it took to reach the sea. And he and his companions boarded their ships and went across to the port of Dover. Then they got on their horses and rode until they came to Logres. There the king found Queen Guenevere, who greeted him most joyfully, and he told her that her father had died. And the king comforted her as well as he knew how. Then he sent his men away and thanked them heartily, and they went into their own countries. King Arthur stayed in Logres with Sir Gawainet his nephew and the knights of the Round Table. And Merlin tarried with them a good long time.

Then Merlin wished to go see his master Blaise, and he would tell him what had happened, although he had not seen it all, and from there he would go see his lady Viviane, for the time he had set with her* was drawing near. So he came to King Arthur and told him that he had to leave. And the king and queen asked him most sweetly to come back soon, for he would be a great comfort to them and most welcome company, for the king loved him very much indeed, because he had helped him in times of great need, and thanks to him and his counsel Arthur had become a king. So the king said to him very affectionately, "Dear friend Merlin, you are going away. I will not keep you here against your will, but I'll be most unhappy until I see you again. For God's sake, hurry [451] back!"

"Sir," said Merlin, "this is for the last time. Farewell, I commend you to God."

When the king heard him say that it was for the last time, he was dumbfounded. And Merlin left without another word, weeping, and he made his way until he came to Blaise, his master, who was very glad at his coming. He asked him what he had done since leaving him, and Merlin told him everything. Then he recounted word for word, all in order, all the things that had happened to King Arthur: about the giant he had killed, his battle with the Romans, and how he had killed the cat. And he told him about the little dwarf the young lady had brought to court and how the king had made him a knight.

"But I'll tell you this much about the dwarf," said Merlin. "He is a most noble man. And he is not a dwarf by birth; rather, a young lady made him so when he was twelve years old, because he did not wish to grant her his love. He was then the most beautiful creature in all the world, but from the sorrow the young lady felt because of him, she turned him into a dwarf, so that nothing on earth would be so ugly or loathsome. But nine weeks from today the spell the lady cast will come to an end, and he will again be the age he ought to be, for from that day twelve years will have passed, but now he appears to be sixty years old or more."

And when Merlin had told all these things and made an account of them, Blaise set them down in writing one after the other, all in order, and this is how we still know them. After Merlin had tarried there a week, he left and told Blaise that it was for the last time, for he was going to stay with his lady, and he would never have the power to leave her or to come and go as he wished.

When Blaise heard Merlin, he was filled with sorrow and heartache, and he said, "Since you cannot ever leave her, don't go!"

"I must go," said Merlin, "for I have sworn an oath to her. And I am so overwhelmed by love for her that I could not leave her. And I have shown her and taught her all the knowledge she has, and she will yet know more, for I cannot leave her."

Then Merlin went away from Blaise, and he made his way a short while until he came to his lady, who was very glad to see him, as he was to see her. And they tarried together for a long time.

And right away she asked him about a great many things he knew how to do, and he taught her so much that he was later taken for a fool—and he still is. And she remembered everything and put it down in writing, for she was good at clerkly learning and knew the seven arts.

---

* That he would return to her in a year.

When Merlin had taught his lady everything she could ask, she began wondering how she could keep him forever. And she began to wheedle Merlin more than she had ever done before, and she said to him, "Sir, there is still something I don't know that I would be very happy to know. And so I beseech you to teach me how I might keep a man imprisoned without a tower or walls or irons, but through wizardry, so that he could never get away but through me."

And when Merlin heard her, he shook his head and began to sigh. And when she saw that, she asked him why he was sighing.

"My lady," he said, "I'll tell you. I know full well what you are thinking, and [452] I know that you want to keep me. And I am so overcome by love of you that I must do your will."

And when the young lady heard him, she put her arms about his neck and said that he had to belong to her, for she was his. "You know very well," she went on, "that the great love I feel for you has even made me leave my father and mother to hold you in my arms day and night All my thoughts, all my longing are for you. Without you I have no joy or happiness; all my hopes are in you, and I can find happiness only in you. And since I love you and you love me, isn't it right that you should do my will and I yours?"

"Indeed, lady," said Merlin, "yes! Now tell me what you want."

"Sir," she said, "I want you to teach me how to make a very beautiful, proper place that I can make so strong with magic that it cannot be undone. And we'll stay there, you and I, in joy and delight whenever we wish."

"Lady," answered Merlin, "I'll gladly do this for you."

"Sir," she said, "I don't want you to do it, but you will teach me how to do it and I'll do it," she went on, "more to my liking."

"I grant you this," said Merlin.

Then he began to explain it, and the lady wrote down everything he said. And when he had told her everything, she was very happy and loved him more and was more cheerful to him than she usually was. Then they tarried together for a long while, until one day came when they were walking hand in hand through the Forest of Broceliande looking for ways to find delight, and they came upon a beautiful bush, green and high, that was a hawthorn loaded with flowers. They sat down in its shade, and Merlin laid his head in the lady's lap, and she began to rub it until he fell asleep. And when the lady felt that he was sleeping, she got up carefully and with her wimple drew a circle all about Merlin and the bush, and she began to cast her spells. Then she sat down again beside him, took his head in her lap, and held him there until he awoke. And he looked about him, and it seemed to him that he was in the most beautiful tower in the world, and he found himself lying in the most beautiful bed he had ever lain in. Then he asked the young lady, "Lady, you have indeed tricked me if you do not stay with me, for no one but you has the power to undo this tower."

And she said to him, "Dear friend, I will come here often, and you will hold me in your arms and I you, and you will do forever whatever you please."

And she kept her oath to him faithfully, for few days or nights went by when she was not with him. Merlin never thereafter left the stronghold where his lady love had put him, but she came and went as she wished.

So the story falls silent right here about Merlin and his lady love, and it speaks about King Arthur.

The story says that from the time Merlin left King Arthur and told him that it was the last time he would see him, King Arthur was filled with sorrow and bewilderment, and he dwelt on the words Merlin had said to him. He waited for him in that state of mind for seven weeks or more, and when he saw that Merlin was not coming back, it was a marvel how sad and worried he was. And one day Sir Gawainet asked him what was wrong.

In truth, [453] dear nephew," answered the king, I am brooding because I think I've lost Merlin, and he'll never come back to me, for he has stayed away longer than he used to. He said that it was for the last time, and I am afraid that he was telling the truth, for he never lied in anything he told me. God help me, I would rather have lost the city of Logres than him. I would like very much to know whether anyone can find him near or far, so I beg you, look for him, if you love me, until you find out the truth about him."

"My lord," said Sir Gawainet, "I am ready to do your will, and you will see me leave at once. And I swear to you on the oath I gave you the day you made me a knight that I will look for him a year and a day or until I have truthful news of him. A year from today you will have me back, God willing and if He keeps me from death and prison, unless I have truthful news about him first."

The same oath was sworn by Sir Yvain, Sagremor, Agravain, Guerrehet, Gaheriet, and twenty-four* knights in their company: they were Doon of Carduel, Caulas the Red, Blois of Casset, Canet of Blay, Amadant of the Hilltop,† Placides the Merry, Laudalis of the Plain, Aiglin of the Vales, Cliacles the Orphan, Guiret of Lambale, Kehedin the Fair, Clarot of the Spur,‡ Yvain of the White Hands, Yvain of Lionel, Gaswain of Estrangort, Alibon of the Spur,§ Segurades of the Perilous Forest, Briamont of Carduel, Ladinel, Ladinas of North Wales, Drian of the Perilous Forest, Satran of the Narrow Borderland, Purades of Carmelide, and Carmaduc the Dark—they all took their oaths after Sir Gawainet. And they rode out of the city of Logres all together as King Arthur willed it, and they undertook their quest for Merlin. And when they were outside the city, they parted ways at a cross they found at the edge of a forest where the road forked into three branches. There they split into three bodies.

But with that the story falls silent from speaking about them and goes back to the lady who led the dwarf knight.

---

*   The text reads *.xxv.* (453, l. 14), but only twenty-four names follow. Counting Gawain, Yvain, Sagremor, Agravain, Guerrehet, and Gaheriet, thirty knights are named in all.

†   Taking the text's *crespe* (453, l.16): "crepe" (?) for *creste*.

‡   Sommer's text has *la broche* (453, l.18): "skewer, quill," etc.

§   Sommer's text again has *la broche* (453, l. 20).

58. Evadeam, the Dwarf Knight.*

Now the story says that after King Arthur had knighted the dwarf at the young lady's behest,† she took him away happily, and they went back to their country. And they made their way the first day until the hour of low vespers. And then they came out of a forest and rode onto a most beautiful heath, which was large and wide. There the lady looked before her and saw an armed knight coming, riding a black and white spotted warhorse, and she pointed him out to her dwarf. And he said, "Lady, don't worry, but ride on unafraid, for you needn't bother about him."

"In God's name," answered the young lady, "he'll want to carry me off with him! That's the only reason he's coming this way!"

And the dwarf said to her, "Ride on unafraid."

The knight shouted to her as soon as he had seen her, loudly enough for her to hear, "Welcome to my lady and my love! Now I have found what I've always been looking for!"

And the dwarf, who heard him very clearly, said to him most kindly, "Sir, don't be in such a hurry, for you might be thwarted before you get started. [454] You do not yet have her in your power, so that you might delight in her."

"Indeed, I ought to take pleasure in her," answered the knight, "for I love her just as if I held her for my own. And I'll have her soon enough."

And all the while the knight was coming closer‡ as fast as he could ride.

When the dwarf saw him coming closer, he fixed his lance in its holder and crouched behind his shield so that only his eye could be seen, and he struck his horse with his spurs through openings cut through the saddle's fenders, for his legs were so short that they did not reach below the saddle. And the horse bore him so fast that you would have thought he was flying, and he shouted to the knight to look out for himself.

And the knight, who was very proud and haughty, found it shameful to joust with such a loathsome creature. He raised his lance and said that, God willing, he would in no wise joust with him, so he held his lance upright. Nevertheless, he put up his shield against the blow. And the dwarf struck him so hard that he drove through his shield and cut through his hauberk, and the tip of his lance grazed his side. And he jolted him so hard with his body and his shield, and his horse was running so fast, that he knocked man and horse to the ground in a heap. As he fell, the knight dislocated his shoulder, and he swooned from the agony he felt.

And when the dwarf saw this, he called the young lady over and asked her to help him down from his horse. She took him in her arms and set him down. And he drew his sword from its scabbard, ran to the knight, and cut his helmet's ties and took it from his head. He threatened to cut him if he did not acknowledge that he was beaten. And the knight, who was sorely wounded, saw the sword he was holding above his head and was afraid of dying. He begged for mercy and said that he would entrust himself wholly to him.

*   Corresponds to Sommer, 453-458.
†   Ch. 52.
‡   Sommer's text reads *saprochoit del cheualier* (454, l. 4): "he was approaching the knight."

And the dwarf said, "Then you will go to King Arthur to be held prisoner. And you will tell him on my behalf that the little knight he dubbed sends you to him, and you will throw yourself on his mercy."

And he swore as much to him.

Then the dwarf told him to mount his horse, but he answered that he lacked the strength, for his shoulder was dislocated. "Instead I'll have to stay here until I find someone who can carry me. But get on your horse and go to the head of this heath, to a valley where you'll find a dwelling of mine, for it is high time for you to find lodging. You will stay there and send some of my men to me to carry me back there. You have nothing to fear."

And the dwarf agreed to this. He went back to the lady, who was holding his warhorse. She leaned down over her palfrey's neck, took him by the arms, and lifted him up until, with much straining, she set him in his saddle. Then they turned back to the knight's retreat.

Six squires who lived there ran out to meet them and helped them dismount.* They disarmed the dwarf and dressed him in a rich cloak, and the dwarf told them that their lord was wounded.

They took a litter, fastened it onto two palfreys, and went to their lord. They put him on the litter and carried him back to the retreat. They disarmed him, then sent for physicians, and they supplied him with what they could. Then they asked him who had done this to him, and he answered that it was a knight he did not know, nor did he dare say, for the shame of it, that it had been the dwarf. Then he welcomed his guests with as much festivity [455] as a wounded knight could muster, and he had them very lavishly served and given their ease. After the meal, they were given two rich beds to sleep in in a beautiful room, and they slept until early the next morning, when they got up and dressed. And the young lady armed her dwarf, for she loved him dearly and wanted no one to put a hand to it but herself. And when she had armed him and got him ready but for his helmet, she took him by the hand and led him to the room where the wounded knight lay. They both said to him, God grant him a good day, and he returned their greeting most meekly. And they commended him to God and heartily thanked him for the honor he had paid them.

Then they went out of the room, and the young lady laced his helmet and helped him get on his horse; then she gave him his shield and lance. Then the squires sprang to life and brought the lady her palfrey and helped her mount. Then they left the knight's retreat and took to the road toward Estrangorre.

And the knight who had been wounded began to think that he had to fulfill his oath, so he had a horse-drawn litter fitted out most lavishly, and it had a most fair and suitable bed, and the litter was covered with a costly silk cloth. The knight was laid on the bed, and the litter was fastened onto two good-tempered palfreys. And they left sorrowfully and took to the road straight to Carduel in Wales, where King Arthur and the queen were spending some time, and that day they were with a great many people. And when they got there King Arthur was seated at his meal, and the knight had himself carried into the hall before the king. And he said, "Sir, in

---

*   Sommer's text appears faulty: *& descendirent & la damoisele & le desarmerent* (454, ll. 36-37): "they alighted and the lady and they disarmed him."

faithfulness and to keep my oath, I have come, filled with shame, to throw myself on your mercy at the behest of the most loathsome creature in the world, who has defeated me in combat."

And when he had said this, he ordered his squires to bear him away. But King Arthur said to him, "What is this, sir knight? You say that you have come to be my prisoner and to beg my mercy?"

"In truth, sir," answered the knight.

Then I beg you," said the king, "to behave like a prisoner and tell me on whose behalf you surrender and how you were defeated."

"Sir," said the knight, "I am well aware that I must tell about my shame and disgrace, and so I shall, since I have come to that, for I must do your will and fulfill my oath. It is true that I have fallen in love with a young lady who is so beautiful and fair that there is not her like in all the world. She is a noble woman, the daughter of a king, and if you wish to know her name, it is the fair Byanne, daughter of King Clamadon, who is very wealthy and powerful. But never, whether by bidding, loving, or knightly service I did on her behalf, never could I bring her to grant me her love. And I would very gladly have taken her for my wife, and her father was most willing and quite happy about it, for I am of highborn stock, the son of a king and a queen, but the lady would not agree to it because of the most loathsome thing ever a mother gave birth to.

"And so the other evening I happened to be riding alone through a heath, wearing my armor, when I met my lady love who was coming back from your court, and [456] that false knight of a dwarf, whose lady she is, was riding with her. And when I saw her coming with such a small escort, I was very glad, and I said that God was to be blessed for bringing her to that place, for I thought I could take her away with me without a fight. But the dwarf who was along with her told me that I was coming too soon, and it would do me no good, for things would go otherwise than I hoped, and it was crazy for me to get so carried away. I thought I could have my way without resistance, so I told him that I was sure to get what I wanted. And so I let my horse run at full speed toward the lady, because I wanted to pick her up and take her away on my horse's neck to a retreat of mine that was not very far away from there.

"But when the dwarf saw that I had started out, he spurred toward me and fastened his lance to its holder, but I was unwilling to joust with him with my own lance, for it seemed a shame and a disgrace to me, so I did not want to strike him. But he hit me so hard that he took me to the ground, and when I fell I dislocated my left shoulder, and I had to faint from the agony. He took off my helmet and would have cut off my head if I hadn't sworn to make myself your prisoner on his behalf, and I am doing all of this."

"In truth, dear friend," said the king, "the one who has sent you here has put you into a good prison. But now tell me whose son the dwarf knight is."

"Sir," he answered, "he is the son of King Brandegorre of the land of Estrangorre, who is a most wealthy and powerful man in lands and friends, and he is faithful to God."

"Indeed," said the king, "he is truly a worthy gentleman, and I wonder that Our Lord could bear it that he should have such offspring."

"Sir," answered the knight, "Our Lord bears many things. And this is not due to a sin of the father or the mother, nor is it anything he has deserved, for at one time there was not in all the world as beautiful a creature as he was. And on Trinity Sunday it will have been nine years since it happened to him, and on that day he will be only twenty-two years old."

And King Arthur said that he could not be just twenty-two years old, "for by his looks he seems to be more than sixty."

"It is true," said the knight, "that he'll be just twenty-two, for King Evadeam, my father, whose name he bears, has told me many times that he is no older than that."

"And how did it happen to him?" asked King Arthur.

"Sir," he answered, "a young lady did this to him because he was unwilling to love her. And there is a time limit to it, so I have been told many times. Now I have told you what I was bound by my oath to say, and so I make myself your prisoner and throw myself on your mercy, for I have been defeated."

"Dear friend," said the king, "you have put yourself in a good prison, for I acquit you of your pledge. But first you must tell me your name."

"Sir," he said, "they call me Tradelmant, and I am godson to the king of North Wales, who in great charity gave me his name. So now I'll go away, by your leave and to my shame."

"Go with God," said the king; "may He guide you."

Then his squires took him up and carried him out of the great hall, and they lifted him up to his litter between two palfreys, and they went back to their own country.

And King Arthur and his barons spoke a great deal about the dwarf and maiden, and they said among themselves that it would be a joyful thing for the dwarf to have his beauty back, and they held the young lady in high esteem, because she never [457] hated her lover for his ugliness.

But with that the story falls silent now about all of them and goes back to speaking about Sagremor, who had left on the quest for Merlin, and he was one of thirty armed knights,* all of whom were worthy and bold.

Now the story says that when Sagremor left Sir Gawainet, he brought with him as many as ten companions of the quest, and they took to the road. And they rode until the sun set. And on the way out of a forest, along the slope of a rock, they happened to be looking about and saw a hut where a hermit lived. So they turned that way to seek lodging. They knocked, and the hermit ran at once to open the door to them, and he made them as comfortable as he could. The next morning he sang Mass for them.

Then they left there and made their way to the edge of a forest. And there Sagremor said to his companions that they should scatter throughout the forest, and so they did. One rode away here, another there, just as they happened to be led;† indeed, many a fair adventure happened on that quest about which the story makes

---

* The text reads *.xxij. sime de chevaliers* (457, l. 3): "a group of twenty-two knights." The reference is to 455, ll. 14-23, where thirty knights are named.

† The text reads *ainsi comme auenture les menoit* (457, l. 14): "just as adventure (happenstance) led them."

no mention now, but they went up and down through various countries until they rounded out the year, and they never learned any news about what they had ridden out for. Then at the end of the year they came back and told their adventures to the king. And there were some among them who recounted their shame more than their honor, but they had to tell, because they were sworn to do so by oath. And people were so faithful at that time that they would not perjure themselves to save their lives. And everything was written down.

So the story falls silent about them and goes back to speaking about Sir Yvain.

This the story says, that Sir Yvain made his way, after he had left Sir Gawainet, until he and his companions came out of a forest. And just as they were riding out of the forest, they met a young lady on a mule, and she was utterly grief-stricken. She was pulling out her hair by the handfuls, and she was screaming in a loud voice, "How wretched I am! What can become of me? For I have lost the one I loved so much, and he loved me so much that to win my love he lost the great beauty he had!"

When Sir Yvain heard her, he felt deeply sorry for her, so he went to her and asked why she was grieving so. And she said, "Noble knight, take pity on me and my lover! Five knights are killing him in that valley beneath that hill!"

"And who is your friend, lady?" asked Sir Yvain.

"Sir," she answered, "it is Evadeam the Dwarf, son of King Brandegorre."

"Stop sorrowing now, lady," said Sir Yvain, "for by the faith I owe you, he won't be harmed if I can help it, provided I get to him in time."

"Sir, God have mercy on you," said the young lady, "but you'll have to hurry."

Then Sir Yvain set out as fast as he could make his horse run on the way to the place the young lady had showed him, and his companions followed behind him. And the lady followed them as best she could, for her mule went very slowly. And Sir Yvain rode until he saw the dwarf, who was fighting lustily with two knights, and he saw three others who were lying in the middle of the field and who did not have the strength to get back up, [458] for one had been wounded through the thigh by a lance, the second had been struck on the shoulder, which was cut off from his body, and the third had been split open down to his teeth by a sword. And the other two were tired out, and both of them were in great fear of dying, for the dwarf kept attacking them with all his might.

And when Sir Yvain saw him behaving thus, he pointed him out to his companions and said what a shame it was that the dwarf was built as he was, "for he is worthy and bold, and he has great heart."

"In truth, sir," said one of his companions, "never has a man with his build fought with such skill. For God's sake, separate them so that nothing bad will happen to him, for it would be a great shame if he happened to be hurt."

"You speak the truth," answered Sir Yvain.

Then he spurred his horse to where they were, but before he could get there the dwarf had sent one of the knights to the ground, and he had ridden over him three or four times with his horse, so that he had nearly killed him. And when the fifth one saw that he was all alone, he was deathly afraid for himself, and he had started to veer away, as he meant to turn in flight, for without a doubt he had deep wounds all over his body. But the dwarf, who was on a very costly horse, kept right on his heels, and he was going so fast that he would surely have killed him if Sir Yvain had not ridden that way at once.

And he said to the dwarf, "Dear sir, don't do any more. Let him go for courtesy's sake, for we can see clearly how he is, for you have fought him long and hard."

And when the dwarf heard him asking him that so meekly, he answered like a man who was more courtly and courteous than any other, "Sir, is it your pleasure that I should give up?"

"Yes," answered Sir Yvain, "and with my thanks. For we can see how he is."

"Then I will do what you ask," said the dwarf, "for you seem to me a most worthy gentleman."

With that the knight who had been fighting with the dwarf* came to Sir Yvain and said to him, "Sir, my thanks to you, for you have saved me from death by coming here. And blessed be God who brought you here!"

Then he surrendered his sword to the dwarf, and the dwarf took it, and the others who were alive did likewise. And he sent all four of them to be King Arthur's prisoners. And they went there and gave themselves over to him on behalf of the dwarf knight.

And Sir Yvain and his companions left the dwarf and the young lady and scattered throughout various countries. They looked for Merlin up and down, but they never found out anything about him, and they were filled with great sorrow and heartache. Then they went back to court at the end of the year, and each one recounted what had happened to him on that quest. And King Arthur had everything put down in writing.

So the story falls silent right here about King Arthur and goes back to speaking about Sir Gawainet.

59. GAWAIN, MERLIN, AND THE DWARF KNIGHT.[†]

When Sir Gawainet had left his companions at the fork in the road, he made his way with about ten others until they came out of the forest. And then Sir Gawainet said to his companions that they should scatter, and each one should go his own way, for he wished to go on alone. And so they scattered, as he had said, and each one went his own way.

Sir Gawainet rode on alone and made his way through most of the land of Logres until one day he happened to be riding, brooding and sad because he could not hear any news of Merlin; and dwelling on these thoughts, he went into a forest. And after he had ridden about two Welsh leagues, a young lady came [459] toward him. She was riding the fairest palfrey in the world. Her saddle was of ivory, her stirrups

---

[*]   Sommer's text reads *li nains qui au cheualier sestoit combatus* (458, l. 24): "the dwarf who had been fighting the knight," which is the opposite of the sense suggested by the subsequent dialogue and action.

[†]   Corresponds to Sommer, 458-465.

of gold, and her saddle blanket was scarlet and had bands that hit the ground, and her reins were of orphrey with gold studs. She was dressed in white samite with linen fastenings, and her head was wrapped in silk against the sun. And all adorned as she was, she passed Sir Gawainet by, but he was so lost in his thoughts that it did not come to his mind to greet her.

And after she had gone by, she drew on her reins, turned her palfrey's head, and said, "Gawainet, Gawainet! It's not true, all they say about you and your great renown that is spread through the kingdom of Logres. They say, and they bear witness to it, that you are the best knight in the world. This much is true. And then they go on to say that you are the most courteous and the noblest in the world. But in this, your renown clashes with the truth, for you are the most boorish knight in the world I've ever seen in my lifetime. You meet me in this forest all by myself, far from other people, and the great wickedness that is rooted in you was not willing to show such kindness or meekness that it would stoop or deign or bear to greet me or even speak to me! You can be sure that as much ill will befall you as you have done to me, and you would give the city of Logres and half of King Arthur's lands not to have it happen to you."

And when Sir Gawainet heard the young lady, he was deeply ashamed, and he turned his horse's head toward her and, heavy-hearted, said to her the words you will hear straightway: "Lady," said Sir Gawainet, "God help me, I was brooding on a thing I am questing for, and I beg you, by your mercy, to forgive me."

"God help me," said the young woman, "first you will pay dearly for it, and you'll be dreadfully shamed and slandered, and you'll remember next time to greet young ladies when you see them, but I'm not saying that it will last you for the rest of your days! But you'll find no one in the kingdom of Logres who can tell you anything about what you're seeking; rather, you'll hear some news about it in Little Brittany. Now I'll go about my business, and you go looking for the thing you set out to find. And may you look like the first man you meet until you see me another time."

Then Sir Gawainet left the young lady, and he had not ridden more than a Welsh league through the forest when he met the dwarf knight and the maiden, who had left Sir Yvain the evening before and sent the four knights to be King Arthur's prisoners. And this happened on Trinity Sunday, right at the hour of midday. And as soon as Sir Gawainet saw the young lady, he thought about the lady he had met before, and he stopped brooding and said to the young lady, God grant happiness to her and her companion, and the lady and the dwarf answered, may God give him good fortune.*

So they passed by, Sir Gawainet on one side and they on the other. And after they had gone a little way past, the dwarf knight came back into the beauty he had had from the first, and his right age was twenty-two years, and he was once again large, well built, and broad of shoulder, and he had to take off the armor he had been wearing, for it was no longer any use to him. [460]

When the young lady saw her lover restored to his beauty, she was happier than anyone could say, and she reached up and put her arms about his neck and

---

* The word is *auenture* (459, l. 38): "adventure".

kissed him more than a hundred times without stopping. And then they went away, rejoicing and happy, side by side, in great gladness. And they thanked Our Lord for the honor He had given them, and they wished Sir Gawainet every happiness and all good luck, for he had said to them God grant them joy, and so He had. And thus they went their way.

But right here the story falls silent about them and will tell about Sir Gawainet.

When Sir Gawainet had gone past the dwarf knight and his lady, he rode a good three arrow-shots before he began to feel that the sleeves of his hauberk were clinging to his hands and that the bottom of his hauberk reached lower than his two feet. For his legs had grown so short that they did not stretch below the fenders of his saddle, and he looked and saw that his mail leggings were drooping over his stirrup tops, and his shield hung down close to the ground. He could see very plainly that he had become a dwarf. And he said to himself that this was what the young lady had sworn would happen to him, and he was so outraged that he nearly killed himself.

And he rode in this state of grief and agony until he reached the edge of the forest. And there he found a cross with a mounting block where he dismounted. And he began to shorten his stirrups, his mail leggings, the trappings of his sword, his shield's straps, and the sleeves of his hauberk, and he fastened straps to his shoulders and fitted himself out as best he could. He was so bewildered and so grief-stricken that he would have preferred to die rather than go on living.

Then he got back on his horse and set out on his way, and he cursed the day and the hour that he had started out on the quest, for he had been shamed and dishonored by it. And he rode on in this way and did not go by a castle or an out-of-the-way dwelling or a wood or a flatland without seeking news about Merlin from every man and woman he met. And he met men and women who said spiteful and loathsome things to him, but he did many knightly deeds, for although he was a dwarf, he had not lost his powers or his heart or his strength; rather, he was bold and enterprising, and he defeated many knights.

And after he had looked up and down throughout the kingdom of Logres, he saw that he would find nothing there, so he took it into his mind to cross over the sea and go to Little Brittany. And so he did. And he looked near and far, but he could learn nothing about Merlin. And he rode on until he neared the time he had set to go back. And so he said to himself, "Alas, what shall I do? The time is growing nearer when I must go back, when I swore an oath to my uncle I would be back, and so I must, for otherwise I'd be a faithless liar. No, I would not! For the oath supposed that I could act of my own free will, but I'm not free to act as I wish, for I am a loathsome and misshapen thing, and I have no mastery of myself. And that's why I can't be bound to go to court. In faith, now I have misspoken! Never in any circumstances, whatever shape I may have, would I perjure myself. And because I'm not locked in a prison, so that I couldn't go wherever I wanted, I would only forswear myself if I didn't go to court. Thus, [461] I must go to court so that I may not prove faithless. And so I beseech God to have mercy on me, for the body is treated shamefully in this world."

As Sir Gawainet uttered this complaint, he turned about to go back to court. As it happened, he was riding through the Forest of Broceliande, and he meant to go that way to come to the sea, and all the time he wailed and moaned as before. All at once he heard a voice not very far away from him, and he turned toward the place where he had heard that voice. He looked up and down and saw nothing but a kind of smoke no thicker than a mist,* and he could not go through it.

Then he heard a voice that said, "Sir Gawainet, do not despair, for everything will happen as it must happen."

And when Sir Gawainet heard the voice that had thus called him by his right name, he answered and said, "For God's sake, who is it that speaks to me?"

"What?" answered the voice. "Don't you recognize me? You used to know me well. This is what happens to something left and forgotten, and the proverb is true that the wise man says: if you leave the court, the court leaves you.† And so it has been with me. While I frequented the court and served King Arthur and his barons, I was known and loved by you and the others. And because I have left the court and no longer know it, I am unknown by you and the others, but I shouldn't be, if only faith and loyalty reigned through the world!"

When Sir Gawainet heard the voice speaking these things to him, the thought came to him that it was Merlin. And so he answered at once, "Indeed, sir, in truth I ought to have recognized you, for I have heard you speak many times. And so I beg you, show yourself to me so that I might see you."

"Sir Gawainet," said Merlin, "you'll never see me, and I am very sorry, for I can do no more about it And after you leave here, I'll never speak to you or to anyone else but my lady, for no one will ever have enough strength to break in here, whatever may happen, and I cannot get out, nor will I ever. For there is no tower in the world so strong as the one where I am locked away, and it is not of wood or iron or stone, but it is enclosed by nothing more than air through enchantment so strong that it cannot be undone at any time. I can't get out, and no one can get in except the lady who has made it and who keeps me company here when it pleases her, and she can come and go at will as she pleases."

"How can this be, dear friend Merlin?" asked Sir Gawainet "So you are held prisoner in this way and cannot free yourself whatever you may do? And you can't come out to me? How can such a thing happen to overwhelm you, who are the wisest man in the world?"

"But I am the most foolish!" said Merlin. "For I was well aware of what would happen to me. And I was so foolish as to love someone else more than myself! And so I taught my lady how she might imprison me, and no one can ever free me!"

"In truth," said Sir Gawainet, "Merlin, I am bitterly sorry about this, and so will be my uncle King Arthur, who has sent men out through all lands in search of you!"

"Then he must bear it," answered Merlin, "for he'll never see me nor I him—this is how things have happened to work out—nor will any ever speak to me after you, and it would be useless to try. And even you, if you had not turned this way, [462] would never have heard me speak. Now go back and greet King Arthur and my lady the queen and all the barons, and tell them all about me. And you will find

---

*   The text reads *vne fumee tout autressi comme air* (461, l. 8): "a smoke just like air."

†   The text reads *Qui eslonge la cort. & la cort luj* (461, l. 14). Cf. Morawski no. 2139: "Qui s'esloigne de cort et cort de lui."

the king at Carduel in Wales, and you'll see him there. And you will find all of your companions with whom you left. You will not be despondent about what has happened to you, for you will find the lady who did this to you in the forest where you met her before; but don't forget to greet her, for that would be a mad thing to do!"

"Sir," said Sir Gawainet, "I won't, God willing!"

"Then farewell, go with God," said Merlin, "and may He keep King Arthur and the kingdom of Logres and you and all the barons, for you are the best men there are in the whole world."

With that Sir Gawainet went away happy and sad— happy because Merlin had reassured him about what had happened to him, but sad because Merlin was lost to the world. And so he went his way and rode until he came to the sea, and he crossed over in all haste and took to the road to Carduel in Wales.

And as he went into the forest he had been riding through when he met the young lady and did not think to greet her, he remembered Merlin, who had told him not to forget to greet her when he met her again. And he was stricken with dread and was sorely afraid that he might go by her without a greeting, so he took off his helmet so that he could see better. He began to look front and back, from side to side, everywhere, until he came to the very spot where he had met the lady and passed her by without greeting her. Then he looked between two clumps of trees, for the forest was thick and deep, and he saw two knights who were fully armed but for their shields and helmets, which they had taken off, and their horses were tied to their lances. And they were holding a young lady between them, and they looked as if they were raping her; yet they did not want to, for the lady was making them do it on purpose to test Sir Gawainet's will and heart, and she thrashed about as if they were indeed trying to rape her.

When Sir Gawainet saw the two knights holding the young lady, one by her hands and the other by her legs as though they meant to lie with her by force, he was deeply angered, and he spurred his horse to where they were, his lance in his hand. And he said to the knights that they were already dead, because they were assaulting a lady in King Arthur's land. "For you know very well," he went on, "that ladies are guaranteed their safety."

When the young lady saw him, she shouted, "Gawainet, now I'll see if you are worthy enough to save me from this shame!"

"Lady," Sir Gawainet then said, "God help me, you will not be shamed where I am there to defend you. I'll die if I don't save you."

And when the knights heard him, it came to them as a stinging rebuke. They sprang to their feet and tied on their helmets, for they were already very much afraid of him. Even so, the young lady had assured them that they would not be hurt by him, and with her knowledge of the arts, she had cast a spell on them to keep them from being harmed by anyone at that time, so they felt better about it. And after they had tied on their helmets, they hung their shields about their necks and said to Sir Gawainet, "God help me, you mad dwarf, you look as if you're dead already. Still, it is a shame to us to attack a loathsome thing like you."

And when Sir Gawainet heard that [463] they were calling him a dwarf and a loathsome thing, he was deeply stricken in his heart. So he said to them, "Loathsome thing that I am, I've come here at a bad time for you! Now get on your horses, for it would seem to me a boorish thing to attack you on horseback while you were on foot."

"Then you have such faith in your own strength," answered the knights, "that you want us to be on our horses?"

"My faith is in God," said Sir Gawainet, "such that when you leave me you will never again do wrong to a lady or a maiden in King Arthur's land."

Then they jumped on their warhorses, took up their lances, and told Sir Gawainet that he was dead. And they went to the road, where the way was more open and moved far apart from each other. And both of the knights together ran against Sir Gawainet and he against them, and they both struck him on his shield and broke their lances, but they did not stir him from his saddle. Then he hit one of them so hard that he sent him sprawling to the ground, and his lance flew into bits, and he ran down the one who had fallen and crushed him under his horse.

Then he drew his sword and made straight for the other one. He was about to strike him on his helmet when the young lady screamed, "Sir Gawainet! Do no more!"

"Lady," he said, "is that what you wish?"

"Yes," she answered.

"Then I'll agree to stop at once for love of you, and may God grant you every happiness, to you and all the ladies of the world. You may be sure that, but for your entreaty, I would have killed him, or he would have killed me, for they have shamed you and wronged you. And they dishonored me when they called me a misshapen dwarf, and yet they spoke the truth, for I am the most loathsome thing in this world: it happened to me in this forest a good six months ago."

And when the young lady and the knights heard this, they began to smile. Then the lady said, "What would you give to the one who could cure you of this?"

"In truth, lady," he answered, "if I could be saved from this, I would give myself first of all and then as much wealth as I could gather in the whole world."

"You won't have to give so much," said the young lady, "but you will swear an oath to me such as I tell you."

"Lady," he said, "I'll do whatever you wish. Just tell me what you will, for I am ready to do it."

"You will swear to me on the oath you gave to King Arthur, your uncle, that you will never fail to help any lady, wed or unwed, and you will never meet a lady without greeting her, if you can, before she greets you."

"Lady," he said, "I swear this to you as a faithful knight."

"And I accept your oath," she answered, "but if you break it, you'll become again what you are now."

"Lady, I agree," he said, "but only if the lady's dispute in which she asks me to help her is just, for I'll have nothing to do with faithlessness, even if it means life or death."

"And so I grant you," answered the lady.

And all at once the straps with which he had tied up his mail leggings broke, because his legs were growing back out, and he was soon back in his own likeness. And when he felt himself restored, he dismounted and knelt before the young lady, and he said that he was her knight forevermore. And the lady thanked him and took him by the hand and stood him back up. And it was the very same young lady who had sent him that unhappy scourge. [464]

Then the young lady took leave of Sir Gawainet; she left with her two knights, and they commended one another to God. And Sir Gawainet went back to where they had fought, let out his body armor so that it was larger, and carefully repaired his shield and other arms. Then he got back on his horse, his shield about his neck, his sword girded, and his lance in his hand, and took to the road for Carduel. And he made his way day by day until he came to Carduel at the end of the year as agreed. And on that same day Sir Yvain, Sagremor, and their companions had come back, and each one had told his adventures and what had happened to him on that quest. And when Sir Gawainet got there, the rejoicing and celebrating were complete. And Sir Gawainet told them all the things that had happened to him on the quest, and the barons were amazed. King Arthur was filled with sorrow for Merlin, but he could do no more about him, so he had to bear it. So they put their minds and hearts to feasting in honor of Sir Gawainet as joyfully as they could.

While they were celebrating, Evadeam came into the great hall. He was twenty-two years old, and he was so fair and comely that no man in two kingdoms was more handsome. He was holding his young lady by her hand, and they came straight before the king and greeted him most courteously.

The king returned his greeting, and the knight said to him, "Sir, you do not know who I am, and it is no wonder, for you have seen me only once before. And then I was wearing clothing that no one would see on me now, and no one would recognize me now who had not seen me when I was a child."

"In truth, dear friend," said King Arthur, "I don't remember ever having seen you before, but you are a most handsome knight."

"Sir," said Evadeam, "do you remember a young lady who brought you a dwarf for you to make a knight?"

"Yes, indeed," answered the king, "and well I should, for he has sent me as prisoners five knights whom he has defeated by his prowess."

"Sir," said Evadeam then, "I am the dwarf whom you dubbed, and this is the lady who asked you to do it. And I am indeed the one who sent you those knights. And Sir Yvain saw everything about the last four, whom he found me fighting the day before Trinity Sunday. And the next day I had the good luck to be riding with my lady through the Forest of Broceliande at the hour of midday, when we met Sir Gawainet, whom I see sitting here. He greeted us and we him, and he said, God grant us happiness. And so He did, for no sooner had the words slid from his mouth than I returned to my own shape and the likeness you see me in now. For then I was a dwarf, ugly and unsightly. And I believe strongly that his words and his prayer availed me that God freed me from my great shame. And for this I thank Our Lord and him!"

Then the king asked him who he was and of what stock, and he told him everything in order, just as you have heard it before now. And when the king, Sir Gawainet, and the others heard this, they were filled with gladness and joy. And the king took him as a companion with those of the Round Table, and the young lady happily and willingly stayed with the queen.

So the story falls silent about King Arthur and his companions, and it goes back to speaking about King Ban [465] of Benoic and King Bors, his brother, king of Gaunes, who were back in their lands.

60. THE BIRTH OF LANCELOT AND THE LOSS OF BENOIC.[*]

The story says that after King Arthur had left King Ban of Benoic and his brother King Bors of Gaunes, the two brothers stayed in Benoic rejoicing with great gladness, and their wives, who were very beautiful and comely, were with them. And so it happened, as it pleased Our Lord, that King Ban and his wife had a son who was named Galahad in baptism, but his surname was Lancelot; he kept the name Lancelot all his life. He brought great joy and happiness to King Ban and his wife, the queen, and the queen loved him so much that she nursed him with her own milk.

And King Bors's wife had a son who was called Lionel, and he was handsome through and through, and twelve months later she had another named Bors. Afterwards these three youths won very great renown in the kingdom of Logres and throughout every land, and they became known for their deeds at arms.

Shortly after the younger of King Bors's two children was born, King Bors fell gravely ill, and he lay for a long time in the city of Gaunes. And King Ban, his brother, was filled with sorrow and heartache, for he could not be with him as he wished, because of a wicked and ruthless neighbor of his, whose land bordered his own. This was King Claudas of the Land Laid Waste, who was so angry and upset about his castle that King Arthur had had pulled down that he nearly went mad, and he could think of no one on whom to avenge himself but King Ban and King Bors, who bordered on his land, because they were King Arthur's men. So he made war on them, and he finally won over a prince of Rome, named Pontius Anthony, to help him. This prince came to him very willingly, because he hated King Arthur and all his men because of his love of the Emperor Lucius, whom they had killed. King Hoel of Nantes died in that dispute, and he had long waged war on King Claudas.

And, for their part, the Romans fought until they had Gaul under their sway, and they sent the men of Gaul and the Land Laid Waste, along with Pontius Anthony's men, against King Ban of Benoic, who defended himself with all his might, for he had a great heart and great skill at arms. Many times he gathered against them on the field of battle, and he lost sometimes and won sometimes. And Leonce of Payerne, Gratian of Trebe, Pharian, and Banin, King Ban's godson, fought wonderfully well there, and they brought down and killed many of King Claudas's men. Gratian died there, but Pharian did not. In the end, King Ban was so weakened from the loss of his men that he could not hold out against the Romans, and they beleaguered him

---

*   Corresponds to Sommer, 465-466.

and day by day took his castles and strongholds. And he could not get help from his brother, King Bors, who lay sick in his bed, from which he never got up.

What gave him the greatest distress was that Pontius Anthony had brought such a great number of men with him that they took his city of Benoic and all his land from him, and he had not one city or castle left that was his own except the castle of Trebe, where Queen Elaine was with Lancelot, her son, who [466] still lay in his cradle. And King Ban had as many men with him there as he could gather, but there were very few of them to withstand such great forces. Banin his godson was there, in whom he had great confidence, and he was right, for he was a good and faithful knight. And he had a seneschal whom he had raised since boyhood, and he had entrusted his land to him after Gratian's death: it was he who betrayed him and made him lose the castle of Trebe, just as the story will recount it to you later.

Here ends the Imprisonment of Merlin. God lead us all to a good end!